The Complete FreeBSD®

The Complete FreeBSD®
FOURTH EDITION

Documentation from the Source

Greg Lehey

O'REILLY®
COMMUNITY PRESS

Beijing · Cambridge · Farnham · Köln · Paris · Sebastopol · Taipei · Tokyo

The Complete FreeBSD®, Fourth Edition

by Greg Lehey (*grog@freebsd.org*)

Printed in the United States of America.

Published by O'Reilly & Associates, Inc., 1005 Gravenstein Highway North, Sebastopol, CA 95472.

O'Reilly & Associates books may be purchased for educational, business, or sales promotional use. Online editions are also available for most titles (*safari.oreilly.com*). For more information, contact our corporate/institutional sales department: 800-998-9938 or *corporate@oreilly.com*.

Editor: Andy Oram

Production Editor: Linley Dolby

Cover Designer: Edie Freedman

Printing History:

May 2003:	Fourth Edition.

ISBN: 0-596-00516-4

[M]   [12/03]

Table of Contents

12: The Vinum Volume Manager 221

13: Writing CD-Rs 243

14: Tapes, backups and floppy disks............................ 251

15: Printers.. 263

16: Networks and the Internet 277

17: Configuring the local network 297

18: Connecting to the Internet 315

21: The Domain Name Service **363**

26: Electronic mail: clients **471**

27: Electronic mail: servers **491**

28: XFree86 in depth 507

29: Starting and stopping the system 527

30: FreeBSD configuration files 551

31: Keeping up to date 581

32: Updating the system software 593

33: Custom kernels 607

A: Bibliography 627

B: The evolution of FreeBSD... 633

Index... 643

Foreword

I have been a long time developer of the Berkeley Software Distributions (BSD). My involvement started in 1976, at the University of California at Berkeley. I got drawn in as an office-mate of Bill Joy, who single-handedly wrote the code for BSD and then started handling its release. Bill went on to run the Computer Systems Research Group (CSRG) which developed and released the first fully complete BSD distributions. After Bill's departure to become a founder of Sun Microsystems, I eventually rose to head the CSRG and oversee the release of the freely redistributable 4.4BSD-Lite. The 4.4BSD-Lite distribution forms the basis for all the freely distributable variants of BSD today as well as providing many of the utilities found in Linux and commercial UNIX distributions.

With the release of 4.4BSD-Lite, the University of California at Berkeley ceased further BSD development. After considering the strengths and weaknesses of different BSD development groups, I decided to do my continued development in FreeBSD because it had the largest user community. For the past ten years, therefore, I have been a member of the FreeBSD developer team.

I have always felt that it is important to use your own product. For this reason, I have always run BSD everywhere: on my workstation, on my Web/file/mail/backup server, on my laptop, and on my firewall. By necessity, I have to find tools to do my job that will run on my BSD systems. It may be easier to just run Windows and PowerPoint to do your presentations, but there are an ever increasing number of fine alternatives out there that run on FreeBSD such as the open source OpenOffice.org suite or MagicPoint.

In the old days, there were not very many people working on the BSD software. This constraint on BSD development made it easy to keep up with what BSD could do and how to manage your system. But the last decade has seen an exponential growth in the open source movement. The result has been a huge increase in the number of people working on FreeBSD and an even larger increase in the number of applications and tools that have been ported to run on FreeBSD. It has become a more than full time job just to keep track of all the system capabilities, let alone to figure out how to use them all.

Greg Lehey has done a wonderful job with this book of helping those of us that want to fully utilize the FreeBSD system to do so without having to devote our entire lives figuring how. He has gone through and figured out each of the different tasks that you might ask your system to do. He has identified the software that you need to do the task. He explains how to configure it for your operational needs. He tells you how to monitor the resulting subsystem to make sure it is working as desired. And, he helps you to identify and fix problems that arise.

The book starts with the basics of getting the FreeBSD system up and running on your hardware, including laptops, workstations, and servers. It then explains how to customize an installation for your personal needs. This personalization includes downloading and operating the most important of the more than 8000 software packages in the FreeBSD ports collection. The book also includes a very comprehensive set of systems administration information, including the setup and operation of printers, local and external networking, the domain name system, the NFS and Samba remote filesystems, electronic mail, web surfing and hosting, and dial-up for FAX, remote login, and point-to-point network connections.

In short, this book provides everything you need to know about the FreeBSD system from the day you first pick up the software through the day you have a full suite of machines. It covers your complete range of computing needs. There is a reason that this book is so popular: as its title says, it is The Complete FreeBSD. I am very happy to see this revision which once again fulfills that mandate.

Marshall Kirk McKusick
Berkeley, California
February 2003

In this chapter:
• The fourth edition
• Conventions used in
  this book
• Acknowledgments
• How this book was
  written

Preface

FreeBSD is a high-performance operating system derived from the *Berkeley Software Distribution* (*BSD*), the version of UNIX developed at the University of California at Berkeley between 1975 and 1993. FreeBSD is not a UNIX clone. Historically and technically, it has greater rights than UNIX System V to be called *UNIX*. Legally, it may not be called UNIX, since UNIX is now a registered trade mark of The Open Group.

This book is intended to help you get FreeBSD up and running on your system and to familiarize you with it. It can't do everything, but plenty of UNIX books and online documentation are available, and a large proportion of them are directly applicable to FreeBSD. In the course of the text, I'll repeatedly point you to other documentation.

I'm not expecting you to be a guru, but I do expect you to understand the basics of using UNIX. If you've come from a Microsoft background, I'll try to make the transition a little less rocky.

The fourth edition

This book has already had quite a history. Depending on the way you count, this is the fourth or fifth edition of *The Complete FreeBSD*: the first edition of the book was called *Installing and Running FreeBSD*, and was published in March 1996. The next edition was called "The Complete FreeBSD", first edition. The first three editions were published by Walnut Creek CDROM, which ceased publishing activities in 2000. This is the first edition to be published by O'Reilly and Associates.

During this time, FreeBSD has changed continually, and it's difficult for a book to keep up with the change. This doesn't mean that FreeBSD has changed beyond recognition, but people have done a great job of working away those little rough edges that make the difference between a usable operating system and one that is a pleasure to use. If you come to FreeBSD from System V, you'll certainly notice the difference.

During the lifetimes of the previous editions of this book, I realised that much of the text becomes obsolete very quickly. For example, in the first edition I went to a lot of trouble to tell people how to install from an ATAPI CD-ROM, since at the time the support was a little wobbly. Almost before the book was released, the FreeBSD team improved the support and rolled it into the base release. The result? Lots of mail messages to the FreeBSD-questions mailing list saying, "Where can I get *ATAPI.FLP*?". Even the frequently posted errata list didn't help much.

This kind of occurrence brings home the difference in time scale between software releases and book publication. FreeBSD CD-ROMs are released several times a year. A new edition of a book every year is considered very frequent, but it obviously can't hope to keep up with the software release cycle. As a result, this book contains less time-sensitive material than previous editions. For example, the chapter on building kernels no longer contains an in-depth discussion of the kernel build parameters. They change too frequently, and the descriptions, though correct at the time of printing, would just be confusing. Instead, the chapter now explains where to find the up-to-date information.

Another thing that we discovered was that the book was too big. The second edition contained 1,100 pages of man pages, the FreeBSD manual pages that are also installed online on the system. These printed pages were easier to read, but they had two disadvantages: firstly they were slightly out of date compared to the online version, and secondly they weighed about 1 kilogram (2.2 lbs). The book was just plain unwieldy, and some people reported that they had physically torn out the man pages from the book to make it more manageable. As a result, the third edition had only the most necessary man pages.

Times have changed since then. At the time, *The Complete FreeBSD* was the only English-language book on FreeBSD. Now there are several—see Appendix A, *Bibliography*, for more detail. In particular, the FreeBSD online handbook is available both in printed form and online at *http://www.freebsd.org/handbook/index.html*, so I have left much of the more time-sensitive issues out of this book. See the online handbook instead. Alternatively, you can print out the man pages yourself—see page 15 for details.

It's very difficult to find a good sequence for presenting that material in this book. In many cases, there is a chicken and egg problem: what do you need to know first? Depending on what you need to do, you need to get information in different sequences. I've spent a lot of time trying to present the material in the best possible sequence, but inevitably you're going to find that you'll have to jump through one of the myriad page cross references.

Conventions used in this book

In this book, I use **bold** for the names of keys on the keyboard. We'll see more about this in the next section.

I use *italic* for the names of UNIX utilities, directories, file names and *URI*s (*Uniform Resource Identifier*, the file naming technology of the World Wide Web), and to emphasize new terms and concepts when they are first introduced. I also use this font for comments in the examples.

I use constant width in examples to show the contents of files, the output from commands, program variables, actual values of keywords, for mail IDs, for the names of *Internet News* newsgroups, and in the text to represent commands.

I use *constant width italic* in examples to show variables for which context-specific substitutions should be made. For example, the variable *filename* would be replaced by an actual file name.

I use **constant width bold** in examples to show commands or text that would be typed in literally by the user.

In this book, I recommend the use of the Bourne shell or one of its descendents (*sh*, *bash*, *pdksh*, *ksh* or *zsh*). *sh* is in the base system, and the rest are all in the Ports Collection, which we'll look at in chapter 9. I personally use the *bash* shell. This is a personal preference, and a recommendation, but it's not the standard shell: the traditional BSD shell is the C shell (*csh*), which FreeBSD has replaced with a fuller-featured descendent, *tcsh*. In particular, the standard installation sets the root user up with a *csh*. See page 136 for details of how to change the shell.

In most examples, I'll show the shell prompt as $, but it doesn't normally matter which shell you use. In some cases, however, it does:

- Sometimes you need to be super-user, the user who can do anything. If this is necessary, I indicate it by using the prompt #.

- Sometimes the commands only work with the Bourne Shell and derivatives (*zsh*, *bash*), and they won't work with *csh*, *tcsh* and friends. In these cases I'll show the *csh* alternative with the standard *csh* prompt %.

> In the course of the text I'll occasionally touch on a subject that is not of absolute importance, but that may be of interest. I'll print such notes in smaller text, like this.

Describing the keyboard

One of the big differences between UNIX and other operating systems concerns the way they treat so-called "carriage control codes." When UNIX was written, the standard interactive terminal was still the Teletype model KSR 35. This mechanical monstrosity printed at 10 characters per second, and the carriage control characters really did cause physical motion of the carriage. The two most important characters were *Carriage Return*, which moved the carriage (which carried the print head) to the left margin, and *Line Feed*, which turned the platen to advance the paper by the height of a line. To get to the beginning of a new line, you needed to issue both control characters. We don't have platens or carriages any more, but the characters are still there, and in many systems, including Microsoft, a line of text is terminated by a carriage return character and a line feed character. UNIX only uses a "new line" character, which corresponds to the line feed. This difference sometimes gives rise to confusion. We'll look at it in more detail on page 267.

It's surprising how many confusing terms exist to describe individual keys on the keyboard. My favourite is the *any* key ("Press any key to continue"). We won't be using the *any* key in this book, but there are a number of other keys whose names need understanding:

- The *Enter* or *Return* key. I'll call this **ENTER**.

- Control characters (characters produced by holding down the **Ctrl** key and pressing a normal keyboard key at the same time). I'll show them as, for example, **Ctrl-D** in the text, but these characters are frequently echoed on the screen as a caret (^) followed by the character entered, so in the examples, you may see things like ^D.

- The **Alt** key, which Emacs aficionados call a **META** key, works in the same way as the **Ctrl** key, but it generates a different set of characters. These are sometimes abbreviated by prefixing the character with a tilde (~) or the characters **A-**. I personally like this method better, but to avoid confusion I'll represent the character generated by holding down the **Alt** key and pressing **D** as **Alt-D**.

- **NL** is the *new line* character. In ASCII, it is **Ctrl-J**, but UNIX systems generate it when you press the **ENTER** key. UNIX also refers to this character as \n, a usage which comes from the C programming language.

- **CR** is the *carriage return* character, in ASCII **Ctrl-M**. Most systems generate it with the **ENTER** key. UNIX also refers to this character as \r—again, this comes from the C programming language.

- **HT** is the ASCII *horizontal tab* character, **Ctrl-I**. Most systems generate it when the **TAB** key is pressed. UNIX and C also refer to this character as \t.

Acknowledgments

This book is based on the work of many people, first and foremost the FreeBSD documentation project. Years ago, I took significant parts from the FreeBSD handbook, in particular Chapter 7, *The tools of the trade*. The FreeBSD handbook is supplied as online documentation with the FreeBSD release—see page 12 for more information. It is subject to the BSD documentation license, a variant of the BSD software license.

Redistribution and use in source (SGML DocBook) and 'compiled' forms (SGML, HTML, PDF, PostScript, RTF and so forth) with or without modification, are permitted provided that the following conditions are met:

1. Redistributions of source code (SGML DocBook) must retain the above copyright notice, this list of conditions and the following disclaimer as the first lines of this file unmodified.

2. Redistributions in compiled form (transformed to other DTDs, converted to PDF, PostScript, RTF and other formats) must reproduce the above copyright notice, this list of conditions and the following disclaimer in the documentation and/or other materials provided with the distribution.

Book reviewers

This book wouldn't be the same without the help of a small group of dedicated critics who tried out what I said and pointed out that it didn't work. In particular, I'd like to thank Jack Velte of Walnut Creek CDROM, who had the idea of this book in the first place, Jordan Hubbard and Gary Palmer for tearing the structure and content apart multiple times, and also Bob Bishop, Julian Elischer, Stefan Esser, John Fieber, Glen Foster, Poul-Henning Kamp, Michael Smith, and Nate Williams for valuable contributions ("What, you expect new users to know that you have to shut down the machine before powering it off?").[1] Finally, special thanks to Josef Möllers, Andreas Ritter, and Jack Velte, who put early drafts of this book through its paces and actually installed FreeBSD with their help.

The second edition had much more review than the first. A number of dedicated reviewers held through for several months as I gradually cranked out usable copy. In particular, special thanks to Annelise Anderson, Sue Blake, Jonathan M. Bresler, William Bulley, Mike Cambria, Brian Clapper, Paul Coyne, Lee Crites, Jerry Dunham, Stefan Esser, Patrick Gardella, Gianmarco Giovannelli, David Kelly, Andreas Klemm, Andrew MacIntyre, Jonathan Michaels, Jörg Micheel, Marco Molteni, Charles Mott, Jay D. Nelson, Daniel J. O'Connor, Andrew Perry, Kai Peters, Wes Peters, Mark Prior, Guido van Rooij, Andrew Rutherford, Thomas Vickery and Don Wilde.

Many of the second edition reviewers came back for the third edition. In addition, thanks to John Birrell for his help with the Alpha architecture, and Michael A. Endsley for ferreting out bugs, some of which had been present since the days of *Installing and Running FreeBSD*.

The following people helped with the fourth edition: Annelise Anderson, Jonathan Arnold, Sue Blake, Doug Barton, Brian Clapper, Jerry Dunham, Matt Geddes, Jeremiah Gowdy, Daniel B. Hemmerich, Justin Heath, Peter N. M. Hansteen, Paul A. Hoadley, Ed Irvine, John Lind, Johannes Lochmann, Warner Losh, Yin Cheung 'Yogesh' Mar, Andrew MacIntyre, Jonathan Michaels, Ove Ruben R. Olsen, Hiten Pandya, Linh Pham, Daniel Phillips, Siegfried P Pietralla. Stephen J. Roznowski, Dan Shearer and Murray Stokely.

In addition, my thanks to the people at O'Reilly and Associates, particularly Andy Oram,

---

1. See page 541 for details on how to shut down the system.

with whom I had discussed this project for years before he was finally able to persuade O'Reilly that it was a good idea. Subsequently it was Andy who coordinated seeing this rather unusual project through O'Reilly channels. Emma Colby designed the cover, and David Futato provided specifications, advice, and examples for the format. Linley Dolby proofread the document after I thought it was ready, and found tens of mistakes on nearly every page, ensuring that the book is better than its predecessors.

Finally, thanks to David Lloyd for the loan of an ATA CD-R drive while writing the ATA section of Chapter 13, *Writing CD-Rs*.

How this book was written

This book was written and typeset entirely with tools supplied as standard with the FreeBSD system, including the Ports Collection. The text of this book was written with the GNU *Emacs* editor, and it was formatted on 30 June 2003 with the GNU *groff* text formatter, Version 1.18, and some heavily modified *mm* macros. The process was performed under FreeBSD 5.0-CURRENT. Even the development versions of FreeBSD are stable enough to perform heavy-duty work like professional text formatting.

The source files for this book are kept under *RCS*, the *Revision Control System* (see the man page *rcs(1)*). Here are the RCS Version IDs for the chapters of this particular book.

```
$Id: title.complete,v 4.2 2003/04/09 19:43:58 grog Exp grog $
$Id: preface.mm,v 4.21 2003/05/25 09:02:19 grog Exp $
$Id: introduction.mm,v 4.26 2003/06/30 06:47:54 grog Exp $
$Id: concepts.mm,v 4.21 2003/04/02 06:37:12 grog Exp $
$Id: quickinstall.mm,v 4.11 2003/04/09 19:26:40 grog Exp $
$Id: shareinstall.mm,v 4.12 2003/04/09 19:26:50 grog Exp $
$Id: install.mm,v 4.22 2003/06/29 04:34:08 grog Exp $
$Id: postinstall.mm,v 4.13 2003/06/29 04:30:44 grog Exp $
$Id: unixref.mm,v 4.16 2003/04/02 06:41:29 grog Exp $
$Id: unixadmin.mm,v 4.13 2003/04/02 06:50:29 grog Exp $
$Id: ports.mm,v 4.12 2003/04/02 06:43:08 grog Exp $
$Id: filesys.mm,v 4.17 2003/04/02 06:43:57 grog Exp $
$Id: disks.mm,v 4.19 2003/06/29 02:54:00 grog Exp $
$Id: vinum.mm,v 4.20 2003/06/29 04:33:42 grog Exp $
$Id: burncd.mm,v 4.14 2003/06/29 04:33:03 grog Exp $
$Id: tapes.mm,v 4.12 2003/06/29 03:06:33 grog Exp $
$Id: printers.mm,v 4.17 2003/04/02 06:48:05 grog Exp $
$Id: netintro.mm,v 4.16 2003/04/02 06:48:55 grog Exp $
$Id: netsetup.mm,v 4.21 2003/06/29 09:05:45 grog Exp $
$Id: isp.mm,v 4.10 2003/04/02 03:09:55 grog Exp $
$Id: modems.mm,v 4.10 2003/04/02 03:11:02 grog Exp $
$Id: ppp.mm,v 4.14 2003/04/02 08:14:21 grog Exp $
$Id: dns.mm,v 4.19 2003/04/02 08:43:25 grog Exp $
$Id: firewall.mm,v 4.13 2003/06/29 04:25:08 grog Exp $
$Id: netdebug.mm,v 4.17 2003/04/03 02:04:14 grog Exp $
$Id: netclient.mm,v 4.18 2003/06/30 06:12:58 grog Exp $
$Id: netserver.mm,v 4.19 2003/04/09 20:42:40 grog Exp $
$Id: mua.mm,v 4.15 2003/04/03 02:07:47 grog Exp $
$Id: mta.mm,v 4.16 2003/04/03 01:18:20 grog Exp $
$Id: xtheory.mm,v 4.14 2003/05/18 02:19:19 grog Exp $
```

```
$Id: starting.mm,v 4.23 2003/06/29 03:13:08 grog Exp $
$Id: configfiles.mm,v 4.19 2003/06/29 04:32:34 grog Exp $
$Id: current.mm,v 4.18 2003/06/29 04:29:20 grog Exp $
$Id: upgrading.mm,v 4.13 2003/06/30 06:52:25 grog Exp $
$Id: building.mm,v 4.18 2003/06/29 04:34:40 grog Exp $
$Id: biblio.mm,v 4.8 2003/06/29 06:27:59 grog Exp $
$Id: evolution.mm,v 4.13 2003/04/02 04:59:47 grog Exp grog $
$Id: tmac.Mn,v 1.18 2003/06/24 07:04:00 grog Exp grog $
```

1

Introduction

FreeBSD is a free operating system derived from AT&T's *UNIX* operating system.[1] It runs on the following platforms:

- Computers based on the Intel i386 CPU architecture, including the 386, 486 and Pentium families of processors, and compatible CPUs from AMD and Cyrix.

- The Compaq/Digital Alpha processor.

- 64 bit SPARC machines from Sun Microsystems.

- In addition, significant development efforts are going towards porting FreeBSD to other hardware, notably the Intel 64 bit architecture and the IBM/Motorola PowerPC architecture.

This book describes the released versions of FreeBSD for Intel and Alpha processors. Current support for SPARC 64 processors is changing too fast for it to be practical to give details specific to this processor, but nearly everything in this book also applies to SPARC 64.

---

1. FreeBSD no longer contains any AT&T proprietary code, so it may be distributed freely. See page 7 for more details.

How to use this book

This book is intended for a number of different audiences. It attempts to present the material without too many forward references. It contains the following parts:

1. The first part, Chapters 1 to 6, tells you how to install FreeBSD and what to do if things go wrong.

2. Chapters 7 to 15 introduce you to life with FreeBSD, including setting up optional features and system administration.

3. Chapters 16 to 27 introduce you to FreeBSD's rich network support.

4. Finally, Chapters 28 to 33 look at system administration topics that build on all the preceding material.

In more detail, we'll discuss the following subjects:

- In the rest of this chapter, we'll look at what FreeBSD is, what you need to run it, and what resources are available, including FreeBSD's features and history, how it compares to other free UNIX-like operating systems, other sources of information about FreeBSD, the world-wide FreeBSD community, and support for FreeBSD. In addition, we'll look at the BSD's daemon emblem.

- Chapter 2, *Before you install*, discusses the installation requirements and theoretical background of installing FreeBSD.

- Chapter 3, *Quick installation*, presents a quick overview of the installation process. If you're reasonably experienced, this may be all you need to install FreeBSD.

- In Chapter 4, *Shared OS installation*, we'll look at preparing to install FreeBSD on a system that already contains another operating system.

- In Chapter 5, *Installing FreeBSD*, we'll walk through a typical installation in detail.

- Chapter 6, *Post-installation configuration*, explains the configuration you need to do after installation to get a complete functional system.

- Chapter 7, *The tools of the trade*, presents a number of aspects of FreeBSD that are of interest to newcomers (particularly from a Microsoft environment). We'll look at setting up a "desktop," the concept of *users* and file naming. We'll also consider the basics of using the *shell* and editor, and how to shut down the machine.

- Chapter 8, *Taking control*, goes into more detail about the specifics of working with UNIX, such as processes, daemons, timekeeping and log files. We'll also look at features unique to FreeBSD, including multiple processor support, removable I/O devices and emulating other systems.

- Chapter 9, *The Ports Collection*, describes the thousands of free software packages that you can optionally install on a FreeBSD system.

- Chapter 10, *File systems and devices*, contains information about the FreeBSD directory structure and device names. You'll find the section on device names (starting on page 195) interesting even if you're an experienced UNIX hacker.

- Chapter 11, *Disks*, describes how to format and integrate hard disks, and how to handle disk errors.

- Managing disks can be a complicated affair. Chapter 12, *The Vinum Volume Manager*, describes a way of managing disk storage.

- In Chapter 13, *Writing CD-Rs*, we'll look at how to use FreeBSD to write CD-Rs.

- FreeBSD provides professional, reliable data backup services as part of the base system. Don't ever let yourself lose data because of inadequate backup provisions. Read all about it in Chapter 14, *Tapes, backups and floppy disks*.

- Chapter 15, *Printers*, describes the BSD spooling system and how to use it both on local and networked systems.

- Starting at Chapter 16, *Networks and the Internet*, we'll look at the Internet and the more important services.

- Chapter 17, *Configuring the local network*, describes how to set up local networking.

- Chapter 18, *Connecting to the Internet*, discusses the issues in selecting an Internet Service Provider (ISP) and establishing a presence on the Internet.

- Chapter 19, *Serial communications*, discusses serial hardware and the prerequisites for PPP and SLIP communications.

- In Chapter 20, *Configuring PPP*, we look at FreeBSD's two PPP implementations and what it takes to set them up.

- In Chapter 21, *The Domain Name Service*, we'll consider the use of names on the Internet.

- Security is an increasing problem on the Internet. In Chapter 22, *Firewalls, IP aliasing and proxies*, we'll look at some things we can do to improve it. We'll also look at *IP aliasing*, since it goes hand-in-hand with firewalls, and *proxy servers*.

- Networks sometimes become *notworks*. In Chapter 23, *Network debugging*, we'll see what we can do to solve network problems.

- Chapter 24, *Basic network access: clients*, describes the client viewpoint of network access, including Web browsers, *ssh*, *ftp*, *rsync* and *nfs* clients for sharing file systems between networked computers.

- Network clients talk to network servers. We'll look at the corresponding server viewpoint in Chapter 25, *Basic network access: servers*.

- Despite the World Wide Web, traditional two-way personal communication is still very popular. We'll look at how to use mail clients in Chapter 26, *Electronic mail: clients*.

- Mail servers are an important enough topic that there's a separate Chapter 27, *Electronic mail: servers*.

- In Chapter 28, *XFree86 in depth*, we'll look at the theory behind getting X11 working.

- Chapter 29, *Starting and stopping the system*, describes how to start and stop a FreeBSD system and all the things you can do to customize it.

- In Chapter 30, *FreeBSD configuration files*, we'll look at the more common configuration files and what they should contain.

- In Chapter 31, *Keeping up to date*, we'll discuss how to ensure that your system is always running the most appropriate version of FreeBSD.

- FreeBSD keeps changing. We'll look at some aspects of what that means to you in Chapter 32, *Updating the system software*.

- Chapter 33, *Custom kernels*, discusses optional kernel features.

- Appendix A, *Bibliography*, suggests some books for further reading.

- Appendix B, *The evolution of FreeBSD*, describes the changes that have taken place in FreeBSD since it was introduced nearly ten years ago.

FreeBSD features

FreeBSD is derived from *Berkeley UNIX*, the flavour of UNIX developed by the Computer Systems Research Group at the University of California at Berkeley and previously released as the *Berkeley Software Distribution* (BSD) of UNIX.

> UNIX is a registered trademark of the Open Group, so legally, FreeBSD may not be called UNIX. The technical issues are different, of course; make up your own mind as to how much difference this makes.

Like commercial UNIX, FreeBSD provides you with many advanced features, including:

- FreeBSD uses *preemptive multitasking* with dynamic priority adjustment to ensure smooth and fair sharing of the computer between applications and users.

- FreeBSD is a *multi-user system*: many people can use a FreeBSD system simultaneously for unrelated purposes. The system shares peripherals such as printers and tape drives properly between all users on the system.

  Don't get this confused with the "multitasking" offered by some commercial systems. FreeBSD is a true multi-user system that protects users from each other.

- FreeBSD is secure. Its track record is borne out by the reports of the *CERT*, the leading organization dealing with computer security. See *http://www.cert.org/* for more information. The FreeBSD project has a team of security officers concerned with maintaining this lead.

- FreeBSD is reliable. It is used by ISPs around the world. FreeBSD systems regularly go several years without rebooting. FreeBSD can fail, of course, but the main causes of outages are power failures and catastrophic hardware failures.

- FreeBSD provides a complete *TCP/IP networking* implementation. This means that your FreeBSD machine can interoperate easily with other systems and also act as an enterprise server, providing vital functions such as NFS (remote file access) and electronic mail services, or putting your organization on the Internet with WWW, FTP, routing and firewall services. In addition, the Ports Collection includes software for communicating with proprietary protocols.

- *Memory protection* ensures that neither applications nor users can interfere with each other. If an application crashes, it cannot affect other running applications.

- FreeBSD includes the *XFree86* implementation of the *X11* graphical user interface.

- FreeBSD can run most programs built for versions of SCO UNIX and UnixWare, Solaris, BSD/OS, NetBSD, 386BSD and Linux on the same hardware platform.

- The FreeBSD Ports Collection includes thousands of ready-to-run applications.

- Thousands of additional and easy-to-port applications are available on the Internet. FreeBSD is source code compatible with most popular commercial UNIX systems and thus most applications require few, if any, changes to compile. Most freely available software was developed on BSD-like systems. As a result, FreeBSD is one of the easiest platforms you can port to.

- Demand paged *virtual memory* (*VM*) and "merged VM/buffer cache" design efficiently satisfies applications with large appetites for memory while still maintaining interactive response to other users.

- The base system contains a full complement of C, C++ and FORTRAN development tools. All commonly available programming languages, such as *perl*, *python* and *ruby*, are available. Many additional languages for advanced research and development are also available in the Ports Collection.

- FreeBSD provides the complete *source code* for the entire system, so you have the greatest degree of control over your environment. The licensing terms are the freest that you will find anywhere ("Hey, use it, don't pretend you wrote it, don't complain to us if you have problems"). Those are just the licensing conditions, of course. As we'll see later in the chapter, there are plenty of people prepared to help if you run into trouble.

- Extensive *online documentation*, including traditional *man pages* and a hypertext-based *online handbook*.

FreeBSD is based on the 4.4BSD UNIX released by the Computer Systems Research Group (CSRG) at the University of California at Berkeley. The FreeBSD Project has spent many thousands of hours fine-tuning the system for maximum performance and reliability. FreeBSD's features, performance and reliability compare very favourably with those of commercial operating systems.

Since the source code is available, you can easily customize it for special applications or projects, in ways not generally possible with operating systems from commercial vendors. You can easily start out small with an inexpensive 386 class PC and upgrade as your needs grow. Here are a few of the applications in which people currently use FreeBSD:

- *Internet Services*: the Internet grew up around Berkeley UNIX. The original TCP/IP implementation, released in 1982, was based on 4.2BSD, and nearly every current TCP/IP implementation has borrowed from it. FreeBSD is a descendent of this implementation, which has been maintained and polished for decades. It is the most mature and reliable TCP/IP available at any price. This makes it an ideal platform for a variety of Internet services such as FTP servers, World Wide Web servers, electronic mail servers, USENET news servers, DNS name servers and firewalls. With the *Samba* suite, you can replace a Microsoft file server.

- *Education:* FreeBSD is an ideal way to learn about operating systems, computer architecture and networking. A number of freely available CAD, mathematical and graphic design packages also make it highly useful to those whose primary interest in a computer is to get *other* work done.

- *Research:* FreeBSD is an excellent platform for research in operating systems as well as other branches of computer science, since the source code for the entire system is available. FreeBSD's free availability also makes it possible for remote groups to collaborate on ideas or shared development without having to worry about special licensing agreements or limitations on what may be discussed in open forums.

- *X Window workstation:* FreeBSD makes an excellent choice for an inexpensive graphical desktop solution. Unlike an X terminal, FreeBSD allows many applications to be run locally, if desired, thus relieving the burden on a central server. FreeBSD can even boot "diskless," making individual workstations even cheaper and easier to administer.

- *Software Development:* The basic FreeBSD system comes with a full complement of development tools including the renowned GNU C/C++ compiler and debugger.

Licensing conditions

As the name suggests, FreeBSD is free. You don't have to pay for the code, you can use it on as many computers as you want, and you can give away copies to your friends. There are some restrictions, however. Here's the BSD license as used for all new FreeBSD code:

Redistribution and use in source and binary forms, with or without modification, are permitted provided that the following conditions are met:

1. Redistributions of source code must retain the above copyright notice, this list of conditions and the following disclaimer.

2. Redistributions in binary form must reproduce the above copyright notice, this list of conditions and the following disclaimer in the documentation and/or other materials provided with the distribution.

This software is provided by the FreeBSD project "as is" and any express or implied warranties, including, but not limited to, the implied warranties of merchantability and fitness for a particular purpose are disclaimed. In no event shall the FreeBSD project or contributors be liable for any direct, indirect, incidental, special, exemplary, or consequential damages (including, but not limited to, procurement of substitute goods or services; loss of use, data, or profits; or business interruption) however caused and on any theory of liability, whether in contract, strict liability, or tort (including negligence or otherwise) arising in any way out of the use of this software, even if advised of the possibility of such damage.

The last paragraph is traditionally written in ALL CAPS, for reasons which don't seem to have anything to do with the meaning. Older versions of the license also contained additional clauses relating to advertising.

A little history

FreeBSD is a labour of love: big commercial companies produce operating systems and charge lots of money for them; the FreeBSD project produces a professional-quality operating system and gives it away. That's not the only difference.

In 1981, when IBM introduced their Personal Computer, the microprocessor industry was still in its infancy. They entrusted Microsoft to supply the operating system. Microsoft already had their own version of UNIX, called XENIX, but the PC had a minimum of 16 kB and no disk. UNIX was not an appropriate match for this hardware. Microsoft went looking for something simpler. The "operating system" they chose was correspondingly primitive: 86/DOS, a clone of Digital Research's successful CP/M operating system, written by Tim Paterson of Seattle Computer Products and originally called *QDOS* (*Quick and Dirty Operating System*). At the time, it seemed just the thing: it ran fine without a hard disk (in fact, the original PC didn't *have* a hard disk, not even as an option), and it didn't use up too much memory. The only thing that they really had to do was to change the name. IBM called its version PC-DOS, while Microsoft marketed its version under the name MS-DOS.

By this time, a little further down the US West Coast, the Computer Systems Research Group (CSRG) of the University of California at Berkeley had just modified AT&T's UNIX operating system to run on the new DEC VAX 11/780 machine, which sported virtual memory, and had turned their attention to implementing some new protocols for the ARPANET: the so-called *Internet Protocols*. The version of UNIX that they had developed was now sufficiently different from AT&T's system that it had been dubbed *Berkeley UNIX*.

As time went on, both MS-DOS and UNIX evolved. Before long, MS-DOS was modified to handle hard disks—not well, but it handled them, and for the PC users, it was so much better than what they had before that they ignored the inefficiencies. After all, the PC gave you your own hard disk on your desk, and you didn't have to share it with all the other people in the department. Microsoft even tried to emulate the UNIX directory structure, but succeeded only in implementing the concept of nested directories. At Berkeley, they were developing a higher performance disk subsystem, the *Fast File System*, now known as the *UNIX File System*.

By the late 80s, it was evident that Microsoft no longer intended to substantially enhance MS-DOS. New processors with support for multitasking and virtual memory had replaced the old Intel 8088 processor of the IBM PC, but they still ran MS-DOS by emulating the 8088 processor, which was now completely obsolete. The 640 kB memory limit of the original PC, which once appeared bigger than anybody would ever need, became a serious problem. In addition, people wanted to do more than one thing at a time with their computers.

A solution to both problems was obvious: move to the 32 bit address mode of the new Intel 80386 processor and introduce real multitasking, which operating systems on larger machines had had for decades. Of course, these larger machines were only physically larger. The average PC of 1990 had more memory, more disk and more processing power than just about any of the large computers of the 70s. Nevertheless, Microsoft didn't solve these problems for its "Windows" platform until much later, and the solutions still leave a lot to be desired.

UNIX, on the other hand, was a relatively mature operating system at the time when the PC was introduced. As a result, Microsoft-based environments have had little influence on the development of UNIX. UNIX development was determined by other factors: changes in legal regulations in the USA between 1977 and 1984 enabled AT&T first to license UNIX to other vendors, noticeably Microsoft, who announced XENIX in 1981, and then to market its own version of UNIX. AT&T developed System III in 1982, and System V in 1983. The differences between XENIX and System V were initially small, but they grew: by the mid-80s, there were four different versions of UNIX: the *Research Version*, used almost only inside AT&T, which from the eighth edition on derived from 4.1cBSD, the *Berkeley Software Distribution* (BSD) from Berkeley, the commercial *System V* from AT&T, and XENIX, which no longer interested Microsoft, and was marketed by the company that had developed it, the *Santa Cruz Operation*, or *SCO*.

One casualty of UNIX's maturity was the CSRG in Berkeley. UNIX was too mature to be considered an object of research, and the writing was on the wall: the CSRG would close down. Some people decided to port Berkeley UNIX to the PC—after all, SCO had ported its version of UNIX to the PC years earlier. In the Berkeley tradition, however, they wanted to give it away. The industry's reaction was not friendly. In 1992, AT&T's subsidiary *USL* (*UNIX Systems Laboratories*) filed a lawsuit against *Berkeley Software Design, Inc.* (*BSDI*), the manufacturer of the BSD/386 operating system, later called BSD/OS, a system very similar to FreeBSD. They alleged distribution of AT&T source code in violation of licence agreements. They subsequently extended the case to the University of California at Berkeley. The suit was settled out of court, and the exact conditions were not all disclosed. The only one that became public was that BSDI would migrate their source base to the newer 4.4BSD-Lite sources, a thing that they were preparing to do in any case. Although not involved in the litigation, it was suggested to FreeBSD that they should also move to 4.4BSD-Lite, which was done with the release of FreeBSD release 2.0 in late 1994.

Now, in the early 21st century, FreeBSD is the best known of the BSD operating systems, one that many consider to follow in the tradition of the CSRG. I can think of no greater honour for the development team. It was developed on a shoestring budget, yet it manages to outperform commercial operating systems by an order of magnitude.

The end of the UNIX wars

In the course of the FreeBSD project, a number of things have changed about UNIX. Sun Microsystems moved from a BSD base to a System V base in the late 80s, a move that convinced many people that BSD was dead and that System V was the future. Things turned out differently: in 1992, AT&T sold USL to Novell, Inc., who had introduced a product based on System V.4 called UnixWare. Although UnixWare has much better specifications than SCO's old System V.3 UNIX, it was never a success, and Novell finally sold their UNIX operation to SCO. SCO itself was then bought out by Caldera (which recently changed its name back to SCO), while the ownership of the UNIX trade mark has passed to the Open Group. System V UNIX is essentially dead: current commercial versions of UNIX have evolved so far since System V that they can't be considered the same system. By contrast, BSD is alive and healthy, and lives on in FreeBSD, NetBSD, OpenBSD and Apple's Mac OS X.

The importance of the AT&T code in the earlier versions of FreeBSD was certainly overemphasized in the lawsuit. All of the disputed code was over 10 years old at the time, and none of it was of great importance. In January 2002, Caldera released all "ancient" versions of UNIX under a BSD license. These specifically included all versions of UNIX from which BSD was derived: the first to seventh editions of Research UNIX and 32V, the predecessor to 3BSD. As a result, all versions of BSD, including those over which the lawsuit was conducted, are now freely available.

Other free UNIX-like operating systems

FreeBSD isn't the only free UNIX-like operating system available—it's not even the best-known one. The best-known free UNIX-like operating system is undoubtedly Linux, but there are also a number of other BSD-derived operating systems. We'll look at them first:

- *386/BSD* was the original free BSD operating system, introduced by William F. Jolitz in 1992. It never progressed beyond a test stage: instead, two derivative operating systems arose, FreeBSD and NetBSD. 386/BSD has been obsolete for years.

- *NetBSD* is an operating system which, to the casual observer, is almost identical to FreeBSD. The main differences are that NetBSD concentrates on hardware independence, whereas FreeBSD concentrates on performance. FreeBSD also tries harder to be easy to understand for a beginner. You can find more information about NetBSD at *http://www.NetBSD.org*.

- *OpenBSD* is a spin-off of NetBSD that focuses on security. It's also very similar to FreeBSD. You can find more information at *http://www.OpenBSD.org*.

- Apple computer introduced Version 10 (X) of its *Mac OS* in early 2001. It is a big deviation from previous versions of Mac OS: it is based on a Mach microkernel with a BSD environment. The base system (Darwin) is also free. FreeBSD and Darwin are compatible at the user source code level.

You could get the impression that there are lots of different, incompatible BSD versions. In fact, from a user viewpoint they're all very similar to each other, much more than the individual distributions of Linux, which we'll look at next.

FreeBSD and Linux

In 1991, Linus Torvalds, then a student in Helsinki, Finland, decided he wanted to run UNIX on his home computer. At that time the BSD sources were not freely available, and so Linus wrote his own version of UNIX, which he called Linux.

Linux is a superb example of how a few dedicated, clever people can produce an operating system that is better than well-known commercial systems developed by a large number of trained software engineers. It is better even than a number of commercial UNIX systems.

Obviously, I prefer FreeBSD over Linux, or I wouldn't be writing this book, but the differences between FreeBSD and Linux are more a matter of philosophy rather than of concept. Here are a few contrasts:

Table 1-1: Differences between FreeBSD and Linux

FreeBSD is a direct descendent of the original UNIX, though it contains no residual AT&T code.	Linux is a clone and never contained any AT&T code.
FreeBSD is a complete operating system, maintained by a central group of software developers under the Concurrent Versions System which maintains a complete history of the project development. There is only one distribution of FreeBSD.	Linux is a kernel, personally maintained by Linus Torvalds and a few trusted companions. The non-kernel programs supplied with Linux are part of a *distribution*, of which there are several. Distributions are not completely compatible with each other.
The FreeBSD development style emphasizes accountability and documentation of changes.	The Linux kernel is maintained by a small number of people who keep track of all changes. Unofficial patches abound.
The kernel supplied with a specific release of FreeBSD is clearly defined.	Linux distributions often have subtly different kernels. The differences are not always documented.

FreeBSD aims to be a stable production environment.

Many versions of Linux are still "bleeding edge" development environments. This is changing rapidly, however.

As a result of the centralized development style, FreeBSD is straightforward and easy to install.

The ease of installation of Linux depends on the *distribution*. If you switch from one distribution of Linux to another, you'll have to learn a new set of installation tools.

FreeBSD is still relatively unknown, since its distribution was initially restricted due to the AT&T lawsuits.

Linux did not have any lawsuits to contend with, so for some time it was thought to be the only free UNIX-type system available.

As a result of the lack of knowledge of FreeBSD, relatively little commercial software is available for it.

A growing amount of commercial software is becoming available for Linux.

As a result of the smaller user base, FreeBSD is less likely to have drivers for brand-new boards than Linux.

Just about any new board will soon have a driver for Linux.

Because of the lack of commercial applications and drivers for FreeBSD, Free-BSD runs most Linux programs, whether commercial or not.

Linux appears not to need to be able to run FreeBSD programs.

FreeBSD is licensed under the BSD license—see page 6. There are very few restrictions on its use.

Linux is licensed under the GNU General Public License. Further details are at *http://www.gnu.org/licenses/gpl.html*. By comparison with the BSD license, it imposes significant restrictions on what you can do with the source code.

FreeBSD has aficionados who are prepared to flame anybody who dares suggest that it's not better than Linux.

Linux has aficionados who are prepared to flame anybody who dares suggest that it's not better than FreeBSD.

In summary, Linux is also a very good operating system. For many, it's better than FreeBSD.

FreeBSD system documentation

FreeBSD comes with a considerable quantity of documentation which we'll look at in the following few pages:

- The FreeBSD Documentation Project maintains a collection of "books," documents in HTML or PDF format which can also be accessed online. They're installed in the directory hierarchy */usr/share/doc*.

- The traditional UNIX document format is *man pages*, individual documents describing specific functionality. They're short and to the point of being cryptic, but if you know what you're looking for, they have just the right amount of detail. They're not a good introduction.

- The GNU project introduced their own document format, *GNU info*. Some GNU programs have no other form of documentation.

Reading online documentation

You'll find a number of HTML documents in the directory */usr/share/doc/en/books*:

- */usr/share/doc/en/books/faq/index.html* contains the FreeBSD *FAQ* (*Frequently Asked Questions*). It's just what it says it is: a list of questions that people frequently ask about FreeBSD, with answers of course.

- */usr/share/doc/en/books/fdp-primer/index.html* is a primer for the *FreeBSD Documentation Project*,

- */usr/share/doc/en/books/handbook/index.html* is the FreeBSD *online handbook*. It contains a lot of information specifically about FreeBSD, including a deeper discussion of many topics in this book.

- */usr/share/doc/en/books/porters-handbook/index.html* is a handbook for contributors to the FreeBSD Ports Collection, which we'll discuss in Chapter 9, *The Ports Collection*.

- */usr/share/doc/en/books/ppp-primer/index.html* contains a somewhat dated document about setting up PPP. If you have trouble with Chapter 20, *Configuring PPP*, you may find it useful.

In addition to the directory */usr/share/doc/en/books*, there's also a directory */usr/share/doc/en/articles* with a number of shorter items of documentation.

Note the component *en* in the pathnames above. That stands for *English*. A number of these books are also installed in other languages: change *en* to *de* for a German version, to *es* for Spanish, to *fr* for French, to *ja* for Japanese, to *ru* for Russian, or to *zh* for Chinese. Translation efforts are continuing, so you may find documentation in other languages as well.

If you're running X, you can use a browser like *mozilla* to read the documents. If you don't have X running yet, use *lynx*. Both of these programs are included in the CD-ROM distribution. To install them, use *sysinstall*, which is described on page 92.

lynx is not a complete substitute for complete web browsers such as *mozilla*: since it is text-only, it is not capable of displaying the large majority of web pages correctly. It's good enough for reading most of the FreeBSD online documentation, however.

In each case, you start the browser with the name of the document, for example:

```
$ lynx /usr/share/doc/en/books/handbook/index.html
$ mozilla /usr/share/doc/en/books/handbook/index.html &
```

Enter the & after the invocation of *mozilla* to free up the window in which you invoke it: *mozilla* opens its own window.

If you haven't installed the documentation, you can still access it from the Live Filesystem CD-ROM. Assuming the CD-ROM is mounted on */cdrom*, choose the file */cdrom/usr/share/doc/en/books/handbook/index.html*.

Alternatively, you can print out the handbook. This is a little more difficult, and of course you'll lose the hypertext references, but you may prefer it in this form. To format the handbook for printing, you'll need a PostScript printer or *ghostscript*. See page 271 for more details of how to print PostScript.

The printable version of the documentation doesn't usually come with the CD-ROM distribution. You can pick it up with *ftp* (see page 433) from *ftp://ftp.FreeBSD.ORG/pub/FreeBSD/doc/*, which has the same directory structure as described above. For example, you would download the handbook in PostScript form from *ftp://ftp.FreeBSD.ORG/pub/FreeBSD/doc/en/books/handbook/book.ps.bz2*.

The online manual

The most comprehensive documentation on FreeBSD is the online manual, usually referred to as the *man pages*. Nearly every program, file, library function, device or interface on the system comes with a short reference manual explaining the basic operation and various arguments. If you were to print it out, it would run to well over 8,000 pages.

When online, you view the man pages with the command *man*. For example, to learn more about the command *ls*, type:

```
$ man ls
LS(1)                        FreeBSD Reference Manual                        LS(1)

NAME
     ls - list directory contents

SYNOPSIS
     ls [-ACFLRTacdfilogrstu1] [ file ... ]

DESCRIPTION
     For each operand that names a file of a type other than directory, ls
```

```
        displays its name as well as any requested, associated information.  For
        each operand that names a file of type directory, ls displays the names.
   (etc)
```

In this particular example, with the exception of the first line, the text in **constant width bold** is not input, it's the way it appears on the screen.

The online manual is divided up into sections numbered:

1. User commands

2. System calls and error numbers

3. Functions in the C libraries

4. Device drivers

5. File formats

6. Games and other diversions

7. Miscellaneous information

8. System maintenance and operation commands

9. Kernel interface documentation

In some cases, the same topic may appear in more than one section of the online manual. For example, there is a user command *chmod* and a system call chmod(). In this case, you can tell the *man* command which you want by specifying the section number:

```
$ man 1 chmod
```

This command displays the manual page for the user command chmod. References to a particular section of the online manual are traditionally placed in parentheses in written documentation. For example, *chmod(1)* refers to the user command *chmod*, and *chmod(2)* means the system call.

This is fine if you know the name of the command and forgot how to use it, but what if you can't recall the command name? You can use *man* to search for keywords in the command descriptions by using the −k option, or by starting the program *apropos*:

```
$ man -k mail
$ apropos mail
```

Both of these commands do the same thing: they show the names of the man pages that have the keyword *mail* in their descriptions.

Alternatively, you may browse through the */usr/bin* directory, which contains most of the system executables. You'll see lots of file names, but you don't have any idea what they do. To find out, enter one of the lines:

```
$ cd /usr/bin; man -f *
$ cd /usr/bin; whatis *
```

Both of these commands do the same thing: they print out a one-line summary of the purpose of the program:

```
$ cd /usr/bin; man -f *
a2p(1)              - Awk to Perl translator
addftinfo(1)        - add information to troff font files for use with groff
apply(1)            - apply a command to a set of arguments
apropos(1)          - search the whatis database
...etc
```

Printing man pages

If you prefer to have man pages in print, rather than on the screen, you can do this in two different ways:

* The simpler way is to redirect the output to the spooler:

  ```
  $ man ls | lpr
  ```

  This gives you a printed version that looks pretty much like the original on the screen, except that you may not get bold or underlined text.

* You can get typeset output with *troff*:

  ```
  $ man -t ls | lpr
  ```

  This gives you a properly typeset version of the man page, but it requires that your spooling system understand PostScript—see page 271 for more details of printing PostScript, even on printers that don't understand PostScript.

GNU info

The Free Software Foundation has its own online hypertext browser called *info*. Many FSF programs come with either no man page at all, or with an excuse for a man page (*gcc*, for example). To read the online documentation, you need to browse the *info* files with the *info* program, or from *Emacs* with the *info* mode. To start *info*, simply type:

```
$ info
```

In *Emacs*, enter **CTRL-h i** or **ALT-x** info. Whichever way you start *info*, you can get brief introduction by typing **h**, and a quick command reference by typing **?**.

Other documentation on FreeBSD

FreeBSD users have access to probably more top-quality documentation than just about any other operating system. Remember that word UNIX is trademarked. Sure, the lawyers tell us that we can't refer to FreeBSD as UNIX, because UNIX belongs to the Open Group. That doesn't make the slightest difference to the fact that nearly every book on UNIX applies more directly to FreeBSD than any other flavour of UNIX. Why?

Commercial UNIX vendors have a problem, and FreeBSD doesn't help them: why should people buy their products when you can get it free from the FreeBSD Project (or, for that matter, from other free UNIX-like operating systems such as NetBSD, OpenBSD and Linux)? One obvious reason would be "value-added features." So they add features or fix weak points in the system, put a copyright on the changes, and help lock their customers in to their particular implementation. As long as the changes are really useful, this is legitimate, but it does make the operating system less compatible with "standard UNIX," and the books about standard UNIX are less applicable.

In addition, many books are written by people with an academic background. In the UNIX world, this means that they are more likely than the average user to have been exposed to BSD. Many general UNIX books handle primarily BSD, possibly with an additional chapter on the commercial System V version.

In Appendix A, *Bibliography*, you'll find a list of books that I find worthwhile. I'd like to single out some that I find particularly good, and that I frequently use myself:

- *UNIX Power Tools*, by Jerry Peek, Tim O'Reilly, and Mike Loukides, is a superb collection of interesting information, including a CD-ROM. Recommended for everybody, from beginners to experts.

- *UNIX for the Impatient*, by Paul W. Abrahams and Bruce R. Larson, is more similar to this book, but it includes a lot more material on specific products, such as shells and the *Emacs* editor.

- The *UNIX System Administration Handbook*, by Evi Nemeth, Garth Snyder, Scott Seebass, and Trent R. Hein, is one of the best books on systems administration I have seen. It covers a number different UNIX systems, including an older version of FreeBSD.

There are also many active Internet groups that deal with FreeBSD. Read about them in the online handbook.

The FreeBSD community

FreeBSD was developed by a world-wide group of developers. It could not have happened without the Internet. Many of the key players have never even met each other in person; the main means of communication is via the Internet. If you have any kind of Internet connection, you can participate as well. If you don't have an Internet connection, it's about time you got one. The connection doesn't have to be complete: if you can receive email, you can participate. On the other hand, FreeBSD includes all the software you need for a complete Internet connection, not the very limited subset that most PC-based "Internet" packages offer you.

Mailing lists

As it says in the copyright, FreeBSD is supplied as-is, without any support liability. If you're on the Internet, you're not alone, however. Liability is one thing, but there are plenty of people prepared to help you, most for free, some for fee. A good place to start is with the mailing lists. There are a number of mailing lists that you can join. Some of the more interesting ones are:

- FreeBSD-questions@FreeBSD.org is the list to which you may send general questions, in particular on how to use FreeBSD. If you have difficulty understanding anything in this book, for example, this is the right place to ask. It's also the list to use if you're not sure which is the most appropriate.

- FreeBSD-newbies@FreeBSD.org is a list for newcomers to FreeBSD. It's intended for people who feel a little daunted by the system and need a bit of reassurance. It's not the right place to ask any kind of technical question.

- FreeBSD-hackers@FreeBSD.org is a technical discussion list.

- FreeBSD-current@FreeBSD.org is an obligatory list for people who run the development version of FreeBSD, called FreeBSD-CURRENT.

- FreeBSD-stable@FreeBSD.org is a similar list for people who run the more recent stable version of FreeBSD, called FreeBSD-STABLE. We'll talk about these versions on page 582. Unlike the case for FreeBSD-CURRENT users, it's not obligatory for FreeBSD-STABLE users to subscribe to FreeBSD-stable.

You can find a complete list of FreeBSD mailing lists on the web site, currently at *http://www.FreeBSD.org/doc/en_US.ISO8859-1/books/handbook/eresources.html*. This address is part of the online handbook and may change when the handbook is modified; follow the link *Mailing Lists* from *http://www.FreeBSD.org/* if it is no longer valid, or if you can't be bothered typing in the URI.

The mailing lists are run by *mailman* (in the Ports Collection). Join them via the web interface mentioned above. You will receive a mail message from *mailman* asking you to confirm your subscription by replying to the message. You don't need to put anything in the reply: the reply address is used once only, and you're the only person who will ever see it, so the system knows that it's you by the fact that you replied at all. You also have the option of confirming via a web interface with a specially generated URI. Similar considerations apply in this case.

FreeBSD mailing lists can have a very high volume of traffic. The FreeBSD-questions mailing list, for example, has thousands of subscribers, and many of them are themselves mailing lists. It receives over a hundred messages every day. That's about a million messages a day in total for just one mailing list, so when you sign up for a mailing list, be sure to read the charter. You can find the URI from the *mailman* confirmation message. It's also a good idea to "lurk" (listen, but not say anything) on the mailing list a while before posting anything: each list has its own traditions.

When submitting a question to `FreeBSD-questions`, consider the following points:

1. Remember that nobody gets paid for answering a FreeBSD question. They do it of their own free will. You can influence this free will positively by submitting a well-formulated question supplying as much relevant information as possible. You can influence this free will negatively by submitting an incomplete, illegible, or rude question. It's perfectly possible to send a message to FreeBSD-questions and not get an answer even if you follow these rules. It's much more possible to not get an answer if you don't.

2. Not everybody who answers FreeBSD questions reads every message: they look at the subject line and decide whether it interests them. Clearly, it's in your interest to specify a subject. "FreeBSD problem" or "Help" aren't enough. If you provide no subject at all, many people won't bother reading it. If your subject isn't specific enough, the people who can answer it may not read it.

3. When sending a new message, well, send a new message. Don't just reply to some other message, erase the old content and change the subject line. That leaves an `In-Reply-To:` header which many mail readers use to thread messages, so your message shows up as a reply to some other message. People often delete messages a whole thread at a time, so apart from irritating people, you also run a chance of having the message deleted unread.

4. Format your message so that it is legible, and PLEASE DON'T SHOUT!!!!!. It's really painful to try to read a message written full of typos or without any line breaks. A lot of badly formatted messages come from bad mailers or badly configured mailers. The following mailers are known to send out badly formatted messages without you finding out about them:

   Eudora
   exmh
   Microsoft Exchange
   Microsoft Internet Mail
   Microsoft Outlook
   Netscape

As you can see, the mailers in the Microsoft world are frequent offenders. If at all possible, use a UNIX mailer. If you must use a mailer under Microsoft environments, make sure it is set up correctly. Try not to use MIME: a lot of people use mailers which don't get on very well with MIME.

For further information on this subject, check out *http://www.lemis.com/email.html*.

5. Make sure your time and time zone are set correctly. This may seem a little silly, since your message still gets there, but many of the people you are trying to reach get several hundred messages a day. They frequently sort the incoming messages by subject and by date, and if your message doesn't come before the first answer, they may assume they missed it and not bother to look.

6. Don't include unrelated questions in the same message. Firstly, a long message tends to scare people off, and secondly, it's more difficult to get all the people who can answer all the questions to read the message.

7. Specify as much information as possible. This is a difficult area: the information you need to submit depends on the problem. Here's a start:

   - If you get error messages, don't say "I get error messages", say (for example) "I get the error message *No route to host*".

   - If your system panics, don't say "My system panicked", say (for example) "my system panicked with the message *free vnode isn't*".

   - If you have difficulty installing FreeBSD, please tell us what hardware you have, particularly if you have something unusual.

   - If, for example, you have difficulty getting PPP to run, describe the configuration. Which version of PPP do you use? What kind of authentication do you have? Do you have a static or dynamic IP address? What kind of messages do you get in the log file? See Chapter 20, *Configuring PPP*, for more details in this particular case.

8. If you don't get an answer immediately, or if you don't even see your own message appear on the list immediately, don't resend the message. Wait at least 24 hours. The FreeBSD mailer offloads messages to a number of subordinate mailers around the world. Usually the messages come through in a matter of seconds, but sometimes it can take several hours for the mail to get through.

9. If you do all this, and you still don't get an answer, there could be other reasons. For example, the problem is so complicated that nobody knows the answer, or the person who does know the answer was offline. If you don't get an answer after, say, a week, it might help to re-send the message. If you don't get an answer to your second message, though, you're probably not going to get one from this forum. Resending the same message again and again will only make you unpopular.

How to follow up to a question

Often you will want to send in additional information to a question you have already sent. The best way to do this is to reply to your original message. This has three advantages:

1. You include the original message text, so people will know what you're talking about. Don't forget to trim unnecessary text, though.

2. The text in the subject line stays the same (you did remember to put one in, didn't you?). Many mailers will sort messages by subject. This helps group messages together.

3. The message reference numbers in the header will refer to the previous message. Some mailers, such as mutt, can thread messages, showing the exact relationships between the messages.

There are more suggestions, in particular for answering questions, at *http://www.lemis.com/questions.html*. See also Chapter 26, *Electronic mail: clients* for more information about sending mail messages. You may also like to check out the FreeBSD web site at *http://www.FreeBSD.org/* and the support page at *http://www.FreeBSD.org/support.html*.

In addition, a number of companies offer support for FreeBSD. See the web page *http://www.FreeBSD.org/commercial/consulting_bycat.html* for some possibilities.

Unsubscribing from the mailing lists

There's a lot of traffic on the mailing lists, particularly on FreeBSD-questions. You may find you can't take it and want to get out again. Again, you unsubscribe from the list either via the web or via a special mail address, ***not*** by sending mail to the the list. Each message you get from the mailing lists finishes with the following text:

```
freebsd-questions@freebsd.org mailing list
http://lists.freebsd.org/mailman/listinfo/freebsd-questions
To unsubscribe, send any mail to "freebsd-questions-unsubscribe@freebsd.org"
```

Don't be one of those people who send the unsubscribe request to the mailing list instead.

User groups

But how about meeting FreeBSD users face to face? There are a number of user groups around the world. If you live in a big city, chances are that there's one near you. Check *http://www.FreeBSD.org/support.html#user* for a list. If you don't find one, consider taking the initiative and starting one.

In addition, USENIX holds an annual conference, the *BSDCon*, which deals with technical aspects of the BSD operating systems. It's also a great opportunity to get to know other users from around the world. If you're in Europe, there is also a BSDCon Europe, which at the time of writing was not run by USENIX. See *http://www.eurobsdcon.org* for more details.

Reporting bugs

If you find something wrong with FreeBSD, we want to know about it, so that we can fix it. To report a bug, use the *send-pr* program to send it as a mail message.

There used to be a web form at *http://www.FreeBSD.org/send-pr.html*, but it has been closed down due to abuse.

The Berkeley daemon

The little daemon at the right symbolizes BSD. It is included with kind permission of Marshall Kirk McKusick, one of the leading members of the former Computer Sciences Research Group at the University of California at Berkeley, and owner of the daemon's copyright. Kirk also wrote the foreword to this book.

The daemon has occasionally given rise to a certain amount of confusion. In fact, it's a joking reference to processes that run in the background—see Chapter 8, *Taking control*, page 150, for a description. The outside world occasionally sees things differently, as the following story indicates:

```
Newsgroups: alt.humor.best-of-usenet
Subject: [comp.org.usenix] A Great Daemon Story

From: Rob Kolstad <kolstad@bsdi.com>
Newsgroups: comp.org.usenix
Subject: A Great Daemon Story
```

Linda Branagan is an expert on daemons. She has a T-shirt that sports the daemon in tennis shoes that appears on the cover of the 4.3BSD manuals and *The Design and Implementation of the 4.3BSD UNIX Operating System* by S. Leffler, M. McKusick, M. Karels, J. Quarterman, Addison Wesley Publishing Company, Reading, MA 1989.

She tells the following story about wearing the 4.3BSD daemon T-shirt:

Last week I walked into a local "home style cookin' restaurant/watering hole" in Texas to pick up a take-out order. I spoke briefly to the waitress behind the counter, who told me my order would be done in a few minutes.

So, while I was busy gazing at the farm implements hanging on the walls, I was approached by two "natives." These guys might just be the original Texas rednecks.

"Pardon us, ma'am. Mind if we ask you a question?"

Well, people keep telling me that Texans are real friendly, so I nodded.

"Are you a Satanist?"

Well, at least they didn't ask me if I liked to party.

"Uh, no, I can't say that I am."

"Gee, ma'am. Are you sure about that?" they asked.

I put on my biggest, brightest Dallas Cowboys cheerleader smile and said, "No, I'm positive. The closest I've ever come to Satanism is watching Geraldo."

"Hmmm. Interesting. See, we was just wondering why it is you have the lord of darkness on your chest there."

I was this close to slapping one of them and causing a scene—then I stopped and noticed the shirt I happened to be wearing that day. Sure enough, it had a picture of a small, devilish-looking creature that has for some time now been associated with a certain operating system. In this particular representation, the creature was wearing sneakers.

They continued: "See, ma'am, we don't exactly appreciate it when people show off pictures of the devil. Especially when he's lookin' so friendly."

These idiots sounded terrifyingly serious.

Me: "Oh, well, see, this isn't really the devil, it's just, well, it's sort of a mascot."

Native: "And what kind of football team has the devil as a mascot?"

Me: "Oh, it's not a team. It's an operating—uh, a kind of computer."

I figured that an ATM machine was about as much technology as these guys could handle, and I knew that if I so much as uttered the word "UNIX" I would only make things worse.

Native: "Where does this satanical computer come from?"

Me: "California. And there's nothing satanical about it really."

Somewhere along the line here, the waitress noticed my predicament—but these guys probably outweighed her by 600 pounds, so all she did was look at me sympathetically and run off into the kitchen.

Native: "Ma'am, I think you're lying. And we'd appreciate it if you'd leave the premises now."

Fortunately, the waitress returned that very instant with my order, and they agreed that it would be okay for me to actually pay for my food before I left. While I was at the cash register, they amused themselves by talking to each other.

Native #1: "Do you think the police know about these devil computers?"

Native #2: "If they come from California, then the FBI oughta know about 'em."

They escorted me to the door. I tried one last time: "You're really blowing this all out of proportion. A lot of people use this 'kind of computers.' Universities, researchers, businesses. They're actually very useful."

Big, big, *big* mistake. I should have guessed at what came next.

Native: "Does the government use these devil computers?"

Me: "Yes."

Another *big* boo-boo.

Native: "And does the government pay for 'em? With our tax dollars?"

I decided that it was time to jump ship.

Me: "No. Nope. Not at all. Your tax dollars never entered the picture at all. I promise. No sir, not a penny. Our good Christian congressmen would never let something like that happen. Nope. Never. Bye."

Texas. What a country.

The daemon tradition goes back quite a way. As recently as 1996, after the publication of the first edition of this book, the following message went through the FreeBSD-chat mailing list:

To: "Jonathan M. Bresler" <jmb@freefall.freebsd.org>
Cc: obrien@antares.aero.org (Mike O'Brien),
    joerg_wunsch@uriah.heep.sax.de,
    chat@FreeBSD.org, juphoff@tarsier.cv.nrao.edu
Date: Tue, 07 May 1996 16:27:20 -0700
Sender: owner-chat@FreeBSD.org

>   details and gifs PLEASE!

If you insist. :-)

Sherman, set the Wayback Machine for around 1976 or so (see Peter Salus' *A Quarter Century of UNIX* for details), when the first really national UNIX meeting was held in Urbana, Illinois. This would be after the "forty people in a Brooklyn classroom" meeting held by Mel Ferentz (yeah I was at that too) and the more-or-less simultaneous West Coast meeting(s) hosted by SRI, but before the UNIX Users Group was really incorporated as a going concern.

I knew Ken Thompson and Dennis Ritchie would be there. I was living in Chicago at the time, and so was comic artist Phil Foglio, whose star was just beginning to rise. At that time I was a bonded locksmith. Phil's roommate had unexpectedly split town, and he was the only one who knew the combination to the wall safe in their apartment. This is the only apartment I've ever seen that had a wall safe, but it sure did have one, and Phil had some stuff locked in there. I didn't hold out much hope, since safes are far beyond where I was (and am) in my locksmithing sphere of competence, but I figured "no guts no glory" and told him I'd give it a whack. In return, I told him, he could do some T-shirt art for me. He readily agreed.

Wonder of wonders, this safe was vulnerable to the same algorithm that Master locks used to be susceptible to. I opened it in about 15 minutes of manipulation. It was my greatest moment as a locksmith and Phil was overjoyed. I went down to my lab and shot some Polaroid snaps of the PDP-11 system I was running UNIX on at the time, and gave it to Phil with some descriptions of the visual puns I wanted: pipes, demons with forks running along the pipes, a "bit bucket" named */dev/null*, all that.

What Phil came up with is the artwork that graced the first decade's worth of "UNIX T-shirts," which were made by a Ma and Pa operation in a Chicago suburb. They turned out transfer art using a 3M color copier in their basement. Hence, the PDP-11 is reversed (the tape drives are backwards) but since Phil left off the front panel, this was hard to tell. His trademark signature was photo-reversed, but was recopied by the T-shirt people and "re-forwardized," which is why it looks a little funny compared to his real signature.

Dozens and dozens of these shirts were produced. Bell Labs alone accounted for an order of something like 200 for a big picnic. However, only four (4) REAL originals were produced: these have a distinctive red collar and sleeve cuff. One went to Ken, one to Dennis, one to me, and one to my then-wife. I now possess the latter two shirts. Ken and Dennis were presented with their shirts at the Urbana conference.

People ordered these shirts direct from the Chicago couple. Many years later, when I was living in LA, I got a call from Armando Stettner, then at DEC, asking about that now-famous artwork. I told him I hadn't talked to the Illinois T-shirt makers in years. At his request I called them up. They'd folded the operation years ago and were within days of discarding all the old artwork. I requested its return, and duly received it back in the mail. It looked strange, seeing it again in its original form, a mirror image of the shirts with which I and everyone else were now familiar.

I sent the artwork to Armando, who wanted to give it to the Ultrix marketing people. They came out with the Ultrix poster that showed a nice shiny Ultrix machine contrasted with the chewing-gum-and-string PDP-11 UNIX people were familiar with. They still have the artwork, so far as I know.

I no longer recall the exact contents of the letter I sent along with the artwork. I did say that as far as I knew, Phil had no residual rights to the art, since it was a 'work made for hire', though nothing was in writing (and note this was decades before the new copyright law). I do not now recall if I explicitly assigned all rights to DEC. What is certain is that John Lassiter's daemon, whether knowingly borrowed from the original, or created by parallel evolution, postdates the first horde of UNIX daemons by at least a decade and probably more. And if Lassiter's daemon looks a lot like a Phil Foglio creation, there's a reason.

I have never scanned in Phil's artwork; I've hardly ever scanned in anything, so I have no GIFs to show. But I have some very very old UNIX T-shirts in startlingly good condition. Better condition than I am at any rate: I no longer fit into either of them.

Mike O'Brien
creaky antique

Note the date of this message: it appeared since the first edition of this book. Since then, the daemon image has been scanned in, and you can find a version at *http://www.mckusick.com/beastie/shirts/usenix.html*.

2

Before you install

FreeBSD runs on just about any modern PC, Alpha or 64 bit SPARC machine. You can skip this chapter and the next and move to chapter 3, and you'll have a very good chance of success. Nevertheless, it makes things easier to know the contents of this chapter before you start. If you do run into trouble, it will give you the background information you need to solve the trouble quickly and simply.

FreeBSD also runs on most Intel-based laptops; in general the considerations above apply for laptops as well. In the course of the book we'll see examples of where laptops require special treatment.

Most of the information here applies primarily to Intel platforms. We'll look at the Compaq Alpha architecture on page 42. The first release of FreeBSD to support the SPARC 64 architecture is 5.0, and support is still a little patchy. At the time of going to press, it's not worth describing, since it will change rapidly. The instructions on the CD-ROM distribution are currently the best source of information on running FreeBSD on SPARC 64.

Using old hardware

FreeBSD runs on all relatively recent machines. In addition, a lot of older hardware that is available for a nominal sum, or even for free, runs FreeBSD quite happily, though you may need to take more care in the installation.

FreeBSD does not support all PC hardware: the PC has been on the market for over 20 years, and it has changed a lot in that time. In particular:

- FreeBSD does not support 8 bit and 16 bit processors. These include the 8086 and 8088, which were used in the IBM PC and PC-XT and clones, and the 80286, used in the IBM PC-AT and clones.

- The FreeBSD kernel no longer supports ST-506 and ESDI drives. You're unlikely to have any of these: they're now so old that most of them have failed. The *wd* driver still includes support for them, but it hasn't been tested, and if you want to use this kind of drive you might find it better to use FreeBSD Release 3. See page 31 to find out how to identify these drives. You can get Release 3 of FreeBSD from *ftp://ftp.FreeBSD.org/pub/FreeBSD/releases/i386/3.x-STABLE*. You'll have to perform a network installation.

- Memory requirements for FreeBSD have increased significantly in the last few years, and you should consider 16 MB a minimum size, though nobody has recently checked whether it wouldn't install in, say, 12 MB. FreeBSD Release 3 still runs in 4 MB, though you need 5 MB for installation.

If you're planning to install FreeBSD on an old machine, consider the following to be an absolute minimum:

- PC with 80386 CPU, Alpha-based machine with SRM firmware.

- 16 MB memory (Intel) or 24 MB (Alpha).

- 80 MB free disk space (Intel). Nobody has tried an installation on an Alpha or SPARC machine with less than 500 MB, though you can probably reduce this value significantly.

You don't absolutely need a keyboard and display board: many FreeBSD machines run server tasks with neither keyboard nor display. Even then, though, you may find it convenient to put a display board in the machine to help in case you run into trouble.

When I say *absolute* minimum, I mean it. You can't do very much with such a minimal system, but for some purposes it might be adequate. You can improve the performance of such a minimal system significantly by adding memory. Before you go to the trouble to even try such a minimal installation, consider the cost of another 16 MB of memory. And you can pick up better machines than this second-hand for $50. Is the hassle worth it?

To get full benefits from a desktop or laptop FreeBSD system (but not from a machine used primarily as a server), you should be running the X Window system. This uses more memory. Consider 32 MB a usable minimum here, though thanks to FreeBSD's virtual memory system, this is not such a hard limit as it is with some other systems.

> The speed of a virtual memory-based system such as FreeBSD depends at least as much on memory performance as on processor performance. If you have, say, a 486DX-33 and 16 MB of memory, upgrading memory to 32 MB will probably buy you more performance than upgrading the motherboard to a Pentium 100 and keeping the 16 MB memory. This applies for a usual mix of programs, in particular, programs that don't perform number crunching.

Any SPARC 64 machine runs FreeBSD acceptably, as the machines are relatively new. If you're running Intel or Alpha, consider the following the minimum for getting useful work done with FreeBSD and X:

- PC with 80486DX/2-66, or Alpha-based machine

- 32 MB memory (i386) or 64 MB (Alpha)

- SVGA display board with 2 MB memory, 1024x768

- Mouse

- 200 MB free disk space

> Your mileage may vary. During the review phase of an earlier edition of this book, one of the reviewers stated that he was very happy with his machine, which has a 486-33 processor, 16 MB main memory, and 1 MB memory on his display board. He said that it ran a lot faster than his Pentium 100 at work, which ran Microsoft. The moral: if your hardware doesn't measure up to the recommended specification, don't be discouraged. Try it out anyway.

Beyond this minimum, FreeBSD supports a large number of other hardware components.

Device drivers

The FreeBSD kernel is the only part of the system that can access the hardware. It includes *device drivers*, which control the function of peripheral devices such as disks, displays and network boards. When you install new hardware, you need a driver for it.

There are two ways to get a driver into the kernel: you can build a kernel that includes the driver code, or you can load a driver module (*Kernel Loadable Module* or *kld*) into the kernel at run time. Not all drivers are available as klds. If you need one of these drivers, and it's not included in the standard kernel, you have to build a new kernel. We look at building kernels in Chapter 33.

The kernel configuration supplied with FreeBSD distributions is called GENERIC after the name of the configuration file that describes it. It contains support for most common devices, though support for some older hardware is missing, usually because it conflicts with more modern drivers. For a full list of currently supported hardware, read the web page *http://www.FreeBSD.org/releases/* and select the link *Hardware Notes* for the release you're interested in. This file is also available on installed FreeBSD systems as */usr/share/doc/en_US.ISO_8859-1/books/faq/hardware.html*. It is also available in other languages; see the subdirectories of */usr/share/doc*.

PC Hardware

This section looks at the information you need to understand to install FreeBSD on the i386 architecture. In particular, in the next section we'll look at how FreeBSD detects hardware, and what to do if your hardware doesn't correspond to the system's expectations. On page 31 we'll see how FreeBSD and other PC operating systems handle disk space, and how to set up your disk for FreeBSD.

Some of this information also applies to the Alpha and SPARC 64 architectures. We'll look at the differences for the Alpha architecture on page 42. Currently the SPARC 64 implementation is changing too fast to describe it in a meaningful manner.

Since the original PC, a number of hardware standards have come, and some have gone:

- The original PC had an 8 bit bus. Very few of these cards are still available, but they are compatible with the ISA bus (see the next item).

- The PC AT, introduced in 1984, had a 16 bit 80286 processor. To support this processor, the bus was widened to 16 bits. This bus came to be known as the *Industry Standard Architecture*, or *ISA*. This standard is still not completely dead, and many new motherboards support it. Most older motherboards have a number of ISA slots.

- The ISA bus has a number of severe limitations, notably poor performance. This became a problem very early. In 1985, IBM introduced the PS/2 system, which addressed this issue with a new bus, the so-called *Microchannel Architecture* or *MCA*. Although successful for IBM, MCA was not adopted by other manufacturers, and FreeBSD does not support it at all. IBM no longer produces products based on MCA.

- In parallel to MCA, other manufacturers introduced a bus called the *Extended Industry Standard Architecture*, or *EISA*. As the name suggests, it is a higher-performance extension of ISA, and FreeBSD supports it. Like MCA, it is obsolete.

- EISA still proved to be not fast enough for good graphics performance. In the late 80s, a number of *local bus* solutions appeared. They had better performance, but some were very unreliable. FreeBSD supported most of them, but you can't rely on it. It's best to steer clear of them.

- Finally, in the early 1990s, Intel brought out a new bus called *Peripheral Component Interconnect*, or *PCI*. PCI is now the dominant bus on a number of architectures. Most modern PC add-on boards are PCI.

  Compared to earlier buses, PCI is much faster. Most boards have a 32 bit wide data bus, but there is also a 64 bit PCI standard. PCI boards also contain enough intelligence to enable the system to configure them, which greatly simplifies installation of the system or of new boards.

- Modern motherboards also have an *AGP* (*Accelerated Graphics Port*) slot specifically designed to support exactly one graphic card. As the name implies, it's faster even than PCI, but it's optimized for graphics only. FreeBSD supports it, of course; otherwise it couldn't run on modern hardware.

- Most laptops have provision for external plug-in cards that conform to the *PC Card* (formerly called *PCMCIA*) or *CardBus* standards. These cards are designed to be inserted into and removed from a running system. FreeBSD has support for these cards; we'll look at them in more detail on page 30.

- More and more, the basic serial and parallel ports installed on early PCs are being replaced by a *Universal Serial Bus* or *USB*. We'll look at it on page 31.

How the system detects hardware

When the system starts, each driver in the kernel examines the system to find any hardware that it might be able to control. This examination is called *probing*. Depending on the driver and the nature of the hardware it supports, the probe may be clever enough to set up the hardware itself, or to recognize its hardware no matter how it has been set up, or it may expect the hardware to be set up in a specific manner in order to find it. In general, you can expect PCI drivers to be able to set up the card to work correctly. In the case of ISA or EISA cards, you may not be as lucky.

Configuring ISA cards

ISA cards are rapidly becoming obsolete, but sometimes they're still useful:

- ISA graphics cards are very slow in comparison with modern graphic cards, but if you just want a card for maintenance on a server machine that normally doesn't display anything, this is an economical alternative.

- Some ISA disk controllers can be useful, but they are sharply limited in performance.

- ISA Ethernet cards may be a choice for low-volume networking.

- Many ISA serial cards and built-in modems are still available.

Most ISA cards require some configuration. There are four main parameters that you may need to set for PC controller boards:

1. The *port address* is the address of the first of possibly several control registers that the driver uses to communicate with the board. It is normally specified in hexadecimal, for example 0x320.

    > If you come from a Microsoft background, you might be more used to the notation 320H. The notation 0x320 comes from the C programming language. You'll see a lot of it in UNIX.

    Each board needs its own address or range of addresses. The ISA architecture has a sharply limited address range, and one of the most frequent causes of problems when installing a board is that the port addresses overlap with those of another board.

    Beware of boards with a large number of registers. Typical port addresses end in (hexadecimal) 0. Don't rely on being able to take any unoccupied address ending in 0, though: some boards, such as Novell NE2000 compatible Ethernet boards, occupy up to 32 registers—for example, from 0x320 to 0x33f. Note also that a number of addresses, such as the serial and parallel ports, often end in 8.

2. Boards use an *Interrupt Request*, also referred to as *IRQ*, to get the attention of the driver when a specific event happens. For example, when a serial interface reads a character, it generates an interrupt to tell the driver to collect the character. Interrupt requests can sometimes be shared, depending on the driver and the hardware. There are even fewer interrupt requests than port addresses: a total of 15, of which a number

are reserved by the motherboard. You can usually expect to be able to use IRQs 3, 4, 5, 7, 9, 10, 11 and 12. IRQ 2 is special: due to the design of the original IBM PC/AT, it is the same thing as IRQ 9. FreeBSD refers to this interrupt as IRQ 9.

As if the available interrupts weren't already restricted enough, ISA and PCI boards use the same set of interrupt lines. PCI cards can share interrupt lines between multiple boards, and in fact the PCI standard only supports four interrupts, called INTA, INTB, INTC and INTD. In the PC architecture they map to four of the 15 ISA interrupts. PCI cards are self-configuring, so all you need to do is to ensure that PCI and ISA interrupts don't conflict. You normally set this up in a BIOS setup menu.

3. Some high-speed devices perform *Direct Memory Access*, also known as *DMA*, to transfer data to or from memory without CPU intervention. To transfer data, they assert a *DMA Request* (DRQ) and wait for the bus to reply with a *DMA Acknowledge* (DACK). The combination of DRQ and DACK is sometimes called a *DMA Channel*. The ISA architecture supplies 7 DMA channels, numbered 0 to 3 (8 bit) and 5 to 7 (16 bit). The floppy driver uses DMA channel 2. DMA channels may not be shared.

4. Finally, controllers may have on-board memory, sometimes referred to as *I/O memory* or *IOmem*. It is usually located at addresses between 0xa0000 and 0xefffff.

If the driver only looks at specific board configurations, you can set the board to match what the driver expects, typically by setting jumpers or using a vendor-supplied diagnostic program to set on-board configuration memory, or you can build a kernel to match the board settings.

PCMCIA, PC Card and CardBus

Laptops don't have enough space for normal PCI expansion slots, though many use a smaller PCI card format. It's more common to see *PC Card* or *CardBus* cards, though. PC Card was originally called *PCMCIA*, which stands for *Personal Computer Memory Card International Association*: the first purpose of the bus was to expand memory. Nowadays memory expansion is handled by other means, and PC Card cards are usually peripherals such as network cards, modems or disks. It's true that you can insert compact flash memory for digital cameras into a PC Card adapter and access it from FreeBSD, but even in this case, the card looks like a disk, not a memory card.

The original PC Card standard already has one foot in the grave: it's a 16 bit bus that doesn't work well with modern laptops. The replacement standard has a 32 bit wide bus and is called *CardBus*. The cards look almost identical, and most modern laptops support both standards. In this book I'll use use the term *PC Card* to include CardBus unless otherwise stated. FreeBSD Release 5 includes completely new PC Card code. It now supports both 16 bit PC Card and 32 bit CardBus cards.

PC Card offers one concept that conventional cards don't: the cards are *hot swappable*. You can insert them and remove them in a running system. This poses a number of potential problems, some of which are only partially solved.

PC Card and CardBus cards

PC Card and CardBus both use the same form factor cards: they are 54 mm wide and at least 85 mm long, though some cards, noticeably wireless networking cards, are up to 120 mm long and project beyond the casing of the laptop. The wireless cards contain an antenna in the part of the card that projects from the machine.

PC Card cards can have one of three standard thicknesses:

- *Type 1* cards are 3.3 mm thick. They're very uncommon.

- *Type 2* cards are 5 mm thick. These are the most common type, and most laptops take two of them.

- *Type 3* cards are 10.5 mm thick. In most laptops you can normally insert either one type 3 card or two type 2 cards.

The GENERIC FreeBSD kernel contains support for PC Card, so you don't need to build a new kernel.

Universal Serial Bus

The *Universal Serial Bus (USB)* is a new way of connecting external peripherals, typically those that used to be connected by serial or parallel ports. It's much faster than the old components: the old serial interface had a maximum speed of 115,200 bps, and the maximum you can expect to transfer over the parallel port is about 1 MB/s. By comparison, current USB implementations transfer data at up to 12 Mb/s, and a version with 480 Mb/s is in development.

As the name states, USB is a *bus*: you can connect multiple devices to a bus. Currently the most common devices are mid-speed devices such as printers and scanners, but you can connect just about anything, including keyboards, mice, Ethernet cards and mass storage devices.

Disks

A number of different disks have been used on PCs:

- *ST-506* disks are the oldest. You can recognize them by the fact that they have two cables: a *control cable* that usually has connections for two disks, and a thinner *data cable* that is not shared with any other disk. They're just about completely obsolete by now, but FreeBSD Release 3 still supports them with the *wd* driver. These disks are sometimes called by their modulation format, *Modified Frequency Modulation* or *MFM*. A variant of MFM that offers about 50% more storage is *RLL* or *Run Length Limited* modulation. From the operating system point of view, there is no difference between MFM and RLL.

- *ESDI* (*Enhanced Small Device Interface*) disks were designed to work around some of the limitations of ST-506 drives. They also use the same cabling as ST-506, but they are not hardware compatible, though most ESDI controllers understand ST-506 commands. They are also obsolete, but the *wd* driver in FreeBSD Release 3 supports them, too.

- *IDE* (*Integrated Device Electronics*), now frequently called *ATA* (*AT Attachment*), is the current low-cost PC disk interface. It supports two disks connected by a single 40 or 80 conductor flat cable. The connectors for both cables are the same, but the 80 conductor cable is needed for the 66 MHz, 100 MHz and 133 MHz transfer rates supported by recent disk drives.

  All modern IDE disks are so-called *EIDE* (*Enhanced IDE*) drives. The original IDE disks were limited by the PC BIOS standard to a size of 504 MB (1024 * 16 * 63 * 512, or 528,482,304 bytes). EIDE drives exceed this limit by several orders of magnitude.

  A problem with older IDE controllers was that they used *programmed I/O* or *PIO* to perform the transfer. In this mode, the CPU is directly involved in the transfer to or from the disk. Older controllers transferred a byte at a time, but more modern controllers can transfer in units of 32 bits. Either way, disk transfers use a large amount of CPU time with programmed I/O, and it's difficult to achieve the transfer rates of modern IDE drives, which can be as high as 100 MB/s. During such transfers, the system appears to be unbearably slow: it "grinds to a halt."

  To solve this problem, modern chipsets offer DMA transfers, which almost completely eliminate CPU overhead. There are two kinds of DMA, each with multiple possible transfer modes. The older *DMA* mode is no longer in use. It handled transfer rates between 2.1 MB/s and 16.7 MB/s. The newer *UDMA* (*Ultra DMA*) mode supports transfer rates between 16.7 MB/s and 133 MB/s. Current disks use UDMA33 (33 MHz transfer rate), which is the fastest rate you can use with a 40 conductor cable, and UDMA66 (66 MHz), UDMA100 (100 MHz) and UDMA-133 (133 MHz) with an 80 conductor cable. To get this transfer rate, both the disk and the disk controller must support the rate. FreeBSD supports all UDMA modes.

  Another factor influencing IDE performance is the fact that most IDE controllers and disks can only perform one transfer at a time. If you have two disks on a controller, and you want to access both, the controller serializes the requests so that a request to one drive completes before the other starts. This results in worse performance than on a SCSI chain, which does not have this restriction. If you have two disks and two controllers, it's better to put one disk on each controller. This situation is gradually changing, so when choosing hardware it's worth checking on current support for *tagged queueing*, which allows concurrent transfers.

- *SCSI* is the *Small Computer Systems Interface*. It's usually pronounced "scuzzy." It is used for disks, tapes, CD-ROMs and also other devices such as scanners and printers. The SCSI controller is more correctly called a *host adapter*. Like IDE, SCSI has evolved significantly over time. SCSI devices are connected by a single flat cable, with 50 conductors ("narrow SCSI," which connects a total of 8 devices) or 68 conductors ("wide SCSI," which also connects up to 16 devices). Some SCSI devices have subdevices, for example CD-ROM changers.

SCSI drives have a reputation for much higher performance than IDE. This is mainly because nearly all SCSI host adapters support DMA, whereas in the past IDE controllers usually used programmed I/O. In addition, SCSI host adapters can perform transfers from multiple units at the same time, whereas IDE controllers can only perform one transfer at a time. Typical SCSI drives are still faster than IDE drives, but the difference is nowhere near as large as it used to be. Narrow SCSI can support transfer rates of up to 40 MB/s (Ultra 2), and wide SCSI can support rates of up to 320 MB/s (Ultra 320). These speeds are not necessarily faster than IDE: you can connect more than seven times as many devices to a wide SCSI chain.

Disk data layout

Before you install FreeBSD, you need to decide how you want to use the disk space available to you. If desired, FreeBSD can coexist with other operating systems on the Intel platform. In this section, we'll look at the way data is laid out on disk, and what we need to do to create FreeBSD file systems on disk.

PC BIOS and disks

The basics of disk drives are relatively straightforward: data is stored on one or more rotating disks with a magnetic coating similar in function to the coating on an audio tape. Unlike a tape, however, disk heads do not touch the surface: the rotating disk produces an air pressure against the head, which keeps it floating very close to the surface. The disk has (usually) one *read/write head* for each surface to transfer data to and from the system. People frequently talk about the number of heads, not the number of surfaces, though strictly speaking this is incorrect: if there are two heads per surface (to speed up access), you're still interested in the number of surfaces, not the number of heads.

While transferring data, the heads are stationary, so data is written on disks in a number of concentric circular *tracks*. Logically, each track is divided into a number of *sectors*, which nowadays almost invariably contain 512 bytes. A single positioning mechanism moves the heads from one track to another, so at any one time all the tracks under the current head position can be accessed without repositioning. This group of tracks is called a *cylinder*.

Since the diameter of the track differs from one track to the other, so does the storage capacity per track. Nevertheless, for the sake of simplicity, older drives, such as ST-506 (MFM and RLL) drives, had a fixed number of sectors per track. To perform a data transfer, you needed to tell the drive which cylinder, head and sector to address. This mode of addressing is thus called *CHS* addressing.

Modern disks have a varying number of sectors per track on different parts of the disk to optimize the storage space, and for the same reason they normally store data on the disk in much larger units than sectors. Externally, they translate the data into units of sectors, and they also optionally maintain the illusion of "tracks" and "heads," though the values have nothing to do with the internal organization of the disk. Nevertheless, BIOS setup routines still give you the option of specifying information about disk drives in terms of the numbers of cylinders, heads and sectors, and some insist on it. In reality, modern disk drives address sectors sequentially, so-called *Logical Block Addressing* or *LBA*. CHS addressing has an additional problem: various standards have limited the size of disks to 504 MB or 8 GB. We'll look at that in more detail on page 39.

SCSI drives are a different matter: the system BIOS normally doesn't know anything about them. They are always addressed in LBA mode. It's up to the host adapter to interrogate the drive and find out how much space is on it. Typically, the host adapter has a BIOS that interrogates the drive and finds its dimensions. The values it determines may not be correct: the PC BIOS 1 GB address limit (see page 39) might bite you. Check your host adapter documentation for details.

Disk partitioning

The PC BIOS divides the space on a disk into up to four *partitions*, headed by a *partition table*. For Microsoft systems, each partition may be either a *primary partition* that contains a file system (a "drive" in Microsoft terminology), or an *extended partition* that contains multiple file systems (or "logical partitions").

FreeBSD does not use the PC BIOS partition table directly. It maintains its own partitioning scheme with its own partition table. On the PC platform, it places this partition table in a single PC BIOS partition, rather in the same way that a PC BIOS extended partition contains multiple "logical partitions." It refers to PC BIOS partitions as "slices."

> This double usage of the word *partition* is really confusing. In this book, I follow BSD usage, but I continue to refer to the PC BIOS partition table by that name.

Partitioning offers the flexibility that other operating systems need, so it has been adopted by all operating systems that run on the PC platform. Figure 2-1 shows a disk with all four slices allocated. The *Partition Table* is the most important data structure. It contains information about the size, location and type of the slices (PC partitions). The PC BIOS allows one of these slices to be designated as *active*: at system startup time, its bootstrap record is used to start the system.

The partition table of a boot disk also contains a *Master Boot Record* (*MBR*), which is responsible for finding the correct slice and booting it. The MBR and the partition table take up the first sector on disk, and many people consider them to be the same thing. You only need an MBR on disks from which you boot the system.

Master Boot Record
Partition Table
Partition (slice) 1   *Idev/da0s1*
Partition (slice) 2   *Idev/da0s2*
Partition (slice) 3   *Idev/da0s3*
Partition (slice) 4   *Idev/da0s4*

Figure 2-1: Partition table

PC usage designates at least one slice as the *primary partition*, the C: drive. Another slice may be designated as an *extended partition* that contains the other "drives" (all together in one slice).

UNIX systems have their own form of partitioning which predates the PC and is not compatible with the PC method. As a result, all versions of UNIX that can coexist with Microsoft implement their own partitioning within a single slice (PC BIOS partition). This is conceptually similar to an extended partition. FreeBSD systems define up to eight partitions per slice. They can be used for the following purposes:

- A partition can be a *file system*, a structure in which UNIX stores files.

- It can be used as a *swap partition*. FreeBSD uses virtual memory: the total addressed memory in the system can exceed the size of physical memory, so we need space on disk to store memory pages that don't fit into physical memory. Swap is a separate partition for performance reasons: you can use files for swap, like Microsoft does, but it is much less efficient.

- The partition may be used by other system components. For example, the *Vinum* volume manager uses special partitions as building blocks for volumes. We'll look at Vinum on page 221.

- The partition may not be a real partition at all. For example, partition c refers to the entire slice, so it overlaps all the rest. For obvious reasons, the partitions that represent file systems and swap space (a, b, and d through h) should not overlap.

Block and character devices

Traditional UNIX treats disk devices in two different ways. As we have seen, you can think of a disk as a large number of sequential blocks of data. Looking at it like this doesn't give you a file system—it's more like treating it as a tape. UNIX calls this kind of access *raw* access. You'll also hear the term *character device*.

Normally, of course, you want files on your disk: you don't care where they are, you just want to be able to open them and manipulate them. In addition, for performance reasons the system keeps recently accessed data in a *buffer cache*. This involves a whole lot more work than raw devices. These devices are called *block devices*.

By contrast with UNIX, Linux originally did not have character disk devices. Starting with Release 4.0, FreeBSD has taken the opposite approach: there are now no user-accessible block devices any more. There are a number of reasons for this:

- Having two different names for devices is confusing. In older releases of FreeBSD, you could recognize block and character devices in an `ls -l` listing by the letters `b` and `c` at the beginning of the permissions. For example, in FreeBSD 3.1 you might have seen:

  ```
  $ ls -l /dev/rwd0s1a   /dev/wd0s1a
  crw-r-----  1 root  operator    3, 131072 Oct 31 19:59 /dev/rwd0s1a
  brw-r-----  1 root  operator    0, 131072 Oct 31 19:59 /dev/wd0s1a
  ```

  wd is the old name for the current *ad* disks. The question is: when do you use which one? Even compared to UNIX System V, the rules were different.

- Nearly all access to disk goes via the file system, and user-accessible block devices add complication.

- If you write to a block device, you don't automatically write to the disk, only into buffer cache. The system decides when to write to disk. If there's a problem writing to disk, there's no way to notify the program that performed the write: it might even already have finished. You can demonstrate this very effectively by comparing the way FreeBSD and Linux write to a floppy disk. It takes 50 seconds to write a complete floppy disk—the speed is determined by the hardware, so the FreeBSD copy program finishes after 50 seconds. With Linux, though, the program runs only for a second or two, after which it finishes and you get your prompt back. In the meantime, the system flushes the data to floppy: you still need to wait a total of 50 seconds. If you remove the floppy in this time, you obviously lose data.

The removal of block devices caused significant changes to device naming. In older releases of FreeBSD, the device name was the name of the block device, and the raw (character) device had the letter `r` at the beginning of the name, as shown in the example above.

Let's look more carefully at how BSD names its partitions:

- Like all other devices, the *device nodes*, the entries that describe the devices, are stored in the directory */dev*. Unlike traditional UNIX and older releases of FreeBSD, FreeBSD Release 5 includes the *device file system* or *devfs*, which creates the device nodes automatically, so you don't need to worry about creating them yourself.

- Next comes the name of the driver. As we have seen, FreeBSD has drivers for IDE and friends (`ad`), SCSI disks (`da`) and floppy disks (`fd`). For SCSI disks, we now have the name */dev/da*.

The original releases of FreeBSD had the abbreviation wd for IDE drives. This abbreviation arose because the most popular of the original MFM controllers were made by Western Digital. Others claim, however, that it's an abbreviation for "Winchester Disk." SCSI disks were originally abbreviated sd. The name da comes from the CAM standard and is short for *direct access*. BSD/OS, NetBSD and OpenBSD still use the old names.

- Next comes the unit number, generally a single digit. For example, the first SCSI disk on the system would normally be called */dev/da0*.

    Generally, the numbers are assigned during the boot probes, but you can reserve numbers for SCSI disks if you want. This prevents the removal of a single disk from changing the numbers of all subsequent drives. See page 574 for more details.

- Next comes the partition information. The so-called *strict slice name* is specified by adding the letter s (for *slice*) and the slice number (1 to 4) to the disk name. BSD systems name partitions by appending the letters a to h to the disk name. Thus, the first partition of the first slice of our disk above (which would typically be a root file system) would be called */dev/da0s1a*.

    Some other versions of BSD do not have the same support for slices, so they use a simpler terminology for the partition name. Instead of calling the root file system */dev/da0s1a*, they refer to it as */dev/da0a*. FreeBSD supports this method as well— it's called *compatibility slice naming*. The compatibility slice is simply the first FreeBSD slice found on the disk, and the partitions in this slice have two different names, for example */dev/ad0s1a* and */dev/ad0a*.

- Partition c is an exception: by convention, it represents the whole BSD disk (in this case, the slice in which FreeBSD resides).

- In addition, NetBSD reserves partition d for the entire disk, including other partitions. FreeBSD no longer assigns any special significance to partition d.

Figure 2-2 shows a typical layout on a system with a single SCSI disk, shared between Microsoft and FreeBSD. You'll note that partition */dev/da0s3c* is missing from the FreeBSD slice, since it isn't a real partition. Like the PC BIOS partition table, the disk label contains information necessary for FreeBSD to manage the FreeBSD slice, such as the location and the lengths of the individual partitions. The bootstrap is used to load the kernel into memory. We'll look at the boot process in more detail in Chapter 29.

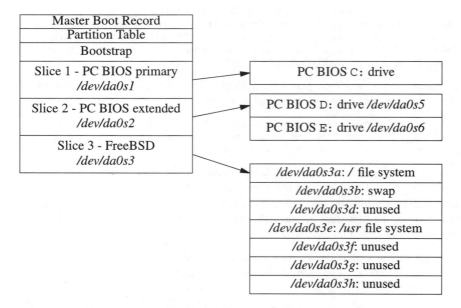

Figure 2-2: Partition table with FreeBSD file system

Table 2-1 gives you an overview of the devices that FreeBSD defines for this disk.

Table 2-1: Disk partition terminology

Slice name	Usage
/dev/da0s1	First slice (PC BIOS C: partition)
/dev/da0s2	Second slice (PC BIOS extended partition)
/dev/da0s3	Third slice (PC BIOS partition), FreeBSD
/dev/da0s5	First drive in extended PC BIOS partition (D:)
/dev/da0s6	Second drive in extended PC BIOS partition (E:)
/dev/da0s3a	Third slice (PC BIOS partition), partition a (root file system)
/dev/da0s3b	Third slice (PC BIOS partition), partition b (swap space)
/dev/da0s3c	Third slice (PC BIOS partition), entire partition
/dev/da0s3e	Third slice (PC BIOS partition), partition e (*usr* file system)
/dev/da0a	Compatibility partition, root file system, same as */dev/da0s1a*
/dev/da0b	Compatibility partition, swap partition, same as */dev/da0s1b*
/dev/da0c	Whole BSD slice, same as */dev/da0s1c*
/dev/da0e	Compatibility partition, *usr* file system, same as */dev/da0s1e*

Making the file systems

Armed with this knowledge, we can now proceed to make some decisions about how to install our systems. First, we need to answer some questions:

- Do we want to share this disk with any other operating system?

- If so, do we have data on this disk that we want to keep?

If you already have another system installed on the disk, it is best to use that system's tools for manipulating the partition table. FreeBSD does not normally have difficulty with partition tables created by other systems, so you can be reasonably sure that the other system will understand what it has left. If the other system is Microsoft, and you have a slice that you don't need, use the MS-DOS *FDISK* program to free up enough space to install FreeBSD. If you don't have a slice to delete, you can use the *FIPS* program to create one—see Chapter 5, *Installing FreeBSD*, page 52.

If for some reason you can't use MS-DOS *FDISK*, for example because you're installing FreeBSD by itself, FreeBSD also supplies a program called *fdisk* that manipulates the partition table. Normally you invoke it indirectly via the *sysinstall* program—see page 63.

Disk size limitations

Disk storage capacity has grown by several orders of magnitude since FreeBSD was first released. As it did so, a number of limits became apparent:

- The first was the BIOS *504 MB limit* on IDE disks, imposed by their similarity with ST-506 disks. We discussed this on page 32. FreeBSD works around this issue by using a loader that understands large disks, so this limit is a thing of the past.

- The next limit was the 1 GB limit, which affected some older SCSI host adapters. Although SCSI drives always use LBA addressing internally, the BIOS needed to simulate CHS addressing for Microsoft. Early BIOSes were limited to 64 heads, 32 sectors and 1024 tracks ($64 \times 32 \times 1024 \times 512 = 1$ GB). This wouldn't be such a problem, except that some old Adaptec controllers offer a 1 GB compatibility option. Don't use it: it's only needed for systems that were installed with the old mapping.

- After that, it's logical that the next limit should come at 2 GB. There are several different problems here. The only one that affects FreeBSD appears to be a bug in some IDE controllers, which don't work beyond this limit. All of them are old, and IDE controllers don't cost anything, so if you are sure you have this problem, you can solve it by replacing the controller. Make sure you get one that supports DMA.

  Other systems, including many versions of UNIX System V, have problems with this limit because 2^{31} is the largest number that can be represented in a 32 bit signed integer. FreeBSD does not have this limitation, as file sizes are represented in 64 bit quantities.

- At 4 GB, some IDE controllers have problems because they convert this to a CHS mapping with 256 heads, which doesn't work: the largest number is 255. Again, if you're sure this is the cause of problems you may be having, a new controller can help.

- At 8 GB the CHS system runs out of steam. It can't describe more than 1024 cylinders, 255 heads or 63 sectors. Beyond this size, you must use LBA addressing—if your BIOS supports it.

- You'd expect more problems at 16 GB, but in fact the next limitation doesn't come until 128 GB. It's due to the limitations in the original LBA scheme, which had only 28 bits of sector address. The new standard extends this to 48 bits, which should be sufficient for the next few years. FreeBSD already uses the new standard, so this limitation has never been an issue.

None of these problems affect FreeBSD directly. The FreeBSD bootstrap no longer uses the system BIOS, so it is not bound by the restrictions of the BIOS and the controller. If you use another operating system's loader, however, you could have problems. If you have the choice, use LBA addressing. Unfortunately, you can't do so if the disk already contains software that uses CHS addressing.

Other things to consider are:

- If you have other software already installed on the disk, and you want to keep it, *do not change the drive geometry*. If you do so, you will no longer be able to run the other software.

- Use LBA addressing if your hardware supports it.

- If you have to use CHS, and you don't have any other software on the drive, use the drive geometry specified on the disk itself or in the manual, if you're lucky enough to get a manual with the disk. Many BIOSes remap the drive geometry in order to get Microsoft to agree to work with the disk, but this can break FreeBSD disk mapping. Check that the partition editor has these values, and change them if necessary.

- If all else fails, install Microsoft in a small slice at the start of the disk. This creates a valid partition table for the drive, and the installation software understands it. Once you have started the installation process, the Microsoft partition has fulfilled its purpose, and you can delete it again.

Display hardware

For years, UNIX users have worked with a single 80x25 character mode display. Many people consider this extremely old-fashioned, but in fact the flexibility of the UNIX system made this quite a good way to work. Still, there's no doubt of the advantage of a system that offers the possibility of performing multiple operations at once, and this is one of the particular advantages of UNIX. But you normally need a terminal to interact with each task. The best way to do this is with the X Window System. You might also want to use a *desktop*, a set of programs that offer commonly used functionality.

In many other environments, the GUI and the graphical display are the same thing, and in some systems, notably Microsoft, there is no clear distinction between the operating system and the GUI. In UNIX, there are at least four levels of abstraction:

- The kernel runs the computer.

- X interfaces with the kernel and runs the display. It doesn't display anything itself except possibly a display background, by default a grey cross-hatch pattern.

- The *window manager* gives you control over the windows, such as moving, resizing and *iconification* (often called *minimizing* in other systems). It provides the windows with *decorations* like frames, buttons and menus.

- The *desktop* provides commonly used applications and ways of starting them. Many people get by without a desktop by using window manager functionality.

Why do it this way? Because it gives you more choice. There are dozens of window managers available, and also several desktops. You're not locked in to a single product. This has its down side, though: you must make the choice, and so setting up X requires a little more thought than installing Microsoft.

The hardware

X runs on almost any hardware. That doesn't mean that all hardware is equal, of course. Here are some considerations:

The keyboard

X uses the keyboard a lot more than Microsoft. Make sure you get a good one.

The mouse

X prefers a three-button mouse, though it has provisions for up to five buttons. It can support newer mice with rollers and side buttons, but most software does not use them. Some mice, such as the Logitech wireless mouse, require undocumented sequences to enable some buttons (the thumb button in the case of Logitech). X does not support this button.

Get the best mouse you can. Prefer a short, light switch. It *must* have at least three buttons. Accept no substitutes. Look for one with an easy-to-use middle button. Frequently mice with both a middle button and a roller make it difficult to use the middle button: it's either misplaced, too heavy in action, or requires pressing on the roller (and thus possibly turning it). All of these prove to be a nuisance over time.

Older mice connected via the serial port or a special card ("bus mouse"). Nowadays most mice are so-called PS/2 mice, and USB mice are becoming more popular.

The display board and monitor

X enables you to do a lot more in parallel than other windowing environments. As a result, screen real estate is at a premium. Use as big a monitor as you can afford, and as high a resolution as your monitor can handle. You should be able to display a resolution of 1600x1200 on a 21" monitor, 1280x1024 on a 17" monitor, and 1024x768 on a 14" monitor. Premium quality 21" monitors can display 2048x1536. If that's not enough, we'll look at multiple monitor configurations on page 523.

Laptop hardware

If you have a laptop, you don't get any choice. The display has a native resolution which you can't change. Most laptops display lower resolutions by interpolation, but the result looks much worse than the native resolution. LCD screens look crisper than CRT monitors, so you can choose higher resolutions—modern laptops have display resolutions of up to 1600x1200.

If you're going to use your laptop for presentations with overhead projectors, make sure you find one that can display both on the internal screen and also on the external output at the same time, while maintaining a display resolution of 1024x768: not many overhead projectors can display at a higher resolution.

Compaq/Digital Alpha machines

FreeBSD also supports computers based on the Compaq (previously Digital) *AXP* processor, commonly called *Alpha*. Much of the information above also applies to the Alpha; notable exceptions are:

- Much of the PC hardware mentioned above was never supplied with the Alpha. This applies particularly to older hardware.

- The PC BIOS is very different from the Alpha console firmware. We'll look at that below.

- Disk partitioning is different. FreeBSD does not support multiple operating systems on the Alpha platform.

In this section we'll look at some additional topics that only apply to the Alpha.

FreeBSD requires the *SRM* console firmware, which is used by *Tru64* (formerly known as *Digital UNIX*). It does not work with the ARC firmware (sometimes called AlphaBIOS) used with Microsoft NT. The SRM firmware runs the machine in 64 bit mode, which is required to run FreeBSD, while the *ARC* firmware sets 32 bit mode. If your system is currently running Tru64, you should be able to use the existing SRM console.

The SRM console commands differ from one version to another. The commands supported by your version are described in the hardware manual that was shipped with your system. The console `help` command lists all supported console commands. If your system has been set to boot automatically, you must type **Ctrl-C** to interrupt the boot process and get to the SRM console prompt (>>>). If the system is not set to boot automatically, it displays the SRM console prompt after performing system checks.

All SRM console versions support the set and show commands, which operate on environment variables that are stored in non-volatile memory. The show command lists all environment variables, including those that are read-only.

Alpha's SRM is picky about which hardware it supports. For example, it recognizes NCR SCSI boards, but it doesn't recognize Adaptec boards. There are reports of some Alphas not booting with particular video boards. The GENERIC kernel configuration (*/usr/src/sys/alpha/conf/GENERIC*) shows what the kernel supports, but that doesn't mean that the SRM supports all the devices. In addition, the SRM support varies from one machine to the next, so there's a danger that what's described here won't work for you.

Other differences for Alpha include:

- The disk layout for SRM is different from the layout for Microsoft NT. SRM looks for its bootstrap where Microsoft keeps its partition table. This means that you cannot share a disk between FreeBSD and Microsoft on an Alpha.

- Most SRM-based Alpha machines don't support IDE drives: you're limited to SCSI.

The CD-ROM distribution

The easiest way to install FreeBSD is from CD-ROM. You can buy them at a discount with the order form at the back of the book, or you can download an *ISO image* from *ftp.FreeBSD.org* and create your own CD-ROM. There are a number of CD-ROMs in a FreeBSD distribution, but the only essential one is the first one, the *Installation* CD-ROM. It contains everything you need to install the system itself. The other CD-ROMs contain mainly installable packages. Individual releases may contain other data, such as a copy of the source code repository. We'll take a more detailed look at the installation CD-ROM here.

Installation CD-ROM

The Installation CD-ROM contains everything you need to install FreeBSD on your system. It supplies two categories of installable software:

- The base operating system is stored as *gzip*ped *tar* archives in the directories *base*, *boot*, *catpages*, *compat1x*, *compat20*, *compat21*, *compat3x*, *compat4x*, *des*, *dict*, *doc*, *games*, *info*, *manpages* and *proflibs*. To facilitate transport to and installation from floppy, the archives have been divided into chunks of 1.44 MB. For example, the only required set is in the files *base/base.??*, in other words, all files whose names start with *base.* and contain two additional characters. This specifically excludes the files *base.inf* and *base.mtree*, which are not part of the archive.

- The directory *packages/All* contains ported, installable software packages as *gzip*ped *tar* archives. They are designed to be installed directly on a running system, so they have not been divided into chunks. Due to size restrictions on the CD-ROM, this directory does not contain all the packages: others are on additional CD-ROMs.

packages/Latest contains the latest versions of the packages.

packages/All contains a large subset of the Ports Collection. To make it easier for you to find your way around them, symbolic links to appropriate packages have been placed in the directories *archivers, astro, audio, benchmarks, biology, cad, chinese, comms, converters, databases, deskutils, devel, editors, emulators, french, ftp, games, german, graphics, hebrew, irc, japanese, java, korean, lang, mail, math, mbone, misc, net, news, palm, picobsd, plan9, print, russian, science, security, shells, sysutils, templates, textproc, ukrainian, vietnamese, www, x11, x11-clocks, x11-fm, x11-fonts, x11-servers, x11-toolkits* and *x11-wm*. Don't get the impression that these are different packages—they are really pointers to the packages in *All*. You will find a list of the currently available packages in the file *packages/INDEX*.

We'll look at the Ports Collection in more detail in Chapter 9.

Table 2-2 lists typical files in the main directory of the installation CD-ROM.

Table 2-2: The installation CD-ROM

File	Contents
ERRATA.TXT	A list of last-minute changes. ***Read this file. It can save you a lot of headaches***.
HARDWARE.TXT	A list of supported hardware.
INSTALL.TXT	Information about installing FreeBSD.
README.TXT	The traditional first file to read. It describes how to use the other files.
RELNOTES.TXT	Release notes.
base	Installation directory: the base distribution of the system. This is the only required directory for installation. See Chapter 5, *Installing FreeBSD*, for more detail.
boot	Files related to booting, including the installation kernel.
catpages	Pre-formatted man pages. See page 13 for more detail.
cdrom.inf	Machine-readable file describing the CD-ROM contents for the benefit of *sysinstall*.
compat1x	Directory containing libraries to maintain compatibility with Release 1.X of FreeBSD.

File	Contents
compat20	Directory containing libraries to maintain compatibility with Release 2.0 of FreeBSD.
compat21	Directory containing libraries to maintain compatibility with Release 2.1 of FreeBSD.
compat22	Directory containing libraries to maintain compatibility with Release 2.2 of FreeBSD.
compat3x	Directory containing libraries to maintain compatibility with Release 3 of FreeBSD.
compat4x	Directory containing libraries to maintain compatibility with Release 4 of FreeBSD.
crypto	Installation directory: cryptographic software.
dict	Installation directory: dictionaries.
doc	Installation directory: documentation.
docbook.css	Style sheet for documentation.
filename.txt	A list of all the files on this CD-ROM.
floppies	A directory containing installation floppy disk images.
games	Installation directory: games.
info	Installation directory: GNU info documents.
kernel	The boot kernel.
manpages	A directory containing the man pages for installation.
packages	A directory containing installable versions of the Ports Collection. See page 168.
ports	The sources for the Ports Collection. See Chapter 9, *The Ports Collection*, page 167.
proflibs	A directory containing profiled libraries, useful for identifying performance problems when programming.
src	A directory containing the system source files.
tools	A directory containing tools to prepare for installation from another operating system.

The *.TXT* files are also supplied in HTML format with a *.HTM* suffix.

The contents of the CD-ROM will almost certainly change from one release to another. Read *README.TXT* for details of the changes.

Live File System CD-ROM

Although the installation CD-ROM contains everything you need to install FreeBSD, the format isn't what you'd like to handle every day. The distribution may include a *Live File System* CD-ROM, which solves this problem: it contains substantially the same data stored in file system format in much the same way as you would install it on a hard disk. You can access the files directly from this CD-ROM.

CVS Repository CD-ROM

One of the disks may also contain the "CVS Repository." The repository is the master source tree of all source code, including all update information. We'll look at it in more detail in Chapter 31, *Keeping up to date*, page 581.

The Ports Collection CD-ROMs

An important part of FreeBSD is the *Ports Collection*, which comprises many thousand popular programs. The Ports Collection automates the process of porting software to FreeBSD. A combination of various programming tools already available in the base FreeBSD installation allows you to simply type *make* to install a given package. The ports mechanism does the rest, so you need only enough disk space to build the ports you want. We'll look at the Ports Collection in more detail in Chapter 9. The files are spread over a number of CD-ROMs:

- You'll find the *ports*, the instructions for building the packages, on the installation CD-ROM.

- The base sources for the Ports Collection fill more than one CD-ROM, even though copyright restrictions mean that not all sources may be included: some source files are freely distributable on the Net, but may not be distributed on CD-ROM.

  Don't worry about the missing sources: if you're connected to the Internet, the Ports Collection automatically retrieves the sources from an Internet server when you type *make*.

- You'll find the most popular *packages*, the precompiled binaries of the ports, on the Installation CD-ROM. A full distribution contains a number of other CD-ROMs with most of the remaining packages.

In this chapter:
- *Making things easy for yourself*
- *FreeBSD on a disk with free space*
- *FreeBSD shared with Microsoft*
- *Configuring XFree86*

3

Quick installation

In Chapters 4 to 6 we'll go into a lot of detail about how to install the system. Maybe this is too much detail for you. If you're an experienced UNIX user, you should be able to get by with significantly less reading. This chapter presents checklists for some of the more usual kinds of installation. Each refers you to the corresponding detailed descriptions in Chapters 4 through 6.

On the following pages we'll look at the simplest installation, where FreeBSD is the only system on the disk. Starting on page 49 we'll look at sharing the disk with Microsoft, and on page 50 we'll look at how to install XFree86. You may find it convenient to photocopy these pages and to mark them up as you go along.

Making things easy for yourself

It is probably easier to install FreeBSD than any other PC operating system, including Microsoft products. Well, most of the time, anyway. Some people spend days trying to install FreeBSD, and finally give up. That happens with Microsoft's products as well, but unfortunately it happens more often with FreeBSD.

Now you're probably saying, "That doesn't make sense. First you say it's easier to install, then you say it's more likely to fail. What's the real story?"

As you might expect, the real story is quite involved. In Chapter 2, *Before you install*, I went into some of the background. Before you start, let's look at what you can do to make the installation as easy as possible:

- Use known, established hardware. New hardware products frequently have undocumented problems. You can be sure that they work under Microsoft, because the manufacturer has tested them in that environment. In all probability, he hasn't tested them under any flavour of UNIX, let alone FreeBSD. Usually the problems aren't serious, and the FreeBSD team solves them pretty quickly, but if you get the hardware before the software is ready, you're the guinea pig.

  At the other end of the scale, you can have more trouble with old hardware as well. It's not as easy to configure, and old hardware is not as well supported as more recent hardware.

- Perform a standard installation. The easiest way to install FreeBSD is by booting from a CD-ROM and installing on an empty hard disk from the CD-ROM. If you proceed as discussed in Chapter 5, *Installing FreeBSD*, you shouldn't have any difficulty.

- If you need to share your hard disk with another operating system, it's easier to install both systems from scratch. If you do already have a Microsoft system on the disk, you can use *FIPS* (see page 52) to make space for it, but this requires more care.

- If you run into trouble, *RTFM*.[1] I've gone to a lot of trouble to anticipate the problems you might encounter, and there's a good chance that you will find something here to help.

- If you do all this, and it still doesn't work, see page 17 for ways of getting external help.

FreeBSD on a disk with free space

This procedure applies if you can install FreeBSD without first having to make space on disk. Perform the following steps:

☐ Boot from CD-ROM. Most systems support booting from CD-ROM, but if yours doesn't:

- Create two boot floppies by copying the images */cdrom/floppies/kern.flp* and */cdrom/floppies/mfsroot.flp* to 3½" diskettes. Refer to page 89 for more details.

- Insert the CD-ROM in the drive before booting.

- Boot from the *kern.flp* floppy. After loading, insert the *mfsroot.flp* floppy when the system prompts you to do so, then press **Enter**.

  If you have a larger floppy, such as 2.88 MB or LS-120, you can copy the image */cdrom/floppies/boot.flp* to it and boot from it. In this case you don't need to change disks.

---

1. Hackerspeak for "Read The Manual"—the **F** is usually silent.

☐ Select the Custom installation. Refer to page 60.

☐ What you do in the partition editor depends on whether you want to share the drive with another operating system or not:

    • If you want to use the drive only for FreeBSD, delete any existing slices, and allocate a single FreeBSD slice that takes up the entire disk. On exiting from the partition editor, select the *Standard* MBR. Refer to page 66.

    • If you want to share the disk with other systems, delete any unwanted slices and use them for FreeBSD. On exiting from the partition editor, select the *BootMgr* MBR. Refer to page 66.

☐ In the disk label editor, delete any existing UNIX partitions. Create the file systems manually. If you don't have any favourite layout, create a root file system with 4 GB, a swap partition with at least 512 MB (make sure it's at least 1 MB larger than the maximum memory you intend to install in your system). Allocate a */home* file system as large as you like, as long as it can fit on a single tape when backed up. If you have any additional space, leave it empty unless you know what to use it for. See page 68 for the rationale of this approach, which is not what *sysinstall* recommends.

☐ Install the complete system, including X and the Ports Collection. This requires about 1 GB of disk space. Refer to page 75 if you want to limit it.

☐ Select CD-ROM as installation medium. Refer to page 76.

☐ Give final confirmation. The system will be installed. Refer to page 77.

☐ After installation, set up at least a user ID for yourself. Refer to page 144.

FreeBSD shared with Microsoft

If you have a disk with Microsoft installed on only part of the disk, and you don't want to change the partition layout, you can proceed as in the instructions above. This is pretty unusual, though: normally Microsoft takes the whole disk, and it's difficult to persuade it otherwise. To install FreeBSD on a disk that currently contains a single Microsoft partition taking up the entire disk, go through the following steps:

☐ *Make a backup!* There's every possibility of erasing your data, and there's absolutely no reason why you should take the risk.

☐ If you have an old machine with an IDE disk larger than 504 MB, you may run into problems. Refer to page 32 for further details.

☐ Boot Microsoft and repartition your disk with *FIPS*. Refer to page 52.

☐ Insert the CD-ROM in the drive before booting.

□ Shut the machine down and reboot from the FreeBSD CD-ROM. If you have to boot from floppy, see page 48 for details.

□ Select the Custom installation.

□ In the partition editor, delete *only the second primary Microsoft partition*. The first primary Microsoft partition contains your Microsoft data, and if there is an extended Microsoft partition, it will also contain your Microsoft data.

□ Create a FreeBSD slice in the space that has been freed. Refer to page 63.

□ On exiting from the partition editor, select the *BootMgr* MBR. Refer to page 66.

□ In the disk label editor, delete any existing UNIX partitions. Create the file systems manually. If you don't have any favourite layout, create a root file system with 4 GB, a swap partition with at least 512 MB (make sure it's at least 1 MB larger than the maximum memory you intend to install in your system). Allocate a */home* file system as large as you like, as long as it can fit on a single tape when backed up. If you have any additional space, leave it empty unless you know what to use it for. See page 68 for the rationale of this approach, which is not what *sysinstall* recommends.

□ Before leaving the disk label editor, also select mount points for your DOS partitions if you intend to mount them under FreeBSD. Refer to page 74.

□ Install the complete system, including X and the Ports Collection. This requires about 1 GB of disk space. Refer to page 75 if you want to limit it.

□ Select CD-ROM as installation medium. Refer to page 76.

□ Give final confirmation. The system will be installed. Refer to page 77.

□ After installation, set up at least a user ID for yourself. Refer to page 144.

Configuring XFree86

You can configure XFree86 during installation or after reboot.

□ Make sure your mouse is connected to the system at boot time. Depending on the hardware, if you connect it later, it may not be recognized.

□ If you have already rebooted the machine, log in as root and restart *sysinstall*.

□ Select the *sysinstall* Configuration menu, XFree86 and then xf86cfg, and follow the instructions. See page 102 for further details.

□ Select the Desktop menu and install the window manager of your choice. See page 108 for further discussion.

In this chapter:
- Separate disks
- Sharing a disk
- Sharing with Linux or another BSD
- Repartitioning with FIPS

4

Shared OS installation

In many cases, you won't want to install FreeBSD on the system by itself: you may need to use other operating systems as well. In this chapter, we'll look at what you need to do to prepare for such an installation. If you're only running FreeBSD on the machine, you don't need to read this chapter, and you can move on to Chapter 5, *Installing FreeBSD*.

> ***Before you start the installation, read this chapter carefully. It's easy to make a mistake, and one of the most frequent results of mistakes is the total loss of all data on the hard disk.***

Currently, only the ia32 (Intel) port of FreeBSD is capable of sharing with other operating systems. We'll concentrate on how to share your system with Microsoft, because that's both the most difficult and the most common, but most of this chapter applies to other operating systems as well. You may want to refer to the discussion of Microsoft and FreeBSD disk layouts on page 34.

Separate disks

The first question is: do you need to share a disk between FreeBSD and the other operating system? It's **much** easier if you don't have to. In this section, we'll look at what you need to do.

Many operating systems will only boot from the first disk identified by the BIOS, usually called the C: disk in deference to Microsoft. FreeBSD doesn't have this problem, so the easiest thing is to install FreeBSD on the entire second disk. BIOS restrictions usually make it difficult to boot from any but the first two disks.

In this case, you don't really need to do anything special, although it's always a good idea to back up your data first. Install FreeBSD on the second disk, and choose the *Boot Manager* option in the partition editor (page 64). This will then give you the choice of booting from the first or second disk. Note that you should not change the order of disks after such an installation; if you do, the system will not be able to find its file systems after boot.

Sharing a disk

If you intend to share a disk between FreeBSD and another operating system, the first question is: is there enough space on the disk for FreeBSD? How much you need depends on what you want to do with FreeBSD, of course, but for the sake of example we'll take 120 MB as an absolute minimum. In the following section, we'll consider what to do if you need to change your partitions. If you already have enough space for a FreeBSD partition (for example, if you have just installed Microsoft specifically for sharing with FreeBSD, and thus have not filled up the disk), continue reading on page 66.

Sharing with Linux or another BSD

Sharing with other free operating systems is relatively simple. You still need to have space for FreeBSD, of course, and unlike Microsoft, there are no tools for shrinking Linux or BSD file systems: you'll have to remove them or recreate them. You can find some information about sharing with Linux in the mini-Howto at *http://www.linux.org/docs/ldp/howto/mini/Linux+FreeBSD.html*.

NetBSD and OpenBSD file systems and slices are very similar to their FreeBSD counterparts. They're not identical, however, and you may find that one of the systems recognizes the partition of another system and complains about it because it's not quite right. For example, NetBSD has a *d* partition that can go outside the boundary of the slice. FreeBSD does not allow this, so you get a harmless error message.

Repartitioning with FIPS

Typically, if you've been running Microsoft on your machine, it will occupy the entire disk. If you need all this space, of course, there's no way to install another operating system as well. Frequently, though, you'll find that you have enough free space in the partition. Unfortunately, that's not where you want it: you want the space in a new partition. There are a number of ways to do so:

- You can reinstall the software. This approach is common in the Microsoft world, but FreeBSD users try to avoid it.

- You can use *FIPS* to shrink a Microsoft partition, leaving space for FreeBSD. *FIPS* is a public domain utility, and it is included on the FreeBSD CD-ROM.

- If you can't use *FIPS*, use a commercial utility like *PartitionMagic*. This is not included on the CD-ROMs, and we won't discuss it further.

In the rest of the section, we'll look at how to shrink a partition with *FIPS*. If you do it with PartitionMagic, the details are different, but the principles are the same. In particular:

Before repartitioning your disk, make a backup. You can shoot yourself in the foot with this method, and the result will almost invariably be loss of data.

If you've been running Microsoft on your system for any length of time, the data in the partition will be spread all around the partition. If you just truncate the partition, you'll lose a lot of data, so you first need to move all the data to the beginning of the partition. Do this with the Microsoft defragmentation utility. Before proceeding, consider a few gotchas:

- The new Microsoft partition needs to be big enough to hold not only the current data, but also anything you will want to put in it in the future. If you make it exactly the current size of the data, it will effectively be full, and you won't be able to write anything to it.

- The second partition is also a Microsoft partition. To install FreeBSD on it, you need to convert it into a FreeBSD partition.

- *FIPS* may result in configuration problems with your Microsoft machine. Since it adds a partition, any automatically assigned partitions that follow will have a different drive letter. In particular, this could mean that your CD-ROM drive will "move." After you delete the second Microsoft partition and change it into a FreeBSD partition, it will "move" back again.

For further information, read the *FIPS* documentation in */cdrom/tools/fips.doc*. In particular, note these limitations:

- *FIPS* works only with Hard Disk BIOSes that use interrupt 0x13 for low-level hard disk access. This is generally not a problem.

- *FIPS* does not split partitions with 12 bit FATs, which were used by older versions of Microsoft. These are less than 10 MB in size and thus too small to be worth splitting.

- *FIPS* splits only Microsoft partitions. The partition table and boot sector must conform to the MS-DOS 3.0+ or Windows 95 conventions. This is marked by the system indicator byte in the partition table, which must have the value 4 (16 bit sector number) or 6 (32 bit sector number). In particular, it will *not* split Linux or Windows 2000 and later partitions.

- *FIPS* does not yet work on extended Microsoft partitions.

- *FIPS* needs a free partition entry. It will not work if you already have four partitions.

- *FIPS* will not reduce the original partition to a size of less than 4085 clusters, because this would involve rewriting the 16 bit FAT to a 12 bit FAT.

Repartitioning—an example

In this section, we'll go through the mechanics of repartitioning a disk. We'll start with a disk containing a single, complete Microsoft system.

First, run the Microsoft error check utility on the partition you want to split. Make sure no "dead" clusters remain on the disk.

Next, prepare a bootable floppy. When you start *FIPS*, you will be given the opportunity to write backup copies of your root and boot sector to a file on drive A:. These will be called *ROOTBOOT.00x*, where *x* represents a digit from 0 to 9. If anything goes wrong while using *FIPS*, you can restore the original configuration by booting from the floppy and running *RESTORRB*.

> If you use *FIPS* more than once (this is normally not necessary, but it might happen), your floppy will contain more than one *ROOTBOOT* file. *RESTORRB* lets you choose which configuration file to restore. The file *RESTORRB.000* contains your original configuration. Try not to confuse the versions.

Before starting *FIPS* you *must* defragment your disk to ensure that the space to be used for the new partition is free. If you're using programs like *IMAGE* or *MIRROR*, note that they store a hidden system file with a pointer to your mirror files in the last sector of the hard disk. You *must* delete this file before using *FIPS*. It will be recreated the next time you run *MIRROR*. To delete it, in the root directory enter:

```
C\:> attrib -r -s -h image.idx        for IMAGE
C\:> attrib -r -s -h mirorsav.fil     for MIRROR
```

Then delete the file.

If *FIPS* does not offer as much disk space for creation of the new partition as you expect, this may mean that:

- You still have too much data in the remaining partition. Consider making the new partition smaller or deleting some of the data. If you delete data, you must defragment and run *FIPS* again.

- There are hidden files in the space of the new partition that have not been moved by the defragmentation program. Make sure which program they belong to. If a file is a swap file of some program (for example NDOS) it is possible that it can be safely deleted (and will be recreated automatically later when the need arises). See your manual for details.

If the file belongs to some sort of copy protection, you must uninstall the program to which it belongs and reinstall it after repartitioning.

If you are running early versions of MS-DOS (before 5.0), or another operating system, such OS/2, or you are using programs like Stacker, SuperStor, or Doublespace, read the FIPS documentation for other possible problems.

Running FIPS

After defragmenting your Microsoft partition, you can run *FIPS*:

```
C:\> D:                              change to CD-ROM
D:\> cd \tools                       make sure you're in the tools directory
D:\tools\> fips                      and start the FIPS program
... a lot of copyright information omitted
Press any key
Which Drive (1=0x80/2=0x81)?         do what the computer says
```

The message *Which Drive* may seem confusing. It refers to BIOS internal numbering. Don't worry about it: if you want to partition the first physical drive in the system, (C:), enter 1, otherwise enter 2. Like the BIOS, *FIPS* handles only two hard disks.

If you start *FIPS* under Windows, it will complain and tell you to boot from a floppy disk. It won't stop you from continuing, but it is a Bad Idea to do so.

Next, *FIPS* reads the root sector of the hard disk and displays the partition table:

Part.	bootable	Start Head	Cyl.	Sector	System	End Head	Cyl.	Sector	Start Sector	Number of Sectors	MB
1	yes	1	0	1	0ch	239	2047	63	63	40083057	19571
2	no	0	0	0	00h	0	0	0	0	0	0
3	no	0	0	0	00h	0	0	0	0	0	0
4	no	0	0	0	00h	0	0	0	0	0	0

This shows that only the first partition is occupied, that it is bootable, and that it occupies the whole disk (19571 MB, from Cylinder 0, Head 1, Sector 1 to Cylinder 2047, Head 238, Sector 63). It also claims that this makes 40083057 sectors. It doesn't: the cylinder number has been truncated, and *FIPS* complains about a partition table inconsistency, which it fixes. After this, we have:

Part.	bootable	Start Head	Cyl.	Sector	System	End Head	Cyl.	Sector	Start Sector	Number of Sectors	MB
1	yes	1	0	1	0ch	239	**2650**	63	63	40083057	19571
2	no	0	0	0	00h	0	0	0	0	0	0
3	no	0	0	0	00h	0	0	0	0	0	0
4	no	0	0	0	00h	0	0	0	0	0	0

Don't worry about the "bootable" flag here—we'll deal with that in the FreeBSD installation. First, *FIPS* does some error checking and then reads and displays the boot sector of the partition:

```
Checking boot sector ... OK
Press any Key
Bytes per sector: 512
Sectors per cluster: 32
Reserved sectors: 32
Number of FATs: 2
Number of rootdirectory entries: 0
Number of sectors (short): 0
Media descriptor byte: f8h
Sectors per FAT: 9784
Sectors per track: 63
Drive heads: 240
Hidden sectors: 63
Number of sectors (long): 40083057
Physical drive number: 80h
Signature: 29h
```

do what it says

After further checking, *FIPS* asks you if you want to make a backup floppy. Enter your
formatted floppy in drive A: and make the backup. Next, you see:

```
Enter start cylinder for new partition (35 - 2650):
Use the cursor keys to choose the cylinder, <enter> to continue
Old partition       Cylinder      New Partition
   258.4 MB            35          19313.4 MB
```

Use the **Cursor Left** and **Cursor Right** keys to adjust the cylinder number at which the
new partition starts. You can also use the keys **Cursor Up** and **Cursor Down** to change
in steps of ten cylinders. *FIPS* updates the bottom line of the display to show the new
values selected. Initially, *FIPS* chooses the smallest possible Microsoft partition, so
initially you can only increase the size of the old partition (with the **Cursor Right** key).
When you're happy with the sizes, press **Enter** to move on to the next step.

> *Be very sure you're happy before you continue. If you make the
> first partition too small, there is no way to make it larger again.
> On the other hand, if you make it too large, you can split it
> again and then use* fdisk *or MS-DOS* FDISK *to remove the
> superfluous partitions.*

In this example, we choose equal-sized partitions:

```
Old partition       Cylinder      New Partition
   251.5 MB            511           251.5 MB
(pressed Enter)
```

Part.	bootable	Start Head	Cyl.	Sector	System	End Head	Cyl.	Sector	Start Sector	Number of Sectors	MB
1	yes	0	0	1	06h	15	511	63	0	515088	251
2	no	0	512	1	06h	15	1023	63	0	515088	251
3	no	0	0	0	00h	0	0	0	0	0	0
4	no	0	0	0	00h	0	0	0	0	0	0

```
Do you want to continue or reedit the partition table (c/r)? c
```

To ensure that the partition is recognized, reboot immediately. Make sure to disable all
programs that write to your disk in *CONFIG.SYS* and *AUTOEXEC.BAT* before
rebooting. It might be easier to to rename the files or to boot from floppy. Be particularly
careful to disable programs like *MIRROR* and *IMAGE*, which might get confused if the

partitioning is not to their liking. After rebooting, use *CHKDSK* or Norton Disk Doctor to make sure the first partition is OK. If you don't find any errors, you may now reboot with your normal *CONFIG.SYS* and *AUTOEXEC.BAT*. Start some programs and make sure you can still read your data.

After that, you have two valid Microsoft partitions on your disk. We'll look at what to do with them in the next chapter. The specific differences from a dedicated install are on page 66, but you'll need to start from the beginning of the chapter to do the install.

5

Installing FreeBSD

In the previous chapters, we've looked at preparing to install FreeBSD. In this chapter, we'll finally do it. If you run into trouble, I'll refer you back to the page of Chapter 2 which discusses this topic. If you want to install FreeBSD on the same disk as Microsoft or another operating system, you should have already read Chapter 4, *Shared OS installation*.

The following discussion relates primarily to installation on the i386 architecture. See page 78 for differences when installing on the AXP ("Alpha") processor.

Installing on the Intel i386 architecture

To install FreeBSD you need the software in a form that the installation software understands. You may also need a boot diskette. Nowadays you will almost invariably install from CD-ROM, so we'll assume that medium. On page 85, we'll look at some alternatives: installation from floppy disk or via the network.

The first step in installing FreeBSD is to start a minimal version of the operating system. The simplest way is to boot directly from the installation CD-ROM. If your system doesn't support this kind of boot, boot from floppy. See page 85 for more details.

The description in this chapter is based on a real-life installation on a real machine. When you install FreeBSD on your machine, a number of things will be different, depending on the hardware you're running, the way you're installing the software and the release of FreeBSD you're installing. Nevertheless, you should be able to recognize what is going on.

Booting from CD-ROM is mainly a matter of setting up your system BIOS and possibly your SCSI BIOS. Typically, you perform one of the following procedures:

- If you're booting from an IDE CD-ROM, you enter your system BIOS setup routines and set the *Boot sequence* parameter to select CD-ROM booting ahead of hard disk booting, and possibly also ahead of floppy disk booting. A typical sequence might be CDROM, C, A.

- On most machines, if you're booting from a SCSI CD-ROM, you also need a host adapter that supports CD-ROM boot. Set up the system BIOS to boot in the sequence, say, SCSI, A, C. On typical host adapters (such as the Adaptec 2940 series), you set the adapter to enable CD-ROM booting, and set the ID of the boot device to the ID of the CD-ROM drive.

These settings are probably not what you want to use for normal operation. If you leave the settings like this, and there is a bootable CD-ROM in your CD-ROM drive, it always boots from that CD-ROM rather than from the hard disk. After installation, change the parameters back again to boot from hard disk before CD-ROM. See your system documentation for further details.

Booting to sysinstall

The boot process itself is very similar to the normal boot process described on page 528. After it completes, though, you are put into the *sysinstall* main menu.

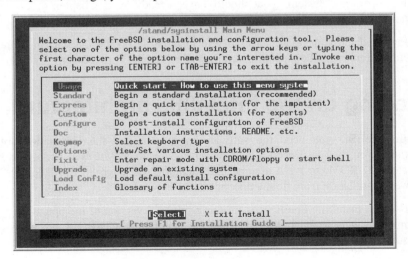

Figure 5-1: Main installation menu

Figure 5-1 shows the main *sysinstall* menu. *sysinstall* includes online help at all stages. Simply press **F1** and you will get appropriate help. Also, if you haven't been here before, the Doc menu gives you a large part of the appropriate information from the handbook.

Kinds of installation

To get started, select one of *Standard*, *Express* or *Custom*. The names imply that the *Standard* installation is the best way to go, the *Express* installation is for people in a hurry, and *Custom* installation is for when you want to specify exactly what is to be done.

In fact, the names are somewhat misleading. There isn't really that much difference between the three forms of installation. They all perform the same steps:

- Possibly set up options.

- Set up disk partitions, which we'll discuss in the next section.

- Set up file systems and swap space within a FreeBSD slice, which we start on page 67.

- Choose what you want to install, which we discuss on page 75.

- Choose where you want to install it from. We'll look at this on page 76.

- Actually install the software. We'll treat this on page 77.

We looked at disk partitions and file systems on page 34. We'll look at the other points when we get to them.

So what's the difference between the kinds of installation?

- The Standard installation takes you through these steps in sequence. Between each step, you get a pop-up window that tells you what is going to happen next.

- The Express installation also takes you through these steps in sequence. The main difference is that you don't get the pop-up window telling you what is going to happen next. This can save a little time. If you do want the information, similar information is available with the F1 key.

- The Custom installation returns you to its main menu after each step. It's up to you to select the next step. You can also select another step, or go back to a previous one. Like the Express installation, you don't get the pop-up information window, but you can get more information with the F1 key.

The big problem with Standard and Express installations is that they don't let you back up: if you pass a specific step and discover you want to change something, you have to abort the installation and start again. With the Custom installation, you can simply go back and change it. As a result, I recommend the Custom installation. In the following discussion, you won't see too much difference: the menus are the same for all three installation forms.

Choose Custom Installation Options
This is the custom installation menu. You may use this menu to specify
details on the type of distribution you wish to have, where you wish
to install it from and how you wish to allocate disk storage to FreeBSD.
X Exit Exit this menu (returning to previous)
2 Options View/Set various installation options
3 Partition Allocate disk space for FreeBSD
4 Label Label allocated disk partitions
5 Distributions Select distribution(s) to extract
6 Media Choose the installation media type
7 Commit Perform any pending Partition/Label/Extract actions
[OK] Cancel
[Press F1 to read the installation guide]

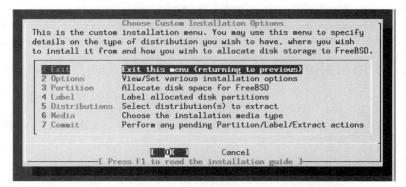

Figure 5-2: Custom Installation options

Setting installation options

The first item on the menu is to set installation options. There's probably not too much you'll want to change. About the only thing of interest might be the editor *ec*, which is a compromise between a simple editor for beginners and more complicated editors like *vi*. If you're planning to edit anything during the installation, for example the file */etc/exports*, which we'll look at on page 566, you may prefer to set an editor with which you are familiar. Select the fields by moving the cursor to the line and pressing the space bar.

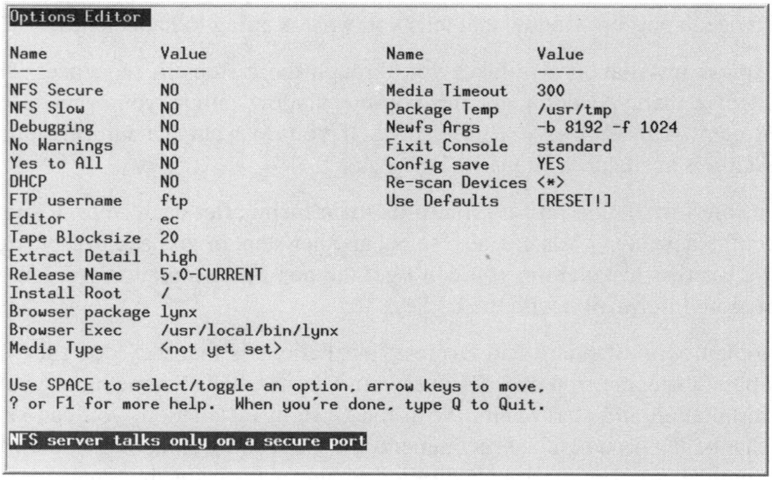

Options Editor
Name Value Name Value
NFS Secure NO Media Timeout 300
NFS Slow NO Package Temp /usr/tmp
Debugging NO Newfs Args -b 8192 -f 1024
No Warnings NO Fixit Console standard
Yes to All NO Config save YES
DHCP NO Re-scan Devices <*>
FTP username ftp Use Defaults [RESET!]
Editor ec
Tape Blocksize 20
Extract Detail high
Release Name 5.0-CURRENT
Install Root /
Browser package lynx
Browser Exec /usr/local/bin/lynx
Media Type <not yet set>
Use SPACE to select/toggle an option, arrow keys to move,
? or F1 for more help. When you're done, type Q to Quit.
NFS server talks only on a secure port

Figure 5-3: Installation options

Partitioning the disk

The first installation step is to set up space for FreeBSD on the disk. We looked at the technical background in Chapter 2, on page 39. In this section only, we'll use the term *partition* to refer to a slice or BIOS partition, because that's the usual terminology.

Even if your disk is correctly partitioned, select the *Partition* menu: the installation routines need to enter this screen in order to read the partition information from the disk. If you like what you see, you can leave again immediately with q (quit), but you must first enter this menu. If you have more than one disk connected to your machine, you will next be asked to choose the drives that you want to use for FreeBSD.

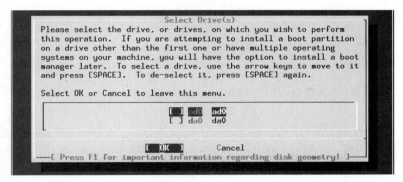

Figure 5-4: Disk selection menu

This screen shows entries for each drive that *sysinstall* has detected; in this example, the system has one ATA (IDE) drive, */dev/ad0*, and one SCSI drive, *da0*. You only get this screen if you have at least two drives connected to your machine; otherwise *sysinstall* automatically goes to the next screen.

If you intend to use more than one disk for FreeBSD, you have the choice of setting up all disks now, or setting the others up after the system is up and running. We'll look at the latter option in Chapter 11, on page 199.

To select the disk on which you want to install FreeBSD, move the cursor to the appropriate line and press the space bar. The screen you get will probably look like Figure 5-5. Table 5-1 explains the meanings of the columns in this display. The first partition contains the Master Boot Record, which is exactly one sector long, and the bootstrap, which can be up to 15 sectors long. The partitioning tools use the complete first track: in this case, the geometry information from BIOS says that it has 63 sectors per track.

In this case, the Microsoft file system uses up the whole disk except for the last track, 1008 sectors (504 kB) at the end of the disk. Clearly there's not much left to share. We have the option of removing the Microsoft partition, which we'll look at here, or we can shorten it with *FIPS*. We looked at *FIPS* in Chapter 4, page 52, and we'll look at what to do with the resultant layout on page 66.

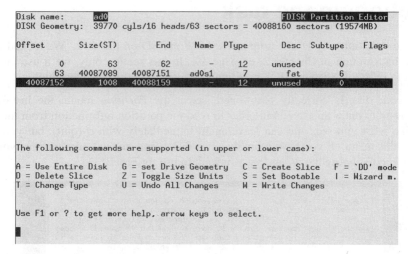

Figure 5-5: Partition editor menu

> *Don't forget that if you remove a partition, you lose all the data*
> *in it. If the partition contains anything you want to keep, make*
> *sure you have a readable backup.*

You remove the partition with the d command. After this, your display looks like:

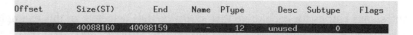

The next step is to allocate a FreeBSD partition. There are two ways to do this: if you want to have more than one partition on the drive (for example, if you share the disk with another operating system), you use the c (create) command. We'll look at that on page 66. In this case, though, you want to use the entire disk for FreeBSD, so you choose the a option. The resultant display is effectively the same as in Figure 5-5: the only difference is that the *Desc* field now shows freebsd instead of fat.

That's all you need to do here: leave *fdisk* by pressing the q key.

> *Don't use the* W *(Write Changes) command here. It's intended*
> *for use only once the system is up and running.*

Table 5-1: fdisk information

Column	Description
Offset	The number of the first sector in the partition.
Size	The length of the partition in sectors.
End	The number of the last sector in the partition.
Name	Where present, this is the device name that FreeBSD assigns to the partition. In this example, only the second entry has a name.
Ptype	The partition type. Partition type 6 is the Master Boot Record, which is exactly one track long (note that the header says that this drive has 63 sectors per track). Type 2 is a regular partition.
Desc	A textual description of the kind of partition. *fat* stands for *File Allocation Table*, a central part of the Microsoft disk space allocation strategy.
Subtype	The partition subtype. This corresponds to the descriptive text.
Flags	Can be one or more of the following characters: = The partition is correctly aligned. > The partition finishes after cylinder 1024, which used to cause problems for Microsoft. A This is the active (bootable) partition. B The partition employs BAD144 bad-spot handling. C This is a FreeBSD compatibility partition. R This partition contains a root file system.

On a PC, the next screen asks what kind of *boot selector* (in other words, *MBR*) you want. You don't get this on an Alpha.

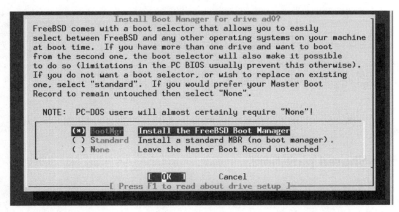

Figure 5-6: Boot selector menu

If you plan to have only one operating system on this disk, select Standard. If you are sharing with another operating system, you should choose *BootMgr* instead. We'll look at this in more detail in the section on booting the system on page 529. Exit by pressing the tab key until the OK tab is highlighted, then press **Enter**.

Table 5-2: MBR choices

Choice	Description
BootMgr	Install the FreeBSD boot manager in the MBR. This will enable you choose which partition to boot every time you start the system.
Standard	Use a standard MBR. You will be able to boot only from the active partition.
None	Don't change the MBR. This is useful if you already have another boot manager installed. If no MBR is installed, though, you won't be able to boot from this disk.

Shared partitions

If you are installing on a disk shared with another operating system, things are a little different. The section continues the example started in Chapter 4. When you enter the partition editor, you will see something like:

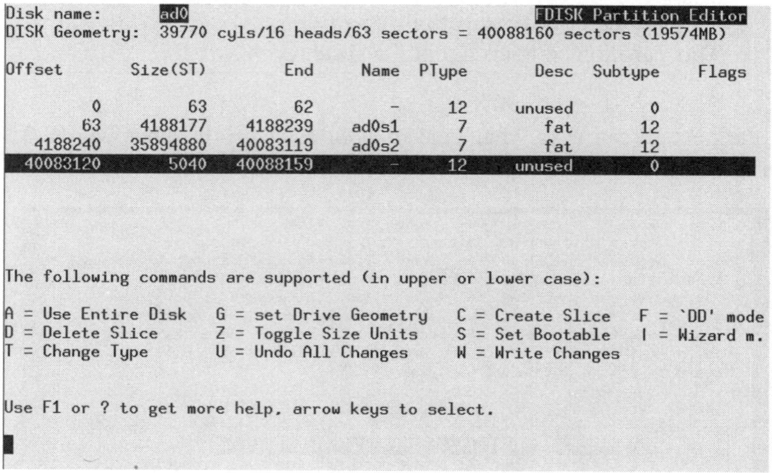

Figure 5-7: Shared partitions

This display shows the two Microsoft partitions, *ad0s1* and *ad0s2*, which is what you see after using *FIPS*; if you have just installed Microsoft on one partition, the partition *ad0s2* will not be present. If it is, you first need to remove it. **Be very careful to remove the correct partition**. It's always the second of the two partitions, in this case *ad0s2*.

Remove the partition by moving the highlight to the second partition and pressing d. After this, the display looks like:

0	63	62	–	12	unused	0
63	4188177	4188239	ad0s1	7	fat	12
4188240	35899920	40088159	–	12	unused	0

The next step is to allocate a FreeBSD partition with the c command. The menu asks for the size of the partition, and suggests a value of 35899920 sectors, the size of the unused area at the end. You can edit this value if you wish, but in this case it's what you want, so just press **ENTER**. You get another window asking you for the partition type, and suggesting type 165, the FreeBSD partition table. When you accept that, you get:

0	63	62	–	12	unused	0
63	4188177	4188239	ad0s1	7	fat	12
4188240	35899920	40088159	ad0s2	8	freebsd	165

The new partition now has a partition type 8 and subtype 165 (0xa5), which identifies it as a FreeBSD partition.

After this, select a boot method as described on page 66 and exit the menu with the q command. There are two operating systems on the disk, so select the BootMgr option.

Defining file systems

The next step is to tell the installation program what to put in your FreeBSD partition. First, we'll look at the simple case of installing FreeBSD by itself. On page 75 we'll look at what differences there are when installing alongside another operating system on the same disk.

When you select *Label*, you get the screen shown in Figure 5-8.

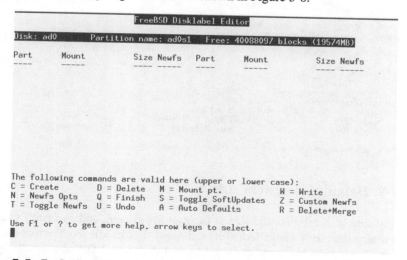

Figure 5-8: Label editor menu

What partitions?

In this example, you have 20 GB of space to divide up. How should you do it? You don't have to worry about this issue, since *sysinstall* can do it for you, but we'll see below why this might not be the best choice. In this section we'll consider how UNIX file systems have changed over the years, and we'll look at the issues in file system layout nowadays.

When UNIX was young, disks were tiny. At the time of the third edition of UNIX, in 1972, the root file system was on a Digital RF-11, a fixed head disk with 512 kB. The system was growing, and it was no longer possible to keep the entire system on this disk, so a second file system became essential. It was mounted on a Digital RK03 with 2 MB of storage. To quote from a paper published in the *Communications of the ACM* in July 1974:

> In our installation, for example, the root directory resides on the fixed-head disk, and the large disk drive, which contains user's files, is mounted by the system initialization program...

As time went on, UNIX got bigger, but so did the disks. By the early 80s, disks were large enough to put / and */usr* on the same disk, and it would have been possible to merge / and */usr*, but they didn't, mainly because of reliability concerns. Since that time, an additional file system, */var*, has come into common use for frequently changed data, and just recently *sysinstall* has been changed to create a */tmp* file system by default. This is what *sysinstall* does if you ask it to partition automatically:

```
                        FreeBSD Disklabel Editor

Disk: ad0         Partition name: ad0s1    Free: 0 blocks (0MB)

Part      Mount          Size Newfs   Part      Mount         Size Newfs
----      -----          ---- -----   ----      -----         ---- -----
ad0s1a    /            128MB UFS1    Y
ad0s1b    swap         244MB SWAP
ad0s1d    /var         256MB UFS1+S Y
ad0s1e    /tmp         256MB UFS1+S Y
ad0s1f    /usr       18690MB UFS1+S Y



The following commands are valid here (upper or lower case):
C = Create       D = Delete    M = Mount pt.           W = Write
N = Newfs Opts   Q = Finish    S = Toggle SoftUpdates  Z = Custom Newfs
T = Toggle Newfs U = Undo      A = Auto Defaults        R = Delete+Merge

Use F1 or ? to get more help, arrow keys to select.
```

Figure 5-9: Default file system sizes

It's relatively simple to estimate the size of the root file system, and *sysinstall*'s value of 128 MB is reasonable. But what about */var* and */tmp*? Is 256 MB too much or too little? In fact, both file systems put together would be lost in the 18.7 GB of */usr* file system. Why are things still this way? Let's look at the advantages and disadvantages:

- If you write to a file system and the system crashes before all the data can be written to disk, the data integrity of that file system can be severely compromised. For performance reasons, the system doesn't write everything to disk immediately, so there's quite a reasonable chance of this happening.

- If you have a crash and lose the root file system, recovery can be difficult.

- If a file system fills up, it can cause lots of trouble. Most messages about file systems on the `FreeBSD-questions` mailing list are complaining about file systems filling up. If you have a large number of small file systems, the chances are higher that one will fill up while space remains on another.

- On the other hand, some file systems are more important than others. If the */var* file system fills up (due to overly active logging, for example), you may not worry too much. If your root file system fills up, you could have serious problems.

- In single-user mode, only the root file system is mounted. With the classical layout, this means that the only programs you can run are those in */bin* and */sbin*. To run other programs, you must first mount the file system on which they are located.

- It's nice to keep your personal files separate from the system files. That way you can upgrade a system much more easily.

- It's very difficult to estimate in advance the size needs of some file systems. For example, on some systems */var* can be very small, maybe only 2 or 3 MB. It's hardly worth making a separate file system for that much data. On the other hand, other systems, such as ftp or web servers, may have a */var* system of 50 or 100 GB. How do you choose the correct size for your system?

- When doing backups, it's a good idea to be able to get a file system on a single tape.

In the early days of UNIX, system crashes were relatively common, and the damage they did to the file systems was relatively serious. Times have changed, and nowadays file system damage is relatively seldom, particularly on file systems that have little activity. On the other hand, disk drives have grown beyond most peoples' wildest expectations. The first edition of this book, only six years ago, showed how to install on a 200 MB drive. The smallest disk drives in current production are 20 GB in size, more than will fit on many tapes.

As a result of these considerations, I have changed my recommendations. In earlier editions of this book, I recommended putting a small root file system and a */usr* file system on the first (or only) disk on the system. */var* was to be a symbolic link to */usr/var*.

This is still a valid layout, but it has a couple of problems:

- In the example we're looking at, */usr* is about 19 GB in size. Not many people have backup devices that can write this much data on a single medium.

- Many people had difficulty with the symbolic link to */usr/var*.

As a result, I now recommend:

- Make a single root file system of between 4 and 6 GB.

- Do not have a separate */usr* file system.

- Do not have a separate */var* file system unless you have a good idea how big it should be. A good example might be a web server, where (contrary to FreeBSD's recommendations) it's a good idea to put the web pages on the */var* file system.

- Use the rest of the space on disk for a */home* file system, as long as it's possible to back it up on a single tape. Otherwise make multiple file systems. */home* is the normal directory for user files.

This layout allows for easy backup of the file systems, and it also allows for easy upgrading to a new system version: you just need to replace the root file system. It's not a perfect fit for all applications, though. Ultimately you need to make your own decisions.

How much swap space?

Apart from files, you should also have at least one swap partition on your disk. It's very difficult to predict how much swap space you need. The *automatic* option gave you 522 MB, slightly more than twice the size of physical memory. Maybe you can get by with 64 MB. Maybe you'll need 2 GB. How do you decide?

It's almost impossible to know in advance what your system will require. Here are some considerations:

- Swap space is needed for all pages of virtual memory that contain data that is not locked in memory and that can't be recreated automatically. This is the majority of virtual memory in the system.

- Some people use rules of thumb like "2.5 times the size of physical memory, or 64 MB, whichever is bigger." These rules work only by making assumptions about your workload. If you're using more than 2.5 times as much swap space as physical memory, performance will suffer.

- Known memory hogs are X11 and integrated graphical programs such as Netscape and StarOffice. If you use these, you will probably need more swap space. Older UNIX-based hogs such as Emacs and the GNU C compiler (*gcc*) are not in the same league.

- You can add additional swap partitions on other disks. This has the additional advantage of balancing the disk load if your machine swaps a lot.

- About the only ways to change the size of a swap partition are to add another partition or to reinstall the system, so if you're not sure, a little bit more won't do any harm, but too little can really be a problem.

- If your system panics, and memory dumping is enabled, it will write the contents of memory to the swap partition. This will obviously not work if your swap partition is smaller than main memory. Under these circumstances, the system refuses to dump, so you will not be able to find the cause of the problems.

  The dump routines can only dump to a single partition, so you need one that is big enough. If you have 512 MB of memory and two swap partitions of 384 MB each, you still will not be able to dump.

- Even with light memory loads, the virtual memory system slowly pages out data in preparation for a possible sudden demand for memory. This means that it can be more responsive to such requests. As a result, you should have at least as much swap as memory.

A couple of examples might make this clearer:

1. Some years ago I used to run *X*, *StarOffice*, *Netscape* and a whole lot of other memory-hungry applications on an old 486 with 16 MB. Sure, it was really slow, especially when changing from one application to another, but it worked. There was not much memory, so it used a lot of swap.

   To view the current swap usage, use *pstat*. Here's a typical view of this machine's swap space:

   ```
   $ pstat -s
   Device            1024-blocks    Used      Avail  Capacity   Type
   /dev/da0s1b          122880     65148      57668    53%      Interleaved
   ```

2. At the time of writing I run much more stuff on an AMD Athlon with 512 MB of memory. It has lots of swap space, but what I see is:

   ```
   $ pstat -s
   Device            1024-blocks    Used      Avail  Capacity   Type
   /dev/ad0s1b         1048576     14644    1033932    1%       Interleaved
   ```

It's not so important that the Athlon is using less swap: it's using less than 3% of its memory in swap, whereas the 486 used 4 times its memory. In a previous edition of this book, I had the example of a Pentium with 96 MB of memory, which used 43 MB of swap. Look at it from a different point of view, and it makes more sense: swap makes up for the lack of real memory, so the 486 was using a total of 80 MB of memory, the Pentium was using 140 MB, and the Athlon is using 526 MB. In other words, there is a tendency to be able to say "the more main memory you have, the less swap you need."

If, however, you look at it from the point of view of acceptable performance, you will hear things like "you need at least one-third of your virtual memory in real memory." That makes sense from a performance point of view, assuming all processes are relatively active. And, of course, it's another way of saying "take twice as much swap as real memory."

In summary: be generous in allocating swap space. If you have the choice, use more. If you really can't make up your mind, take 512 MB of swap space or 1 MB more than the maximum memory size you are likely to install.

For the file systems, the column *Mount* now shows the mount points, and the *Newfs* column contains the letters UFS1 for *UNIX File System*, Version 1, and the letter Y, indicating that you need to create a new file system before you can use it. At this point, you have two choices: decide for yourself what you want, or let the disk label editor do it for you. Let's look at both ways:

Creating the file systems

With these considerations in mind, we'll divide up the disk in the following manner:

- 4 GB for the root file system, which includes */usr* and */var*

- 512 MB swap space

- The rest of the disk for the */home* file system

To create a file system, you press c. You get a prompt window asking for the size of the file system, and offering the entire space. Enter the size of the root file system:

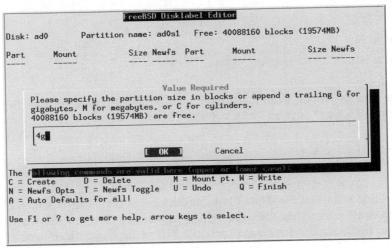

Figure 5-10: Specifying partition size

When you press **ENTER**, you see another prompt asking for the kind of partition. Select A File System:

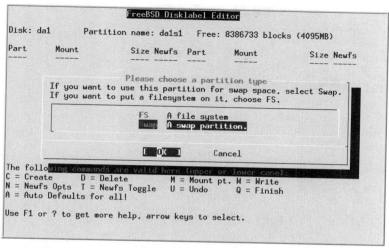

Figure 5-11: Selecting partition type

When you press **ENTER**, you see another prompt asking for the mount point for the file system. Enter / for the root file system, after which the display looks like:

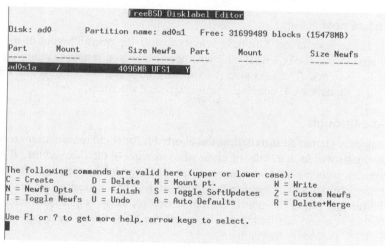

Figure 5-12: Allocated root file system

It's not immediately obvious at this point that soft updates are not enabled for this file system. Press s to enable them, after which the entry in the Newfs column changes from UFS1 to UFS1+S. See page 191 for reasons why you want to use soft updates.

Next, repeat the operation for the swap partition and the */home* file system, entering the appropriate values each time. Don't change the value offered for the length of */home*: just use all the remaining space. At the end, you have:

```
                         ┌─────────────────────────┐
                         │ FreeBSD Disklabel Editor │
                         └─────────────────────────┘
Disk: ad0        Partition name: ad0s1   Free: 0 blocks (0MB)

Part        Mount          Size Newfs  Part      Mount         Size Newfs
----        -----          ---- -----  ----      -----         ---- -----
ad0s1a      /            4096MB UFS1+S Y
ad0s1b      swap          512MB SWAP
ad0s1d      /home       14966MB UFS1+S Y




The following commands are valid here (upper or lower case):
C = Create          D = Delete   M = Mount pt.      W = Write
N = Newfs Opts      Q = Finish   S = Toggle SoftUpdates   Z = Custom Newfs
T = Toggle Newfs    U = Undo     A = Auto Defaults   R = Delete+Merge

Use F1 or ? to get more help, arrow keys to select.
```

Figure 5-13: Completed partition allocation

You don't need to enable soft updates for /home; that happens automatically.

That's all you need to do. Exit the menu by pressing q.

Where you are now

At this point in the installation, you have told *sysinstall* the overall layout of the disk or disks you intend to use for FreeBSD, and whether or how you intend to share them with other operating systems. The next step is to specify how you want to use the FreeBSD partitions. First, though, we'll consider some alternative scenarios.

Second time through

If you have already started an installation and aborted it for some reason after creating the file systems, things will look a little different when you get to the label editor. It will find the partitions, but it won't know the name of the mount points, so the text under Mount will be <none>. Under Newfs, you will find an asterisk (*) instead of the text UFS1 Y. The label editor has found the partitions, but it doesn't know where to mount the file systems. Before you can use them, you *must* tell the label editor the types and mount points of the UFS partitions. To do this:

- Position the cursor on each partition in turn.

- Press m (Mount). A window pops up asking for the mount point. Enter the name, in this example, first /, then press **Enter**. The label editor enters the name of the mount point under *Mount*, and under *Newfs* it enters UFS1 N—it knows that this is a UFS file system, so it just checks its consistency and doesn't overwrite it. Repeat this procedure for /home, and you're done. If you are sharing your disk with another system, you can also use this method to specify mount points for your Microsoft file systems. Select the Microsoft partition and specify the name of a mount point.

- Unless you are very sure that the file system is valid, and you really want to keep the data in the partitions, press t to specify that the file system should be created. The text UFS1 N changes to UFS1 Y. If you leave the N there, the commit phase will check the integrity of the file system with *fsck* rather than creating a new one.

File systems on shared disks

If you have another operating system on the disk, you'll notice a couple of differences. In particular, the label editor menu of Figure 5-8 (on page 68) will not be empty: instead, you'll see something like this:

Be careful at this point. The file system shown in the list is the active Microsoft partition, *not* a FreeBSD file system. The important piece of information here is the fact that we have 17529 MB of free space on the disk. We'll create the file systems in that free space in the same way we saw on page 72.

Selecting distributions

The next step is to decide what to install. Figure 5-14 shows you the menu you get when you enter *Distributions*. A complete installation of FreeBSD uses about 1 GB of space, so there's little reason to choose anything else. Position the cursor on the line All, as shown, and press the space bar.

> Why press the space bar when so far you have been pressing **ENTER**? Because in this particular menu, **ENTER** will return you to the upper level menu or simply continue to the media selection menu, depending on the type of installation you're doing. It's one of the strangenesses of *sysinstall*.

Next, *sysinstall* asks you if you want to install the Ports Collection. We'll look at the Ports Collection in Chapter 9. You don't have to install it now, and it takes much more time than you would expect from the amount of space that it takes: the Ports Collection consists of over 150,000 very small files, and copying them to disk can take as long as the rest of the installation put together. On the other hand, it's a lot easier to do now, so if you have the time, you should install them.

Whatever you answer to this question, you are returned to the distribution menu of Figure 5-14. Select Exit, and you're done selecting your distributions.

> Earlier versions of *sysinstall* asked you questions about XFree86 at this point. Nowadays you do that after completing the installation.

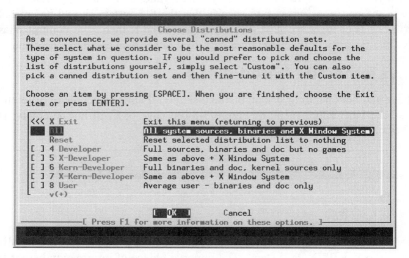

Figure 5-14: Distribution selection menu

Where you are now

Now *sysinstall* knows the layout of the disk or disks you intend to use for FreeBSD, and what to put on them. Next, you specify where to get the data from.

Selecting the installation medium

The next thing you need to specify is where you will get the data from. Where you go now depends on your installation medium. Figure 5-15 shows the *Media* menu. If you're installing from anything except an ftp server or NFS, you just need to select your medium and then commit the installation, which we look at on page 77. If you're installing from media other than CD-ROM, see page 85.

At this point, *sysinstall* knows everything it needs to install the software. It's just waiting for you to tell it to go ahead.

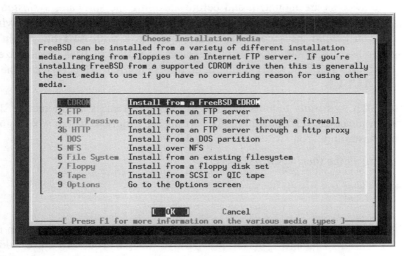

Figure 5-15: Installation medium menu

Performing the installation

So far, everything you have done has had no effect on the disk drives. If you change your mind, you can just abort the installation, and the data on your disks will be unchanged. That changes completely in the next step, which you call *committing* the installation. Now is the big moment. You've set up your partitions, decided what you want to install and from where. Now you do it.

If you are installing with the Custom installation, you need to select *Commit* explicitly. The Standard installation asks you if you want to proceed:

```
Last Chance!  Are you SURE you want continue the installation?

If you're running this on an existing system, we STRONGLY
encourage you to make proper backups before proceeding.
We take no responsibility for lost disk contents!
```

When you answer yes, *sysinstall* does what we've been preparing for:

- It creates the partitions and disk partitions.

- It creates the file system structures in the file system partitions, or it checks them, depending on what you chose in the label editor.

- It mounts the file systems and swap space.

- It installs the software on the system.

After the file systems are mounted, and before installing the software, *sysinstall* starts processes on two other virtual terminals.[1] On */dev/ttyv1* you get log output showing you what's going on behind the scenes. You can switch to it with **ALT-F2**. Right at the beginning you'll see a whole lot of error messages as *sysinstall* tries to initialize every device it can think of. Don't worry about them, they're normal. To get back to the install screen, press **ALT-F1**.

In addition, after *sysinstall* mounts the root file system, it starts an interactive shell on */dev/ttyv3*. You can use it if something goes wrong, or simply to watch what's going on while you're installing. You switch to it with **ALT-F4**.

After installing all the files, *sysinstall* asks:

```
Visit the general configuration menu for a chance to set
any last options?
```

You really have the choice here. You can answer Yes and continue, or you can reboot: the system is now runnable. In all probability, though, you will have additional installation work to do, so it's worth continuing. We'll look at that in the following chapter.

Installing on an Alpha system

Installing FreeBSD on an Alpha (officially Compaq AXP) has a few minor differences due to the hardware itself. In principle, you perform the same steps to install FreeBSD on the Alpha architecture that you perform for the Intel architecture. See page 42 for some differences.

The easiest type of installation is from CD-ROM. If you have a supported CD-ROM drive and a FreeBSD installation CD for Alpha, you can start the installation by building a set of FreeBSD boot floppies from the files *floppies/kern.flp* and *floppies/mfsroot.flp* as described for the Intel architecture on page 85. Use the CD-ROM marked "Alpha installation." From the SRM console prompt, insert the *kern.flp* floppy and type the following command to start the installation:

```
>>>boot dva0
```

Insert the *mfsroot.flp* floppy when prompted and you will end up at the first screen of the install program. You can then continue as for the Intel architecture on page 59.

To install over the Net, fetch the floppy images from the ftp site, boot as above, then proceed as for the Intel architecture.

---

1. See page 197 for an explanation of virtual terminals.

Once the install procedure has finished, you will be able to start FreeBSD/Alpha by typing something like this to the SRM prompt:

```
>>>boot dkc0
```

This instructs the firmware to boot the specified disk. To find the SRM names of disks in your machine, use the show device command:

```
>>>show device
dka0.0.0.4.0            DKA0        TOSHIBA CD-ROM XM-57  3476
dkc0.0.0.1009.0         DKC0                    RZ1BB-BS  0658
dkc100.1.0.1009.0       DKC100         SEAGATE ST34501W   0015
dva0.0.0.0.1            DVA0
ewa0.0.0.3.0            EWA0            00-00-F8-75-6D-01
pkc0.7.0.1009.0         PKC0                SCSI Bus ID 7  5.27
pqa0.0.0.4.0            PQA0                    PCI EIDE
```

This example comes from a Digital Personal Workstation 433au and shows three disks attached to the machine. The first is a CD-ROM called *dka0* and the other two are disks and are called *dkc0* and *dkc100* respectively.

You can specify which kernel file to load and what boot options to use with the -file and -flags options to boot:

```
>>>boot -file kernel.old -flags s
```

To make FreeBSD/Alpha boot automatically, use these commands:

```
>>>set boot_osflags a
>>>set bootdef_dev dkc0
>>>set auto_action BOOT
```

Upgrading an old version of FreeBSD

Paradoxically, upgrading an old version of FreeBSD is more complicated than installing from scratch. The reason is that you almost certainly want to keep your old configuration. There's enough material in this topic to fill a chapter, so that's what I've done: see Chapter 31, for more details on how to upgrade a system.

How to uninstall FreeBSD

What, you want to remove FreeBSD? Why would you want to do that?

Seriously, if you decide you want to completely remove FreeBSD from the system, this is no longer a FreeBSD issue, it's an issue of whatever system you use to replace it. For example, on page 63 we saw how to remove a Microsoft partition and replace it with FreeBSD; no Microsoft software was needed to remove it. In the same way, you don't need any help from FreeBSD if you want to replace it with a different operating system.

If things go wrong

In this section, we'll look at the most common installation problems. Many of these are things that once used to happen and haven't been seen for some time: *sysinstall* has improved considerably, and modern hardware is much more reliable and easy to configure. You can find additional information on this topic in the section *Known Hardware Problems* in the file *INSTALL.TXT* on the first CD-ROM.

Problems with sysinstall

sysinstall is intended to be easy to use, but it is not very tolerant of errors. You may well find that you enter something by mistake and can't get back to where you want to be. In case of doubt, if you haven't yet committed to the install, you can always just reboot.

Problems with CD-ROM installation

If you select to install from CD-ROM, you may get the message:

```
No CD-ROM device found
```

This might even happen if you have booted from CD-ROM! The most common reasons for this problem are:

- You booted from floppy and forgot to put the CD-ROM in the drive before you booted. Sorry, this is a current limitation of the boot process. Restart the installation (press **Ctrl-Alt-DEL** or the reset button, or power cycle the computer).

- You are using an ATAPI CD-ROM drive that doesn't quite fit the specification. In this case you need help from the FreeBSD developers. Send a message to FreeBSD-questions@FreeBSD.org and describe your CD-ROM as accurately as you can.

Can't boot

One of the most terrifying things after installing FreeBSD is if you find that the machine just won't boot. This is particularly bad if you have important data on the disk (either another operating system, or data from a previous installation of FreeBSD).

At this point, seasoned hackers tend to shrug their shoulders and point out that you still have the backup you made before you did do the installation. If you tell them you didn't do a backup, they tend to shrug again and move on to something else.

Still, all is probably not lost. The most frequent causes of boot failure are an incorrect boot installation or geometry problems. In addition, it's possible that the system might hang and never complete the boot process. All of these problems are much less common than they used to be, and a lot of the information about how to address them is a few years old, as they haven't been seen since.

Incorrect boot installation

It's possible to forget to install the bootstrap, or even to wipe it the existing bootstrap. That sounds like a big problem, but in fact it's easy enough to recover from. Refer to the description of the boot process on page 529, and boot from floppy disk or CD-ROM. Interrupt the boot process with the space bar. You might see:

```
BTX loader 1.00  BTX version is 1.01
BIOS drive A: is disk0
BIOS drive C: is disk1
BIOS drive D: is disk1
BIOS 639kB/130048kB available memory

FreeBSD/i386 bootstrap loader, Revision 0.8
(grog@freebie.example.com, Thu Jun 13 13:06:03 CST 2002)
Loading /boot/defaults/loader.conf

Hit [Enter] to boot immediately, or any other key for command prompt.
Booting [kernel] in 6 seconds...       press space bar here
ok unload                              unload the current kernel
ok set currdev disk1s1a                and set the location of the new one
ok load /boot/kernel/kernel            load the kernel
ok boot                                then start it
```

This boots from the drive */dev/ad0s1a*, assuming that you are using IDE drives. The correspondence between the name */dev/ad0s1a* and *disk1s1a* goes via the information at the top of the example: BTX only knows the BIOS names, so you'd normally be looking for the first partition on drive *C:*. After booting, install the correct bootstrap with bsdlabel -B or *boot0cfg*, and you should be able to boot from hard disk again.

Geometry problems

Things might continue a bit further: you elect to install *booteasy*, and when you boot, you get the Boot Manager prompt, but it just prints F? at the boot menu and won't accept any input. In this case, you may have set the hard disk geometry incorrectly in the partition editor when you installed FreeBSD. Go back into the partition editor and specify the correct geometry for your hard disk. You may need to reinstall FreeBSD from the beginning if this happens.

It used to be relatively common that *sysinstall* couldn't calculate the correct geometry for a disk, and that as a result you could install a system, but it wouldn't boot. Since those days, *sysinstall* has become a lot smarter, but it's still barely possible that you'll run into this problem.

If you can't figure out the correct geometry for your machine, and even if you don't want to run Microsoft on your machine, try installing a small Microsoft partition at the beginning of the disk and install FreeBSD after that. The install program sees the Microsoft partition and tries to infer the correct geometry from it, which usually works. After the partition editor has accepted the geometry, you can remove the Microsoft partition again. If you are sharing your machine with Microsoft, make sure that the Microsoft partition is before the FreeBSD partition.

Alternatively, if you don't want to share your disk with any other operating system, select the option to use the entire disk (a in the partition editor). You're less likely to have problems with this option.

System hangs during boot

A number of problems may lead to the system hanging during the boot process. All the known problems have been eliminated, but there's always the chance that something new will crop up. In general, the problems are related to hardware probes, and the most important indication is the point at which the boot failed. It's worth repeating the boot with the verbose flag: again, refer to the description of the boot process on page 529. Interrupt the boot process with the space bar and enter:

```
Hit [Enter] to boot immediately, or any other key for command prompt.
Booting [kernel] in 6 seconds...      press space bar here
ok set boot_verbose                   set a verbose boot
ok boot                               then continue
```

This flag gives you additional information that might help diagnose the problem. See Chapter 29 for more details of what the output means.

If you're using ISA cards, you may need to reconfigure the card to match the kernel, or change the file */boot/device.hints* to match the card settings. See the example on page 608. Older versions of FreeBSD used to have a program called *UserConfig* to perform this function, but it is no longer supported.

System boots, but doesn't run correctly

If you get the system installed to the point where you can start it, but it doesn't run quite the way you want, *don't reinstall*. In most cases, reinstallation won't help. Instead, try to find the cause of the problem—with the aid of the FreeBSD-questions mailing list if necessary—and fix the problem.

Root file system fills up

You might find that the installation completes successfully, and you get your system up and running, but almost before you know it, the root file system fills up. This is relatively unlikely if you follow my recommendation to have one file system for /, */usr* and */var*, but if you follow the default recommendations, it's a possibility. It could be, of course, that you just haven't made it big enough—FreeBSD root file systems have got bigger over the years. In the first edition of this book I recommended 32 MB "to be on the safe side." Nowadays the default is 128 MB.

On the other hand, maybe you already have an 128 MB root file system, and it still fills up. In this case, check where you have put your */tmp* and */var* file systems. There's a good chance that they're on the root file system, and that's why it's filling up.

Panic

Sometimes the system gets into so much trouble that it can't continue. It should notice this situation and stop more or less gracefully. You might see a message like:

```
panic: free vnode isn't

Syncing disks 14 13 9 5 5 5 5 5 5 5 giving up

dumping to dev 20001 offset 0
dump 16 32 48 64 80 96 112 128 succeeded
Automatic reboot in 15 seconds - press a key on the console to abort
Reboooting...
```

Just because the system has panicked doesn't mean that you should panic too. It's a sorry fact of life that software contains bugs. Many commercial systems just crash when they hit a bug, and you never know why, or they print a message like General protection fault, which doesn't tell you very much either. When a UNIX system panics, it usually gives you more detailed information—in this example, the reason is *free vnode isn't*. You may not be any the wiser for a message like this (it tells you that the file system handling has got confused about the current state of storage on a disk), but other people might. In particular, if you *do* get a panic and you ask for help on FreeBSD-questions, please don't just say "My system panicked, what do I do?" The first answer—if you get one—will be "What was the panic string?" The second will be "Where's the dump?"

After panicking, the system tries to write file system buffers back to disk so that they don't get lost. This is not always possible, as we see on the second line of this example. It started off with 14 buffers to write, but it only managed to write 9 of them, possibly because it was confused about the state of the disk. This can mean that you will have difficulties after rebooting, but it might also mean that the system was wrong in its assumptions about the number of buffers needed to be written.

In addition to telling you the cause of the panic, FreeBSD will optionally copy the current contents of memory to the swap file for post-mortem analysis. This is called *dumping* the system, and is shown on the next two lines. To enable dumping, you need to specify where the dump should be written. In */etc/defaults/rc.conf*, you will find:

```
dumpdev="NO"              # Device name to crashdump to (if enabled).
```

To enable dumping, put something like this in */boot/loader.conf*:

```
dumpdev="/dev/ad0s1b"
```

This enables the dumps to be taken even if a panic occurs before the system reads the */etc/rc.conf* file. Make sure that the name of the dumpdev corresponds to a swap partition with at least as much space as your total memory. You can use *pstat* to check this:

```
# pstat -s
Device          1024-blocks       Used    Avail Capacity   Type
/dev/ad0s1b          51200       50108     1028      98%    Interleaved
/dev/da0s1b          66036       51356    14616      78%    Interleaved
/dev/da2s1b         204800       51220   153516      25%    Interleaved
Total               321844      152684   169160      47%
```

As long as this machine doesn't have more than about 192 MB of memory, it will be possible to take a dump on */dev/da2s1b*.

In addition, ensure that you have a directory called */var/crash*. After rebooting, the system first checks the integrity of the file systems, then it checks for the presence of a dump. If it finds one, it copies the dump and the current kernel to */var/crash*.

It's always worth enabling dumping, assuming your swap space is at least as large as your memory. You can analyze the dumps with *gdb*—see page 622 for more details.

To get the best results from a dump analysis, you need a *debug kernel*. This kernel is identical to a normal kernel, but it includes a lot of information that can be used for dump analysis. See page 614 for details of how to build a debug kernel. You never know when you might run into a problem, so I highly recommend that you use a debug kernel at all times. It doesn't have any effect on the performance of the system.

Fixing a broken installation

A really massive crash may damage your system to such an extent that you need to reinstall the whole system. For example, if you overwrite your hard disk from start to finish, you don't have any other choice. In many cases, though, the damage is repairable. Sometimes, though, you can't start the system to fix the problems. In this case, you have two possibilities:

- Boot from the second CD-ROM (*Live Filesystem*). It will be mounted as the root file system.

- Boot from the *Fixit* floppy. The Fixit floppy is in the distribution in the same directory as the boot diskette, *floppies*. Just copy *floppies/fixit.flp* to a disk in the same way as described for boot diskettes on page 85. To use the fixit floppy, first boot with the boot diskette and select "Fixit floppy" from the main menu. The Fixit floppy will be mounted under the root MFS as */mnt2*.

In either case, the hard disks aren't mounted; you might want to do repair work on them before any other access.

Use this option only if you have a good understanding of the system installation process. Depending on the damage, you may or may not be successful. If you have a recent backup of your system, it might be faster to perform a complete installation than to try to fix what's left, and after a reinstallation you can be more confident that the system is correctly installed.

Alternative installation methods

The description at the beginning of this chapter applied to the most common installation method, from CD-ROM. In the following sections we'll look at the relatively minor differences needed to install from other media. The choices you have are, in order of decreasing attractiveness:

- Over the network. You have the choice of *ftp* or NFS connection. If you're connected to the Internet and you're not in a hurry, you can load directly from one of the distribution sites described in the FreeBSD handbook.

- From a locally mounted disk partition, either FreeBSD (if you have already installed it) or Microsoft.

- From floppy disk. This is only for masochists or people who really have almost no hardware: depending on the extent of the installation, you will need up to 250 disks, and at least one of them is bound to have an I/O error. And don't forget that a CD-ROM drive costs a lot less than 250 floppies.

Preparing boot floppies

If your machine is no longer the youngest, you may be able to read the CD-ROM drive, but not boot from it. In this case, you'll need to boot from floppy. If you are using 1.44 MB floppies, you will need two or three of them, the *Kernel Disk* and the *MFS Root Disk* and possibly the *Drivers Disk* to boot the installation programs. If you are using 2.88 MB floppies or a LS-120 disk, you can copy the single *Boot Disk*, which is 2.88 MB long, instead of the kernel and MFS root disks. The images of these floppies are on the CD-ROM distribution in the files *floppies/kern.flp*, *floppies/mfsroot.flp*, *floppies/drivers.flp* and *floppies/boot.flp* respectively. If you have your CD-ROM mounted on a Microsoft system, they may be called *FLOPPIES\KERN.FLP*, *FLOPPIES\MFS-ROOT.FLP*, *FLOPPIES\DRIVERS.FLP* and *FLOPPIES\BOOT.FLP* respectively. The bootstrap does not recover bad blocks, so the floppy must be 100% readable.

The way you get the boot disk image onto a real floppy depends on the operating system you use. If you are using any flavour of UNIX, just perform something like:

```
# dd if=/cdrom/floppies/kern.flp of=/dev/fd0 bs=36b
```
change the floppy
```
# dd if=/cdrom/floppies/mfsroot.flp of=/dev/fd0 bs=36b
```
change the floppy
```
# dd if=/cdrom/floppies/drivers.flp of=/dev/fd0 bs=36b
```

This assumes that your software is on CD-ROM, and that it is mounted on the directory */cdrom*. It also assumes that your floppy drive is called */dev/fd0*. This is the FreeBSD name as of Release 5.0, and it's also the name that Linux uses. Older FreeBSD and other BSD systems refer to it as */dev/fd0c*.

The *dd* implementation of some versions of UNIX, particularly older System V variants, may complain about the option bs=36b. If this happens, just leave it out. It might take up to 10 minutes to write the floppy, but it will work, and it will make you appreciate FreeBSD all the more.

If you have to create the boot floppy from Microsoft, use the program *FDIMAGE.EXE*, which is in the *tools* directory of the first CD-ROM.

Booting from floppy

In almost all cases where you don't boot from CD-ROM, you'll boot from floppy, no matter what medium you are installing from. If you are installing from CD-ROM, *put the CD-ROM in the drive* before booting. The installation may fail if you boot before inserting the CD-ROM.

Boot the system in the normal manner from the first floppy (the one containing the *kern.flp* image). After loading the kernel, the system will print the message:

```
Please insert MFS root floppy and press enter:
```

After you replace the floppy and press enter, the boot procedure carries on as before.

If you're using the 2.88 MB image on a 2.88 MB floppy or an LS-120 drive, you have everything you need on the one disk, so you don't get the prompt to change the disk. Depending on your hardware, you may later get a prompt to install additional drivers from the driver floppy.

Installing via ftp

The fun way to install FreeBSD is via the Internet, but it's not always the best choice. There's a lot of data to transfer, and unless you have a really high-speed, non-overloaded connection to the server, it could take forever. On the other hand, of course, if you have the software on another machine on the same LAN, and the system on which you want to install FreeBSD doesn't have a CD-ROM drive, these conditions are fulfilled, and this could be for you. Before you decide, though, read about the alternative of NFS installation below: if you don't have an ftp server with the files already installed, it's a lot easier to set up an NFS installation.

There are two ftp installation modes you can use:

- Regular *ftp* mode does not work through most firewalls but will often work best with older ftp servers that do not support passive mode. Use this mode if your connection hangs with passive mode.

- If you need to pass through firewalls that do not allow incoming connections, try *passive ftp*.

Whichever mode of installation and whichever remote machine you choose, you need to have access to the remote machine. The easiest and most common way to ensure access is to use anonymous ftp. If you're installing from another FreeBSD machine, read how to install anonymous ftp on page 450. This information is also generally correct for other UNIX systems.

Setting up the ftp server

Put the FreeBSD distribution in the public ftp directory of the ftp server. On BSD systems, this will be the home directory of user ftp, which in FreeBSD defaults to */var/spool/ftp*. The name of the directory is the name of the release, which in this example we'll assume to be *5.0-RELEASE*. You can put this directory in a subdirectory of */var/spool/ftp*, for example */var/spool/ftp/FreeBSD/5.0-RELEASE*, but the only optional part in this example is the parent directory *FreeBSD*.

This directory has a slightly different structure from the CD-ROM distribution. To set it up, assuming you have your distribution CD-ROM mounted on */cdrom*, and that you are installing in the directory */var/spool/ftp/FreeBSD/5.0-RELEASE*, perform the following steps:

```
# cd /var/spool/ftp/FreeBSD/5.0-RELEASE
# mkdir floppies
# cd floppies
# cp /cdrom/floppies/* .                    don't omit the . at the end
# cd /cdrom                                 the distribution directory on CD-ROM
# tar cf - . | (cd /var/spool/ftp/FreeBSD/5.0-RELEASE; tar xvf -)
```

This copies all the directories of */cdrom* into */var/spool/ftp/FreeBSD/5.0-RELEASE*. For a minimal installation, you need only the directory *base*. To just install *base* rather than all of the distribution, change the last line of the example above to:

```
# mkdir base
# cp /cdrom/base/* base
```

Installing via ftp

On page 77 we saw the media select menu. Figure 5-16 shows the menu you get when you select *FTP* or *FTP Passive*. To see the remainder of the sites, use the **PageDown** key. Let's assume you want to install from *presto*, a system on the local network. *presto* isn't on this list, of course, so you select URL. Another menu appears, asking for an ftp pathname in the URL form ftp://*hostname/pathname*. *hostname* is the name of the system, in this case *presto.example.org*, and *pathname* is the path relative to the anonymous ftp directory, which on FreeBSD systems is usually */var/spool/ftp*. The install program knows its version number, and it attaches it to the name you supply.

> You can change the version number from the options menu, for example to install a snapshot of a newer release of FreeBSD.

In this case, we're installing Release 5.0 of FreeBSD, and it's in the directory */var/spool/ftp/pub/FreeBSD/5.0-RELEASE*. *sysinstall* knows the *5.0-RELEASE*, so you enter only *ftp://presto.example.org/pub/FreeBSD*. The next menu asks you to configure your network. This is the same menu that you would normally fill out at the end of the installation—see page 98 for details.

This information is used to set up the machine after installation, so it pays to fill out this information correctly. After entering this information, continue with *Commit* (on page 77).

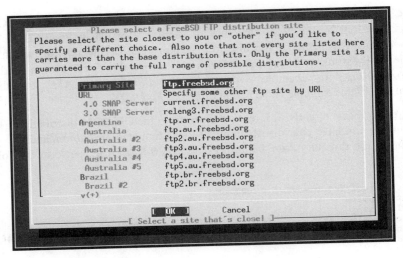

Figure 5-16: Selecting ftp server

Installing via NFS

If you're installing from a CD-ROM drive on another system in the local network, you might find an installation via ftp too complicated for your liking. Installation is a lot easier if the other system supports NFS. Before you start, make sure you have the CD-ROM mounted on the remote machine, and that the remote machine is exporting the file system (in System V terminology, exporting is called *sharing*). When prompted for the name of the directory, specify the name of the directory on which the CD-ROM is mounted. For example, if the CD-ROM is mounted on directory */cdrom* on the system *presto.example.org*, enter `presto.example.org:/cdrom`. That's all there is to it!

> Older versions of FreeBSD stored the distribution on a subdirectory *dists*. Newer versions store it in the root directory of the CD-ROM.

Next, you give this information to *sysinstall*, as shown in Figure 5-17. After entering this information, *sysinstall* asks you to configure an interface. This is the same procedure that you would otherwise do after installation—see page 98. After performing this configuration, you continue with *Commit* (on page 77).

Installing from a Microsoft partition

On the Intel architecture you can also install from a primary Microsoft partition on the first disk. To prepare for installation from a Microsoft partition, copy the files from the distribution into a directory called *C:\FREEBSD*. For example, to do a minimal installation of FreeBSD from Microsoft using files copied from a CD-ROM, copy the directories *floppies* and *base* to the Microsoft directories *C:\FREEBSD\FLOPPIES* and *C:\FREEBSD\BIN* respectively. You need the directory *FLOPPIES* because that's where *sysinstall* looks for the *boot.flp*, the first image in every installation.

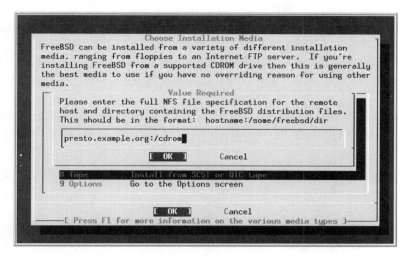

Figure 5-17: Specifying NFS file system

The only required directory is *base*. You can include as many other directories as you want, but be sure to maintain the directory structure. In other words, if you also wanted to install *XF86336* and *manpages*, you would copy them to *C:\FREEBSD\XF86336* and *C:\FREEBSD\MANPAGES*.

Creating floppies for a floppy installation

Installation from floppy disk is definitely the worst choice you have. You will need nearly 50 floppies for the minimum installation, and about 250 for the complete installation. The chance of one of them being bad is high. Most problems on a floppy install can be traced to bad media, or differences in alignment between the media and the drive in which they are used, so:

> *Before starting, format all floppies in the drive you intend to use, even if they are preformatted.*

The first two floppies you'll need are the Kernel floppy and the MFS Root floppy, which were described earlier.

In addition, you need at minimum as many floppies as it takes to hold all files in the *base* directory, which contains the binary distribution. Read the file *LAYOUT.TXT* paying special attention to the "Distribution format" section, which describes which files you need.

If you're creating the floppies on a FreeBSD machine, you can put *ufs* file systems on the floppies instead:

```
# fdformat -f 1440 fd0.1440
# bsdlabel -w fd0.1440 floppy3
# newfs -t 2 -u 18 -l 1 -i 65536 /dev/fd0
```

Next, copy the files to the floppies. The distribution files are split into chunks that will fit exactly on a conventional 1.44MB floppy. Copy one file to each floppy. Make very sure to put the file *base.inf* on the first floppy; it is needed to find out how many floppies to read.

The installation itself is straightforward enough: follow the instructions starting on page 63, select *Floppy* in the installation medium menu on page 76, then follow the prompts.

In this chapter:
- Installing additional
  software
- Adding users
- Time zone
- Network services
- Startup preferences
- Configuring the
  mouse
- Configuring X
- Rebooting the new
  system

6

Post-installation
configuration

In the last chapter we looked at the installation of the basic system, up to the point where it could be rebooted. It's barely possible that this could be enough. Almost certainly, though, you'll need to perform a number of further configuration steps before the system is useful. In this chapter we roughly follow the final configuration menu, but there are a few exceptions. The most important things to do are:

- Install additional software.

- Create accounts for normal users.

- Set up networking support.

- Configure the system to start all the services you need.

- Configure the X Window System and desktop.

In this chapter, we'll concentrate on getting the system up and running as quickly as possible. Later on in the book we'll go into more detail about these topics.

At the end of the previous chapter, we had a menu asking whether we wanted to visit the "last options" menu. If you answer YES, you get the configuration menu shown in Figure 6-1. If you have rebooted the machine, log in as root and start *sysinstall*. Then select Configure, which gets you into the same menu.

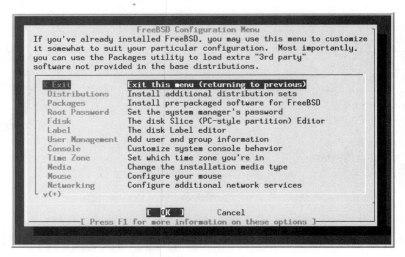

Figure 6-1: Configuration menu

As the markers under the word Networking indicate, this menu is larger than the window in which it is displayed. We'll look at some of the additional entries below. Only some of these entries are of interest in a normal install; we'll ignore the rest.

There may be some reasons to deviate from the sequence in this chapter. For example, if your CD-ROM is mounted on a different system, you may need to set up networking before installing additional software.

Installing additional software

The first item of interest is Packages. These are some of the ports in the Ports Collection, which we'll look at in more detail in Chapter 9.

The Ports Collection contains a large quantity of software that you may want to install. In fact, there's so much that just making up your mind what to install can be a complicated process: there are over 8,000 ports in the collection. Which ones are worth using? I recommend the following list:

- *acroread* is the Acrobat reader, a utility for reading and printing PDF files. We look at it briefly on page 276.

- *bash* is the shell recommended in this book. We'll look at it in more detail on page 113. Other popular shells are *tcsh* and *csh*, both in the base system.

- *cdrecord* is a utility to burn SCSI CD-Rs. We'll discuss it in chapter Chapter 13, *Writing CD-Rs*. You don't need it if you have an IDE CD-R drive.

- *Emacs* is the GNU Emacs editor recommended in this book. We'll look at it on page 139. Other popular editors are *vi* (in the base system) and *vim* (in the Ports Collection).

- *fetchmail* is a program for fetching mail from POP mailboxes. We look at it on page 504.

- *fvwm2* is a window manager that you may prefer to a full-blown desktop. We look at it on page 118.

- *galeon* is a web browser. We'll look at it briefly on page 418.

- *ghostscript* is a PostScript interpreter. It can be used to display PostScript on an X display, or to print it out on a non-PostScript printer. We'll look at it on page 273.

- *gpg* is an encryption program.

- *gv* is a utility that works with *ghostscript* to display PostScript on an X display. It allows magnification and paging, both of which *ghostscript* does not do easily. We'll look at it on page 273.

- *ispell* is a spell check program.

- *kde* is the desktop environment recommended in this book. We'll look at it in more detail in Chapter 7, *The tools of the trade*.

- *mkisofs* is a program to create CD-R images. We look at it in chapter Chapter 13, *Writing CD-Rs*.

- *mutt* is the mail user agent (MUA, or mail reader) recommended in Chapter 26, *Electronic mail: clients*.

- *postfix* is the mail transfer agent (MTA) recommended in chapter Chapter 27, *Electronic mail: servers*.

- *xtset* is a utility to set the title of an *xterm* window. It is used by the *.bashrc* file installed with the *instant-workstation* package.

- *xv* is a program to display images, in particular *jpeg* and *gif*.

Why do I recommend these particular ports? Simple: because I like them, and I use them myself. That doesn't mean they're the only choice, though. Others prefer the *Gnome* window manager to *kde*, or the *pine* or *elm* MUAs to *mutt*, or the *vim* editor to *Emacs*. This is the stuff of holy wars. See *http://www.tuxedo.org/~esr/jargon/html/entry/holy-wars.html* for more details.

Instant workstation

The ports mentioned in the previous section are included in the *misc/instant-workstation* port, which installs typical software and configurations for a workstation and allows you to be productive right away. At a later point you may find that you prefer other software, in which case you can install it.

It's possible that the CD set you get will not include *instant-workstation*. That's not such a problem: you just install the individual ports from this list. You can also do this if you don't like the list of ports.

Changing the default shell for root

After installation, you may want to change the default shell for existing users to *bash*. If you have installed *instant-workstation*, you should copy the file */usr/share/skel/dot.bashrc* to root's home directory and call it *.bashrc* and *.bash_profile*. First, start

```
presto# cp /usr/share/skel/dot.bashrc .bashrc
presto# ln .bashrc .bash_profile
presto# bash
=== root@presto (/dev/ttyp2) ~ 1 -> chsh
```

The last command starts an editor with the following content:

```
#Changing user database information for root.
Login: root
Password:
Uid [#]: 0
Gid [# or name]: 0
Change [month day year]:
Expire [month day year]:
Class:
Home directory: /root
Shell: /bin/csh
Full Name: Charlie &
Office Location:
Office Phone:
Home Phone:
Other information:
```

Change the Shell line to:

```
Shell: /usr/local/bin/bash
```

Note that the *bash* shell is in the directory */usr/local/bin*; this is because it is not part of the base system. The standard shells are in the directory */bin*.

Adding users

A freshly installed FreeBSD system has a number of users, nearly all for system components. The only login user is root, and you shouldn't log in as root. Instead you should add at least one account for yourself. If you're transferring a *master.passwd* file from another system, you don't need to do anything now. Otherwise select this item and then the menu item User, and fill out the resulting menu like this:

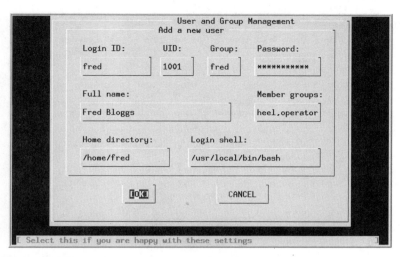

Figure 6-2: Adding a user

You should not need to enter the fields UID and Home directory: *sysinstall* does this for you. It's important to ensure that you are in group wheel so that you can use the *su* command to become root, and you need to be in group operator to use the *shutdown* command.

Don't bother to add more users at this stage; you can do it later. We'll look at user management in Chapter 8, on page 112.

Setting the root password

Next, select Root Password. We'll talk about passwords more on page 144. Select this item to set the password in the normal manner.

Time zone

Next, select the entry time zone. The first entry asks you if the machine CMOS clock (i.e. the hardware clock) is set to UTC (sometimes incorrectly called GMT, which is a British time zone). If you plan to run only FreeBSD or other UNIX-like operating systems on this machine, you should set the clock to UTC. If you intend to run other software that doesn't understand time zones, such as many Microsoft systems, you have to set the time to local time, which can cause problems with daylight savings time.

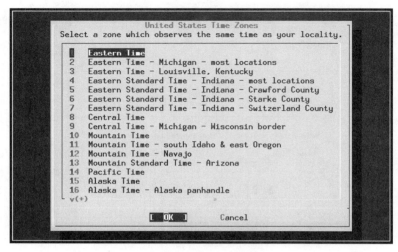

Figure 6-3: Time zone select menu: USA

The next menu asks you to select a "region," which roughly corresponds with a continent. Assuming you are living in Austin, TX in the United States of America, you would select America -- North and South and then (after scrolling down) United States of America. The next menu then looks like this: Select Central Time and select Yes when the system asks you whether the abbreviation CST sounds reasonable.

This particular step is relatively cumbersome. You may find it easier to look in the directory */usr/share/zoneinfo* after installation. There you find:

```
# cd /usr/share/zoneinfo/
# ls
Africa          Australia       Etc             MET             WET
America         CET             Europe          MST             posixrules
Antarctica      CST6CDT         Factory         MST7MDT         zone.tab
Arctic          EET             GMT             PST8PDT
Asia            EST             HST             Pacific
Atlantic        EST5EDT         Indian          SystemV
```

If you want to set the time zone to, say, Singapore, you could enter:

```
# cd Asia/
# ls
Aden            Chungking       Jerusalem       Novosibirsk     Tehran
Almaty          Colombo         Kabul           Omsk            Thimbu
Amman           Dacca           Kamchatka       Phnom_Penh      Tokyo
Anadyr          Damascus        Karachi         Pyongyang       Ujung_Pandang
Aqtau           Dili            Kashgar         Qatar           Ulaanbaatar
Aqtobe          Dubai           Katmandu        Rangoon         Ulan_Bator
Ashkhabad       Dushanbe        Krasnoyarsk     Riyadh          Urumqi
Baghdad         Gaza            Kuala_Lumpur    Saigon          Vientiane
Bahrain         Harbin          Kuching         Samarkand       Vladivostok
Baku            Hong_Kong       Kuwait          Seoul           Yakutsk
Bangkok         Hovd            Macao           Shanghai        Yekaterinburg
Beirut          Irkutsk         Magadan         Singapore       Yerevan
```

```
Bishkek      Istanbul      Manila      Taipei
Brunei       Jakarta       Muscat      Tashkent
Calcutta     Jayapura      Nicosia     Tbilisi
# cp Singapore /etc/localtime
```

Note that the files in */usr/share/zoneinfo/Asia* (and the other directories) represent specific towns, and these may not correspond with the town in which you are located. Choose one in the same country and time zone.

You can do this at any time on a running system.

Network services

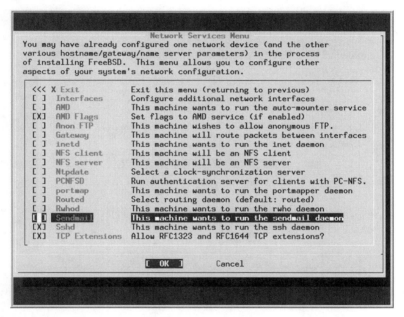

Figure 6-4: Network services menu

The next step is to configure your networking equipment. Figure 6-4 shows the Network Services Menu. There are a number of ways to get to this menu:

- If you're running the recommended Custom installation, you'll get it automatically after the end of the installation.

- If you're running the Standard and Express installations, you don't get it at all: after setting up your network interfaces, *sysinstall* presents you with individual items from the Network Services Menu instead.

- If you're setting up after rebooting, or if you missed it during installation, select
  Configure from the main menu and then Networking.

The first step should always be to set up the network interfaces, so this is where you find
yourself if you are performing a Standard or Express installation.

Setting up network interfaces

Figure 6-5 shows the network setup menu. On a standard 80x25 display it requires
scrolling to see the entire menu. If you installed via FTP or NFS, you will already have
set up your network interfaces, and *sysinstall* won't ask the questions again. The only
real network board on this list is *xl0*, the Ethernet board. The others are standard
hardware that can also be used as network interfaces. Don't try to set up PPP here;
there's more to PPP configuration than *sysinstall* can handle. We'll look at PPP
configuration in Chapter 20.

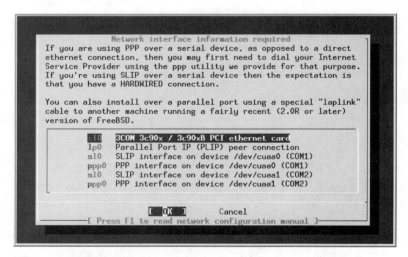

Figure 6-5: Network setup menu

In our case, we choose the Ethernet board. The next menu asks us to set the internet
parameters. Figure 6-6 shows the network configuration menu after filling in the values.
Specify the fully qualified local host name; when you tab to the Domain: field, the
domain is filled in automatically. The names and addresses correspond to the example
network that we look at in Chapter 16, on page 294. We have chosen to call this machine
presto, and the domain is *example.org*. In other words, the full name of the machine is
presto.example.org. Its IP address is 223.147.37.2. In this configuration, all access to
the outside world goes via gw.example.org, which has the IP address 223.147.37.5.
The name server is located on the same host, *presto.example.org*. The name server isn't
running when this information is needed, so we specify all addresses in numeric form.

What happens if you don't have a domain name? If you're connecting to the global Internet, you should go out and get one—see page 318. But in the meantime, don't fake it. Just leave the fields empty. If you're not connecting to the Internet, of course, it doesn't make much difference what name you choose.

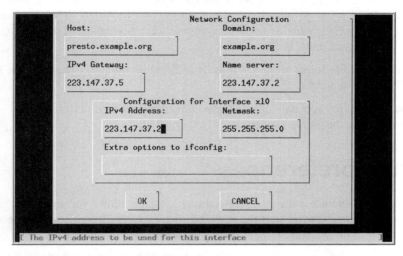

Figure 6-6: Network configuration menu

As is usual for a class C network, the net mask is 255.255.255.0. You don't need to fill in this information—if you leave this field without filling it in, *sysinstall* inserts it for you. Normally, as in this case, you wouldn't need any additional options to *ifconfig*.

Other network options

It's up to you to decide what other network options you would like to use. None of the following are essential, and none need to be done right now, but you may possibly find some of the following interesting:

- *inetd* allows connections to your system from outside. We'll look at it in more detail on page 448. Although it's very useful, it's also a security risk if it's configured incorrectly. If you don't want to accept any connections from outside, you can disable *inetd* and significantly reduce possible security exposures.

- *NFS client.* If you want to mount NFS file systems located on other machines, select this box. An X appears in the box, but nothing further happens. See Chapters 24 and 25 for further details of NFS.

- *NFS server.* If you want to allow other systems to mount file systems located on this machine, select this box. You get a prompt asking you to create the file */etc/exports*, which describes the conditions under which other systems can mount the file systems on this machine. You must enter the editor, but there is no need to change anything at this point. We'll look at */etc/exports* in more detail on page 463.

- *ntpdate* and *ntpd* are programs that automatically set the system time from time servers located on the Internet. See page 156 for more details. If you wish, you can select the server at this point.

- *rwhod* broadcasts information about the status of the systems on the network. You can use the *ruptime* program to find the uptime of all systems running *rwhod*, and *rwho* to find who is running on these systems. On a normal-sized display, you need to scroll the menu down to find this option.

- You don't need to select sshd: it's already selected for you. See page 453 for further details of *ssh* and *sshd*.

You don't need to specify any of the remaining configuration options during configuration. See the online handbook for further details.

Startup preferences

The next step of interest is the Startup submenu, which allows you to choose settings that take effect whenever you start the machine. See Chapter 29 for details of the startup files.

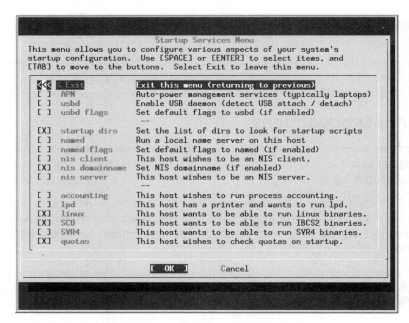

Figure 6-7: Startup configuration menu

The most important ones are:

- Select APM if you're running a laptop. It enables you to power the system down in *suspend to RAM* or *suspend to disk* mode, preserving the currently running system, and to resume execution at a later date.

- If you have USB peripherals, select usbd to enable the *usbd* daemon, which recognizes when USB devices are added or removed.

- named starts a name daemon. Use this if you're connecting to the Internet at all, even if you don't have a DNS configuration: the default configuration is a *caching name server*, which makes name resolution faster. Just select the box; you don't need to do anything else. We'll look at *named* in Chapter 21.

- Select lpd, the *line printer daemon*, if you have a printer connected to the machine. We'll look at *lpd* in Chapter 15.

- Select linux if you intend to run Linux binaries. This is almost certainly the case, and by default the box is already ticked for you.

- Select SVR4 and SCO if you intend to run UNIX System V.4 (SVR4) or SCO OpenDesktop or OpenServer (SCO) binaries respectively.

Configuring the mouse

FreeBSD detects PS/2 mice at boot time only, so the mouse must be plugged in when you boot. If not, you will not be able to use it. To configure, select Mouse from the configuration menu. The menu in Figure 6-8 appears.

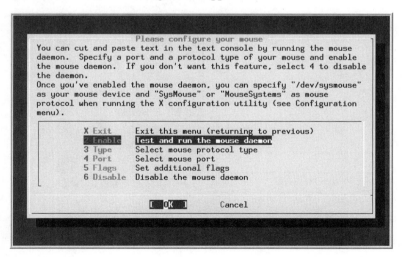

Figure 6-8: Mouse menu

With a modern PS/2 mouse, you don't need to do any configuration at all. You just enable the *mouse daemon* or *moused*. Select the menu item Enable: you have the chance to move the mouse and note that the cursor follows. The keys don't work in this menu: select Yes and exit the menu. That's all you need to do.

If you're running a serial mouse, choose the item Select mouse port and set it to correspond with the port you have; if you have an unusual protocol, you may also need to set it with the Type menu. For even more exotic connections, read the man page for *moused* and set the appropriate parameters.

Configuring X

You should have installed X along with the rest of the system—see page 75. If you haven't, install the package *x11/XFree86*. In this section, we'll look at what you need to do to get X up and running.

X configuration has changed a lot in the course of time, and it's still changing. The current method of configuring X uses a program called *xf86cfg*, which is still under development, and it shows a few strangenesses. Quite possibly the version you get will not behave identically with the following description. The differences should be relatively clear, however.

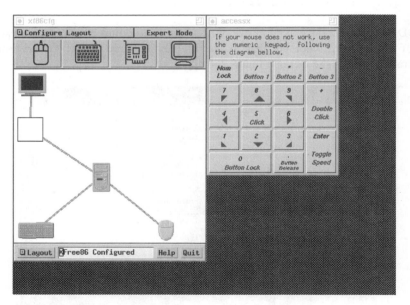

Figure 6-9: xf86cfg main menu

The configuration is stored in a file called *XF86Config*, though the directory has changed several times in the last few years. It used to be in */etc/X11/XF86Config* or

/etc/XF86Config, but the current preferred place is */usr/X11R6/lib/X11/XF86Config*. The server looks for the configuration file in multiple places, so if you're upgrading from an earlier version, make sure you remove any old configuration files. We'll look at the contents of the file in detail in Chapter 28. In this section, we'll just look at how to generate a usable configuration.

From the configuration menu, select XFree86 and then xf86cfg. There is a brief delay while *xf86cfg* creates an initial configuration file, then you see the main menu of Figure 6-9. This application runs without knowing what the hardware is, so the rendering is pretty basic. The window on the left shows the layout of the hardware, and the window on the right is available in case your mouse isn't working. Select the individual components with the mouse or the numeric keypad. For example, to configure the mouse, select the image at top left:

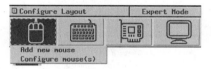

Figure 6-10: xf86cfg mouse menu

In all likelihood that won't be necessary. The configuration file that *xf86cfg* has already created may be sufficient, so you could just exit and save the file. You'll probably want to change some things, though. In the following, we'll go through the more likely changes you may want to make.

Configuring the keyboard

You can select a number of options for the keyboard, including alternative key layouts. You probably won't need to change anything here.

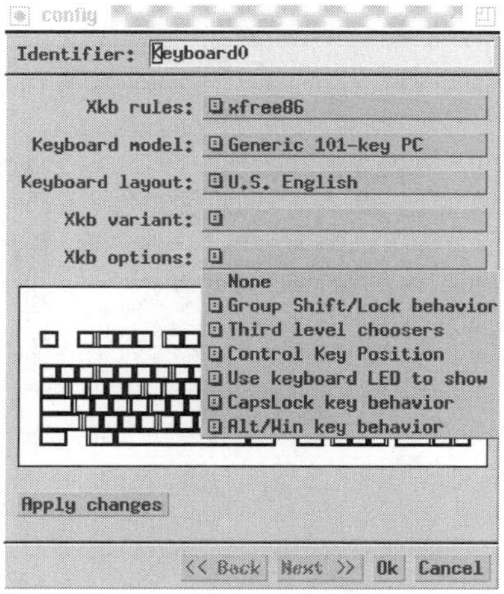

Figure 6-11: xf86cfg keyboard menu

Describing the monitor

Probably the most important thing you need to change are the definitions for the monitor and the display card. Some modern monitors and most AGP display cards supply the information, but older devices do not. In this example we'll configure a Hitachi CM813U monitor, which does not identify itself to *xf86cfg*. Select the monitor image at the top right of the window, then Configure Monitor(s). You see:

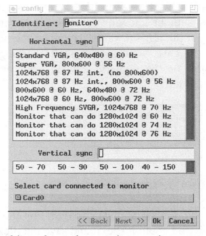

xf86cfg doesn't know anything about the monitor, so it assumes that it can only display standard VGA resolutions at 640x480. The important parameters to change are the horizontal and vertical frequencies. You can select one of the listed possibilities, but unless you don't know your's monitor specifications, you should set exactly the frequencies it can do. In this case, the monitor supports horizontal frequencies from 31 kHz to 115 kHz and vertical frequencies from 50 Hz to 160 Hz, so that's what we enter. At the same time, we change the identifier to indicate the name of the monitor:

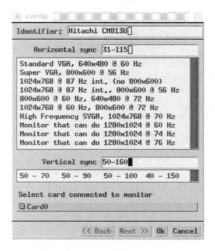

Figure 6-12: xf86cfg monitor menu

Select OK to return to the previous menu.

Configuring the display card

xf86cfg recognizes most modern display cards, including probably all AGP cards, so you probably don't need to do anything additional to configure the display card. If you find that the resultant configuration file doesn't know about your card, you'll have to select the card symbol at the top of the screen. Even if the card has been recognized, you get this display:

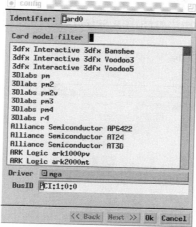

The only indication you have that *xf86cfg* has recognized the card (here a Matrox G200) is that it has selected mga for the driver name. If you need to change it, scroll down the list until you find the card:

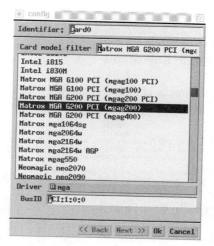

Figure 6-13: xf86cfg card select menu

Selecting display resolutions

The display resolution is defined by *Mode Lines*, which we'll look at in detail on page 513. The names relate to the resolution they offer. By default, *xf86cfg* only gives you 640x480, so you'll certainly want to add more. First, select the field at the top left of the screen:

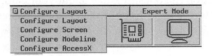

Figure 6-14: xf86cfg configuration selection

From this menu, select `Configure ModeLine`. You see:

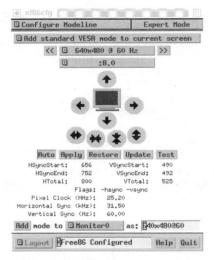

Figure 6-15: xf86cfg mode line menu

If you pass the cursor over the image of the screen, you'll see this warning:

Figure 6-16: xf86cfg mode line warning

Take it seriously. We'll look at this issue again in Chapter 28 on page 510. For an initial setup, you shouldn't use this interface. Instead, select `Add standard VESA mode` at the top. We get another menu:

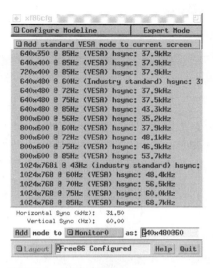

Figure 6-17: xf86cfg VESA mode lines

Select the resolutions you want with the highest frequency that your hardware can handle. In this case, you might select 1024x768 @ 85 Hz, because it's still well within the range of the monitor. Answer Yes to the question of whether you want to add it. You can select as many resolutions as you want, but the ModeLine window does not show them.

You can also use the ModeLine window to tune the display, but it's easier with another program, *xvidtune*. We'll look at those details in Chapter 28.

Finally, select Quit at the bottom right of the display. You get this window:

Figure 6-18: xf86cfg quit

When you answer Yes, you get a similar question asking whether you want to save the keyboard definition. Once you've done that, you're finished.

Desktop configuration

Next, select Desktop from the Configuration menu. You get this menu:

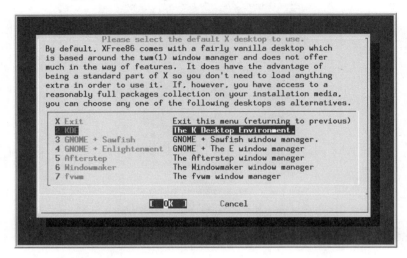

Figure 6-19: Desktop select menu

Which one do you install? You have the choice. If you know what you want, use it. There are many more window managers than shown here, so if you don't see what you're looking for, check the category *x11-wm* in the Ports Collection. The select menu gives you the most popular ones: *Gnome*, *Afterstep*, *Enlightenment*, *KDE*, *Windowmaker* and *fvwm2*. In this book, we'll consider the *KDE* desktop and the *fvwm2* window manager. KDE is comfortable, but it requires a lot of resources. Gnome is similar in size to KDE. By contrast, *fvwm2* is much faster, but it requires a fair amount of configuration. We'll look at KDE and *fvwm2* in Chapter 7.

Additional X configuration

At this point, we're nearly done. A few things remain to be done:

- Decide how you want to start X. You can do it explicitly with the *startx* command, or you can log in directly to X with the *xdm* display manager. If you choose *startx*, you don't need to do any additional configuration.

- For each user who runs X, create an X configuration file.

Configuring xdm

To enable *xdm*, edit the file */etc/ttys*. By default it contains the following lines:

```
ttyv8    "/usr/X11R6/bin/xdm -nodaemon"   xterm    off secure
```

Using an editor, change the text off to on:

```
ttyv8    "/usr/X11R6/bin/xdm -nodaemon"   xterm    on secure
```

If you do this from a running system, send a HUP signal to *init* to cause it to re-read the configuration file and start *xdm*:

```
# kill -1 1
```

This causes an *xdm* screen to appear on */dev/ttyv8*. You can switch to it with **Alt-F9**.

User X configuration

If you're starting X manually with *startx*, create a file *.xinitrc* in your home directory. This file contains commands that are executed when X starts. Select the line that corresponds to your window manager or desktop from the following list, and put it in *.xinitrc*:

```
startkde                                          for kde
exec gnome-session                                for Gnome
fvwm2                                             for fvwm2
```

If you're using *xdm*, you put the same content in the file *.xsession* in your home directory.

Rebooting the new system

When you get this far, you should have a functional system. If you're still installing from CD-ROM, you reboot by exiting *sysinstall*. If you have already rebooted, you exit *sysinstall* and reboot with:

```
# shutdown -r now
```

Don't just press the reset button or turn the power off. That can cause data loss. We'll look at this issue in more detail on page 541.

7

The tools of the trade

So now you have installed FreeBSD, and it successfully boots from the hard disk. If you're new to FreeBSD, your first encounter with it can be rather puzzling. You probably didn't expect to see the same things you know from other platforms, but you might not have expected what you see either:

```
FreeBSD (freebie.example.org) (ttyv0)

login:
```

If you have installed *xdm*, you'll at least get a graphical display, but it still asks you to log in and provide a password. Where do you go from here?

There isn't space in this book to explain everything there is about working with FreeBSD, but in the following few chapters I'd like to make the transition easier for people who have prior experience with Microsoft platforms or with other flavours of UNIX. You can find a lot more information about these topics in *UNIX for the Impatient*, by Paul W. Abrahams and Bruce R. Larson, *UNIX Power Tools*, by Jerry Peek, Tim O'Reilly, and Mike Loukides, and *UNIX System Administration Handbook*, by Evi Nemeth, Garth Snyder, Scott Seebass, and Trent R. Hein. The third edition of this book also covers FreeBSD Release 3.2. See Appendix A, *Bibliography*, for more information.

If you've come from Microsoft, you will notice a large number of differences between UNIX and Microsoft, but in fact the two systems have more in common than meets the eye. Indeed, back in the mid-80s, one of the stated goals of MS-DOS 2.0 was to make it more UNIX-like. You be the judge of how successful that attempt was, but if you know the MS-DOS command-line interface, you'll notice some similarities in the following sections.

In this chapter, we'll look at FreeBSD from the perspective of somebody with computer experience, but with no UNIX background. If you *do* have a UNIX background, you may still find it interesting.

If you're coming from a Microsoft platform, you'll be used to doing just about everything with a graphical interface. In this book I recommend that you use X and possibly a desktop, but the way you use it is still very different. FreeBSD, like other UNIX-like systems, places much greater emphasis on the use of text. This may seem primitive, but in fact the opposite is true. It's easier to point and click than to type, but you can express yourself much more accurately and often more quickly with a text interface.

As a result, the two most important tools you will use with FreeBSD are the *shell* and the *editor*. Use the shell to issue direct commands to the system, and the editor to prepare texts. We'll look at these issues in more detail in this chapter. In Chapter 8, *Taking control*, we'll look at other aspects of the system. First, though, we need to get access to the system.

Users and groups

Probably the biggest difference between most PC operating systems and FreeBSD also takes the longest to get used to: FreeBSD is a multi-user, multi-tasking system. This means that many people can use the system at once, and each can do several things at the same time. You may think "Why would I want to do that?" Once you've got used to this idea, though, you'll never want to do without it again. If you use the X Window System, you'll find that all windows can be active at the same time—you don't have to select them. You can monitor some activity in the background in another window while writing a letter, testing a program, or playing a game.

Before you can access a FreeBSD system, you must be registered as a *user*. The registration defines a number of parameters:

• A *user name*, also often called *user ID*. This is a name that you use to identify yourself to the system.

• A *password*, a security device to ensure that other people don't abuse your user ID. To log in, you need to specify both your user ID and the correct password. When you type in the password, nothing appears on the screen, so that people looking over your shoulder can't read it.

It might seem strange to go to such security measures on a system that you alone use. The incidence of Internet-related security problems in the last few years has shown that it's not strange at all, it's just common sense. Microsoft systems are still subject to a never-ending series of security exploits. FreeBSD systems are not.

- A *shell*, a program that reads in your commands and executes them. MS-DOS uses the program *COMMAND.COM* to perform this function. UNIX has a large choice of shells: the traditional UNIX shells are the Bourne shell *sh* and the C shell *csh*, but FreeBSD also supplies *bash*, *tcsh*, *zsh* and others. I personally use the *bash* shell, and the examples in this book are based on it.

- A *home directory*. The system can have multiple users, so each one needs a separate directory in which to store his private files. Typically, users have a directory */home/username*, where **username** is the name they use to log in. When you log in to the system, the shell sets the current directory to your home directory. In it, you can do what you want, and normally it is protected from access by other users. Many shells, including the *bash* shell used in these examples, use the special notation ~ (tilde) to represent the name of the home directory.

- A *group* number. UNIX collects users into *groups* who have specific common access permissions. When you add a user, you need to make him a member of a specific group, which is entered in the password information. Your group number indirectly helps determine what you are allowed to do in the system. As we'll see on page 181, your user and group determine what access you have to the system. You can belong to more than one group.

  Group numbers generally have names associated with them. The group names and numbers are stored in the file */etc/group*. In addition, this file may contain user IDs of users who belong to another group, but who are allowed to belong to this group as well.

  If you find the concept of groups confusing, don't worry about them. You can get by quite happily without using them at all. You'll just see references to them when we come to discuss file permissions. For further information, look at the man page for *group(5)*.

By the time you get here, you should have defined a user name, as recommended on page 94. If you haven't, you'll have to log in as root and create one as described there.

Gaining access

Once you have a user name, you can log in to the system. Already you have a choice: FreeBSD offers both *virtual terminals* and the X Window System. The former displays plain text on the monitor, whereas the latter uses the system's graphics capabilities. Once running, you can switch from one to the other, but you have the choice of which interface you use first. If you don't do anything, you get a virtual terminal. If you run *xdm*, you get X.

It's still relatively uncommon to use *xdm*, and in many instances you may not want X at all, for example if you're running the system as a server. As a result, we'll look at the "conventional" login first.

If you're logging in on a virtual terminal, you'll see something like this:

```
login: grog
Password:                                      password doesn't show on the screen
Last login: Fri Apr 11 16:30:04 from canberra
Copyright (c) 1980, 1983, 1986, 1988, 1990, 1991, 1993, 1994
        The Regents of the University of California.  All rights reserved.

FreeBSD 5.0-RELEASE (FREEBIE) #0: Tue Dec 31 19:08:24 CST 2002

Welcome to FreeBSD!

You have mail.
erase ^H, kill ^U, intr ^C, status ^T
Niklaus Wirth has lamented that, whereas Europeans pronounce his name
correctly (Ni-klows Virt), Americans invariably mangle it into
(Nick-les Worth).  Which is to say that Europeans call him by name, but
Americans call him by value.
=== grog@freebie (/dev/ttyv0) ~ 1 ->
```

There's a lot of stuff here. It's worth looking at it in more detail:

- The program that asks you to log in on a terminal window is called *getty*. It reads in your user ID and starts a program called *login* and passes the user ID to it.

- *login* asks for the password and checks your user ID.

- If the user ID and password are correct, *login* starts your designated shell.

- While starting up, the shell looks at a number of files. See the man page for your particular shell for details of what they are for. In this case, though, we can see the results: one file contains the time you last logged in, another one contains the *Message of the day* (*/etc/motd*), and a third one informs you that you have mail. The shell prints out the message of the day verbatim—in this case, it contains information about the name of the kernel and a welcome message. The shell also prints information on last login time (in this case, from a remote system) and whether you have mail.

- The line "erase ^H, kill ^U, intr ^C, status ^T" looks strange. It's telling you the current editing control characters. We'll look at these on page 131. At this point, the shell changes the current directory to your *home directory*. There is no output on the screen to indicate this.

- The shell runs the *fortune* program, which prints out a random quotation from a database of "fortune cookies." In this case, we get a message about Niklaus Wirth, the inventor of the Pascal programming language.

- Finally, the last line is a prompt, the information that tells you that the shell is ready for input.

The prompt illustrates a number of things about the UNIX environment. By default, *sh* and friends prompt with a $, and *csh* and friends prompt with a %. You can change it to just about anything you want with the UNIX shells. You don't have to like my particular version, but it's worth understanding what it's trying to say.

The first part, ===, is just to make it easier to find in a large list on an X display. An *xterm* window on a high resolution X display can contain up to 120 lines, and searching for command prompts can be non-trivial.

Next, grog@freebie is my user ID and the name of system on which I am working, in
the RFC 2822 format used for mail IDs. Multiple systems and multiple users can all be
present on a single X display. This way, I can figure out which user I am and what
system I am running on.

/dev/ttyv0 is the name of the terminal device. This can sometimes be useful.

~ is the name of the home directory. Most shells, but not all of them, support this
symbolism.

1 is the prompt number. Each time you enter a command, it is associated with this
number, and the prompt number is incremented. One way to re-execute the command is
to enter !!1 (two exclamation marks and the number of the command). We'll look at
more comfortable ones on page 131.

To start X from a virtual terminal shell, use the *startx* command:

```
$ startx
```

If you use *xdm*, you bypass the virtual terminals and go straight into X. Enter your user
name and password to the login prompt or the *xdm* login screen, and press **Enter**. If you
use the *xdm* login, you'll go straight into X.

Figure 7-1: KDE display

Either way, assuming that you've installed and configured *kde*, you'll get a display similar to that in Figure 7-1. This example includes four windows that are not present on startup. On startup the central part of the screen is empty. We'll look at the windows further below.

The KDE desktop

KDE is a complicated system, and good documentation is available at *http://www.kde.org/documentation/*. Once you have KDE running, you can access the same information via the help icon on the panel at the bottom (the life ring icon). The following description gives a brief introduction.

The KDE display contains a number of distinct areas. At the top is an optional menu, at the bottom an almost optional *panel*, and the middle of the screen is reserved for windows.

The Desktop Menu

The *Desktop Menu* is at the very top of the screen. It provides functionality that is not specific to a particular application. Select the individual categories with the mouse. For example, the New menu looks like this:

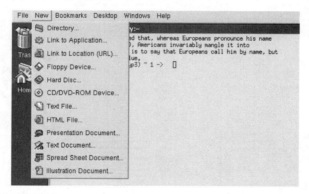

Figure 7-2: KDE desktop menu

As the menu indicates, you can use these menus to create new files.

The Panel

At the bottom of the screen is the panel, which consists of a number of fields. The left-hand section is used for starting applications.

The stylized letter K at the extreme left is the *Application Starter*. When you select it, a long vertical menu appears at the left of the screen and allows you to start programs ("applications") or access just about any other function.

Next comes an icon called "show desktop." This is a convenient way to iconify all the windows currently on the desktop.

The remaining icons on this part of the panel represent various applications.

- The *konsole* terminal emulator.

- The *command center*, which you use to configure KDE.

- The help system.

- Access to the home directory with the browser *konqueror*.

- Access to the Web, also with the browser *konqueror*.

- The *Kmail* MUA.

- The *KWord* word processor, which can understand Microsoft Word documents.

- The *Kspread* spreadsheet.

- The *Kpresenter* presentation package.

- The *Kate* editor.

The next section of the panel contains some control buttons and information about the current desktop layout:

The section at the left shows the current contents of four screens, numbered 1 to 4. Screen 1 is the currently displayed screen; you can select one of the others by moving the cursor in the corresponding direction, or by selecting the field with the mouse.

To the right of that are icons for the currently active windows. The size expands and contracts depending on the number of different kinds of window active. If you select one of these icons with the left mouse button, it will iconify or deiconify ("minimize" or "maximize") the window. If you have multiple *xterms* active, you will only have one icon. In this case, if you select the icon, you will get another pop-up selection menu to allow you to choose the specific window.

The right part of the panel contains a further three fields:

- The first one shows a stylized padlock (for locking the session when you leave the machine; unlock by entering your password) and a stylized off switch, for logging out of the session.

- The next section shows a stylized power connector, which displays the current power status of the machine, and a clipboard.

- The right side shows a digital clock.

Probably the most useful part of this section of the panel is not very obvious: the right-pointing arrow allows you to remove the panel if you find it's in the way. The entire panel is replaced by a single left-pointing arrow at the extreme right of the display.

Using the mouse

By default, *kde* only uses the left and the right mouse buttons. In general, the left button is used to select a particular button, and the right button is used for an auxiliary menu.

Manipulating windows

You'll notice that each window has a frame around it with a number of features. In X terminology, they're called *decorations*. Specifically:

- There's a *title bar* with the name of the program. If you select the bar itself, you raise the window above all others. If you hold down the button on the title bar, you can move the window.

- At the left of the title bar there is an X logo. If you select this logo, you get a menu of window operations.

- At the right of the title bar, there are three buttons that you can select. The left one iconifies the window, the middle one *maximizes* the window, making it take up the entire screen, and the one on the right kills the application. If the window is already maximized, the middle button restores it to its previous size.

- You can select any corner of the window, or any of the other edges, to change the size of the window.

The fvwm2 window manager

If you come from a conventional PC background, you shouldn't have much difficulty with KDE. It's a relatively complete, integrated environment. But it isn't really UNIX. If you come from a UNIX environment, you may find it too all-encompassing. You may also find that there are significant delays when you start new applications.

UNIX has a very different approach to windows. There is no desktop, just a window manager. It takes up less disk space, less processor time, and less screen real estate. By default, XFree86 comes with the *twm* window manager, but that's really a little primitive. With modern machines, there's no reason to choose such a basic window manager. You may, however, find that *fvwm2* is more your style than KDE.

Starting fvwm2

Like KDE, you install *fvwm2* from the Ports Collection. It's not designed to work completely correctly out of the box, though it does work. As with KDE, the first thing you need to do is to create a *.xsession* or *.xinitrc* file, depending on whether you're running *xdm*. It must contain at least the line:

```
fvwm2
```

Start X the same way you did for KDE. This time you see, after starting the same applications as before:

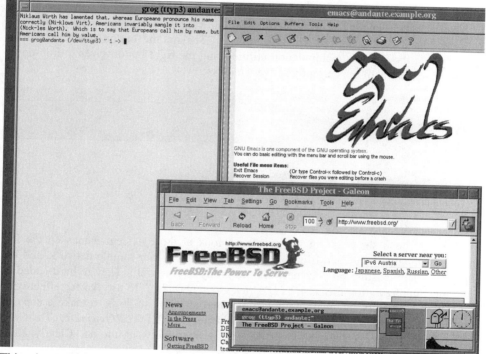

This picture shows both similarities with and differences from KDE. The similarities include:

- Each window has a frame and a title. The exact form of the decorations is different, but the purpose is the same. There is no "close application" button: for most UNIX applications, you should get the program to exit rather than killing it.

- There is a task bar at the bottom right, taking up only half the width of the screen. The currently active window (the *xterm* at the left in this example) is highlighted.

- The default *fvwm2* display also has four screens, and the task bar shows the position of the windows on the task bar.

Still, there are a number of differences as well:

- Unless you have a top-end machine, it's *much* faster in what it does.

- The background (the *root window*) doesn't have any pattern; it's just a grey cross-hatch.

- You can move from one screen to the other using the cursor, and windows can overlap. In this example, the *galeon* web browser window goes down to the screen below, and the Emacs window goes over all four screens, as the display on the task bar shows. With KDE, the only way to display the rest of these windows is to move the window.

- Paradoxically, you can do a lot more with the mouse. On the root window, the left mouse button gives you a menu for starting various programs, both locally and remotely, and also various window utilities. The middle button gives you direct access to the window manipulation utilities, and the right button gives a drop-down list to select any of the currently active windows:

The menus above show one of the problems: look at those system names on the left submenu (*dopey*, *snoopy* and friends). They don't exist on our sample network, and the chance of them existing on your network are pretty low as well. They're hard-coded in the sample configuration file, */usr/X11R6/etc/system.fvwm2rc*. To use *fvwm2* effectively, you'll have to modify the configuration file. The best thing to do is to make a copy of */usr/X11R6/etc/system.fvwm2rc* in your own directory, as *˜/.fvwm2/.fvwm2rc*. Then you can have lots of fun tweaking the file to do exactly what you want it to do. Clearly, KDE is easier to set up.

Changing the X display

When you set up your *XF86Config* file, you may have specified more than one resolution. For example, on page 107 we selected the additional resolution 1024x768 pixels. When you start X, it automatically selects the first resolution, in this case 640x480. You can change to the previous resolution (the one to the left in the list) by pressing the **Ctrl-Alt-Keypad -** key, and to the following resolution (the one to the right in the list) with **Ctrl-Alt-Keypad +**. *Keypad +* and *Keypad -* refer to the **+** and **-** symbols on the numeric keypad at the right of the keyboard; you can't use the **+** and **-** symbols on the main keyboard for this purpose. The lists wrap around: in our example, if your current resolution is 640x480, and you press **Ctrl-Alt-Keypad -**, the display changes to 1024x768. It's a very good idea to keep the default resolution at 640x480 until you have debugged your *XF86Config* parameters: 640x480 almost always works, so if your display is messed up, you can just switch back to a known good display with a single keystroke.

Selecting pixel depth

You can configure most display boards to display a number of different pixel depths (a different number of bits per pixel, which translates to a different number of colours). When you start X, however, it defaults to 8 bits per pixel (256 colours), which is a very poor rendition. To start it with a different number, specify the number of planes. For example, to start with 32 bits per pixel (4,294,967,296 colours), enter:

```
$ startx -- -bpp 32
```

With older display boards, which had relatively limited display memory, there was a tradeoff between maximum resolution and maximum pixel depth. Modern display cards no longer have this limitation. We'll look at this issue in more detail on page 522.

Getting a shell

As we saw at the beginning of the chapter, your main tools are the shell and the editor, and that's what we saw on the sample screens. But when you start X, they're not there: you need to start them.

In KDE, you have two ways to start a terminal window:

* You can select the icon showing a monitor with a shell in front of it, third from the left at the bottom of the example above. This starts the *konsole* terminal emulator.

* You can start an *xterm* by pressing **Alt-F2**. You see a window like the one in the centre left of Figure 7-1, enter the text xterm (as shown) and press Run or the **Enter** key.

Obviously the first is the intended approach, and it's easier. Nevertheless, I recommend using *xterm* at least until you're sure you want to stick with *kde*: there are some subtle differences, and *konsole* is intended to work with *kde* only. If you do stick with KDE, you should change the configuration of the *konsole* button to start *xterm* instead; that's relatively straightforward.

In *fvwm2*, you start an *xterm* from the left mouse menu, as shown above.

Shell basics

The most basic thing you can do with the shell is to start a program. Consider program names to be commands: like you might ask somebody to "wash the dishes" or "mow the lawn," you can tell the shell to "remove those files":

```
$ rm file1 file2 file3
```

This starts a program called *rm* (remove), and gives it a list of three file names to remove.

If you're removing a whole lot of files, this could take a while. Consider removing the entire directory hierarchy */usr/obj*, which is created when building a new version of the system (see page 595). This directory hierarchy contains about 15,000 files and directories, and it'll take a while to remove it. You can do this with the following command:

```
# rm -rf /usr/obj &
```

In this example, we have a couple of options led in by a hyphen (-) and also the character & at the end of the line.

- The r option tells *rm* to *recursively* descend into subdirectories. If you didn't specify this, it would remove all files in the directory */usr/obj* and then exit, complaining that it can't delete directories.

- The f (*force*) option tells *rm* to continue on error; otherwise if anything goes wrong, it will stop.

- The & character at the end of the line tells the shell (not *rm*) to continue after starting the program. It can run for some time, and there's no need to wait for it.

Options

In the previous example, we saw a couple of options. By convention, they come between the command name and other parameters, and they're identified because they start with a hyphen character (-). There's a lot of variation, though, depending on the individual program.

- Sometimes, as in the previous example, options consist of a single letter and can often be joined together.

- Some programs, like *tar* and *ps*, don't insist on the hyphen lead-in. In Chapter 8, we'll see the command:

```
# ps waux
```

This command could equally well be written:

```
# ps -waux
```

You may also come across programs that refuse to accept the hyphen at all.

- Sometimes options can have values. For example, in Chapter 23 we'll see:

```
# tcpdump -i ppp0 host hub.freebsd.org
```

Here, ppp0 is an argument to the i option. In some cases, it must be written with a space; in others, it must be written without a space; and in others again, it can be written either way. Pay attention to this detail when reading man pages.

- In other cases, they can be keywords, in which case they need to be written separately. The GNU project is particularly fond of this kind of option. For example, when building the system you may see compiler invocations like these:

```
cc -O -pipe -Dinline=rpcgen_inline -Wall -Wno-format-y2k -Wno-uninitialized \
-D__FBSDID=__RCSID -c /usr/src/usr.bin/rpcgen/rpc_main.c
```

With the exception of the last parameter, all of these texts are options, as the hyphen suggests.

- Options are specific to particular commands, though often several commands attempt to use the same letters to mean the same sort of thing. Typical ones are v for verbose output, q for quiet output (i.e. less than normal).

- Sometimes you can run into problems when you supply a parameter that looks like an option. For example, how do you remove a file called *-rf*? There are a number of solutions for this problem. In this example, you could write:

```
$ rm ./-rf
```

This is an alternative file naming convention that we'll look at again on page 126.

Shell parameters

When you invoke a program with the shell, it first *parses* the input line before passing it to the program: it turns the line into a number of parameters (called *arguments* in the C programming language). Normally the parameters are separated by *white space*, either a space or a tab character. For example, consider the previous example:

```
$ rm file1 file2 file3
```

the program receives four arguments, numbered 0 to 3:

Table 7-1: Program arguments

Argument	Value
0	rm
1	file1
2	file2
3	file3

What happens if you want to pass a name with a space? For example, you might want to look for the text "Mail rejected" in a log file. UNIX has a standard program for looking for text, called *grep*. The syntax is:

```
grep expression files
```

Argument 1 is the expression; all additional arguments are the names of files to search. We could write:

```
$ grep Mail rejected /var/log/maillog
```

but that would try to look for the text Mail in the files *rejected* (probably causing an error message that the file did not exist) and */var/log/maillog* (where just about every line contains the text Mail). That's not what we want. Instead, we do pretty much what I wrote above:

```
$ grep "Mail rejected" /var/log/maillog
```

In other words, if we put quote characters " " around a group of words, the shell will interpret them as a single parameter. The first parameter that is passed to *grep* is Mail rejected, not "Mail rejected".

This behaviour of the shell is a very good reason not to use file names with spaces in them. It's perfectly legitimate to embed spaces into UNIX file names, but it's a pain to use. If you want to create a file name that contains several words, for example *All files updated since last week*, consider changing the spaces to underscores: *All_files_updated_since_last_week*.

It's even more interesting to see what happens when you pass a globbing character to a program, for example:

```
$ cc -o foo *.c
```

This invocation compiles all C source files (**.c*) and creates a program *foo*. If you do this with Microsoft, the C compiler gets four parameters, and it has to find the C source files itself. In UNIX, the shell expands the text **.c* and replaces it with the names of the source files. If there are thirty source files in the directory, it will pass a total of 33 parameters to the compiler.

Fields that can contain spaces

The solution to the "Mail rejected" problem isn't ideal, but it works well enough as long as you don't have to handle fields with blanks in them too often. In many cases, though, particularly in configuration files, fields with blanks are relatively common. As a result, a number of system configuration files use a colon (:) as a delimiter. This looks very confusing at first, but it turns out not to be as bad as the alternatives. We'll see some examples in the PATH environment variable on page 130, in the password file on page 144, and in the login class file on page 570.

Files and file names

Both UNIX and Microsoft environments store disk data in *files*, which in turn are placed in *directories*. A file may be a directory: that is, it may contain other files. The differences between UNIX and Microsoft start with *file names*. Traditional Microsoft file names are rigid: a file name consists of eight characters, possibly followed by a period and another three characters (the so-called *file name extension*). There are significant restrictions on which characters may be used to form a file name, and upper and lower case letters have the same meaning (internally, Microsoft converts the names to UPPER CASE). Directory members are selected with a backslash (\), which conflicts with other meanings in the C programming language—see page 138 for more details.

FreeBSD has a very flexible method of naming files. File names can contain any character except /, and they can be up to 255 characters long. They are *case-sensitive*: the names *FOO*, *Foo* and *foo* are three different names. This may seem silly at first, but any alternative means that the names must be associated with a specific character set. How do you upshift the German name *ungleichmäßig*? What if the same characters appear in a Russian name? Do they still shift the same? The exception is because the / character represents directories. For example, the name */home/fred/longtext-with-a-long-name* represents:

1. First character is a /, representing the *root file system*.

2. *home* is the name of a directory in the root file system.

3. *fred* is the name of a directory in */home*.

4. The name suggests that *longtext-with-a-long-name* is probably a file, not a directory, though you can't tell from the name.

As a result, you can't use / in a file name. In addition, binary 0s (the ASCII NUL character) can confuse a lot of programs. It's almost impossible to get a binary 0 into a file name anyway: that character is used to represent the end of a string in the C programming language, and it's difficult to input it from the keyboard.

Case sensitivity no longer seems as strange as it once did: web browsers have made UNIX file names more popular with *Uniform Resource Indicators* or *URIs*, which are derived from UNIX names.

File names and extensions

The Microsoft naming convention (name, period and extension) seems similar to that of
UNIX. UNIX also uses extensions to represent specific kinds of files. The difference is
that these extensions (and their lengths) are implemented by convention, not by the file
system. In Microsoft, the period between the name and the extension is a typographical
feature that only exists at the display level: it's not part of the name. In UNIX, the period
is part of the name, and names like *foo.bar.bazzot* are perfectly valid file names. The
system doesn't assign any particular meaning to file name extensions; instead, it looks for
magic numbers, specific values in specific places in the file.

Relative paths

Every directory contains two directory entries, . and .. (one and two periods). These are
relative directory entries: . is an alternative way to refer to the current directory, and ..
refers to the parent directory. For example, in */home/fred*, . refers to */home/fred*, and ..
refers to */home*. The root directory doesn't have a parent directory, so in this directory
only, .. refers to the same directory. We'll see a number of cases where this is useful.[1]

Globbing characters

Most systems have a method of representing groups of file names and other names,
usually by using special characters for representing an abstraction. The most common in
UNIX are the characters *, ? and the square brackets []. UNIX calls these characters
globbing characters. The Microsoft usage comes from UNIX, but the underlying file
name representation makes for big differences. Table 7-2 gives some examples.

Table 7-2: Globbing examples

Name	Microsoft meaning	UNIX meaning
CONFIG.*	All files with the name *CONFIG*, no matter what their extension.	All files whose name starts with *CONFIG.*, no matter what the rest is. Note that the name contains a period.
CONFIG.BA?	All files with the name *CONFIG* and an extension that starts with *BA*, no matter what the last character.	All files that start with *CONFIG.BA* and have one more character in their name.
*	Depending on the Microsoft version, all files without an extension, or all files.	All files.
.	All files with an extension.	All files that have a period in the middle of their name.

---

1. Interestingly, the Microsoft file systems also have this feature.

foo[127]	In older versions, invalid. In newer versions with long file name support, the file with the name *foo[127]*.	The three files *foo1*, *foo2* and *foo7*.

Input and output

Most programs either read input data or write output data. To make it easier, the shell usually starts programs with at least three open files:

- *Standard input*, often abbreviated to *stdin*, is the file that most programs read to get input data.

- *Standard output*, or *stdout*, is the normal place for programs to write output data.

- *Standard error output*, or *stderr*, is a separate file for programs to write error messages.

With an interactive shell (one that works on a terminal screen, like we're seeing here), all three files are the same device, in this case the terminal you're working on.

Why two output files? Well, you may be collecting something important, like a backup of all the files on your system. If something goes wrong, you want to know about it, but you don't want to mess up the backup with the message.

Redirecting input and output

But of course, even if you're running an interactive shell, you don't want to back up your system to the screen. You need to change *stdout* to be a file. Many programs can do this themselves; for example, you might make a backup of your home directory like this:

```
$ tar -cf /var/tmp/backup ~
```

This creates (option c) a file (option f) called */var/tmp/backup*, and includes all the files in your home directory (~). Any error messages still appear on the terminal, as *stderr* hasn't been changed.

This syntax is specific to *tar*. The shell provides a more general syntax for redirecting input and output streams. For example, if you want to create a list of the files in your current directory, you might enter:

```
$ ls -l
drwxr-xr-x   2 root  wheel    512 Dec 20 14:36 CVS
-rw-r--r--   1 root  wheel   7928 Oct 23 12:01 Makefile
-rw-r--r--   5 root  wheel    209 Jul 26 07:11 amd.map
-rw-r--r--   5 root  wheel   1163 Jan 31  2002 apmd.conf
-rw-r--r--   5 root  wheel    271 Jan 31  2002 auth.conf
-rw-r--r--   1 root  wheel    741 Feb 19  2001 crontab
-rw-r--r--   5 root  wheel    108 Jan 31  2002 csh.cshrc
-rw-r--r--   5 root  wheel    482 Jan 31  2002 csh.login
(etc)
```

You can redirect this output to a file with the command:

```
$ ls -l > /var/tmp/etclist
```

This puts the list in the file */var/tmp/etclist*. The symbol > tells the shell to redirect *stdout* to the file whose name follows. Similarly, you could use the < to redirect *stdin* to that file, for example when using *grep* to look for specific texts in the file:

```
$ grep csh < /var/tmp/etclist
 -rw-r--r--   5 root  wheel    108 Jan 31  2002 csh.cshrc
 -rw-r--r--   5 root  wheel    482 Jan 31  2002 csh.login
 -rw-r--r--   5 grog  lemis    110 Jan 31  2002 csh.logout
```

In fact, though, there's a better way to do that: what we're doing here is feeding the output of a program into the input of another program. That happens so often that there's a special method of doing it, called *pipes*:

```
$ ls -l | grep csh
 -rw-r--r--   5 root  wheel    108 Jan 31  2002 csh.cshrc
 -rw-r--r--   5 root  wheel    482 Jan 31  2002 csh.login
 -rw-r--r--   5 grog  lemis    110 Jan 31  2002 csh.logout
```

The | symbol causes the shell to start two programs. The first has a special file, a *pipe*, as the output, and the second has the same pipe as input. Nothing gets written to disk, and the result is much faster.

A typical use of pipes are to handle quantities of output data in excess of a screenful. You can pipe to the *less*[1] program, which enables you to page backward and forward:

```
$ ls -l | less
```

Another use is to sort arbitrary data:

```
$ ps aux | sort -n +1
```

This command takes the output of the *ps* command and sorts it by the numerical (-n) value of its *second* column (+1). The first column is numbered 0. We'll look at *ps* on page 148.

Environment variables

The UNIX programming model includes a concept called *environment variables*. This rather unusual sounding name is simply a handy method of passing relatively long-lived information of a general nature from one program to another. It's easier to demonstrate the use than to describe. Table 7-3 takes a look at some typical environment variables. To set environment variables from Bourne-style shells, enter:

---

1. Why *less*? Originally there was a program called *more*, but it isn't as powerful. *less* is a new program with additional features, which proves beyond doubt that *less* is *more*.

```
$ export TERM=xterm
```

This sets the value of the TERM variable to xterm. The word export tells the shell to pass this information to any program it starts. Once it's exported, it stays exported. If the variable isn't exported, only the shell can use it.

Alternatively, if you want to set the variable only once when running a program, and then forget it, you can set it at the beginning of a command line:

```
$ TERM=xterm-color mutt
```

This starts the *mutt* mail reader (see page 474) with *xterm*'s colour features enabled.

For *csh* and *tcsh*, set environment variables with:

```
% setenv TERM xterm
```

To start a process with these variables, enter:

```
% env xterm-color mutt
```

Table 7-3: Common environment variables

Name	Purpose
BLOCKSIZE	The size of blocks that programs like *df* count. The default is 512 bytes, but it's often more convenient to use 1024 or even 1048576 (1 MB).
DISPLAY	When running X, the name of the X server. For a local system, this is typically unix:0. For remote systems, it's in the form *system-name*:*server-number*.*screen-number*. For the system *bumble.example.org*, you would probably write bumble.example.org:0.
EDITOR	The name of your favourite editor. Various programs that start editors look at this variable to know which editor to start.
HOME	The name of your home directory.
LANG	The *locale* that you use. This should be the name of a directory in */usr/share/locale*.
MAIL	Some programs use this variable to find your incoming mail file.
MANPATH	A list of path names, separated by colons (:), that specifies where the *man* program should look for man pages. A typical string might be /usr/share/man:/usr/local/man, and specifies that there are man pages in each of the directories */usr/share/man* and */usr/local/man*.
NTAPE	The name of the non-rewinding tape device. See page 252 for more details.

Name	Purpose
PATH	A list of path names, separated by colons (`:`), that specifies where the shell should look for executable programs if you specify just the program name.
PS1	In Bourne-style shells, this is the prompt string. It's usually set to **$**, but can be changed. See page 114 for a discussion of a possible prompt for *bash*.
PS2	In Bourne-style shells, this is the prompt string for continuation lines. It's usually set to **>**.
SHELL	The name of the shell. Some programs use this for starting a shell.
TAPE	The name of the rewinding tape device. See page 252 for more details.
TERM	The type of terminal emulation you are using. This is very important: there is no other way for an application to know what the terminal is, and if you set it to the wrong value, full-screen programs will behave incorrectly.
TZ	Time zone. This is the name of a file in */usr/share/zoneinfo* that describes the local time zone. See the section on timekeeping on page 155 for more details.

Note particularly the PATH variable. One of the most popular questions in the FreeBSD-questions mailing list is "I have compiled a program, and I can see it in my directory, but when I try to run it, I get the message "command not found." This is usually because PATH does not include the current directory.

> It's good practice *not* to have your current directory or your home directory in the PATH: if you do, you can be subject to security compromises. For example, somebody could install a program called *ps* in the directory */var/tmp*. Despite the name, the program might do something else, for example remove all files in your home directory. If you change directory to */var/tmp* and run *ps*, you will remove all files in your home directory. Obviously much more subtle compromises are possible.
>
> Instead, run the program like this:
>
> $ ./program

You should set your PATH variable to point to the most common executable directories. Add something like this to your *.profile* file (for Bourne-style shells):

```
PATH=/usr/bin:/usr/local/bin:/usr/sbin:/bin:/sbin:/usr/X11R6/bin
export PATH
```

This variable is of great importance: one of the leading problems that beginners have is to have an incorrect PATH variable.

Printing out environment variables

So you can't start a program, and you're wondering whether your PATH environment variable is set correctly. You can find out with the *echo* command:

```
$ echo $PATH
/bin:/usr/bin
```

The $ at the beginning of $PATH tells the shell to substitute the value of the environment variable for its name. Without this, the shell has no way of knowing that it's an environment variable, so it passes the text PATH to *echo*, which just prints it out.

If you want to print out all the environment variables, use the *printenv* command:

```
$ printenv | sort
BLOCKSIZE=1048576
CLASSPATH=/usr/local/java/lib:/usr/local/java/lib/classes.zip:/home/grog/netscape/
CVSROOT=/home/ncvs
DISPLAY=freebie:0
EDITOR=emacs
HOME=/home/grog
PAGER=less
PATH=.:/usr/bin:/usr/sbin:/bin:/sbin:/usr/X11R6/bin:/usr/local/bin:/usr/local/sbin
XAUTHORITY=/home/grog/.Xauthority
```

This example sorts the variables to make it easier to find them. In all probability, you'll find many more variables.

Command line editing

Typing is a pain. If you're anything like me, you're continually making mistakes, and you may spend more time correcting typing errors than doing the typing in the first place. It's particularly frustrating when you enter something like:

```
$ groff -rex=7.5 -r$$ -rL -rW -rN2 -mpic tmac.M unixerf.mm
troff: fatal error: can't open 'unixerf.mm': No such file or directory
```

This command *should* create the PostScript version of this chapter, but unfortunately I messed up the name of the chapter: it should have been *unixref.mm*, and I typed *unixerf.mm*.

> Yes, I know this looks terrible. In fact, UNIX has ways to ensure you almost never need to write commands like this. The command I really use to format this chapter is "make unixref".

It would be particularly frustrating if I had to type the whole command in again. UNIX offers a number of ways to make life easier. The most obvious one is so obvious that you tend to take it for granted: the **Backspace** key erases the last character you entered. Well, most of the time. What if you're running on a machine without a **Backspace** key? You won't have that problem with a PC, of course, but a lot of workstations have a **DEL** key instead of a **Backspace** key. UNIX lets you specify what key to use to erase the last character entered. By default, the erase character really is **DEL**, but the shell startup changes it and prints out a message saying what it has done:

```
erase ^H, kill ^U, intr ^C, status ^T
```

in the example on page 113. **^H (Ctrl-H)** is an alternative representation for **Backspace**.

The three other functions kill, intr, and status perform similar editing functions. kill erases the whole line, and intr stops a running program.

> More correctly, intr sends a *signal* called SIGINT to the process. This normally causes a program to stop.

You'll notice that it is set to **Ctrl-C**, so its function is very similar to that of the MS-DOS **Break** key. status is an oddball function: it doesn't change the input, it just displays a statistics message. *bash* doesn't in fact use it: it has a better use for **Ctrl-T**.

In fact, these control characters are just a few of a large number of control characters that you can set. Table 7-4 gives an overview of the more common control characters. For a complete list, see the man page *stty(1)*.

Table 7-4: Terminal control characters

Name	Default	Function
CR	\r	Go to beginning of line. Normally, this also terminates input (in other words, it returns the complete line to the program, which then acts on the input).
NL	\n	End line. Normally, this also terminates input.
INTR	Ctrl-C	Generate a SIGINT signal. This normally causes the process to terminate.
QUIT	Ctrl-|	Generate a SIGQUIT signal. This normally causes the process to terminate and *core dump*, to save a copy of its memory to disk for later analysis.
ERASE	DEL	Erase last character. FreeBSD sets this to **Backspace** on login, but under some unusual circumstances you might find it still set to **DEL**.
KILL	Ctrl-U	Erase current input line.
EOF	Ctrl-D	Return end-of-file indication. Most programs stop when they receive an EOF.
STOP	Ctrl-S	Stop output. Use this to examine text that is scrolling faster than you can read.
START	Ctrl-Q	Resume output after stop.
SUSP	Ctrl-Z	Suspend process. This key generates a SIGTSTP signal when typed. This normally causes a program to be suspended. To restart, use the *fg* command.

Name	Default	Function
DSUSP	Ctrl-Y	Delayed suspend. Generate a SIGTSTP signal when the character is read. Otherwise, this is the same as SUSP.
REPRINT	Ctrl-R	Redisplay all characters in the input queue (in other words, characters that have been input but not yet read by any process). The term "print" recalls the days of harcopy terminals. Many shells disable this function.
DISCARD	Ctrl-O	Discard all terminal output until another DISCARD character arrives, more input is typed or the program clears the condition.

To set these characters, use the *stty* program. For example, if you're used to erasing the complete input line with **Ctrl-X**, and specifying an end-of-file condition with **Ctrl-Z**, you could enter:

```
$ stty susp \377 kill ^X eof ^Z
```

You need to set SUSP to something else first, because by default it is Ctrl-Z, so the system wouldn't know which function to perform if you press ^Z.

> The combination \377 represents the character octal 377 (this notation comes from the C programming language, and its origin is lost in the mists of time, back in the days when UNIX ran on PDP-11s). This character is the "null" character that turns off the corresponding function. System V uses the character \0 for the same purpose.

In this particular case, ^X really does mean the character ^ followed by the letter X, and not **Ctrl-X**, the single character created by holding down the **Control** character and pressing **X** at the same time.

Command history and other editing functions

Nowadays, most shells supply a *command history* function and additional functionality for editing it. We'll take a brief look at these features here—for more details, see the man pages for your shell.

Shell command line editing has been through a number of evolutionary phases. The original Bourne shell supplied no command line editing at all, though the version supplied with FreeBSD gives you many of the editing features of more modern shells. Still, it's unlikely that you'll want to use the Bourne shell as your shell: *bash*, *ksh*, and *zsh* are all compatible with the Bourne shell, but they also supply better command line editing.

The next phase of command line editing was introduced with the C shell, *csh*. By modern standards, it's also rather pitiful. It's described in the *csh* man page if you really want to know. About the only part that is still useful is the ability to repeat a previous command with the !! construct. Modern shells supply command line editing that resembles the editors *vi* or *Emacs*. In *bash*, *sh*, *ksh*, and *zsh* you can make the choice by entering:

```
$ set -o emacs          for Emacs-style editing
$ set -o vi             for vi-style editing
```

In *tcsh*, the corresponding commands are:

```
% bind emacs
% bind vi
```

Normally you put one of these commands in your startup file.

In *Emacs* mode, you enter the commands simply by typing them in. In *vi* mode, you have to press **ESC** first. Table 7-5 shows an overview of the more typical Emacs-style commands in *bash*. Many other shells supply similar editing support.

As the name suggests, the *Emacs* editor understands the same editing characters. It also understands many more commands than are shown here. In addition, many X-based commands, including web browsers, understand some of these characters.

Table 7-5: Emacs editing characters

Key	Function
Ctrl-A	Move to the beginning of the line.
LeftArrow	Move to previous character on line.
Ctrl-B	Move to previous character on line (alternative).
Ctrl-D	Delete the character under the cursor. Be careful with this character: it's also the shell's end-of-file character, so if you enter it on an empty line, it stops your shell and logs you out.
Ctrl-E	Move to the end of the line.
RightArrow	Move to next character on line.
Ctrl-F	Move to next character on line (alternative).
Ctrl-K	Erase the rest of the line. The contents are saved to a *ring buffer* of erased text and can be restored, possibly elsewhere, with **Ctrl-Y**.
Ctrl-L	Erase screen contents (shell) or redraw window (*Emacs*).
DownArrow	Move to next input line.
Ctrl-N	Move to next input line (alternative).
UpArrow	Move to previous input line.
Ctrl-P	Move to previous input line (alternative).
Ctrl-R	Incremental search backward for text.
Ctrl-S	Incremental search forward for text.
Ctrl-T	Transpose the character under the cursor with the character before the cursor.
Ctrl-Y	Insert previously erased with **Ctrl-K** or **Alt-D**.
Ctrl-_	Undo the last command.
Alt-C	Capitalize the following word.
Alt-D	Delete the following word.
Alt-F	Move forward one word.
Alt-L	Convert the following word to lower case.

Key	Function
Alt-T	Transpose the word before the cursor with the one after it.
Alt-U	Convert the following word to upper case.
Ctrl-X Ctrl-S	Save file (*Emacs* only).
Ctrl-X Ctrl-C	Exit the *Emacs* editor.

You'll note a number of alternatives to the cursor keys. There are two reasons for them: firstly, the shell and *Emacs* must work on systems without arrow keys on the keyboard. The second reason is not immediately obvious: if you're a touch-typer, it's easier to type **Ctrl-P** than take your hands away from the main keyboard and look for the arrow key. The arrows are good for beginners, but if you get used to the control keys, you'll never miss the arrow keys.

File name completion

As we have seen, UNIX file names can be much longer than traditional Microsoft names, and it becomes a problem to type them correctly. To address this problem, newer shells provide *file name completion*. In *Emacs* mode, you typically type in part of the name, then press the **Tab** key. The shell checks which file names begin with the characters you typed. If there is only one, it puts in the missing characters for you. If there are none, it beeps (rings the "terminal bell"). If there are more than one, it puts in as many letters as are common to all the file names, and then beeps. For example, if I have a directory *docco* in my home directory, I might enter:

```
=== grog@freebie (/dev/ttyp4) ~ 14 -> cd docco/
=== grog@freebie (/dev/ttyp4) ~/docco 15 -> ls
freebsd.faq  freebsd.fbc  freeware
=== grog@freebie (/dev/ttyp4) ~/docco 16 -> emacs freebeepbsd.fbeepaq
```

Remember that my input is in **constant width bold** font, and the shell's output is in constant width font. On the first line, I entered the characters cd doc followed by a **Tab** character, and the shell completed with the text co/. On the last line, I entered the characters emacs f and a **Tab**. In this case, the shell determined that there was more than one file name that started like this, so it added the letters ree and rang the bell. I entered the letter b and pressed **Tab** again, and the shell added the letters sd.f and beeped again. Finally, I added the letters aq to complete the file name *freebsd.faq*.

Command line completion in *vi* mode is similar: instead of pressing **Tab**, you press **ESC** twice.

Shell startup files

As we saw above, there are a lot of ways to customize your shell. It would be inconvenient to have to set them every time, so all shells provide a means to set them automatically when you log in. Nearly every shell has its own startup file. Table 7-6 gives an overview.

Table 7-6: Shell startup files

Shell	startup file
bash	*.profile*, then *.bashrc*
csh	*.login* on login, always *.cshrc*
sh	*.profile*
tcsh	*.login* on login, always *.tcshc*, *.cshrc* if *.tcshrc* not found

These files are shell scripts—in other words, straight shell commands. Figure 7-3 shows a typical *.bashrc* file to set the environment variables we discussed.

```
umask 022
export BLOCKSIZE=1024   # for df
export CVSROOT=/src/ncvs
export EDITOR=/opt/bin/emacs
export MANPATH=/usr/share/man:/usr/local/man
export MOZILLA_HOME=/usr/local/netscape
export PAGER=less
export PATH=/usr/bin:/usr/local/bin:/usr/sbin:/bin:/sbin:/usr/X11R6/bin
PS1="=== \u@\h ('tty') \w \# -> "
PS2="\u@\h \w \! ++ "
export SHELL=/usr/local/bin/bash
export TAPE=/dev/nsa0   # note non-rewinding as standard
if [ "$TERM" = "" ]; then
  export TERM=xterm
fi
if [ "$DISPLAY" = "" ]; then
  export DISPLAY=:0
fi
/usr/games/fortune                    # print a fortune cookie
```

Figure 7-3: Minimal .bashrc file

It would be tedious for every user to put settings in their private initialization files, so the shells also read a system-wide default file. For the Bourne shell family, it is */etc/profile*, while the C shell family has three files: */etc/csh.login* to be executed on login, */etc/csh.cshrc* to be executed when a new shell is started after you log in, and */etc/csh.logout* to be executed when you stop a shell. The start files are executed before the corresponding individual files.

In addition, login classes (page 570) offer another method of setting environment variables at a global level.

Changing your shell

The FreeBSD installation gives root a C shell, *csh*. This is the traditional BSD shell, but it has a number of disadvantages: command line editing is very primitive, and the script language is significantly different from that of the Bourne shell, which is the *de facto* standard for shell scripts: if you stay with the C shell, you may still need to understand the Bourne shell. The latest version of the Bourne shell *sh* also includes some command line editing. See page 133 for details of how to enable it.

If you want to stay with a *csh*-like shell, you can get better command line editing with *tcsh*, which is also in the base system. You can get both better command line editing and Bourne shell syntax with *bash*, in the Ports Collection.

If you have `root` access, you can use *vipw* to change your shell, but there's a more general way: use *chsh* (*Change Shell*). Simply run the program. It starts your favourite editor (as defined by the `EDITOR` environment variable). Here's an example before:

```
#Changing user database information for velte.
Shell: /bin/csh
Full Name: Jack Velte
Location:
Office Phone:
Home Phone:
```

You can change anything after the colons. For example, you might change this to:

```
#Changing user database information for velte.
Shell: /usr/local/bin/bash
Full Name: Jack Velte
Location: On the road
Office Phone: +1-408-555-1999
Home Phone:
```

chsh checks and updates the password files when you save the modifications and exit the editor. The next time you log in, you get the new shell. *chsh* tries to ensure you don't make any mistakes—for example, it won't let you enter the name of a shell that isn't mentioned in the file */etc/shells*—but it's a *very* good idea to check the shell before logging out. You can try this with *su*, which you normally use to become super user:

```
bumble# su velte
Password:
su-2.00$                           note the new prompt
```

You might hear objections to using *bash* as a root shell. The argument goes something like this: *bash* is installed in */usr/local/bin*, so it's not available if you boot into single-user mode, where only the root file system is available. Even if you copy it to, say, */bin*, you can't run it in single-user mode because it needs libraries in */usr/lib*.

In fact, this isn't a problem. If you install the system the way I recommend in Chapter 5, */usr is* on the root file system. Even if it isn't, though, you don't have to use *bash* in single-user mode. When you boot to single-user mode, you get a prompt asking you which shell to start, and suggesting */bin/sh*.

Differences from Microsoft

If you're coming from a Microsoft background, there are a few gotchas that you might trip over.

Slashes: backward and forward

/ (slash) and \ (backslash) are confusing. As we've seen, UNIX uses / to delimit directories. The backslash \ is called an *escape character*. It has several purposes:

- You can put it in front of another special character to say "don't interpret this character in any special way." We've seen that the shell interprets a space character as the end of a parameter. In the previous example we changed Mail rejected to "Mail rejected" to stop the shell from interpreting it. We could also have written: Mail\ rejected.

  A more common use for this *quoting* is to tell the shell to ignore the end of a line. If a command line in a shell script gets too long, you might like to split it up into several lines; but the shell sees the end of a line as a go-ahead to perform the command. Stop it from doing so by putting a backslash *immediately* before the end of the line:

  ```
  $ grep \
    "Mail rejected" \
    /var/log/maillog
  ```

  Don't put any spaces between the \ and the end of the line; otherwise the shell will interpret the first space as a parameter by itself, and then it will interpret the end of line as the end of the command.

- In the C programming language, the backslash is used to represent several *control characters*. For example, \n means "new line." This usage appears in many other places as well.

- Using \ as an escape character causes problems: how do we put a \ character on a line? The answer: quote it. Write \\ when you mean \. This causes particular problems when interfacing with Microsoft: if you give a Microsoft path name to a shell, it needs the doubled backslashes: *C:\\WINDOWS*.

Tab characters

We've seen that the shell treats "white space," either spaces or tab characters, as the same. Unfortunately, some other programs do not. *make*, *sendmail* and *syslogd* make a distinction between the two kinds of characters, and they all require tabs (not spaces) in certain places. This is a *real* nuisance, because hardly any editor makes a distinction between them.

Carriage control characters

In the olden days, the standard computer terminal was a Teletype, a kind of computer-controlled electric typewriter. When the carriage, which contained the print head, got to the end of a line, it required two mechanical operations to move to the beginning of the next line: the *carriage return* control character told it to move the carriage back to the beginning of the line, and the *line feed* character told it turn the platen to the next line.

Generations of computer systems emulated this behaviour by putting both characters at the end of each text line. This makes it more difficult to recognize the end of line, it uses up more storage space, and normally it doesn't buy you much. The implementors of UNIX decided instead to use a single character, which it calls the *new line* character. For some reason, they chose the line feed to represent new line, though the character generated by **Enter** is a carriage return. As we saw above, the C programming language represents it as \n.

This causes problems transferring data between FreeBSD and Microsoft, and also when printing to printers that still expect both characters. We'll look at the file transfer issues on page 260 and the printer issues on page 267.

The Emacs editor

Apart from the shell, your second most important tool is the *editor*, a program that creates and changes texts. Another divergence of concept between UNIX and Microsoft environments is that UNIX gives you a choice of editors in just about anything you do. Microsoft products frequently try to redefine the whole environment, so if you change mailers, you may also have to change the editor you use to write mail. This has a profound effect on the way you work. In particular, the Microsoft way makes it uninteresting to write a really good editor, because you can't use it all the time.

The standard BSD editor is *vi*, about which people speak with a mixture of admiration, awe and horror. *vi* is one of the oldest parts of BSD. It is a very powerful editor, but nobody would say that it is easy to learn. There are two reasons to use *vi*:

1. If you're already an experienced *vi* hacker, you probably won't want to change.

2. If you do a lot of work on different UNIX systems, you can rely on *vi* being there. It's about the only one on which you can rely.

If, on the other hand, you don't know *vi*, and you only work on systems whose software you can control, you probably shouldn't use *vi*. *Emacs* is much easier to learn, and it is more powerful than *vi*.

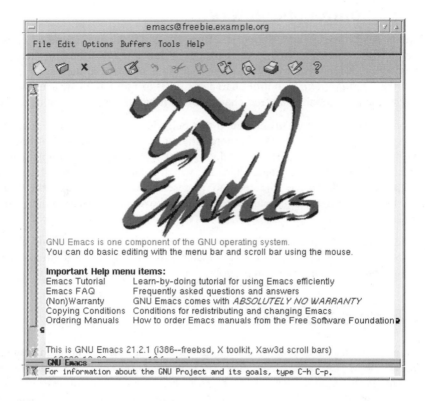

Figure 7-4: Emacs main menu

When running under X, *Emacs* displays its own window (*vi* uses an *xterm* under these circumstances). As a result, if you start *Emacs* from an *xterm*, you should use the & character to start it in the background:

```
$ emacs &
```

Figure 7-4 shows the resulting display. As you can see, the first thing that *Emacs* offers you is a tutorial. You should take it. You'll also notice the menu bars at the top. Although they look primitive compared to graphics toolbars, they offer all the functionality of graphics-oriented menus. In addition, they will tell you the keystrokes that you can use to invoke the same functions. Figure 7-5 gives an example of the *Files* menu.

There is a lot of documentation for *Emacs*, much of it on line. The complete *Emacs* handbook is available via the *info* mode of *Emacs*, which is described in the tutorial. If that's not enough, read *Learning GNU Emacs*, by Debra Cameron, Bill Rosenblatt and Eric Raymond.

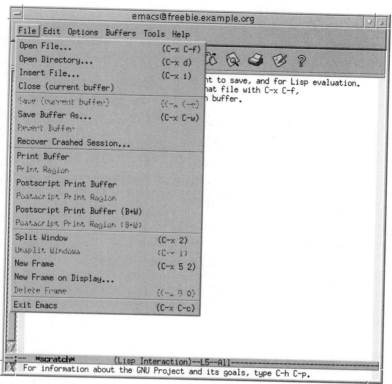

Figure 7-5: Emacs files menu

Stopping the system

To stop X, press the key combination **Ctrl-Alt-Backspace**, which is deliberately chosen to resemble the key combination **Ctrl-Alt-Delete** used to reboot the machine. **Ctrl-Alt-Backspace** stops X and returns you to the virtual terminal in which you started it. If you run from *xdm*, it redisplays a login screen.

To stop the system, use the *shutdown* program. To do so, you need to be a member of group operator.

By default, KDE uses the *halt* program. Only root can use this program, so you should reconfigure KDE to use *shutdown*. After this, you can shut down from KDE with the keystroke combination **Ctrl-Alt-PageDown**.

8

Taking control

In Chapter 7 we saw the basics of working with FreeBSD. In this part of the book, we'll look at some more system-specific issues. This chapter discusses the following topics:

- UNIX is a multi-user operating system. We've already skimmed over creating user accounts, but on page 144 we'll look at it in more detail.

- Not all users are created equal. In particular, the system administration login root has power over all other users. We'll look at root on page 146.

- UNIX implements multi-tasking via a mechanism called *processes*. We'll look at them on page 148.

- Timekeeping is extremely important in a networking system. If your system has the wrong time, it can cause all sorts of strange effects. On page 155 we'll look at how to ensure that your system is running the correct time.

- A number of events are of interest in keeping a machine running smoothly. The system can help by keeping track of what happens. One mechanism for this is *log files*, files that contain information about what has happened on the machine. We'll look at them on page 157.

- On page 159, we'll look at how FreeBSD handles systems with more than one processor. This is also called *Symmetrical Multi-Processor* or *SMP* support.

- Nearly every modern laptop has as special bus for plugin cards. It used to be called *PCMCIA*, an acronym for the rather unlikely name *Personal Computer Memory Card International Association*. Nowadays it's called *PC Card*. It was later upgraded to a 32 bit bus called *CardBus*. We'll look at how FreeBSD supports PC Card and CardBus on page 159.

- Starting on page 162, we'll look at FreeBSD's support for emulating other operating systems.

- Other aspects of FreeBSD are so extensive that we'll dedicate separate chapters to them. We'll look at them in Chapters 9 to 15.

- Starting and stopping the system is straightforward, but there are a surprising number of options. Many of them are related to networking, so Chapter 29 is located after the networking section.

Users and groups

We've already looked at users in Chapter 7. In this chapter, we'll take a deeper look.

In traditional UNIX, information about users was kept in the file */etc/passwd*. As the name suggests, it included the passwords, which were stored in encrypted form. Any user could read this file, but the encryption was strong enough that it wasn't practical to decrypt the passwords. Nowadays processors are much faster, and it's too easy to crack a password. As a result, FreeBSD keeps the real information in a file called */etc/master.passwd*, and for performance reasons it also makes it available in database form in */etc/pwd.db* and */etc/spwd.db*. None of these file are user-readable. */etc/passwd* remains for compatibility reasons: some third-party programs access it directly to get information about the environment in which they are running.

Choosing a user name

So what user name do you choose? User names are usually related to your real name and can be up to eight characters long. Like file names, they're case-sensitive. By convention, they are in all lower case, even when they represent real names. Typical ways to form a user name are:

- First name. In my personal case, this would be greg.

- Last name (lehey).

- First name and initial of last name (gregl).

- Initial of first name, and last name (glehey).

- Initials (gpl).

- Nickname (for example, grog).

I choose the last possibility, as we will see in the following discussion.

Adding users

We've already seen how to use *sysinstall* to create a user. It's not the only way. There are at least two other methods. One is the program *adduser*:

```
# adduser
Use option ''-verbose'' if you want see more warnings & questions
or try to repair bugs.

Enter username [a-z0-9]: yana
Enter full name []: Yana Lehey
Enter shell bash csh date no sh [bash]:          accept the default
Uid [1000]:                                       accept the default
Enter login class: default []:                    accept the default
Login group yana [yana]: home
Login group is ''home''. Invite yana into other groups: no
[no]: wheel                                       to be able to use su
Enter password []:                                no echo
Enter password again []:                          no echo

Name:      yana
Password:  ****
Fullname:  Yana Lehey
Uid:       1000
Gid:       1001 (home)
Class:
Groups:    home wheel
HOME:      /home/yana
Shell:     /bin/bash
OK? (y/n) [y]:                                    accept the default
Added user ''yana''
Add another user? (y/n) [y]: n
```

An alternative way of adding or removing users is with the *vipw* program. This is a more typical UNIX-hackish approach: *vipw* starts your favourite editor and allows you to edit the contents of the file */etc/master.passwd*. After you have finished, it checks the contents and rebuilds the password database. Figure 8-1 shows an example.

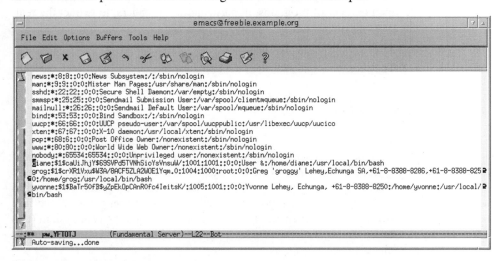

Figure 8-1: vipw display

You might be wondering why would you ever want to do things this way, and you might find it funny that most experienced UNIX administrators prefer it. The reason is that you get more of an overview than with a peephole approach that graphical environments give you, but of course you need to understand the format better. It's less confusing once you know that each line represents a single user, that the lines are divided into *fields* (which may be empty), and that each field is separated from the next by a colon (:). Table 8-1 describes the fields you see on the line on which the cursor is positioned. You can read more about the format of */etc/master.passwd* in the man page *passwd(5)*.

Table 8-1: /etc/master.passwd format

Field	Meaning
yvonne	User name.
(gibberish)	Encrypted password. When adding a new user, leave this field empty and add it later with the *passwd* program.
1005	User number.
1001	Group number.
(empty)	Login class, which describes a number of parameters for the user. We'll look at it in Chapter 29, on page 570. This field is not included in */etc/passwd*.
0	Password change time. If non-0, it is the time in seconds after which the password must be changed. This field is not included in */etc/passwd*.
0	Account expiration time. If non-0, it is the time in seconds after which the user expires. This field is not included in */etc/passwd*.
Yvonne Lehey	The so-called *gecos* field, which describes the user. This field is used by a number of programs, in particular mail readers, to extract the real name of the user.
/home/yvonne	The name of the home directory.
/bin/bash	The shell to be started when the user logs in.

The super user

FreeBSD has a number of privileged users for various administration functions. Some are just present to be the owners of particular files, while others, such as daemon and uucp, exist to run particular programs. One user stands above all others, however: root may do just about anything. The kernel gives root special privileges, and you need to become root to perform a number of functions, including adding other users. Make sure root has a password if there is any chance that other people can access your system (this is a must if you have any kind of dialup access). Apart from that, root is a user like any other, but to quote the man page *su(1)*:

*By default (unless the prompt is reset by a startup file) the super user prompt is
set to # to remind one of its awesome power.*

Becoming super user

Frequently when you're logged in normally, you want to do something that requires you
to be root. You can log out and log in again as root, of course, but there's an easier
way:

```
$ su                          become super user
Password:                     as usual, it doesn't echo
#                             root prompt
```

To use *su*, you must be a member of the group wheel. Normally you do this when you
add the user, but otherwise just put the name of the user at the end of the line in
/etc/group:

```
wheel:*:0:root,grog           add the text in bold face
```

> BSD treats *su* somewhat differently from System V. First, you need to be a member of the group
> wheel, and secondly BSD gives you more of the super user environment than System V. See the
> man page for further information.

Having a single root password is a security risk on a system where multiple people
know the password. If one of them leaves the project, you need to change the password.
An alternative is the *sudo* port (*/usr/ports/security/sudo*). It provides fine-grained access
to root privileges, all based on the user's own password. Nobody needs to know the
root password. If a user leaves, you just remove his account, and that cancels his access.

Adding or changing passwords

If your system has any connection with the outside world, it's a good idea to change your
password from time to time. Do this with the *passwd* program. The input doesn't look
very interesting:

```
$ passwd
Changing local password for yana.
Old password:                 doesn't echo
New password:                 doesn't echo
Retype new password:          doesn't echo
passwd: rebuilding the database...
passwd: done
```

You have to enter the old password to make sure that some passer-by doesn't change it
for you while you're away from your monitor, and you have to enter the new password
twice to make sure that you don't mistype and lock yourself out of your account. If this
does happen anyway, you can log in as root and change the password: root doesn't
have to enter the old password, and it can change anybody's password. For example:

```
# passwd yana
Changing local password for yana.
New password:                                  doesn't echo
Retype new password:                           doesn't echo
passwd: rebuilding the database...
passwd: done
```

In this case, you specify the name of the user for whom you change the password.

If you are changing the root password, be careful: it's easy enough to lock yourself out of the system if you mess things up, which could happen if, for example, you mistyped the password twice in the same way (don't laugh, it happens). If you're running X, open another window and use *su* to become root. If you're running in character mode, select another virtual terminal and log in as root there. Only when you're sure you can still access root should you log out.

If you *do* manage to lose the root password, all may not be lost. Reboot the machine to single-user mode (see page 540), and enter:

```
# mount -u /                     mount root file system read/write
# mount /usr                     mount /usr file system (if separate)
# passwd root                    change the password for root
Enter new password:
Enter password again:
# ^D                             enter ctrl-D to continue with startup
```

If you have a separate */usr* file system (the normal case), you need to mount it as well, since the *passwd* program is in the directory */usr/bin*. Note that you should explicitly state the name root: in single-user mode, the system doesn't have the concept of user IDs.

Processes

As we have seen, UNIX is a multi-user, multi-tasking operating system. In particular, you can run a specific program more than once. We use the term *process* to refer to a particular instance of a running program. Each process is given a *process ID*, more frequently referred to as *PID*, a number between 0 and 99999 that uniquely identifies it. There are many things that you might like to know about the processes that are currently running, such as:

• How many processes are running?

• Who is running the processes?

• Why is the system so slow?

• Which process is blocking my access to the modem?

Your primary tool for investigating process behaviour is the *ps* (*process status*) command. It has a large number of command options, and it can tell you a whole lot of things that you will only understand when you have investigated how the kernel works, but it can be very useful for a number of things. Here are some typical uses:

What processes do I have running?

After starting a large number of processes in a number of windows under X, you probably can't remember what is still running. Maybe processes that you thought had stopped are still running. To display a brief summary of the processes you have running, use the *ps* command with no options:

```
$ ps
  PID  TT  STAT      TIME COMMAND
  187  p0  Is+    0:01.02 -bash (bash)
  188  p1  Ss     0:00.62 -bash (bash)
  453  p1  R+     0:00.03 ps
```

This display shows the following information:

- The PID of the process.

- TT is short for *teletype*, and shows the last few letters of the name of the *controlling terminal*, the terminal on which the process is running. In this example, the terminals are */dev/ttyp0* and */dev/ttyp1*.

- STAT shows the current process status. It's involved and requires a certain amount of understanding of how the kernel runs to interpret it—see the man page for *ps* for more details.

- TIME is the CPU time that the process has used in minutes, seconds and hundredths of a second. Note that many other UNIX systems, particularly System V, only show this field to the nearest second.

- COMMAND is normally the command you entered, but don't rely on this. In the next section, you'll see that *sendmail* has changed its COMMAND field to tell you what it is doing. You'll notice that the command on the last line is the *ps* that performs the listing. Due to some complicated timing issue in the kernel, this process may or may not appear in the listing.

What processes are running?

There are many more processes in the system than the list above shows. To show them all, use the a option to *ps*. To show daemons as well (see the next section for a definition of *daemon*), use the x option. To show much more detail, use the u or l options. For example:

```
$ ps waux
USER     PID %CPU %MEM   VSZ  RSS  TT  STAT STARTED       TIME COMMAND
root      12 95.7  0.0     0   12  ??  RL   1Jan70  1406:43.85 (idle: cpu0)
root      11 95.1  0.0     0   12  ??  RL   1Jan70  1406:44.64 (idle: cpu1)
root       1  0.0  0.0   708   84  ??  ILs  1Jan70     0:09.10 /sbin/init --
root      12  0.0  0.0     0   12  ??  WL   1Jan70    15:04.95 (swi1: net)
root      13  0.0  0.0     0   12  ??  WL   1Jan70    21:30.29 (swi6: tty:sio clock)
root      15  0.0  0.0     0   12  ??  DL   1Jan70     2:17.27 (random)
root      18  0.0  0.0     0   12  ??  WL   1Jan70     0:00.00 (swi3: cambio)
root      20  0.0  0.0     0   12  ??  WL   1Jan70     0:00.00 (irq11: ahc0 uhci0++)
root      21  0.0  0.0     0   12  ??  WL   1Jan70    39:00.32 (irq5: rl0)
root      22  0.0  0.0     0   12  ??  WL   1Jan70     7:12.92 (irq14: ata0)
root      23  0.0  0.0     0   12  ??  WL   1Jan70     0:47.99 (irq15: ata1)
```

```
root       24  0.0  0.0      0   12  ??  DL    1Jan70   0:00.08  (usb0)
root       25  0.0  0.0      0   12  ??  DL    1Jan70   0:00.00  (usbtask)
root       26  0.0  0.0      0   12  ??  DL    1Jan70   0:00.07  (usb1)
root       27  0.0  0.0      0   12  ??  DL    1Jan70   0:00.08  (usb2)
root      340  0.0  0.1   1124  280  ??  S     18Dec02 16:41.11 nfsd: server (nfsd)
root      375  0.0  0.0   1192   12  ??  Ss    18Dec02  0:01.70 /usr/sbin/lpd
daemon    408  0.0  0.0   1136  152  ??  Ss    18Dec02  0:11.41 /usr/sbin/rwhod
root      420  0.0  0.1   2648  308  ??  Ss    18Dec02  0:04.20 /usr/sbin/sshd
root      491  0.0  0.1   2432  368  ??  Ss    18Dec02  0:38.61 /usr/local/sbin/httpd
root      551  0.0  0.0   1336   12  ??  Ss    18Dec02  0:02.71 /usr/sbin/inetd -wW
root      562  0.0  0.0   1252  216  ??  Is    18Dec02  0:15.50 /usr/sbin/cron
root      572  0.0  0.0   1180    8  v2  IWs+  -        0:00.00 /usr/libexec/getty Pc
www       582  0.0  0.0   2432    8  ??  IW    -        0:00.00 /usr/local/sbin/httpd
grog      608  0.0  0.1   1316  720  v0  I     18Dec02  0:00.04 -bash (bash)
root     2600  0.0  0.0   1180    8  v1  IWs+  -        0:00.00 /usr/libexec/getty Pc
root    33069  0.0  0.3   5352 1716  ??  Ss    29Dec02  0:01.30 xterm -name xterm
grog    33081  0.0  0.1   1328  752  p8  Is+   29Dec02  0:00.09 /usr/local/bin/bash
```

This list is just an excerpt. Even on a freshly booted system, the real list of processes will be much larger, about 50 processes.

We've seen a number of these fields already. The others are:

- USER is the *real user ID* of the process, the user ID of the person who started it.

- %CPU is an approximate count of the proportion of CPU time that the process has been using in the last few seconds. This is the column to examine if things suddenly get slow.

- %MEM is an approximate indication of the amount of physical memory that the process is using.

- VSZ (*virtual size*) is the amount of virtual memory that the process is using, measured in kilobytes.

- RSS (*resident segment size*) is the amount of physical memory currently in use, measured in kilobytes.

- STARTED is the time or date when the process was started.

In addition, a surprising number of processes don't have a controlling terminal. They are *daemons*, and we'll look at them in the next section.

Daemons

A significant part of the work in a FreeBSD system is performed by *daemons*. A daemon is not just the BSD mascot described on page 20—it's also a process that goes around in the background and does routine work such as sending mail (*sendmail*), handling incoming Internet connections (*inetd*), or starting jobs at particular times (*cron*).

> To quote the *Oxford English Dictionary*: **Demon** Also **dæmon**. ME [In form, and in sense I, a. L. *dæmon* (med. L. *demon*)...] 1a. In ancient Greek mythology (= δαίμων): A supernatural being of a nature intermediate between that of gods and men, an inferior divinity, spirit, genius (including the souls of deceased persons, *esp* deified heros). Often written *dæmon* for distinction.

You can recognize daemons in a ps waux listing by the fact that they don't have a controlling terminal—instead you see the characters ??. Each daemon has a man page that describes what it does.

Normally, daemons are started when the system is booted and run until the system is stopped. If you stop one by accident, you can usually restart them. One exception is *init*, which is responsible for starting other processes. If you kill it, you effectively kill the system. Unlike traditional UNIX systems, FreeBSD does not allow *init* to be killed.

cron

One of the more useful daemons is *cron*, named after Father Time. *cron* performs functions at specific times. For example, the system runs the script */etc/periodic/daily* every day at 2:00 am, the script */etc/periodic/weekly* every Saturday at 3:30 am, and the script */etc/periodic/monthly* on the first day of every month at 5:30 am.

To tell *cron* to perform a function at a particular time, you need a file called a *crontab*. The system keeps the real *crontab* where you can't get at it, but you can keep a copy. It's a good idea to call it *crontab* as well.

Let's look at the format of the default system *crontab*, located in */etc/crontab*:

```
# /etc/crontab - root's crontab for FreeBSD
#
# $Id: crontab,v 1.10 1995/05/27 01:55:21 ache Exp $
# From: Id: crontab,v 1.6 1993/05/31 02:03:57 cgd Exp
#
SHELL=/bin/sh
PATH=/etc:/bin:/sbin:/usr/bin:/usr/sbin
HOME=/var/log
#
#minute hour    mday    month   wday    who     command
#
*/5     *       *       *       *       root    /usr/libexec/atrun
#
# rotate log files every hour, if necessary
#0      *       *       *       *       root    /usr/bin/newsyslog
#
# do daily/weekly/monthly maintenance
0       2       *       *       *       root    /etc/daily 2>&1
30      3       *       *       6       root    /etc/weekly 2>&1
30      5       1       *       *       root    /etc/monthly 2>&1
#
# time zone change adjustment for wall cmos clock,
# See adjkerntz(8) for details.
1,31    0-4     *       *       *       root    /sbin/adjkerntz -a
```

As usual, lines starting with # are comments. The others have seven fields. The first five fields specify the minute, the hour, the day of the month, the month, and the day of the week on which an action should be performed. The character * means "every." Thus, 0 2 * * * (for */etc/daily*) means "0 minutes, 2 o'clock (on the 24 hour clock), every day of the month, every month, every weekday."

Field number six is special: it only exists in */etc/crontab*, not in private *crontab*s. It specifies the user for whom the operation should be performed. When you write your own *crontab* file, don't use this field.

The remaining fields define the operation to be performed. *cron* doesn't read your shell initialization files. In particular, this can mean that it won't find programs you expect it to find. It's a good idea to put in explicit PATH definitions, or specify an absolute pathname for the program, as is done in this example. *cron* mails the output to you, so you should check root's mail from time to time.

To install or list a *crontab*, use the *crontab* program:

```
$ crontab crontab                    install a crontab
$ crontab -l                         list the contents of an installed crontab
# DO NOT EDIT THIS FILE - edit the master and reinstall.
# (crontab installed on Wed Jan  1 15:15:10 1997)
# (Cron version -- $Id: crontab.c,v 1.7 1996/12/17 00:55:12 pst Exp $)
0 0 * * * /home/grog/Scripts/rotate-log
```

Processes in FreeBSD Release 5

Some of the processes in the example above are specific to FreeBSD Release 5:

- FreeBSD Release 5 has an *idle process* to use up the excess processor time and perform certain activities needed when no process is active. This example machine has two processors, so there are two of them:

```
root  12 95.7  0.0  0  12  ??  RL   1Jan70 1406:43.85  (idle: cpu0)
root  11 95.1  0.0  0  12  ??  RL   1Jan70 1406:44.64  (idle: cpu1)
```

- A number of the processes have names starting with irq or swi:

```
root  12  0.0  0.0   0  12  ??  WL   1Jan70 15:04.95  (swi1: net)
root  13  0.0  0.0   0  12  ??  WL   1Jan70 21:30.29  (swi6: tty:s
root  18  0.0  0.0   0  12  ??  WL   1Jan70  0:00.00  (swi3: cambi
root  20  0.0  0.0   0  12  ??  WL   1Jan70  0:00.00  (irq11: ahc0
root  21  0.0  0.0   0  12  ??  WL   1Jan70 39:00.32  (irq5: rl0)
root  22  0.0  0.0   0  12  ??  WL   1Jan70  7:12.92  (irq14: ata0)
root  23  0.0  0.0   0  12  ??  WL   1Jan70  0:47.99  (irq15: ata1)
```

These processes handle hardware interrupts (irq) or software interrupts (swi). The text which follows gives an idea of which devices or software services they support.

top

Another tool for investigating system performance is *top*, which shows a number of performance criteria, including the status of the processes are using the most resources. Start it with the number of processes you want displayed. Figure 8-2 gives an example.

```
$ top -S 10
last pid: 3992; load averages: 0.59, 0.17, 0.06 up 0+23:54:49  17:25:13
87 processes: 3 running, 73 sleeping, 8 waiting, 3 lock
CPU states: 10.2% user, 0.0% nice, 18.8% system, 1.7% interrupt, 69.4% idle
Mem: 43M Active, 36M Inact, 31M Wired, 7460K Cache, 22M Buf, 2996K Free
Swap: 512M Total, 512M Free

  PID USER   PRI NICE   SIZE   RES STATE  C   TIME  WCPU     CPU COMMAND
   12 root   -16    0    0K    12K RUN    0  23.7H 55.32% 55.32% idle: cpu0
   11 root   -16    0    0K    12K CPU1   1  23.7H 54.49% 54.49% idle: cpu1
 2854 grog    97    0  4940K 3932K *Giant 1   0:04  3.88%  3.86% xterm
   20 root   -64 -183    0K    12K WAIT   1   0:08  0.83%  0.83% irq14: ata0
 2925 root    96    0   712K  608K select 1   0:01  0.15%  0.15% make
 3193 grog    96    0  2220K 1304K CPU0   0   0:01  0.15%  0.15% top
 3783 root    96    0   520K  416K select 1   0:00  0.10%  0.05% make
  167 root    96    0 13876K 2112K select 0   1:02  0.00%  0.00% xcpustate
   25 root   -68 -187    0K    12K WAIT   0   0:28  0.00%  0.00% irq9: xl0
  110 root    96    0  1528K  956K select 1   0:26  0.00%  0.00% ntpd
```

Figure 8-2: top display

By default, the display is updated every two seconds and contains a lot of information about the system state:

- The first line gives information about the last PID allocated (you can use this to follow the number of processes being created) and the *load average*, which gives information about how many processes are waiting to be scheduled.

- The next line gives an overview of process statistics, and in what state they are. A process waits for external events to complete; it waits on a lock if some other process has a kernel resource which it wants.

- The third line shows the percentage of time used in user mode, in system (kernel) mode and by interrupts.

- The fourth line shows memory usage.

- The fifth line shows swap statistics. When swapping activity occurs, it also appears on this line.

- The remaining lines show the ten most active processes (because the parameter 10 was specified on the command line). The -S option tells *top* to include system processes, such as the idle and the interrupt processes. The state can be:

  - RUN, when the process is waiting for a processor to run on.

  - CPU0 or CPU1, when the process is actively executing.

  - *lock*, where *lock* is the name of a kernel lock. In this example, the *xterm* is waiting on the lock Giant.

  - A *wait string*, which indicates an event on which the process is waiting.

See the man page *top(1)* for more details.

Stopping processes

Sometimes you may find that you want to stop a currently running process. There are a number of ways to do this, but the easiest are:

- If the process is running on a terminal, and it's accepting input, hitting the EOF key (usually **Ctrl-D**) will often do it.

- If EOF doesn't do it, try the INTR key (usually **Ctrl-C**).

- If the process is ignoring INTR, or if it is not associated with a terminal, use the *kill* command. For example, to find who is using all the CPU time, use *ps* and look at the %CPU field:

```
# ps waux | grep cron
root   105  97.3  1.1  236  340  ??  Is    9:11AM 137:14.29 cron
```

Here, *cron* is using 97% of the CPU time, and has accumulated over 2 hours of CPU time since this morning. It's obviously sick, and we should put it out of its misery. To stop it, enter:

```
# kill 105
```

This command sends a signal called SIGTERM (terminate) to the process. This signal gives the process time to tidy up before exiting, so you should always try to use it first. The 105 is *cron*'s PID, which we got from the *ps* command.

If the process doesn't go away within a few seconds, it's probably ignoring SIGTERM. In this case, you can use the ultimate weapon:

```
# kill -9 105
```

The -9 is the number of SIGKILL, a signal that cannot be caught or ignored. You can find a list of the signals and their numeric values in */usr/include/sys/signal.h*, which is part of the software development package.

FreeBSD also has a script called *killall*. As the name implies, it kills a group of processes, by name. If you find that you have, say, a whole lot of runaway *sendmail* processes, you might save the day by writing:

```
# killall sendmail
```

As we'll see elsewhere, you can also use *killall* to send a signal to a single process when you know that only one is present. For example, to cause *inetd* to re-read its configuration file, you could write:

```
# killall -1 inetd
```

Timekeeping

FreeBSD is a networking system, so keeping the correct time is more important than on a standalone system. Apart from the obvious problem of keeping the same time as other local systems, it's also important to keep time with systems in other time zones.

Internally, FreeBSD keeps the time as the number of seconds since the *epoch*, the beginning of recorded history: 00:00:00 UTC, 1 January 1970. *UTC* is the international base time zone, and means *Universal Coordinated Time*, despite the initials. It corresponds very closely, but not exactly, to Greenwich Mean Time (GMT), the local time in England in the winter. It would be inconvenient to keep all dates in UTC, so the system understands the concept of time zones. For example, in Walnut Creek, CA, the time zone in the winter is called *PST* (*Pacific Standard Time*), and in the summer it is *PDT* (*Pacific Daylight Time*). FreeBSD comes with a set of time zone description files in the directory hierarchy */usr/share/zoneinfo*. We've already seen on page 95 that when you install the system, it stores information about the local time zone in the file */etc/localtime*. If you move time zones, you should change the time zone, not the time, either by running the *tzsetup* program, or simply by copying the file. For example, if you travel with a laptop from Adelaide, South Australia, to San Francisco CA, you would do:

```
# cp /usr/share/zoneinfo/America/Los_Angeles /etc/localtime
```

When you get home again, you would do:

```
# cp /usr/share/zoneinfo/Australia/Adelaide /etc/localtime
```

At no time do you need to change the date or time directly.

Why `Los_Angeles` and not `San_Francisco`? The developers of the time zone package chose the largest city in the time zone. You need to have a certain understanding of the time zones to choose the correct one.

The TZ environment variable

An alternate means of describing the time zone is to set the environment variable `TZ`, which we looked at on page 128. You might use this form if you're connected to a remote system in a different time zone, or maybe just to find the time at some other place. For example, in Adelaide, SA I might find:

```
$ date
Sun Apr 14 13:31:15 CST 2002
$ TZ=America/Los_Angeles date
Sat Apr 13 21:01:15 PDT 2002
```

Set the `TZ` variable to the name of the time zone info file in the */usr/share/zoneinfo* hierarchy. For example, the value of `TZ` for Berlin, Germany is `Europe/Berlin` in FreeBSD.

This is not the same as the usage of the TZ variable in UNIX System V. System V doesn't have the time zone definition files in */usr/share/zoneinfo*, so the TZ variable tells it information about the time zone. If you were using System V in Berlin, you would set your TZ variable to MEZ1MSZ2, indicating time zone names and offsets from UTC.

Keeping the correct time

If you're connected to the Internet on a reasonably regular basis, there are a number of programs which can help you synchronize your time via the *ntp (Network Time Protocol)* service.

A number of systems around the world supply time information via the *ntp* service. Look at *http://www.eecis.udel.edu/~mills/ntp/servers.html* to find one near you.

Your choice of program depends on the nature of your connection to the Internet. If you're connected full time, you'll probably prefer *ntpd*, which keeps the system synchronized. Otherwise you can use *ntpdate*, which you can run as you feel like it.

ntpd

ntpd performs periodic queries to keep the system synchronized with a time server. There are many ways to run it—see the man page *ntpd(8)*. In most cases, you can set up one system on the network to connect to an external time reference, and the other systems on the same Ethernet can get the time information from the first system.

To get the time from an external source and broadcast it to the other systems on the network, create a file */etc/ntp.conf* with a content like this:

```
server     227.21.37.18              this address is invalid; check what's near you
driftfile  /etc/ntp.drift
broadcast  223.147.37.255  ·
```

The first line defines the server. The value in this example is invalid , so don't try to use it. It's important to get one near you: network delays can significantly impair the accuracy of the results. *ntpd* uses the file */etc/ntp.drift* to record information about the (in)accuracy of the local system's clock. You only need the final line if you have other systems on the network which wait for a broadcast message. It specifies the broadcast address for the network and also tells *ntpd* to broadcast on this address.

After setting up this file, you just need to start *ntpd*:

```
# ntpd
```

To ensure that *ntpd* gets started every time you reboot, make sure that you have the following lines in */etc/rc.conf*:

```
ntpd_enable="YES"                # Run ntpd Network Time Protocol (or NO).
```

The comment on the first line is misleading: the value of ntpd_enable must be YES. You don't need any flags. You put exactly the same text in the */etc/rc.conf* on the other machines, and simply omit the file */etc/ntp.conf*. This causes *ntpd* on these machines to monitor broadcast messages.

In previous versions of FreeBSD, *ntpd* was called *xntpd*, so you may find things like `xntpd_enable` in your */etc/rc.conf*. If you do, you'll have to change the name.

ntpdate

If you connect to the Internet infrequently, *ntpd* may become discouraged and not keep good time. In this case, it's better to use *ntpdate*. Simply run it when you want to set the time:

```
# ntpdate server
```

You can't use both *ntpdate* and *ntpd* at the same time: they both use the same port. *ntpd* takes quite some time to synchronize, and if the time is wildly out, it won't even try, so it's often a good idea to run *ntpdate* on startup and then start *ntpd* manually.

Log files

Various components of FreeBSD report problems or items of interest as they happen. For example, there can always be problems with mail delivery, so a mail server should keep some kind of record of what it has been doing. If hardware problems occur, the kernel should report them. If somebody tries to break into the machine, the components affected should report the fact.

FreeBSD has a generalized system for *logging* such events. The *syslogd* daemon takes messages from multiple sources and writes them to multiple destinations, usually log files in the directory */var/log*. You can change this behaviour by modifying the file */etc/syslog.conf*. See *syslog.conf(5)* for further details. In addition to *syslogd*, other programs write directly to files in this directory. The following files are of interest:

- *XFree86.0.log* contains the log file for the last (or current) X session started on display 0. This is a prime source of information if you run into problems with X.

- *auth.log* contains information about user authentication. For example, you might see:

```
Dec 10 10:55:11 bumble su: grog to root on /dev/ttyp0
Dec 10 12:00:19 bumble sshd[126]: Server listening on :: port 22.
Dec 10 12:00:19 bumble sshd[126]: Server listening on 0.0.0.0 port 22.
Dec 10 12:06:52 bumble sshd[167]: Accepted publickey for grog from 223.147.37.80
  port 49564 ssh2
Dec 10 12:06:58 bumble su: BAD SU grog to root on /dev/ttyp0
```

The first line is a successful *su* invocation; the last line is an unsuccessful one (because the password was mistyped). The messages at 12:00:19 are from *sshd* startup, and the message at 12:06:52 is a successful remote login with *ssh*.

- *cron* is a log file for *cron*. It's relatively uninteresting:

```
Jan  5 16:00:00 bumble newsyslog[2668]: logfile turned over
Jan  5 16:05:00 bumble /usr/sbin/cron[2677]: (root) CMD (/usr/libexec/atrun)
Jan  5 16:05:00 bumble /usr/sbin/cron[2678]: (root) CMD (/usr/libexec/atrun)
Jan  5 16:10:00 bumble /usr/sbin/cron[2683]: (root) CMD (/usr/libexec/atrun)
```

  If you have problems with *cron*, that could change rapidly.

- *dmesg.today* and *dmesg.yesterday* are created by a *cron* job at 2 am every day. The *dmesg* message buffer wraps around, overwriting older entries, so they can be of use.

- *lastlog* is a binary file recording last login information. You don't normally access it directly.

- *maillog* contains information about mail delivery.

- *messages* is the main log file.

- The files *mount.today* and *mount.yesterday* show the currently mounted file systems in the format needed for */etc/fstab*.

- The file *ppp.log* contains information on PPP connections. We look at it on page 353.

- The files *setuid.today* and *setuid.yesterday* contain a list of *setuid* files. The daily security check compares them and sends a mail message if there are any differences.

- The file *vinum_history* contains information about *vinum* activity.

- The file *wtmp* contains information about logins to the system. Like *lastlog*, it's in binary form. See *utmp(5)* for the format of both *lastlog* and *wtmp*.

A number of the more important log files are kept through several cycles. As the example above shows, *cron* runs the *newsyslog* command every hour. *newsyslog* checks the size of the files, and if they are larger than a certain size, it renames the old ones by giving them a numerical extension one higher than the current one, then renames the base file with an extension *.0* and compresses it. The result looks like this:

```
-rw-r--r--  1 root  wheel  31773 Jan  5 13:01 messages
-rw-r--r--  1 root  wheel   8014 Jan  2 01:00 messages.0.bz2
-rw-r--r--  1 root  wheel  10087 Dec 15 14:00 messages.1.bz2
-rw-r--r--  1 root  wheel   9940 Dec  3 17:00 messages.2.bz2
-rw-r--r--  1 root  wheel   9886 Nov 16 11:00 messages.3.bz2
-rw-r--r--  1 root  wheel   9106 Nov  5 18:00 messages.4.bz2
-rw-r--r--  1 root  wheel   9545 Oct 15 17:00 messages.5.bz2
```

newsyslog has a configuration file */etc/newsyslog.conf*, which we discuss on page 572.

Multiple processor support

FreeBSD Release 5 can support most current Intel and AMD multiprocessor motherboards with the ia32 architecture. It also supports some Alpha, SPARC64 and Intel ia64
motherboards. Documentation on SMP support is currently rather scanty, but you can find
some information at *http://www.freebsd.org/~fsmp/SMP/SMP.html*.

The GENERIC kernel does not support SMP, so you must build a new kernel before you
can use more than one processor. The configuration file */usr/src/sys/i386/conf/GENERIC*
contains the following commented-out entries:

```
# To make an SMP kernel, the next two are needed
#options        SMP                 # Symmetric MultiProcessor Kernel
#options        APIC_IO             # Symmetric (APIC) I/O
```

For other platforms, you don't need APIC_IO. See Chapter 33 for information on how to
build a new kernel.

PC Card devices

As we have already seen, PC Card devices are special because they can be hot-plugged.
They are also intended to be recognized automatically. Starting with Release 5, FreeBSD
recognizes card insertion and removal in the kernel and invokes the appropriate driver to
handle the event. When you insert a card you will see something like this on the system
console:

```
ata2 at port 0x140-0x14f irq 11 function 0 config 1 on pccard0
ad4: 7MB <LEXAR ATA FLASH> [251/2/32] at ata2-master BIOSPIO
```

This is a compact flash memory card, which the system sees as an ATA disk. The kernel
has created the necessary structures, but it can't know how to mount the device, for
example. We'll look at what we can do about this in the next section.

devd: The device daemon

The device daemon, *devd*, provides a way to run userland programs when certain kernel
events happen. It is intended to handle userland configuration of PC Card devices such as
Ethernet cards, which it can do automatically. We'll look at this automatic usage on page
304.

devd reads the kernel event information from the device */dev/devctl* and processes it
according to rules specified in the configuration file */etc/devd.conf*, which is installed
with the system. If you want to use it for other devices, you must modify */etc/devd.conf*.
This file contains a number of sections, referred to as *statements* in the man page:

- The *options* statement describes file paths and a number of regular expressions (patterns) to look for in the messages it reads from */dev/devctl*.

- *attach* statements specify what action to perform when a device is attached. For example:

```
attach 0 {
        device-name "$scsi-controller-regex";
        action "camcontrol rescan all";
};
```

  The device-name entry uses the regular expression $scsi-controller-regex to recognize the name of a SCSI controller in the attach message. The action entry then specifies what action to take when such a device is attached to the system. In this case, it runs the *camcontrol* program to rescan the SCSI buses and recognize any new devices that have been added.

  Multiple *attach* statements can match a specific event, but only one will be executed. The order in which they are checked is specified by a *priority*, a numerical value after the keyword action. The statements are checked in order of highest to lowest numerical priority.

- *detach* statements have the same syntax as *attach* statements. As the name suggests, they are executed when a device is detached.

  It's not always possible or necessary to perform any actions when a device is removed. In the case of SCSI cards, there is no *detach* statement. We'll look at this issue in more detail below.

- Finally, if the kernel was unable to locate a driver for the card, it generates a *no match* event, which is handled by the *nomatch* statement.

So what does *devd* do when we insert the compact flash card? By default, nothing. The ATA driver recognizes and configures the card. It would be nice to get *devd* to mount it as well. That's relatively simple:

- Ensure that you have an entry for the device in */etc/fstab*. Digital cameras create a single MS-DOS file system on flash cards. An appropriate entry in */etc/fstab* for this device might be:

```
/dev/ad4s1              /camera       msdos   rw,noauto       0       0
```

  This is a removable device, so you should use the noauto keyword to stop the system trying to mount it on system startup.

- In the *options* section of */etc/devd.conf*, add an expression to recognize the names of ATA controllers:

```
      set ata-controller-regex
           "ata[0-9]+";
```

- Add an *attach* section for the device:

```
attach 0 {
      device-name "$ata-controller-regex";
      action "mount /camera";
};
```

- Restart *devd*:

```
# killall devd
# devd
```

After this, the file system will be automatically mounted when you insert the card.

Removing PC Card devices

The next thing we'd like to do is to unmount the file system when you remove the flash card. Unfortunately, that isn't possible. Unmounting can involve data transfer, so you have to do it before you remove the card. If you forget, and remove the card without unmounting, the system may panic next time you try to access the card.

After unmounting, you can remove the card. On the console you'll see something like:

```
ad4: removed from configuration
ad4: no status, reselecting device
ad4: timeout sending command=e7 s=ff e=04
ad4: flushing cache on detach failed
ata2: detached
```

Alternate PC Card code

The PC Card implementation described here, called *NEWCARD*, is new in FreeBSD Release 5. At the time of writing, the older implementation, called *OLDCARD*, is still included in the system. It's possible that you might have an older card that is supported by OLDCARD but not by NEWCARD. In that case, you will need to build a kernel with OLDCARD support. Check the *NOTES* files in */usr/src/sys/conf* and */usr/src/sys/arch/conf*, where *arch* is the architecture of your system, and the man pages *pccardd* and *pccard.conf*.

Configuring PC Card devices at startup

A number of entries in */etc/rc.conf* relate to the use of PC Card devices, but nearly all of them are for OLDCARD. You only need one for NEWCARD:

```
devd_enable="YES"
```

This starts *devd* at system startup.

Emulating other systems

A large number of operating systems run on Intel hardware, and there is a lot of software that is available for these other operating systems, but not for FreeBSD.

Emulators and simulators

There are a number of ways to execute software written for a different platform. The most popular are:

- *Simulation* is a process where a program executes the functions that are normally performed by the native instruction set of another machine. They simulate the low-level instructions of the target machine, so simulators don't have to run on the same kind of machine as the code that they execute. A good example is the port *emulators/p11*, which simulates a PDP-11 minicomputer, the machine for which most early versions of UNIX were written.

  Simulators run much more slowly than the native instruction set: for each simulated instruction, the simulator may execute hundreds of machine instructions. Amusingly, on most modern machines, the *p11* emulator still runs faster than the original PDP-11: modern machines are over 1,000 times faster than the PDP-11.

- In general, *emulators* execute the program instructions directly and only simulate the operating system environment. As a result, they have to run on the same kind of hardware, but they're not noticeably slower than the original. If there is any difference in performance, it's because of differences between the host operating system and the emulated operating system.

- Another use for the term *emulator* is where the hardware understands a different instruction set than the native one. Obviously this is not the kind of emulator we're talking about here.

FreeBSD can emulate many other systems to a point where applications written for these systems will run under FreeBSD. Most of the emulators are in the Ports Collection in the directory */usr/ports/emulators*.

In a number of cases, the emulation support is in an experimental stage. Here's an overview:

- FreeBSD will run most BSD/OS programs with no problems. You don't need an emulator.

- FreeBSD will also run most NetBSD and OpenBSD executables, though not many people do this: it's safer to recompile them under FreeBSD.

- FreeBSD runs Linux executables with the aid of the *linux kld* (*loadable kernel module*). We'll look at how to use it in the next section.

- FreeBSD can run SCO COFF executables with the aid of the *ibcs2 kld*. This support is a little patchy: although the executables will run, you may run into problems caused by differences in the directory structure between SCO and FreeBSD. We'll look at it on page 164.

- A *Microsoft Windows* emulator is available. We'll look at it on page 165.

Emulating Linux

Linux is a UNIX-like operating system that in many ways is very similar to FreeBSD. We discussed it on page 10. Although it looks very UNIX-like, many of the internal kernel interfaces are different from those of FreeBSD or other UNIX-based systems. The Linux compatibility package handles these differences, and most Linux software will run on FreeBSD. Most of the exceptions use specific drivers that don't run on FreeBSD, though there is a considerable effort to minimize even this category.

To install the Linux emulator, you must:

- Install the compatibility libraries. These are in the port */usr/ports/emulators/linux_base*.

- Run the Linux emulator kld, *linux*.

Running the Linux emulator

Normally you load the Linux emulator when you boot the system. Put the following line in your */etc/rc.conf*:

```
linux_enable="YES"
```

If you don't want to do this for some reason, you can start it from the command line:

```
# kldload linux
```

You don't interact directly with the emulator module: it's just there to supply kernel functionality, so you get a new prompt immediately when you start it.

linux is a kld, so it doesn't show up in a *ps* listing. To check whether it is loaded, use *kldstat*:

```
$ kldstat
Id Refs Address    Size     Name
 1    5 0xc0100000 1d08b0   kernel
 2    2 0xc120d000 a000     ibcs2.ko
 3    1 0xc121b000 3000     ibcs2_coff.ko
 5    1 0xc1771000 e000     linux.ko
```

This listing shows that the SCO UNIX emulation (*ibcs2*) has also been loaded.

The Linux emulator and many Linux programs are located in the directory hierarchy */usr/compat/linux*. You won't normally need to access them directly, but if you get a Linux program that includes libraries destined for */lib*, you will need to manually place them in */usr/compat/linux/lib*. Be **very** careful not to replace any files in the */usr/lib* hierarchy with Linux libraries; this would make it impossible to run FreeBSD programs that depend on them, and it's frequently very difficult to recover from such problems. Note that FreeBSD does not have a directory */lib*, so the danger is relatively minor.

Linux procfs

Linux systems have a file system called *procfs*, or *Process File System*, which contains information used by many programs. FreeBSD also has a *procfs*, but it is completely different. To be able to run Linux programs which refer to *procfs*, place the following entry in your */etc/fstab* file:

```
linproc         /compat/linux/proc  linprocfs   rw      0       0
```

Problems executing Linux binaries

One of the problems with the ELF format used by older Linux binaries is that they may contain no information to identify them as Linux binaries. They might equally well be BSD/OS or UnixWare binaries. That's normally not a problem, unless there are library conflicts: the system can't decide which shared library to use. If you have this kind of binary, you must *brand* the executable using the program *brandelf*. For example, to brand the StarOffice program *swriter3*, you would enter:

```
# brandelf -t Linux /usr/local/StarOffice-3.1/linux-x86/bin/swriter3
```

This example deliberately shows a very old version of StarOffice: it's not clear that there are any modern binaries that cause such problems.

Emulating SCO UNIX

SCO UNIX, also known as *SCO OpenDesktop* and *SCO Open Server*, is based on UNIX System V.3.2. This particular version of UNIX was current in the late 1980s. It uses an obsolete binary format called *COFF* (*Common Object File Format*).

Like Linux support, SCO support for FreeBSD is supplied as a loadable kernel module. It's not called *sco*, though: a number of older System V.3.2 systems, including Interactive UNIX, also support the *ibcs2*[1] standard. As a result, the kld is called *ibcs2*.

Run ibcs2 support like Linux support: start it manually, or modify */etc/rc.conf* to start it automatically at bootup:

---

1. *ibcs2* stands for *Intel Binary Compatibility System 2*.

```
ibcs2_enable="YES"        # Ibcs2 (SCO) emulation loaded at startup (or NO).
```

Alternatively, load the kld:

```
# kldload ibcs2
```

One problem with SCO emulation is the SCO shared libraries. These are required to execute many SCO executables, and they're not supplied with the emulator. They *are* supplied with SCO's operating systems. Check the SCO license to determine whether you are allowed to use them on FreeBSD. You may also be eligible for a free SCO license—see the SCO web site for further details.

Emulating Microsoft Windows

The *wine* project has been working for some time to provide an emulation of Microsoft's *Windows* range of execution environments. It's changing continually, so there's little point describing it here. You can find up-to-date information at *http://www.winehq.com/about/*, and you can install it from the port *emulators/wine*. Be prepared for a fair amount of work.

Accessing Microsoft files

Often you're not as interested in running Microsoft applications as decoding their proprietary formats. For example, you might get a mail message with an attachment described only as

```
[-- Attachment #2: FreeBSD.doc --]
[-- Type: application/octet-stream, Encoding: x-unknown, Size: 15K --]

[-- application/octet-stream is unsupported (use 'v' to view this part) --]
```

This attachment has an unspecific MIME type,[1] but you might guess that it is Microsoft Word format because the file name ends in *.doc*. That doesn't make it any more legible. To read it, you need something that understands the format. A good choice is *OpenOffice.org*, a clone of Microsoft's "Office" product. Install from the Ports Collection (*/usr/ports/editors/openoffice*).

OpenOffice.org is not a good example of the UNIX way. It breaks a number of conventions, and in general it's a lot more difficult to use than normal FreeBSD tools. Its only real advantage is that you can process Microsoft document formats.

---

1. See Chapter 26, *Electronic mail: clients*, page 489, for more information about MIME.

9

The Ports Collection

The Internet is full of free software that is normally distributed in source form. That can be a problem in itself: the way from the source archive that you get free from the Internet to the finished, installed, running program on your machine—normally called *porting*—can be a long and frustrating one. See my book *Porting UNIX Software* for more details of the porting process.

To get a software package up and running on your system, you need to go through most of these steps:

1. Get the source files on your machine. They are usually contained in an *archive*, a file containing a number of other files. Archives used for the ports collection are generally *gzipped tar* files, packaged with *tar* and compressed with *gzip*, but other formats are also possible. Whatever the format, you'll typically use *ftp* to get them to your machine.

2. Unpack the archive into a *source tree*, in this case using *gunzip* and *tar*.

3. Configure the package. Most packages include shell scripts to do this. Configuration performs a threefold adaptation of the package:

   1. It adapts it to the system hardware.

   2. It adapts it to the software environment you're running (in this case, FreeBSD).

   3. It adapts it to your personal preferences.

4. Build the package. For most packages, this involves compiling the source files and creating executables. The main tool for this purpose is *make*, which uses a set of rules, traditionally stored in a file called *Makefile*, to decide how to build the package.

There is nearly always a *Makefile* in the sources, but the Ports Collection includes a second one that controls the build at a higher level.

5. Install the package. This involves mainly copying the executables, configuration files and documentation created by a build to the correct place in the directory hierarchy.

6. Configure the installed software. This is similar in concept to package configuration, except that it occurs in the run-time environment. The package configuration may perform all the necessary configuration for you.

These are a lot of steps, and you'll often find they're laid through a minefield: one false move, and everything blows up. To make porting and installing software easier, the FreeBSD team created a framework called the *Ports Collection*, which makes it trivial to perform these steps. It also provides a method of packaging and installing the resultant ported software, called *packages*. The CD-ROM edition of FreeBSD includes a large number of pre-built packages that can be installed directly.

In this chapter, we'll consider the following points as they relate to the FreeBSD ports collection:

*   How to install a pre-compiled package. We'll look at this in the next section.

*   What the ports tree is, and how to compile and install ("build") a package. We'll look at this on page 169.

*   How to create and submit a new port, on page 174.

How to install a package

In FreeBSD parlance, a package is simply a special archive that contains those files (usually executable binary files) that are installed when you build and install a port. Effectively it's a snapshot of the port build process that we saw above, taken after step 4 has completed. Compared to the full-blown port, packages are much faster to install—it's usually a matter of seconds. On the other hand, they don't give you the choice of configuration that the complete port does. The distribution CD-ROMs contain a directory *packages* with a large number of pre-compiled software packages. Alternatively, you can find FreeBSD packages on many servers on the Internet—check the online handbook for some places to look.

To help maintain an overview, both ports and packages are divided into categories. They are stored in directories named after the category. See the file */usr/ports/INDEX* for a list. For example, *emacs* under *editors* is currently in the file *packages/editors/emacs-21.2.tgz*, though this name will change with updated versions of *emacs*. For the latest version of the packages only, you'll find another copy without the extension in *packages/Latest/emacs.tgz*. To install it, you enter:

```
# pkg_add /cdrom/packages/Latest/emacs.tgz
```

Alternatively, you can install packages from the *sysinstall* final configuration menu shown in Figure 6-1 on page 92.

Building a port

The more general way to install third-party software is with a *port*. The FreeBSD project uses the term *port* to describe the additional files needed to adapt a package to build under FreeBSD. It does *not* include the source code itself, though the CD-ROM distribution includes many code archives in the directory */ports/distfiles*, spread over several of the CD-ROMs.

Before you get started with the ports, you need to install the port information on your system. Normally this will be in */usr/ports*. This directory tree is frequently called the *Ports Tree*. There are a number of ways to install them.

Installing ports during system installation

The simplest way to install the Ports Collection is when you install the system. When you choose the components to install, *sysinstall* offers to install the Ports Collection for you as well.

Installing ports from the first CD-ROM

The file *ports/ports.tgz* on the first CD-ROM is a *tar* archive containing all the ports. If you didn't install it during system installation, use the following method to install the complete collection (about 200 MB). Make sure your CD-ROM is mounted (in this example on */cdrom*), and enter:

```
# cd /usr
# tar xzvf /cdrom/ports/ports.tgz
```

If you only want to extract a single package, say *inn*, which is in the category *news*, enter:

```
# cd /usr
# tar xzvf /cdrom/ports/ports.tgz  ports/news/inn
```

It takes a surprisingly long time to install the ports; although there isn't much data in the archive, there are about 250,000 files in it, and creating that many files takes a lot of disk I/O.

Installing ports from the live file system CD-ROM

Alternatively, the files are also on the live file system CD-ROM. This is not much of an advantage for installation, but you may find it convenient to browse through the source trees in the directory *ports* on the CD-ROM. Let's assume you have found a directory */usr/ports/graphics/hpscan* on the CD-ROM, and it is your current working directory.

You can move the data across with the following:

```
# cd /cdrom/ports/graphics
# mkdir -p /usr/ports/graphics
# tar cf - . | (cd /usr/ports/graphics; tar xvf -)
```

Getting new ports

What happens when a new version of a port comes out? For example, you've been using
Emacs Version 20 forever, and now Version 21.2 becomes available? It's brand new, so
it's obviously not on your CD-ROM.

One way to get the port is via *ftp*. This used to be quite convenient: you could download
a tarball directly and extract it locally. That is unfortunately no longer possible: currently
you must download files a directory at a time. If you're following the Ports Collection at
all closely, you should consider using *cvsup*, which can keep your sources up to date
automatically. See Chapter 31, page 585, for more details.

All ports are kept in subdirectories of the URL *ftp://ftp.FreeBSD.org/pub/FreeBSD/ports/*.
This directory has the following contents:

```
drwxr-xr-x    6 1006   1006        512 Jun  8 13:18 alpha
drwxr-xr-x  209 1006   1006     401408 May 28 14:08 distfiles
drwxr-xr-x    6 1006   1006       1536 May 28 17:53 i386
drwxr-xr-x    3 1006   1006        512 Apr  6 13:45 ia64
drwxr-xr-x   83 1006   1006       3072 May 20 15:35 local-distfiles
lrwxrwxrwx    1 root   wheel        13 Jun  1  2001 packages -> i386/packages
lrwxrwxrwx    1 root   wheel        24 Jun  1  2001 ports -> ../FreeBSD-current/ports
lrwxrwxrwx    1 root   wheel         5 Jun  1  2001 ports-current -> ports
lrwxrwxrwx    1 root   wheel         5 Jun  1  2001 ports-stable -> ports
drwxr-xr-x    4 1006   1006        512 Apr  9 10:37 sparc64
```

The directories *alpha*, *i386*, *ia64* and *sparc64* contain packages (not ports) for the
corresponding architecture. *distfiles* contains a large number of the original sources for
the third-party packages; it's intended as a "last resort" location if you can't find them at
other locations.

The directory *local-distfiles* is used by people working on the Ports Collection; you don't
normally need anything from these directories. The important directories for you are
ports, *ports-current* and *ports-stable*. Currently these are really all the same directory,
but things may not remain like that.

Getting back to your *emacs* port: you would find it in the directory */pub/Free-
BSD/ports/ports/editors/*. Note the final / in that directory name: if you leave it out, *ftp*
prints an error message and exits. Here's what might happen:

```
$ ftp ftp://ftp.FreeBSD.org/pub/FreeBSD/ports/ports/editors/
Connected to ftp.beastie.tdk.net.
220 ftp.beastie.tdk.net FTP server (Version 6.00LS) ready.
331 Guest login ok, send your email address as password.
230- The FreeBSD mirror at Tele Danmark Internet.
...much blurb omitted
250 CWD command successful.
250 CWD command successful.
ftp> ls
```

```
229 Entering Extended Passive Mode (||||55649||)
150 Opening ASCII mode data connection for '/bin/ls'.
total 704
...
drwxr-xr-x  3 1006  1006     512 May 20 10:07 emacs
drwxr-xr-x  4 1006  1006     512 May 20 10:08 emacs20
drwxr-xr-x  4 1006  1006     512 May 20 10:08 emacs20-dl
drwxr-xr-x  4 1006  1006     512 May 20 10:08 emacs20-mule-devel
drwxr-xr-x  3 1006  1006     512 May 20 10:08 emacs21
drwxr-xr-x  2 1006  1006     512 May 20 10:08 eshell-emacs20
...
```

This shows that your files will be in the directory *emacs21*. You can get them with the *ftp* mget command:

```
ftp> mget emacs21
mget emacs21/files [anpqy?]? a              answer a for all files
Prompting off for duration of mget.
ftp: local: emacs21/files: No such file or directory
ftp: local: emacs21/Makefile: No such file or directory
(etc)
```

This happens because you need to create the destination directory manually. Try again:

```
ftp> !mkdir emacs21                                  create the local directory
ftp> mget emacs21
mget emacs21/files [anpqy?]? a
Prompting off for duration of mget.
229 Entering Extended Passive Mode (||||57074||)
550 emacs21/files: not a plain file.
229 Entering Extended Passive Mode (||||57085||)
150 Opening BINARY mode data connection for 'emacs21/Makefile' (2185 bytes).
100% |***********************************|  2185        2.34 MB/s    00:00 ETA
226 Transfer complete.
(etc)
```

You get one of these for each file transferred. But note the error message: *not a plain file*. *emacs21/files* is a directory, so we need to get it separately:

```
ftp> !mkdir emacs21/files
ftp> mget emacs21/files
mget emacs21/files/patch-lib-src:Makefile.in [anpqy?]? a
Prompting off for duration of mget.
229 Entering Extended Passive Mode (||||57258||)
150 Opening BINARY mode data connection for 'emacs21/files/patch-lib-src:Makefile.in
' (908 bytes).
100% |***********************************|   908        1.64 MB/s    00:00 ETA
226 Transfer complete.
(etc)
```

Note that the *ftp* command specifies the URL of the directory. It must have a trailing /, otherwise *ftp* will complain. This form is supported by FreeBSD *ftp*, but many other *ftp* clients will require you to do it in two steps:

```
# ftp ftp.FreeBSD.org
Connected to ftp.beastie.tdk.net.
(etc)
ftp> cd /pub/FreeBSD/ports/ports/editors
250 CWD command successful.
```

What's in that port?

One problem with the Ports Collection is the sheer number. It can be difficult just to find out what they're supposed to do. If you build all the ports, you'll be busy for weeks, and there's no way you could read all the documentation in one lifetime. Where can you get an overview? Here are some suggestions. In each case, you should have the directory */usr/ports* as your current working directory.

- There's an index in */usr/ports/INDEX*. If you have updated the ports tree, you can make the index with the following commands:

```
# cd /usr/ports
# make index
```

index is the name of a *target*, the part of a rule that identifies it. It's usually either a file name or an abbreviation for an operation to perform. We'll see a number of *make* targets in the course of the book.

The index is intended for use by other programs, so it's written as a single long line per package, with fields delimited by the vertical bar character (|). Here are two lines as an example, wrapped over three lines to fit on the page:

```
mp3asm-0.1.3|/usr/ports/audio/mp3asm|/usr/local|MP3 frame level editor|/usr/port
s/audio/mp3asm/pkg-descr|ports@FreeBSD.org|audio| autoconf213-2.13.000227_1||htt
p://mp3asm.sourceforge.net/
mp3blaster-3.0p8|/usr/ports/audio/mp3blaster|/usr/local|MP3 console ncurses-base
d player|/usr/ports/audio/mp3blaster/pkg-descr|greid@FreeBSD.org|audio|||http://
www.stack.nl/~brama/mp3blaster.html
```

You'll probably want to process it with other tools.

- You can print the index with the following commands:

```
# cd /usr/ports
# make print-index | lpr
```

Note that there are about 1,000 pages of output, which look like this:

```
Port:   zip-2.3_1
Path:   /usr/ports/archivers/zip
Info:   Create/update ZIP files compatible with pkzip
Maint:  ache@FreeBSD.org
Index:  archivers
B-deps: unzip-5.50
R-deps:
```

- You can search for a specific keyword with the search target. For example, to find ports related to *Emacs*, you might enter:

```
# cd /usr/ports
# make search key=Emacs | less
```

Pipe the output through *less*: it can be quite a lot.

• You can build a series of nearly 10,000 *html* pages like this:

```
# cd /usr/ports
# make readmes
```

You can then browse them at the URL *file:///usr/ports/README.html*.

Getting the source archive

You'll see from the above example that there are not many files in the port. Most of the files required to build the software are in the original source code archive (the "tarball"), but that's not part of the port.

There are a number of places from which you can get the sources. If you have a CD-ROM set, many of them are scattered over the CD-ROMs, in the directory */cdrom/ports/distfiles* on each CD-ROM. The Ports Collection Makefiles look for them in this directory (another good reason to mount your CD-ROM on */cdrom*) and also in */usr/ports/distfiles*.

If you don't have the source tarball, that's not a problem. Part of the function of the Ports Collection is to go out on the Net and get them for you. This is completely automatic: you just type make, and the build process gets the source archive for you and builds it. Of course, you must be connected to the Internet for this to work.

If you mount your CD-ROM elsewhere (maybe because you have more than one CD-ROM drive, and so you have to mount the CD-ROM on, say, */cd4*), the Makefiles will not find the distribution files and will try to load the files from the Internet. One way to solve this problem is to create a symbolic link from */cd4/ports/distfiles* to */usr/ports/distfiles*. The trouble with this approach is that you will then no longer be able to load new distribution files into */usr/ports/distfiles*, because it will be on CD-ROM. Instead, do:

```
# cd /cd4/ports/distfiles
# mkdir -p /usr/ports/distfiles          make sure you have a distfiles directory
# for i in *; do
>   ln -s /cd4/ports/distfiles/$i /usr/ports/distfiles/$i
> done
```

If you're using *csh* or *tcsh*, enter:

```
# cd /cd4/ports/distfiles
# mkdir -p /usr/ports/distfiles          make sure you have a distfiles directory
# foreach i (*)
?   ln -s /cd4/ports/distfiles/$i /usr/ports/distfiles/$i
? end
```

This creates a symbolic link to each distribution file, but if the file for a specific port isn't there, the Ports Collection can fetch it and store it in the directory.

Building the port

Once you have the skeleton files for the port, the rest is simple. Just enter:

```
# cd /usr/ports/editors/emacs21
# make
# make install
====>
====> To enable menubar fontset support, define WITH_MENUBAR_FONTSET
====>
>> emacs-21.2.tar.gz doesn't seem to exist in /usr/ports/distfiles/.
>> Attempting to fetch from ftp://ftp.gnu.org/gnu/emacs/.
===>   Extracting for emacs-21.2_1
>> Checksum OK for emacs-21.2.tar.gz.
===>    emacs-21.2_1 depends on executable: gmake - found
===>    emacs-21.2_1 depends on executable: autoconf213 - not found
===>    Verifying install for autoconf213 in /usr/ports/devel/autoconf213
===>   Extracting for autoconf213-2.13.000227_2
>> Checksum OK for autoconf-000227.tar.bz2.
===>    autoconf213-2.13.000227_2 depends on executable: gm4 - not found
===>    Verifying install for gm4 in /usr/ports/devel/m4
===>   Extracting for m4-1.4_1
>> Checksum OK for m4-1.4.tar.gz.
===>   Patching for m4-1.4_1
===>   Applying FreeBSD patches for m4-1.4_1
===>   Configuring for m4-1.4_1
creating cache ./config.cache
checking for mawk... no
(etc)
```

It's a good idea to perform the *make* step first: *make install* does not always build the package.

Port dependencies

Sometimes, it's not enough to build a single port. Many ports depend on other ports. If you have the complete, up-to-date ports tree installed on your system, the Ports Collection will take care of this for you: it will check if the other port is installed, and if it isn't, it will install it for you. For example, *tkdesk* depends on *tk*. *tk* depends on *tcl*. If you don't have any of them installed, and you try to build *tkdesk*, it will recursively install *tk* and *tcl* for you.

Package documentation

Once you have installed your port, you'll want to use it. In almost every case, that requires documentation. Most packages have documentation, but unfortunately it's not always obvious where it is. In some cases, the port doesn't install all the documentation.

More generally, there are the following possibilities:

* If the port includes man pages, they will be installed in */usr/X11R6/man* if the package is related to X, and */usr/local/man* if they are not. Typically installing the man pages is the last thing that happens during the installation, so you should see it on the screen. If not, or if you want to check, you can have a look at the package list:

```
$ cd /var/db/pkg
$ pkg_info -L emacs-21.2_1|grep /man/
/usr/local/man/man1/ctags.1.gz
/usr/local/man/man1/emacs.1.gz
/usr/local/man/man1/etags.1.gz
/usr/local/man/man1/gfdl.1.gz
```

You don't need to change the directory to */var/db/pkg*, but if you do, you can use file name completion to finish the name of the package. We use /man/ as the search string, and not simply man, because otherwise other files might match as well.

- If the package includes GNU *info* pages, you can use the same method to look for them:

```
$ pkg_info -L emacs-21.2_1|grep /info/
/usr/local/info/ada-mode
/usr/local/info/autotype
/usr/local/info/ccmode
/usr/local/info/cl
(many more)
```

This isn't normally necessary, though: if you're using GNU *info*, the index page will be updated to include the package.

- If the package includes hardcopy documentation, it may or may not be included in the port. The *Emacs* documentation also includes a user's guide and a programmer's guide. The user's guide, all 640 pages of it, is in the directory *man* of the *Emacs* build directory, but it doesn't get built during installation. This is typical of most ports. In this case you'll have to build the documentation yourself.

Getting binary-only software

A lot of software doesn't need to be ported. For example, if you want *Netscape*, you can just download it from *ftp.netscape.com*. But how do you install it? Netscape's installation procedures are getting better, but they still leave something to be desired.

The answer's simple: take the port! Although Netscape comes only in binary form, the port handles getting the correct version and installing it for you. Another advantage to using a port instead of installing the package manually is that the port installs the software as a FreeBSD package, which makes it much easier to remove the software later.

This method can be used to install some other software as well, for example StarOffice. The moral is simple: always check the Ports Collection before getting a software package from the Net.

Maintaining ports

Once you install a port, you might consider that to be the end of the story. That's seldom the case. For example:

- You might need to replace a port with a newer version. How do you do it? We'll look at that below.

- One day, you might find your disk fills up, so you go looking for old ports you don't use any more. We'll look at some utility commands on page 178.

Upgrading ports

From time to time, new versions of software will appear. There are a number of approaches to upgrading:

- You can remove the old version of the port and install a new version. The trouble here is that removing the old version might remove any configuration files as well.

- You can install a new version without removing the old version. The trouble here is that you end up with two entries in the packages database */var/db/pkg*:

```
$ pkg_info | grep emacs
emacs-21.1_5          GNU editing macros
emacs-21.2_1          GNU editing macros
```

Clearly you don't need *emacs-21.1_5* any more. In fact, it's not complete any more, because the program */usr/local/bin/emacs* has been overwritten by the new version. But you can't remove it either: that would remove components of *emacs-21.2_1*, which you want to keep. On the other hand, if you don't remove it, you are left with nearly 50 MB of disk space used up in the directory */usr/local/share/emacs/21.1*.

- You can use *portupgrade*, a program that does some of the upgrading automatically. We'll look at this below.

Using portupgrade

Portupgrade is—what else?—a port. Install it in the usual manner:

```
# cd /usr/ports/sysutils/portupgrade
# make install
```

Before you can perform the upgrade, you should first back up */var/db/pkg*, then build a ports database with *pkgdb*. A typical build might look like this:

```
# cd /var/db
# tar czvf db.pkg.tar.gz pkg/
# pkgdb -F
[Updating the pkgdb <format:bdb1_btree> in /var/db/pkg ... - 181 packages
found (-5 +92) (...)...................................... done]
Checking the origin of AbiWord-1.0.3
Checking the origin of ImageMagick-5.5.1.1
Checking the origin of ORBit-0.5.17
...
Checking the origin of xv-3.10a_3
Checking the origin of zip-2.3_1
Checking for origin duplicates
Checking AbiWord-1.0.3
Checking ImageMagick-5.5.1.1
Stale dependency: ImageMagick-5.5.1.1 -> ghostscript-gnu-7.05_3:
ghostscript-gnu-6.52_4 (score:64%) ? ([y]es/[n]o/[a]ll) [no] y
Fixed. (-> ghostscript-gnu-6.52_4)
Checking ORBit-0.5.17
Checking XFree86-4.2.0_1,1
...
Checking bonobo-1.0.21_1
Stale dependency: bonobo-1.0.21_1 -> ghostscript-gnu-7.05_3:
ghostscript-gnu-6.52_4 ? ([y]es/[n]o/[a]ll) [yes] Enter pressed
Fixed. (-> ghostscript-gnu-6.52_4)
Checking cdrtools-1.11.a28
...
Checking xv-3.10a_3
Checking zip-2.3_1
Regenerating +REQUIRED_BY files
Checking for cyclic dependencies
```

In this example, the port *ghostscript-gnu-7.05_3* had been replaced by the earlier version *ghostscript-gnu-6.52_4*, since *ghostscript* Release 7 has some annoying bugs. The dialogue shows how *pkgdb* recognized the discrepancy, and how it recovered from it.

Now you can start the upgrade. To upgrade a specific port, simply specify its base name, without the version number. This example uses the -v option to show additional information:

```
# portupgrade -v bison
--->  Upgrade of devel/bison started at: Mon, 04 Nov 2002 13:20:52 +1030
--->  Upgrading 'bison-1.35_1' to 'bison-1.75' (devel/bison)
--->  Build of devel/bison started at: Mon, 04 Nov 2002 13:20:52 +1030
... normal port build output
===>    Registering installation for bison-1.75
make clean issued by portupgrade
===>  Cleaning for libiconv-1.8_2
===>  Cleaning for gettext-0.11.5_1
...
--->  Removing the temporary backup files
--->  Installation of devel/bison ended at: Mon, 04 Nov 2002 13:23:00 +1030 (consume
d 00:00:06)
--->  Removing the obsoleted dependencies
--->  Cleaning out obsolete shared libraries
--->  Upgrade of devel/bison ended at: Mon, 04 Nov 2002 13:23:01 +1030 (consumed 00:
02:08)
--->  Reporting the results (+:succeeded / -:ignored / *:skipped / !:failed)
        + devel/bison (bison-1.35_1)
```

If the port is already up to date, you'll see something like this:

```
# portupgrade -v perl-5.8.0_3
** No need to upgrade 'perl-5.8.0_3' (>= perl-5.8.0_3). (specify -f to force)
---> Reporting the results (+:succeeded / -:ignored / *:skipped / !:failed)
        - lang/perl5.8 (perl-5.8.0_3)
```

To upgrade all ports, use the command:

```
# portupgrade -a
```

Controlling installed ports

We've already seen the program *pkg_add* when installing pre-compiled packages. There are a number of other *pkg_* programs that can help you maintain installed ports, whether they have been installed by *pkg_add* or by *make install* from the Ports Collection:

- *pkg_info* tells you which ports are installed. For example:

```
$ pkg_info | less
AbiWord-1.0.3          An open-source, cross-platform WYSIWYG word proces
ImageMagick-5.5.1.1    Image processing tools (interactive optional--misc
ORBit-0.5.17           High-performance CORBA ORB with support for the C
XFree86-4.2.0_1,1      X11/XFree86 core distribution (complete, using min
... etc
bash-2.05b.004         The GNU Bourne Again Shell
bison-1.75             A parser generator from FSF, (mostly) compatible w
bonobo-1.0.21_1        The component and compound document system for GNO
cdrtools-1.11.a28      Cdrecord, mkisofs and several other programs to re
... etc
elm-2.4ME+22           ELM Mail User Agent
elm-2.4ME+32           ELM Mail User Agent
```

  Note that the last two entries in this example show that two versions of *elm* are installed. This can't be right; it happens when you install a new version without removing the old version and without running *portupgrade*. We'll discuss this matter further below.

- If you have the ports tree installed, you can use *pkg_version* to check whether your ports are up to date. *pkg_version* is a little cryptic in its output:

```
AbiWord-gnome                      =
ImageMagick                        <
ORBit                              <
Wingz                              =
XFree86                            <
...
x2x-1.28                           ?
```

  The symbols to the right of the package names have the following meanings:

=	The installed version of the package is current.
<	The installed version of the package is older than the current version.
>	The installed version of the package is newer than the current version. This situation can arise with an out-of-date index file, or when testing new ports.
?	The installed package does not appear in the index. This could be due to an out of date index or a package that has not yet been committed.
*	There are multiple versions of a particular software package listed in the index file.
!	The installed package exists in the index but for some reason, *pkg_version* was unable to compare the version number of the installed package with the corresponding entry in the index.

- There are two ways to remove a port: if you've built it from source, and you're in the build directory, you can write:

```
# make deinstall
```

Alternatively, you can remove any installed package with *pkg_delete*. For example, the list above shows two versions of the *elm* mail user agent. To remove the older one, we enter:

```
# pkg_delete elm-2.4ME+22
File '/usr/local/man/man1/answer.1' doesn't really exist.
Unable to completely remove file '/usr/local/man/man1/answer.1'
File '/usr/local/man/man1/checkalias.1' doesn't really exist.
Unable to completely remove file '/usr/local/man/man1/checkalias.1'
... etc
Couldn't entirely delete package (perhaps the packing list is
incorrectly specified?)
```

In this case, it looks as if somebody has tried to remove the files before, so *pkg_delete* couldn't do so.

Another problem with *pkg_delete* is that it might delete files of the same name that have been replaced by newer packages. After performing this operation, we try:

```
$ elm
bash: elm: command not found
```

Oops! We tried to delete the old version, but we deleted at least part of the new version. Now we need to install it again.

The moral of this story is that things aren't as simple as they might be. When you install a new version of a package, you may want to test it before you commit to using it all the time. You can't just go and delete the old version. One possibility would be to install the new package, and try it out. When you've finished testing, delete *both* packages and re-install the one you want to keep.

Keeping track of updates

The best way to find out about updates is to subscribe to the FreeBSD-ports mailing list. That way, you will get notification every time something changes. If you're tracking the ports tree with *CVSup*, you also get the updates to the ports tree automatically. Otherwise you will have to download the port. In either case, to update your installed port, just repeat the build.

Submitting a new port

The Ports Collection is constantly growing. Hardly a day goes by without a new port being added to the list. Maybe you want to submit the next one? If you have something interesting that isn't already in the Ports Collection, you can find instructions on how to prepare the port in the *FreeBSD Porter's Handbook*. The latest version is available on the FreeBSD web site, but you'll also find it on your system as */usr/share/doc/en/porters-handbook/index.html*.

10

File systems and devices

One of the most revolutionary concepts of the UNIX operating system was its *file system*, the way in which it stores data. Although most other operating systems have copied it since then, including Microsoft's platforms, none have come close to the elegance with which it is implemented. Many aspects of the file system are not immediately obvious, some of them not even to seasoned UNIX users.

We've already looked at file naming conventions on page 125. In the next section, we'll look at the file system access, structure and hierarchy, and on page 195 we'll look at how the file system treats hardware devices as files.

File permissions

A UNIX system may potentially be used by many people, so UNIX includes a method of protecting data from access by unauthorized persons. Every file has three items of information associated with it that describe who can access it in what manner:

- The *file owner*, the user ID of the person who owns the file.

- The *file group*, the group ID of the group that "owns" the file.

- A list of what the owner, the group and other people can do with the file. The possible actions are reading, writing or executing.

For example, you might have a program that accesses private data, and you want to be sure that only you can execute it. You do this by setting the permissions so that only the owner can execute it. Or you might have a text document in development, and you want to be sure that you are the only person who can change it. On the other hand, the people who work with you have a need to be able to refer to the document. You set the permissions so that only the owner can write it, that the owner and group can read it, and, because it's not ready for publication yet, you don't allow anybody else to access it.

Traditionally, the permissions are represented by three groups of rwx: r stands for *read* permission, w stands for *write* permission, and x stands for *execute* permission. The three groups represent the permissions for the owner, the group and others respectively. If the permission is not granted, it is represented by a hyphen (-). Thus, the permissions for the program I discussed above would be r-x------ (I can read and execute the program, and nobody else can do anything with it). The permissions for the draft document would be rw-r----- (I can read and write, the group can read, and others can't access it).

Typical FreeBSD file access permissions are rwxr-xr-x for programs and rw-r--r-- for other system files. In some cases, however, you'll find that other permissions are *required*. For example, the file *.rhosts*, which is used by some network programs for user validation, may contain the user's password in legible form. To help ensure that other people don't read it, the network programs refuse to read it unless its permissions are rw-------. The vast majority of system problems in UNIX can be traced to incorrect permissions, so you should pay particular attention to them.

Apart from these access permissions, executables can also have two bits set to specify the access permissions of the process when it is run. If the *setuid (set user ID)* bit is set, the process always runs as if it had been started by its owner. If the *setgid (set group ID)* bit is set, it runs as if it had been started by its group. This is frequently used to start system programs that need to access resources that the user may not access directly. We'll see an example of this with the *ps* command on page 185. *ls* represents the *setuid* bit by setting the third letter of the permissions string to s instead of x; similarly, it represents the *setgid* bit by setting the sixth letter of the permissions string to s instead of x.

In addition to this access information, the permissions contain a character that describes what kind of file it represents. The first letter may be a - (hyphen), which designates a regular file, the letter d for directory, or the letters b or c for a device node. We'll look at device nodes in Chapter 11, page 195. There are also a number of other letters that are less used. See the man page *ls(1)* for a full list.

To list files and show the permissions, use the *ls* command with the -l option:

```
$ ls -l
total 2429
-rw-rw-r--  1 grog    wheel      28204 Jan  4 14:17 %backup%~
drwxrwxr-x  3 grog    wheel        512 Oct 11 15:26 2.1.0-951005-SNAP
drwx------  4 grog    wheel        512 Nov 25 17:23 Mail
-rw-rw-r--  1 grog    wheel        149 Dec  4 14:18 Makefile
-rw-rw-r--  1 grog    wheel        108 Dec  4 12:36 Makefile.bak
-rw-rw-r--  1 grog    wheel        108 Dec  4 12:36 Makefile~
-rw-rw-r--  1 grog    wheel          0 Dec  4 12:36 depend
-rw-rw-r--  1 daemon  wheel    1474560 Dec 14 17:03 deppert.floppy
```

```
-rwxr-xr-x   1 grog     wheel          100 Dec 19 15:24 doio
-rwxrwxr-x   1 grog     wheel          204 Dec 19 15:25 doiovm
-rwxrwxr-x   1 grog     wheel          204 Dec 19 15:16 doiovm~
-rwxr-xr-x   1 grog     wheel          115 Dec 26 08:42 dovm
-rwxr-xr-x   1 grog     wheel          114 Dec 19 15:30 dovm~
drwxr-xr-x   2 grog     wheel          512 Oct 16  1994 emacs
drwxrwxrwx   2 grog     wheel          512 Jan  3 14:07 letters
```

This format shows the following information:

- First, the permissions, which we've already discussed.

- Then, the *link count*. This is the number of hard links to the file. For a regular file, this is normally 1, but directories have at least 2. We look at links on page 186.

- Next come the names of the owner and the group, and the size of the file in bytes. You'll notice that the file *deppert.floppy* belongs to daemon. This was probably an accident, and it could lead to problems. Incidentally, looking at the name of the file and its size, it's fairly obvious that this is an *image* of a 3½" floppy, that is to say, a literal copy of the data on the complete floppy.

- The date is normally the date that the file was last modified. With the -u option to *ls*, you can list the last time the file was accessed.

- Finally comes the name of the file. As you can see from this example, the names can be quite varied.

A couple of the permissions are of interest. The directories all have the x (execute) permission bit set. This enables accessing (i.e. opening) files in the directory—that's the way the term *execute* is defined for a directory. If I reset the execute permission, I can still list the names of the files, but I can't access them.

I am the only person who can access the directory *Mail*. This is the normal permission for a mail directory.

Changing file permissions and owners

Often enough, you may want to change file permissions or owners. UNIX supplies three programs to do this:

- To change the file owner, use *chown*. For example, to change the ownership of the file *deppert.floppy*, which in the list above belongs to daemon, root would enter:

  ```
  # chown grog deppert.floppy
  ```

  Note that only root may perform this operation.

- To change the file group, use *chgrp*, which works in the same way as *chown*. To change the group ownership to *lemis*, you would enter:

```
# chgrp lemis deppert.floppy
```

chown can also change both the owner and the group. Instead of the two previous examples, you could enter:

```
# chown grog:lemis deppert.floppy
```

This changes the owner to grog, as before, and also changes the group to lemis.

- To change the permissions, use the *chmod* program. *chmod* has a number of different formats, but unfortunately the nine-character representation isn't one of them. Read the man page *chmod(1)* for the full story, but you can achieve just about anything you want with one of the formats shown in table 10-1:

Table 10-1: chmod permission codes

Specification	Effect
go-w	Deny write permission to group and others
=rw,+X	Set the read and write permissions to the usual defaults, but retain any execute permissions that are currently set
+X	Make a directory or file searchable/executable by everyone if it is already searchable/executable by anyone
u=rwx,go=rx	Make a file readable/executable by everyone and writable by the owner only
go=	Clear all mode bits for group and others
g=u-w	Set the group bits equal to the user bits, but clear the group write bit

Permissions for new files

None of this tells us what the permissions for new files are going to be. The wrong choice could be disastrous. For example, if files were automatically created with the permissions rwxrwxrwx, anybody could access them in any way. On the other hand, creating them with r-------- could result in a lot of work setting them to what you really want them to be. UNIX solves this problem with a thing called *umask* (*User mask*). This is a default non-permission: it specifies which permission bits *not* to allow.

As if this weren't confusing enough, it's specified in the octal number system, in which the valid digits are 0 to 7. Each octal digit represents 3 bits. By contrast, the more common hexadecimal system uses 16 digits, 0 to 9 and a to f. The original versions of UNIX ran on machines that used the octal number system, and since the permissions come in threes, it made sense to leave the *umask* value in octal.

An example: by default, you want to create files that anybody can read, but only you can write. You set the mask to 022. This corresponds to the binary bit pattern 000010010.

The leading 0 is needed to specify that the number is in octal, not to make up three digits. If you want to set the permissions so that by default nobody can read, you'd set it to 0222. Some shells automatically assume that the number is octal, so you *may* be able to omit the 0, but it's not good practice.

The permissions are allowed where the corresponding bit is 0:

```
rwxrwxrwx        Possible permissions
000010010        umask
rwxr-xr-x        resultant permissions
```

By default, files are created without the x bits, whereas directories are created with the allowed x bits, so with this *umask*, a file would be created with the permissions rw-r--r--.

umask is a shell command. To set it, just enter:

```
$ umask 022
```

It's preferable to set this in your shell initialization file—see page 135 for further details.

Beware of creating a too restrictive umask. For example, you will get into a lot of trouble with a umask like 377, which creates files that you can only read, and that nobody else can access at all. If you disallow the x (executable) bit, you will not be able to access directories you create, and you won't be able to run programs you compile.

Making a program executable

File permissions enable one problem that occurs so often that it's worth drawing attention to it. Many operating systems require that an executable program have a special naming convention, such as *COMMAND.COM* or *FOO.BAT*, which in MS-DOS denotes a specific kind of binary executable and a script file, respectively. In UNIX, executable programs don't need a special suffix, but they must have the x bit set. Sometimes this bit gets reset (turned off), for example if you copy it across the Net with *ftp*. The result looks like this:

```
$ ps
bash: ps: Permission denied
$ ls -l /bin/ps
-r--r--r--  1 bin   kmem   163840 May  6 06:02 /bin/ps
$ su                                            you need to be super user to set ps permission
Password:                                       password doesn't echo
# chmod +x /bin/ps                              make it executable
# ps                                            now it works
  PID  TT  STAT     TIME COMMAND
  226  p2  S      0:00.56 su (bash)
  239  p2  R+     0:00.02 ps
  146  v1  Is+    0:00.06 /usr/libexec/getty Pc ttyv1
  147  v2  Is+    0:00.05 /usr/libexec/getty Pc ttyv2
# ^D                                            exit su
$ ps
ps: /dev/mem: Permission denied                 hey! it's stopped working
```

Huh? It only worked under *su*, and stopped working when I became a mere mortal again? What's going on here?

There's a second problem with programs like *ps*: some versions need to be able to access special files, in this case */dev/mem*, a special file that addresses the system memory. To do this, we need to set the *setgid* bit, s, which requires becoming superuser again:

```
$ su                                          you need to be super user to set ps permission
Password:                                     password doesn't echo
# chmod g+s /bin/ps                           set the setgid bit
# ls -l /bin/ps                               see what it looks like
-r-xr-sr-x  1 bin  kmem  163840 May  6 06:02 /bin/ps
# ^D                                          exit su
$ ps                                          now it still works
  PID  TT  STAT     TIME COMMAND
  226  p2  S      0:00.56 su (bash)
  239  p2  R+     0:00.02 ps
  146  v1  Is+    0:00.06 /usr/libexec/getty Pc ttyv1
  147  v2  Is+    0:00.05 /usr/libexec/getty Pc ttyv2
```

In this example, the permissions in the final result really are the correct permissions for *ps*. It's impossible to go through the permissions for every standard program. If you suspect that you have the permissions set incorrectly, use the permissions of the files on the Live Filesystem CD-ROM as a guideline.

setuid and *setgid* programs can be a security issue. What happens if the program called *ps* is really something else, a Trojan Horse? We set the permissions to allow it to break into the system. As a result, FreeBSD has found an alternative method for *ps* to do its work, and it no longer needs to be set *setgid*.

Mandatory Access Control

For some purposes, traditional UNIX permissions are insufficient. Release 5.0 of FreeBSD introduces *Mandatory Access Control*, or *MAC*, which permits loadable kernel modules to augment the system security policy. MAC is intended as a toolkit for developing local and vendor security extensions, and it includes a number of sample policy modules, including Multi-Level Security (MLS) with compartments, and a number of augmented UNIX security models including a file system firewall. At the time of writing it is still considered experimental software, so this book doesn't discuss it further. See the man pages for more details.

Links

In UNIX, files are defined by *inodes*, structures on disk that you can't access directly. They contain the *metadata*, all the information about the file, such as owner, permissions and timestamps. What they don't contain are the things you think of as making up a file: they don't have any data, and they don't have names. Instead, the inode contains information about where the data blocks are located on the disk. It doesn't know anything about the name: that's the job of the directories.

A directory is simply a special kind of file that contains a list of names and inode numbers: in other words, they assign a name to an inode, and thus to a file. More than one name can point to the same inode, so files can have more than one name. This connection between a name and an inode is called a *link*, sometimes confusingly *hard link*. The inode numbers relate to the file system, so files must be in the same file system as the directory that refers to them.

Directory entries are independent of each other: each points to the inode, so they're completely equivalent. The inode contains a *link count* that keeps track of how many directory entries point to it: when you remove the last entry, the system deletes the file data and metadata.

Alternatively, *symbolic links*, sometimes called *soft links*, are not restricted to the same file system (not even to the same system!), and they refer to another file name, not to the file itself. The difference is most evident if you delete a file: if the file has been hard linked, the other names still exist and you can access the file by them. If you delete a file name that has a symbolic link pointing to it, the file goes away and the symbolic link can't find it any more.

It's not easy to decide which kind of link to use—see *UNIX Power Tools* (O'Reilly) for more details.

Directory hierarchy

Although Microsoft platforms have a hierarchical directory structure, there is little standardization of the directory names: it's difficult to know where a particular program or data file might be. UNIX systems have a standard directory hierarchy, though every vendor loves to change it just a little bit to ensure that they're not absolutely compatible. In the course of its evolution, UNIX has changed its directory hierarchy several times. It's still better than the situation in the Microsoft world. The most recent, and probably most far-reaching changes, occurred over ten years ago with System V.4 and 4.4BSD, both of which made almost identical changes.

Nearly every version of UNIX prefers to have at least two file systems, / (the *root file system*) and */usr*, even if they only have a single disk. This arrangement is considered more reliable than a single file system: it's possible for a file system to crash so badly that it can't be mounted any more, and you need to read in a tape backup, or use programs like *fsck* or *fsdb* to piece them together. We have already discussed this issue on page 68, where I recommend having */usr* on the same file system as /.

Standard directories

The physical layout of the file systems does not affect the names or contents of the directories, which are standardized. Table 10-2 gives an overview of the standard FreeBSD directories; see the man page hier(7) for more details.

Table 10-2: FreeBSD directory hierarchy

Directory name	Usage
/	Root file system. Contains a couple of system directories and mount points for other file systems. It should not contain anything else.
/bin	Executable programs of general use needed at system startup time. The name was originally an abbreviation for *binary*, but many of the files in here are shell scripts.
/boot	Files used when booting the system, including the kernel and its associated *klds*.
/cdrom	A mount point for CD-ROM drives.
/compat	A link to */usr/compat*: see below.
/dev	Directory of device nodes. The name is an abbreviation for *devices*. From FreeBSD 5.0 onward, this is normally a mount point for the *device file system, devfs*. We'll look at the contents of this directory in more detail on page 195.
/etc	Configuration files used at system startup. Unlike System V, */etc* does not contain kernel build files, which are not needed at system startup. Unlike earlier UNIX versions, it also does not contain executables—they have been moved to */sbin*.
/home	By convention, put user files here. Despite the name, */usr* is for system files.
/mnt	A mount point for floppies and other temporary file systems.
/proc	The *process file system*. This directory contains pseudo-files that refer to the virtual memory of currently active processes.
/root	The home directory of the user root. In traditional UNIX file systems, root's home directory was /, but this is messy.
/sbin	System executables needed at system startup time. These are typically system administration files that used to be stored in */etc*.
/sys	If present, this is usually a symbolic link to */usr/src/sys*, the kernel sources. This is a tradition derived from 4.3BSD.
/tmp	A place for temporary files. This directory is an anachronism: normally it is on the root file system, though it is possible to mount it as a separate file system or make it a symbolic link to */var/tmp*. It is maintained mainly for programs that expect to find it.
/usr	The "second file system." See the discussion above.

Directory name	Usage
/usr/X11R6	The X Window System.
/usr/X11R6/bin	Executable X11 programs.
/usr/X11R6/include	Header files for X11 programming.
/usr/X11R6/lib	Library files for X11.
/usr/X11R6/man	Man pages for X11.
/usr/bin	Standard executable programs that are not needed at system start. Most standard programs you use are stored here.
/usr/compat	A directory containing code for emulated systems, such as Linux.
/usr/games	Games.
/usr/include	Header files for programmers.
/usr/lib	Library files. FreeBSD does not have a directory */lib*.
/usr/libexec	Executable files that are not started directly by the user, for example the phases of the C compiler (which are started by */usr/bin/gcc*) or the *getty* program, which is started by *init*.
/usr/libdata	Miscellaneous files used by system utilities.
/usr/local	Additional programs that are not part of the operating system. It parallels the */usr* directory in having subdirectories *bin*, *include*, *lib*, *man*, *sbin*, and *share*. This is where you can put programs that you get from other sources.
/usr/obj	Object files created when building the system. See Chapter 33.
/usr/ports	The Ports Collection.
/usr/sbin	System administration programs that are not needed at system startup.
/usr/share	Miscellaneous read-only files, mainly informative. Subdirectories include *doc*, the FreeBSD documentation, *games*, *info*, the GNU *info* documentation, *locale*, internationization information, and *man*, the man pages.
/usr/src	System source files.
/var	A file system for data that changes frequently, such as mail, news, and log files. If */var* is not a separate file system, you should create a directory on another file system and symlink */var* to it.
/var/log	Directory with system log files
/var/mail	Incoming mail for users on this system

Directory name	Usage
/var/spool	Transient data, such as outgoing mail, print data and anonymous ftp.
/var/tmp	Temporary files.

File system types

FreeBSD supports a number of file system types. The most important are:

- *UFS* is the *UNIX File System.*[1] All native disk file systems are of this type. Since FreeBSD 5.0, you have a choice of two different versions, *UFS 1* and *UFS 2*. As the names suggest, UFS 2 is a successor to UFS 1. Unlike UFS 1, UFS 2 file systems are not limited to 1 TB (1024 GB) in size. UFS 2 is relatively new, so unless you require very large file systems, you should stick to UFS 1.

- *cd9660* is the ISO 9660 CD-ROM format with the so-called *Rock Ridge Extensions* that enable UNIX-like file names to be used. Use this file system type for all CD-ROMs, even if they don't have the Rock Ridge Extensions.

- *nfs* is the *Network File System*, a means of sharing file systems across a network. We'll look at it in Chapter 25.

- FreeBSD supports a number of file systems from other popular operating systems. You mount the file systems with the *mount* command and the -t option to specify the file system type. For example:

```
# mount -t ext2fs /dev/da1s1 /linux      mount a Linux ext2 file system
# mount -t msdos /dev/da2s1 /C:           mount a Microsoft FAT file system
```

Here's a list of currently supported file systems:

Table 10-3: File system support

File system	mount option
CD-ROM	cd9660
DVD	udf
Linux ext2	ext2fs
Microsoft MS-DOS	msdosfs
Microsoft NT	ntfs
Novell Netware	nwfs
Microsoft CIFS	smbfs

---

1. Paradoxically, although BSD may not be called UNIX, its file system *is* called the UNIX File System. The UNIX System Group, the developers of UNIX System V.4, adopted UFS as the standard file system for System V and gave it this name. Previously it was called the Berkeley *Fast File System*, or *ffs*.

Soft updates

Soft updates change the way the file system performs I/O. They enable *metadata* to be written less frequently. This can give rise to dramatic performance improvements under certain circumstances, such as file deletion. Specify soft updates with the −U option when creating the file system. For example:

```
# newfs -U /dev/da1s2h
```

If you forget this flag, you can enable them later with *tunefs*:

```
# tunefs -n enable /dev/da1s2h
```

You can't perform this operation on a mounted file system.

Snapshots

One of the problems with backing up file systems is that you don't get a consistent view of the file system: while you copy a file, other programs may be modifying it, so what you get on the tape is not an accurate view of the file at any time. *Snapshots* are a method to create a unified view of a file system. They maintain a relatively small file in the file system itself containing information on what has changed since the snapshot was taken. When you access the snapshot, you get this data rather than the current data for the parts of the disk which have changed, so you get a view of the file system as it was at the time of the snapshot.

Creating snapshots

You create snapshots with the *mount* command and the −o snapshot option. For example, you could enter

```
# mount -u -o snapshot /var/snapshot/snap1 /var
```

This command creates a snapshot of the */var* file system called */var/snapshot/snap1*.

Snapshot files have some interesting properties:

- You can have multiple snapshots on a file system, up to the current limit of 20.

- Snapshots have the schg flag set, which prevents anybody writing to them.

- Despite the schg flag, you can still remove them.

- They are automatically updated when anything is written to the file system. The view of the file system doesn't change, but this update is necessary in order to maintain the "old" view of the file system.

- They look like normal file systems. You can mount them with the *md* driver. We'll look at that on page 193.

Probably the most useful thing you can do with a snapshot is to take a backup of it. We'll look at backups on page 253.

At the time of writing, snapshots are still under development. It's possible that you might still have trouble with them, in particular with deadlocks that can only be cleared by rebooting.

It takes about 30 seconds to create a snapshot of an 8 GB file system. During the last five seconds, file system activity is suspended. If there's a lot of soft update activity going on in the file system (for example, when deleting a lot of files), this suspension time can become much longer, up to several minutes. To remove the same snapshot takes about two minutes, but it doesn't suspend file system activity at all.

Mounting file systems

Microsoft platforms identify partitions by letters that are assigned at boot time. There is no obvious relation between the partitions, and you have little control over the way the system assigns them. By contrast, all UNIX partitions have a specific relation to the *root file system*, which is called simply /. This flexibility has one problem: you have the choice of where in the overall file system structure you put your individual file systems. You specify the location with the *mount* command. For example, you would typically mount a CD-ROM in the directory */cdrom*, but if you have three CD-ROM drives attached to your SCSI controller, you might prefer to mount them in the directories */cd0*, */cd1*, and */cd2*. To mount a file system, you need to specify the device to be mounted, where it is to be mounted, and the type of file system (unless it is ufs). The *mount point*, (the directory where it is to be mounted) must already exist. To mount your second CD-ROM on */cd1*, you enter:

```
# mkdir /cd1                                only if it doesn't exist
# mount -t cd9660 -o ro /dev/cd1a /cd1
```

When the system boots, it calls the startup script */etc/rc*, which among other things automatically mounts the file systems. All you need to do is to supply the information: what is to be mounted, and where? This is in the file */etc/fstab*. If you come from a System V environment, you'll notice significant difference in format—see the man page *fstab(5)* for the full story. A typical */etc/fstab* might look like:

```
/dev/ad0s1a   /                    ufs        rw   1 1   root file system
/dev/ad0s1b   none                 swap       sw   0 0   swap
/dev/ad0s1e   /usr                 ufs        rw   2 2   /usr file system
/dev/da1s1e   /src                 ufs        rw   2 2   additional file system
/dev/da2s1    /linux               ext2fs     rw   2 2   Linux file system
/dev/ad1s1    /C:                  msdos      rw   2 2   Microsoft file system
proc          /proc                procfs     rw   0 0   proc pseudo-file system
linproc       /compat/linux/proc   linprocfs  rw   0 0
/dev/cd0a     /cdrom               cd9660     ro   0 0   CD-ROM
presto:/      /presto/root         nfs        rw   0 0   NFS file systems on other systems
presto:/usr   /presto/usr          nfs        rw   0 0
presto:/home  /presto/home         nfs        rw   0 0
presto:/S     /S                   nfs        rw   0 0
//guest@samba/public   /smb        smbfs      rw,noauto   0 0   SMB file system
```

The format of the file is reasonably straightforward:

- The first column gives the name of the device (if it's a real file system), a keyword for some file systems, like proc, or the name of the remote file system for NFS mounts.

- The second column specifies the mount point. Swap partitions don't have a mount point, so the mount point for the swap partition is specified as none.

- The third column specifies the type of file system. Local file systems on hard disk are always *ufs*, and file systems on CD-ROM are *cd9660*. Remote file systems are always *nfs*. Specify swap partitions with *swap*, and the *proc* file system with *proc*.

- The fourth column contains rw for file systems that can be read or written, ro for file systems (like CD-ROM) that can only be read, and sw for swap partitions. It can also contain options like the noauto in the bottom line, which tells the system startup scripts to ignore the line. It's there so that you can use the shorthand notation mount /smb when you want to mount the file system.

- The fifth and sixth columns are used by the *dump* and fsck programs. You won't normally need to change them. Enter 1 for a root file system, 2 for other UFS file systems, and 0 for everything else.

Mounting files as file systems

So far, our files have all been on devices, also called *special files*. Sometimes, though, you may want to access the contents of a file as a file system:

- It's sometimes of interest to access the contents of a snapshot, for example to check the contents.

- After creating an ISO image to burn on CD-R, you should check that it's valid.

- Also, after downloading an ISO image from the Net, you may just want to access the contents, and not create a CD-R at all.

In each case, the solution is the same: you mount the files as a *vnode* device with the *md* driver.

The *md* driver creates a number of different kinds of pseudo-device. See the man page *md(4)*. We use the *vnode* device, a special file that refers to file system files. Support for *md* is included in the GENERIC kernel, but if you've built a kernel without the *md* drive, you can load it as a *kld*. If you're not sure, try loading the kld anyway.

In the following example, we associate a vnode device with the ISO image *iso-image* using the program *mdconfig*:

```
# kldload md                          load the kld module if necessary
kldload: can't load md: File exists   already loaded or in the kernel
# mdconfig -a -t vnode -f iso-image   and configure the device
md0                                   this is the name assigned in directory /dev
# mount -t cd9660 /dev/md0 /mnt       then mount it
```

After this, you can access the image at */mnt* as a normal file system. You specify -t cd9660 in this case because the file system on the image is a CD9660 file system. You don't specify this if you're mounting a UFS file system, for example a snapshot image.

Older versions of FreeBSD used the *vn* driver, which used different syntax. Linux uses *loop mounts*, which FreeBSD doesn't support.

Unmounting file systems

When you mount a file system, the system assumes it is going to stay there, and in the interests of efficiency it delays writing data back to the file system. This is also the reason why you can't just turn the power off when you shut down the system. If you want to stop using a file system, you must tell the system about it so that it can flush any remaining data. You do this with the *umount* command. Note the spelling of this command—there's no **n** in the command name.

You need to do this even with read-only media such as CD-ROMs: the system assumes it can access the data from a mounted file system, and it gets quite unhappy if it can't. Where possible, it locks removable media so that you can't remove them from the device until you unmount them.

Using *umount* is straightforward: just tell it what to unmount, either the device name or the directory name. For example, to unmount the CD-ROM we mounted in the example above, you could enter one of these commands:

```
# umount /dev/cd1a
# umount /cd1
```

Before unmounting a file system, *umount* checks that nobody is using it. If somebody is using it, it refuses to unmount it with a message like umount: /cd1: Device busy. This message often occurs because you have changed your directory to a directory on the file system you want to remove. For example (which also shows the usefulness of having directory names in the prompt):

```
=== root@freebie (/dev/ttyp2) /cd1 16 -> umount /cd1
umount: /cd1: Device busy
=== root@freebie (/dev/ttyp2) /cd1 17 -> cd
=== root@freebie (/dev/ttyp2) ~ 18 -> umount /cd1
=== root@freebie (/dev/ttyp2) ~ 19 ->
```

After unmounting a vnode file system, don't forget to unconfigure the file:

```
# umount /mnt
# mdconfig -d -u 0
```

The parameter 0 refers to *md* device 0, in other words */dev/md0*.

FreeBSD devices

UNIX refers to devices in the same manner as it refers to normal files. By contrast to normal ("regular") files, they are called *special files*. They're not really files at all: they're information about device support in the kernel, and the term *device node* is more accurate. Conventionally, they are stored in the directory */dev*. Some devices don't have device nodes, for example Ethernet interfaces: they are treated differently by the *ifconfig* program.

Traditional UNIX systems distinguish two types of device, *block devices* and *character devices*. FreeBSD no longer has block devices; we discussed the reasons for this on page 35.

In traditional UNIX systems, including FreeBSD up to Release 4, it was necessary to create device nodes manually. This caused a number of problems when they didn't match what was in the system. Release 5 of FreeBSD has solved this problem with the *device file system*, also known as *devfs*. *devfs* is a pseudo-file system that dynamically creates device nodes for exactly those devices that are in the kernel, which makes it unnecessary to manually create devices.

Overview of FreeBSD devices

Every UNIX system has its own peculiarities when it comes to device names and usage. Even if you're used to UNIX, you'll find the following table useful.

Table 10-4: FreeBSD device names

Device	Description
acd0	First ata (IDE) CD-ROM drive.
ad0	First ata (IDE or similar) disk drive. See Chapter 2, page 38, for a complete list of disk drive names.
bpf0	Berkeley packet filter.
cd0	First SCSI CD-ROM drive.
ch0	SCSI CD-ROM changer (juke box)
console	System console, the device that receives console messages. Initially it is */dev/ttyv0*, but it can be changed.
cuaa0	First serial port in callout mode.
cuaia0	First serial port in callout mode, initial state. Note the letter i for *initial*.
cuala0	First serial port in callout mode, lock state. Note the letter l for *lock*.
da0	First SCSI disk drive. See Chapter 2, page 38, for a complete list of disk drive names.
esa0	First SCSI tape drive, eject on close mode.

Device	Description
fd	File descriptor pseudo-devices: a directory containing pseudo-devices that, when opened, return a duplicate of the file descriptor with the same number. For example, if you open */dev/fd/0*, you get another handle on your *stdin* stream (file descriptor 0).
fd0	The first floppy disk drive, accessed as a file system.
kmem	Kernel virtual memory pseudo-device.
lpt0	First parallel printer.
mem	Physical virtual memory pseudo-device.
nsa0	First SCSI tape drive, no-rewind mode.
null	The "bit bucket." Send data to this device if you never want to see it again.
psm0	PS/2 mouse.
ptyp0	First master pseudo-terminal. Master pseudo-terminals are named */dev/ptyp0* through */dev/ptypv*, */dev/ptyq0* through */dev/ptyqv*, */dev/ptyr0* through */dev/ptyrv*, */dev/ptys0* through */dev/ptysv*, */dev/ptyP0* through */dev/ptyPv*, */dev/ptyQ0* through */dev/ptyQv*, */dev/ptyR0* through */dev/ptyRv* and */dev/ptyS0* through */dev/ptySv*.
random	Random number generator.
sa0	First SCSI tape drive, rewind on close mode.
sysmouse	System mouse, controlled by *moused*. We'll look at this again on page 519.
tty	Current controlling terminal.
ttyd0	First serial port in callin mode.
ttyid0	First serial port in callin mode, initial state.
ttyld0	First serial port in callin mode, lock state.
ttyp0	First slave pseudo-terminal. Slave pseudo-terminals are named */dev/ttyp0* through */dev/ttypv*, */dev/ttyq0* through */dev/ttyqv*, */dev/ttyr0* through */dev/ttyrv*, */dev/ttys0* through */dev/ttysv*, */dev/ttyP0* through */dev/ttyPv*, */dev/ttyQ0* through */dev/ttyQv*, */dev/ttyR0* through */dev/ttyRv* and */dev/ttyS0* through */dev/ttySv*. Some processes, such as *xterm*, only look at */dev/ttyp0* through */dev/ttypv*.
ttyv0	First virtual tty. This is the display with which the system starts. Up to 10 virtual ttys can be activated by adding the appropriate *getty* information in the file */etc/ttys*. See Chapter 19, page 338, for further details.
ugen0	First generic USB device.
ukbd0	First USB keyboard.
ulpt0	First USB printer.

Device	Description
umass0	First USB mass storage device.
ums0	First USB mouse.
uscanner0	First USB scanner.
vinum	Directory for Vinum device nodes. See Chapter 12, for further details.
zero	Dummy device that always returns the value (binary) 0 when read.

You'll note a number of different modes associated with the serial ports. We'll look at them again in Chapter 19.

Virtual terminals

As we have seen, UNIX is a multitasking operating system, but a PC generally only has one screen. FreeBSD solves this problem with *virtual terminals*. When in text mode, you can change between up to 16 different screens with the combination of the **Alt** key and a function key. The devices are named */dev/ttyv0* through */dev/ttyv15*, and correspond to the keystrokes **Alt-F1** through **Alt-F16**. By default, three virtual terminals are active: */dev/ttyv0* through */dev/ttyv2*. The system console is the virtual terminal */dev/ttyv0*, and that's what you see when you boot the machine. To activate additional virtual terminals, edit the file */etc/ttys*. There you find:

```
ttyv0   "/usr/libexec/getty Pc"      cons25  on  secure
ttyv1   "/usr/libexec/getty Pc"      cons25  on  secure
ttyv2   "/usr/libexec/getty Pc"      cons25  on  secure
ttyv3   "/usr/libexec/getty Pc"      cons25  off secure
```

The keywords on and off refer to the state of the terminal: to enable one, set its state to on. To enable extra virtual terminals, add a line with the corresponding terminal name, in the range */dev/ttyv4* to */dev/ttyv15*. After you have edited */etc/ttys*, you need to tell the system to re-read it in order to start the terminals. Do this as root with this command:

```
# kill -1 1
```

Process 1 is *init* —see page 528 for more details.

Pseudo-terminals

In addition to virtual terminals, FreeBSD offers an additional class of terminals called *pseudo-terminals*. They come in pairs: a *master device*, also called a *pty* (pronounced *pity*) is used only by processes that use the interface, and has a name like */dev/ptyp0*. The *slave device* looks like a terminal, and has a name like */dev/ttyp0*. Any process can open it without any special knowledge of the interface. These terminals are used for network connections such as *xterm*, *telnet* and *rlogin*. You don't need a *getty* for pseudo-terminals. Since FreeBSD Release 5.0, pseudo-terminals are created as required.

11

Disks

One of the most important parts of running any computer system is handling data on disk. We have already looked at UNIX file handling in Chapter 10. In this chapter, we'll look at two ways to add another disk to your system, and what you should put on them. In addition, we'll discuss disk error recovery on page 218.

Adding a hard disk

When you installed FreeBSD, you created file systems on at least one hard disk. At a later point, you may want to install additional drives. There are two ways to do this: with *sysinstall* and with the traditional UNIX command-line utilities.

There was a time when it was dangerous to use *sysinstall* after the system had been installed: there was a significant chance of shooting yourself in the foot. There's always a chance of doing something wrong when initializing disks, but *sysinstall* has become a lot better, and now it's the tool of choice. It's good to know the alternatives, though. In this section we'll look at *sysinstall*, and on page 209 we'll see how to do it manually if *sysinstall* won't cooperate.

We've been through all the details of disk layout and slices and partitions in Chapter 2, so I won't repeat them here. Basically, to add a new disk to the system, you need to:

- Install the disk physically. This usually involves power cycling the machine.

- Barely possibly, format the disk. Without exception, modern disks come pre-formatted, and you only need to format a disk if it has defects or if it's ancient. In many cases the so-called "format" program doesn't really format at all.

- If you want to share with other operating systems, create a PC style partition table on the disk. We looked at the concepts on page 63.

- Define a FreeBSD slice (which the PC BIOS calls a "partition").

- Define the partitions in the FreeBSD slice.

- Tell the system about the file systems and where to mount them.

- Create the file systems.

These are the same operations that we performed in Chapter 5.

Disk hardware installation

Before you can do anything with the disk, you have to install it in the system. To do this, you must normally shut down the system and turn the power off, though high-end SCSI enclosures allow *hot-swapping*, changing disks in a running system. If the disk is IDE, and you already have an IDE disk on the controller, you need to set the second disk as "slave" drive. *And* you may have to set the first disk as "master" drive: if you only have one drive, you don't set any jumpers, but if you have two drives, some disks require you to set jumpers on both disks. If you don't do this, the system will appear to hang during the power-on self test, and will finally report some kind of disk error.

Adding a SCSI disk is more complicated. You can connect up to 15 SCSI devices to a host adapter, depending on the interface. Many systems restrict the number to 7 for compatibility with older SCSI interfaces. Typically, your first SCSI disk will have the SCSI ID 0, and the host adapter will have the SCSI ID 7. Traditionally, the IDs 4, 5, and 6 are reserved for tape and CD-ROM drives, and the IDs 0 to 3 are reserved for disks, though FreeBSD doesn't impose any restrictions on what goes where.

Whatever kind of disk you're adding, look at the boot messages, which you can retrieve with the *dmesg* command. For example, if you're planning to add a SCSI device, you might see:

```
sym0: <875> port 0xc400-0xc4ff mem 0xec002000-0xec002fff,0xec003000-0xec0030ff irq 10
  at device 9.0 on pci0
sym0: Symbios NVRAM, ID 7, Fast-20, SE, NO parity
sym0: open drain IRQ line driver, using on-chip SRAM
sym0: using LOAD/STORE-based firmware.
sym0: SCAN FOR LUNS disabled for targets 0.
sym1: <875> port 0xc800-0xc8ff mem 0xec001000-0xec001fff,0xec000000-0xec0000ff irq 9
at device 13.0 on pci0
sym1: No NVRAM, ID 7, Fast-20, SE, parity checking
further down...
Waiting 3 seconds for SCSI devices to settle
sa0 at sym0 bus 0 target 3 lun 0
sa0: <EXABYTE EXB-8505SMBANSH2 0793> Removable Sequential Access SCSI-2 device
sa0: 5.000MB/s transfers (5.000MHz, offset 11)
sa1 at sym0 bus 0 target 4 lun 0
sa1: <ARCHIVE Python 28849-XXX 4.CM> Removable Sequential Access SCSI-2 device
sa1: 5.000MB/s transfers (5.000MHz, offset 15)
sa2 at sym0 bus 0 target 5 lun 0
sa2: <TANDBERG TDC 3800 -03:> Removable Sequential Access SCSI-CCS device
sa2: 3.300MB/s transfers
pass4 at sym0 bus 0 target 4 lun 1
pass4: <ARCHIVE Python 28849-XXX 4.CM> Removable Changer SCSI-2 device
```

```
pass4: 5.000MB/s transfers (5.000MHz, offset 15)
cd0 at sym0 bus 0 target 6 lun 0
cd0: <NRC MBR-7 110> Removable CD-ROM SCSI-2 device
cd0: 3.300MB/s transfers
cd0: cd present [322265 x 2048 byte records]
da0 at sym1 bus 0 target 3 lun 0
da0: <SEAGATE ST15230W SUN4.2G 0738> Fixed Direct Access SCSI-2 device
da0: 20.000MB/s transfers (10.000MHz, offset 15, 16bit), Tagged Queueing Enabled
da0: 4095MB (8386733 512 byte sectors: 255H 63S/T 522C)
```

This output shows two Symbios SCSI host adapters /dev/(*sym0* and /dev/*sym1*), three tape drives /dev/(*sa0*, /dev/*sa1* and /dev/*sa2*), a CD-ROM drive /dev/(*cd0*), a tape changer /dev/(*pass4*), and also a disk drive /dev/da0 on ID 3, which is called a *target* in these messages. The disk is connected to the second host adapter, and the other devices are connected to the first host adapter.

Installing an external SCSI device

External SCSI devices have two cable connectors: one goes towards the host adapter, and the other towards the next device. The order of the devices in the chain does not have to have anything to do with the SCSI ID. This method is called *daisy chaining*. At the end of the chain, the spare connector may be plugged with a *terminator*, a set of resistors designed to keep noise off the bus. Some devices have internal terminators, however. When installing an external device, you will have to do one of the following:

- If you are installing a first external device (one connected directly to the cable connector on the backplane of the host adapter), you will have to ensure that the device provides termination. If you already have at least one internal device, the host adapter will no longer be at one end of the chain, so you will also have to stop it from providing termination. Modern SCSI host adapters can decide whether they need to terminate, but older host adapters have resistor packs. In the latter case, remove these resistor packs.

- If you are adding an additional external device, you have two choices: you can remove a cable in the middle of the daisy chain and plug it into your new device. You then connect a new cable from your device to the device from which you removed the original cable.

  Alternatively, you can add the device at the end of the chain. Remove the terminator or turn off the termination, and plug your cable into the spare socket. Insert the terminator in your device (or turn termination on).

You can add external SCSI devices to a running system if they're hot-pluggable. It might even work if they're not hot-pluggable, but it's not strictly the correct thing to do, and there's the risk that you might damage something, possibly irreparably. After connecting the devices, powering them up and waiting for them to come ready, run *camcontrol rescan*. For example, if you added a second disk drive to the second host adapter in the example above, you might see:

```
# camcontrol rescan 1
da1 at sym1 bus 0 target 0 lun 0
da1: <SEAGATE ST15230W SUN4.2G 0738> Fixed Direct Access SCSI-2 device
da1: 20.000MB/s transfers (10.000MHz, offset 15, 16bit), Tagged Queueing Enabled
da1: 4095MB (8386733 512 byte sectors: 255H 63S/T 522C)
Re-scan of bus 1 was successful
```

There's a problem with this approach: note that */dev/da1* has ID 0, and the already present */dev/da0* has ID 3. If you now reboot the system, they will come up with the device names the other way round. We'll look at this issue in more detail in the next section.

Installing an internal SCSI device

Installing an internal SCSI device is much the same as installing an external device. Instead of daisy chains, you have a flat band cable with a number of connectors. Find one that suits you, and plug it into the device. Again, you need to think about termination:

- If you are installing the device at the end of the chain, it should have termination enabled. You should also disable termination for the device that was previously at the end of the chain. Depending on the device, this may involve removing the physical terminators or setting a jumper.

- If you are installing the device in the middle of the chain, make sure it does not have termination enabled.

In this chapter, we'll look at two ways of installing a drive in an existing SCSI chain. We could be in for a surprise: the device ID we get for the new drive depends on what is currently on the chain. For example, consider our example above, where we have a chain with a single drive on it:

```
da0 at sym1 bus 0 target 3 lun 0
da0: <SEAGATE ST15230W SUN4.2G 0738> Fixed Direct Access SCSI-2 device
da0: 20.000MB/s transfers (10.000MHz, offset 15, 16bit), Tagged Queueing Enabled
da0: 4095MB (8386733 512 byte sectors: 255H 63S/T 522C)
```

This drive on target (ID) 2. If we put our new drive on target 0 and reboot, we see:

```
da0 at sym1 bus 0 target 0 lun 0
da0: <SEAGATE ST15230W SUN4.2G 0738> Fixed Direct Access SCSI-2 device
da0: 20.000MB/s transfers (10.000MHz, offset 15, 16bit), Tagged Queueing Enabled
da0: 4095MB (8386733 512 byte sectors: 255H 63S/T 522C)
da1 at sym1 bus 0 target 3 lun 0
da1: <SEAGATE ST15230W SUN4.2G 0738> Fixed Direct Access SCSI-2 device
da1: 20.000MB/s transfers (10.000MHz, offset 15, 16bit), Tagged Queueing Enabled
da1: 4095MB (8386733 512 byte sectors: 255H 63S/T 522C)
```

At first glance, this looks reasonable, but that's only because both disks are of the same type. If you look at the target numbers, you'll notice that the new disk is */dev/da0*, not */dev/da1*. The target ID of the new disk is lower than the target ID of the old disk, so the system recognizes the new disk as */dev/da0*, and our previous */dev/da0* has become */dev/da1*.

This change of disk ID can be a problem. One of the first things you do with a new disk is to create new disk labels and file systems. Both offer excellent opportunities to shoot yourself in the foot if you choose the wrong disk: the result would almost certainly be the complete loss of data on that disk. Even apart from such catastrophes, you'll have to edit */etc/fstab* before you can mount any file systems that are on the disk. The alternatives are to wire down the device names, or to change the SCSI IDs. In FreeBSD 5.0, you wire down device names and busses by adding entries to the boot configuration file */boot/device.hints*. We'll look at that on page 574.

Formatting the disk

Formatting is the process of rewriting every sector on the disk with a specific data pattern, one that the electronics find most difficult to reproduce: if they can read this pattern, they can read anything. Microsoft calls this a *low-level format*.[1] Obviously it destroys any existing data, so

> *If you have anything you want to keep, back it up before formatting.*

Most modern disks don't need formatting unless they're damaged. In particular, formatting will not help if you're having configuration problems, if you can't get PPP to work, or you're running out of disk space. Well, it *will* solve the disk space problem, but not in the manner you probably desire.

If you do need to format a SCSI disk, use *camcontrol*. *camcontrol* is a control program for SCSI devices, and it includes a lot of useful functions that you can read about in the man page. To format a disk, use the following syntax:

```
# camcontrol format da1
```

> *Remember that formatting a disk destroys all data on the disk. Before using the command, make sure that you need to do so: there are relatively few cases that call for formatting a disk. About the only reasons are if you want to change the physical sector size of the disk, or if you are getting "medium format corrupted" errors from the disk in response to read and write requests.*

FreeBSD can format only floppies and SCSI disks. In general it is no longer possible to reformat ATA (IDE) disks, though some manufacturers have programs that can recover from some data problems. In most cases, though, it's sufficient to write zeros to the entire disk:

```
# dd if=/dev/zero of=/dev/ad1 bs=128k
```

If this doesn't work, you may find formatting programs on the manufacturer's web site. You'll probably need to run them under a Microsoft platform.

---

1. Microsoft also uses the term *high-level format* for what we call creating a file system.

Using sysinstall

If you can, use *sysinstall* to partition your disk. Looking at the *dmesg* output for our new disk, we see:

```
da1 at sym1 bus 0 target 0 lun 0
da1: <SEAGATE ST15230W SUN4.2G 0738> Fixed Direct Access SCSI-2 device
da1: 20.000MB/s transfers (10.000MHz, offset 15, 16bit), Tagged Queueing Enabled
da1: 4095MB (8386733 512 byte sectors: 255H 63S/T 522C)
```

You see the standard installation screen (see Chapter 5, page 60). Select Index, then Partition, and you see the following screen:

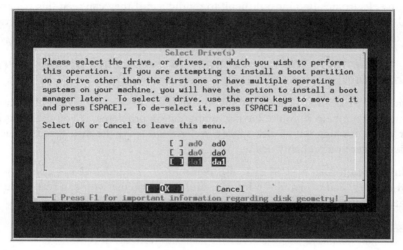

Figure 11-1: Disk selection menu

In this case, we want to partition */dev/da1*, so we position the cursor on da1 (as shown) and press **Enter**. We see the disk partition menu, which shows that the disk currently contains three partitions:

- The first starts at offset 0, and has a length of 63. This is *not* unused, no matter what the description says. It's the partition table, padded to the length of a "track."

- The next partition takes up the bulk of the drive and is a Microsoft partition.

- Finally, we have 803 sectors left over as a result of the partitioning scheme. Sometimes this can be much larger—I have seen values as high as 35 MB. This is the price we pay for compatibility with PC BIOS partitioning.

We want a FreeBSD partition, not a Microsoft partition. At this point, we have a number of choices:

```
Disk name:      da1                                    FDISK Partition Editor
DISK Geometry:  522 cyls/255 heads/63 sectors = 8385930 sectors (4094MB)

Offset        Size(ST)        End     Name  PType        Desc  Subtype    Flags

        0          63         62        -      6      unused     0
       63     8385867    8385929     da1s1     2         fat     6
  8385930         803    8386732        -      6      unused     0




The following commands are supported (in upper or lower case):

A = Use Entire Disk   G = set Drive Geometry   C = Create Slice
D = Delete Slice      Z = Toggle Size Units    S = Set Bootable
T = Change Type       U = Undo All Changes     W = Write Changes

Use F1 or ? to get more help, arrow keys to select.
```

Figure 11-2: Disk partition menu

- We can change the partition type (called "Subtype" in the menu). It's currently 6, and we would need to change it to 165. Do this with the t command.

- We could delete the partition by positioning the cursor on the partition information and pressing d, then create a new partition, either with a if we want a single partition, or with c if we want more than one partition.

- If we're using this disk for FreeBSD only, we don't have to waste even this much space. There is an option "use whole disk for FreeBSD," the so-called "dangerously dedicated" mode. This term comes partially from superstition and partially because some BIOSes expect to find a partition table on the first sector of a disk, and they can't access the disk if they don't find one. If your BIOS has this bug, you'll find this one out pretty quickly when you try to boot. If it doesn't fail on the first boot, it won't fail, though it's barely possible that you might have trouble if you move it to a system with a different BIOS. If you want to use this method, use the undocumented f command.

To use the whole disk, we first delete the current partition: we press the cursor down key until it highlights the FreeBSD partition. Then we press **d**, and the three partitions are joined into one, marked unused.

The next step is to create a new partition using the entire disk. If we press f, we get the
following message:

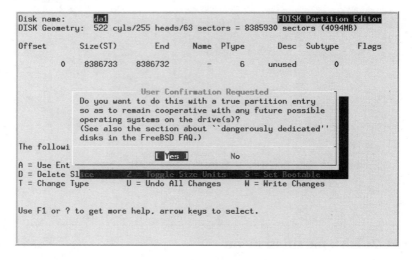

We don't get this message if we use the a command: it just automatically assumes Yes.
In this case we've decided to use the whole disk, so we move the cursor right to No and
press **Enter**. That gives us a boot manager selection screen:

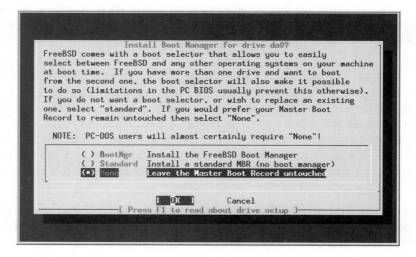

This isn't a boot disk, so we don't need any boot record, and it doesn't make any difference what we select. It's tidier, though, to select None as indicated. Then we press q to exit the partition editor, get back to the function index, and select Label. We see:

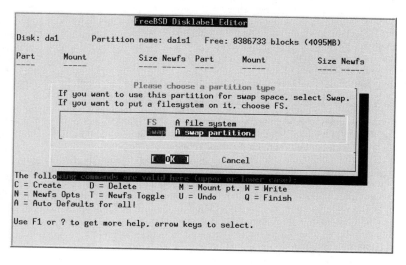

The important information on this rather empty looking menu is the information at the top about the free space available. We want to create two partitions: first, a swap partition of 512 MB, and then a file system taking up the rest of the disk. We press C, and are shown a submenu offering us all 8386733 blocks on the disk. We erase that and enter 512m, which represents 512 MB. Then we press **Enter**, and another submenu appears, asking us what kind of slice it is. We move the cursor down to select A swap partition:

Next, we press c again to create a new partition. This time, we accept the offer of the rest
of the space on the disk, 7338157 sectors, we select A file system, and we are
presented with yet another menu asking for the name of the file system. We enter the
name, in this case */S*:

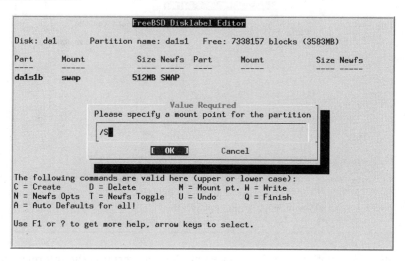

After pressing **Enter**, we see:

```
                        FreeBSD Disklabel Editor
Disk: da1        Partition name: da1s1   Free: 0 blocks (0MB)

Part    Mount        Size Newfs Part      Mount         Size Newfs
----    -----        ---- ----- ----      -----         ---- -----
da1s1b  swap         512MB SWAP
da1s1e  /S           3583MB UFS Y




The following commands are valid here (upper or lower case):
C = Create      D = Delete       M = Mount pt. W = Write
N = Newfs Opts  T = Newfs Toggle U = Undo      Q = Finish
A = Auto Defaults for all!

Use F1 or ? to get more help, arrow keys to select.
```

Finally, we press W to tell the disk label editor to perform the function. We get an additional warning screen:

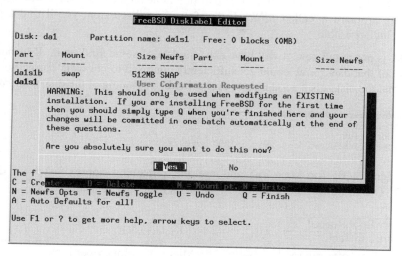

We're doing this online, so that's OK. We select Yes, and *sysinstall* creates the file system and mounts both it and the swap partition. This can take quite a while. Don't try to do anything with the drive until it's finished.

Doing it the hard way

Unfortunately, sometimes you may not be able to use the *sysinstall* method. You may not have access to *sysinstall*, or you may want to use options that *sysinstall* doesn't offer. That leaves us with the old way to add disks. The only difference is that this time we need to use different tools. In the following sections, we'll look at what we have to do to install this same 4 GB Seagate drive manually. This time we'll change the partitioning to contain the following partitions:

- A Microsoft file system.

- The */newhome* file system for our FreeBSD system.

- Additional swap for the FreeBSD system.

We've called this file system */newhome* to use it as an example of moving file systems to new disks. On page 218 we'll see how to move the data across.

Creating a partition table

The first step is to create a PC BIOS style partition table on the disk. As in Microsoft, the partitioning program is called *fdisk*. In the following discussion, you'll find a pocket calculator indispensable.

If the disk is not brand new, it will have existing data of some kind on it. Depending on the nature of that data, *fdisk* could get sufficiently confused to not work correctly. If you don't format the disk, it's a good idea to overwrite the beginning of the disk with *dd*:

```
# dd if=/dev/zero of=/dev/da1 count=100
100+0 records in
100+0 records out
51200 bytes transferred in 1 secs (51200 bytes/sec)
```

We'll assign 1 GB for Microsoft and use the remaining approximately 3 GB for FreeBSD. Our resulting partition table should look like:

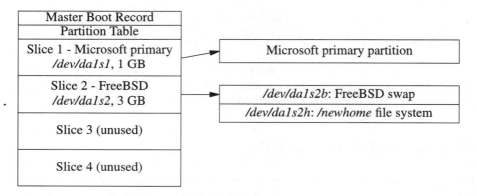

Figure 11-3: Partition table on second FreeBSD disk

The Master Boot Record and the Partition Table take up the first sector of the disk, but many of the allocations are track oriented, so the entire first track of the disk is not available for allocation. The rest, up to the end of the last entire cylinder, can be divided between the partitions. It's easy to make a mistake in specifying the parameters, and *fdisk* performs as good as no checking. You can easily create a partition table that has absolutely no relationship with reality, so it's a good idea to calculate them in advance. For each partition, we need to know three things:

- The *partition type*, which *fdisk* calls *sysid*. This is a number describing what the partition is used for. FreeBSD partitions have partition type 165, and modern (MS-DOS Release 4 and later) Microsoft partitions have type 6.

- The *start sector*, the first sector in the partition.

- The *end sector* for the partition.

In addition, we need to decide which partition is the *active* partition, the partition from which we want to boot. In this case, it doesn't make any difference, because we won't be booting from the disk, but it's always a good idea to set it anyway.

We specify the partitions we don't want by giving them a type, start sector and end sector of 0. Our disk has 8386733 sectors, numbered 0 to 8386732. Partitions should start and end on a cylinder boundary, and we want the Microsoft partition to be about 1 GB. 1 GB is 1024 MB, and 1 MB is 2048 sectors of 512 bytes each, so theoretically we want 1024 × 2048, or 2197152 sectors. Because of the requirement that partitions begin and end on a "cylinder" boundary, we need to find the closest number of "cylinders" to this value. First we need to find out how big a "cylinder" is. We can do this by running *fdisk* without any options:

```
# fdisk da1
******* Working on device /dev/da1 *******
parameters extracted from in-core disklabel are:
cylinders=13726 heads=13 sectors/track=47 (611 blks/cyl)

Figures below won't work with BIOS for partitions not in cyl 1
parameters to be used for BIOS calculations are:
cylinders=13726 heads=13 sectors/track=47 (611 blks/cyl)

fdisk: invalid fdisk partition table found
Media sector size is 512
Warning: BIOS sector numbering starts with sector 1
Information from DOS bootblock is:
The data for partition 1 is:
<UNUSED>
The data for partition 2 is:
<UNUSED>
The data for partition 3 is:
<UNUSED>
The data for partition 4 is:
sysid 165,(FreeBSD/NetBSD/386BSD)
    start 47, size 8386539 (4094 Meg), flag 80 (active)
        beg: cyl 0/ head 1/ sector 1;
        end: cyl 413/ head 12/ sector 47
```

You'll notice that *fdisk* has decided that there is a FreeBSD partition in partition 4. That happens even if the disk is brand new. In fact, this is a less desirable feature of *fdisk*: it "suggests" this partition, it's not really there, which can be really confusing. This printout does, however, tell us that *fdisk* thinks there are 611 sectors per cylinder, so we divide 2197152 by 611 and get 3423.327 cylinders. We round down to 3423 cylinders, which proves to be 2091453 sectors. This is the length we give to the first partition.

We use the remaining space for the FreeBSD partition. How much? Well, *dmesg* tells us that there are 8386733 sectors, but if you look at the geometry that *fdisk* outputs, there are 13726 cylinders with 13 heads (tracks) per cylinder and 47 sectors per track. 13726 × 13 × 47 is 8386586. This rounding down is the explanation for the missing data at the end of the disk that we saw on page 204. The best way to calculate the size of the FreeBSD partition is to take the number of cylinders and multiply by the number of tracks per cylinder. The FreeBSD partition starts behind the Microsoft partition, so it goes from cylinder 3423 to cylinder 13725 inclusive, or 10303 cylinders. At 611 sectors per cylinder, we have a total of 6295133 sectors in the partition. Our resulting information is:

Table 11-1: sample *fdisk* parameters

Partition number	Partition type	Start sector	Size
1	6	1	2091453
2	165	2091453	6295133
3	0	0	
4	0	0	

Next we run *fdisk* in earnest by specifying the -i option. During this time, you may see messages on the console:

```
da1: invalid primary partition table: no magic
```

The message *no magic* doesn't mean that *fdisk* is out of purple smoke. It refers to the fact that it didn't find the so-called *magic number*, which identifies the partition table. We don't have a partition table yet, so this message isn't surprising. It's also completely harmless.

fdisk prompts interactively when you specify the -i flag:

```
# fdisk -i da1
****** Working on device /dev/da1 ******
parameters extracted from in-core disklabel are:
cylinders=13726 heads=13 sectors/track=47 (611 blks/cyl)

Figures below won't work with BIOS for partitions not in cyl 1
parameters to be used for BIOS calculations are:
cylinders=13726 heads=13 sectors/track=47 (611 blks/cyl)

Do you want to change our idea of what BIOS thinks ? [n]   Enter pressed
Media sector size is 512
Warning: BIOS sector numbering starts with sector 1
Information from DOS bootblock is:
The data for partition 1 is:
sysid 165,(FreeBSD/NetBSD/386BSD)
    start 0, size 8386733 (4095 Meg), flag 80 (active)
        beg: cyl 0/ head 0/ sector 1;
        end: cyl 522/ head 12/ sector 47
Do you want to change it? [n] y
Supply a decimal value for "sysid (165=FreeBSD)" [0] 6
Supply a decimal value for "start" [0]   Enter pressed
Supply a decimal value for "size" [0] 2091453
Explicitly specify beg/end address ? [n]   Enter pressed
sysid 6,(Primary 'big' DOS (> 32MB))
    start 0, size 2091453 (1021 Meg), flag 0
        beg: cyl 0/ head 0/ sector 1;
        end: cyl 350/ head 12/ sector 47
Are we happy with this entry? [n] y
The data for partition 2 is:
<UNUSED>
Do you want to change it? [n] y
Supply a decimal value for "sysid (165=FreeBSD)" [0] 165
Supply a decimal value for "start" [0] 2091453
Supply a decimal value for "size" [0] 6295133
Explicitly specify beg/end address ? [n]   Enter pressed
sysid 165,(FreeBSD/NetBSD/386BSD)
```

```
            start 2091453, size 6295133 (3073 Meg), flag 0
               beg: cyl 351/ head 0/ sector 1;
               end: cyl 413/ head 12/ sector 47
  Are we happy with this entry? [n] y
  The data for partition 3 is:
  <UNUSED>
  Do you want to change it? [n] Enter pressed
  The data for partition 4 is:
  sysid 165,(FreeBSD/NetBSD/386BSD)
            start 47, size 8386539 (4094 Meg), flag 80 (active)
               beg: cyl 0/ head 1/ sector 1;
               end: cyl 413/ head 12/ sector 47
  Do you want to change it? [n] y

  The static data for the DOS partition 4 has been reinitialized to:
  sysid 165,(FreeBSD/NetBSD/386BSD)
            start 47, size 8386539 (4094 Meg), flag 80 (active)
               beg: cyl 0/ head 1/ sector 1;
               end: cyl 413/ head 12/ sector 47
  Supply a decimal value for "sysid (165=FreeBSD)" [165] 0
  Supply a decimal value for "start" [47] 0
  Supply a decimal value for "size" [8386539] 0
  Explicitly specify beg/end address ? [n] Enter pressed
  <UNUSED>
  Are we happy with this entry? [n] y
  Do you want to change the active partition? [n] y
  Supply a decimal value for "active partition" [1] 2
  Are you happy with this choice [n] y

  We haven't changed the partition table yet.  This is your last chance.
  parameters extracted from in-core disklabel are:
  cylinders=13726 heads=13 sectors/track=47 (611 blks/cyl)

  Figures below won't work with BIOS for partitions not in cyl 1
  parameters to be used for BIOS calculations are:
  cylinders=13726 heads=13 sectors/track=47 (611 blks/cyl)

  Information from DOS bootblock is:
  1: sysid 6,(Primary 'big' DOS (> 32MB))
            start 0, size 2091453 (1021 Meg), flag 0
               beg: cyl 0/ head 0/ sector 1;
               end: cyl 350/ head 12/ sector 47
  2: sysid 165,(FreeBSD/NetBSD/386BSD)
            start 2091453, size 6295133 (3073 Meg), flag 80 (active)
               beg: cyl 351/ head 0/ sector 1;
               end: cyl 413/ head 12/ sector 47
  3: <UNUSED>
  4: <UNUSED>
  Should we write new partition table? [n] y
```

You'll notice a couple of things here:

- Even though we created valid partitions 1 and 2, which cover the entire drive, *fdisk* gave us the phantom partition 4 which covered the whole disk, and we had to remove it.

- The cylinder numbers in the summary at the end don't make any sense. We've already calculated that the Microsoft partition goes from cylinder 0 to cylinder 3422 inclusive, and the FreeBSD partition goes from cylinder 3423 to cylinder 13725. But *fdisk* says that the Microsoft partition goes from cylinder 0 to cylinder 350 inclusive, and the FreeBSD partition goes from cylinder 351 to cylinder 413. What's that all about?

The problem here is overflow: once upon a time, the maximum cylinder value was 1023, and *fdisk* still thinks this is the case. The numbers we're seeing here are the remainder left by dividing the real cylinder numbers by 1024.

Labelling the disk

Once we have a valid PC BIOS partition table, we need to create the file systems. We won't look at the Microsoft partition in any more detail, but we still need to do some more work on our FreeBSD slice (slice or PC BIOS partition 2). It'll make life easier here to remember a couple of things:

- From now on, we're just looking at the slice, which we can think of as a logical disk. Names like *disk label* really refer to the slice, but many standard terms use the word *disk*, so we'll continue to use them.

- All offsets are relative to the beginning of the slice, not the beginning of the disk. Sizes also refer to the slice and not the disk.

The first thing we need is the disk (slice) label, which supplies general information about the slice:

- The fact that it's a FreeBSD slice.

- The size of the slice.

- The sizes, types and layout of the file systems.

- Some obsolete information about details like rotational speed of the disk and the track-to-track switching time. This is still here for historical reasons only. It may go away soon.

The only information we need to input is the kind, size and locations of the partitions. In this case, we have decided to create a file system on partition h (*/dev/da1s2h*) and swap space on partition b (*/dev/da1s1b*). The swap space will be 512 MB, and the file system will take up the rest of the slice. This is mainly tradition: traditionally data disks use the h partition and not the a partition, so we'll stick to that tradition, though there's nothing to stop you from using the a partition if you prefer. In addition, we need to define the c partition, which represents the whole slice. In summary, the FreeBSD slice we want to create looks like:

/dev/da1s2b: FreeBSD swap, 512 MB
/dev/da1s2h: */newhome* file system, 2.5 GB

Figure 11-4: FreeBSD slice on second disk

bsdlabel

The program that writes the disk label used to be called *disklabel*. As FreeBSD migrated to multiple platforms, this proved to be too generic: many hardware platforms have their own disk label formats. For example, FreeBSD on SPARC64 uses the Sun standard labels. On platforms which use the old BSD labels, such as the PC, the name was changed to *bsdlabel*. On SPARC64 it is called *sunlabel*. On each platform, the appropriate file is linked to the name *disklabel*, but some of the options have changed. In addition, the output format now normally ignores a number of historical relics. It's not as warty as *fdisk*, but it can still give you a run for your money. You can usually ignore most of the complexity, though. You can normally create a disk label with the single command:

```
# bsdlabel -w /dev/da1s2 auto
```

This creates the label with a single partition, c. You can look at the label with *bsdlabel* without options:

```
# bsdlabel /dev/da1s2
# /dev/da0s2:
8 partitions:
#        size   offset    fstype   [fsize bsize bps/cpg]
  c:  6295133        0    unused        0     0            # "raw" part, don't edit
```

At this point, the only partition you have is the "whole disk" partition c. You still need to create partitions b and h and specify their location and size. Do this with *bsdlabel -e*, which starts an editor with the output you see above. Simply add additional partitions:

```
8 partitions:
#        size    offset    fstype   [fsize bsize bps/cpg]
  c:  6295133         0    unused        0     0           # "raw" part, don't edit
  b:  1048576         0    swap          0     0
  h:  5246557   1048576    unused        0     0
```

You don't need to maintain any particular order, and you don't need to specify that partition h will be a file system. In the next step, *newfs* does that for you automatically.

Problems running bsdlabel

Using the old *disklabel* program used to be like walking through a minefield. Things have got a lot better, but it's possible that some problems are still hiding. Here are some of the problems that have been encountered in the past, along with some suggestions about what to do if you experience them:

• When writing a label (the –w option), you may find:

```
# bsdlabel -w da1s2
bsdlabel: /dev/da1s2c: Undefined error: 0
```

This message may be the result of the kernel having out-of-date information about the slice in memory. If this is the case, a reboot may help.

- No disk label on disk is straightforward enough. You tried to use *bsdlabel* to look at the label before you had a label to look at.

- Label magic number or checksum is wrong! tells you that *bsdlabel* thinks it has a label, but it's invalid. This could be the result of an incorrect previous attempt to label the disk. It can be difficult to get rid of an incorrect label. The best thing to do is to repartition the disk with the label in a different position, and then copy */dev/zero* to where the label used to be:

  ```
  # dd if=/dev/zero of=/dev/da1 bs=128k count=1
  ```

  Then you can repartition again the way you want to have it.

- Open partition would move or shrink probably means that you have specified incorrect values in your slice definitions. Check particularly that the c partition corresponds with the definition in the partition table.

- write: Read-only file system means that you are trying to do something invalid with a valid disk label. FreeBSD write protects the disk label, which is why you get this message.

- In addition, you might get kernel messages like:

  ```
  fixlabel: raw partition size > slice size
  ```
  or
  ```
  fixlabel: raw partitions offset != slice offset
  ```

  The meanings of these messages should be obvious.

Creating file systems

Once we have a valid label, we need to create the file systems. In this case, there's only one file system, on */dev/da1s2h*. Mercifully, this is easier:

```
# newfs -U /dev/da1s2h
/dev/vinum/da1s2h: 2561.8MB (5246556 sectors) block size 16384, fragment size 2048
        using 14 cylinder groups of 183.77MB, 11761 blks, 23552 inodes.
        with soft updates
super-block backups (for fsck -b #) at:
 160, 376512, 752864, 1129216, 1505568, 1881920, 2258272, 2634624, 3010976, 3387328,
 3763680, 4140032, 4516384, 4892736
```

The -U flag tells *newfs* to enable soft updates, which we looked at on page 191.

Mounting the file systems

Finally the job is done. Well, almost. You still need to mount the file system, and to tell the system that it has more swap. But that's not much of a problem:

```
# mkdir /newhome                        make sure we have a directory to mount on
# mount /dev/da1s2h /newhome            and mount it
# swapon /dev/da1s2b
# df                                    show free capacity and mounted file systems
Filesystem      1024-blocks     Used    Avail Capacity  Mounted on
/dev/ad0s1a          19966     17426      944     95%    /
/dev/ad0s1e        1162062    955758   113340     89%    /usr
procfs                   4         4        0    100%    /proc
presto:/             15823      6734     8297     45%    /presto/root
presto:/usr         912271    824927    41730     95%    /presto/usr
presto:/home       1905583   1193721   521303     70%    /presto/home
presto:/S          4065286   3339635   563039     86%    /S
/dev/da1s2h        2540316         2  2337090      0%    /newhome
# pstat -s                              show swap usage
Device          1K-blocks        Used    Avail Capacity  Type
/dev/ad0s4b        524160           0   524160      0%    Interleaved
/dev/da1s2b        524160           0   524160      0%    Interleaved
Total             1048320           0  1048320      0%
```

This looks fine, but when you reboot the system, */newhome* and the additional swap will be gone. To ensure that they get mounted after booting, you need to add the following lines to */etc/fstab*:

```
/dev/da1s2b                none            swap    sw      0       0
/dev/da1s2h                /newhome        ufs     rw      0       0
```

Moving file systems

Very frequently, you add a new disk to a system because existing disks have run out of space. Let's consider the disk we have just added and assume that currently the files in */home* are physically located on the */usr* file system, and that */home* is a symbolic link to */usr/home*. We want to move them to the new file system and then rename it to */home*. Here's what to do:

- Copy the files:

  ```
  # cd /home
  # tar cf - . | (cd /newhome; tar xvf - 2>/var/tmp/tarerrors)
  ```

  This writes any error messages to the file */var/tmp/tarerrors*. If you don't do this, any errors will get lost.

- *Check /var/tmp/tarerrors and make sure that the files really made it to the right place!*

- Remove the old files:

  ```
  # rm -rf /usr/home
  ```

- In this case, */home* was a symbolic link, so we need to remove it and create a directory called */home*:

  ```
  # rm /home
  # mkdir /home
  ```

  You don't need to do this if */home* was already a directory (for example, if you're moving a complete file system).

- Modify */etc/fstab* to contain a line like:

  ```
  /dev/da1s2h              /home          ufs    rw    0       0
  ```

- Unmount the */newhome* directory and mount it as */home*:

  ```
  # umount /newhome
  # mount /home
  ```

Recovering from disk data errors

Modern hard disks are a miracle in evolution. Today you can buy a 200 GB hard disk for under $200, and it will fit in your shirt pocket. Thirty years ago, a typical disk drive was the size of a washing machine and stored 20 MB. You would need 10,000 of them to store 200 GB.

At the same time, reliability has gone up, but disks are still relatively unreliable devices. You can achieve maximum reliability by keeping them cool, but sooner or later you are going to run into some kind of problem. One kind is due to surface irregularities: the disk can't read a specific part of the surface.

Modern disks make provisions for recovering from such errors by allocating an alternate sector for the data. IDE drives do this automatically, but with SCSI drives you have the option of enabling or disabling reallocation. Usually reallocation is enabled when you buy the disk, but occasionally it is not. When installing a new disk, you should check that the parameters *ARRE* (*Auto Read Reallocation Enable*) and *AWRE* (*Auto Write Reallocation Enable*) are turned on. For example, to check and set the values for disk */dev/da1*, you would enter:

```
# camcontrol modepage da1 -m 1 -e
```

This command will start up your favourite editor (either the one specified in the EDITOR environment variable, or *vi* by default) with the following data:

```
AWRE (Auto Write Reallocation Enbld):  0
ARRE (Auto Read Reallocation Enbld):  0
TB (Transfer Block):  1
EER (Enable Early Recovery):  0
PER (Post Error):  1
DTE (Disable Transfer on Error):  0
DCR (Disable Correction):  0
Read Retry Count:  41
Write Retry Count:  24
```

The values for AWRE and ARRE should both be 1. If they aren't, as in this case, where AWRE is 0, change the data with the editor, write it back, and exit. *camcontrol* writes the data back to the disk and enables the option.

Note the last two lines in this example. They give the number of actual retries that this drive has performed. You can reset these values too if you want; they will be updated if the drive performs any additional retries.

12

The Vinum Volume Manager

Vinum is a *Volume Manager*, a virtual disk driver that addresses these three issues:

- Disks can be too small.

- Disks can be too slow.

- Disks can be too unreliable.

From a user viewpoint, Vinum looks almost exactly the same as a disk, but in addition to the disks there is a maintenance program.

Vinum objects

Vinum implements a four-level hierarchy of objects:

- The most visible object is the virtual disk, called a *volume*. Volumes have essentially the same properties as a UNIX disk drive, though there are some minor differences. They have no size limitations.

- Volumes are composed of *plexes*, each of which represents the total address space of a volume. This level in the hierarchy thus provides redundancy. Think of plexes as individual disks in a mirrored array, each containing the same data.

• Vinum exists within the UNIX disk storage framework, so it would be possible to use UNIX partitions as the building block for multi-disk plexes, but in fact this turns out to be too inflexible: UNIX disks can have only a limited number of partitions. Instead, Vinum subdivides a single UNIX partition (the *drive*) into contiguous areas called *subdisks*, which it uses as building blocks for plexes.

• Subdisks reside on Vinum *drives*, currently UNIX partitions. Vinum drives can contain any number of subdisks. With the exception of a small area at the beginning of the drive, which is used for storing configuration and state information, the entire drive is available for data storage.

Plexes can include multiple subdisks spread over all drives in the Vinum configuration, so the size of an individual drive does not limit the size of a plex, and thus of a volume.

Mapping disk space to plexes

The way the data is shared across the drives has a strong influence on performance. It's convenient to think of the disk storage as a large number of data sectors that are addressable by number, rather like the pages in a book. The most obvious method is to divide the virtual disk into groups of consecutive sectors the size of the individual physical disks and store them in this manner, rather like the way a large encyclopaedia is divided into a number of volumes. This method is called *concatenation*, and sometimes *JBOD* (*Just a Bunch Of Disks*). It works well when the access to the virtual disk is spread evenly about its address space. When access is concentrated on a smaller area, the improvement is less marked. Figure 12-1 illustrates the sequence in which storage units are allocated in a concatenated organization.

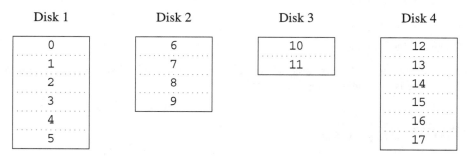

Figure 12-1: Concatenated organization

An alternative mapping is to divide the address space into smaller, equal-sized components, called *stripes*, and store them sequentially on different devices. For example, the first stripe of 292 kB may be stored on the first disk, the next stripe on the next disk and so on. After filling the last disk, the process repeats until the disks are full. This mapping is called *striping* or RAID-0,[1] though the latter term is somewhat misleading: it provides no redundancy. Striping requires somewhat more effort to locate

---

1. *RAID* stands for *Redundant Array of Inexpensive Disks* and offers various forms of fault tolerance.

the data, and it can cause additional I/O load where a transfer is spread over multiple disks, but it can also provide a more constant load across the disks. Figure 12-2 illustrates the sequence in which storage units are allocated in a striped organization.

Disk 1	Disk 2	Disk 3	Disk 4
0	1	2	3
4	5	6	7
8	9	10	11
12	13	14	15
16	17	18	19
20	21	22	23

Figure 12-2: Striped organization

Data integrity

Vinum offers two forms of redundant data storage aimed at surviving hardware failure: *mirroring*, also known as RAID level 1, and *parity*, also known as RAID levels 2 to 5.

Mirroring maintains two or more copies of the data on different physical hardware. Any write to the volume writes to both locations; a read can be satisfied from either, so if one drive fails, the data is still available on the other drive. It has two problems:

- The price. It requires twice as much disk storage as a non-redundant solution.

- The performance impact. Writes must be performed to both drives, so they take up twice the bandwidth of a non-mirrored volume. Reads do not suffer from a performance penalty: you only need to read from one of the disks, so in some cases, they can even be faster.

The most interesting of the parity solutions is RAID level 5, usually called *RAID-5*. The disk layout is similar to striped organization, except that one block in each stripe contains the parity of the remaining blocks. The location of the parity block changes from one stripe to the next to balance the load on the drives. If any one drive fails, the driver can reconstruct the data with the help of the parity information. If one drive fails, the array continues to operate in *degraded* mode: a read from one of the remaining accessible drives continues normally, but a read request from the failed drive is satisfied by recalculating the contents from all the remaining drives. Writes simply ignore the dead drive. When the drive is replaced, Vinum recalculates the contents and writes them back to the new drive.

In the following figure, the numbers in the data blocks indicate the relative block numbers.

Disk 1	Disk 2	Disk 3	Disk 4
0	1	2	Parity
3	4	Parity	5
6	Parity	7	8
Parity	9	10	11
12	13	14	Parity
15	16	Parity	17

Figure 12-3: RAID-5 organization

Compared to mirroring, RAID-5 has the advantage of requiring significantly less storage space. Read access is similar to that of striped organizations, but write access is significantly slower, approximately 25% of the read performance.

Vinum also offers *RAID-4*, a simpler variant of RAID-5 which stores all the parity blocks on one disk. This makes the parity disk a bottleneck when writing. RAID-4 offers no advantages over RAID-5, so it's effectively useless.

Which plex organization?

Each plex organization has its unique advantages:

- Concatenated plexes are the most flexible: they can contain any number of subdisks, and the subdisks may be of different length. The plex may be extended by adding additional subdisks. They require less CPU time than striped or RAID-5 plexes, though the difference in CPU overhead from striped plexes is not measurable. They are the only kind of plex that can be extended in size without loss of data.

- The greatest advantage of striped (RAID-0) plexes is that they reduce hot spots: by choosing an optimum sized stripe (between 256 and 512 kB), you can even out the load on the component drives. The disadvantage of this approach is the restriction on subdisks, which must be all the same size. Extending a striped plex by adding new subdisks is so complicated that Vinum currently does not implement it. A striped plex must have at least two subdisks: otherwise it is indistinguishable from a concatenated plex. In addition, there's an interaction between the geometry of UFS and Vinum that makes it advisable not to have a stripe size that is a power of 2: that's the background for the mention of a 292 kB stripe size in the example above.

- RAID-5 plexes are effectively an extension of striped plexes. Compared to striped plexes, they offer the advantage of fault tolerance, but the disadvantages of somewhat higher storage cost and significantly worse write performance. Like striped plexes, RAID-5 plexes must have equal-sized subdisks and cannot currently be extended. Vinum enforces a minimum of three subdisks for a RAID-5 plex: any smaller number would not make any sense.

• Vinum also offers RAID-4, although this organization has some disadvantages and no advantages when compared to RAID-5. The only reason for including this feature was that it was a trivial addition: it required only two lines of code.

The following table summarizes the advantages and disadvantages of each plex organization.

Table 12-1: Vinum plex organizations

Plex type	Minimum subdisks	Can add subdisks	Must be equal size	Application
concatenated	1	yes	no	Large data storage with maximum placement flexibility and moderate performance.
striped	2	no	yes	High performance in combination with highly concurrent access.
RAID-5	3	no	yes	Highly reliable storage, primarily read access.

Creating Vinum drives

Before you can do anything with Vinum, you need to reserve disk space for it. Vinum drive objects are in fact a special kind of disk partition, of type *vinum*. We've seen how to create disk partitions on page 215. If in that example we had wanted to create a Vinum volume instead of a UFS partition, we would have created it like this:

```
8 partitions:
#        size    offset    fstype   [fsize bsize bps/cpg]
  c:   6295133        0    unused       0     0    # (Cyl.    0 - 10302)
  b:   1048576        0    swap         0     0    # (Cyl.    0 - 10302)
  h:   5246557  1048576    vinum        0     0    # (Cyl.    0 - 10302)
```

Starting Vinum

Vinum comes with the base system as a *kld*. It gets loaded automatically when you run the *vinum* command. It's possible to build a special kernel that includes Vinum, but this is not recommended: in this case, you will not be able to stop Vinum.

FreeBSD Release 5 includes a new method of starting Vinum. Put the following lines in
/boot/loader.conf:

```
vinum_load="YES"
vinum.autostart="YES"
```

The first line instructs the loader to load the Vinum kld, and the second tells it to start
Vinum during the device probes. Vinum still supports the older method of setting the
variable start_vinum in */etc/rc.conf*, but this method may go away soon.

Configuring Vinum

Vinum maintains a *configuration database* that describes the objects known to an
individual system. You create the configuration database from one or more configuration
files with the aid of the *vinum* utility program. Vinum stores a copy of its configuration
database on each Vinum drive. This database is updated on each state change, so that a
restart accurately restores the state of each Vinum object.

The configuration file

The configuration file describes individual Vinum objects. To define a simple volume,
you might create a file called, say, *config1*, containing the following definitions:

```
drive a device /dev/da1s2h
volume myvol
  plex org concat
    sd length 512m drive a
```

This file describes four Vinum objects:

- The drive line describes a disk partition (*drive*) and its location relative to the
  underlying hardware. It is given the symbolic name *a*. This separation of the
  symbolic names from the device names allows disks to be moved from one location
  to another without confusion.

- The volume line describes a volume. The only required attribute is the name, in this
  case myvol.

- The plex line defines a plex. The only required parameter is the organization, in this
  case concat. No name is necessary: the system automatically generates a name from
  the volume name by adding the suffix .p*x*, where *x* is the number of the plex in the
  volume. Thus this plex will be called *myvol.p0*.

- The sd line describes a subdisk. The minimum specifications are the name of a drive
  on which to store it, and the length of the subdisk. As with plexes, no name is
  necessary: the system automatically assigns names derived from the plex name by
  adding the suffix .s*x*, where *x* is the number of the subdisk in the plex. Thus Vinum
  gives this subdisk the name *myvol.p0.s0*

After processing this file, *vinum(8)* produces the following output:

```
vinum -> create config1
1 drives:
D a                         State: up         /dev/da1s2h       A: 3582/4094 MB (87%)

1 volumes:
V myvol                     State: up         Plexes:       1 Size:        512 MB

1 plexes:
P myvol.p0          C State: up               Subdisks:     1 Size:        512 MB

1 subdisks:
S myvol.p0.s0               State: up         D: a              Size:      512 MB
```

This output shows the brief listing format of *vinum*. It is represented graphically in Figure 12-4.

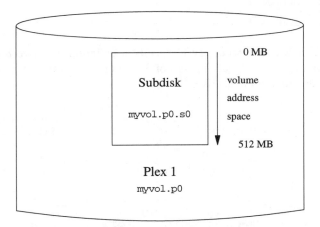

Figure 12-4: A simple Vinum volume

This figure, and the ones that follow, represent a volume, which contains the plexes, which in turn contain the subdisks. In this trivial example, the volume contains one plex, and the plex contains one subdisk.

Creating a file system

You create a file system on this volume in the same way as you would for a conventional disk:

```
# newfs -U /dev/vinum/myvol
/dev/vinum/myvol: 512.0MB (1048576 sectors) block size 16384, fragment size 2048
        using 4 cylinder groups of 128.02MB, 8193 blks, 16512 inodes.
super-block backups (for fsck -b #) at:
 32, 262208, 524384, 786560
```

This particular volume has no specific advantage over a conventional disk partition. It contains a single plex, so it is not redundant. The plex contains a single subdisk, so there is no difference in storage allocation from a conventional disk partition. The following sections illustrate various more interesting configuration methods.

Increased resilience: mirroring

The resilience of a volume can be increased either by mirroring or by using RAID-5 plexes. When laying out a mirrored volume, it is important to ensure that the subdisks of each plex are on different drives, so that a drive failure will not take down both plexes. The following configuration mirrors a volume:

```
drive b device /dev/da2s2h
volume mirror
  plex org concat
    sd length 512m drive a
  plex org concat
    sd length 512m drive b
```

In this example, it was not necessary to specify a definition of drive *a* again, because Vinum keeps track of all objects in its configuration database. After processing this definition, the configuration looks like:

```
2 drives:
D a                    State: up        /dev/da1s2h    A: 3070/4094 MB (74%)
D b                    State: up        /dev/da2s2h    A: 3582/4094 MB (87%)

2 volumes:
V myvol                State: up        Plexes:      1 Size:        512 MB
V mirror               State: up        Plexes:      2 Size:        512 MB

3 plexes:
P myvol.p0          C State: up         Subdisks:    1 Size:        512 MB
P mirror.p0         C State: up         Subdisks:    1 Size:        512 MB
P mirror.p1         C State: initializing  Subdisks:     1 Size:          512 MB

3 subdisks:
S myvol.p0.s0          State: up        D: a           Size:        512 MB
S mirror.p0.s0         State: up        D: a           Size:        512 MB
S mirror.p1.s0         State: empty     D: b           Size:        512 MB
```

Figure 12-5 shows the structure graphically.

In this example, each plex contains the full 512 MB of address space. As in the previous example, each plex contains only a single subdisk.

Note the state of *mirror.p1* and *mirror.p1.s0*: initializing and empty respectively. There's a problem when you create two identical plexes: to ensure that they're identical, you need to copy the entire contents of one plex to the other. This process is called *reviving*, and you perform it with the *start* command:

```
vinum -> start mirror.p1
vinum[278]: reviving mirror.p1.s0
Reviving mirror.p1.s0 in the background
vinum -> vinum[278]: mirror.p1.s0 is up
```

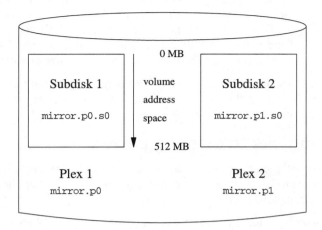

Figure 12-5: A mirrored Vinum volume

During the start process, you can look at the status to see how far the revive has progressed:

```
vinum -> list mirror.p1.s0
S mirror.p1.s0          State: R 43%     D: b              Size:          512 MB
```

Reviving a large volume can take a very long time. When you first create a volume, the contents are not defined. Does it really matter if the contents of each plex are different? If you will only ever read what you have first written, you don't need to worry too much. In this case, you can use the setupstate keyword in the configuration file. We'll see an example of this below.

Adding plexes to an existing volume

At some time after creating a volume, you may decide to add additional plexes. For example, you may want to add a plex to the volume *myvol* we saw above, putting its subdisk on drive *b*. The configuration file for this extension would look like:

```
plex name myvol.p1 org concat volume myvol
    sd size 1g drive b
```

To see what has happened, use the recursive listing option -r for the *list* command:

```
vinum -> l -r myvol
V myvol               State: up       Plexes:      2 Size:        1024 MB
P myvol.p0        C State: up         Subdisks:    1 Size:         512 MB
P myvol.p1        C State: initializing  Subdisks:    1 Size:        1024 MB
S myvol.p0.s0         State: up       D: a            Size:         512 MB
S myvol.p1.s0         State: empty    D: b            Size:        1024 MB
```

The command *l* is a synonym for *list*, and the -r option means *recursive*: it displays all subordinate objects. In this example, plex *myvol.p1* is 1 GB in size, although *myvol.p0* is only 512 MB in size. This discrepancy is allowed, though it isn't very useful by itself: only the first half of the volume is protected against failures. As we'll see in the next section, though, this is a useful stepping stone to extending the size of a file system.

Note that you can't use the setupstate keyword here. Vinum can't know whether the existing volume contains valid data or not, so you *must* use the *start* command to synchronize the plexes.

Adding subdisks to existing plexes

After adding a second plex to *myvol*, it had one plex with 512 MB and another with 1024 MB. It makes sense to have the same size plexes, so the first thing we should do is add a second subdisk to the plex *myvol.p0*.

If you add subdisks to striped, RAID-4 or RAID-5 plexes, you will change the mapping of the data to the disks, which effectively destroys the contents. As a result, you must use the -f option. When you add subdisks to concatenated plexes, the data in the existing subdisks remains unchanged. In our case, the plex is concatenated, so we create and add the subdisk like this:

```
sd name myvol.p0.s1 plex myvol.p0 size 512m drive c
```

After adding this subdisk, the volume looks like this:

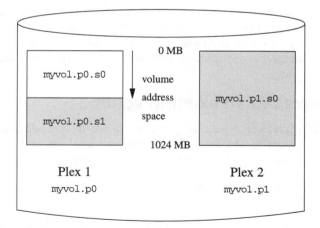

Figure 12-6: An extended Vinum volume

It doesn't look too happy, however:

```
vinum -> l -r myvol
V myvol              State: up          Plexes:       2 Size:        1024 MB
P myvol.p0         C State: corrupt     Subdisks:     2 Size:        1024 MB
P myvol.p1         C State: initializing  Subdisks:    1 Size:          1024 MB
S myvol.p0.s0        State: up          D: a          Size:         512 MB
S myvol.p0.s1        State: empty       D: c          Size:         512 MB
S myvol.p1.s0        State: stale       D: b          Size:        1024 MB
```

In fact, it's in as good a shape as it ever has been. The first half of *myvol* still contains the file system that we put on it, and it's as accessible as ever. The trouble here is that there is *nothing* in the other two subdisks, which are shown shaded in the figure. Vinum can't know that that is acceptable, but we do. In this case, we use some maintenance commands to set the correct object states:

```
vinum -> setstate up myvol.p0.s1 myvol.p0
vinum -> l -r myvol
V myvol              State: up          Plexes:       2 Size:        1024 MB
P myvol.p0         C State: up          Subdisks:     2 Size:        1024 MB
P myvol.p1         C State: faulty      Subdisks:     1 Size:        1024 MB
S myvol.p0.s0        State: up          D: a          Size:         512 MB
S myvol.p0.s1        State: up          D: c          Size:         512 MB
S myvol.p1.s0        State: stale       D: b          Size:        1024 MB
vinum -> saveconfig
```

The command *setstate* changes the state of individual objects without updating those of related objects. For example, you can use it to change the state of a plex to up even if all the subdisks are down. If used incorrectly, it can can cause severe data corruption. Unlike normal commands, it doesn't save the configuration changes, so you use *saveconfig* for that, *after* you're sure you have the correct states. Read the man page before using them for any other purpose.

Next you start the second plex:

```
vinum -> start myvol.p1
Reviving myvol.p1.s0 in the background
vinum[446]: reviving myvol.p1.s0
vinum -> vinum[446]: myvol.p1.s0 is up        some time later
l                                             command for previous prompt
3 drives:
D a                  State: up      /dev/da1s2h    A: 3582/4094 MB (87%)
D b                  State: up      /dev/da2s2h    A: 3070/4094 MB (74%)
D c                  State: up      /dev/da3s2h    A: 3582/4094 MB (87%)

1 volumes:
V myvol              State: up      Plexes:       2 Size:        1024 MB

2 plexes:
P myvol.p0         C State: up      Subdisks:     2 Size:        1024 MB
P myvol.p1         C State: up      Subdisks:     1 Size:        1024 MB

3 subdisks:
S myvol.p0.s0        State: up      D: a          Size:         512 MB
S myvol.p1.s0        State: up      D: b          Size:        1024 MB
S myvol.p0.s1        State: up      D: c          Size:         512 MB
```

The message telling you that *myvol.p1.s0* is up comes after the prompt, so the next command doesn't have a prompt. At this point you have a fully mirrored, functional volume, 1 GB in size. If you now look at the contents, though, you see:

```
# df /mnt
Filesystem         1048576-blocks Used Avail Capacity  Mounted on
/dev/vinum/myvol              503    1   461      0%    /mnt
```

The volume is now 1 GB in size, but the file system on the volume is still only 512 MB. To expand it, use *growfs*:

```
# umount /mnt
# growfs /dev/vinum/myvol
We strongly recommend you to make a backup before growing the Filesystem

 Did you backup your data (Yes/No) ? Yes
new file systemsize is: 524288 frags
Warning: 261920 sector(s) cannot be allocated.
growfs: 896.1MB (1835232 sectors) block size 16384, fragment size 2048
        using 7 cylinder groups of 128.02MB, 8193 blks, 16512 inodes.
super-block backups (for fsck -b #) at:
 1048736, 1310912, 1573088
# mount /dev/vinum/myvol /mnt
# df /mnt
Filesystem         1048576-blocks Used Avail Capacity  Mounted on
/dev/vinum/myvol              881    1   809      0%    /mnt
```

Optimizing performance

The mirrored volumes in the previous example are more resistant to failure than unmirrored volumes, but their performance is less: each write to the volume requires a write to both drives, using up a greater proportion of the total disk bandwidth. Performance considerations demand a different approach: instead of mirroring, the data is striped across as many disk drives as possible. The following configuration shows a volume with a plex striped across four disk drives:

```
drive c device /dev/da3s2h
drive d device /dev/da4s2h
volume stripe
  plex org striped 480k
    sd length 128m drive a
    sd length 128m drive b
    sd length 128m drive c
    sd length 128m drive d
```

When creating striped plexes for the UFS file system, ensure that the stripe size is a multiple of the file system block size (normally 16 kB), but not a power of 2. UFS frequently allocates cylinder groups with lengths that are a power of 2, and if you allocate stripes that are also a power of 2, you may end up with all inodes on the same drive, which would significantly impact performance under some circumstances. Files are allocated in blocks, so having a stripe size that is not a multiple of the block size can cause significant fragmentation of I/O requests and consequent drop in performance. See the man page for more details.

Vinum requires that a striped plex have an integral number of stripes. You don't have to calculate the size exactly, though: if the size of the plex is not a multiple of the stripe size, Vinum trims off the remaining partial stripe and prints a console message:

```
vinum: removing 256 blocks of partial stripe at the end of stripe.p0
```

As before, it is not necessary to define the drives that are already known to Vinum. After processing this definition, the configuration looks like:

```
4 drives:
D a                       State: up        /dev/da1s2h      A: 2942/4094 MB (71%)
D b                       State: up        /dev/da2s2h      A: 2430/4094 MB (59%)
D c                       State: up        /dev/da3s2h      A: 3966/4094 MB (96%)
D d                       State: up        /dev/da4s2h      A: 3966/4094 MB (96%)

3 volumes:
V myvol                   State: up        Plexes:       2 Size:       1024 MB
V mirror                  State: up        Plexes:       2 Size:        512 MB
V stripe                  State: up        Plexes:       1 Size:        511 MB

5 plexes:
P myvol.p0                C State: up           Subdisks:   1 Size:        512 MB
P mirror.p0               C State: up           Subdisks:   1 Size:        512 MB
P mirror.p1               C State: initializing Subdisks:     1 Size:         512 MB
P myvol.p1                C State: up           Subdisks:   1 Size:       1024 MB
P stripe.p0               S State: up           Subdisks:   4 Size:        511 MB

8 subdisks:
S myvol.p0.s0             State: up        D: a        Size:        512 MB
S mirror.p0.s0           State: up        D: a        Size:        512 MB
S mirror.p1.s0           State: empty     D: b        Size:        512 MB
S myvol.p1.s0            State: up        D: b        Size:       1024 MB
S myvol.p0.s1            State: up        D: c        Size:        512 MB
S stripe.p0.s0           State: up        D: a        Size:        127 MB
S stripe.p0.s1           State: up        D: b        Size:        127 MB
S stripe.p0.s2           State: up        D: c        Size:        127 MB
S stripe.p0.s3           State: up        D: d        Size:        127 MB
```

This volume is represented in Figure 12-7. The darkness of the stripes indicates the position within the plex address space: the lightest stripes come first, the darkest last.

Resilience and performance

With sufficient hardware, it is possible to build volumes that show both increased resilience and increased performance compared to standard UNIX partitions. Mirrored disks will always give better performance than RAID-5, so a typical configuration file might be:

```
drive e device /dev/da5s2h
drive f device /dev/da6s2h
drive g device /dev/da7s2h
drive h device /dev/da8s2h
drive i device /dev/da9s2h
drive j device /dev/da10s2h
volume raid10 setupstate
  plex org striped 480k
    sd length 102480k drive a
    sd length 102480k drive b
```

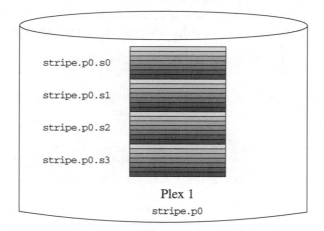

stripe.p0.s0

stripe.p0.s1

stripe.p0.s2

stripe.p0.s3

Plex 1

stripe.p0

Figure 12-7: A striped Vinum volume

```
      sd length 102480k drive c
      sd length 102480k drive d
      sd length 102480k drive e
plex org striped 480k
      sd length 102480k drive f
      sd length 102480k drive g
      sd length 102480k drive h
      sd length 102480k drive i
      sd length 102480k drive j
```

In this example, we have added another five disks for the second plex, so the volume is spread over ten spindles. We have also used the setupstate keyword so that all components come up. The volume looks like this:

```
vinum -> l -r raid10
V raid10                State: up        Plexes:      2 Size:      499 MB
P raid10.p0      S State: up             Subdisks:    5 Size:      499 MB
P raid10.p1      S State: up             Subdisks:    5 Size:      499 MB
S raid10.p0.s0          State: up        D: a           Size:       99 MB
S raid10.p0.s1          State: up        D: b           Size:       99 MB
S raid10.p0.s2          State: up        D: c           Size:       99 MB
S raid10.p0.s3          State: up        D: d           Size:       99 MB
S raid10.p0.s4          State: up        D: e           Size:       99 MB
S raid10.p1.s0          State: up        D: f           Size:       99 MB
S raid10.p1.s1          State: up        D: g           Size:       99 MB
S raid10.p1.s2          State: up        D: h           Size:       99 MB
S raid10.p1.s3          State: up        D: i           Size:       99 MB
S raid10.p1.s4          State: up        D: j           Size:       99 MB
```

This assumes the availability of ten disks. It's not essential to have all the components on different disks. You could put the subdisks of the second plex on the same drives as the subdisks of the first plex. If you do so, you should put corresponding subdisks on different drives:

```
plex org striped 480k
   sd length 102480k drive a
   sd length 102480k drive b
   sd length 102480k drive c
   sd length 102480k drive d
   sd length 102480k drive e
plex org striped 480k
   sd length 102480k drive c
   sd length 102480k drive d
   sd length 102480k drive e
   sd length 102480k drive a
   sd length 102480k drive b
```

The subdisks of the second plex are offset by two drives from those of the first plex: this helps ensure that the failure of a drive does not cause the same part of both plexes to become unreachable, which would destroy the file system.

Figure 12-8 represents the structure of this volume.

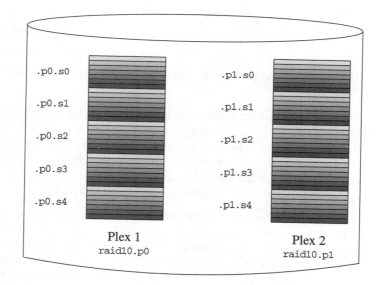

Figure 12-8: A mirrored, striped Vinum volume

Vinum configuration database

Vinum stores configuration information on each drive in essentially the same form as in the configuration files. You can display it with the *dumpconfig* command. When reading from the configuration database, Vinum recognizes a number of keywords that are not allowed in the configuration files, because they would compromise data integrity. For example, after adding the second plex to *myvol*, the disk configuration would contain the following text:

```
vinum -> dumpconfig
Drive a:        Device /dev/da1s2h
                Created on bumble.example.org at Tue Nov 26 14:35:12 2002
                Config last updated Tue Nov 26 16:12:35 2002
                Size:       4293563904 bytes (4094 MB)
volume myvol state up
plex name myvol.p0 state up org concat vol myvol
plex name myvol.p1 state up org concat vol myvol
sd name myvol.p0.s0 drive a plex myvol.p0 len 1048576s driveoffset 265s state up ple
xoffset 0s
sd name myvol.p1.s0 drive b plex myvol.p1 len 2097152s driveoffset 265s state up ple
xoffset 0s
sd name myvol.p0.s1 drive c plex myvol.p0 len 1048576s driveoffset 265s state up ple
xoffset 1048576s

Drive /dev/da1s2h: 4094 MB (4293563904 bytes)

Drive b:        Device /dev/da2s2h
                Created on bumble.example.org at Tue Nov 26 14:35:27 2002
                Config last updated Tue Nov 26 16:12:35 2002
                Size:       4293563904 bytes (4094 MB)
volume myvol state up
plex name myvol.p0 state up org concat vol myvol
plex name myvol.p1 state up org concat vol myvol
sd name myvol.p0.s0 drive a plex myvol.p0 len 1048576s driveoffset 265s state up ple
xoffset 0s
sd name myvol.p1.s0 drive b plex myvol.p1 len 2097152s driveoffset 265s state up ple
xoffset 0s
sd name myvol.p0.s1 drive c plex myvol.p0 len 1048576s driveoffset 265s state up ple
xoffset 1048576s
```

The obvious differences here are the presence of explicit location information and naming (both of which are also allowed, but discouraged, for use by the user) and the information on the states (which are not available to the user). Vinum does not store information about drives in the configuration information: it finds the drives by scanning the configured disk drives for partitions with a Vinum label. This enables Vinum to identify drives correctly even if they have been assigned different UNIX drive IDs.

When you start Vinum with the *vinum start* command, Vinum reads the configuration database from one of the Vinum drives. Under normal circumstances, each drive contains an identical copy of the configuration database, so it does not matter which drive is read. After a crash, however, Vinum must determine which drive was updated most recently and read the configuration from this drive. It then updates the configuration, if necessary, from progressively older drives.

Installing FreeBSD on Vinum

Installing FreeBSD on Vinum is complicated by the fact that *sysinstall* and the loader don't support Vinum, so it is not possible to install directly on a Vinum volume. Instead, you need to install a conventional system and then convert it to Vinum. That's not as difficult as it might sound.

Normal disk installations lay out overlapping disk partitions: the *c* partition overlaps all the other partitions. You can do the same thing with a Vinum drive, which is also a partition. You can then create subdisks in the Vinum drive corresponding in length and position to the partitions. In the following diagram, each column represents the entire disk. On the left there are four normal partitions. In the middle is the *c* partition, and on the right is a Vinum drive partition:

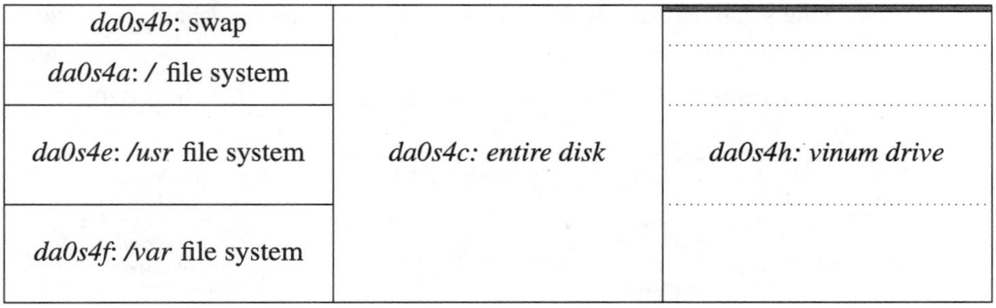

da0s4b: swap		
da0s4a: / file system	*da0s4c*: entire disk	*da0s4h*: vinum drive
da0s4e: /usr file system		
da0s4f: /var file system		

Figure 12-9: Partition layout with Vinum

This layout shows three file system partitions and a swap partition, which is not the layout recommended on page 68. We'll look at the reasons for this below.

The shaded area at the top of the Vinum partition represents the configuration information, which cuts into the swap partition and the bootstrap. To fix that, we redefine the swap partition to start after the Vinum configuration information and to be a total of 281 sectors shorter, 265 sectors for the Vinum configuration and 16 sectors for the bootstrap.

The swap partition isn't normally the first partition on a drive, but you can create this layout with *sysinstall* simply by creating the swap partition before any other partition. Consider installing FreeBSD on a 4 GB drive. Create, in sequence, a swap partition of 256 MB, a root file system of 256 MB, a */usr* file system of 2 GB, and a */var* file system to take up the rest. It's important to create the swap partition at the beginning of the disk, so you create that first. After installation, the output of *bsdlabel* looks like this:

```
a:   524288    524288     4.2BSD    2048 16384 32776          root file system
b:   524288         0     swap                                swap partition
c:  8385867         0     unused       0     0      # "raw"   part, don't edit
d:  4194304   1048576     4.2BSD    2048 16384 28512          /usr file system
e:  3142987   5242880     4.2BSD    2048 16384 28512          /var file system
```

This corresponds to the left and centre columns in the figure above. To convert to Vinum, you need to:

• create a volume of type *vinum* that starts after the bootstrap in the *c* partition.

• shorten the swap partition by 281 sectors at the beginning.

Boot in single user mode and remount the root file system (to make it read/write), mount the */usr* directory and run *bsdlabel* with the –e (edit label) option:

```
# mount -u /
# mount /usr
# bsdlabel -e da0s4
```

See page 215 for more information about *bsdlabel*. You need to boot in single user mode because otherwise the swap partition would be mounted, and you can't change the size of the swap partition when it's mounted.

When you finish, the partition table should look like this (changed values in **bold**):

```
#         size    offset    fstype    [fsize bsize bps/cpg]
   a:   524288    524288    4.2BSD     2048 16384 32776              root file system
   b:   524007       281    swap                                     swap partition
   c:  8385867         0    unused        0     0       # "raw" part, don't edit
   d:  4194304   1048576    4.2BSD     2048 16384 28512             /usr file system
   e:  3142987   5242880    4.2BSD     2048 16384 28512             /var file system
   h:  8385851        16    vinum                                   Vinum drive
```

Be sure to shorten the length of the swap partition by 281 sectors, or it will overlap the root partition and cause extreme data corruption when swap gets full, which might not happen until months later.

The next step is to create the Vinum objects. The plexes and volumes are straightforward: each plex is concatenated with a single subdisk, and the volume has a single plex. It makes sense to give the volumes names that relate to the mount point.

Creating the subdisks requires a little more care. You can use the size values from the *bsdlabel* output above directly in a Vinum configuration file, but since the Vinum drive starts after the bootstrap, you need to subtract 16 (the length of the bootstrap) from the offset values:

```
drive rootdev device /dev/da0s4h
volume root
  plex org concat
# a:        524288                    524288    4.2BSD     2048 16384 32776
    sd len 524288s   driveoffset 524272s drive rootdev
volume swap
  plex org concat
# b:        524007                       281       swap
    sd len 524007s   driveoffset 265s drive rootdev
volume usr
  plex org concat
# d:       4194304                   1048576    4.2BSD     2048 16384 28512
    sd len 4194304s  driveoffset 1048560s drive rootdev
volume var
  plex org concat
# e:       3142987                   5242880    4.2BSD     2048 16384 28512
    sd len 3142987s  driveoffset 5242864s drive rootdev
```

The comments are the corresponding lines from the *bsdlabel* output. They show the corresponding values for size and offset. Run *vinum create* against this file, and confirm that you have the volumes */, /usr* and */var*.

Next, ensure that you are set up to start Vinum with the new method. Ensure that you have the following lines in */boot/loader.conf*, creating it if necessary:

```
vinum_load="YES"
vinum.autostart="YES"
```

Then reboot to single-user mode, start Vinum and run *fsck* against the volumes, using the −n option to tell *fsck* not to correct any errors it finds. You should see something like this:

```
# fsck -n -t ufs /dev/vinum/usr
** /dev/vinum/usr (NO WRITE)
** Last Mounted on /usr
** Phase 1 - Check Blocks and Sizes
** Phase 2 - Check Pathnames
** Phase 3 - Check Connectivity
** Phase 4 - Check Reference Counts
** Phase 5 - Check Cyl groups
35323 files, 314115 used, 718036 free (4132 frags, 89238 blocks, 0.4% fragmentation)
```

If there are any errors, they will probably be because you have miscalculated size or offset. You'll see something like this:

```
# fsck -n -t ufs /dev/vinum/usr
** /dev/vinum/usr (NO WRITE)
Cannot find file system superblock
/dev/vinum/usr: CANNOT FIGURE OUT FILE SYSTEM PARTITION
```

You need to do this in single-user mode because the volumes are shadowing file systems, and it's normal for open file systems to fail *fsck*, since some of the state is in buffer cache.

If all is well, remount the root file system read-write:

```
# mount -u /
```

Then edit */etc/fstab* to point to the new devices. For this example, */etc/fstab* might initially contain:

```
# Device        Mountpoint    FStype  Options   Dump   Pass#
/dev/da0s4a     /             ufs     rw        1      1
/dev/da0s4b     none          swap    sw        0      0
/dev/da0s4e     /usr          ufs     rw        1      1
/dev/da0s4f     /var          ufs     rw        1      1
```

Change it to reflect the Vinum volumes:

```
# Device         Mountpoint    FStype  Options   Dump   Pass#
/dev/vinum/swap  none          swap    sw        0      0
/dev/vinum/root  /             ufs     rw        1      1
/dev/vinum/usr   /usr          ufs     rw        1      1
/dev/vinum/var   /var          ufs     rw        1      1
```

Then reboot again to mount the root file system from */dev/vinum/root*. You can also optionally remove all the UFS partitions *except the root partition*. The loader doesn't know about Vinum, so it must boot from the UFS partition.

Once you have reached this stage, you can add additional plexes to the volumes, or you can extend the plexes (and thus the size of the file system) by adding subdisks to the plexes, as discussed on page 229.

Recovering from drive failures

One of the purposes of Vinum is to be able to recover from hardware problems. If you have chosen a redundant storage configuration, the failure of a single component will not stop the volume from working. In many cases, you can replace the components without down time.

If a drive fails, perform the following steps:

1. Replace the physical drive.

2. Partition the new drive. Some restrictions apply:

    •   If you have hot-plugged the drive, it must have the same ID, the Vinum drive must be on the same partition, and it must have the same size.

    •   If you have had to stop the system to replace the drive, the old drive will not be associated with a device name, and you can put it anywhere. Create a Vinum partition that is at least large enough to take all the subdisks *in their original positions on the drive*. Vinum currently does not compact free space when replacing a drive. An easy way to ensure this is to make the new drive at least as large as the old drive.

        If you want to have this freedom with a hot-pluggable drive, you must stop Vinum and restart it.

3. If you have restarted Vinum, create a new drive. For example, if the replacement drive *data3* is on the physical partition */dev/da3s1h*, create a configuration file, say *configfile*, with the single line

    ```
    drive data3 device /dev/da3s1h
    ```

    Then enter:

    ```
    # vinum create configfile
    ```

4. Start the plexes that were down. For example, *vinum list* might show:

    ```
    vinum -> l -r test
    V test                 State: up        Plexes:     2 Size:      30 MB
    P test.p0         C State: up        Subdisks:   1 Size:      30 MB
    P test.p1         C State: faulty    Subdisks:   1 Size:      30 MB
    S test.p0.s0        State: up        PO:       0  B Size:      30 MB
    S test.p1.s0        State: obsolete  PO:       0  B Size:      30 MB
    vinum -> start test.p1.s0
    Reviving test.p1.s0 in the background
    vinum -> vinum[295]: reviving test.p1.s0      this message appears after the prompt
    vinum[295]: test.p1.s0 is up                  (some time later)
    ```

Failed boot disk

If you're running your root file system on a Vinum volume, you can survive the failure of the boot volume if it is mirrored with at least two concatenated plexes each containing only one subdisk. Under normal circumstances, you can carry on running as if nothing had happened, but obviously you will no longer be able to reboot from that disk. Instead, boot from the other disk.

The root file system also has individual UFS partitions, so you have a choice of what you mount. For example, if your root file system has UFS partitions */dev/da0s4a* and */dev/da1s4a*, you can mount either of these partitions or */dev/vinum/root*. Never mount more than one of them, otherwise you can cause data corruption.

An even more insidious way to corrupt the root file system is to mount */dev/da0s4a* or */dev/da1s4a* and modify it. In this case, the two partitions are no longer the same, but there's no way for Vinum to know that. If this happens, you *must* mark the other subdisk as crashed with the *vinum stop* command.

Migrating Vinum to a new machine

Sometimes you might want to move a set of Vinum disks to a different FreeBSD machine. This is simple, as long as there are no name conflicts between the objects on the Vinum disks and any other Vinum objects you may already have on the system. Simply connect the disks and start Vinum. You don't need to put the disks in any particular location, and you don't need to run *vinum create*: Vinum stores the configuration on the drives themselves, and when it starts, it locates it accordingly.

Things you shouldn't do with Vinum

The *vinum* command offers a large number of subcommands intended for specific purposes. It's easy to abuse them. Here are some things you should not do:

- Do not use the *resetconfig* command unless you genuinely don't want to see any of your configuration again. There are other alternatives, such as *rm*, which removes individual objects or groups of objects.

- Do not re-run the *create* command for objects that already exist. Vinum already knows about them, and the *start* command should find them.

- Do not name your drives after the disk device on which they are located. The purpose of having drive names is to be device independent. For example, if you have two drives *a* and *b*, and they are located on devices */dev/da1s1h* and */dev/da2s1h* respectively, you can remove the drives, swap their locations and restart Vinum. Vinum will still correctly locate the drives. If you had called the drives *da1* and *da2*, you would then see something confusing like this:

```
  2 drives:
D da2                    State: up      /dev/da1s1h    A: 3582/4094 MB (87%)
D da1                    State: up      /dev/da1s2h    A: 3582/4094 MB (87%)
```

This is clearly not helpful.

• Don't put more than one drive on a physical disk. Each drive contains two copies of
  the Vinum configuration, and both updating the configuration and starting Vinum
  slow down as a result. If you want more than one file system to occupy space on a
  physical drive, create subdisks, not drives.

In this chapter:
- Creating an ISO-9660 image
- Burning the CD-R
- Copying CD-ROMs

13

Writing CD-Rs

Under FreeBSD, data on conventional hard disks is stored in the *UNIX File System* or *UFS* format. CD-ROMs and CD-Rs use a different file system, the *ISO 9660* format, which is compatible with other systems. This is not a problem when you mount a CD-ROM: FreeBSD includes a read-only ISO 9660 file system. When you want to write a CD-R, however, things are a little more complicated: the medium requires you to write the entire file system at once, and since the file system is stored in a different format, you can't just copy the UFS file system. Instead, you must first create an *image* of the file system that you want to put on the CD-R, and then you copy it. We'll look at these steps in more detail below.

Creating an ISO-9660 image

The first step is to create the *ISO 9660* file system image, frequently simply called an *ISO image*. There are a number of ports available in the Ports Collection; here we'll look at *mkisofs*, which is part of the *cdrtools* port. Installation isn't quite as straightforward as you might expect: you need a special flag to install *mkisofs*:

```
# cd /usr/ports/sysutils/cdrtools
# make install -DMKISOFS
```

mkisofs has a bewildering number of parameters. Here are the important ones:

- The -A option specifies the *application ID*, a text string written to the header of the file system to describe the "application" on the image. It can be up to 128 characters long.

- Use -b if you want to be able to boot from the CD, such as a FreeBSD bootable CD. In the case of FreeBSD, use the 2.88 MB image *floppies/boot.flp* which is built as part of the release process. Note that this file *must* be in one of the directories included in the image, and the name is relative to the root directory of the CD.

- The -f option tells *mkisofs* to follow symbolic links. If you don't specify this option and you have symbolic links in the directory from which you create the image, the resultant CD-ROM image will contain only a symbolic link instead of the file itself. If the file to which the symbolic link points is below the top-level (root) directory, this is the preferred way to do things, because it saves space, but if it points outside the CD-ROM, the file will not appear on the CD-ROM at all. Use this option if you have symbolic links to files outside the directory that you're using for the root of the CD-ROM file system.

- The -J option makes the CD compatible with Microsoft's *Joliet* format. You don't need it for FreeBSD, but it doesn't cost much, so it's a good idea to include it if there's a chance the CD will be used in a Microsoft environment.

- Use the -o option to specify the name of the resultant ISO image. This image is the size of the resultant CD, so it could be up to 700 MB.

- The -p option specifies the *preparer ID*, another ISO 9660 header field to specify who made the CD-ROM.

- The -r option specifies the *Rock Ridge Extensions* that are used to store UNIX file names. It makes a number of assumptions about permissions and owners; see the man page for details. It takes no parameters.

- The -T option tells *mkisofs* to include a translation file *TRANS.TBL* in each directory for use by systems that don't support the Rock Ridge extensions. For each file name in the directory, *TRANS.TBL* contains a Microsoft-compatible name (up to eight characters, a period (.) and up to three more characters). The names bear a slight resemblance to the original names.

- If you don't like the name *TRANS.TBL*, you can specify a different name with the -table-name option, which implies -T. For example, if you write -table-name .MAP you will generate names that won't show up with a normal *ls* command.

- The -V option specifies the *volume ID* for the file system. This will normally be more specific than the application ID; for example, each CD in a set of CDs might have the same application ID and a different volume ID.

- The final parameters are the names of the directories that will be included in the image. You can specify multiple directories. In each case, the entire directory hierarchy will be included.

This is a lot of stuff to type in every time. It's easier to write a *Makefile* and use *make*:

```
APPLID   =       "Dummy application"
BOOT     =
# To make it bootable, put in something like this:
# Note that the -b option is there as well
# BOOT   =       "-b floppies/boot.flp"
ISO      =       /var/tmp/isoimage
PREPARER =       "me"
VOLID    =       "Volume 0000"
DIR      =       .

cdrom:
        mkisofs -A ${APPLID} ${BOOT} -J -o ${ISO} -f \
        -p ${PREPARER} -r -T -V ${VOLID} ${DIR}
```

For example, to make a bootable CD-R of the FreeBSD release, you would first perform the *make world* and *make release*. Assuming that the release directory is */home/release*, you will find the directory trees for the first two CD-ROMs in */home/release/R/cdrom/disc1* and */home/release/R/cdrom/disc2*. You could do this:

```
# make cdrom DIR=/home/release/R/cdrom/disc1
mkisofs -A "Dummy application"  -J -o ../iso -table-name .MAP  -p "Greg Lehey" -r -T
-V "Volume 0000" .
  6.40% done, estimate finish Sun Aug 27 13:34:54 2000
 12.79% done, estimate finish Sun Aug 27 13:35:02 2000
 19.19% done, estimate finish Sun Aug 27 13:35:05 2000
 25.57% done, estimate finish Sun Aug 27 13:35:10 2000
 31.97% done, estimate finish Sun Aug 27 13:35:10 2000
 38.36% done, estimate finish Sun Aug 27 13:35:10 2000
 44.75% done, estimate finish Sun Aug 27 13:35:10 2000
 51.15% done, estimate finish Sun Aug 27 13:35:12 2000
 57.54% done, estimate finish Sun Aug 27 13:35:12 2000
 63.94% done, estimate finish Sun Aug 27 13:35:12 2000
 70.34% done, estimate finish Sun Aug 27 13:35:11 2000
 76.72% done, estimate finish Sun Aug 27 13:35:13 2000
 83.12% done, estimate finish Sun Aug 27 13:35:12 2000
 89.52% done, estimate finish Sun Aug 27 13:35:13 2000
 95.90% done, estimate finish Sun Aug 27 13:35:13 2000
Total translation table size: 35119
Total rockridge attributes bytes: 59724
Total directory bytes: 104448
Path table size(bytes): 256
Max brk space used 86224
78211 extents written (152 Mb)
```

The progress reports are rather boring nowadays, considering that the whole process only takes a couple of minutes, but the summary information at the bottom can be of interest.

Testing the CD-R

So now you have an ISO image. How do you know it's correct? It's just a single file, and it could have just about anything on it. You can burn a CD, of course, but if it's junk, you have another coaster. If you're not sure, it's better to look inside first. You can do that by using it as the basis for an *md vnode* device.

The *md* driver creates a number of different kinds of pseudo-device. See the man page *md(4)* for more details. We use the *vnode* device, a special file that refers to file system files. Support for *md* is included in the GENERIC kernel, but if you've built a kernel without the *md* driver, you can load it as a *kld*. If you're not sure, try loading the kld anyway. Then you associate a vnode device with the ISO image *iso-image* using the program *mdconfig*:

```
# kldload md                          load the kld module if necessary
kldload: can't load md: File exists   already loaded or in the kernel
# mdconfig -a -t vnode -f iso-image   configure the device
md0                                   this is the name assigned
# mount -t cd9660 /dev/md0 /mnt       mount it
```

After this, you will be able to access the image at */mnt* as a normal file system. Don't forget to unmount and unconfigure the file when you're finished:

```
# umount /mnt
# mdconfig -d -u 0
```

Older releases of FreeBSD used the *vn* driver, which used different syntax.

Burning the CD-R

Once you have created and tested an ISO image, you can copy it to CD-R. For SCSI burners, you use *cdrecord*; ATA (IDE) CD-R burners you use *burncd*. In the following sections we'll look at both programs.

Burning a CD-R on an ATA burner

To burn a CD-R in an ATA (or IDE) burner, use *burncd*, which is part of the base system. Typically you'll only have one CD-R burner on the system, so it will be called */dev/acd0*. You'll have something like this in your *dmesg* output:

```
acd0: CD-RW <RWD RW4224> at ata1-slave BIOSPIO
```

burncd has both flags and commands. For our purposes, the most important flags are:

- The -f *device* option specifies the device to use for the burning process.

- The -m option tells *burncd* to close the disk in multisession mode.

- The -q option tells *burncd* to be quiet and not to print progress messages. In fact, it's not very verbose anyway.

- The -s *speed* option specifies the speed of the burner device. It defaults to 1, so you'll save a lot of time using this.

- The -t option specifies a test write: *burncd* does not actually write on the medium.

- The -v (verbose) option prints a few extra progress messages.

The most important commands for writing ISO 9660 CD-ROMs are:

- data or mode1 write data tracks, also known as *mode1* tracks, for the image files named on the command line.

- fixate fixates the medium by generating the table of contents. This should be the last command to *burncd*.

If *burncd* doesn't recognize a command, it assumes it's a file name. If it does, it assumes it isn't a file name. This can be confusing: there are other commands not mentioned in the list above, for example raw. If you have an ISO file called *raw*, you'll have to rename it before you can burn it with *burncd*.

Before you start, you should decide on the recording speed. If your machine is fast enough, use the rated recording speed. In the case of the example machine, that's an 8x speed (i.e. it records at eight times the speed at which a normal audio CD is played). Before you do this, though, you should make sure that your system can keep a sufficient data rate so that there is always data available to transfer to the CD-R. If it can't keep up, you'll get an *underrun*, a gap in the data, and your CD-R is worthless (a *coaster*).

To make sure you don't make coasters, you should do a test run. The system goes through all the motions, but it doesn't actually write anything to the CD-R blank. Nevertheless, it tests all aspects of the burn, so you must have a valid CD-R blank in the drive, otherwise the attempt will fail. To test burn an image called *iso*, enter:

```
# burncd -f /dev/acd0c -t -v -s 8 data iso fixate
adding type 0x08 file iso size 184576 KB 92288 blocks
next writeable LBA 0
addr = 0 size = 189005824 blocks = 92288
writing from file iso size 184576 KB
written this track 6880 KB (3%) total 6880 KB
```

At this point, *burncd* overwrites the line with progress indications until it is finished. Finally, you see:

```
written this track 184576 KB (100%) total 184576 KB
fixating CD, please wait..
burncd: ioctl(CDRIOCFIXATE): Input/output error
```

This last line appears a little alarming. It's not really serious, though: the CD has not really been written, so it's not possible to read from it. A number of CD-R drives return error conditions under these circumstances.

If everything was OK in the test run, you can repeat the command without the -t flag:

```
# burncd -f /dev/acd0c -v -s 8 data iso fixate
```

The output is identical, but this time you should not get the error message.

Burning a CD-R on a SCSI burner

If you have a SCSI burner, use *cdrecord*, which is part of the *cdrtools* port we installed on page 243. *cdrecord* has a rather strange habit of not using device names: instead, it accesses the device directly by its SCSI parameters (bus, unit and LUN). You can get these parameters from the *dmesg* output in */var/run/dmesg.boot*, but there's an easier way:

```
# cdrecord -scanbus
Cdrecord 1.9 (i386-unknown-freebsd4.1) Copyright (C) 1995-2000 Jörg Schilling
Using libscg version 'schily-0.1'
scsibus0:
        0,0,0     0) 'MATSHITA' 'CD-R    CW-7503 ' '1.06' Removable CD-ROM
cdrecord: Warning: controller returns zero sized CD capabilities page.
cdrecord: Warning: controller returns wrong size for CD capabilities page.
cdrecord: Warning: controller returns wrong page 0 for CD capabilities page (2A).
        0,1,0     1) 'TEAC   ' 'CD-ROM CD-532S ' '1.0A' Removable CD-ROM
        0,2,0     2) *
        0,3,0     3) *
        0,4,0     4) 'SONY   ' 'SDT-10000     ' '0101' Removable Tape
        0,5,0     5) *
        0,6,0     6) *
        0,7,0     7) *
        0,8,0     8) 'QUANTUM ' 'QM318000TD-SW ' 'N491' Disk
```

This output doesn't tell you exactly which devices are CD-Rs, and it also doesn't look at any except the first SCSI bus. Alternatively, you can use the standard system utility *camcontrol*:

```
# camcontrol devlist
<MATSHITA CD-R   CW-7503 1.06>      at scbus0 target 0 lun 0 (pass0,cd0)
<TEAC CD-ROM CD-532S 1.0A>          at scbus0 target 1 lun 0 (pass1,cd1)
<SONY SDT-10000 0101>               at scbus0 target 4 lun 0 (sa0,pass2)
<QUANTUM QM318000TD-SW N491>        at scbus0 target 8 lun 0 (pass3,da0)
<EXABYTE EXB-8505SMBANSH2 0793>     at scbus1 target 1 lun 0 (sa1,pass4)
<Quantum DLT4000 CC1E>              at scbus1 target 3 lun 0 (sa2,pass5)
<AIWA GD-8000 0119>                 at scbus1 target 4 lun 0 (sa3,pass6)
<NRC MBR-7 110>                     at scbus1 target 6 lun 0 (pass7,cd2)
<NRC MBR-7 110>                     at scbus1 target 6 lun 1 (pass8,cd3)
<NRC MBR-7 110>                     at scbus1 target 6 lun 2 (pass9,cd4)
<NRC MBR-7 110>                     at scbus1 target 6 lun 3 (pass10,cd5)
<NRC MBR-7 110>                     at scbus1 target 6 lun 4 (pass11,cd6)
<NRC MBR-7 110>                     at scbus1 target 6 lun 5 (pass12,cd7)
<NRC MBR-7 110>                     at scbus1 target 6 lun 6 (pass13,cd8)
```

Either way, you need to recognize the CD-R device, which in this case is relatively easy: it's the Matsushita CW-7503 ("MATSHITA") at the very beginning of each list. *cdrecord* refers to this device as 0,0,0 (bus 0, target 0, LUN 0).

The next thing to look at is the recording speed. If your machine is fast enough, use the rated recording speed. In the case of the example machine, that's an 8x speed (i.e. it records at 8 times the speed at which a normal audio CD is played). Before you do this, though, you should make sure that your system can keep a sufficient data rate so that there is always data available when to go on the CD. If you can't keep up, you'll get an *underrun*, a gap in the data, and your CD-R is worthless (a *coaster*).

To make sure you don't make coasters, you should do a dummy run. The system goes through all the motions, but it doesn't actually write anything to the CD-R blank. Nevertheless, it tests all aspects of the burn, so you must have a valid CD-R blank in the drive, otherwise the attempt will fail. To burn an image called *iso*, enter:

```
# cdrecord -dummy -v dev=0,0,0 -speed=8 iso
Cdrecord 1.9 (i386-unknown-freebsd5.0) Copyright (C) 1995-2000 Jörg Schilling
TOC Type: 1 = CD-ROM
scsidev: '0,0,0'
scsibus: 0 target: 0 lun: 0
Using libscg version 'schily-0.1'
atapi: 0
Device type    : Removable CD-ROM
Version        : 2
Response Format: 2
Capabilities   : SYNC LINKED
Vendor_info    : 'MATSHITA'
Identifikation : 'CD-R    CW-7503  '
Revision       : '1.06'
Device seems to be: Generic mmc CD-R.
Using generic SCSI-3/mmc CD-R driver (mmc_cdr).
Driver flags   : SWABAUDIO
FIFO size      : 4194304 = 4096 KB
Track 01: data  152 MB
Total size:      175 MB (17:22.84) = 78213 sectors
Lout start:      175 MB (17:24/63) = 78213 sectors
Current Secsize: 2048
ATIP info from disk:
  Indicated writing power: 5
  Is not unrestricted
  Is not erasable
  ATIP start of lead in:  -11080 (97:34/20)
  ATIP start of lead out: 335100 (74:30/00)
Disk type:    Long strategy type (Cyanine, AZO or similar)
Manuf. index: 11
Manufacturer: Mitsubishi Chemical Corporation
Blocks total: 335100 Blocks current: 335100 Blocks remaining: 256887
RBlocks total: 342460 RBlocks current: 342460 RBlocks remaining: 264247
Starting to write CD/DVD at speed 8 in dummy mode for single session.
Last chance to quit, starting dummy write in 1 seconds.
Waiting for reader process to fill input buffer ... input buffer ready.
Starting new track at sector: 0
Track 01: 0 of 152 MB written (fifo 100%).
```

At this point, *cdrecord* overwrites the last line with progress indications until it is finished. If you're watching, keep an eye on the *fifo* information at the end of the line. This gives you an idea how well the system is keeping up with the burner. If the utilization drops to 0, you will get an underrun, and the blank would have become a coaster if this were for real.

Finally, you see:

```
Track 01: 152 of 152 MB written (fifo 100%).
Track 01: Total bytes read/written: 160176128/160176128 (78211 sectors).
Writing  time:  136.918s
Fixating...
WARNING: Some drives don't like fixation in dummy mode.
Fixating time:   35.963s
cdrecord: fifo had 2523 puts and 2523 gets.
cdrecord: fifo was 0 times empty and 2451 times full, min fill was 96%.
```

The summary information at the end shows that at some point the fifo dropped below 100% full, but this is far from being a problem. If, on the other hand, there was a lot of disk activity at the same time, you might find the fifo level dropping much lower.

When you're sure that you won't have any problems, you can do the real thing: just repeat the command without the −dummy option. The output looks almost identical.

Copying CD-ROMs

Frequently you'll want to make a verbatim copy of another CD. There are copyright implications here, of course, but many CD-ROMs are not restricted. In particular, you may make copies of FreeBSD CD-ROMs for your personal use.

CD-ROMs are already in ISO format, of course, so to get a file *iso*, as in the examples above, you could just perform a literal copy with *dd*:

```
# dd if=/dev/cd0c of=iso bs=128k
```

The bs=128k tells *dd* to copy in blocks of 128 kB. It's not strictly necessary, but if you omit it, it will perform a separate transfer for every sector, and on a slow machine it can be much less efficient.

There's an even easier way, though, if you have two CD-ROM drives: you can frequently copy directly from one drive to the other, without storing on disk at all. To do this, of course, you need to be very sure that your CD-ROM drive is fast enough. In particular, if it spins down during the copy, you will almost certainly have underruns and a useless copy. Be very sure to do a dummy run first. Let's assume that your second CD-ROM drive is */dev/cd1c* (a SCSI drive). For IDE drives, write:

```
# burncd -f /dev/acd0c -t -v -s 8 data /dev/cd1c fixate
```

In this example, the −f option indicates that */dev/acd0c* is the (IDE) CD-R burner. */dev/cd1c* is the (SCSI) CD-ROM drive with the original CD-ROM. You don't need to mount */dev/cd1c*, since it's being accessed as raw data, not a file system.

When you're sure this will work, remove the −t flag and repeat.

For SCSI, enter

```
# cdrecord -dummy -v dev=0,0,0 -speed=8 /dev/cd1c
```

When it completes satisfactorily, remove the −dummy and repeat.

14

Tapes, backups and floppy disks

In Chapter 11 we looked at hard disks. In this chapter, we'll consider how to guard against data loss, and how to transfer data from one location to another. These are functions that UNIX traditionally performs with tapes, and we'll look at them in the next sections. Because FreeBSD runs on PCs, however, you can't completely escape floppy disks, though it would be an excellent idea. We'll look at floppies on page 256.

Backing up your data

No matter how reliable your system, you are never completely protected against loss of data. The most common reasons are hardware failure and human error. By comparison, it's *very* seldom that a software error causes data loss, but this, too, can happen.

UNIX talks about *archives*, which are copies of disk data in a form suitable for writing on a serial medium such as tape. You can, however, write them to disk files as well, and that's what people do when they want to move a source tree from one system to another. You'll also hear the term *tarball* for an archive made by the *tar* program, which we discuss below.

What backup medium?

Traditionally, PCs use floppy disks as a removable storage medium. We'll look at floppies below, but you can sum the section up in one statement: don't use floppy disks.

Floppy disks are particularly unsuited as a backup medium for modern computers. Consider even a minimal system with a 2 GB hard disk. Storing 2 GB of data on floppies requires about 1,500 floppies, which, at $0.30 each, would cost you $450. Copying the data to a floppy takes about 50 seconds per floppy, so the raw backup time would be about 21 hours, plus the time it takes you to change the floppies, which could easily take another three or more hours. During this time you have to sit by the computer playing disk jockey, a total of three days' work during which you could hardly do anything else. When you try to read in the data again, there's a virtual certainty that one of the floppies has a data error, especially if you read them with a different drive.

By contrast, a single DDS or Exabyte cassette stores several gigabytes and costs about $6. The backup time for 2 GB is about 90 minutes, and the operation can be performed completely unattended.

A number of cheaper tape drives are also available, such as Travan tapes. FreeBSD supports them, but for one reason or another, they are not popular. FreeBSD once used to have support for "floppy tape," run off a floppy controller, but these tapes were very unreliable, and they are no longer supported.

You can also use writeable "CD-ROMs" (*CD-R*s) for backup purposes. By modern standards, the media are small (up to 700 MB), but they have the advantage of being readily accessible on other systems. We looked at CD-Rs in Chapter 13.

Tape devices

FreeBSD tape devices have names like */dev/nsa0* (see page 196). Each letter has a significance:

- n means *non-rewinding*. When the process that accesses the tape closes it, the tape remains at the same position. This is inconvenient if you want to remove the tape (before which you should rewind it), but it's the only way if you want to handle multiple archives on the tape. The name of the corresponding *rewind device* has no n (for example, the rewind device corresponding to */dev/nsa0* is */dev/sa0*). A rewind device rewinds the tape when it is closed.

  > Older releases of FreeBSD used the names */dev/nrsa0* and */dev/rsa0*. r stands for *raw*, in other words a character device. Since the removal of block devices, this letter is superfluous, but you might see it occasionally in older documents.

- sa stands for *serial access*, and is always SCSI. You can also get ATAPI tape drives, which are called */dev/ast0* and */dev/nast0*, and the older QIC-02 interface tapes are called */dev/wst0* and */dev/nwst0*.

- 0 is the *unit number*. If you have more than one tape, the next will be called */dev/nsa1*, and so on.

Backup software

FreeBSD does not require special "backup software." The base operating system supplies all the programs you need. The tape driver is part of the kernel, and the system includes a number of backup programs. The most popular are:

- *tar*, the *tape archiver*, has been around longer than anybody can remember. It is particularly useful for data exchange, since everybody has it. There are even versions of *tar* for Microsoft platforms. It's also an adequate backup program.

- *cpio* is an alternative backup program. About its only advantage over *tar* is that it can read *cpio* format archives.

- *pax* is another alternative backup program. It has the advantage that it can also read and write *tar* and *cpio* archives.

- *dump* is geared more towards backups than towards archiving. It can maintain multiple levels of backup, each of which backs up only those files that have changed since the last backup of the next higher (numerically lower) level. It is less suited towards data exchange because its formats are very specific to BSD. Even older releases of FreeBSD cannot read dumps created under FreeBSD Release 5.

- *amanda*, in the Ports Collection, is another popular backup program.

Backup strategies are frequently the subject of religious wars. I personally find that *tar* does everything I want, but you'll find plenty of people who recommend *dump* or *amanda* instead. In the following section, we'll look at the basics of using *tar*. See the man page *dump(8)* for more information on *dump*.

tar

tar, the *tape archiver*, performs the following functions:

- Creating an *archive*, which can be a serial device such as a tape, or a disk file, from the contents of a number of directories.

- Extracting files from an archive.

- Listing the contents of an archive.

tar does not compress the data. The resulting archive is slightly larger than the sum of the files that it contains, since it also contains a certain amount of header information. You can, however, use the *gzip* program to compress a *tar* archive, and *tar* invokes it for you automatically with the -z option. The size of the resultant archives depends strongly on the data you put in them. JPEG images, for example, hardly compress at all, while text compresses quite well and can be as much as 90% smaller than the original file.

Creating a tar archive

Create an archive with the c option. Unlike most UNIX programs, *tar* does not require a hyphen (–) in front of the options. For example, to save your complete kernel source tree, you could write:

```
# tar cvf source-archive.tar /usr/src/sys
tar: Removing leading / from absolute path names in the archive.
usr/src/sys/
usr/src/sys/CVS/
usr/src/sys/CVS/Root
usr/src/sys/CVS/Repository
usr/src/sys/CVS/Entries
usr/src/sys/compile/
usr/src/sys/compile/CVS/
(etc)
```

The parameters have the following meaning:

- cvf are the options. c stands for *create* an archive, v specifies *verbose* operation (in this case, this causes *tar* to produce the list of files being archived), and f specifies that the next parameter is the name of the archive file.

- source-archive.tar is the name of the archive. In this case, it's a disk file.

- /usr/src/sys is the name of the directory to archive. *tar* archives all files in the directory, including most devices. For historical reasons, *tar* can't back up devices with minor numbers greater than 65536, and changing the format would make it incompatible with other systems.

The message on the first line (Removing leading / ...) indicates that, although the directory name was specified as /usr/src/sys, *tar* treats it as *usr/src/sys*. This makes it possible to restore the files into another directory at a later time.

You can back up to tape in exactly the same way:

```
# tar cvf /dev/nsa0 /usr/src/sys
```

There is a simpler way, however: if you don't specify a file name, *tar* looks for the environment variable TAPE. If it finds it, it interprets it as the name of the tape drive. You can make things a lot easier by setting the following line in the configuration file for your shell (*.profile* for *sh*, *.bashrc* for *bash*, *.login* for *csh* and *tcsh*):

```
TAPE=/dev/nsa0 export TAPE              for sh and bash
setenv TAPE /dev/nsa0                   for csh and tcsh
```

After this, the previous example simplifies to:

```
# tar cv /usr/src/sys
```

Listing an archive

To list an archive, use the option t:

```
# tar t                                         from tape
usr/src/sys/
usr/src/sys/CVS/
usr/src/sys/CVS/Root
usr/src/sys/CVS/Repository
usr/src/sys/CVS/Entries
usr/src/sys/compile/
usr/src/sys/compile/CVS/
usr/src/sys/compile/CVS/Root
(etc)
# tar tvf source-archive.tar                    from disk
drwxrwxrwx root/bin          0 Oct 25 15:07 1997 usr/src/sys/
drwxrwxrwx root/bin          0 Oct 25 15:08 1997 usr/src/sys/CVS/
-rw-rw-rw- root/wheel        9 Sep 30 23:13 1996 usr/src/sys/CVS/Root
-rw-rw-rw- root/wheel       17 Sep 30 23:13 1996 usr/src/sys/CVS/Repository
-rw-rw-rw- root/bin        346 Oct 25 15:08 1997 usr/src/sys/CVS/Entries
drwxrwxrwx root/bin          0 Oct 27 17:11 1997 usr/src/sys/compile/
drwxrwxrwx root/bin          0 Jul 30 10:52 1997 usr/src/sys/compile/CVS/
(etc)
```

This example shows the use of the v (*verbose*) option with t. If you don't use it, *tar* displays only the names of the files (first example, from tape). If you do use it, *tar* also displays the permissions, ownerships, sizes and last modification date in a form reminiscent of *ls -l* (second example, which is from the disk file *source-archive.tar*).

Extracting files

To extract a file from the archive, use the x option:

```
# tar xv usr/src/sys/Makefile                   from tape
usr/src/sys/Makefile                            confirms that the file was extracted
```

As with the c option, if you don't use the v option, *tar* does not list any file names. If you omit the names of the files to extract, *tar* extracts the complete archive.

Compressed archives

You can combine *gzip* with *tar* by specifying the z option. For example, to create the archive *source-archive.tar.gz* in compressed format, write:

```
# tar czf source-archive.tar.gz /usr/src/sys
```

You *must* specify the z option when listing or extracting compressed archives, and you must not do so when listing or extracting non-compressed archives. Otherwise you get messages like:

```
# tar tzvf source-archive.tar
gzip: stdin: not in gzip format
tar: child returned status 1
# tar tvf source-archive.tar.gz
tar: only read 2302 bytes from archive source-archive.tar.gz
```

Using floppy disks under FreeBSD

I don't like floppy disks. UNIX doesn't like floppy disks. Probably you don't like floppy disks either, but we occasionally have to live with them.

FreeBSD uses floppy disks for one thing only: for initially booting the system on systems that can't boot from CD-ROM. We've already seen that they're unsuitable for archival data storage and data transfer. For this purpose, FreeBSD uses tapes and CD-ROMs, which are much more reliable, and for the data volumes involved in modern computers, they're cheaper and faster.

So why use floppies? The only good reasons are:

- You have a floppy drive. You may not have a tape drive. Before you go out and buy all those floppies, though, consider that it might be cheaper to buy a tape drive and some tapes instead.

- You need to exchange data with people using Microsoft platforms, or with people who don't have the same kind of tape as you do.

In the following sections, we'll look at how to handle floppies under FreeBSD, with particular regard to coexisting with Microsoft. Here's an overview:

- Always format floppies before using them on your system for the first time, even if they've been formatted before. We'll look at that in the next section.

- Just occasionally, you need to create a UNIX file system on floppy. We'll look at that on page 257.

- When exchanging with Microsoft users, you need to create a Microsoft file system. We'll look at that on page 259.

- When exchanging with other UNIX users, whether FreeBSD or not, use *tar* or *cpio*. We'll look at how to do that on page 259.

Formatting a floppy

Even if you buy preformatted floppies, it's a good idea to reformat them. Track alignment can vary significantly between individual floppy drives, and the result can be that your drive doesn't write quite on top of the pre-written tracks. I have seen read failure rates as high as 2% on pre-formatted floppies: in other words, after writing 100 floppies with valuable data, the chances are that two of them have read errors. You can reduce this problem by reformatting the floppy in the drive in which it is to be written, but you can't eliminate it.

On Microsoft platforms, you format floppies with the *FORMAT* program, which performs two different functions when invoked on floppies: it performs both a *low-level* format, which rewrites the physical sector information, and then it performs what it calls a *high-level* format, which writes the information necessary for Microsoft platforms to use it as a file system. UNIX calls the second operation creating a file system. It's not always necessary to have a file system on the diskette—in fact, as we'll see, it can be a disadvantage. In addition, FreeBSD offers different kinds of file system, so it performs the two functions with different programs. In this section, we'll look at *fdformat*, which performs the low-level format. We'll look at how to create a *UFS* or Microsoft file system in the next section.

To format a diskette in the first floppy drive, */dev/fd0*, you would enter:

```
$ fdformat /dev/fd0
Format 1440K floppy '/dev/fd0'? (y/n): y
Processing -------------------------------------
```

Each hyphen character (-) represents two tracks. As the format proceeds, the hyphens change to an **F** (Format) and then to **V** (Verify) in turn, so at the end the line reads

```
Processing VVVVVVVVVVVVVVVVVVVVVVVVVVVVVVVVVVVVV done.
```

File systems on floppy

It's possible to use floppies as file systems under FreeBSD. You can create a *UFS* file system on a floppy just like on a hard disk. This is not necessarily a good idea: the *UFS* file system is designed for performance, not maximum capacity. By default, it doesn't use the last 8% of disk space, and it includes a lot of structure information that further reduces the space available on the disk. Here's an example of creating a file system, mounting it on the directory */A*, and listing the remaining space available on an empty 3½" floppy. Since release 5, FreeBSD no longer requires a partition table on a floppy, so you don't need to run *bsdlabel* (the replacement for the older *disklabel* program).

```
# newfs -O1 /dev/fd0                            create a new file system
/dev/fd0: 1.4MB (2880 sectors) block size 16384, fragment size 2048
        using 2 cylinder groups of 1.00MB, 64 blks, 128 inodes.
super-block backups (for fsck -b #) at:
 32, 2080
# mount /dev/fd0 /A                              mount the floppy on /A
# df -k /A                                       display the space available
Filesystem  1024-blocks     Used    Avail Capacity  Mounted on
/dev/fd0           1326        2     1218    0%      /A
```

Let's look at this in a little more detail:

- *newfs* creates the *UFS* file system on the floppy. We use the -O1 flag to force the older UFS1 format, which leaves more usable space than the default UFS2.

- We have already seen *mount* on page 192. In this case, we use it to mount the floppy on the file system */A*.

- The *df* program shows the maximum and available space on a file system. By default, *df* displays usage in blocks of 512 bytes, an inconvenient size. In this example we use the -k option to display it in kilobytes. You can set a default block size via the environment variable BLOCKSIZE. If it had been set to 1024, we would see the same output without the -k option. See page 128 for more details of environment variables.

The output of *df* looks terrible! Our floppy only has 1218 kB left for normal user data, even though there is nothing on it and even *df* claims that it can really store 1326 kB. This is because *UFS* keeps a default of 8% of the space free for performance reasons. You can change this, however, with *tunefs*, the file system tune program:[1]

```
# umount /A                                first unmount the floppy
# tunefs -m 0 /dev/fd0                      and change the minimum free to 0
tunefs: minimum percentage of free space changes from 8% to 0%
tunefs: should optimize for space with minfree < 8%
# tunefs -o space /dev/fd0                  change the optimization
tunefs: optimization preference changes from time to space
# mount /dev/fd0 /A                         mount the file system again
# df /A                                     and take another look
Filesystem  1024-blocks    Used    Avail Capacity  Mounted on
/dev/fd0            1326       2     1324      0%    /A
```

Still, this is a far cry from the claimed data storage of a Microsoft disk. In fact, Microsoft disks can't store the full 1.4 MB either: they also need space for storing directories and allocation tables. The moral of the story: only use file systems on floppy if you don't have any alternative.

Microsoft file systems

To create a Microsoft FAT12, FAT16 or FAT32 file system, use the *newfs_msdos* command:

```
$ newfs_msdos -f 1440 /dev/fd0
```

The specification -f 1440 tells *newfs_msdos* that this is a 1.4 MB floppy. Alternatively, you can use the *mformat* command:

```
$ mformat A:
```

You can specify the number of tracks with the -t option, and the number of sectors with the -s option. To explicitly specify a floppy with 80 tracks and 18 sectors (a standard 3½" 1.44 MB floppy), you could enter:

```
$ mformat -t 80 -s 18 A:
```

mformat is one of the *mtools* that we look at in the next section.

Other uses of floppies

Well, you could take the disks out of the cover and use them as a kind of frisbee. But there is one other useful thing you can do with floppies: as an archive medium, they don't need a file system on them. They just need to be low-level formatted. For example, to write the contents of the current directory onto a floppy, you could enter:

---

1. To quote the man page: *You can tune a file system, but you can't tune a fish.*

```
$ tar cvfM /dev/fd0 .
./
.xfmrc
.x6530modkey
.uwmrc
.twmrc
.rnsoft
.rnlast
...etc
Prepare volume #2 for /dev/fd0 and hit return:
```

Note also the solitary dot (.) at the end of the command line. That's the name of the current directory, and that's what you're backing up. Note also the option M, which is short for --multi-volume. There's a very good chance that you'll run out of space on a floppy, and this option says that you have a sufficient supply of floppies to perform the complete backup.

To extract the data again, use *tar* with the x option:

```
$ tar xvfM /dev/fd0
./
.xfmrc
.x6530modkey
.uwmrc
...etc
```

See the man page *tar(1)* for other things you can do with *tar*.

Accessing Microsoft floppies

Of course, most of the time you get data on a floppy, it's not in *tar* format: it has a Microsoft file system on it. We've already seen the Microsoft file system type on page 190, but that's a bit of overkill if you just want to copy files from floppy. In this case, use the *mtools* package from the Ports Collection. *mtools* is an implementation of the MS-DOS programs *ATTRIB*, *CD*, *COPY*, *DEL*, *DIR*, *FORMAT*, *LABEL*, *MD*, *RD*, *READ*, *REN*, and *TYPE* under UNIX. To avoid confusion with existing utilities, the UNIX versions of these commands start with the letter m. They are also written in lower case. For example, to list the contents of a floppy and copy one of the files to the current (FreeBSD) directory, you might enter:

```
$ mdir                                          list the current directory on A:
 Volume in drive A is MESSED OS
 Directory for A:/

IO       SYS      33430   4-09-91   5:00a
MSDOS    SYS      37394   4-09-91   5:00a
COMMAND  COM      47845  12-23-92   5:22p
NFS             <DIR>    12-24-92  11:03a
DOSEDIT  COM       1728  10-07-83   7:40a
CONFIG   SYS        792  10-07-94   7:31p
AUTOEXEC BAT        191  12-24-92  11:10a
MOUSE           <DIR>    12-24-92  11:09a
        12 File(s)     82944 bytes free
$ mcd nfs                                       change to directory A:\NFS
$ mdir                                          and list the directory
 Volume in drive A is MESSED OS
 Directory for A:/NFS
```

```
.               <DIR>     12-24-92  11:03a
..              <DIR>     12-24-92  11:03a
HOSTS            5985     10-07-94   7:34p
NETWORK   BAT     103     12-24-92  12:28p
DRIVES    BAT      98     11-07-94   5:24p
...and many more
      51 File(s)       82944 bytes free
$ mtype drives.bat                          type the contents of DRIVES.BAT
net use c: presto:/usr/dos
c:
cd \nfs
# net use f: porsche:/dos
# net use g: porsche:/usr
$ mcopy a:hosts .                           copy A:HOSTS to local UNIX directory
Copying HOSTS
$ ls -l hosts                               and list it
-rw-rw-rw-   1 root       wheel        5985 Jan 28 18:04 hosts
```

You must specify the drive letter to *mcopy*, because it uses this indication to decide whether the file name is a UNIX or a Microsoft file name. You can copy files from FreeBSD to the floppy as well, of course.

A word of warning. UNIX uses a different text data format from Microsoft: in UNIX, lines end with a single character, called **Newline**, and represented by the characters \n in the C programming language. It corresponds to the ASCII character **Line Feed** (represented by ^J). Microsoft uses two characters, a **Carriage Return** (^M) followed by a **Line Feed**. This unfortunate difference causes a number of unexpected compatibility problems, since both characters are usually invisible on the screen.

In FreeBSD, you won't normally have many problems. Occasionally a program complains about non-printable characters in an input line. Some, like *Emacs*, show them. For example, Emacs shows our last file, *drives.bat*, like this:

```
net use c: presto:/usr/dos^M
c:^M
cd \nfs^M
# net use f: porsche:/dos^M
# net use g: porsche:/usr^M
```

This may seem relatively harmless, but it confuses some programs, including the C compiler and pagers like *more*, which may react in confusing ways. You can remove them with the -t option of *mcopy*:

```
$ mcopy -t a:drives.bat .
```

Transferring files in the other direction is more likely to cause problems. For example, you might edit this file under FreeBSD and then copy it back to the diskette. The results depend on the editor, but assuming we changed all occurrences of the word porsche to freedom, and then copied the file back to the diskette, Microsoft might then find:

```
C:> type drives.bat
net use c: presto:/usr/dos
                    c:
                      cd \nfs
                          # net use f: freedom:/dos
                                  # net use g: freedom:/usr
```

This is a typical result of removing the **Carriage Return** characters. The -t option to *mcopy* can help here, too. If you use it when copying *to* a Microsoft file system, it reinserts the **Carriage Return** characters.

15

Printers

In this chapter, we'll look at some aspects of using printers with FreeBSD. As a user, you don't access printers directly. Instead, a series of processes, collectively called the *spooler*, manage print data. One process, *lpr*, writes user print data to disk, and another, *lpd*, copies the print data to the printers. This method enables processes to write print data even if the printers are busy and ensures optimum printer availability.

In this section, we'll look briefly at what you need to do to set up printers. For more details, look in the online handbook section on printing.

lpd is the central spooler process. It is responsible for a number of things:

- • It controls access to attached printers and to printers attached to other hosts on the network.

- • It enables users to submit files to be printed. These submissions are known as jobs.

- • It prevents multiple users from accessing a printer at the same time by maintaining a queue for each printer.

- • It can print header pages, also known as banner or burst pages, so users can easily find jobs they have printed in a stack of printouts.

- • It takes care of communications parameters for printers connected on serial ports.

- • It can send jobs over the network to another spooler on another host.

- • It can run special filters to format jobs to be printed for various printer languages or printer capabilities.

- It can account for printer usage.

Through a configuration file, and by providing the special filter programs, you can enable the spooler to do all or some subset of the above for a great variety of printer hardware.

This may sound like overkill if you are the only user on the system. It *is* possible to access the printer directly, but it's not a good idea:

- The spooler prints jobs in the background. You don't have to wait for data to be copied to the printer.

- The spooler can conveniently run a job to be printed through filters to add headers or convert special formats (such as PostScript) into a format the printer will understand.

- Most programs that provide a print feature expect to talk to the spooler on your system.

Printer configuration

There are three commonly used ways to connect a printer to a computer:

- Older UNIX systems frequently used serial printers, but they are no longer in common use. Serial printers seldom transmit more than 1,920 characters per second, which is too slow for modern printers.

- Most printers are still connected by a *parallel port*. Parallel ports enable faster communication with the printer, up to about 100,000 bytes per second. Such speeds may still not be enough for complex PostScript or bit-mapped images. Most parallel ports require CPU intervention via an interrupt for each character transmitted, and 100,000 interrupts per second can use the entire processing power of a fast machine.

- More modern printers have USB or Ethernet interfaces, which enable them to connect to several machines at once at much higher speeds. The load on the host computer is also much lower.

It's pretty straightforward to connect a parallel printer. You don't need to do anything special to configure the line printer driver *lpt*: it's in the kernel by default. All you need to do is to plug in the cable between the printer and the computer. If you have more than one parallel interface, of course, you'll have to decide which one to use. Parallel printer devices are called /dev/lpt*n*, where *n* is the number, starting with 0. USB devices have names like */dev/ulptn*. See Table 10-4 on page 195 for further details.

Configuring an Ethernet-connected printer is more complicated. You obviously need an IP address, which you configure on the printer. Most modern printers then appear like a remote computer to the spooler. We look at spooling to remote computers on page 266.

Testing the printer

When you have connected and powered on a parallel port printer, run the built-in test if one is supplied: typically there's a function that produces a printout describing the printer's features. After that, check the communication between the computer and the printer.

```
# lptest > /dev/lpt0
```

If you have a pure PostScript printer, one which can't print anything else, you won't get any output. Even here, though, you should see some reaction on the status display.

Configuring /etc/printcap

The next step is to configure the central configuration file, */etc/printcap*. This file is not the easiest to read, but after a while you'll get used to it. Here are some typical entries:

```
lp|lj|ps|local LaserJet 6MP printer:\
        :lp=/dev/lpt0:sd=/var/spool/output/lpd:lf=/var/log/lpd-errs:sh:mx#0:\
        :if=/usr/local/libexec/lpfilter:

rlp|sample remote printer:\
        :rm=freebie:sd=/var/spool/output/freebie:lf=/var/log/lpd-errs:\
        :rp=lp:
```

Let's look at this in detail:

- All fields are delimited by a colon (:).

- Continuation lines require a backslash character (\). Note particularly that you require a colon at the end of a continued line, and another at the beginning of the following line.

- The first line of each entry specifies a number of names that you can use to specify this printer when talking to *lpr* or *lpd*. The names are separated by vertical bar symbols |. By tradition, the last name is a more verbose description, and you wouldn't normally use it to talk to programs.

- The following fields describe *capabilities*, descriptions of how to do something. Capabilities are described by a two-letter keyword and optionally a parameter, which is separated by a delimiter indicating the type of parameter. If the field takes a string parameter, the delimiter is =, and if it takes a numeric value, the delimiter is #. You'll find a full description in the man page.

- The first entry defines a local printer, called lp, lj, ps and local LaserJet 6MP printer. Why so many names? lp is the default, so you should have it somewhere. lj is frequently used to talk to printers that understand HP's LaserJet language (now PCL), and ps might be used to talk to a printer that understands PostScript. The final name is more of a description.

- The entry `lp=/dev/lpt0` tells the spooler the name of the physical device to which the printer is connected. Remote printers don't have physical devices.

- `sd` tells the spooler the directory in which to store jobs awaiting printing. This directory must exist; the spooler doesn't create it.

- `lf=/var/log/lpd-errs` specifies the name of a file in which to log errors.

- `sh` is a flag telling *lpd* to omit a header page. If you don't have that, every job will be preceded by a descriptor page. In a small environment, this doesn't make sense and is just a waste of paper.

- The parameter `mx` tells *lpd* the maximum size of a spool job in kilobytes. If the job is larger than this value, *lpd* refuses to print it. In our case, we don't want to limit the size. We do this by setting `mx` to 0.

- `if` tells *lpd* to apply a *filter* to the job before printing. We'll look at this below.

- In the remote printer entry, `rm=freebie` tells *lpd* to send the data to the machine called `freebie`. This could be a fully qualified domain name, of course.

- In the remote printer entry, `rp=lp` tells *lpd* the name of the printer on the remote machine. This doesn't have to be the same name as the name on the local machine.

Remote printing

In a network, you don't need to have a printer on every machine; you can print on another machine (which may be a printer) on the same network. There are a couple of things to consider:

- There are two machines involved in remote printing, the client ("local") machine and the server ("remote") machine.

- On the client, you specify the name of the server machine with the `rm` capability, and you specify the name of the printer with the `rp` capability. You don't specify any `lp` (device name) capability. A typical entry might look like this:

```
lp|HP LaserJet 6MP on freebie:\
        :rm=freebie:sd=/var/spool/output/freebie:lf=/var/log/lpd-errs:mx#0:
```

- On the client machine, you must also create the spool directory, */var/spool/output/freebie* in the example above.

- On the server machine, you don't need to do anything special with the */etc/printcap* file. You need an entry for the printer specified in the client machine's `rp` entry, of course.

- On the server machine you must allow spooler access from the client machine. For a BSD machine, you add the name of the machine to the file */etc/hosts.lpd* on a line by itself.

Spooler filters

Probably the least intelligible entry in the configuration file on page 265 was the `if` entry. It specifies the name of an *input filter*, a program through which *lpd* passes the complete print data before printing.

What does it do that for? There can be a number of reasons. Maybe you have data in a format that isn't fit to print. For example, it might be PostScript, and your printer might not understand PostScript. Or it could be the other way around: your printer understands *only* PostScript, and the input isn't PostScript.

There's a more likely reason to require a filter, though: most printers still emulate the old teletypes, so they require a carriage return character (**Ctrl-M** or **^M**) to start at the beginning of the line, and a new line character (**Ctrl-J** or **^J**) to advance to the next line. UNIX uses only **^J**, so if you copy data to it, you're liable to see a *staircase effect*. For example, *ps* may tell you:

```
$ ps
  PID  TT  STAT      TIME COMMAND
  2252 p1  Ss     0:01.35 /bin/bash
  2287 p1  IW     0:04.77 e /etc/printcap
  2346 p1  R+     0:00.05 ps
```

When you try to print it, however, you get:

```
  PID  TT  STAT      TIME COMMAND
                           2252  p1  Ss   0:01.35 /bin/bash
                                                        2287  p1  IW   0
```

The rest of the page is empty: you've gone off the right margin.

There are a number of ways to solve this problem:

- You may be able to configure your printer to interpret **Ctrl-J** as both new line and return, and to ignore **Ctrl-M**. Check your printer handbook.

- You may be able to issue a control sequence to your printer to tell it to interpret **Ctrl-J** as both new line and return to the beginning of the line, and to ignore **Ctrl-M**. For example, HP LaserJets and compatibles will do this if you send them the control sequence **ESC**&k2G.

- You can write an *input filter* that transforms the print job into a form that the printer understands. We'll look at this option below.

There are a couple of options for the print filter. One of them, taken from the online handbook, sends out a LaserJet control sequence before every job. Put the following shell script in */usr/local/libexec/lpfilter*:

```
#!/bin/sh
printf "\033&k2G" && cat && printf "\f" && exit 0
exit 2
```

Figure 15-1: Simple print filter

This approach does not work well with some printers, such as my HP LaserJet 6MP, which can print both PostScript and LaserJet (natural) formats at random. They do this by recognizing the text at the beginning of the job. This particular filter confuses them by sending a LaserJet command code, so the printer prints the PostScript as if it were plain text.

In this kind of situation, the standard filters are no longer sufficient. You can solve the problem with the port *apsfilter*, which is in the Ports Collection.

Starting the spooler

As we saw above, the line printer daemon *lpd* is responsible for printing spooled jobs. By default it isn't started at boot time. If you're root, you can start it by name:

```
# lpd
```

Normally, however, you will want it to be started automatically when the system starts up. You do this by setting the variable lpd_enable in */etc/rc.conf*:

```
lpd_enable="YES"                          # Run the line printer daemon
```

See page 552 for more details of */etc/rc.conf*.

You can also add another line referring to the line printer daemon to */etc/rc.conf*:

```
lpd_flags=""                              # Flags to lpd (if enabled).
```

You don't normally need this line. See the man page for *lpd* for details of the flags.

Testing the spooler

To test the spooler, you can run the *lptest* program again. This time, however, instead of sending it directly to the printer, you send it to the spooler:

```
$ lptest 80 5 | lpr
```

The results should look like:

```
!"#$%&'()*+,-./0123456789:;<=>?@ABCDEFGHIJKLMNOPQRSTUVWXYZ[\]^_`abcdefghijklmnop
"#$%&'()*+,-./0123456789:;<=>?@ABCDEFGHIJKLMNOPQRSTUVWXYZ[\]^_`abcdefghijklmnopq
#$%&'()*+,-./0123456789:;<=>?@ABCDEFGHIJKLMNOPQRSTUVWXYZ[\]^_`abcdefghijklmnopqr
$%&'()*+,-./0123456789:;<=>?@ABCDEFGHIJKLMNOPQRSTUVWXYZ[\]^_`abcdefghijklmnopqrs
%&'()*+,-./0123456789:;<=>?@ABCDEFGHIJKLMNOPQRSTUVWXYZ[\]^_`abcdefghijklmnopqrst
```

Troubleshooting

Here's a list of the most common problems and how to solve them.

Table 15-1: Common printer problems

Problem	Cause
The printer prints, but the last page doesn't appear. The status shows that the printer still has data in the buffer. After several minutes, the last page may appear.	Your output data is not ejecting the last page. The printer is configured to either wait for an explicit eject request (the ASCII *Form feed* character, **Ctrl-L**) or to eject after a certain period of time. You have a choice as to what you do about this. Usually you can configure the printer, or you could get the print filter to print a form feed character at the end of the job. Figure 15-1 already does this—that's the `printf "\f"`.
The lines wander off to the right edge of the paper and are never seen again.	This is the *staircase effect*. Refer to page 268 for a couple of solutions.
Individual characters or whole sections of text are missing.	This problem occurs almost only on serial printers. It's a result of incorrect handshaking—see page 330 and the online handbook for more details.
The output contained completely unintelligible random characters.	On a serial printer, if the characters appear slowly, and there's a predominance of the characters { | } ~, this probably means that you have set up the communication parameters incorrectly. Check the online handbook for a solution. Make sure you don't confuse this problem with the following one.

Problem	Cause
The text was legible, but it bore no relationship to what you wanted to print.	One possibility is that you are sending PostScript output to your printer. See the discussion on page 271 to check if it is PostScript. If it is, your printer is not interpreting it correctly, either because it doesn't understand PostScript, or because it has been confused (see the discussion on page 268 for one reason).
The display on the printer shows that data are arriving, but the printer doesn't print anything.	You might be sending normal text to a PostScript printer that doesn't understand normal text. In this case, too, you will need a filter to convert the text to PostScript—the opposite of the previous problem.
	Alternatively, your printer port may not be interrupting correctly. This will not stop the printer from printing, but it can take up to 20 minutes to print a page. You can fix this by issuing the following command, which puts the printer */dev/lpt0* into polled mode:
	<pre># **lptcontrol -p**</pre>
You get the message `lpr: cannot create freebie/.seq`	You have forgotten to create the spool directory */var/spool/output/freebie*.

Using the spooler

Using the spooler is relatively simple. Instead of outputting data directly to the printer, you *pipe* it to the spooler *lpr* command. For example, here is the same print command, first printing directly to the printer, and secondly via the spooler:

```
# ps waux > /dev/lpt0
$ ps waux | lpr
```

Note the difference in prompt: you have to be root to write directly to the printer, but normally anybody can write to the spooler. The spooler creates a *job* from this data. You can look at the current print queue with the *lpq* program:

```
$ lpq
waiting for lp to become ready (offline ?)
Rank   Owner    Job  Files                      Total Size
1st    grog     313  (standard input)           9151 bytes
2nd    grog     30   (standard input)           3319 bytes
3rd    yvonne   31   (standard input)           3395 bytes
4th    root     0    (standard input)           2611 bytes
```

The first line is a warning that *lpd* can't currently print. Take it seriously. In this example, the printer was deliberately turned off so that the queue did not change from one example to the next.

Normally, the job numbers increase sequentially: this particular example came from three different machines. You can get more detail with the −l option:

```
$ lpq -l
waiting for lp to become ready (offline ?)

grog: 1st                                   [job 313freebie.example.org]
        (standard input)                    9151 bytes

grog: 2nd                                   [job 030presto.example.org]
        (standard input)                    3319 bytes

yvonne: 3rd                                 [job 031presto.example.org]
        (standard input)                    3395 bytes

root: 4th                                   [job 000bumble.example.org]
        (standard input)                    2611 bytes
```

Removing print jobs

Sometimes you may want to delete spool output without printing it. You don't need to do this because of a printer configuration error: just turn the printer off, fix the configuration error, and turn the printer on again. The job should then be printed correctly. But if you discover that the print job itself contains garbage, you can remove it with the *lprm* program. First, though, you need to know the job number. Assuming the list we have above, we might want to remove job 30:

```
# lprm 30
dfA030presto.example.org dequeued
cfA030presto.example.org dequeued
# lpq
waiting for lp to become ready (offline ?)
Rank   Owner    Job  Files                           Total Size
1st    grog     313  (standard input)                9151 bytes
2nd    yvonne   31   (standard input)                3395 bytes
3rd    root     0    (standard input)                2611 bytes
```

If the printer is offline, it may take some time for the *lprm* to complete.

PostScript

We've encountered the term *PostScript* several times already. It's a *Page Description Language*. With it, you can transmit detailed documents such as this book electronically and print them out in exactly the same form elsewhere.[1] PostScript is a very popular format on the World Wide Web, and web browsers like Netscape usually print in PostScript format.

---

1. This is in fact the way this book was sent to the printers.

Most other document formats describe special print features with *escape sequences*, special commands that start with a special character. For example, the HP LaserJet and PCL formats use the ASCII **ESC** character (0x1b) to indicate the beginning of an escape sequence. PostScript uses the opposite approach: unless defined otherwise, the contents of a PostScript file are commands, and the printable data is enclosed in parentheses. PostScript documents start with something like:

```
%!PS-Adobe-3.0
%%Creator: groff version 1.10
%%CreationDate: Fri Oct 31 18:36:45 1997
%%DocumentNeededResources: font Symbol
%%+ font Courier
%%+ font Times-Roman
%%DocumentSuppliedResources: file images/vipw.ps
%%Pages: 32
%%PageOrder: Ascend
%%Orientation: Portrait
%%EndComments
%%BeginProlog
```

This is the *prologue* (the beginning) of the PostScript output for this chapter. The *prologue* of such a program can be several hundred kilobytes long if it includes embedded fonts or images. A more typical size is about 500 lines.

You can do a number of things with PostScript:

- You can look at it with *gv*, which is in the Ports Collection. We'll look at this option below.

- Many printers understand PostScript and print it directly. If yours does, you probably know about it, since it's an expensive option. In case of doubt, check your printer manual.

- If your printer doesn't understand PostScript, you can print with the aid of ghostscript. The *apsfilter* port does this for you.

Viewing with gv

gv is part of the instant workstation port that we discussed on page 93. To view a file with *gv*, simply start it:

```
$ gv filename &
```

If you don't specify a file name, you get a blank display. You can then open a file window by pressing o, after which you can select files and display them. Figure 15-2 shows the display of a draft version of this page with an overlaid open window at the top right. The *Open File* window contains a field at the top into which you can type the name of a file. Alternatively, the columns below, with scroll bars, allow you to browse the current directory and the parent directories.

The window below shows the text of the previous page (roughly) on the right hand side. Instead of scroll bars, there is a scroll area below the text Save Marked. You can scroll the image in all directions by selecting the box with the left mouse button and moving around. At top left are menu buttons that you can select with the left mouse button. Note also the button 1.414 at the top of the window: this is the magnification of the image. You can change it by selecting this button: a menu appears and gives you a range of magnifications to choose from.

The column to the right of these buttons is a list of page numbers. You can select a page number with the middle mouse button. You can also get an enlargement display of the text area around the mouse cursor by pressing the left button.

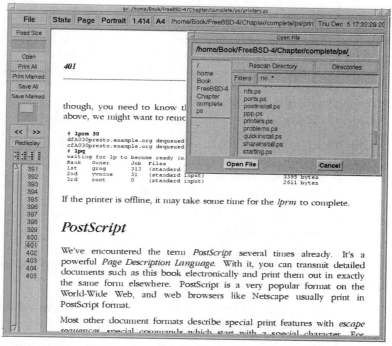

Figure 15-2: gv display

Printing with ghostscript

If your printer doesn't support PostScript, you can still print some semblance of the intended text with the help of *ghostscript*. The results are very acceptable with modern laser and inkjet printers, less so with older dot matrix printers.

To print on your particular printer, you first need to find a *driver* for it in *ghostscript*. In this context, the term *driver* means some code inside *ghostscript* that converts the data into something that the printer can print.

We've already seen how to use */etc/printcap*. In this case, we'll need an *input filter*, a script or program that transforms the PostScript data into a form that the printer understands. The entry in */etc/printcap* is pretty much the same for all printers:

```
ps|HP OfficeJet 725 with PostScript:\
     :lp=/dev/lpt0:sd=/var/spool/output/colour:lf=/var/log/lpd-errs:sh:mx#0:\
     :if=/usr/local/libexec/psfilter:
```

This entry defines a printer called *ps*. The comment states that it's an HP OfficeJet, but that's only a comment. Obviously you should choose a comment that matches the printer you really have.

The printer is connected to */dev/lpt0*, the first parallel printer. Spool data is collected in the directory */var/spool/output/colour*. You must create this directory, or printing will fail, and depending on what you use to print, you may not even see any error messages. They also don't appear on the log file, which in this case is */var/log/lpd-errs*.

The important entry is in the last line, which refers to the input filter */usr/local/libexec/ps-filter*. This file contains the instructions to convert the PostScript into something that the printer can understand. For example, for the HP OfficeJet we're talking about here, it contains:

```
#!/bin/sh
/usr/local/bin/gs -sDEVICE=pcl3 -q -sPaperSize=a4 -dNOPAUSE -sOutputFile=- -
```

These options state:

- Use *ghostscript* device *pcl3*. This is the driver to choose for most Hewlett Packard inkjet printers. We'll see alternatives for other printers below.

- The output file is *stdin* (see page 127). By convention, a number of programs use the character – to represent the *stdout* stream.

- -q means *quiet*. Normally *ghostscript* outputs a message on startup, and it often outputs other informative messages as well. In this case, we're using it as a filter, so we don't want any output except what we print.

- Don't pause between pages. If you don't specify this parameter, *ghostscript* waits for a key press at the end of each page.

- The paper size is the international A4 format. By default, *ghostscript* produces output for American standard 8.5 × 10 inch "letter" paper.

- The character – by itself tells *ghostscript* that the input is from *stdin*. Together with the output to *stdout*, this makes *ghostscript* function as a filter.

Which driver?

The previous example used the driver for the HP DeskJet. Well, to be more precise, it used one of a plethora of drivers available. You can find more information in the HTML driver documentation at */usr/local/share/ghostscript/7.05/doc/Devices.htm*. The *7.05* in the name refers to the release of *ghostscript*, which will change.

The documentation isn't the easiest to read. It's probably older than your printer, so there's a good chance that it won't mention your specific printer model. You may need to experiment a little before you get things working the way you want.

Printer drivers for DeskJets

There are at least six sets of drivers for HP DeskJets. They're all described in *Devices.htm*, but the following summary may help:

- Hewlett Packard supply their own drivers. In addition to *ghostscript*, they require server software that you can install from the Ports collection (*/usr/ports/print/hpijs*).

- Next come three different independently written drivers for specific models of DeskJet, probably all now obsolete. If you recognize your printer or something similar in one of them, that's a good first choice.

- Next comes the generic *pcl3* driver that was used in the example above. It's not mentioned in the documentation.

- Finally, *uniprint* is a completely different driver framework for a number of different makes of printer. It requires a slightly different command line, and we'll look at it separately below.

If you're using a DeskJet, you have the choice. Unfortunately, there's no way to know which is best until you've tried them all. Similar considerations apply to other makes of printer.

uniprint drivers

The *uniprint* drivers have a somewhat different kind of interface. They're described towards the end of the same *Devices.htm* file. To use them, change the driver specification as in the following example, that refers to an Epson

```
#!/bin/sh
/usr/local/bin/gs @stc500ph.upp -q -sPaperSize=a4 -dNOPAUSE -sOutputFile=- - -c quit
```

The differences here are:

- The name of the driver (*stc500ph.upp*) is specified differently.

- The line ends with a command to the driver itself (-c quit). The exact meaning is not documented, though it's easy to guess.

Which drivers?

Another problem you might encounter is that it's possible to specify the drivers you want in your *ghostscript* executable when you build the port. It's quite possible that the drivers described in *Devices.htm* don't exist on your system. To find out, run *ghostscript* interactively with the -h (help) option:

```
$ gs -h
GNU Ghostscript 7.05 (2002-04-22)
Copyright (C) 2002 artofcode LLC, Benicia, CA.  All rights reserved.
Usage: gs [switches] [file1.ps file2.ps ...]
Most frequently used switches: (you can use # in place of =)
  -dNOPAUSE            no pause after page    | -q        'quiet', fewer messages
  -g<width>x<height>  page size in pixels     | -r<res>   pixels/inch resolution
  -sDEVICE=<devname>  select device           | -dBATCH   exit after last file
  -sOutputFile=<file> select output file: - for stdout, |command for pipe,
```

```
                                    embed %d or %ld for page #
Input formats: PostScript PostScriptLevel1 PostScriptLevel2 PDF
Available devices:
    x11 x11alpha x11cmyk x11gray2 x11gray4 x11mono x11rg16x x11rg32x md2k
    md5k md50Mono md50Eco md1xMono bj10e bj10v bj10vh bj200 bjc600 bjc800
    lips2p lips3 lips4 bjc880j lips4v uniprint dmprt epag escpage lp2000
    alc8600 alc8500 alc2000 alc4000 lp8800c lp8300c lp8500c lp3000c lp8200c
    lp8000c epl5900 epl5800 epl2050 epl2050p epl2120 lp7500 lp2400 lp2200
    lp9400 lp8900 lp8700 lp8100 lp7700 lp8600f lp8400f lp8300f lp1900 lp9600s
    lp9300 lp9600 lp8600 lp1800 mjc180 mjc360 mjc720 mj500c deskjet djet500
    cdeskjet cdjcolor cdjmono cdj550 cdj670 cdj850 cdj880 cdj890 cdj1600
    cdj970 laserjet ljetplus ljet2p ljet3 ljet3d ljet4 ljet4d cljet5 cljet5c
    cljet5pr lj5mono lj5gray pj pjxl pjxl300 pxlmono pxlcolor pcl3 hpdj ijs
    npdl rpdl gdi bmpmono bmpgray bmp16 bmp256 bmp16m bmp32b bmpsep1 bmpsep8
    faxg3 faxg32d faxg4 jpeg jpeggray pcxmono pcxgray pcx16 pcx256 pcx24b
    pcxcmyk pdfwrite bit bitrgb bitcmyk pbm pbmraw pgm pgmraw pgnm pgnmraw
    pnm pnmraw ppm ppmraw pkm pkmraw pksm pksmraw pngmono pnggray png16
    png256 png16m psmono psgray psrgb pswrite epswrite tiffcrle tiffg3
    tiffg32d tiffg4 tiff12nc tiff24nc tifflzw tiffpack nullpage
Search path:
    . : /opt/lib/ghostscript : /opt/lib/ghostscript/fonts :
    /opt/lib/ghostscript/garamond : /usr/local/share/ghostscript/7.05/lib :
    /usr/local/share/ghostscript/fonts
For more information, see /usr/local/share/ghostscript/7.05/doc/Use.htm.
Report bugs to bug-gs@ghostscript.com, using the form in Bug-form.htm.
```

PDF

PDF, or *Page Description Format*, is a newer format for transferring print documents. Like PostScript, it comes from Adobe, and it is becoming increasingly important as a document interchange format on the Internet.

There are two ways to handle PDF:

- Use *Acrobat Reader*, available in the Ports Collection as */usr/src/print/acroread5*. The *5* refers to the version of Acrobat Reader and may change. Acrobat Reader is proprietary, but it's available for free, unfortunately only in binary form. It is quite a convenient way to view PDF documents, and it can print them in PostScript formats. This means that you can also use it to convert PDF to PostScript.

- *ghostscript* also understands PDF, and it is capable of converting between PostScript and PDF in both directions. *ghostscript* provides two scripts, *pdf2ps* and *ps2pdf*, which act as a front end to *ghostscript* to make the job easier.

Unlike PostScript, an editor is available for PDF (*Acrobat*, the big brother of Acrobat Reader). Unfortunately, it's proprietary and not free, and worse still, it's not available for FreeBSD.

16

Networks and the Internet

In this part of the book we'll look at the fastest-growing part of the industry: *networks*, and in particular the *Internet*.

The industry has seen many different kinds of network software:

- Years ago, the *CCITT* started a group of recommendations for individual protocols. The CCITT is now called the ITU-T, and its data communications recommendations have not been wildly successful. The best known is probably recommendation *X.25*, which still has a large following in some parts of the world. An X.25 package was available for FreeBSD, but it died for lack of love. If you need it, you'll need to invest a lot of work to get it running.

- IBM introduced their *Systems Network Architecture*, *SNA*, decades ago. It's still going strong in IBM shops. FreeBSD has minimal support for it in the Token Ring package being developed in FreeBSD-CURRENT.

- Early UNIX machines had a primitive kind of networking called *UUCP*, for *UNIX to UNIX Copy*. It ran over dialup phone lines or dedicated serial connections. System V still calls this system *Basic Networking Utilities*, or *BNU*. Despite its primitiveness, and despite the Internet, there are still some applications where UUCP makes sense, but this book discusses it no further.

- The *Internet Protocols* were developed by the US *Defense Advanced Research Projects Agency* (*DARPA*) for its *ARPANET* network. The software was originally developed in the early 80s by BBN and the CSRG at the University of California at Berkeley. The first widespread release was with the 4.2BSD operating system—the granddaddy of FreeBSD. After the introduction of IP, the ARPANET gradually changed its name to *Internet*.

The Internet Protocol is usually abbreviated to *IP*. People often refer to it as *TCP/IP*, which stands for *Transmission Control Protocol/Internet Protocol*. In fact, TCP is just one of many other protocols that run on top of IP. In this book, I refer to the IP protocol, but of course FreeBSD includes TCP and all the other standard protocols. The IP implementation supplied with FreeBSD is the most mature technology you can find anywhere, at any price.

In this part of the book, we'll look only at the Internet Protocols. Thanks to its background, FreeBSD is a particularly powerful contender in this area, and we'll go into a lot of detail about how to set up and operate networks and network services. In the chapters following, we'll look at:

- How the Internet works, which we'll look at in the rest of this chapter.

- How to set up local network connections in Chapter 17, *Configuring the local network*.

- How to select an Internet Service Provider in Chapter 18, *Connecting to the Internet*.

- How to use the hardware in Chapter 19, *Serial communications*.

- How to use PPP in Chapter 20, *Configuring PPP*.

- How to set up domain name services in Chapter 21, *The Domain Name Service*.

- How to protect yourself from intruders in Chapter 22, *Firewalls, IP aliasing and proxies*. This chapter also describes *proxy servers* and *Network Address Translation*.

- How to solve network problems in Chapter 23, *Network debugging*.

- Most network services come in pairs, a *client* that requests the service, and a *server* that provides it. In Chapter 24, *Basic network access: clients* we'll look at the client side of the World Wide Web ("web browser"), command execution over the net, including *ssh* and *telnet*, copying files across the network, and mounting remote file systems with NFS.

- In Chapter 25, *Basic network access: servers* we'll look at the server end of the same services. In addition, we'll look at *Samba*, a server for Microsoft's *Common Internet File System*, or *CIFS*.

- Electronic mail is so important that we dedicate two chapters to it, Chapter 26, *Electronic mail: clients* and Chapter 27, *Electronic mail: servers*.

The rest of this chapter looks at the theoretical background of the Internet Protocols and Ethernet. You can set up networking without understanding any of it, as long as you and your hardware don't make any mistakes. This is the approach most commercial systems take. It's rather like crossing a lake on a set of stepping stones, blindfolded. In this book, I take a different approach: in the following discussion, you'll be inside with the action, not on the outside looking in through a window. It might seem unusual at first, but once you get used to it, you'll find it much less frustrating.

Network layering

One of the problems with networks is that they can be looked at from a number of different levels. End-users of PCs access the World Wide Web (WWW), and often enough they call it the *Internet*. That's just plain wrong. At the other end of the scale is the *Link Layer*, the viewpoint you'll take when you first create a connection to another machine.

Years ago, the International Standards Organization came up with the idea of a seven-layered model of networks, often called the *OSI reference model*. Why *OSI* and not *ISO*? *OSI* stands for *Open Systems Interconnect*. Since its introduction, it has become clear that it doesn't map very well to modern networks. W. Richard Stevens presents a better layering in *TCP/IP Illustrated*, Volume 1, page 6, shown here in Figure 16-1.

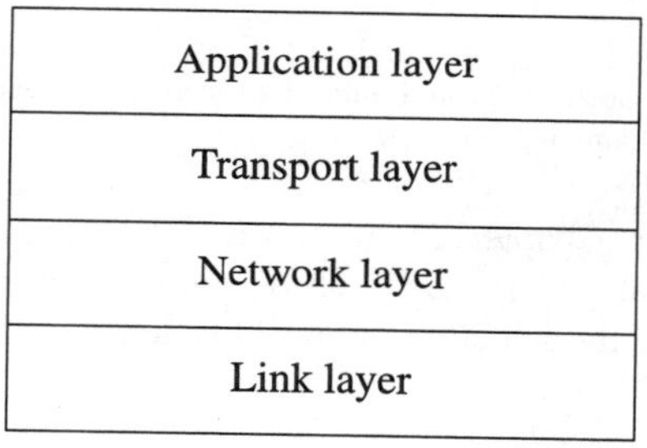

Application layer
Transport layer
Network layer
Link layer

Figure 16-1: Four-layer network model

We'll look at these layers from the bottom up:

- The *Link layer* is responsible for the lowest level of communication, between machines that are physically connected. The most common kinds of connection are Ethernet and telephone lines. This is the only layer associated with hardware.

- The *Network layer* is responsible for communication between machines that are not physically connected. For this to function, the data must pass through other machines that are not directly interested in the data. This function is called *routing*. We'll look at how it works in Chapter 17.

- The *Transport Layer* is responsible for communication between any two processes, regardless of the machines on which they run.

- The *Application Layer* defines the format used by specific applications, such as email or the Web.

The link layer

Data on the Internet is split up into *packets*, also called *datagrams*, which can be transmitted independently of each other. The *link layer* is responsible for getting packets between two systems that are connected to each other. The most trivial case is a point-to-point network, a physical connection where any data sent down the line arrives at the other end. More generally, though, multiple systems are connected to the network, as in an Ethernet. This causes a problem: how does each system know what is intended for it?

IP solves this problem by including a *packet header* in each IP packet. Consider the header something like the information you write on the outside of a letter envelope: address to send to, return address, delivery instructions. In the case of IP, the addresses are 32-bit digits that are conventionally represented in *dotted decimal* notation: the value of each byte is converted into decimal. The four values are written separated by dots. Thus the hexadecimal address 0xdf932501 would normally be represented as 223.147.37.1.

> UNIX uses the notation 0x in a number to represent a hexadecimal number. The usage comes from the C programming language.

As we will see in Chapter 23, it makes debugging much easier if we understand the structure of the datagrams, so I'll show some of the more common ones in this chapter. Figure 16-2 shows the structure of an IP header.

	0			31
0	Version	IP Header length	Type of service	Total length in bytes
4	identification		flags	fragment offset
8	Time to live		Protocol	Header Checksum
12	Source IP address			
16	Destination IP address			

Figure 16-2: IP Header

We'll only look at some of these fields; for the rest, see *TCP/IP Illustrated*, Volume 1.

- The *Version* field specifies the current version of IP. This is currently 4. A newer standard is *IPv6*, Version number 6, which is currently in an early implementation stage. IPv6 headers are very different from those shown here.

- The *time to live* field specifies how many times the packet may be passed from one system to another. Each time it is passed to another system, this value is decremented. If it reaches 0, the packet is discarded. This prevents packets from circulating in the net for ever as the result of a routing loop.

- The *protocol* specifies the kind of the packet. The most common protocols are TCP and UDP, which we'll look at in the section on the network layer.

- Finally come the *source address*, the address of the sender, and the *destination address*, the address of the recipient.

The network layer

The main purpose of the network layer is to ensure that packets get delivered to the correct recipient when it is not directly connected to the sender. This function is usually called *routing*.

Imagine routing to be similar to a postal system: if you want to send a letter to somebody you don't see often, you put the letter in a letter box. The people or machines who handle the letter look at the address and either deliver it personally or forward it to somebody else who is closer to the recipient, until finally somebody delivers it.

Have you ever received a letter that has been posted months ago? Did you wonder where they hid it all that time? Chances are it's been sent round in circles a couple of times. That's what can happen in the Internet if the routing information is incorrect, and that's why all packets have a *time to live* field. If it can't deliver a packet, the Internet Protocol simply drops (forgets about) it. You may find parallels to physical mail here, too.

It's not usually acceptable to lose data. We'll see how we avoid doing so in the next section.

The transport layer

The *transport layer* is responsible for end-to-end communication. The IP address just identifies the interface to which the data is sent. What happens when it gets there? There could be a large number of processes using the link. The IP header doesn't contain sufficient information to deliver messages to specific users within a system, so two additional protocols have been implemented to handle the details of communications between "end users."[1] These end users connect to the network via *ports*, or communication end points, within individual machines.

TCP

The *Transmission Control Protocol*, or *TCP*, is a so-called *reliable protocol*: it ensures that data gets to its destination, and if it doesn't, it sends another copy. If it can't get through after a large number of tries (14 tries and nearly 10 minutes), it gives up, but it doesn't pretend the data got through. To perform this service, TCP is also *connection oriented*: before you can send data with TCP, you must establish a connection, which is conceptually similar to opening a file.

To implement this protocol, TCP packets include a *TCP header* after the IP header, as shown in Figure 16-3. This figure ignores the possible options that follow the IP header. The offset of the TCP header, shown here as 20, is really specified by the value of the IP

---

1. In practice, these end users are processes.

Header length field in the first byte of the packet. This is only a 4 bit field, so it is counted in words of 32 bits: for a 20 byte header, it has the value 5.

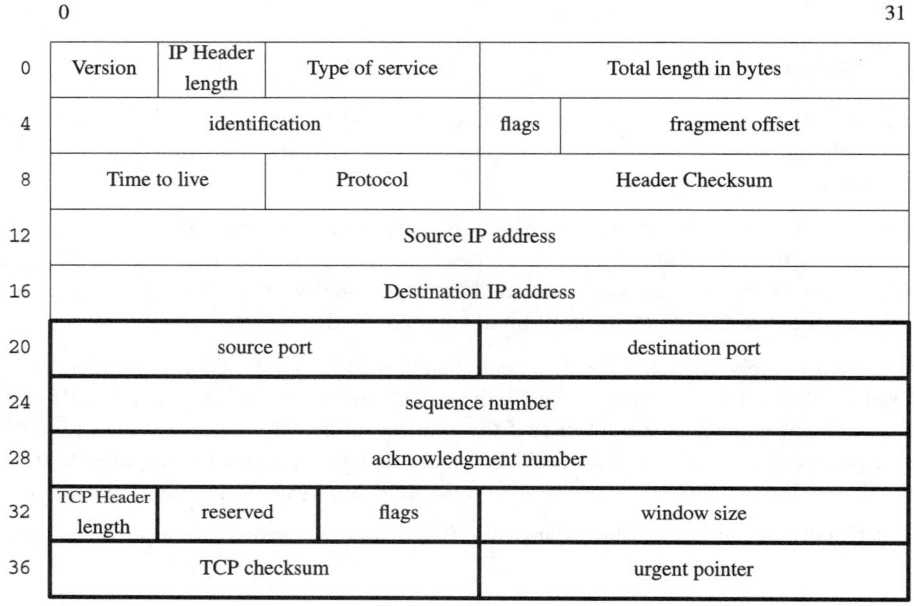

0				31

0	Version	IP Header length	Type of service	Total length in bytes
4	identification		flags	fragment offset
8	Time to live		Protocol	Header Checksum
12	Source IP address			
16	Destination IP address			
20	source port		destination port	
24	sequence number			
28	acknowledgment number			
32	TCP Header length	reserved	flags	window size
36	TCP checksum		urgent pointer	

Figure 16-3: TCP Header with IP header

A number of fields are of interest when debugging network connections:

- The *sequence number* is the byte offset of the last byte that has been sent to the other side.

- The *acknowledgment number* is the byte offset of the last byte that has received from the other side.

- The *window size* is the number of bytes that can be sent before an acknowledgment is required.

These three values are used to ensure efficient and reliable transmission of data. For each connection, TCP maintains a copy of the highest acknowledgment number received from the other side and a copy of all data that the other side has not acknowledged receiving. It does not send more than *window size* bytes of data beyond this value. If it does not receive an acknowledgment of transmitted data within a predetermined time, usually one second, it sends all the unacknowledged data again and again at increasingly large intervals. If it can't transmit the data after about ten minutes, it gives up and closes the connection.

UDP

The *User Datagram Protocol*, or *UDP*, is different: it's an *unreliable protocol*. It sends data out and never cares whether it gets to its destination or not. So why do we use it if it's unreliable? It's faster, and thus cheaper. Consider it a junk mail delivery agent: who cares if you get this week's AOL junk CD-ROM or not? There will be another one in next week's mail. Since it doesn't need to reply, UDP is connectionless: you can just send a message off with UDP without worrying about establishing a connection first. For example, the *rwhod* daemon broadcasts summary information about a system on the LAN every few minutes. In the unlikely event that a message gets lost, it's not serious: another one will come soon.

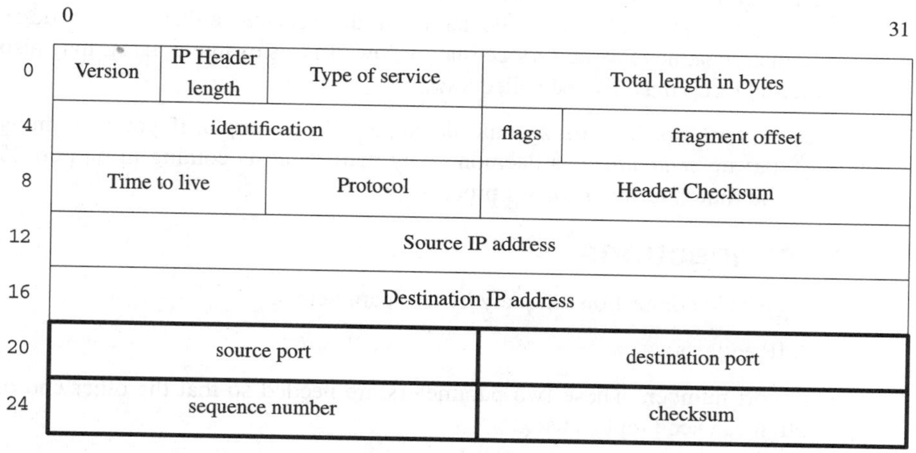

	0			31

0	Version	IP Header length	Type of service	Total length in bytes
4	identification		flags	fragment offset
8	Time to live	Protocol		Header Checksum
12	Source IP address			
16	Destination IP address			
20	source port		destination port	
24	sequence number		checksum	

Figure 16-4: UDP Header with IP header

Port assignment and Internet services

A *port* is simply a 16 bit number assigned to specific processes and which represents the source and destination end points of a specific connection. A process can either request to be connected to a specific port, or the system can assign one that is not in use.

RFC 1700 defines a number of *well-known ports* that are used to request specific services from a machine. On a UNIX machine, these are provided by daemons that *listen* on this port number—in other words, when a message comes in on this port number, the IP software passes it to them, and they process it. These ports are defined in the file */etc/services*. Here's an excerpt:

```
# Network services, Internet style
#
# WELL KNOWN PORT NUMBERS
#
ftp              21/tcp      #File Transfer [Control]
ssh        22/tcp    #Secure Shell Login
ssh        22/udp    #Secure Shell Login
telnet           23/tcp
smtp             25/tcp    mail          #Simple Mail Transfer
smtp             25/udp    mail          #Simple Mail Transfer
domain           53/tcp    #Domain Name Server
domain           53/udp    #Domain Name Server
...
http       80/tcp    www www-http        #World Wide Web HTTP
http       80/udp    www www-http        #World Wide Web HTTP
```

This file has a relatively simple format: the first column is a service name, and the second column contains the port number and the name of the service (either tcp or udp). Optionally, alternative names for the service may follow. In this example, smtp may also be called mail, and http may also be called www.

When the system starts up, it starts specific daemons. For example, if you're running mail, you may start up *sendmail* as a daemon. Any mail requests coming in on port 25 (smtp) will then be routed to *sendmail* for processing.

Network connections

You can identify a TCP connection uniquely by five parameters:

• The source IP address.

• The source port number. These two parameters are needed so that the other end of the connection can send replies back.

• The destination IP address.

• The destination port number.

• The protocol (TCP).

When you set up a connection, you specify the destination IP address and port number, and implicitly also the protocol. Your system supplies the source IP address; that's obvious enough. But where does the source port number come from? The system literally picks one out of a hat; it chooses an unused port number somewhere above the "magic" value 1024. You can look at this information with *netstat*:

```
$ netstat
Proto Recv-Q Send-Q  Local Address    Foreign Address        (state)
tcp4       0      0  presto.smtp      203.130.236.50.1825    ESTABLISHED
tcp4       0      0  presto.3312      andante.ssh            ESTABLISHED
tcp4       0      0  presto.2593      hub.freebsd.org.ssh    ESTABLISHED
tcp4       0      0  presto.smtp      www.auug.org.au.3691   ESTABLISHED
```

As you can see, this is the view on a system called *presto*. We'll see *presto* again in our sample network below. Normally you'll see a lot more connections here. For each connection, the protocol is tcp4 (TCP on IPv4). The first line shows a connection to the port smtp on *presto* from port 1825 on a machine with the IP address 203.130.236.50.

netstat shows the IP address in this case because the machine in question does not have reverse DNS mapping. This machine is sending a mail message to *presto*. The second and third lines show outgoing connections from *presto* to port ssh on the systems *andante* and *hub.freebsd.org*. The last is another incoming mail message from *www.auug.org.au*. Graphically, you could display the connection between *presto* and *www.auug.org.au* like this:

```
┌─────────┬──────────────────────────┬───────┬────────────────────────┬──────┐
│         │ IP 223.147.37.2          │       │ IP 150.101.248.57      │      │
│ presto  ├──────────────────────────┤       ├────────────────────────┤ www  │
│         │ Port 25                  │ TCP   │ Port 3691              │      │
└─────────┴──────────────────────────┴───────┴────────────────────────┴──────┘
```

Note that the port number for smtp is 25.

For various reasons, it's not always possible to connect directly in this manner:

- The Internet standards define a number of IP address blocks as *non-routable*. In these cases, we'll have to translate at least the IP addresses to establish connection. This technique is accordingly called *Network Address Translation* or *NAT*, and we'll look at it in Chapter 22, on page 393.

- For security reasons, it may not be advisable to make direct connections to servers via the Internet. Instead, the only access may be via an encrypted session on a different port. This technique is called *tunneling*, and we'll look at it in Chapter 24, on page 424.

The physical network connection

The most obvious thing about your network connection is what it looks like. It usually involves some kind of cable going out of your computer,[1] but there the similarity ends. FreeBSD supports most modern network interfaces:

- The most popular choice for *Local Area Networks* is *Ethernet*, which transfers data between a number of computers at speeds of 10 Mb/s, 100 Mb/s or 1000 Mb/s (1 Gb/s). We'll look at it in the following section.

- An increasingly popular alternative to Ethernet is *wireless networking*, specifically local networks based on the IEEE 802.11 standard. We'll look at them on page 291.

- *FDDI* stands for *Fiber Distributed Data Interface*, and was originally run over glass fibres. In contrast to Ethernet, it ran at 100 Mb/s instead of 10 Mb/s. Nowadays Ethernet runs at 100 Mb/s as well, and FDDI runs over copper wire, so the biggest difference is the protocol. FreeBSD does support FDDI, but we won't look at it here.

- *Token Ring* is yet another variety of LAN, introduced by IBM. It has never been very popular in the UNIX world. FreeBSD does have some support for it, but it's a little patchy, and we won't look at it in this book.

---

1. Maybe it won't. For example, you might use wireless Ethernet, which broadcasts in the microwave radio spectrum.

- Probably the most common connection to a *Wide-Area Network* is via a telephone with a modem or with DSL. Modems have the advantage that you can also use them for non-IP connections such as UUCP and direct dial up (see page 338), but they're much slower than DSL. If you use a modem to connect to the Internet, you'll almost certainly use the *Point to Point Protocol*, *PPP*, which we look at on page 339. In some obscure cases you may need to use the *Serial Line Internet Protocol*, *SLIP*, but it's really obsolete.

- An alternative to ADSL or modem lines is *cable networking*, which uses TV cable services to supply Internet connectivity. In many ways, it looks like Ethernet.

- In some areas, *Integrated Services Digital Networks* (*ISDNs*) are an attractive alternative to modems. They are much faster than modems, both in call setup time and in data transmission capability, and they are also much more reliable. FreeBSD includes the *isdn4bsd* package, which was developed in Germany and allows the direct connection of low-cost German ISDN boards to FreeBSD. In other parts of the world, ISDN is not cost effective, and it's also much slower than ADSL and cable.

- In some parts of the world, *satellite links* are of interest. In most cases, they are unidirectional: they transfer data from the Internet to your system (the *downlink*) and require some other connection to get data back to the Internet (the *uplink*).

- If you have a large Internet requirement, you may find it suitable to connect to the Internet via a *Leased Line*, a telephone line that is permanently connected. This is a relatively expensive option, of course, and we won't discuss it here, particularly as the options vary greatly from country to country and from region to region.

The decision on which WAN connection you use depends primarily on the system you are connecting to, in many cases an *Internet Service Provider* or *ISP*. We'll look at ISPs in Chapter 18.

Ethernet

In the early 1970s, the Xerox Company chartered a group of researchers at its Palo Alto Research Center (*PARC*) to brainstorm the *Office of the Future*. This innovative group created the mouse, the window interface metaphor and an integrated, object-oriented programming environment called *Smalltalk*. In addition, a young MIT engineer in the group named Bob Metcalfe came up with the concept that is the basis of modern local area networking, the *Ethernet*. The Ethernet protocol is a low-level broadcast packet-delivery system that employed the revolutionary idea that it was easier to resend packets that didn't arrive than it was to make sure all packets arrived. There are other network hardware systems out there, IBM's Token Ring architecture and Fiber Channel, for example, but by far the most popular is the Ethernet system in its various hardware incarnations. Ethernet is by far the most common local area network medium. There are three types:

1. Originally, Ethernet ran at 10 Mb/s over a single thick coaxial cable, usually bright yellow in colour. This kind of Ethernet is often referred to as *thick Ethernet*, also called *10B5*, and the line interface is called *AUI*. You may also hear the term *yellow string* (for tying computers together), though this term is not limited to thick Ethernet. Thick Ethernet is now obsolete: it is expensive, difficult to lay, and relatively unreliable. It requires 50 Ω resistors at each end of the cable to transmit signals correctly. If you leave these out, you won't get degraded performance: the network Will Not Work at all.

2. As the name suggests, *thin Ethernet* is thin coaxial cable, and otherwise quite like thick Ethernet. It is significantly cheaper (thus the term *Cheapernet*), and the only disadvantage over thick Ethernet is that the cables can't be quite as long. The cable is called *RG58*, and the cable connectors are called *BNC*. Both terms are frequently used to refer to this kind of connection, as is *10 Base 2*. You'll still see thin Ethernet around, but since it's effectively obsolete. Performance is poor, and it's no cheaper than 100 Mb/s Ethernet. Like thick Ethernet, all machines are connected by a single cable with terminators at each end.

3. Modern Ethernets run at up to 1000 Mb/s over multi-pair cables called *UTP*, for *Unshielded Twisted Pair*. *Twisted pair* means that each pair of wires are twisted to minimize external electrical influence—after all, the frequencies on a 1000 Mb/s Ethernet are way up in the UHF range. Unlike coaxial connections, where all machines are connected to a single cable, UTP connects individual machines to a *hub* or a *switch*, a box that distributes the signals. We'll discuss the difference between a hub and a switch on page 288. You'll also hear the terms *10BaseTP*, *100BaseTP* and *1000BaseTP*.

Compared to coaxial Ethernet, UTP cables are much cheaper, and they are more reliable. If you damage or disconnect a coaxial cable, the whole network goes down. If you damage a UTP cable, you only lose the one machine connected to it. On the down side, UTP requires switches or hubs, which cost money, though the price has decreased to the point where it's cheaper to buy a cheap switch and UTP cables rather than the RG58 cable alone. UTP systems employ a star architecture rather than the string of coaxial stations with terminators. You can connect many switches together simply by reversing the connections at one end of a switch-to-switch link. In addition, UTP is the only medium currently available that supports 100 Mb/s Ethernet.

How Ethernet works

A large number of systems can be connected to a single Ethernet. Each system has a 48 bit address, the so-called *Ethernet address*. Ethernet addresses are usually written in bytes separated by colons (:), for example 0:a0:24:37:0d:2b. All data sent over the Ethernet contains two addresses: the Ethernet address of the sender and the Ethernet address of the receiver. Normally, each system responds only to messages sent to it or to a special broadcast address.

You'll also frequently hear the term *MAC address*. *MAC* stands for *Media Access Control* and thus means the address used to access the network link layer. For Ethernets I prefer to use the more exact term *Ethernet address*.

The fact that multiple machines are on the same network gives rise to a problem: obviously only one system can transmit at any one time, or the data will be garbled. But how do you synchronize the systems? In traditional Ethernets, the answer is simple, but possibly surprising: trial and error. Before any interface transmits, it checks that the network is idle—in the Ethernet specification, this is called *Carrier Sense*. Unfortunately, this isn't enough: two systems might start sending at the same time. To solve this problem, while it sends, each system checks that it can still recognize what it is sending. If it can't, it assumes that another system has started sending at the same time—this is called a *collision*. When a collision occurs, both systems stop sending, wait a random amount of time, and try again. You'll see this method referred to as *CSMA/CD* (*Carrier Sense Multiple Access/Collision Detect*).

There are a number of problems with this approach:

- The interface needs to listen while sending, so it can't receive anything while it's sending: it's running in *half-duplex* mode. If it could send and receive at the same time (*full-duplex* mode), the network throughput could be doubled.

- The more active the network, the more likely collisions will be. This slows things down too, sometimes to a point where the network hardly transmits any traffic.

- The more systems on the network, the less bandwidth is available for each system.

With the point-to-point connections on a UTP-based network, you would think it would be possible to change some of this. After all, the connections look pretty much like the same wire that joins two modems together, and modems don't have collisions, and they do run in full-duplex mode. The problem is the hub: if you send a packet out to a hub, it doesn't know which connector to send it down, so it sends it down all of them, thus imitating the old Ethernet. To send it just to the destination, it would need to analyze the Ethernet address in every packet and know where to send it.

This is what a switch does: it learns the Ethernet addresses of each interface on the network and uses this information to send packets to only the line to which that interface is connected. There could be more than one if switches are cascaded. This also means that the line can run in full-duplex mode.

Nowadays the price differential between switches and hubs is very small; go into a computer market and you'll see that the prices overlap. If at all possible, buy a switch.

Transmitting Internet data across an Ethernet has another problem. Ethernet evolved independently of the Internet standards. As a result, Ethernets can carry different kinds of traffic. In particular, Microsoft uses a protocol called *NetBIOS*, and Novell uses a protocol called *IPX*. In addition, Internet addresses are only 32 bits, and it would be impossible to map them to Ethernet addresses even if they were the same length. The result? You guessed it, another header. Figure 16-5 shows an Ethernet packet carrying an IP datagram.

Finding Ethernet addresses

So we send messages to Ethernet interfaces by setting the correct Ethernet address in the header. But how do we find the Ethernet address? All our IP packets use IP addresses. And it's not a good solution to just statically assign Ethernet addresses to IP addresses: first, there would be problems if an interface board or an IP address was changed, and secondly multiple boards can have the same IP address.

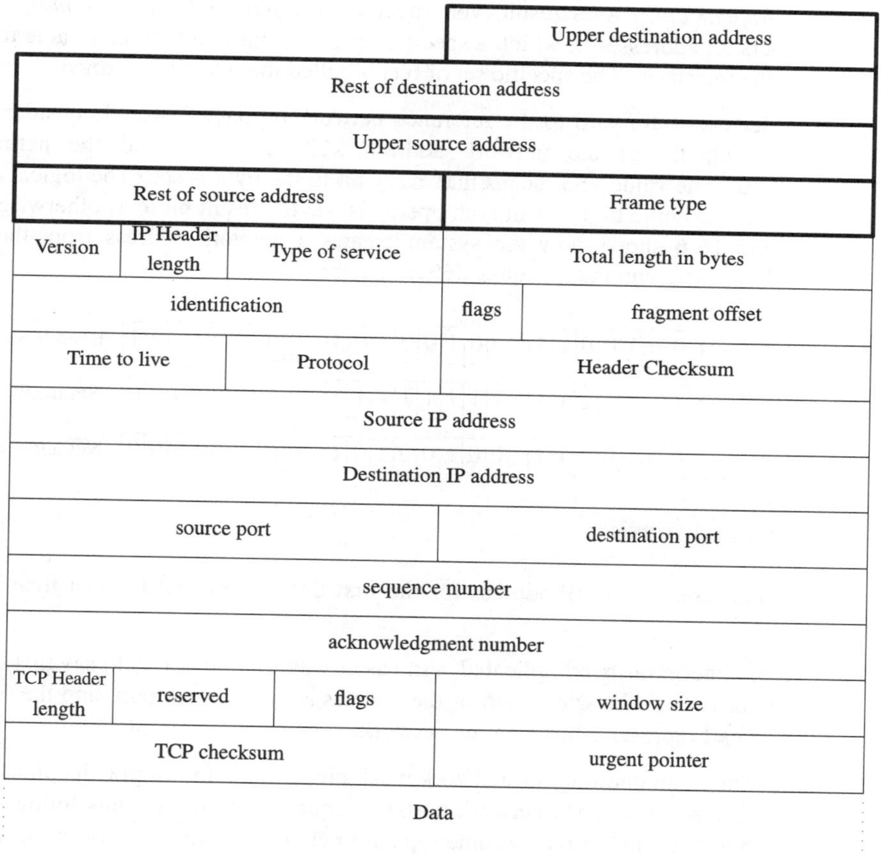

	Upper destination address	
Rest of destination address		
Upper source address		
Rest of source address		Frame type
Version	IP Header length	Type of service	Total length in bytes
identification		flags	fragment offset
Time to live	Protocol		Header Checksum
Source IP address		
Destination IP address		
source port		destination port
sequence number		
acknowledgment number		
TCP Header length	reserved	flags	window size
TCP checksum		urgent pointer

Data

Figure 16-5: Ethernet frame with TCP datagram

The chosen solution is the *Address Resolution Protocol*, usually called *ARP*. ARP sends out a message on the Ethernet broadcast address saying effectively "Who has IP address 223.147.37.1? Tell me your Ethernet address." The message is sent on the broadcast address, so each system on the net receives it. In each machine, the ARP protocol checks the specified IP address with the IP address of the interface that received the packet. If they match, the machine replies with the message "I am IP 223.147.37.1, my Ethernet address is 00:a0:24:37:0d:2b"

What systems are on that Ethernet?

Multiple systems can be accessed via an Ethernet, so there must be some means for a system to determine which other systems are present on the network. There might be a lot of them, several hundred for example. You could keep a list, but the system has to determine the interface for every single packet, and a list that long would slow things down. The preferred method is to specify a *range* of IP addresses that can be reached via a specific interface. The computer works in binary, so one of the easiest functions to perform is a *logical and*. As a result, you specify the range by a *network mask*: the system considers all addresses in which a specific set of bits have a particular value to be reachable via the interface. The specific set of bits is called the *interface address*.

For example, let's look forward to the reference network on page 294 and consider the local network, which has the network address 223.147.37.0 and the netmask 255.255.255.0. The value 255 means that every bit in the byte is set. The logical *and* function says "if a specific bit is set in both operands, set the result bit to 1; otherwise set it to 0." Figure 16-6 shows how the system creates a network address from the IP address 223.147.37.5 and the net mask 255.255.255.0.

1 1 0 1 1 1 1 1	1 0 0 1 0 0 1 1	0 0 1 0 0 1 0 1	0 0 0 0 0 1 0 1	IP address
1 1 1 1 1 1 1 1	1 1 1 1 1 1 1 1	1 1 1 1 1 1 1 1	0 0 0 0 0 0 0 0	Net mask
1 1 0 1 1 1 1 1	1 0 0 1 0 0 1 1	0 0 1 0 0 1 0 1	0 0 0 0 0 0 0 0	Net address

Figure 16-6: Net mask

The result is the same as the IP address for the first three bytes, but the last byte is 0: 223.147.37.0.

This may seem unnecessarily complicated. An easier way to look at it is to say that the *1* bits of the net mask describe which part of the address is the network part, and the *0* bits describe which part represents hosts on the network.

Theoretically you could choose your network mask bits at random. In practice, it's clear that it makes more sense to make network masks a sequence of binary 1 bits followed by a sequence of binary 0 bits. It has become typical to abbreviate the network mask to the number of 1 bits. Thus the network mask 255.255.255.0, with 24 bits set and 8 bits not set, is abbreviated to /24. The / character is always part of the abbreviation.

Address classes

When the Internet Protocols were first introduced, they included the concept of a default netmask. These categories of address were called *address classes*. The following classes are defined in RFC 1375:

Table 16-1: Address classes

Class	Address range	Network mask	Network address bits	Host address bits	Number of systems
A	0–127	255.0.0.0	/8	24	16777216
B	128–191	255.255.0.0	/16	16	65536
C	192–207	255.255.255.0	/24	8	256
F	208–215	255.255.255.240	/28	4	16
G	216–219	*(reserved)*			
H	220–221	255.255.255.248	/29	3	8
K	222–223	255.255.255.254	/31	1	2
D	224–239	*(multicast)*			
E	240–255	*(reserved)*			

This method is no longer used for specifying net masks, though the software still defaults to these values, but it is used for allocating networks. In addition you will frequently hear the term *Class C network* to refer to a network with 256 addresses in the range 192–223. This usage goes back to before RFC 1375.

Unroutable addresses

On occasion you may want to have addresses which are not visible on the global Internet, either for security reasons or because you want to run Network Address Translation (see page 393). RFC 1918 provides for three address ranges that should not be routed: 10.0.0.0/8 (with last address 10.255.255.255), 172.16.0.0/12 (with last address 172.31.255.255), and 192.168.0.0/16 (with last address 192.168.255.255).

Wireless LANs

An obvious problem with Ethernet is that you need a cable. As more and more machines are installed, the cabling can become a nightmare. It's particularly inconvenient for laptops: the network cable restricts where you can use the machine.

Wireless network cards have been around for some time, but in the last few years they have become particularly popular. Modern cards are built around the IEEE 802.11 series of standards.

> The 802 series of standards cover almost all networking devices; don't let the number 802 suggest wireless networking. Ethernet is 802.3, for example.

They are usually PCMCIA (PC Card) cards, though some PCI cards are also available. Currently you're liable to come across the following kinds of cards:

- *802.11 FHSS* (*Frequency Hopping Spread Spectrum*) cards, which run at up to 2 Mb/s. These are now obsolete, but FreeBSD still supports the WebGear Aviator card with the *ray* driver.

- *802.11 DSSS* (*Discrete Sequence Spread Spectrum*) cards, which also run at up to 2 Mb/s. These are also obsolete.

- *802.11b DSSS* cards, which run at up to 11 Mb/s. They can interoperate with the slower 802.11 DSSS cards, but not with FHSS cards.

- *802.11a* cards, which run at 54 Mb/s. They use a modulation called *Orthogonal Frequency Division Multiplexing* or *OFDM*, and run in the 5 GHz band. They are not compatible with older cards. At the time of writing, they have not achieved significant market penetration. FreeBSD does not support them yet, though that may have changed by the time you read this.

- *802.11g* cards are the newest. Like 802.11a, they which run at 54 Mb/s, and they're not supported. Again, that may have changed by the time you read this. Like 802.11b, they run in the 2.4 GHz band.

Most current cards are 802.11b and run at up to 11 Mb/s. We'll concentrate on them in the rest of this section. They operate in the 2.4 GHz band, which is shared with a number of other services, including some portable telephones and microwave ovens. This kind of portable telephone can completely disrupt a wireless network. Interference and range are serious issues: wireless networks are generally not as reliable as wired networks.

Wireless cards can operate in up to three different modes:

- Normally, they interoperate with an *access point*, also called a *base station*. The base station is normally connected to an external network, so it also doubles as a gateway. Unlike Ethernets, however, all traffic in the network goes via the base station. This arrangement is called a *Basic Service Set* or *BSS*.

  Networks can have multiple base stations which are usually interconnected via a wired Ethernet. If the machine with the wireless card moves around, the base stations negotiate with the machine to decide which base station handles the card. In this manner, the machines can cover large distances without losing network connection. This arrangement is called an *Extended Basic Service Set* or *EBSS*.

  This mode of operation, with or without an EBSS, is called *managed mode*, *infrastructure mode* or *BSS mode*.

- In smaller networks, the cards can interact directly. This mode of operation is called *peer-to-peer mode*, *ad-hoc mode* or *IBSS mode* (for *Independent Basic Service Set*).

- Finally, some cards support a method called *Lucent demo ad-hoc mode*, which some BSD implementations used to call *ad-hoc mode*. But it's not the same as the previous method, and though the principle is the same, they can't interoperate. This mode is not standardized, and there are significant interoperability issues with it, so even if it's available you should use IBSS mode.

How wireless networks coexist

Wireless networks have a number of issues that don't affect Ethernets. In particular, multiple networks can share the same geographical space. In most large cities you'll find that practically the entire area is shared by multiple networks. This raises a number of issues:

- There's only so much bandwidth available. As the number of networks increase, the throughput drops.

  There's no complete solution to this problem, but it's made a little easier by the availability of multiple operating frequencies. Depending on the country, 802.11b cards can have between 11 and 14 frequency channels. If your area has a lot of traffic on the frequency you're using, you may be able to solve the problem by moving to another frequency. That doesn't mean that this many networks can coexist in the same space: as the name *spread spectrum* indicates, the signal wanders off to either side of the base frequency, and in practice you can use only three or four distinct channels.

- Cards on a given network need to have a way to identify each other.

  802.11 solves this issue by requiring a network identification, called a *Service Set Identifier* or *SSID*. All networks have an SSID, though frequently base stations will accept connections from cards that supply a blank SSID. SSIDs don't offer any improvement in security: their only purpose is identifying the network.

- Cards on a given network need to protect themselves against snooping by people who don't belong to the network.

  The 802.11 standard offers a partial solution to this issue by optionally encrypting the packets. We'll look at this issue below.

Encryption

As mentioned above, security is a big issue in wireless networks. The encryption provided is called *Wired Equivalent Privacy* or *WEP*, and it's not very good. Everybody connecting to the network needs to know the WEP key, so if anybody loses permission to access the network (for example, when changing jobs), the WEP keys need to be changed, which is a serious administrative problem. In some cases it's completely impractical: if you want to access a wireless network in an airport or a coffee shop (where they're becoming more and more common), it's not practical to use a WEP key. In fact, nearly all such public access networks don't use encryption at all.

As if that weren't bad enough, the WEP algorithm is flawed. Depending on the circumstances, it can take less than 10 minutes to crack it. Don't trust it.

So how do you protect yourself? The best solution is, of course, don't use wireless networks for confidential work. If you have to use a wireless network, make sure that anything confidential is encrypted end-to-end, for example with an *ssh* tunnel, which we'll look at on page 424.

The reference network

One of the problems in talking about networks is that there are so many different kinds of network connection. To simplify things, this book bases on one of the most frequent environments: a number of computers connected together by an Ethernet LAN with a single gateway to the Internet. Figure 16-7 shows the layout of the network to which we will refer in the rest of this book.

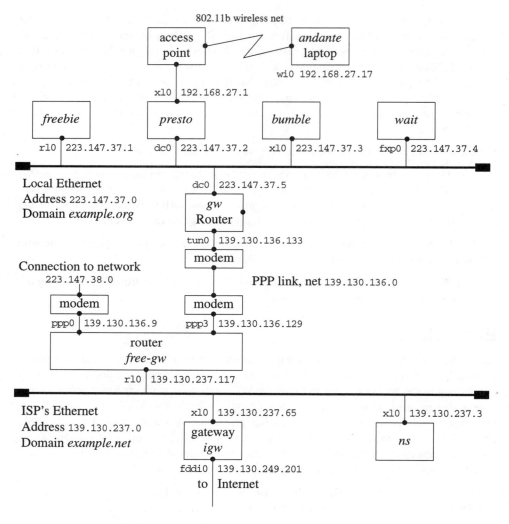

Figure 16-7: Reference network

This figure contains a lot of information, which we will examine in detail in the course of the text:

- The boxes in the top row represent the systems in the local network example.org: *freebie, presto, bumble*, and *wait*.

- The line underneath is the local Ethernet. The network has the address 223.147.37.0. It has a full 256 addresses ("Class C"), so the network mask is 255.255.255.0.

- The machines on this Ethernet belong to the domain *example.org*. Thus, the full name of *bumble* is *bumble.example.org*. We'll look at these names in Chapter 21.

- The connections from the systems to the Ethernet are identified by two values: on the left is the *interface name*, and on the right the address associated with the interface name.

- Further down the diagram is the router, gw. It has two interfaces: dc0 interfaces to the Ethernet, and tun0 interfaces to the PPP line to the ISP. Each interface has a different addresses.

- The lower half of the diagram shows part of the ISP's network. It also has an Ethernet, and its router looks very much like our own. On the other hand, it interfaces to a third network via the machine *igw*. To judge by the name of the interface, it is a *FDDI* connection—see page 285 for more details.

- The ISP runs a name server on the machine ns, address 139.130.237.3.

- The ends of the Ethernets are thickened. This represents the *terminators* required at the end of a coaxial Ethernet. We talked about them on page 287. In fact this network is a 100 Mb/s switched network, but they are still conventionally represented in this form. You can think of the Ethernets as the switches that control each network.

- *presto* has a wireless access point connected to it. The diagram shows one laptop, *andante*, connected via a NAT interface.

17

Configuring the local network

In Chapter 16 we looked at the basic concepts surrounding BSD networking. In this chapter and the following two, we'll look at what we need to do to configure a network, first manually, then automatically. Configuring *PPP* is still a whole lot more difficult than configuring an Ethernet, and they require more prerequisites, so we'll dedicate Chapter 20, to that issue.

In this chapter, we'll first look at *example.org* in the reference network on page 294, since it's the easiest to set up. After that, we'll look at what additional information is needed to configure machines on *example.net*.

Network configuration with sysinstall

To configure a network, you must describe its configuration to the system. The system initialization routines that we discussed on page 528 include a significant portion that sets up the network environment. In addition, the system contains a number of standard IP configuration files that define your system's view of the network. If you didn't configure the network when you installed your system, you can still do it now. Log in as root and start *sysinstall*. Select the Index, then Network Interfaces. You will see the menu of Figure 17-1, which is the same as in Figure 6-4 on page 97. On a standard 80x25 display it requires scrolling to see the entire menu. The only real network board on this list is *xl0*, the Ethernet board. The others are standard hardware that can also be used as network interfaces.

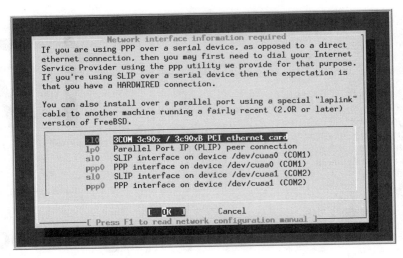

Figure 17-1: Network setup menu

Choose the Ethernet board, *xl0* You get a question about whether you want to use IPv6 configuration. In this book we doesn't discuss IPv6, so answer No. Next you get a question about DHCP configuration. We discuss DHCP configuration on page 302. If you already have a DHCP server set up, you may prefer to answer Yes to this question, which is all you need to do. If you answer No, the next menu asks us to set the internet parameters. Figure 17-2 shows the network configuration menu after filling in the values.

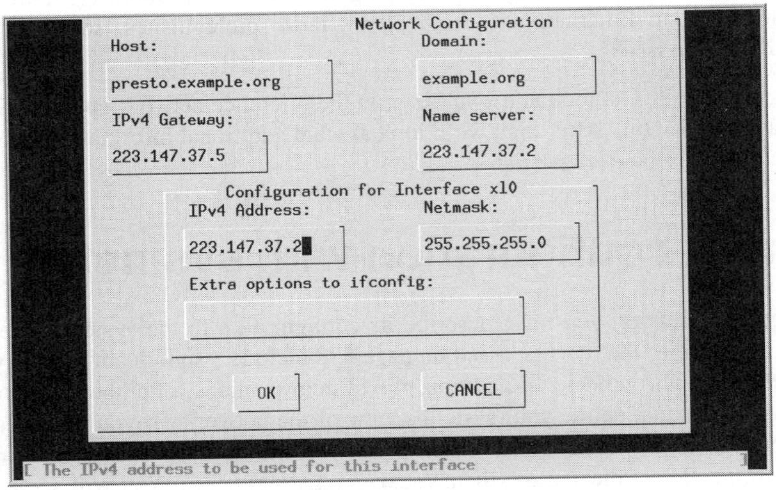

Figure 17-2: Network configuration menu

Specify the fully qualified local host name. When you tab to the Domain: field, the domain is filled in automatically. We have chosen to call this machine *presto*, and the domain is *example.org*. In other words, the full name of the machine is *presto.example.org*. Its IP address is 223.147.37.2. In this configuration, all access to the outside world goes via *gw.example.org*, which has the IP address 223.147.37.5. The name server is located on the same host, *presto.example.org*. If the name server isn't running when this information is needed, we must specify all addresses in numeric form, as shown.

What happens if you don't have a domain name? If you're connecting to the global Internet, you should go out and get one—see page 318. But in the meantime, don't fake it. Just leave the fields empty. If you're not connecting to the Internet, of course, it doesn't make much difference what name you choose.

As is usual for a class C network, the net mask is 255.255.255.0. You don't need to fill in this information—if you leave this field without filling it in, *sysinstall* inserts it for you. Normally, as in this case, you wouldn't need any additional options to *ifconfig*.

sysinstall saves configuration information in */etc/rc.conf*. When the system starts, the startup scripts use this information to configure the network. It also optionally starts the interface immediately. In the next section we'll look at the commands it uses to perform this function.

Manual network configuration

Usually FreeBSD configures your network automatically when it boots. To do so, it uses the configuration files in */etc*. So why do it manually? There are several reasons:

- It makes it easier to create and maintain the configuration files if you know what's going on behind the scenes.

- It makes it easier to modify something "on the fly." You don't have to reboot just because you have changed your network configuration.

- With this information, you can edit the configuration files directly rather than use the menu interface, which saves a lot of time.

> We spend a lot of time discussing this point on the FreeBSD mailing lists. One thing's for sure: neither method of configuration is perfect. Both menu-based and text-file–based configuration schemes offer you ample opportunity to shoot yourself in the foot. But at the moment, the configuration file system is easier to check *if you understand what's going on*. That's the reason for the rest of this chapter.

In this section, we'll look at the manual way to do things first, and then we'll see how to put it in the configuration files so that it gets done automatically next time. You can find a summary of the configuration files and their contents on page 551.

Describing your network

In Table 16-7 on page 294, we saw that systems connect to networks via *network interfaces*. The kernel detects the interfaces automatically when it starts, but you still need to tell it what interfaces are connected to which networks, and even more importantly, which address your system has on each network. In addition, if the network is a *broadcast* network, such as an Ethernet, you need to specify a range of addresses that can be reached directly on that network. As we saw on page 290, we perform this selection with the *network mask*.

Ethernet interfaces

Once we have understood these concepts, it's relatively simple to use the *ifconfig* program to set them. For example, for the Ethernet interface on system *gw*, with IP address 223.147.37.5, we need to configure interface *dc0*. The network mask is the standard value for a class C network, 255.255.255.0. That's all we need to know:

```
# ifconfig dc0 inet 223.147.37.5 netmask 255.255.255.0 up
```

In fact, this is more than you usually need. The inet tells the interface to use Internet protocol Version 4 (the default), and up tells it to bring it up (which it does anyway). In addition, this is a class C network address, so the net mask defaults to 255.255.255.0. As a result, you can abbreviate this to:

```
# ifconfig dc0 223.147.37.5
```

Note that this is different from what Linux requires. With Linux you must supply explicit netmask and broadcast address specifications.

As we saw on page 290, it has become typical to abbreviate net masks to the character / followed by the number of 1 bits set in the network mask. *ifconfig* understands this usage, so if you wanted to set a non-standard network mask of, say, 255.255.255.240, which has 28 bits set, you could write:

```
# ifconfig dc0 223.147.37.5/28
```

Point-to-point interfaces

With a point-to-point interface, the software currently requires you to specify the IP address of the other end of the link as well. As we shall see in Chapter 20, there is no good reason to do this, but *ifconfig* insists on it. In addition, we need the network mask for a non-broadcast medium. The value is obvious:[1] you can reach exactly one address at the other end, so it must be 255.255.255.255. With this information, we could configure the PPP interface on *gw*:

```
# ifconfig tun0 139.130.136.133 139.130.136.129 netmask 255.255.255.255
```

---

1. Well, you'd think it was obvious. We'll see on page 345 that some people think it should be something else.

In fact, this is almost never necessary; in Chapter 20 we'll see that the PPP software usually sets the configuration automatically.

The loopback interface

The IP protocols require you to use an address to communicate with every system—even your own system. Theoretically, you could communicate with your system via the an Ethernet interface, but this is relatively slow: the data would have to go through the network stack. Instead, there is a special interface for communicating with other processes in the same system, the *loopback interface*. Its name is *lo0*, and it has the address 127.0.0.1. It's straightforward enough to configure:

```
# ifconfig lo0 127.0.0.1
```

In fact, though, you don't even need to do this much work: the system automatically sets it up at boot time.

Checking the interface configuration

ifconfig doesn't just set the configuration: you can also use it to check the configuration. It's a good idea to do this after you change something:

```
$ ifconfig
dc0: flags=8843<UP,BROADCAST,RUNNING,SIMPLEX,MULTICAST> mtu 1500
        inet 223.147.37.5 netmask 0xffffff00 broadcast 223.147.37.255
        inet6 fe80::280:c6ff:fef9:d3fa%dc0 prefixlen 64 scopeid 0x1
        ether 00:80:c6:f9:d3:fa
        media: Ethernet autoselect (100baseTX <full-duplex>)
        status: active
lp0: flags=8810<POINTOPOINT,SIMPLEX,MULTICAST> mtu 1500
lo0: flags=8049<UP,LOOPBACK,RUNNING,MULTICAST> mtu 16384
        inet6 ::1 prefixlen 128
        inet6 fe80::1%lo0 prefixlen 64 scopeid 0x3
        inet 127.0.0.1 netmask 0xff000000
tun0: flags=8051<UP,POINTOPOINT,RUNNING,MULTICAST> mtu 1500
        inet 139.130.136.133 --> 139.130.136.129 netmask 0xffffffff
```

> Other BSD systems require you to write *ifconfig -a.* to list the configuration of all interfaces, and FreeBSD still accepts it. Some commercial UNIX systems don't understand even this flag.

There are a number of things to note here:

- The *dc0* interface has both an IPv4 address (inet) and a corresponding IPv6 address (inet6). It also specifies the Ethernet address (ether 00:80:c6:f9:d3:fa). It is capable of negotiating 10 Mb/s, 100 Mb/s half duplex and 100 Mb/s full duplex. It's connected to a switch, so it's currently running 100 Mb/s full duplex.

- The interface *lp0* is the the *PLIP* interface for connections via the parallel port. It is not configured (in other words, it has not been set up for operation).

- We've already seen the loopback interface *lo0*.

- There is also a *tun0* interface for PPP.

The configuration files

The system startup scripts summarize this configuration information in a number of *configuration variables*. See Chapter 29 for more details. At the moment, the following variables are of interest to us:

- hostname is the name of the host. You should have set it when you installed the system (see page 87). You can also set it manually with the *hostname* command:

  ```
  # hostname -s gw.example.org
  ```

- For each interface, a variable of the form ifconfig_*interface* contains the parameters to be passed to *ifconfig* to configure that interface.

Previously, FreeBSD also required you to set a variable network_interfaces, a list of the names of the interfaces to be configured. This variable now defaults to the value auto to specify that all interfaces should be configured. You only need to change it if you specifically want to exclude an interface from configuration.

For *gw*, we put the following information in */etc/rc.conf*:

```
hostname="gw.example.org"
ifconfig_dc0="inet 223.147.37.5"
```

We don't configure the *tun0* interface here; as we'll see in Chapter 20, the PPP setup works differently.

Automatic configuration with DHCP

Maintaining the network configurations for a number of machines can be a pain, especially if they're laptops that come and go. There's an alternative for larger networks: use *DHCP*, the *Dynamic Host Configuration Protocol*. DHCP enables a machine to get configuration information automatically from the network. The concept is expandable, but typically you get an IP address and net mask and the names of the default name servers and routers. In terms of the configuration we've seen so far, this replaces running the *ifconfig* and *route* programs, and also the file */etc/resolv.conf*, which describes the locations of name servers. We'll look at it on page 366.

There are two parts to DHCP: the client and the server.

DHCP client

To get a configuration, you run *dhclient*. In previous releases of FreeBSD, *dhclient* printed out information about the addresses it received. In Release 5, it does not print anything. Simply start it with the name of the interface:

```
# dhclient dc0
```

To assign an address automatically at boot time, put the special value DHCP in the ifconfig_dc0 variable:

```
ifconfig_dc0=DHCP
```

DHCP server

DHCP requires a server. The server is not included as part of the base system; instead, install the *net/isc-dhcp3* port:

```
# cd /usr/ports/net/isc-dhcp3
# make install
```

To configure *dhcpd*, edit the configuration file */usr/local/etc/isc-dhcpd.conf*. Here's an example:

```
ddns-update-style ad-hoc;

# 100 Mb/s Ethernet
subnet 223.147.37.0 netmask 255.255.255.0 {
   range 223.147.37.90 223.147.37.110;
   option domain-name-servers freebie.example.com, presto.example.com;
   option domain-name "example.com";
   option routers gw.example.com;
   option subnet-mask 255.255.255.0;
   option broadcast-address 223.147.37.255;
   default-lease-time 86400;
   max-lease-time 259200;
   use-host-decl-names on;                         use the specified name as host name
   host andante {
      hardware ethernet 0:50:da:cf:7:35;
   }
}
```

This configuration file tells *dhcpd*:

- To dynamically allocate IP addresses in the range 223.147.37.90 to 223.147.37.110 (range keyword).

- That the domain name servers are *freebie.example.com* and *andante.example.com*. We'll look at domain name servers in Chapter 21.

- The net mask and the broadcast address.

The variables default-lease-time and max-lease-time, which are specified in seconds, determine how long it will be before a system checks its configuration. The values here represent one day and three days respectively.

use-host-decl-names tells *dhcpd* to use the name on the host line as the host name of the system. Otherwise you would need an additional option host-name specification for every system. For one machine it doesn't make much difference, but if you have twenty such machines, you'll notice the difference.

One of the problems with *dhcpd* is that by default it doesn't allocate a static IP address. Theoretically you could attach a laptop to the same DHCP server and get a different address every time, but in fact *dhcpd* does its best to keep the same address, and sometimes you may find it impossible to change its mind. In this configuration file, though, we have explicitly told *dhcpd* about *andante*, which is recognized by its Ethernet address. This works relatively well for fixed machines, but there's a problem with laptops and PC Card: *dhcpd* recognizes the network interface, not the machine, and if you swap the interface card, the IP address moves to the new machine.

Starting dhcpd

The *dhcpd* port installs a sample startup file in the directory */usr/local/etc/rc.d*. It's called *isc-dhcpd.sh.sample*, a name which ensures that it won't get executed. This file doesn't normally require any configuration; simply copy it to *isc-dhcpd.sh* in the same directory. This enables the system startup to find it and start *dhcpd*.

To start *dhcpd* during normal system operation, just run this same script:

```
# /usr/local/etc/rc.d/isc-dhcpd.sh start
Mar 14 15:45:09 freebie dhcpd: Internet Software Consortium DHCP Server V3.0rc10
Mar 14 15:45:09 freebie dhcpd: Copyright 1995-2001 Internet Software Consortium.
Mar 14 15:45:09 freebie dhcpd: All rights reserved.
Mar 14 15:45:09 freebie dhcpd: For info, please visit http://www.isc.org/products/DHCP
Mar 14 15:45:09 freebie dhcpd: Wrote 0 deleted host decls to leases file.
Mar 14 15:45:09 freebie dhcpd: Wrote 0 new dynamic host decls to leases file.
Mar 14 15:45:09 freebie dhcpd: Wrote 14 leases to leases file.
Mar 14 15:45:09 freebie dhcpd: Listening on BPF/xl0/00:50:da:cf:07:35/223.147.37.0/24
Mar 14 15:45:09 freebie dhcpd: Sending on   BPF/xl0/00:50:da:cf:07:35/223.147.37.0/24
Mar 14 15:45:09 freebie dhcpd: Sending on   Socket/fallback/fallback-net
```

When you change the configuration file */usr/local/etc/isc-dhcpd.conf*, you must restart *dhcpd*:

```
# /usr/local/etc/rc.d/isc-dhcpd.sh restart
```

Configuring PC Card networking cards

We've looked at PC Card devices on page 159, but there are some special issues involved in configuring networking cards. Of course, *ifconfig* works with PC Card networking cards in exactly the same way as it does with PCI and ISA cards, but you can't configure them in the same manner at startup, because they might not yet be present.

On inserting a PC Card device, you will see something like this on the console:

```
Manufacturer ID: 01015751
Product version: 5.0
Product name: 3Com Corporation | 3CCFE575BT | LAN Cardbus Card | 001 |
Functions: Network Adaptor, Memory
CIS reading done
cardbus0: Resource not specified in CIS: id=14, size=80
cardbus0: Resource not specified in CIS: id=18, size=80
xl0: <3Com 3c575B Fast Etherlink XL> port 0x1080-0x10bf mem 0x88002400-0x8800247
```

```
f,0x88002480-0x880024ff irq 11 at device 0.0 on cardbus0
xl0: Ethernet address: 00:10:4b:f8:fd:20
miibus0: <MII bus> on xl0
tdkphy0: <TDK 78Q2120 media interface> on miibus0
tdkphy0: 10baseT, 10baseT-FDX, 100baseTX, 100baseTX-FDX, auto
```

After this, *ifconfig* shows:

```
$ ifconfig xl0
xl0: flags=8802<BROADCAST,SIMPLEX,MULTICAST> mtu 1500
        ether 00:10:4b:f8:fd:20
        media: Ethernet autoselect (100baseTX <full-duplex>)
```

The card is there, but it's not configured. FreeBSD uses the *devd* daemon to perform userland configuration after a card has been attached. We've already looked at *devd* on page 159. When *devd* establishes that the card is a networking card, it calls */etc/pccard_ether* to configure it. In the following, we'll see how */etc/pccard_ether* configures our *xl0* interface. It performs the following steps:

- It reads the configuration from */etc/defaults/rc.conf* and */etc/rc.conf*.

- If the interface is already up, it exits.

- If a file */etc/start_if.xl0* exists, it executes it. After doing so, it continues.

- It checks whether the variable `removable_interfaces` exists and contains the name of the interface, *xl0*. If not, it continues.

- If the value of `ifconfig_xl0` is NO, it exits.

- If the value of `ifconfig_xl0` is DHCP, it attempts to set up the interface with DHCP.

- Otherwise it performs the *ifconfig* commands specified in the variable `ifconfig_xl0`.

That's a lot of choice. What do you use when? That depends on what you want to do. The first thing to note is that nothing happens unless your interface name is in the variable `removable_interfaces`, and the variable `ifconfig_xl0` exists. The question is, what do you put in `ifconfig_xl0`?

In principle, it's the same as with other network cards: either IP address and other options, or DHCP. The third alternative is important, though. Let's consider the case where you want to start a number of services when the system is connected. You might want to run *ntpdate*, then start *ntpd* and *rwhod*, and you may want to mount some NFS file systems. You can do all this at startup with normal network cards, but */etc/pccard_ether* isn't clever enough to do all that. Instead, create a file called */etc/start_if.xl0* and give it the following contents:

```
dhclient xl0
ntpdate freebie
killall ntpd
ntpd &
killall rwhod
rwhod &
mount -t nfs -a
```

Don't forget to start DHCP or otherwise set the IP address, because this method bypasses the standard startups.

In addition, you put this in */etc/rc.conf*:

```
devd_enable=YES
ifconfig_xl0=NO
removable_interfaces="wi0 xe0 xl0"
```

The values in the last line only need to include *xl0*, of course, but it's good to put in every interface name that you would possibly use.

Detaching network cards

When you remove a network card, *devd* invokes */etc/pccard_ether* again. The actions are similar to the one it performs when the card is attached:

- If a file */etc/stop_if.xl0* exists, it is executed.

- If the variable ifconfig_xl0 is set to DHCP, */etc/pccard_ether* stops the *dhclient* process, which would otherwise loop forever.

- If ifconfig_xl0 contains normal *ifconfig* parameters, */etc/pccard_ether* removes any static routes for that interface.

If you travel elsewhere with a laptop and suspend the system, make sure you unmount any NFS file systems first. You can't do it once you're no longer connected to the network, and it's possible that things will hang trying to access NFS-mounted files.

Setting up wireless networking

We saw in Chapter 16 that wireless cards have a few more tricks up their sleeves than conventional Ethernets. To set them up correctly, you need to know:

- Does the network you are joining accept connections with a blank SSID? If not, what is its SSID?

- What mode are you running in? Is it BSS mode, IBSS mode, or Lucent demo ad-hoc?

- If you're running in IBSS or Lucent demo ad-hoc mode, you'll need to know the frequency (channel) on which the network is running.

- If you're running in IBSS mode, do you already have an IBSS, or is your machine going to be the IBSS?

- Are you worried about power consumption? If you're running in BSS mode, you can significantly reduce the power consumption of the card by turning on power save mode, but it can slow some things down.

• Are you using WEP? If so, what's the key?

Each of these translates into an *ifconfig* command. Here are some typical examples:

```
ifconfig wi0 ssid Example                         join Example network
ifconfig wi0 media autoselect mediaopt -adhoc     set BSS mode
ifconfig wi0 channel 3                            select channel 3 (if not in BSS mode)
ifconfig wi0 wepmode on                           turn encryption on (if using WEP)
ifconfig wi0 wepkey 0x42726f6b21                  encryption key (for WEP)
```

When setting media options, you must also select the media, even if it is unchanged; thus the `media autoselect` in the example above.

You have a choice of where to put these specifications. For example, if you were connecting to the *Example* network, which is IBSS, you could put this in your */etc/rc.conf*:

```
devd_enable=YES
ifconfig_wi0="192.168.27.4 ssid Example media autoselect mediaopt adhoc \
            channel 3 wepmode on wepkey 0x42726f6b21
removable_interfaces="wi0 xe0 xl0"
```

You don't need to do anything special to become an IBSS master in an IBSS network: if there is no master already, and your card supports it, your system will become the IBSS master.

If, on the other hand, you were connecting to a non-encrypted network, you would not need the WEP key, and you might enter:

```
ifconfig_wi0="192.168.27.4 ssid Example media autoselect mediaopt ibss-master channe
1 3 wepmode off"
```

What we can do now

At this point, we have configured the link layer. We can communicate with directly connected machines. To communicate with machines that are not directly connected, we need to set up *routing*. We'll look at that next.

Routing

Looking back at our example network on page 294, we'll reconsider a problem we met there: when a system receives a normal data packet, what does it do with it? There are four possibilities:

1. If the packet is a broadcast packet, or if it's addressed to one of its interface addresses, it delivers it locally.

2. If it's addressed to a system to which it has a direct connection, it sends it to that system.

3. If it's not addressed to a system to which it is directly connected, but it knows a system that knows what to do with the packet, it sends the packet to that system.

4. If none of the above apply, it discards the packet.

Table 17-1: The routing table

Destination	Gateway	Net mask	Type	Interface
127.0.0.1	127.0.0.1	255.0.0.0	Host	lo0
223.147.37.0		255.255.255.0	Direct	dc0
139.130.136.129	139.130.136.133	255.255.255.255	Host	tun0
default	139.130.136.129	0.0.0.0	Gateway	tun0

These decisions are the basis of *routing*. The implementation performs them with the aid of a *routing table*, which tells the system which addresses are available where. We've already seen the *net mask* in Chapter 16, on page 290. We'll see that it also plays a significant role in the routing decision. Table 17-1 shows a symbolic view of the routing table for *gw.example.org*. It looks very similar to the *ifconfig* output in the previous section:

- The first entry is the *loopback* entry: it shows that the local host can be reached by the interface *lo0*, which is the name for the loopback interface on all UNIX systems. Although this entry specifies a single host, the net mask allows for 16,276,778 hosts. The other addresses aren't used.

- The second entry is for the local Ethernet. In this case, we have a direct connection, so we don't need to specify a gateway address. Due to the net mask 255.255.255.0, this entry accounts for all addresses from 223.147.37.0 to 223.147.37.255.

  This entry also emphasizes the difference between the output of *ifconfig* and the routing table. *ifconfig* shows the address of the interface, the address needed to reach our system. For the Ethernet interface, it's 223.147.37.5. The routing table shows the addresses that can be reached *from* this system, so it shows the base address of the Ethernet, 223.147.37.0.

- The third entry represents the PPP interface. It is a host entry, like the loopback entry. This entry allows access to the other end of the PPP link only, so the net mask is set to 255.255.255.255 (only one system).

- Finally, the fourth entry is the big difference. It doesn't have a counterpart in the *ifconfig* listing. It specifies how to reach any address not already accounted for—just about the whole Internet. In this case, it refers to the other end address of the PPP link.

And that's all there is to it! Well, sort of. In our example configuration, we're hidden in one corner of the Internet, and there's only one way out to the rest of the network. Things look different when you are connected to more than one network. On page 310 we'll look at the differences we need for the ISP *example.net*. In the middle of the Internet, things are even more extreme. There may be dozens of interfaces, and the choice of a route for a particular address may be much more complicated. In such an environment, two problems occur:

- The concept of a default route no longer has much significance. If each interface carries roughly equal traffic, you really need to specify the interface for each network or group of networks. As a result, the routing tables can become enormous.

- There are probably multiple ways to route packets destined for a specific system. Obviously, you should choose the best route. But what happens if it fails or becomes congested? Then it's not the best route any more. This kind of change happens frequently enough that humans can't keep up with it—you need to run *routing software* to manage the routing table.

Adding routes automatically

FreeBSD comes with all the currently available routing software, primarily the daemon *routed*. The newer *gated* used to be included as well, but it is no longer available for free. It is available from *http://www.nexthop.com/products/howto_order.shtml*. An alternative in the Ports Collection is *zebra*.

All these daemons have one thing in common: you don't need them. At any rate, you don't need them until you have at least two different connections to the Internet, and even then it's not sure. As a result, we won't discuss them here. If you do need to run routing daemons, read all about them in *TCP/IP Network Administration*, by Craig Hunt.

From our point of view, however, the routing protocols have one particular significance: the system expects the routing table to be updated automatically. As a result, it is designed to use the information supplied by the routing protocols to perform the update. This information consists of two parts:

- The address and netmask of the network (in other words, the address range).

- The address of the *gateway* that forwards data for this address range. The gateway is a directly connected system, so it also figures in the routing table.

Adding routes manually

As we saw in the previous section, the routing software uses only addresses, and not the interface name. To add routes manually, we have to give the same information.

The program that adds routes manually is called *route*. We need it to add routes to systems other than those to which we are directly connected.

To set up the routing tables for the systems connected only to our reference network (*freebie*, *presto*, *bumble* and *wait*), we could write:

```
# route add default gw
```

During system startup, the script */etc/rc.network* performs this operation automatically if you set the following variable in */etc/rc.conf*:

```
defaultrouter="223.147.37.5"      # Set to default gateway (or NO).
```

Note that we enter the address of the default router as an IP address, not a name. This command is executed before the name server is running. We can't change the sequence in which we start the processes: depending on where our name server is, we may need to have the route in place to access the name server.

On system *gw*, the default route goes via the *tun0* interface:

```
# defaultrouter="139.130.136.129" # Set to default gateway (or NO).
gateway_enable="YES"              # Set to YES if this host will be a gateway.
```

This is a PPP interface, so you don't need a `defaultrouter` entry; if you did, it would look like the commented-out entry above. On page 347 we'll see how PPP sets the default route.

We need to enable gateway functionality on this system, since it receives data packets on behalf of other systems. We'll look at this issue in more depth on page 313.

ISP's route setup

At the ISP site, things are slightly more complicated than at *example.org*. Let's look at the gateway machine *free-gw.example.net*. It has three connections, to the global Internet, to *example.org* and to another network, *biguser.com* (the network serviced by interface *ppp0*). To add the routes requires something like the following commands:

```
# route add default 139.130.237.65          igw.example.net
# route add -net 223.147.37.0 139.130.136.133   gw.example.org
# route add -net 223.147.38.0 -iface ppp0       local ppp0 interface
```

The first line tells the system that the default route is via *gw.example.org*. The second shows that the network with the base IP address 223.147.37.0 (*example.org*) can be reached via the gateway address 139.130.136.133, which is the remote end of the PPP link connected via *ppp3*. In the case of *biguser.com*, we don't know the address of the remote end; possibly it changes every time it's connected. As a result, we specify the name of the interface instead: we know it's always connected via *ppp0*.

The procedure to add this information to */etc/rc.conf* is similar to what we did for the interface addresses:

- The variable `static_routes` contains a list of the static routes that are to be configured.

- For each route, a variable corresponding to the route name specified in `static_routes`, with the text `route_` prepended. Unlike the interfaces, you can assign any name you want to them, as long as it starts with `route_`. It makes sense for them to be related to the domain name, but they don't have to. For example, we would have liked to have called our network *freebie.org*, but there's a good chance that this name has been taken, so we called it *example.org* instead. The old name lives on in the name of the route, `route_freebie`. In the case of *biguser.com*, we have called the route variable `route_biguser`.

We put the following entries into *free-gw*'s */etc/rc.conf*:

```
defaultrouter="139.130.237.65" # Set to default gateway (or NO).
static_routes="freebie biguser" # list of static routes
route_freebie="-net 223.147.37.0 139.130.237.129"
route_biguser="-net 223.147.38.0 139.130.237.9"
```

Looking at the routing tables

You can show the routing tables with the *netstat* tool. Option `-r` shows the routing tables. For example, on `freebie` you might see:

```
# netstat -r
Routing tables

Internet:
Destination    Gateway             Flags    Refs      Use    Netif Expire
default        gw                  UGSc        9     8732    rl0
localhost      localhost           UH          0     1255    lo0
223.147.37     link#2              UC          0        0
presto         0:0:c0:44:a5:68     UHLW       13   139702    rl0   1151
freebie        0:a0:24:37:d:2b     UHLW        3    38698    lo0
wait           0:60:97:40:fb:e1    UHLW        6     1062    rl0    645
bumble         8:0:20:e:2c:98      UHLW        2       47    rl0   1195
gw             0:60:97:40:fb:e1    UHLW        6     1062    rl0    645
broadcast      ff:ff:ff:ff:ff:ff   UHLWb       2     5788    rl0
```

There's a lot to notice about this information:

- The first column is the name of a host or a network to which packets can be sent, or the keyword `default`.

- The second column, the *gateway*, indicates the path to the destination. This field differs significantly even from older versions of UNIX. It can be the name of a host (for example, *gw*), a pointer to an interface (`link#2`, which means the second Internet interface; the output from *ifconfig* is in the same sequence), or an Ethernet address (`8:0:20:e:2c:98`). Older versions of UNIX do not use the last two forms.

- We'll look at the flags below. The most important ones to note are G (gateway) and H (host).

- The fields Refs, Use and Expire are only of interest when you're running a routing protocol. See the man page *netstat(1)* for more details.

- Netif is the name of the interface by which the gateway can be reached. In the case of a link, this is the interface, so the Netif field is empty.

- The order of the entries is not important. The system searches the table for a best fit, not a first fit.

- The default entry points to *gw*, as we would expect. The interface, *rl0*, is the interface by which *gw* can be reached.

- You will also get some additional output for IPv6 ("Internet6"). If you're not using IPv6, you can ignore it. If it gets on your nerves, you can limit your view to IPv4 by entering the command netstat -rfinet. The -f flag specifies which *address family* you're interested in, and inet specifies IPv4.

Flags

Compared to earlier versions of *netstat*, the current version displays many more flags. The following table gives you an overview.

Table 17-2: netstat -r flags values

Flag	Name	Meaning
1	RTF_PROTO1	Protocol specific routing flag 1
2	RTF_PROTO2	Protocol specific routing flag 2
3	RTF_PROTO3	Protocol specific routing flag 3
B	RTF_BLACKHOLE	Just discard pkts (during updates)
b	RTF_BROADCAST	The route represents a broadcast address
C	RTF_CLONING	Generate new routes on use
c	RTF_PRCLONING	Protocol-specified generate new routes on use
D	RTF_DYNAMIC	Created dynamically (by redirect)
G	RTF_GATEWAY	Destination requires forwarding by intermediary
H	RTF_HOST	Host entry (net otherwise)
L	RTF_LLINFO	Valid protocol to link address translation
M	RTF_MODIFIED	Modified dynamically (by redirect)
R	RTF_REJECT	Host or net unreachable
S	RTF_STATIC	Manually added
U	RTF_UP	Route usable
W	RTF_WASCLONED	Route was generated as a result of cloning
X	RTF_XRESOLVE	External daemon translates proto to link address

Packet forwarding

We saw above that when a system receives a packet that is not intended for itself, it looks for a route to the destination. In fact, this is not always the case: by default, FreeBSD just silently drops the packet. This is desirable for security reasons, and indeed it's required by RFC 1122, but if you want to access the Internet via another machine on your local net, it's less than convenient.

The rationale for this is that most systems are only connected to one network, and it doesn't make sense to have packet forwarding enabled. Earlier systems made this a kernel option, so that disabling packet forwarding also made the kernel fractionally smaller. In current versions of FreeBSD, the code is always there, even if it is disabled.

It's straightforward enough to set up your machine as a router (or *gateway*): you can set it with the *sysctl* command:

```
# sysctl -w net.inet.ip.forwarding=1
net.inet.ip.forwarding: 0 -> 1
```

In */etc/rc.conf*, you can set this with the variable gateway_enable:

```
gateway_enable="YES"              # Set to YES if this host will be a gateway.
```

Configuration summary

In the course of this chapter, we've discussed a number of different configurations. In this section we'll summarize the configuration for for *free-gw.example.net*, since it is the most complicated. You enter the following information in your */etc/rc.conf*:

- Set your host name:

  ```
  hostname="free-gw.example.net"
  ```

- For each interface, specify IP addresses and possibly net masks for each interface on the machine:

  ```
  ifconfig_rl0="inet 139.130.237.117"
  ```

  The PPP interfaces are configured independently, so we won't look at them here, but we might need their addresses for static routes. The local interface address for *ppp0* is 139.130.136.9, and the local address for *ppp3* is 139.130.136.129.

- Decide on a default route. In this case, it is the gateway machine *igw.example.net*, with the address 139.130.237.65:

```
        defaultrouter="139.130.237.65" # Set to default gateway (or NO).
```

- Decide on other routes. In this case, we have two, to *example.org* and *biguser.com*. List them in the variable static_routes:

```
    static_routes="freebie biguser" # Set to static route list
```

- For each static route, create a variable describing the route:

```
    route_freebie="-net 223.147.37.0 139.130.136.133"
    route_biguser="-net 223.147.38.0 -iface ppp0"
```

- Enable IP forwarding:

```
    gateway_enable="YES"                    # Set to YES if this host will be a gateway.
```

Without the comments, this gives the following entries:

```
hostname="free-gw.example.net"
ifconfig_rl0="inet 139.130.237.117"
defaultrouter="139.130.237.65" # Set to default gateway (or NO).
static_routes="freebie biguser" # Set to static route list
route_freebie="-net 223.147.37.0 139.130.136.133"
route_biguser="-net 223.147.38.0 -iface ppp0"
gateway_enable="YES"                    # Set to YES if this host will be a gateway.
```

For a machine configured with DHCP, you might have:

```
hostname="andante.example.net"
ifconfig_wi0=DHCP
```

18

Connecting to the Internet

To implement the reference network shown in the previous chapter, we need to do a lot of things that interface with the outside world. They can take some time, so we should look at them first:

• What kind of physical connection should we use? We'll consider that in the next section.

• We may want to *register a domain*. Many people don't, but I strongly recommend it. Find out about that on page 317.

• We may also want to *register a network*. In our example, we have used the network 223.147.37.0. In real life, we can't choose our own network: we take what is given to us. We'll look at this on page 318.

• We need to find an *Internet Service Provider*. We'll look at what that entails on page 319.

The physical connection

Just two or three years ago, the way to connect to the outside world was simple: a phone line. Since then, things have changed quite a bit, and you may have quite a choice:

- Analogue telephone line connections are still the most common way of connecting small networks in most countries, but their bandwidth is limited to about 7 kB/s at best. You can run PPP or SLIP over this kind of line, though nowadays most ISPs support only PPP.

- *ISDN* stands for *Integrated Systems Digital Network*. It's the new, better, washes-whiter telephone system that is replacing POTS (*Plain Old Telephone Service*) in some countries, notably in Europe. FreeBSD supports ISDN with the *isdn4bsd* driver. We won't look at ISDN further in this book.

- *Leased lines* form the backbone of the Internet. They're invariably more expensive than dialup lines, but they can provide quite high speeds—in the USA, a *T1* line will give you 1,536 kbps, and in the rest of the world an *E1* will give you 2,048 kbps. Leased lines are becoming less interesting, and we won't look at them in more detail in this book.

- *Cable modems* use existing cable TV networks to deliver a high speed connection, up to several megabits per second. They use the cable as a broadcast medium, rather like an Ethernet, and suffer from the same load problems: you share the speed with the other users of the cable. There are also some security issues to consider, but if you have a cable service in your area, you'll probably find it superior to telephones. The cable modem is effectively a bridge between the cable and an Ethernet. From the FreeBSD point of view, the cable modem looks like just another Ethernet device.

- *DSL (Digital Subscriber Line)* is the telephone companies' reaction to cable modems.

  > Until recently, the *L* stood for *Loop*, not *Line*. A loop is the telco term for the pair of wires between the exchange (or *Central Office*) and the subscriber premises.

  There are a number of variants on DSL: *ADSL (Asynchronous Digital Subscriber Line)* has different speeds for the uplink and the downlink, while *SDSL (Symmetric Digital Subscriber Line)* and *HDSL (High-speed Digital Subscriber Line)* have the same speed in each direction. Speeds and capabilities differ widely from one location to another. By modifying the way they transmit data over normal phone wires, including the use of special modems, ADSL can get speeds of up to 6 Mb/s downstream (towards the end user), and about 640 kbps upstream. HDSL has similar speeds, but the speed is the same in each direction. In contrast to cable modems, you don't have to share this bandwidth with anybody. Technical considerations limit the loop length to about four miles, so even in big cities you may not be able to get it. Many DSL services are plagued by technical problems. There are a number of different ways to connect to a DSL service, but most of them involve a conversion to Ethernet.

- In some parts of the world, *satellite connections* are a viable alternative. These usually use a telephone line for outgoing data and a satellite receiver for incoming data. Pricing varies from very cheap to quite expensive, but if you can't get cable or DSL, this might be your only choice.

Establishing yourself on the Internet

The first thing you need to decide is the extent of your presence on the Net. There are various possibilities:

- You could get a dialup service where you use your computer just to connect to the ISP, and perform network functions such as reading mail and news on the ISP's machine (a *shell account*). It's a lot faster to perform these functions on your own machine, and you have all the software you need to do so, so this option isn't very desirable. This option is becoming increasingly uncommon.

- You could perform all the functions on your machine, but using names and addresses assigned to you by the ISP.

- You could perform all the functions on your machine, using addresses assigned to you by the ISP, but you would use your own domain name.

- You get your own address space and use your own domain name.

Does it matter? That's for you to decide. It's certainly a very good idea to have your own domain name. As time goes on, your email address will become more and more important. If you get a mail address like 4711@flybynight.net, and Flybynight goes broke, or you decide to change to a different ISP, your mail address is gone, and you have to explain that to everybody who might want to contact you. If, on the other hand, your name is Jerry Dunham, and you register a domain dunham.org, you can assign yourself any mail address in that domain.

But how do you go about it? One way would be to pay your ISP to do it for you. You don't need to do that: it's easy enough to do yourself on the World-Wide Web. You must be connected to the Internet to perform these steps. This implies that you should first connect using your ISP's domain name, then establish your domain name, and change to that domain.

Which domain name?

We'll continue to assume that your name is Jerry Dunham. If you live in, say, Austin, Texas, you have a number of domain names you can choose from: dunham.org, dunham.com, dunham.net, or even dunham.tx.us if you want to use the geographical domain.

If you live in, say, Capetown, people will probably suggest that you get the domain dunham.za, the geographical domain for South Africa. The problem with that is that you are limiting yourself to that country. If you move to, say, Holland, you would have to change to dunham.nl—a situation only fractionally better than being bound to an ISP. The same considerations apply to dunham.tx.us, of course.

Your choice of domain name also affects the way you apply. In the following sections, I assume you take my advice and apply for an organizational rather than a geographical domain.

Preparing for registration

Once upon a time, registration was handled by InterNIC, a professional body. Since then it has been delegated to commercial companies, and the quality of service has suffered correspondingly: they don't even appear to know the technical terms. For example, you may find them referring to a domain name as a "Web Address." Things are still deteriorating at the time of writing: additional companies are being allowed to register domain names, and the field seems to attract a lot of cowboys.

Registering a domain name

The only prerequisites for registering a domain name are:

- The name must be available, though there are some legal implications that suggest that, though you might be able to register a domain such as *microsoft.edu*, it might not be good for you if you do. In fact, *microsoft.edu* was once registered to the BISPL business school in Hyderabad, India, presumably not in agreement with Microsoft.

- You must be able to specify two name servers for it—see Chapter 21 for further details about name servers.

First, check that the name is available:

```
$ whois dunham.org
No match for "DUNHAM.ORG".

The InterNIC Registration Services Host contains ONLY Internet Information
(Networks, ASN's, Domains, and POC's).
Please use the whois server at nic.ddn.mil for MILNET Information.
```

Next, try to find a reputable registrar. Immediately after the transfer of registrars from InterNIC, the only company to offer this service was Network Solutions, but now there are many. I do not recommend Network Solutions: they're expensive and incompetent. If, as I recommend, you set up your mail server to refuse mail from servers without reverse mapping, you will not be able to communicate with them, since they do not have reverse DNS on their mail servers, and they use unregistered names for them. Judge for yourself what this says about their technical competence.

One registrar that many FreeBSD people use is Gandi (*http://www.gandi.net/*), which is slightly associated with the FreeBSD project. So far nobody has found anything negative to say about them. Unlike Network Solutions, their web pages are also relatively simple to understand.

Getting IP addresses

Once upon a time, it was possible to get IP addresses from InterNIC, but this practice is now restricted to large allocations for ISPs. Instead, get the addresses from your ISP. Routing considerations make it impractical to move IP addresses from one place to another. If you move a long distance, you should expect to change your IP addresses in the same way as you would change your telephone number.

Choosing an Internet Service Provider

In most cases, you will get your connection to the Internet from an *Internet Service Provider*, or *ISP*. As the name suggests, an ISP will supply the means for you to connect your system or your local network to the Internet. They will probably also supply other services: most ISPs can't live on Internet connections alone.

In this chapter we'll look at the things you need to know about ISPs, and how to get the best deal. We'll concentrate on what is still the most common setup, PPP over a dialup line with a V.90 modem (56 kbps), which will give you a peak data transfer rate of about 7 kB/s.

Who's that ISP?

As the Internet, and in particular the number of dialup connections, explodes, a large number of people have had the idea to become involved. In the early days of public Internet access, many ISPs were small companies run by very technical people who have seen a market opportunity and have grabbed it. Other ISPs were small companies run by not-so technical people who have jumped on the bandwagon. Still other ISPs are run by large companies, in particular the cable TV companies and the telephone companies. Which is for you? How can you tell to which category an ISP belongs? Do you care?

You *should* care, of course. Let's consider what you want from an ISP, and what the ISP wants. You want a low-cost, high-reliability, high speed connection to the Internet. You may also want technical advice and value-added services such as DNS (see Chapter 21) and web pages.

The main priority of a small ISP (or any other ISP, for that matter) is to get a good night's sleep. Next, he wants to ensure the minimum number of nuisance customers. After that, he wants to ensure that he doesn't go out of business. Only *then* is he interested in the same things that you are.

In the last few years, a large number of ISPs have gone out of business, and many more have merged with other companies. In particular, large companies frequently bought out small techie ISPs and then ran them into the ground with their incompetence. For a humorous view of this phenomenon, see the "User Friendly" cartoon series starting at *http://ars.userfriendly.org/cartoons/?id=19980824.*

Questions to ask an ISP

So how do you choose an ISP? Don't forget the value of word-of-mouth—it's the most common way to find an ISP. If you know somebody very technical, preferably a FreeBSD user, who is already connected, ask him—he'll certainly be able to tell you about his ISP. Otherwise, a lot depends on your level of technical understanding. It's easy to know more about the technical aspects of the Internet than your ISP, but it doesn't often help getting good service. Here are a few questions to ask any prospective ISP:

☐   What kind of connections do you provide?

See the discussion on page 315.

☐   How do you charge? By volume, by connect time, or flat rate?

Once most ISPs charged by connect time: you paid whether you transfer data or not. This
made it unattractive to an ISP to provide good performance, since that would have meant
that you could finish your session more quickly. Nowadays, flat rates are becoming more
popular: you pay the same no matter how much you use the service. The disadvantage of
the flat rate is that there is no incentive to disconnect, so you might find it difficult to
establish connections.

When comparing connect time and volume rates, expect an average data transfer rate of
about 600 bytes per second for most connections via a 56 kbps modem. You'll get up to 7
kB per second with traffic-intensive operations like file downloading, but normally, you'll be
doing other things as well, and your data rate over the session is more likely to be 600 bytes
per second if you're reasonably active, and significantly less if not. Faster lines typically
don't charge by connect time: in particular, DSL lines are permanently connected and thus
charge by data volume or at a flat rate.

Another alternative that is again becoming more popular is a "download limit." Your flat
monthly fee allows you to download up to a certain amount of data, after which additional
data costs money. This may seem worse than a flat rate, but it does tend to keep people from
abusing the service.

☐   Do you have a cheaper charge for data from your own network?

Many ISPs maintain web proxy caches, ftp archives and network news. If they charge by
volume, some will give you free access to their own net. Don't overestimate the value of
this free data.

☐   What speed connections do you offer?

ADSL connections have two different rates, a faster one for downloads and a slower one for
the uplink. That's fine if you're planning to use the system as a client. If you intend to run
servers on your system, things can look very different.

If you are using a modem connection, they should be the fastest, of course, which are
currently 56 kbps.

☐   What uplink connections do you have?

The purpose of this question is twofold: first, see if he understands the question. An uplink
connection is the connection that the ISP has to the rest of the Internet. If it's inadequate,
your connection to the Internet will also be inadequate. To judge whether the link is fast
enough, you also need to know how many people are connected at any one time. See the
question about dialup modems below.

☐   How many hops are there to the backbone?

Some ISPs are a long way from the Internet backbone. This can be a disadvantage, but it
doesn't have to be. If you're connected to an ISP with T3 all the way to the backbone,
you're better off than somebody connected directly to the backbone by an ISDN Basic Rate
connection. All other things being equal, though, the smaller the number of hops, the better.

☐ **How many dialup modems do you have?**

> This question has two points to make as well. On the one hand, the total bandwidth of these modems should not exceed the uplink bandwidth by too much—let's say it shouldn't be more than double the uplink bandwidth. On the other hand, you want to be able to get a free line when you dial in. Nothing is more frustrating than having to try dozens of times before you can get a connection. This phenomenon also causes people not to disconnect when they're finished, especially if there is no hourly rate. This makes the problem even worse. Of course, the problem depends on the number of subscribers, so ask the next question too.

☐ **How many subscribers do you have? What is the average time they connect per week?**

> Apart from the obvious information, check whether they keep this kind of statistics. They're important for growth.

☐ **What's your up-time record? Do you keep availability statistics? What are they?**

> ISPs are always nervous to publish their statistics. They're never as good as *I* would like. But if they publish them, you can assume that that fact alone makes them better than their competitors.

☐ **What kind of hardware and software are you running?**

> This question will sort out the good techie ISPs from the wannabes. The real answers aren't quite as important as the way they explain it. Nevertheless, consider that you'll be better off with an ISP who also runs FreeBSD or BSD/OS.[1] Only small ISPs can afford to use UNIX machines (including FreeBSD) as routers; the larger ones will use dedicated routers.
>
> Next, in my personal opinion, come other UNIX systems (in decreasing order of preference, Solaris 2.X, Linux and IRIX), and finally, a long way behind, Windows NT. If you're looking for technical support as well, you'll be a lot better off with an ISP who uses FreeBSD or BSD/OS. You'll also be something special to them: most ISPs hate trying to solve problems for typical Windows users.

☐ **How many name servers do you run?**

> The answer should be at least 2. You'll probably be accessing them for your non-local name server information, because that will be faster than sending requests throughout the Internet.

☐ **Can you supply primary or secondary DNS for me? How much does it cost?**

> I strongly recommend using your own domain name for mail. That way, if your ISP folds, or you have some other reason for wanting to change, you don't need to change your mail ID. To do this, you need to have the information available from a name server 24 hours per day. DNS can generate a lot of traffic, and unless you're connected to the network 100% of the time, mail to you can get lost if a system can't find your DNS information. Even if you are connected 100% of the time, it's a good idea to have a backup DNS on the other side of the link. Remember, though, that it doesn't have to be your ISP. Some ISPs supply free secondaries to anybody who asks for them, and you might have friends who will also do it for you.
>
> The ISP may also offer to perform the domain registration formalities for you—for a fee.

---

1. BSD/OS is a commercial operating system closely related to FreeBSD. If you have a few thousand dollars to spare, you may even find it better than FreeBSD. Check out *http://www.wrs.com/* for further details.

You can just as easily do this yourself: see page 318 for more details. Check the fee, though: in some countries, the ISP may get a discount for the domain registration fees. If it's big enough, registering via the ISP may possibly be cheaper than doing it yourself.

☐   Can you route a class C network for me? What does it cost?

If you're connecting a local area network to the Internet, routing information must be propagated to the Net. ISPs frequently consider this usage to be "commercial," and may jack up the prices considerably as a result.

Alternatives to a full class C network are a group of static addresses (say, 8 or 16) out of the ISP's own assigned network addresses. There's no particular problem with taking this route. If you change ISPs, you'll have to change addresses, but as long as you have your own domain name, that shouldn't be a problem.

Another possibility might be to use *IP aliasing*. See page 393 for more details.

☐   Can you supply me with a static address? How much does it cost?

It's highly desirable to have static addresses. See page 346 for more details. Unfortunately, many ISPs use static IPs to distinguish links for commercial use from those for home use, and may charge significantly more for a static address.

☐   Do you give complete access to the Internet, or do you block some ports?

This is a complicated question. Many ISPs block services like smtp (mail) or http (web servers). If they do, you can't run a mail or web server on your own machines. In the case of mail, this is seldom a problem: they will provide you with their own mail server through which you must relay your mail. This also allows the ISP to limit spam, which might otherwise come from any system within the network.

For http, the situation is different. Usually ISPs charge money for supplying access to their own web servers. On the other hand, this arrangement can provide much faster web access, especially if you are connected by a slow link, and you may also save volume charges. Ultimately it's a choice you need to make.

☐   Do you have complete reverse DNS?

In previous editions of this book, I didn't ask this question: it seemed impossible that any ISP would answer "no." Unfortunately, times have changed, and a number of ISPs not only don't supply DNS, they seem to think it unnecessary. Don't have anything to do with them: firstly, it shows complete incompetence, and secondly it will cause trouble for you accessing a number of sites, including sending mail to the FreeBSD mailing lists.

Making the connection

After calling a few ISPs, you should be able to make a decision based on their replies to these questions. The next step is to gather the information needed to connect. Use Table 18-1 to collect the information you need. See Chapter 20 for information about authentication, user name and password.

Table 18-1: Information for ISP setup

Information	Fill in specific value
IP address of your end of the link	
IP address of the other end of the link	
Kind of authentication (CHAP, PAP, login)	
User or system name	
Password or key	
Primary Name Server name	
Primary Name Server IP address	
Secondary Name Server name	
Secondary Name Server IP address	
Pop (Mail) Server Name	
News Server Name	

19

Serial communications

UNIX has always had a high level of support for serial lines, but their purpose has changed dramatically. In the early 70s, the standard "terminal" was a Teletype KSR35, a 10-character-per-second serial printer with keyboard. Early UNIX serial line support was geared towards supporting these devices, either directly connected, or via a modem.

Even in the early 80s, when 4.2BSD introduced network support, things didn't change much: the network support used different hardware. By this time, the Teletypes had been replaced with *glass ttys*, in other words serial terminals with a monitor instead of a printer. The speeds had gone up from the 110 bps of the Teletype to 9600 bps, but the underlying principles hadn't changed.

It wasn't until the last 10 years that the glass ttys were replaced by display boards directly connected to the system bus, or by other machines connected by Ethernet. The role of the serial port has changed completely: nowadays, they're used mainly for mice and dialup Internet connections.

This change in use has invalidated a few basic concepts. Only a few years ago, the standard "high-speed" modem was a V.22bis 2400 bps modem, even then too slow for an Internet connection. The standard data communication line was 56 kb/s, and it was invariably a leased line. As a result, the Internet grew up assuming that connections were leased lines, and therefore permanently connected. Even today, the Internet protocols do not deal well with dialup access.

On the other hand, *UUCP* did use dialup access. As a result, provisions for dialup access in UNIX tend to be derived from *UUCP*. This doesn't make for smooth integration.

In this chapter, we'll look at the way FreeBSD handles serial communications, at how modems work, and how the two fit together.

Terminology

Any serial connection has two ends, which may be computers, terminals, printers or modems. In modem terminology, the computers are *Data Terminal Equipment* or *DTE* (this terminology arose at a time when the device connected to a modem was usually a terminal), and modems are *Data Communication Equipment* or *DCE*. You'll also sometimes hear the name *dataset* for a modem.

Asynchronous and synchronous communication

There are two different ways to transmit serial data, called *synchronous* and *asynchronous* communication. They grew up in different worlds:

Asynchronous communication

Asynchronous communication predates computers. It was originally developed to run *teletypewriters*, electrical typewriters that were run off a serial data stream, the best-known of which were made by the Teletype corporation. These machines were frequently used to provide a remote transcript of what somebody was typing miles away, so they would typically print one character at a time, stop, and wait for the next. In the early days of UNIX, the standard terminal was a Teletype model KSR35, commonly just called *teletype* or *tty* (pronounced "titty").

Here's a picture of a typical byte encoding:

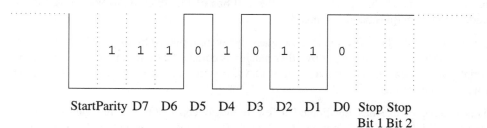

StartParity D7 D6 D5 D4 D3 D2 D1 D0 Stop Stop
                                                Bit 1 Bit 2

Figure 19-1: Asynchronous byte encoding

This figure shows an encoding for the letter j, in binary 01101011. We'll see a number of things about it:

- Before the character starts, the line is idle, which shows as a *high* level: this indicates to the teletype that the line is still connected.

- First comes a *start bit*. In the olden days, this bit started the motor of the teletype mechanism. Now it signals that data is coming.

- Next comes a *parity bit*. To detect any transmission errors, this character is encoded with *even parity*. The parity bit is set to 1 if the character contains an odd number of bits, and to 0 otherwise, which ensures that the character, including the parity bit, always has an even number of bits. If a single bit is corrupted during transmission, the character will arrive with odd parity, and the receiver will detect an error.

- Next come the bits of the character, last bit first. We represent 1 with a low level and 0 with a high level.

- Finally come one or two *stop bits*. The stop bits were originally intended to give the teletype time to stop the motor, but they are now largely superfluous. You needed two stop bits for a teletype, but nowadays you should always use one.

- This example also shows something else of importance: there are a number of ways to encode the character. How many bits? How many stop bits? Odd parity? Even parity? No parity? Mark parity (always a 1 bit)? Space parity (always a 0 bit)? How much time from one bit to the next (what bit rate)? They're all set with the *stty* program (see man page *stty(1)*), but if you set them wrongly, you'll run into trouble.

- The encoding isn't very efficient. For every character you send, you also send a start bit and a stop bit. Most communications no longer use the parity bit, but this still means that you have a 25% overhead on communication: for every 8 bits, you send 10, and you could send up to 12, as in this example. We'll see that synchronous communication doesn't have this problem. Users of synchronous communication protocols often refer to asynchronous communication as *start-stop* communication.

Synchronous communication

By contrast with asynchronous communication, synchronous communication comes from the mainframe world, and it assumes that data does not come one byte at a time. Instead, it transmits data in *blocks*. Each block is preceded by one or two *SYN* characters that tell the receiver that data is coming, and that enable it to determine the correct orientation of the bits in the data.

All modern modems use synchronous communication on the phone line, because it is more efficient, and it's the basis of protocols such as SNA and X.25, but you will almost never see any other use of it in UNIX systems.

Serial ports

Nowadays, all PCs come equipped with two serial ports, which are called COM1: and COM2: in the DOS world. UNIX names are different, and FreeBSD calls these same devices sio0 and sio1. It's possible to connect up to four direct serial ports on a standard PC, but due to the design of the board, each one requires a separate IRQ line. If you put two serial ports on the same interrupt line, neither of them will work.

The first two devices, *sio0* and *sio1*, normally use the default IRQs 4 and 3. By default, however, PC manufacturers put *COM3:* and *COM4:* also at IRQs 4 and 3. How can this work? It can't, if you also have *COM1:* and *COM2:* enabled at those IRQs. However, DOS tends to do only one thing at a time, so you can use different ports at different times on the same IRQ, as long as the interrupts aren't enabled on more than one of the ports at a time. This restriction is unacceptable for UNIX, so we have to put them somewhere else. The only unused interrupt available to 8-bit boards is IRQ 5, originally intended for a second parallel printer port.

There's a very good chance that IRQ 5 will already be occupied. What can you do? If one of the boards has a 16-bit or better interface, you can check if one of the interrupts 10 to 15 is available. All EISA and PCI boards fit into this category, and so do ISA boards with two connectors to the motherboard. Unfortunately, a lot of ISA serial cards only have an 8-bit interface. The only alternative is an intelligent serial board that only occupies a single interrupt. In this case, you will probably have to build a custom kernel. See the man page *sio(4)*.

Connecting to the port

Theoretically, a serial line can consist of only three wires: a *Receive Data* line, often abbreviated to *RxD*, a *Transmit Data* line (*TxD*), and a *Signal Ground* line (*SG*). In fact, it is possible to get a link to work like this, but there are a number of problems:

• How do we know when the other end is able to accept data? It may be busy processing data it has already received.

• How do we know when it's even switched on?

• In the case of a modem, how do we know when it is connected to the modem at the other end?

We solve these questions, and more, by the use of additional lines. The most common standard is *RS-232*, also known as *EIA-232*, a standard for DCE to DTE connection. In Europe, it is sometimes confused with the *CCITT V.24* standard, though V.24 does not in fact correspond exactly to RS-232. Most external modems display some of these signals on LED, but modem manufacturers love to create alternative abbreviations for signal names. Here are the signals that RS-232 defines, with some of the more common abbreviations that you may see on external modems.

Table 19-1: RS-232 signals and modem LEDs

RS-232 name	Pin	Modem LED	Purpose
PG	1		Protective ground. Used for electrical grounding only.
TxD	2	TD D1	Transmitted data: data coming from the DTE to the modem.
RxD	3	RD D2	Received data: data coming from the modem to the DTE.
RTS	4		Request to send. Indicates that the device has data to output.
CTS	5		Clear to send. Indicates that the device can receive input.
DSR	6	MR PW ON	Data set ready. Indicates that the modem is powered on and has passed self-test. On some modems, PW indicates that power is on, and MR indicates that it is operative.
SG	7		Signal ground. Return for the other signals.
DCD	8	CD M5	Carrier detect. Indicates that the modem has connection with another modem.
DTR	20	DTR S1	Data terminal ready. Indicates that the terminal or computer is ready to talk to the modem.
RI	22	AA	Ring indicator. Raised by a modem to indicate that an incoming call is ringing. The AA indicator on a modem will usually flash when the incoming call is ringing.
		AA	"Auto Answer." Indicates that the modem will answer an incoming call.
		HS	"High Speed." Indicates that the modem is running at a higher speed than its minimum. Individual modems interpret this differently, but you can assume that something is wrong if your modem has this indicator and it's off during transmission.
		MNP	Indicates that error correction is active.
		OH	"Off hook." Indicates that the modem has some connection with the phone line.
		PW	Indicates that modem power is on. May or may not imply DSR.

The line *DCD* tells the DTE that the modem has established a connection. We'll look at how to use this information on page 335.

In addition to these signals, synchronous modems supply *clocks* on pins 17 and 19. For more details about RS-232, see *RS-232 Made easy* by Martin Seyer.

When can I send data?

There are two ways to determine if the other end is prepared to accept data: *hardware handshaking* and *software handshaking*. Both are also referred to as *flow control*. In each case, the handshaking is symmetrical. We'll look at it from the point of view of the DTE, because this is the more common viewpoint.

In hardware handshaking, the DCE raises *CTS* (*Clear to Send*) when it's ready to accept input. The DTE only transmits data when CTS is asserted from the other end. You'll often see that the DTE asserts RTS (*Request to send*) when it wants to send data. This is a throwback to the days of *half-duplex* modems, which could only transmit in one direction at a time: *RTS* was needed to switch the modem into send mode.

Software handshaking is also called *X-on/X-off*. The DCE sends a character (*X-off*, which corresponds to **Ctrl-S**) when the buffer is full, and another (*X-on*, corresponding to **Ctrl-Q**) when there is space in the buffer again. You can also use this method on a terminal to temporarily stop the display of a lot of data, and then restart it. It's no longer a good choice for modems.

For hardware handshake to work, your modem must be configured correctly, and you must have the correct cables. If it isn't, the symptoms will be very slow response when transferring large quantities of data: at a higher level, TCP can recover from these overruns, but it takes at least a second to do so every time. We'll see how to check that your modem has the correct kind of flow control on page 333.

Modems

A *modem* is a device that transfers digital data into a form suitable for transmission over a transmission line, which is usually a telephone line. Telephone lines are limited to a frequency of about 3.6 kHz, and this limited the speed of older modems to about 1200 bits per second. Modern modems use many sophisticated techniques to increase the speed way beyond this. Current modems transmit at 56 kilobits per second.

Let's consider the modem connection in the reference network on page 294, which is repeated in figure 19-2. As we can see, there are three connections:

* The connection from the router gw to the local modem, connected at 57,600 bits per second.

* The connection between the modems, at 56,000 bits per second.

* The connection from the ISP's modem to his router, at 115,200 bits per second.

You'll also note another value specified here: the connection between the modems is 2,400 baud. Isn't a *baud* the same thing as a bit per second? No, not always. The term *baud* is a representation of the frequency of data on a serial line. On the connections between the systems and the modem, which handle raw digital data, it corresponds to the bit rate. On the modem line, it doesn't. Here, it indicates that 2,400 units of data are sent per second.

Unfortunately, many people use the term *baud* where *bit rate* should be used. This didn't make any difference in the old days with simple modems where the bit rate and baud rate were the same, but nowadays it's confusing.

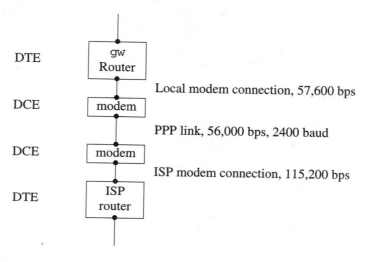

Figure 19-2: Network modem connection

Modem speeds

Two factors determine the data transmission speed of a modem: the *protocol* and the use of *data compression*. Table 19-2 on page 332 gives an overview of modem protocols and their speeds.

Currently, the most popular modem protocol is V.90. V.90 pushes modem technology to the limit, and it only works when the other end of the link is a digital (ISDN) connection. You can't get a 56 kb/s connection with any kind of analogue modem at the other end. As a result, they're really only suitable for connection to a large ISP site. In addition, the actual speed of the connection depends greatly on the telephone line quality, so the difference between a V.90 and a V.34bis modem may not be as much as it appears.

Data compression

In addition, you usually have a choice of data compression: *V.42bis* or *MNP-5*. The choice depends on what the modem at the other end of the line does. You can set most modems to negotiate either protocol. These protocols include related error correction standards, called *V.42* or *MNP2-4* respectively. If you believe the sales claims, these compression protocols will give you up to 100% increase in data throughput. Consider this the upper limit; a lot of data is binary, and when ftp'ing a typical gzipped tar archive, you will probably get almost no speed improvement.

Data compression has one negative side: it increases the data rate, but it also increases *latency*, the time it takes for data to get from the local DTE to the remote DTE. The data doesn't take as long on the line, but it spends more time in the modems being compressed and uncompressed. If you're running a protocol like PPP that supplies optional compression in the software, you may find it advantageous to turn off compression. We'll look at that again in Chapter 20, *Configuring PPP*.

Table 19-2: Modem protocols and speeds

Protocol	Speed (bps)
Bell 203	300
V.21	300
Bell 212	1200
V.22	1200
V.22bis	2400
V.32	9600
V.32bis	14400
V.34	28800
V.34bis	33600
V.90	56000

The link speed

The standard PC serial hardware can run at speeds that are a fraction of 115,200 bps (in other words, 115200 divided by a small integer). This gives the following combinations:

Table 19-3: Serial line speeds

Divisor	Speed (bps)
1	115200
2	57600
3	38400
4	28800
5	23040
6	19200

You'll notice that it can't run at 33600 or 56000 bps. Also, looking at the example above, you'll note that all three links run at different speeds. How can that work? Only a few years ago, it wouldn't, but modern modems can *buffer* data. For example, the ISP can send data to the modem far faster than the modem can send it to the other modem. It stores the data in internal memory until it can be transmitted. This can also happen at the other end. If you misconfigure your line so that the local link runs at 9600 bps, things will still work, but of course the total speed is the speed of the slowest link, in this case 9600 bps.

This flexibility brings a problem with it: the modem can't know in advance how fast the connection to the computer is. It needs a way to find out. The modem solves the question of local line speed by a trick: all commands start with AT or at (you're not allowed to mix cases, like aT or At). It can recognize these characters even if they arrive at the wrong speed, and thus it can establish the speed of the connection.

Dialing out

Nowadays, all modems are capable of dialing. That wasn't always the case, and in some old documentation you may find references to an *Auto-Call Unit* or *ACU*, which is simply the dialler part of a modem connected via a separate port. Typically, one ACU could serve multiple modems.

Nearly every modern modem uses a command set designed by Hayes Corporation, which is thus called the *Hayes Command Set*. We'll look at it in the following section. It is also sometimes called the *AT command set*, because nearly all the commands start with the sequence AT. The CCITT also created an autodial recommendation, *V.25*, which was occasionally implemented, but now appears to be dead.

Modem commands

Modern modems store their state in a number of registers, called *S registers*. The register use varies somewhat from manufacturer to manufacturer, but most modems have a number in common. They each store a one-byte value, ranging between 0 and 255. Here's a list of the more important ones for a Rockwell V.34 chip set. The name of the chip set is not the same as the name of the modem. You'll note that one of the commands enables you to find out the chip set version, as we'll see in the example that follows.

Table 19-4: Selected S registers

Register number	Purpose
S0	Number of rings until auto-answer. 0 disables auto-answer. Set to 0 for no automatic answer, or 1 for auto-answer.
S2	The *escape character*, which lets you return from online mode to command mode. Normally, this character is a +. To return to command mode, wait a second after any previous input, enter +++, and wait a second, after which the modem should reply with OK.
S6	The time, in seconds, to wait before *blind dialing*. If you have set your modem to not wait for a dial tone (maybe because it doesn't understand the dial tone), it will wait this long and then try to dial anyway.

Register number	Purpose
S7	The number of seconds to wait after dialing before DCD must be asserted (before a connection is established). If this is set too short, you will not be able to establish a connection. If it's too long, you will waste time when there is no answer or the line is busy.
S11	The duration of DTMF (dialing) tones. If these are set incorrectly, the telephone exchange may not understand the number you dial.

The AT command set tells the modem to do something specific. Here are some of the more important ones.

Table 19-5: Selected AT commands

Command	Meaning
A/	Redial the last number.
ATA	Answer an incoming call manually. This is an alternative to auto-answer by setting S0.
ATD*number*	Dial *number*. This command has a large number of options, but if your modem is set up correctly, you probably won't need any of them.
ATE*number*	Enable command echo if *number* is 1, disable it if *number* is 0. The setting of this parameter can be important for some chat scripts, which may not respond correctly otherwise.
ATH0	Disconnect the line.
ATI*number*	Display modem identification. The values of *number* vary from one modem to the next. See the examples below.
ATL*number*	Set the speaker volume. *number* ranges from 0 to 3. 0 means "speaker off," 3 is the loudest.
ATM*number*	Determine when the speaker is on. 0 means "always off," 1 means "speaker on until connect," 2 means "speaker always on," and 3 means "speaker off during dialing and receiving."
ATO0	Go back online from command mode. You don't need this command when dialing: the modem automatically goes online when the connection is established.
ATP	Select pulse dial. If your exchange doesn't understand DTMF (tone) dialing, you should set this mode. Never use it if your exchange understands DTMF: pulse dialing (also known as *steam dialing*) is *much* slower.
ATQ*number*	If *number* is 0, suppress result codes (like OK after every command). If *number* is 1, enable them. This value can be of importance for chat scripts.

Command	Meaning
ATS*r*=*n*	Set the value of S register *r* to *n*.
ATS*number*?	Display the contents of an *S* register. See the example below.
ATT	Set tone (DTMF) dialing.
ATV*number*	If **number** is 0, return result codes in numeric form. If it's 1, return text. Don't rely on either form to be consistent from one modem to the next.
ATX*number*	Determine the form of the result codes. This depends a lot on the manufacturer, but it's important for chat scripts. If you run into trouble, with chat scripts, check your modem documentation.
ATZ	Reset modem configuration to default values.
AT&K*number*	Select flow control method. Normally, 3 enables RTS/CTS flow control, which is what you want.
AT&R*number*	If **number** is 0, CTS is only asserted if the DTE asserts RTS, even if the modem is able to receive data. If it's set to 1, it behaves normally. Make sure this value is set to 1.
AT&T*number*	Perform modem-specific test **number**. This command is the origin of the statement: "UNIX is a trademark of AT&T in the USA and other countries. AT&T is a modem test command."
AT&V	View the current configuration. See the example below.
AT&W*number*	Store the current configuration as *profile* **number**. Most external modems can store two *profiles*, or configurations. If *number* is not specified, write the profile specified in a previous AT&Y command. See the example below.
AT&Y*number*	Decide which profile (0 or 1) will be loaded when the modem is reset, and which will be written by the command AT&W

Dialing out manually

In this section, we'll look at what needs to be done to establish a dial-out connection. You don't normally do this yourself: some software will do it for you automatically. It's useful to know what goes on, though: it can be of immense help in solving connection problems.

There are two distinct things that you want to do with the modem: first, you send commands to the modem to set up the link. Once the link is established, you don't want to talk to the modem any more, you want to talk to the system at the other end of the link.

In the old days, the system used a separate ACU to establish the connection, and the solution was simple: the system issued the dialing commands to the ACU and opened the modem in such a manner that the open did not complete until a connection had been established. Nowadays, the modem handles both dialing and the establishment of connection. But to do so, the system has to open the modem before communication has been established.

The terminal parameter clocal enables communication with a device that is not asserting *DCD* (such as a modem that hasn't established a connection yet). When it starts, the software sets clocal. When it has finished talking to the modem and wants to wait for the connection to be established, it resets (turns off) clocal and waits for *DCD*. You can check this with the *stty* command:

```
# stty -f /dev/cuaa2 -a
ppp disc; speed 57600 baud; 0 rows; 0 columns;
lflags: -icanon -isig -iexten -echo -echoe -echok -echoke -echonl
        -echoctl -echoprt -altwerase -noflsh -tostop -flusho -pendin
        -nokerninfo -extproc
iflags: -istrip -icrnl -inlcr -igncr -ixon -ixoff -ixany -imaxbel ignbrk
        -brkint -inpck ignpar -parmrk
oflags: -opost -onlcr -oxtabs
cflags: cread cs8 -parenb -parodd hupcl -clocal -cstopb crtscts -dsrflow
        -dtrflow -mdmbuf
cchars: discard = ^O; dsusp = ^Y; eof = ^D; eol = <undef>;
        eol2 = <undef>; erase = ^?; intr = ^C; kill = ^U; lnext = ^V;
        min = 1; quit = ^\; reprint = ^R; start = ^Q; status = ^T;
        stop = ^S; susp = ^Z; time = 0; werase = ^W;
```

This example, taken when the modem is connected, shows clocal reset. As you can see, this is indicated by the text -clocal.

There's a problem here: what if this line is also enabled for dialup? As we shall see on page 338, there will be a *getty* process in the process of opening the line. It won't succeed until *DCD* is asserted, so we can dial with no problem. But when the connection is established, how do we stop *getty* from being there first?

The FreeBSD solution is to create separate devices for each case. For the second serial port, *sio1*, the system creates a file */dev/cuaa1* for dialing out, and */dev/ttyd1* for dialing in. If *cuaa1* is open, an open on *ttyd1* does not complete when connection is established.

Dialing out—an example

For an example of what you might look at, let's consider a manual dialup to an ISP. This assumes that you are using user PPP (see page 348) and that have an entry ISP in your */etc/ppp/ppp.conf*. If you don't have an entry for an ISP, you can still test the modem, but in this case you won't be able to dial. In this case, simply omit the text ISP.

```
# ppp ISP
User Process PPP. Written by Toshiharu OHNO.
Using interface: tun0
Interactive mode
ppp ON freebie> term                        go into direct connect mode
Enter to terminal mode.
Type '~?' for help.
at                                          synchronize with the modem
OK
at&v                                        look at the modem profile
ACTIVE PROFILE:
B0 E1 L0 M1 N1 Q0 T V1 W0 X4 Y0 &C1 &D2 &G0 &J0 &K4 &Q5 &R1 &S0 &T5 &X0 &Y0
S00:000 S01:000 S02:043 S03:013 S04:010 S05:008 S06:002 S07:060 S08:002 S09:006
S10:014 S11:090 S12:050 S18:000 S25:005 S26:001 S36:007 S37:000 S38:020 S44:020
S46:138 S48:007 S95:000

STORED PROFILE 0:
B0 E1 L0 M1 N1 Q0 T V1 W0 X4 Y0 &C1 &D2 &G0 &J0 &K4 &Q5 &R1 &S0 &T5 &X0
S00:000 S02:043 S06:002 S07:060 S08:002 S09:006 S10:014 S11:090 S12:050 S18:000
```

```
S36:007 S37:000 S40:104 S41:195 S46:138 S95:000

STORED PROFILE 1:
B0 E1 L1 M1 N1 Q0 T V1 W0 X4 Y0 &C1 &D2 &G0 &J0 &K3 &Q5 &R1 &S0 &T5 &X0
S00:000 S02:043 S06:002 S07:060 S08:002 S09:006 S10:014 S11:090 S12:050 S18:000
S36:007 S37:000 S40:104 S41:195 S46:138 S95:000

TELEPHONE NUMBERS:
0=T1234567890                        1=
2=                                   3=

OK
```

The term *profile* refers to a set of the complete configuration information for the modem. External modems can usually store two different profiles. Some modems may not have any stored profiles, or they may have a different number. The AT&V command shows the current configuration ("active profile") and the two stored profiles. The first line reflects the parameters set with AT commands (for example, L0 means that the command ATL0, turn off the speaker, has been issued). The next two or three lines reflect the values of the S registers. In addition, this modem can store up to four telephone numbers, a feature that is seldom of great interest.

If you look at this profile, you'll notice that the active profile includes the parameter &K4. This means "use XON/XOFF flow control." This is not desirable: it's better to use RTS/CTS flow control. To fix it,

at&k3	*set RTS/CTS flow control*
OK	
at&w	*write the active profile*
OK	
at&v	*and check*

```
ACTIVE PROFILE:
B0 E1 L0 M1 N1 Q0 T V1 W0 X4 Y0 &C1 &D2 &G0 &J0 &K3 &Q5 &R1 &S0 &T5 &X0 &Y0
S00:000 S01:000 S02:043 S03:013 S04:010 S05:008 S06:002 S07:060 S08:002 S09:006
S10:014 S11:090 S12:050 S18:000 S25:005 S26:001 S36:007 S37:000 S38:020 S44:020
S46:138 S48:007 S95:000

STORED PROFILE 0:
B0 E1 L0 M1 N1 Q0 T V1 W0 X4 Y0 &C1 &D2 &G0 &J0 &K3 &Q5 &R1 &S0 &T5 &X0
S00:000 S02:043 S06:002 S07:060 S08:002 S09:006 S10:014 S11:090 S12:050 S18:000
S36:007 S37:000 S40:104 S41:195 S46:138 S95:000

STORED PROFILE 1:
B0 E1 L1 M1 N1 Q0 T V1 W0 X4 Y0 &C1 &D2 &G0 &J0 &K3 &Q5 &R1 &S0 &T5 &X0
S00:000 S02:043 S06:002 S07:060 S08:002 S09:006 S10:014 S11:090 S12:050 S18:000
S36:007 S37:000 S40:104 S41:195 S46:138 S95:000

TELEPHONE NUMBERS:
0=T1234567890                        1=
2=                                   3=

OK
```

The active profile includes the parameter **&Y0**, so the AT&W command writes back to stored profile 0.

The **AT&V** command doesn't show all the S registers. Some of them relate to the current state of the modem, and aren't part of the configuration. For example, my modem includes an S register S86, the *Call Failure Reason Code*. If a call fails, it could be interesting to look at it. To do so:

```
ats86?                                    show contents of S86
012                                       Connection dropped by other end
```

With this background, we can now proceed to establish a connection:

```
atd1234567                                just dial
CONNECT 57600
ppp ON freebie>
PPP ON freebie>
```

Dialing in

Traditionally, UNIX distinguishes between local serial terminals and terminals connected by modem by whether they assert the *DCD* signal. It starts a *getty* (for *Get TTY*) process for each line. *getty* opens the line, but for modems the line state is set in such a way that the call to open does not complete until the DCE asserts *DCD*. This is done by resetting the flag clocal. If you look at the line state with the *stty* program, it will show -clocal if the flag is reset.

To set up a line for dialing in, add information about the line in the file */etc/ttys*. The default file contains a number of lines like:

```
ttyd0    "/usr/libexec/getty std.9600"   unknown off secure
```

This information has the following meaning:

* The first column is the name of the terminal special file, relative to */dev*. In other words, this entry represents the file */dev/ttyd0*.

* The next field consists of the text /usr/libexec/getty std.9600. This is the invocation for *getty*: the *getty* program is */usr/libexec/getty*, and it is invoked with the parameter std.9600. This is a label in the file */etc/gettytab*, and describes a standard 9600 bps connection. You'll probably want to upgrade to std.57600.

* unknown refers to the terminal type. This is the value to which *getty* sets the environment variable TERM. If you know that only people with VT100 terminals dial in, you might change this string to vt100, but you should do this with care. It can cause a real mess on the screen, and even make it impossible to work with it.

* The remaining fields can occur in any order. off means "don't start the *getty* after all." If you want to run a *getty* on this line, change this string to on.

  secure means that only people you trust can access this line, so you can allow a root login on this line. That's fine for a direct connect terminal in the same room, for example. It's not a good idea for a modem to which anybody can dial up. If the line is not secure, just omit the string.

After changing */etc/ttys*, send *init* (process 1) a HUP signal to tell it to re-read */etc/ttys*:

```
# kill -1 1
```

20

Configuring PPP

Two protocols support connection to the Internet via modem: *SLIP* (*Serial Line Internet Protocol*) and *PPP* (*Point to Point Protocol*). As the name suggests, SLIP supports only IP. It is an older, less rugged protocol. Its only advantage is that it may be available where PPP isn't. If you have the choice, always take PPP: it differs from SLIP in being able to handle multiple protocols simultaneously, and it's also used on many DSL links (*PPP over Ethernet* or *PPPoE*). In this chapter, we'll look only at PPP.

PPP can perform a number of functions:

- It dials and establishes a phone connection if necessary. Strictly speaking, this isn't part of the PPP specification, but it is supported by most PPP implementations.

- It performs *authentication* to ensure that you are allowed to use the connection.

- It performs *negotiation* to decide what kind of protocol to use over the link. You might think, "that's OK, I'm just using IP," but in fact there are a number of different ways to transmit IP datagrams over a PPP link. In addition, the other end may be able to handle non-Internet protocols such as X.25, SNA and Novell's IPX.

- It can perform *line quality monitoring* to ensure that the modems are able to understand each other.

FreeBSD provides two versions of PPP:

- Traditional BSD implementations of IP are located in the kernel, which makes for more efficiency. The corresponding implementation of PPP is referred to as *kernel PPP*. We'll look at it on page 355.

- Although kernel PPP is more efficient, it's also frequently more difficult to debug. As a result, FreeBSD also supplies an implementation known as *user PPP* or *iijppp*, after the *Internet Institute of Japan*, which supplied the original base code. It uses the *tunnel driver* to pass IP packets up to a user process. It's easier to configure and debug, and though it's not as efficient, the difference is not usually a problem. We'll look at this implementation on page 348.

If you have a DSL link, you don't have a choice of version: currently, only User PPP supports PPPoE.

Quick setup

The following sections go into some detail about how PPP works. It's not completely necessary to know it all to set up PPP. If you're in a hurry, you can move on to the configuration summaries on page 348 for user PPP, or page 359 for kernel PPP.

How PPP works

The following steps are necessary to set up a PPP connection:

- Set up a serial connection between the two systems. This could be a direct wire connection, but normally it's a dialup modem or an ISDN or DSL link.

- For a modem link, establish connection, traditionally called *dialing* the other end. The modems then set up a link and assert *DCD* (*Data Carrier Detect*) to tell the machines to which they are connected that the modem connection has been established.

- Start PPP. PPP selects a network interface to use for this connection.

- The two PPP processes negotiate details like IP address, protocol, and authentication protocols.

- Establish routes to the systems at the other end of the link.

On the following pages, we'll look at these points in detail.

The interfaces

Most network interfaces are dedicated to networking. For example, an Ethernet adapter can't be used for anything else. Serial lines are different: you could also use them to connect a mouse or even a remote terminal. There's another difference, too: you access serial lines via their device names. You access network interfaces via the *ifconfig* program, because they don't usually have device names—in technical jargon, they're in a separate *name space* from files. How do we solve this conflict?

The solution may seem a little surprising: PPP uses two different devices for each connection. You decide which serial line you want to use, and the software chooses a network interface for you, though you can override this choice if you're using user PPP.

For example, your serial line might be called */dev/cuaa0*, */dev/cuaa1* or */dev/cuaa2*, while your interface will be called *tun0* or *tun1* (for user PPP), or *ppp0* or *ppp1* (for kernel PPP). It's possible to connect to a DSL line without PPP, but when you use PPPoE, you also have two devices, the Ethernet interface and *tun0* (Kernel PPP does not support PPPoE).

The tunnel device uses a device interface called */dev/tunn*, where *n* is a digit, to read and write to the other side of the corresponding network interface.

User PPP runs in user space, so it *does* require a device name for the network interface, for example *tun0*. It uses this device to read and write to the back end of the tunnel interface.

Dialing

If you're running a PPP connection over a dial-up link, you'll need to establish a telephone connection, which is still called *dialing*. That's a modem function, of course, and it's not defined in the PPP standard.

User PPP includes both built-in dialing support and external dialing support, while kernel PPP supplies only the latter. In practice, the only difference is the way your configuration files look. We'll look at these when we discuss the individual implementations.

You don't need to dial for a DSL connection.

Negotiation

Once the connection is established and the PPP processes can talk to each other, they negotiate what PPP features they will use.[1] The negotiation is successful if the two sides can agree on a functional subset of the features both would like to have.

For each feature of the link, PPP negotiation can perform up to two actions. User PPP uses the following terms to describe them, viewed from the local end of a link:

- To *enable* a feature means: "request this feature."

- To *disable* a feature means: "do not request this feature."

- To *accept* a feature means: "if the other side requests this feature, use it."

- To *deny* a feature means: "if the other side requests this feature, refuse it."

Negotiation is successful if each end accepts all the features that the other end has enabled. In some cases, however, PPP systems have an alternative. For example, if you accept PAP and deny CHAP, a router may first request CHAP, and when you deny it, it may then request PAP. You do this by enabling both PAP and CHAP in your PPP configuration files.

---

1. Years ago, you might have first have had to perform a normal UNIX login ("login authentication"). This was usually handled by the dialing script ("chat script"). Microsoft didn't support this kind of authentication, so it's practically obsolete now, though there's nothing wrong with the idea.

Who throws the first stone?

The first step in negotiation is to decide which side starts. One of them starts the negotiation, and the other one responds. If you configure your end incorrectly, one of these things can happen:

1. You both wait for the other end to start. Nothing happens. After a while, one of you times out and drops the connection.

2. You both fire away and place your demands, and listen for the other one to reply. The software should recognize that the other end is talking, too, and recover, but often enough both ends give up and drop the connection.

3. One side initiates negotiations before the other, and things work normally despite the misconfiguration. This is the most difficult kind to recognize: sometimes the connection will work, and sometimes it won't, apparently dependent on the phase of the moon.

In general, systems with login authentication also initiate the negotiation. ISPs with *PAP* or *CHAP* authentication tend to expect the end user to start first, because that's the way Microsoft does it. It's easier for debugging to assume that the other end will start. If it doesn't, and you have an external modem, you'll notice that there is no traffic on the line, and that the line has dropped. Then you can switch to active mode negotiation.

It makes more sense for the called system to start the negotiation: the calling system is ready to use the link immediately, but the called system often takes a certain amount of time execute its PPP server program. A common cause of problems is when the server machine is busy and it takes a while to invoke the PPP process. In this case the caller sends its initial configuration data and the called system's tty device may echo it back, resulting in a lot of confusion at the caller's end. User PPP can typically survive about three reflections of this type before getting too confused to recover.

Typical features that require negotiation are:

• *What kind of authentication?* Login authentication doesn't count here, because it's not part of PPP. You may choose to offer *CHAP* or *PAP* negotiation. You may also require the other end to authenticate itself. You can accept both *CHAP* and *PAP* authentication—that way, you can accept whichever the other end asks for. If the other end is an ISP, you will probably not be able to authenticate him, but you should check with the ISP.

A common configuration problem is when a user enables some form of authentication without first agreeing this with the ISP. For example, very few ISPs perform authentication from their end (to prove to you that they're really the ISP you dialed). You can specify this type of authentication in your configuration file, but if the ISP refuses to authenticate, you will never establish a connection.

• *LQR, Link Quality Requests*, give you an overview of your line quality, *if* your modem doesn't use error correction. If it does use error correction, it will hide any LQR problems. Occasionally LQR packets can confuse a PPP implementation, so don't enable it if you don't intend to use it.

- *Data and header compression.* You have a choice here: modern modems offer various kinds of data compression, and so do the PPP implementations. As we saw on page 331, modem compression increases the data throughput, but also increases the latency. If your ISP supports the same kind of data compression as your PPP software, you might find that it improves matters to disable modem data compression. Both implementations support *Van Jacobson*, *deflate* and *Predictor 1* compression, and kernel PPP also supports *BSD compression*.

  Which do you choose? *Van Jacobson* compression works at the TCP level. It compresses only the headers (see page 280 for more details), and the other compression schemes work at the frame level. You can always enable Van Jacobson compression. As far as the others are concerned, use whatever the other side offers. In case of doubt, enable all available compression types and allow PPP to negotiate the best combination.

  Compression negotiation is handled by the *Compression Control Protocol*, usually known as *CCP*. It uses its own protocol number so that it can be distinguished from other protocols that the remote system might offer, such as IP, X.25, SNA and IPX.

- *IP addresses.* In many cases, the server machine allocates a dynamic IP address. We'll look at the implications below.

- *Proxy ARP.* Some systems can't understand being at the other end of a PPP link. You can fool them by telling the router to respond to *ARP* requests for machines at the other end of the link. You don't need this subterfuge in FreeBSD.

Authentication

Nearly every PPP link requires some kind of identification to confirm that you are authorized to use the link. On UNIX systems, the authentication traditionally consisted of the UNIX *login* procedure, which also allows you to dialup either to a shell or to a PPP session, depending on what user ID you use. Login authentication is normally performed by the dial-up chat script.

Microsoft has changed many things in this area. Their platforms don't normally support daemons, and in some cases not even multiple users, so the UNIX login method is difficult to implement. Instead, you connect directly to a PPP server and perform authentication directly with it. There are two different authentication methods currently available, *PAP* (*Password Authentication Protocol*) and *CHAP* (*Challenge Handshake Authentication Protocol*). Both perform similar functions. From the PPP point of view, you just need to know which one you are using. Your ISP should tell you this information, but a surprising number don't seem to know. In case of doubt, accept either of them.

Just to confuse matters, Microsoft has implemented authentication protocols of its own, such as MS LanMAN, MS CHAP Version 1 (also known as CHAP type 0x80) and MS CHAP Version 2, also known as CHAP type 0x81. User PPP supports both kinds.

If you're using *PAP* or *CHAP*, you need to specify a system name and an authentication key. These terms may sound complicated, but they're really just a fancy name for a user name and a password. We'll look at how to specify these values when we look at the individual software.

How do you decide whether you use *PAP* or *CHAP*? You don't need to—accept both and let the other end decide which kind to use.

Which IP addresses on the link?

After passing authentication, you may need to negotiate the addresses on the link. At first sight, you'd think that the IP addresses on the link would be very important. In fact, you can often almost completely ignore them. To understand this, we need to consider what the purpose of the IP addresses is.

An IP address is an address placed in the source or the destination field in an IP packet to enable the software to route it to its destination. As we saw in Chapter 17, *Configuring the local network*, it is not necessarily the address of the interface to which the packet is sent. If your packet goes through 15 nodes on the way through the Internet, quite a normal number, it will be sent to 14 nodes whose address is not specified in the packet.

The first node is the router at the other end of the PPP link. This is a point-to-point link, so it receives all packets that are sent down the line, so you don't need to do anything special to ensure it gets them. This is in marked contrast to a router on a broadcast medium like an Ethernet: on an Ethernet you must specify the IP address of the router for it to receive the packets.

> On an Ethernet, although the IP address in the packets doesn't mention the router, the Ethernet headers do specify the Ethernet address of the router as the destination address. Your local system needs the IP address to determine the Ethernet address with the aid of *ARP*, the *Address Resolution Protocol*.

In either case, except for testing, it's very unlikely that you will ever want to address a packet directly to the router, and it's equally unlikely that the router would know what to do with most kinds of packets if they are addressed to itself. So we don't really need to care about the address.

What if we set up the wrong address for the other end of the link? Look at the router gw.example.com in the reference network on page 294. Its PPP link has the local address 139.130.136.133, and the other end has the address 139.130.136.129. What happens if we get the address mixed up and specify the other end as 139.130.129.136? Consider the commands we might enter if we were configuring the interface manually (compare with page 300):

```
# ifconfig tun0  139.130.136.133  139.130.129.136  netmask 255.255.255.255
# route add default 139.130.129.133
```

Figure 20-1: Configuring an interface and a route

You need to specify the netmask, because otherwise *ifconfig* chooses one based on the network address. In this case, it's a class B address, so it would choose 255.255.0.0. This tells the system that the other end of the link is 139.130.129.136, which is incorrect. It then tells the system to route all packets that can't be routed elsewhere to this address (the default route). When such a packet arrives, the system checks the routing table, and find that 139.130.129.136 can be reached by sending the packet out from interface *tun0*. It sends the packet down the line.

At this point any memory of the address 139.130.129.136 (or, for that matter, 139.130.136.129) is gone. The packet arrives at the other end, and the router examines it. It still contains only the original destination address, and the router routes it accordingly. In other words, the router never finds out that the packet has been sent to the incorrect "other end" address, and things work just fine.

What happens in the other direction? That depends on your configuration. For any packet to get to your system from the Internet, the routing throughout the Internet must point to your system. Now how many IP addresses do you have? If it's only a single IP address (the address of your end of the PPP link), it must be correct. Consider what would happen if you accidentally swapped the last two octets of your local IP address:

```
# ifconfig tun0   139.130.133.136   139.130.129.136
```

If gw sends out a packet with this source address, it does not prevent it from getting to its destination, because the source address does not play any part in the routing. But when the destination system replies, it sends it to the address specified in the source field, so it will not get back.

So how can this still work? Remember that routers don't change the addresses in the packets they pass. If system bumble sends out a packet, it has the address 223.147.37.3. It passes through the incorrectly configured system gw unchanged, so the reply packet gets back to its source with no problems.

In practice, of course, it doesn't make sense to use incorrect IP addresses. If you don't specify an address at either end of the link, PPP can negotiate one for you. What this does mean, though, is that you shouldn't worry too much about what address you get. There is one exception, however: the issue of *dynamic addressing*. We'll look at that below.

The net mask for the link

As we saw on page 290, with a broadcast medium you use a net mask to specify which range of addresses can be addressed directly via the interface. This is a different concept from *routing*, which specifies ranges of addresses that can be addressed indirectly via the interface. By definition, a point-to-point link only has one address at the other end, so the net mask must be 255.255.255.255.

Static and dynamic addresses

Traditionally, each interface has had a specific address. With the increase in the size of the Internet, this has caused significant problems: a few years ago, people claimed that the Internet was running out of addresses. As a solution, Version 6 of the Internet Protocol (usually called *IPv6*) has increased the length of an address from 32 bits to 128 bits, increasing the total number of addresses from 4,294,967,296 to 3.4×10^{38}—enough to assign multiple IP addresses to every atom on Earth (though there may still be a limitation when the Internet grows across the entire universe). FreeBSD contains full support for IPv6, but unfortunately that's not true of most ISPs, so at present, IPv6 is not very useful. This book doesn't discuss it further.

ISPs don't use IPv6 because they have found another "solution" to the address space issue: *dynamic IP addresses*. With dynamic addresses, every time you dial in, you get a free IP address from the ISP's address space. That way, an ISP only needs as many IP addresses as he has modems. He might have 128 modems and 5000 customers. With static addresses, he would need 5000 addresses, but with dynamic addresses he only needs 128. Additionally, from the ISPs point of view, routing is trivial if he assigns a block of IP addresses to each physical piece of hardware.

Dynamic addresses have two very serious disadvantages:

1. IP is a peer-to-peer protocol: there is no master and no slave. Theoretically, any system can initiate a connection to any other, as long as it knows its IP address. This means that your ISP could initiate the connection if somebody was trying to access your system. With dynamic addressing, it is absolutely impossible for anybody to set up a connection: there is no way for any other system to know in advance the IP address that you will get when the link is established.

   This may seem unimportant—maybe you consider the possibility of the ISP calling you even dangerous—but consider the advantages. If you're travelling somewhere and need to check on something on your machine at home, you can just connect to it with *ssh*. If you want to let somebody collect some files from your system, there's no problem. In practice, however, very few ISPs are prepared to call you, though that doesn't make it a bad idea.

2. Both versions of PPP support an *idle timeout* feature: if you don't use the link for a specified period of time, it may hang up. Depending on where you live, this may save on phone bills and ISP connect charges. It only disconnects the phone link, and not the TCP sessions. Theoretically you can reconnect when you want to continue, and the TCP session will still be active. To continue the session, however, you need to have the same IP address when the link comes up again. Otherwise, though the session isn't dead, you can't reconnect to it.

Setting a default route

Very frequently, the PPP link is your only connection to the Internet. In this case, you should set the *default route* to go via the link. You can do this explicitly with the *route add* command, but both versions of PPP can do it for you.

When you set your default route depends on what kind of addressing you're using. If you're using static addressing, you can specify it as one of the configuration parameters. If you're using dynamic addressing, this isn't possible: you don't know the address at that time. Both versions have a solution for this, which we'll look at when we get to them.

Autodial

A PPP link over modem typically costs money. You will normally pay some or even all of the following charges:

- Telephone call setup charges, a charge made once per call. Unlike the other charges, these make it advantageous to stay connected as long as possible.

- Telephone call duration charges. In some countries, you pay per time unit (for example, per minute), or you pay a fixed sum for a variable unit of time.

- ISP connect charges, also per time unit.

- ISP data charges, per unit of data.

Typically, the main cost depends on the connection duration. To limit this cost, both PPP implementations supply methods to dial automatically and to disconnect when the line has been idle for a predetermined length of time.

The information you need to know

Whichever PPP implementation you decide upon, you need the following information:

- Which physical device you will use for the connection. For a modem, it's normally a serial port like */dev/cuaa0*. For PPPoE, it's an Ethernet adapter, for example *xl0*.

- If it's a modem connection, whom are you going to call? Get the phone number complete with any necessary area codes, in exactly the format the modem needs to dial. If your modem is connected to a PABX, be sure to include the access code for an external line.

- The user identification and password for connection to the ISP system.

- The kind of authentication used (usually CHAP or PAP).

In addition, some ISPs may give you information about the IP addresses and network masks, especially if you have a static address. You should have collected all this information in the table on page 323.

Setting up user PPP

This chapter contains a lot of information about PPP setup. If you're in a hurry, and you have a "normal" PPP connection, the following steps may be enough to help you set it up. If it doesn't work, just read on for the in-depth explanation.

- Edit */etc/ppp/ppp.conf.* Find these lines lines:

  ```
  papchap:
    (comments omitted)
    set phone PHONE_NUM                          only for modem connections
    set authname USERNAME
    set authkey PASSWORD
  ```

  Replace the texts `PHONE_NUM`, `USERNAME` and `PASSWORD` with the information supplied by the ISP. If you're using PPPoE, remove the `set phone` line.

- Still in */etc/ppp/ppp.conf*, check that the device is correct. The default is */dev/cuaa1.* If you're connecting to a different serial line, change the device name accordingly. If you're running PPPoE, say over the Ethernet interface *xl0*, change it to:

  ```
  set device PPPoE:xl0
  ```

- Modify */etc/rc.conf.* First, check the PPP settings in */etc/defaults/rc.conf.* Currently they are:

  ```
  # User ppp configuration.
  ppp_enable="NO"          # Start user-ppp (or NO).
  ppp_mode="auto"          # Choice of "auto", "ddial", "direct" or "dedicated".
                           # For details see man page for ppp(8). Default is auto.
  ppp_nat="YES"            # Use PPP's internal network address translation or NO.
  ppp_profile="papchap"    # Which profile to use from /etc/ppp/ppp.conf.
  ppp_user="root"          # Which user to run ppp as
  ```

  Don't change this file: just add the following line to */etc/rc.conf*:

  ```
  ppp_enable=YES           # Start user-ppp (or NO).
  ```

- If you have a permanent connection (in other words, you don't ever want to disconnect the line), you should also add the following line to */etc/rc.conf*:

  ```
  ppp_mode=ddial           # Choice of "auto", "ddial", "direct" or "dedicated".
  ```

  This tells PPP not to disconnect at all.

- After this, PPP will start automatically on boot and will connect whenever necessary. If you are not planning to reboot, you can start PPP immediately with the following command:

  ```
  # /usr/sbin/ppp -quiet -auto papchap
  ```

If that works for you, you're done. Otherwise, read on.

Setting up user PPP: the details

The user PPP configuration files are in the directory */etc/ppp*. In addition to them, you probably want to modify */etc/rc.conf* to start PPP and possibly to include global Internet information. The main configuration file is */etc/ppp/ppp.conf*. It contains a number of multi-line entries headed by a label. For example, the `default` entry looks like:

```
default:
 set log Phase Chat LCP IPCP CCP tun command
 ident user-ppp VERSION (built COMPILATIONDATE)

 # Ensure that "device" references the correct serial port
 # for your modem. (cuaa0 = COM1, cuaa1 = COM2)
 #
 set device /dev/cuaa1                      device to use

 set speed 115200                           connect at 115,200 bps
 set dial "ABORT BUSY ABORT NO\\sCARRIER TIMEOUT 5 \
         \"\" AT OK-AT-OK ATE1Q0 OK \\dATDT\\T TIMEOUT 40 CONNECT"
 set timeout 180                            # 3 minute idle timer (the default)
 enable dns                                 # request DNS info (for resolv.conf)
```

Let's look at this entry in detail.

- Note the format: labels begin at the beginning of the line, and other entries must be indented by one character.

- The line `default:` identifies the default entry. This entry is always run when PPP starts.

- The `set log` line specifies which events to log. This can be helpful if you run into problems.

- The `ident` line specifies what identification the system will present to the other end of the connection. You don't need to change it.

- The `set device` line specifies the device that PPP should use to establish the connection, in this case the second serial port, */dev/cuaa1*. For PPPoE connections, use the name of the Ethernet interface, prepended by the text PPPoE.

    ```
    set device PPPoE:xl0
    ```

- For modem connections, the `set speed` line sets the speed of the link between the modem and the computer. Some older PCs had problems at 115,200 bps, but you shouldn't have any need to change it any more, especially since the next lower speed for conventional PC hardware is 57,600 bps, which is too slow to use the full bandwidth when compression is enabled.

- Also for modems only, `set dial` describes a *chat script*, a series of responses and commands to be exchanged with the modem.

- `enable dns` tells PPP to get information about name servers when setting up the link. If the remote site supplies this information, you don't need to set it manually. You should remove this line if you're running a local name server, which I strongly recommend. See Chapter 21, *The Domain Name Service*, for more details.

The default entry alone does not supply enough information to create a link. In particular, it does not specify who to call or what user name or password to use. In addition to the default entry, you need an entry describing how to connect to a specific site. The bare minimum would be the first three set lines of the papchap entry in *ppp.conf*:

```
papchap:
  #
  # edit the next three lines and replace the items in caps with
  # the values which have been assigned by your ISP.
  #

  set phone PHONE_NUM
  set authname USERNAME
  set authkey PASSWORD

  set ifaddr 10.0.0.1/0 10.0.0.2/0 255.255.255.0 0.0.0.0
  add default HISADDR                      # Add a (sticky) default route
```

PPP calls this entry a *profile*. papchap is the profile supplied in the default installation. You can change the name, for example to the name of your ISP. This is particularly useful if you connect to more than one ISP (for example, with a laptop). In these examples, we'll stick with papchap.

As the comment states, replace the texts PHONE_NUM, USERNAME and PASSWORD with your specific information. If you are using PPPoE, replace the set phone line with a set device line as discussed above.

The last two lines may or may not be needed. The line set ifaddr specifies addresses to assign to each end of the link, and that they can be overridden. This line is seldom needed, even for static addressing: the ISP will almost always allocate the correct address. We'll look at this issue again below when we discuss dynamic addresses.

Finally, the last line tells *ppp* to set a default route on this interface when the line comes up. HISADDR is a keyword specifying the other end of the link. This is the only way to specify the route for dynamic addressing, but it works just as well for static addressing. If your primary connection to the Internet is via a different interface, remove this entry.

Negotiation

As we saw on page 342, you need to decide who starts negotiation. By default, user PPP starts negotiation. If the other end needs to start negotiation, add the following line to your */etc/ppp/ppp.conf*:

```
  set openmode passive
```

User PPP uses four keywords to specify how to negotiate:

- To *enable* a feature means: "request this feature."

- To *disable* a feature means: "do not request this feature."

- To *accept* a feature means: "if the other side requests this feature, accept it."

- To *deny* a feature means: "if the other side requests this feature, refuse it."

We'll see examples of this in the following sections.

Requesting LQR

By default, user PPP disables LQR, because it has been found to cause problems under certain circumstances, but it accepts it for modem lines. If you want to enable it, include the following line in your dial entry:

```
enable lqr
```

Authentication

The configuration file syntax is the same for PAP and CHAP. Normally, your ISP assigns you both system name and authorization key. Assuming your system name is *FREEBIE*, and your key is *X4dWg9327*, you would include the following lines in your configuration entry:

```
set authname FREEBIE
set authkey  X4dWg9327
```

User PPP accepts requests for PAP and CHAP authentication automatically, so this is all you need to do unless you intend to authenticate the other end, which is not normal with ISPs.

/etc/ppp/ppp.secret

The PPP system name and authentication key for PAP or CHAP are important data. Anybody who has this information can connect to your ISP and use the service at your expense. Of course, you should set the permissions of your */etc/ppp/ppp.conf* to -r-------- and the owner to root, but it's easy and costly to make a mistake when changing the configuration. There is an alternative: store the keys in the file */etc/ppp/ppp.secret*. Here's a sample:

```
# Sysname      Secret Key     Peer's IP address
oscar          OurSecretKey   192.244.184.34/24
FREEBIE        X4dWg9327      192.244.184.33/32
gw             localPasswdForControl
```

There are a few things to note here:

- As usual, lines starting with # are comments.

- The other lines contain three values: the system name, the authentication key, and possibly an IP address.

- The last line is a password for connecting to the *ppp* process locally: you can connect to the process by starting:

  ```
  # telnet localhost 3000
  ```

  The local password entry matches the host name. See the man page *ppp(8)* for further details.

Dynamic IP configuration

If you have to accept dynamic IP addresses, user PPP can help. In fact, it provides fine control over which addresses you accept and which you do not. To allow negotiation of IP addresses, you specify how many bits of the IP addresses at each end are of interest to you. For static addresses, you can specify them exactly:

```
set ifaddr 139.130.136.133  139.130.136.129
```

You can normally maintain some control over the addressing, for example to ensure that the addresses assigned don't conflict with other network connections. The addresses assigned to you when the link comes up are almost invariably part of a single subnet. You can specify that subnet and allow negotiation of the host part of the address. For example, you may say "I don't care what address I get, as long as the first three bytes are 139.130.136, and the address at the other end starts with 139." You can do this by specifying the number of bits that interest you after the address:

```
set ifaddr 139.130.136.133/24  139.130.136.129/8
```

This says that you would prefer the addresses you state, but that you require the first 24 bits of the local interface address and the first eight bits of the remote interface address to be as stated.

If you really don't care which address you get, specify the local IP address as 0:

```
set ifaddr 0 0
```

If you do this, you can't use the -auto modes, because you need to send a packet to the interface to trigger dialing. Use one of the previous methods in this situation.

Running user PPP

After setting up your PPP configuration, run it like this:

```
$ ppp
Working in interactive mode
Using interface: tun0
ppp ON freebie> dial papchap          this is the name of the entry in ppp.conf
Dial attempt 1 of 1
Phone: 1234567                         the phone number
dial OK!                               modem connection established
login OK!                              authentication complete
ppp ON freebie> Packet mode.          PPP is running
ppp ON freebie>
PPP ON freebie>                        and the network connection is complete
```

You'll notice that the prompt (ppp) changes to upper case (PPP) when the connection is up and running. At the same time, *ppp* writes some messages to the log file */var/log/ppp.log*:

```
Sep  2 15:12:38 freebie ppp[23679]: Phase: Using interface: tun0
Sep  2 15:12:38 freebie ppp[23679]: Phase: PPP Started.
Sep  2 15:12:47 freebie ppp[23679]: Phase: Phone: 1234567
Sep  2 15:13:08 freebie ppp[23679]: Phase: *Connected!
Sep  2 15:13:11 freebie ppp[23679]: Phase: NewPhase: Authenticate
Sep  2 15:13:11 freebie ppp[23679]: Phase:  his = c223, mine = 0
Sep  2 15:13:11 freebie ppp[23679]: Phase:  Valsize = 16, Name = way3.Adelaide
Sep  2 15:13:11 freebie ppp[23679]: Phase: NewPhase: Network
Sep  2 15:13:11 freebie ppp[23679]: Phase: Unknown protocol 0x8207
Sep  2 15:13:11 freebie ppp[23679]: Link:  myaddr = 139.130.136.133  hisaddr = 139.1
30.136.129
Sep  2 15:13:11 freebie ppp[23679]: Link: OsLinkup: 139.130.136.129
Sep  2 15:14:11 freebie ppp[23679]: Phase: HDLC errors -> FCS: 0 ADDR: 0 COMD: 0 PRO
TO: 1
```

You'll notice a couple of messages that look like errors. In fact, they're not: Unknown protocol 0x8207 means that the other end requested a protocol that *ppp* doesn't know (and, in fact, is not in the RFCs. This is a real example, and the protocol is in fact Novell's IPX). The other message is HDLC errors -> FCS: 0 ADDR: 0 COMD: 0 PROTO: 1. In fact, this relates to the same "problem."

How long do we stay connected?

The following entries in */etc/defaults/rc.conf* relate to user ppp:

```
# User ppp configuration.
ppp_enable="NO"          # Start user-ppp (or NO).
ppp_mode="auto"          # Choice of "auto", "ddial", "direct" or "dedicated".
                         # For details see man page for ppp(8). Default is auto.
ppp_nat="YES"            # Use PPP's internal network address translation or NO.
ppp_profile="papchap"    # Which profile to use from /etc/ppp/ppp.conf.
ppp_user="root"          # Which user to run ppp as
```

Now our PPP connection is up and running. How do we stop it again? There are two possibilities:

- To stop the connection, but to leave the *ppp* process active, enter close:

```
PPP ON freebie> close
ppp ON freebie>
```

- To stop the connection and the *ppp* process, enter q or quit:

```
PPP ON freebie> q
#
```

There are a couple of problems with this method: first, a connection to an ISP usually costs money in proportion to the time you are connected, so you don't want to stay connected longer than necessary. On the other hand, you don't want the connection to drop while you're using it. User PPP approaches these problems with a compromise: when the line has been idle for a certain time (in other words, when no data has gone in either direction during this time), it disconnects. This time is called the *idle timeout*, and by default it is set to 180 seconds. You can set it explicitly:

```
set timeout 300
```

This sets the idle timeout to 300 seconds (5 minutes).

Automating the process

Finally, setting up the connection this way takes a lot of time. You can automate it in a number of ways:

- If you have a permanent connection, you can tell user PPP to stay up all the time. Use the -ddial modifier:

```
$ ppp -ddial papchap
```

Again, papchap is the name of the PPP profile. This version dials immediately and keeps the connection up regardless of whether traffic is passing or not.

- If you want to be able to connect to the Net automatically whenever you have something to say, use the -auto modifer:

```
$ ppp -auto papchap
```

In this case, user PPP does not dial immediately. As soon as you attempt to send data to the Net, however, it dials automatically. When the line has been idle for the idle timeout period, it disconnects again and waits for more data before dialing. This only makes sense for static addresses or when you know that no IP connections remain alive after the line disconnects.

- Finally, you can just write

```
$ ppp -background papchap
```

The -background option tells user PPP to dial immediately and stay in the background. After the idle timeout period, the user PPP process disconnects and exits. If you want to connect again, you must restart the process.

Actions on connect and disconnect

If you don't have a permanent connection, there are some things that you might like to do every time you connect, like flush your outgoing mail queue. User PPP provides a method for doing this: create a */etc/ppp/ppp.linkup* with the same format as */etc/ppp/ppp.conf*. If it exists, PPP looks for the profile you used to start PPP (papchap in our examples) and executes the commands in that section. Use the exclamation mark (!) to specify that the commands should be performed by a shell. For example, to flush your mail queue, you might write:

```
papchap:
 ! sendmail -q
```

Similarly, you can create a file */etc/ppp/ppp.linkdown* with commands to be executed when the link goes down. You can find sample files in the directory */usr/share/examples/ppp*.

If things go wrong

Things don't always work "out of the box." You could run into a number of problems. We'll look at the more common ones on page 361.

Setting up kernel PPP

It makes more sense to run PPP in the kernel than in user space: in the kernel it's more efficient and theoretically less prone to error. The implementation has fewer features than user PPP, and it's not quite as easy to debug, so it is not used as much.

The configuration files for kernel PPP are in the same directory as the user PPP configuration files. You can also set up your own *˜/.ppprc* file, though I don't recommend this: PPP is a system function and should not be manipulated at the user level.

Kernel PPP uses a daemon called *pppd* to monitor the line when it is active. Kernel PPP interface names start with *ppp* followed by a number. You need one for each concurrent link. You don't need to specifically build a kernel for the *ppp* interface: FreeBSD Release 5 loads the PPP module */boot/kernel/if_ppp.ko* dynamically and adds interfaces as required. This also means that you can no longer check for ppp support with the *ifconfig* command. The interface won't be there until you need it.

Kernel PPP used to provide a number of build options to enable some features, including the compression options described below. The options are still there, but they're set by default, so you don't need to do anything there either.

When kernel PPP starts, it reads its configuration from the file */etc/ppp/options*. Here is a typical example:

```
# Options file for PPPD
defaultroute                    set the default route here when the line comes up
crtscts                         use hardware flow control
modem                           use modem control lines
deflate 12,12                   use deflate compression
predictor1                      use predictor 1 compression
vj-max-slots 16                 Van Jacobson compression slots
user FREEBIE                    our name (index in password file)
lock                            create a UUCP lock file
```

This is quite a short file, but it's full of interesting stuff:

- The `defaultroute` line tells the kernel PPP to set the default route via this interface after it establishes a connection.

- The `crtscts` line tells it to use hardware flow control (necessary to prevent loss of characters). You could also specify `xonxoff`, which uses software flow control, but hardware flow control is preferable.

- The `modem` line says to monitor the modem *DCD* (Carrier detect) line. If the connection is lost without proper negotiation, the only way that kernel PPP can know about it is because of the drop in *DCD*.

- The line *deflate* tells kernel PPP to request *deflate* compression, which can increase the effective bandwidth.

- `predictor1` tells PPP to use *Predictor 1* compression where possible.

- `vj-max-slots` specifies how many slots to use for *Van Jacobson* header compression. Having more slots can speed things up.

- The `user` line tells kernel PPP the user ID to use. If you don't specify this, it takes the system's name.

- `lock` tells kernel PPP to create a UUCP-style lock on the serial line. This prevents other programs, such as *getty*, from trying to open the line while it is running PPP.

None of these options are required to run *pppd*, though you'll probably need a `user` entry to establish connection. It's a good idea to set the indicated options, however.

Authentication

We've seen that */etc/ppp/options* contains a user name, but no password. The passwords are stored in separate files, */etc/ppp/chap-secrets* for *CHAP*, or */etc/ppp/pap-secrets* for *PAP*. The format of either file is:

username systemname password

To match any system name, set *systemname* to *. For example, to authenticate the *FREEBIE* we saw on page 351, we would enter the following in the file:

```
FREEBIE * X4dWg9327
```

In addition, you should add a `domain` line to specify your domain for authentication purposes:

```
domain example.org
```

Dialing

Kernel PPP does not perform dialing, so you need to start a program that does the dialing. In the following example, we use *chat*, a program derived from UUCP intended exactly for this purpose. Some people use *kermit*, which is in fact a complete communications program for a PC protocol, to perform this function, but this requires manual intervention. *chat* does the whole job for you.

Chat scripts

chat uses a *chat script* to define the functions to perform when establishing a connection. See the man page *chat(8)* for further details. The chat script consists primarily of alternate *expect strings*, which *chat* waits to receive, followed by *send* strings, which *chat* sends when it receives the *expect* string.

In addition to these strings, the chat script can contain other commands. To confuse things, they are frequently written on a single line, though this is not necessary: *chat* does not pay any attention to line breaks. Our chat script, which we store in */etc/ppp/dial.chat*, looks more intelligible written in the following manner:

```
# Abort the chat script if the modem replies BUSY or NO CARRIER
ABORT BUSY
ABORT 'NO CARRIER'
# Wait up to 5 seconds for the reply to each of these
TIMEOUT 5
'' ATZ
OK ATDT1234567
# Wait 40 seconds for connection
TIMEOUT 40
CONNECT
```

This script first tells *chat* to abort dial-up on a BUSY or NO CARRIER response from the modem. The next line waits for nothing ('') and resets the modem with the command ATZ. The following line waits for the modem to reply with OK, and dials the ISP.

Call setup can take a while, almost always more than five seconds for real (analogue) modems, so we need to extend the timeout, in this case to 40 seconds. During this time we must get the reply CONNECT from the modem.

Who throws the first stone?

On page 342 we saw how to specify whether we should start negotiating or whether we should wait for the other end to start. By default, kernel PPP starts negotiation. If you want the other end to start, add the keyword passive in your */etc/ppp/options* file.

Dynamic IP configuration

By default, kernel PPP performs dynamic address negotiation, so you don't need to do anything special for dynamic IP. If you have static addresses, add the following line to */etc/ppp/conf*:

```
139.130.136.133:139.130.136.129
```

These are the addresses that you would use on machine gw.example.org to set up the PPP link in the middle of Figure 16-7 on page 294. The first address is the local end of the link (the address of the *pppn* device), and the second is the address of the remote machine (free-gw.example.net).

Running kernel PPP

To run *pppd*, enter:

```
# pppd /dev/cuaa1 115200 connect 'chat -f /etc/ppp/dial.chat'
```

This starts kernel PPP on the serial line */dev/cuaa1* at 115,200 bps. The option connect tells kernel PPP that the following argument is the name of a program to execute: it runs *chat* with the options -f /etc/ppp/dial.chat, which tells *chat* the name of the chat file.

After you run *pppd* with these arguments, the modem starts dialing and then negotiates a connection with your provider, which should complete within 30 seconds. During negotiation, you can observe progress with the *ifconfig* command:

```
$ ifconfig ppp0
ppp0: flags=8010<POINTOPOINT,MULTICAST> mtu 1500
         at this point, the interface has not yet started
$ ifconfig ppp0
ppp0: flags=8810<POINTOPOINT,RUNNING,MULTICAST> mtu 1500
      now the interface has been started
$ ifconfig ppp0
ppp0: flags=8811<UP,POINTOPOINT,RUNNING,MULTICAST> mtu 1500
      inet 139.130.136.133 --> 139.130.136.129 netmask 0xffffffff
      now the connection has been established
```

Automating the process

You can automate connection setup and disconnection in a number of ways:

- If you have a permanent connection, you can tell kernel PPP to stay up all the time. Add the following line to */etc/ppp/options*:

  ```
  persist
  ```

  If this option is set, kernel PPP dials immediately and keeps the connection up regardless of whether traffic is passing or not.

- If you want to be able to connect to the Net automatically whenever you have something to say, use the demand option:

  ```
  demand
  ```

  In this case, kernel PPP does not dial immediately. As soon as you attempt to send data to the net, however, it dials automatically. When the line has been idle for the idle timeout period, it disconnects again and waits for more data before dialing.

- Finally, you can start kernel PPP without either of these options. In this case, you are connected immediately. After the idle timeout period, kernel PPP disconnects and exits. If you want to connect again, you must restart the process.

Timeout parameters

A number of options specify when kernel PPP should dial and disconnect:

- The idle parameter tells kernel PPP to disconnect if the line has been idle for the specified number of seconds, and if persist (see above) has not been specified. For example, to disconnect after five minutes, you could add the following line to the */etc/ppp/options* file:

  ```
  idle 300
  ```

- The active-filter parameter allows you to specify which packets to count when determining whether the line is idle. See the man page for more details.

- The holdoff parameter tells kernel PPP how long to wait before redialing when the line has been disconnected for reasons other than being idle. If the line is disconnected because it was idle, and you have specified demand, it dials as soon as the next valid packet is received.

Configuration summary

To summarize the examples above, we'll show the kernel PPP versions of the user PPP examples on page 348. As before, we assume that the reference network on page 294 uses *CHAP* authentication, and we have to initiate. The */etc/ppp/options* looks like:

```
# Options file for PPPD
defaultroute                          set the default route here when the line comes up
crtscts                               use hardware flow control
modem                                 use modem control lines
domain example.org                    specify your domain name
persist                               stay up all the time
deflate 12,12                         use deflate compression
predictor1                            use predictor 1 compression
vj-max-slots 16                       Van Jacobson compression slots
user FREEBIE                          name to present to ISP
139.130.136.133:139.130.136.129       specify IP addresses of link
```

/etc/ppp/dial.chat is unchanged from the example on page 357:

```
# Abort the chat script if the modem replies BUSY or NO CARRIER
ABORT BUSY
ABORT 'NO CARRIER'
# Wait up to 5 seconds for the reply to each of these
TIMEOUT 5
'' ATZ
OK ATDT1234567
# Wait 40 seconds for connection
TIMEOUT 40
CONNECT
```

/etc/ppp/chap-secrets contains:

```
FREEBIE * X4dWg9327
```

With kernel PPP, there's no need to disable *PAP*: that happens automatically if it can't find an authentication for *FREEBIE* in */etc/pap-secrets*.

The change for dynamic addressing is even simpler. Remove the line with the IP addresses from the */etc/ppp/options* file:

```
# Options file for PPPD
defaultroute                          set the default route here when the line comes up
crtscts                               use hardware flow control
modem                                 use modem control lines
domain example.org                    specify your domain name
persist                               stay up all the time
deflate 12,12                         use deflate compression
predictor1                            use predictor 1 compression
vj-max-slots 16                       Van Jacobson compression slots
user FREEBIE                          name to present to ISP
```

Actions on connect and disconnect

If you don't have a permanent connection, there are some things that you might like to do every time you connect, like flush your outgoing mail queue. We've seen that user PPP provides a method for doing this with the */etc/ppp/ppp.linkup* and */etc/ppp/ppp.linkdown* files. Kernel PPP supplies similar functionality with */etc/ppp/auth-up* and */etc/ppp/auth-down*. Both of these files are shell scripts. For example, to flush your mail queue, you might put the following line in */etc/ppp/auth-up*:

```
sendmail -q
```

Things that can go wrong

Setting up PPP used to be a pain. Two things have made it easier than it used to be. Firstly, the widespread adoption of dialup Internet connections has consolidated the procedure, so one size fits nearly everybody. Secondly, the software has had some of the rough edges taken off, so now it almost works out of the box. Still there are a number of things that can go wrong.

Problems establishing a connection

The first thing you need to do is to dial the connection. If you have an external modem, you can follow the process via the indicator LEDs. The following steps occur:

- First, the OH LED ("off hook") goes on, indicating that the modem is dialing. If this doesn't happen, check the cables and that you're talking to the right device.

- Next you should see a brief flicker of the RD and TD LEDs. If that doesn't happen, you may also have cable problems, or it could be a problem with the chat script.

- When the CD (or DCD) LED goes on, you have a connection to the remote system. If you don't get that, check the phone number.

- If you get this far, but you still don't get a connection, check the system log files. It's most likely to be an authentication failure. See page 353 for an example of the messages from user PPP. Kernel PPP is much less verbose.

21

The Domain Name Service

Ever since the beginning of the ARPAnet, systems have had both names and IP addresses. UNIX systems, as well as many others who have copied the BSD IP implementation, used the file */etc/hosts* to convert between names and addresses. This file contains a list of IP addresses and the corresponding host names, one per line.

It's clearly impossible to have an */etc/hosts* file that describes the complete Internet. Even if you had disk space, the number of updates would overload your network. The solution is a distributed database, the *Domain Name System*, or *DNS*. The most common implementation of DNS is *BIND*, the *Berkeley Internet Name Domain*.[1] You'll notice the word *Berkeley* in there. BIND is part of BSD, and it's about the only game in town. Despite these names, the daemon that performs the resolution is called *named* (the *name daemon*, pronounced "name-dee").

DNS provides the information needed to connect to remote systems in the form of *Resource Records*, or *RRs*. Unfortunately, the names of the records aren't overly intuitive.

• *A (Address) records* translate host names to IP addresses. For example, one A record tells you that *www.FreeBSD.org* (currently) has the IP address 216.136.204.117. These are what most people think of when they hear the name DNS. The name specified in the A record is called the *canonical* name of the interface, and it should be the one to which the PTR record (see below) refers.

---

1. Does this sound like an acronym in search of a name?

- *PTR (Pointer) records* provide a translation from IP address to name. This process is also called *reverse lookup*.

- *MX (Mail Exchange) records* specify the IP addresses of mail servers for a domain.

- *SOA (Start Of Authority) records* define *zones*, which roughly correspond to domains. We'll look at the distinction between zones and domains below.

- *NS (Name Server) records* describe name servers for a zone.

- *HINFO (Hardware Information) records* describe the hardware and software that runs on a particular system.

- *CNAME (Canonical Name) records* describe alternative names for a system.

FreeBSD allows you to use both */etc/hosts* and DNS. One reason for this might be to have name resolution of local hosts at startup time: there's a chicken-and-egg problem with mounting NFS file systems before *named* is running.

The common objections to using DNS include:

- It's supposedly difficult to set up DNS configuration files.

- DNS supposedly generates a lot of network traffic.

- DNS supposedly causes a dial-on-demand system to dial all the time.

These statements are all untrue. We'll look at them in the rest of this chapter as we set up DNS for our reference network.

Domains and zones

In Internet parlance, a *domain* is a group of names ending with a specific *domain name*. We looked at domain names in Chapter 18, *Connecting to the Internet*, page 318. Note that, like file names, there are two kinds of domain names:

- A *fully qualified domain name* (*FQDN*) ends in a period (.). This domain name relates to the root domain . (a single period).

- A *relative domain name* relates to the current domain. You'll see them occasionally in the configuration files.

Most times, when you write a domain name, you intend it to be fully qualified. But if you write it without the terminating period, DNS will frequently append your own domain name. For example, if you specify a name like *freebie.example.org*, DNS won't find a fully qualified name: it's a misspelling of *freebie.example.org.*. As a result, it will look for the name *freebie.example.org.example.org*. It won't find it, of course, but it may spend a long time trying. The moral is simple: when writing DNS configuration files, always put a period (full stop) at the end of names that are fully qualified.

Zones

In many ways, a *zone* is the same thing as a domain: it's the subset of the DNS name space that is maintained by a specific set of name servers—in DNS-speak, name servers are *authoritative* for the zone. The difference is mainly in the way it's used. There is one exception, however: usually, a *subdomain* will have a different name server. This subdomain is part of the domain, but not of the zone.

For example, in our reference network, the name servers on *freebie* and *presto* are authoritative for *example.org*. The owner of the domain might give permission for somebody, maybe in a different country, to run a subdomain *china.example.org*, with name servers *beijing.china.example.org* and *xianggang.china.example.org*. Because there are different name servers, there are two zones: *freebie.example.org* would be authoritative for the zone *example.org*, but not for *china.example.org*. *beijing.china.example.org* and *xianggang.china.example.org* would be authoritative for the zone *china.example.org*, but not for *example.org*.

Setting up a name server

DNS service is supplied by the *name daemon*, called *named*. *named* can be run in a number of different modes. In this chapter, we'll concentrate on setting the appropriate configurations for our reference network. If you want to go further, check the following documents:

- The *BIND Online Documentation*, in the source distribution in the directory */usr/src/contrib/bind/doc/html/index.html*.

- *TCP/IP Network Administration*, by Craig Hunt (O'Reilly).

- *DNS and BIND*, by Paul Albitz and Cricket Liu (O'Reilly).

In the last few years, BIND has undergone some significant changes, mainly as a result of abuse on the net. The current release is Version 9, but FreeBSD still ships with Version 8. The differences are relatively minor: Version 9 introduces a number of new features, but the contents of this chapter should also apply to Version 9. The previous version was Version 4, and you'll still find a lot of old documentation referring to it. There were no Versions 5, 6 or 7, and the main configuration file changed its format completely in Version 8; even the name changed. We'll look at how to convert the formats on page 380. Before using the documentation above, make sure that it refers to the correct version of BIND.

Passive DNS usage

Not every system needs to run its own name daemon. If you have another machine on the same network, you can send requests to it. For example, in the reference network, *freebie* and *presto* may be running name servers. There's no particular reason for *bumble* and *wait*, both presumably slower machines, to do so as well. Instead, you can tell them to use the name servers on the other two machines.

To do this, make sure that you don't enable *named* in your */etc/rc.conf*, and create a file */etc/resolv.conf* with the following contents:

```
domain example.org
nameserver 223.147.37.1          # freebie
nameserver 223.147.37.2          # presto
```

Specify the IP addresses, not the names, of the name servers here. This is a classic chicken-and-egg problem: you can't access the name server to get its address until you know its address.

With this file in place, this machine will send all name server requests to *freebie* or *presto*. We'll look at how to configure them later.

Name server on a standalone system

If you only have a single machine connected to the network, and your own machine is part of the ISP's zone, you can use the *resolv.conf* method as well. This is a fairly typical situation if you're using a PPP or DSL link. It's still not a good idea, however. Every lookup goes over the link, which is relatively slow. The results of the lookup aren't stored anywhere locally, so you can end up performing the same lookup again and again. DNS has an answer to the problem: save the information locally. You can do this with a *caching-only name server*. As the name suggests, the caching-only name server doesn't have any information of its own, but it stores the results of any queries it makes to other systems, so if a program makes the same request again—which happens frequently—it presents the results much more quickly on subsequent requests. Set up a caching-only name server like this:

- Either rename or remove */etc/resolv.conf*, and create a new one with the following contents:

  ```
  nameserver 127.0.0.1                           local name server
  ```

- Put this line in */etc/rc.conf*:

  ```
  named_enable="YES"                    # Run named, the DNS server (or NO).
  ```

  If */etc/rc.conf* doesn't exist, just create one with this content.

- Create a file */etc/namedb/localhost.rev* containing:

```
$TTL 1d
@          IN SOA     @host@. root.@host@.  (
                                 @date@  ; Serial
                                 1h      ; Refresh
                                 5m      ; Retry
                                 100d    ; Expire
                                 1h )    ; Negative cache
           IN NS      @host@.
1          IN PTR     localhost.@domain@.
```

We'll look at the meaning of this file in the next section. To create it, you can start with the file */etc/namedb/PROTO.localhost.rev*, which contains a template for this file. Replace @host@ with the FQDN of your host (*freebie.example.org* in this example), @date@ (the serial number) with the date in the form *yyyymmddxx*, where *xx* are a small integer such as 01,[1] and @domain@ with *example.org.*. Make sure that the FQDNs end with a trailing period. Alternatively, you can run the script */etc/namedb/make-localhost*.

- Edit the file */etc/namedb/named.conf* to contain:

```
options {
        directory "/etc/namedb";

        forwarders {
                139.130.237.3;   139.130.237.17;
        };
zone "0.0.127.in-addr.arpa" {
        type master;
        file "localhost.rev";
};
```

/etc/namedb/named.conf should already be present on your system as well. It contains a lot of comments, but at the end there's a similar zone definition, which you can edit if you want. The addresses 139.130.237.3 and 139.130.237.17. are the ISP's name server addresses. The forwarders line contains up to ten name server addresses.

- Start *named*:

```
# ndc start
```

---

1. We'll look at the serial number on page 368.

Name server on an end-user network

Of course, a simple caching-only name server won't work when you have your own domain. In fact, most of the authorities who allocate domain names won't even let you register an Internet domain unless you specify two functional name servers, and they'll check them before the registration can proceed. In this section, we'll look at what you need to do to run a "real" name server.

The first thing we need to do is to create a zone file for our zone *example.org*. We'll put it and all other zone files in a directory */etc/namedb* and call it */etc/namedb/db.example.org* after the name of the zone it describes.

The SOA record

The first thing we need is a record describing the *Start of Authority*. This defines a new zone. Write:

```
$TTL 1d
example.org.     IN SOA      freebie.example.org. grog.example.org. (
                                2003031801 ; Serial (date, 2 digits version of day)
                                1d    ; refresh
                                2h    ; retry
                                100d ; expire
                                1h ) ; negative cache expiry
```

The first line, $TTL 1d, is relatively new. It's not strictly part of the SOA record, but it's now required to fully define the SOA. It specifies the length of time that remote name servers should cache records from this zone. During this time they will not attempt another lookup. In older versions of BIND, this value was stored in the last field of the SOA record below.

The remaining lines define a single SOA record. the name on the left is the name of the zone. The keyword IN means *Internet*, in other words the Internet Protocols. The BIND software includes support for multiple network types, most of which have now been forgotten. The keyword SOA defines the type of record. *freebie.example.org* is the master name server.

The next field, *grog.example.org*, is the mail address of the DNS administrator. "Wait a minute," you may say, "that's not a mail address. There should be an @ there, not a . ." That's right, but unfortunately DNS uses the @ sign for other purposes, and it would be a syntax error in this position. So the implementors resorted to this kludge. To generate the mail ID, replace the first . with an @, to give you *grog@example.org*.

The *serial number* identifies this version of the zone configuration. Remote name servers first retreive the SOA record and check if the serial number has incremented before deciding whether to access the rest of the zone, which could be large. Make sure you increment this field every time you edit the file. If you don't, your updates will not propagate to other name servers. It's a good idea to use a format that reflects the date, as here: the format gives four digits for the year, two digits for the month, two for the day, and two for the number of the modification on a particular day. The serial number in this example shows it to be the second modification to the zone configuration on 18 March 2003.

The remaining parameters describe the timeout characteristics of the zone. Use the values in the example unless you have a good reason to change them. The data formats for the records require all times to be specified in seconds, and in previous versions of BIND, this was the only choice you had. In current versions of BIND, you can use scale factors like d for day and h for hours in the configuration file. *named* converts them to seconds before transmission.

- The *refresh* time is the time after which a remote name server will check whether the zone configuration has changed. 1 day is reasonable here unless you change your configuration several times per day.

- The *retry* time is the time to wait if an attempt to load the zone fails.

- The *expire* time is the time after which a slave name server will drop the information about a zone if it has not been able to reload it from the master name server. You probably want to make this large.

- In previous versions of BIND, the last field was the *minimum time to live*. Now the $TTL parameter sets that value, and the last parameter specifies the *negative caching* time. If an authoritative name server (one that maintains the zone) reports that a record doesn't exist, it returns an SOA record as well to indicate that it's authoritative. The local name server maintains this information for the period of time specified by this field of the returned SOA record and it doesn't retry the query until the time has expired. The only way things can change here is if the remote hostmaster changes the DNS configuration, so it's reasonable to keep the negative cache time to about an hour.

The A records

The most obvious requirement are the IP addresses of the systems on the network. In the zone *example.org*, define the A records like this:

```
localhost     IN A      127.0.0.1           local machine, via loopback interface
freebie       IN A      223.147.37.1
presto        IN A      223.147.37.2
bumble        IN A      223.147.37.3
wait          IN A      223.147.37.4
gw            IN A      223.147.37.5
```

In practice, as we will see in the completed configuration file, we tend to put the A records further towards the end of the list, because they are usually the most numerous. It makes the file easier to read if we put them after the shorter groups of entries.

The NS records

DNS uses a special kind of record to tell where your name servers are. In our case, we're running name servers on *freebie* and *presto*. We could write:

```
IN NS       freebie.example.org.
IN NS       presto.example.org.
```

This would work just fine, but in fact we'll do it a little differently, as we'll see in the next section.

Nicknames

We're running a whole lot of services on the reference network, in particular a web server and an ftp server. By convention, a web server machine is called *www*, an ftp server is called *ftp*, and a name server is called *ns*. But they're both running on machines with different names. What do we do? We give our machines nicknames:

```
www         IN CNAME        freebie
ftp         IN CNAME        presto
```

We'd like to do the same with the name servers, but unfortunately DNS doesn't like that, and will complain about your DNS configuration all over the world if you make *ns* a CNAME. There's a good reason for this: if you use CNAME records to define your name servers, remote systems have to perform two lookups to find the address of the name server, one to retreive the CNAME and one to get the corresponding A record for the CNAME. Define new A records for them:

```
            IN NS       ns
            IN NS       ns1

ns          IN A        223.147.37.1
ns1         IN A        223.147.37.2
```

You'll note that we're using relative domain names in these examples. They are taken to be relative to the name that starts the SOA record.

The MX records

As we will see on page 493, you could send mail to hosts listed in an A record, but it's not a good idea. Instead, you should have at least two MX records to tell SMTP what to do with mail for your domain. This method has an added advantage: it allows you to rename individual machines without having to change the users' mail IDs. We'll take this advice and assume that all mail is sent to *user@example.org*. In addition, we'll use the ISP's mail server *mail.example.net* as a backup in case our mail server is down. That way, when it comes back up, the delivery will be expedited. The resulting MX records look like:

```
IN MX       50  bumble.example.org.
IN MX       100 mail.example.net.
```

The numbers 50 and 100 are called *preferences*. Theoretically you could make them 1 and 2, except that you might want to put others in between. A mail transfer agent sends mail to the system with the lowest preference unless it does not respond—then it tries the MX record with the next-lowest preference, and so on.

The HINFO records

Finally, you may want to tell the world about your hardware and this great operating system you're running. You can do that with the HINFO record:

```
freebie       IN HINFO    "Pentium/133"      "FreeBSD 4.0-CURRENT (4.4BSD)"
presto        IN HINFO    "Pentium II /233"  "FreeBSD 3.2 (4.4BSD)"
bumble        IN HINFO    "Pentium/133"      "SCO OpenServer"
wait          IN HINFO    "Pentium Pro 266"  "Microsoft Windows 95%"
gw            IN HINFO    "486/33"           "FreeBSD 3.2 (4.4BSD)"
```

Of course, telling the world the truth about your hardware also helps crackers choose the tools to use if they want to break into your system. If this worries you, don't use HINFO. It's still the exception to see HINFO records.

Putting it all together

In summary, our configuration file */etc/namedb/db.example.org* looks like:

```
; Definition of zone example.org
$TTL 1d
example.org.    IN SOA    freebie.example.org. grog.example.org.  (
                          2003031801 ; Serial (date, 2 digits version of day)
                          1d   ; refresh
                          2h   ; retry
                          100d ; expire
                          1h ) ; negative cache expiry

; name servers
                IN NS     ns
                IN NS     ns1

; MX records
                IN MX     50  bumble.example.org.
                IN MX     100 mail.example.net.

ns              IN A      223.147.37.1
ns1             IN A      223.147.37.2

; Hosts
localhost       IN A      127.0.0.1
freebie         IN A      223.147.37.1
presto          IN A      223.147.37.2
bumble          IN A      223.147.37.3
wait            IN A      223.147.37.4
gw              IN A      223.147.37.5

; nicknames
www             IN CNAME  freebie
ftp             IN CNAME  presto

; System information
freebie         IN HINFO  "Pentium/133"      "FreeBSD 4.0-CURRENT (4.4BSD)"
presto          IN HINFO  "Pentium II/233"   "FreeBSD 3.2 (4.4BSD)"
bumble          IN HINFO  "Pentium/133"      "SCO OpenServer"
```

```
wait            IN HINFO    "Pentium Pro 266"  "Microsoft Windows 95%"
gw              IN HINFO    "486/33"           "FreeBSD 3.2 (4.4BSD)"
```

You'll notice that comment lines start with ;, and not with the more usual #. Also, we have rearranged the MX records and the A records for the name servers. If we placed the MX records below the A records for the name servers, they would refer to *ns1.example.org*.

That's all the information we need for our zone *example.org*. But we're not done yet—we need another zone. Read on.

Reverse lookup

It's not immediately apparent that you might want to perform *reverse lookup*, to find the name associated with a specific IP address. In fact, it's used quite a bit, mainly to confirm that a system is really who it says it is. Many mail servers, including *FreeBSD.org*, insist on valid reverse lookup before accepting mail. We'll look at that in more detail in Chapter 27, on page 501. It's not difficult, but many systems, particularly those using Microsoft, don't have their reverse lookup set up correctly.

/etc/hosts is a file, so you can perform lookup in either direction. Not so with DNS: how can you know which name server is authoritative for the domain if you don't know its name? You can't, of course, so DNS uses a trick: it fabricates a name from the address. For the address 223.147.37.4, it creates a domain name *37.147.223.in-addr.arpa*. The digits of the address are reversed, and the last digit is missing: it's the host part of the address. It asks the name server for this domain to resolve the name *4.37.147.223.in-addr.arpa*.

To resolve the names, we need another zone. That means another file, which we'll call */etc/namedb/example-reverse*. It's not quite as complicated as the forward file:

```
$TTL 1d
@               IN SOA      freebie.example.org. grog.example.org.  (
                            2003022601 ; Serial (date, 2 digits version of day)
                            1d     ; refresh
                            2h     ; retry
                            100d   ; expire
                            2h )   ; negative cache
                IN NS       ns.example.org.
                IN NS       ns1.example.org.

1               IN PTR      freebie.example.org.
2               IN PTR      presto.example.org.
3               IN PTR      bumble.example.org.
4               IN PTR      wait.example.org.
5               IN PTR      gw.example.org.
```

In this case, the SOA record is identical to that in */etc/namedb/db.example.org*, with two exceptions: instead of the zone name at the beginning of the line, we have the @ symbol, and the serial number is different—you don't normally need to update reverse lookup domains so often. This @ symbol represents the name of the zone, in this case *37.147.223.in-addr.arpa.*. We'll see how that works when we make the

/etc/named/named.root file below. We also use the same name server entries. This time they need to be fully qualified, because they are in a different zone.

Finally, we have the PTR (reverse lookup) records. They specify only the last digit (the host part) of the IP address, so this will be prepended to the zone name. The host name at the end of the line is in fully qualified form, because it's in another zone. For example, in fully qualified form, the entry for *wait* could be written:

```
4.37.147.223.in-addr.arpa.             IN PTR     wait.example.org.
```

The distant view: the outside world

So far, we have gone to a lot of trouble to describe our own tiny part of the Internet. What about the rest? How can the name server find the address of, say, *freefall.Free-BSD.org*? So far, it can't.

What we need now is some information about other name servers who can help us, specifically the 13 *root name servers*. These are named *A.ROOT-SERVERS.NET.* through *M.ROOT-SERVERS.NET.*. They are described in a file that you can get from *ftp://ftp.rs.internic.net/domain/named.root* if necessary, but you shouldn't need to: after installing FreeBSD, it should be present in */etc/namedb/named.root*. This file has hardly changed in years—the names have changed once, but most of the addresses have stayed the same. Of course, it's always a good idea to check from time to time.

The named.conf file

So far, we have two files, one for each zone for which our name server is authoritative. In a large system, there could be many more. What we need now is to tell the name server which files to use. That's the main purpose of *named.conf*. There's already a skeleton in */etc/namedb/named.conf*. With the comments removed, it looks like:

```
options {
        directory "/etc/namedb";
        forwarders {
                127.0.0.1;
        };
zone "." {
        type hint;
        file "named.root";
};

zone "0.0.127.IN-ADDR.ARPA" {
        type master;
        file "localhost.rev";
};

zone "domain.com" {
        type slave;
        file "s/domain.com.bak";
        masters {
                192.168.1.1;
        };
};
```

```
zone "0.168.192.in-addr.arpa" {
        type slave;
        file "s/0.168.192.in-addr.arpa.bak";
        masters {
                192.168.1.1;
        };
};
```

Each entry consists of a keyword followed by text in braces ({}). These entries have the following significance:

- The `directory` entry tells *named* where to look for the configuration files.

- The first zone is the top-level domain, .. It's a hint: it tells *named* to look in the file *named.root* in its configuration directory. *named.root* contains the IP addresses of the 13 top-level name servers.

- We've seen the entry for `0.0.127.IN-ADDR.ARPA` already on page 367: it's the reverse lookup for the localhost address.

- The `hint` entry specifies the name of the file describing the root servers (domain .).

- The zone entries for *domain.com* and *0.168.192.in-addr.arpa* define *slave name servers*. A slave name server addresses all queries to one of the specified *master name servers*. In earlier versions of DNS, a slave name server was called a *secondary name server*, and the master name server was called a *primary name server*. This is still current usage outside BIND, but you should expect this to change.

This file already contains most of the information we need. The only things we need to add are the information about the names of our zones and the location of the description file:

```
zone "example.org" {
        type master;
        file "db.example.org";
};
zone "37.147.223.in-addr.arpa" {
        type master;
        file "example-reverse";
};
```

When we've done that, we can start the name server with *ndc*, the *named* control program:[1]

```
# ndc start
new pid is 86183
```

If it's already running, we can restart it:

```
# ndc reload
Reload initiated.
```

---

1. In Release 9 of *named* it will change its name to *rndc*.

Starting or restarting the name server doesn't mean it will work, of course. If you make a mistake in your configuration files, it may not work at all. Otherwise it might start, but refuse to load specific zones. *named* logs messages with *syslog*, and if you are using the standard *syslog* configuration, the messages will be written to the console and to the file */var/log/messages*. After starting *named*, you should check what it said. *named* produces a number of messages, including:

```
Mar 18 15:01:57 freebie named[69751]: starting (/etc/namedb/named.conf).  named 8.3.
4-REL Wed Dec 18 13:38:28 CST 2002 grog@freebie.example.org:/usr/obj/src/FreeBSD/5-S
TABLE-FREEBIE/src/usr.sbin/named
Mar 18 15:01:57 freebie named[69751]: hint zone "" (IN) loaded (serial 0)
Mar 18 15:01:57 freebie named[69751]: master zone "example.org" (IN) loaded (serial
2003031801)
Mar 18 15:01:57 freebie named[69751]: Zone "0.0.127.in-addr.arpa" (file localhost.re
verse): No default TTL ($TTL <value>) set, using SOA minimum instead
Mar 18 15:01:57 freebie named[69751]: master zone "0.0.127.in-addr.arpa" (IN) loaded
(serial 97091501)
Mar 18 15:01:57 freebie named[69751]: listening on [223.147.37.1].53 (rl0)
Mar 18 15:01:57 freebie named[69751]: listening on [127.0.0.1].53 (lo0)
Mar 18 15:01:57 freebie named[69752]: Ready to answer queries.
```

Note the warning output for *0.0.127.in-addr.arpa*: this is obviously an old-style zone file, as the serial number also suggests. It doesn't have a $TTL entry, so *named* defaults to the old-style behaviour and uses the last field (which used to be called "minimum") of the SOA record instead. This warning is not very serious, but you probably want a longer default TTL than you do for caching failed lookups, which is what the field is used for now.

What you don't want to see are error messages like:

```
May 10 14:26:37 freebie named[1361]: db.example.org: Line 28: Unknown type: System.
May 10 14:26:37 freebie named[1361]: db.example.org:28: Database error (System)
May 10 14:26:37 freebie named[1361]: master zone "example.org" (IN) rejected due to
errors (serial 1997010902)
```

As the last message states, this error has caused the zone to be rejected. Funny: if you look at line 28 of */etc/namedb/db.example.org*, it looks straightforward enough:

```
# System information
freebie        IN HINFO          "Pentium/133"      "FreeBSD 3.0-CURRENT (4.4BSD)"
presto         IN HINFO          "Pentium II/233"  "FreeBSD 2.2.5 (4.4BSD)"
```

The problem here is that *named* doesn't use the standard UNIX convention for comments: the comment character is a semicolon (;), not a hash mark (#).

Most other configuration errors should be self-explanatory. On page 379 we'll look at messages that *named* produces during normal operation.

Slave name servers

A lot of software relies on name resolution. If for any reason a name server is not accessible, it can cause serious problems. This is one of the reasons why most registrars insist on at least two name servers before they will register a domain.

If you run multiple name servers, it doesn't really matter which one answers. So why a distinction between *master* and *slave* name servers? It's purely organizational: a master name server loads its data from the configuration files you create, as we saw above. A slave name server loads its data from a master name server if it is running. It saves the information in a private file so that if it is restarted while the master name server isn't running, it can reload information about the zones it is serving from this file. This makes it a lot easier to configure a slave name server, of course; everything we need is in */etc/namedb/named.conf*:

```
zone "." {
        type hint;
        file "named.root";
};

zone "example.org" {
        type slave;
        file "backup.example.org";
        masters {
                223.147.37.1;
        };
};

zone "37.147.223.in-addr.arpa" {
        type slave;
        file "backup.example-reverse";
        masters {
                223.147.37.1;
        };
};

zone "0.0.127.in-addr.arpa" {
        type master;
        file "localhost.rev";
};
```

Although this is a slave name server, there's no point in being a slave for *localhost*'s reverse mapping, so the last entry is still a master.

The numerical address is for *freebie.example.org*, the name server from which the zone is to be loaded. We use the numerical address because the name server needs the address before it can perform resolution. You can specify multiple name servers if you want. The *backup file* is the name of the file where the zone information should be saved in case the name server is restarted when the master name server is not accessible.

The next level down: delegating zones

In the previous example, we configured a name server for a single zone with no subzones. We did briefly consider what would happen if we created a subdomain *china.example.org*. In this section, we'll create the configuration files for this subzone and see how to link it to the parent zone, a process called *delegation*.

china.example.org

For the subdomain *china.example.org*, the same considerations apply as in our previous example: we have a domain without subdomains. Only the names and the addresses change.

In the following examples, let's assume that *china.example.org* has two name servers, *beijing.china.example.org* and *xianggang.china.example.org*. Let's look at the files we might have on these systems, starting with */etc/namedb/db.china.example.org*:

```
; Definition of zone china.example.org
$TTL 1d
@                       IN SOA   beijing.china.example.org. zhang.china.example.org.  (
                                 2001061701 ; Serial (date, 2 digits version of day)
                                 1d    ; refresh
                                 2h    ; retry
                                 100d  ; expire
                                 2h )  ; negative cache

; name servers
                        IN NS    ns
                        IN NS    ns1
ns                      IN A     223.169.23.1
ns1                     IN A     223.169.23.2
; MX records
                        IN MX    50  xianggang.china.example.org.
                        IN MX    70  bumble.example.org.
                        IN MX    100 mail.example.net.

; Hosts
beijing                 IN A     223.169.23.1
xianggang               IN A     223.169.23.2
shanghai                IN A     223.169.23.3
guangzhou               IN A     223.169.23.4
gw                      IN A     223.169.23.5

; nicknames
www                     IN CNAME shanghai
ftp                     IN CNAME shanghai
```

Then, */etc/namedb/china-reverse*:

```
; Definition of zone china.example.org
@                       IN SOA   beijing.china.example.org. zhang.china.example.org.  (
                                 1997090501 ; Serial (date, 2 digits version of day)
                                 86400   ; refresh (1 day)
                                 7200    ; retry (2 hours)
                                 8640000 ; expire (100 days)
                                 86400 ) ; minimum (1 day)
```

```
; name servers
                IN NS       ns.china.example.org.
                IN NS       ns1.china.example.org.

; Hosts
1               IN PTR      beijing
2               IN PTR      xianggang
3               IN PTR      shanghai
4               IN PTR      guangzhou
5               IN PTR      gw
```

and finally */etc/namedb/named.conf*:

```
zone "." {
        type hint;
        file "named.root";
};

zone "0.0.127.IN-ADDR.ARPA" {
        type master;
        file "localhost.rev";
};

zone "china.example.org" {
        type master;
        file "db.china.example.org";
};

zone "23.169.233.IN-ADDR.ARPA" {
        type master;
        file "china-reverse";
};
```

These files look very much like the corresponding files for *example.org*. The real difference happens in the configuration for *example.org*, not for *china.example.org*. We'll look at that next.

example.org with delegation

What does *example.org*'s name server need to know about *china.example.org*? You might think, "nothing, they're separate zones," but that's not completely true. For a remote name server to find *china.example.org*, it first goes to *example.org*, so the parent domain must maintain enough information to find the child domain. This process is called *delegation*. The parent name server maintains NS records ("delegation records") and corresponding A records ("glue records") for the child zone. It might also be a good idea for the name servers for *example.org* to maintain a secondary name server for *china*: that way we can save a lookup to the master name servers for *china.example.org* most of the time. To do so, we add the following line to */etc/namedb/named.conf*:

```
zone "china.example.org" {
        type slave;
        file "backup.china";
        masters {
                223.169.23.1;
                223.169.23.2;
        };
};
```

```
zone "23.169.223.in-addr.arpa" {
        type slave;
        file "backup.china-reverse";
        masters {
                223.169.23.1;
                223.169.23.2;
        };
};
```

We add the following information to */etc/namedb/db.example.org*:

```
@               IN SOA    freebie.example.org. grog.example.org.  (
                          1997090501 ; Serial (date, 2 digits version of day)
                          86400    ; refresh (1 day)
                          7200     ; retry (2 hours)
                          8640000 ; expire (100 days)
                          86400 )  ; minimum (1 day)

china           IN NS     ns.china.example.org.
china           IN NS     ns1.china.example.org.

ns.china        IN A      223.169.23.1
ns1.china       IN A      223.169.23.2
```

We changed the information, so we also change the serial number of the SOA record so that the secondary name servers for *example.org* will reload the updated information.

We need to specify the addresses of the name servers as well. Strictly speaking they belong to the zone *china*, but we need to keep them in the parent zone *example.org*: these are the addresses to which we need to send any kind of query.

After changing the configuration like this, we restart the name server:

```
# ndc reload
```

We check the output, either by looking on the system console or by using the command tail /var/log/messages. We'll see something like:

```
Mar 18 15:23:40 freebie named[69752]: reloading nameserver
Mar 18 15:23:40 freebie named[69752]: master zone "china.example.org" (IN) loaded (s
erial 2001061701)
Mar 18 15:23:40 freebie named[69752]: Forwarding source address is [0.0.0.0].4673
Mar 18 15:23:40 freebie named[69752]: Ready to answer queries.
```

Messages from named

Once your *named* is up and running, it may still produce a number of messages. Here are some examples:

```
May 10 15:09:06 freebie named[124]: approved AXFR from [223.147.37.5].2872 for "exam
ple.org"
May 10 15:09:06 freebie named[124]: zone transfer of "example.org" (IN) to [192.109.
197.137].2872
```

These messages indicate that another name server has loaded the zone specified. This will typically be one of your secondary name servers. This should happen about as often as you have specified in your *refresh* parameter for the zone.

```
Mar 18 19:21:53 freebie named[69752]: ns_forw: query(tsolyani.com) contains our add
ress (freebie.example.org:223.147.37.1) learnt (A=example.org:NS=66.47.255.122)
```

This message indicates that the server indicated by the A record has asked us to forward a query whose name server list includes our own names or address(es). This used to be called a *lame delegation*. It's interesting that the address in this (real) message was *a.root-servers.net*, one of the 13 base servers for the whole Internet, which was probably forwarding a query from some other system. The server doesn't check the validity of the queries it forwards, so it's quite possible for them to be in error.

```
Mar 19 14:53:32 freebie named[13822]: Lame server on '182.201.184.212.relays.osirus
oft.com' (in 'relays.osirusoft.com'?): [195.154.210.134].53 'ns1-relays.osirusoft.c
om': learnt (A=216.102.236.44,NS=216.102.236.44)
```

This message indicates that a name server, listed as authoritative for a particular zone, is in fact not authoritative for that zone.

```
Sep 14 03:33:18 freebie named[55]: ns_forw: query(goldsword.com) NS points to CNAME
(ns-user.goldsword.com:) learnt (CNAME=199.170.202.100:NS=199.170.202.100)
```

As we saw above, a name server address should be an A record. The administrator of this system didn't know this, and pointed it to a CNAME record.

```
Sep 14 15:55:52 freebie named[55]: ns_forw: query(219.158.96.202.in-addr.arpa) A RR
negative cache entry (ns.gz.gdpta.net.cn:) learnt (NODATA=202.96.128.68:NS=202.12.28
.129)
```

This message indicates that the name server has already determined that the name server specified cannot be found, and has noted that fact in a *negative cache entry*.

Upgrading a Version 4 configuration

What we've seen so far applies to Versions 8 and 9 of *named*. The previous version was Version 4 (don't ask what happened to 5, 6 and 7; until Version 9 came along, there were rumours that the next version would be 16). Version 8 of *named* introduced a completely new configuration file format. If you have an existing DNS configuration from Version 4, the main configuration file will be called */etc/named.boot* or */etc/named/named.boot*. You can convert it to the *named.conf* format with the script */usr/sbin/named-bootconf*:

```
# named-bootconf < /etc/namedb/named.boot > /etc/namedb/named.conf
```

Looking up DNS information

You can use *dig*, *host* or *nslookup* to look up name information. It's largely a matter of preference which you use, but you should note that *nslookup* uses the resolver interface, which can result in you getting different results from what your name server would get. The output format of *dig* gets on my nerves, so I use *host*. Others prefer *dig* because it formulates the queries exactly the same way the name server does, and its output is more suited as input to *named*. For example, the command `dig @a.root-servers.net .` `axfr` produces a *named.root* file that *named* understands. We'll look briefly at *host*. Here are some examples:

```
$ host hub.freebsd.org                                 look up an A record
hub.freebsd.org has address 216.136.204.18
hub.freebsd.org mail is handled (pri=10) by mx1.freebsd.org
$ host 216.136.204.18                                  perform a reverse lookup
18.204.136.216.IN-ADDR.ARPA domain name pointer hub.freebsd.org
$ host ftp.freebsd.org                                 another one
ftp.freebsd.org is a nickname for ftp.beastie.tdk.net   this is a CNAME
ftp.beastie.tdk.net has address 62.243.72.50            and the corresponding A record
ftp.beastie.tdk.net mail is handled (pri=20) by mail-in1.inet.tele.dk
ftp.beastie.tdk.net mail is handled (pri=30) by mail-in2.inet.tele.dk
$ host -v -t soa freebsd.org                           Get an SOA record
Trying null domain
rcode = 0 (Success), ancount=1
The following answer is not authoritative:
freebsd.org            3066 IN SOA      ns0.freebsd.org hostmaster.freebsd.org(
                                        103031602    ;serial (version)
                                        1800      ;refresh period
                                        900       ;retry refresh this often
                                        604800    ;expiration period
                                        1800      ;minimum TTL
                       )
For authoritative answers, see:
freebsd.org            3066 IN NS       ns0.freebsd.org
freebsd.org            3066 IN NS       ns1.iafrica.com
freebsd.org            3066 IN NS       ns1.downloadtech.com
freebsd.org            3066 IN NS       ns2.downloadtech.com
Additional information:
ns0.freebsd.org        92727 IN A       216.136.204.126
ns1.iafrica.com        92727 IN A       196.7.0.139
ns1.downloadtech.com   92727 IN A       170.208.14.3
ns2.downloadtech.com   92727 IN A       66.250.75.2
ns2.iafrica.com        22126 IN A       196.7.142.133
```

There are a number of things to look at in the last example:

- We used the -v (verbose) option to get more information.

- Note the message `Trying null domain`. This comes because the name supplied was not a fully qualified domain name: the period at the end was missing. *host* decides that it looks like a fully qualified name, so it doesn't append a domain name to the name.

- The local name server at *example.org* already had the SOA record for *FreeBSD.org* in its cache; as a result, it didn't need to ask the name server that was authoritative for the zone. Instead, it tells you that the answer was not authoritative and tells you where you can get a valid answer.

- The output is in pretty much the same format as we discussed earlier in the chapter, but there are some numbers in front of IN in all the resource records. These are the *time-to-live* values for each individual record, in seconds. You can put these in the zone files, too, if you want, and they'll override the TTL value for the zone. In this printout, they specify how long it will be before the cached entry expires. Try it again and you'll see that the value is lower.

To get an answer from one of the authoritative name servers, we simply specify its name at the end of the request:

```
$ host -v -t soa freebsd.org. ns0.freebsd.org.
host -v -t soa freebsd.org. ns0.sd.org.
Using domain server:
Name: ns0.freebsd.org
Addresses: 216.136.204.126

rcode = 0 (Success), ancount=1
freebsd.org                3600 IN SOA    ns0.freebsd.org hostmaster.freebsd.org(
                                          103031602     ;serial (version)
                                          1800     ;refresh period
                                          900      ;retry refresh this often
                                          604800   ;expiration period
                                          1800     ;minimum TTL

                       )
```

This time we specified the names as FQDNs, so the message about the null domain no longer appears. Also, the TTL value is now the correct value for the record, and it won't change. Apart from that, the only difference is the missing message that the answer is not authoritative. The rest of the printout is the same.

You can also use the -t option to look for a specific record:

```
$ host -t mx freebsd.org.                    get the MX records
freebsd.org mail is handled (pri=10) by mx1.freebsd.org
$ host -t hinfo hub.freebsd.org.             get HINFO records
$ host -t hinfo freefall.freebsd.org.
freefall.freebsd.org host information Intel FreeBSD
```

These invocations don't use the -v (*verbose*) option, so they're much shorter. In particular, *hub.freebsd.org* doesn't have any HINFO records, so we got no output at all.

Checking DNS for correctness

Several programs are available for diagnosing DNS configuration problems. They're outside the scope of this book, but if you're managing large DNS configurations, take a look at the collection at *http://www.isc.org/*.

DNS security

named was written at a time when the Internet was run by gentlemen. In the last few years, a relatively large number of security issues have been found in it. The FreeBSD project fixes these problems quickly, and you can expect that the version you get will have no known security issues. That can change, though: keep an eye on the security advisories from the FreeBSD project and update your name server if necessary.

22

Firewalls, IP aliasing and proxies

The Internet was developed by a relatively small community of computer scientists, who were for the most part responsible people who often did not take security issues very seriously. Since the Internet has been opened to the general public, three problems have become evident:

- A large number of people have sought to abuse its relatively lax security.

- The address space is no longer adequate for the number of machines connecting to the network.

- Much bandwidth is used by people downloading the same web pages multiple times.

What do these problems have to do with each other? Nothing much, but the solutions are related, so we'll look at them together. More specifically, we'll consider:

- How to set up an *Internet firewall* to keep intruders out of your network.

- Security tools that ensure that nobody can steal your password from a node through which it passes.

- Tools for *IP aliasing*, which translate IP addresses to make them appear to come from the gateway machine. The way this is done makes it impossible to set up connections from outside, so they also represent a kind of security device.

- *Caching proxy servers*, which both address the multiple download issues and provide some additional security.

Security and firewalls

Recall from Chapter 16 that incoming packets need to connect to an IP port, and that some process on the machine must accept them. By default, this process is *inetd*. You can limit the vulnerability of your machine by limiting the number of services it supports. Do you need to supply *telnet* and *rlogin* services? If not, don't enable the service. By default, */etc/inetd.conf* no longer enables any services, so this should not be a problem. Obviously, careful system configuration can minimize your vulnerability, but it also reduces your accessibility: intruders can't get in, but neither can the people who need to access the machine.

A better solution is a tool that passes authorized data and refuses to pass unauthorized data. Such a tool is called a *firewall*. In this section, we'll look at *packet filtering firewalls*: the firewall examines each incoming packet and uses a set of predefined walls to decide whether to pass it unchanged, change it, or simply discard it. An alternative approach is a *proxy firewall*, which analyzes each packet and creates new requests based on its content. On page 396 we'll look at *squid*, a caching proxy server that provides some of this functionality.

FreeBSD supports three different firewalls, *ipf*, *ipfilter* and *ipfw*. We consider *ipfw* here; you can find details about *ipf* and *ipfilter* and in the respective man pages.

The DEFAULT FreeBSD kernel does not include firewall support. If you wish, you can build a kernel with firewall support—see the file */usr/src/sys/conf/NOTES* for a list of parameters—but you don't need to build a new kernel. You can load the KLD */boot/kernel/ipfw.ko* instead:

```
# kldload ipfw
ipfw2 initialized, divert disabled, rule-based forwarding enabled, default to deny
, logging disabled
```

Before you do so, make sure you have direct local connection to the system. If you start this command remotely, you will instantly lose access to the system. Read the following section before loading the firewall.

ipfw: defining access rules

The program *ipfw* processes access rules for the firewall. Each rule relates to specific kinds of packet and describes what to do with them. On receiving a packet, *ipfw* examines each rule in a predetermined order until it finds one which matches the packet. It then performs the action that the rule specifies. In most cases, the rule accepts or denies the packet, so *ipfw* does not need to continue processing the remaining rules, though sometimes processing can continue after a match. If no rule matches, the default is to allow no traffic.

Table 22-1 shows the keywords you can use to define the packets and the forms that the *IP address range* can take:

Table 22-1: *ipfw* packet types

Keyword	Description
ip	All IP packets.
tcp	TCP packets.
udp	UDP packets.
icmp	ICMP packets.
service name or number	A packet destined for one of the services described in */etc/services*.
src *IP address range*	A packet with a source address that matches *IP address*. See below for the interpretation of *IP address range*.
dst *IP address range*	A packet with a destination address that matches *IP address*.
via *interface*	All packets going by the specified interface. *interface* may be an interface name or an IP address associated with only one interface.
recv *interface*	All packets arriving by the specified interface. *interface* may be an interface name or an IP address associated with only one interface.
xmit *interface*	All packets going out by the specified interface. *interface* may be an interface name or an IP address associated with only one interface.
IP address	This is an IP address. It specifies a match for exactly this address.
IP address/bits	*bits* is a value between 0 and 32. This form matches the first *bits* bits of *IP address*.
IP address:mask	*mask* is a 32-bit value. This form matches those bits of *IP address* specified in *mask*. This is the same concept as a net mask—see Chapter 16, page 290, for a description of net masks.

These options can be combined with a few restrictions:

- The recv interface can be tested on either incoming or outgoing packets, while the xmit interface can be tested only on outgoing packets. This means that you must specify the keyword out (and you may not specify in) when you use xmit. You can't specify via together with xmit or recv.

- A packet that originates from the local host does not have a receive interface. A packet destined for the local host has no transmit interface.

Actions

When *ipfw* finds a rule which matches a packet, it performs the specified action. Table 22-2 shows the possibilities.

Table 22-2: Actions on packets

Keyword	Description
allow	Allow a packet to pass. Stop processing the rules.
deny	Discard the packet. Stop processing the rules.
unreach	Discard the packet and send an ICMP *host unreachable* message to the sender. Stop processing the rules.
reset	Discard the packet and send a TCP reset message. This can apply only to TCP packets. Stop processing the rules.
count	Count the packet and continue processing the rules.
divert *port*	Divert the packet to the *divert socket* bound to port *port*. See the man page *ipfw(8)* for more details. Stop processing the rules.
tee *port*	Send a copy of the packet to the *divert socket* bound to port *port*. Continue processing the rules.
skipto *rule*	Continue processing the rules at rule number *rule*.

Writing rules

The sequence in which rules are applied is not necessarily the sequence in which they are read. Instead, each rule can have a *line number* between 1 and 65534. Rules are applied from the lowest to the highest line number. If you enter a rule without a line number, however, it receives a number 100 higher than the previous rule.

The highest-numbered rule is number 65535, which is always present. Normally it has the form:

```
65535 deny all from any to any
```

In other words, if no other rules are present, or they don't match the packet, *ipfw* drops the packet. If you build a kernel with the option IPFIREWALL_DEFAULT_TO_ACCEPT, this rule changes to its opposite:

```
65535 allow all from any to any
```

These two rulesets implicitly illustrate two basic security strategies. You may note parallels to certain political systems:

- The first takes the attitude "everything is forbidden unless explicitly allowed."

- The second takes the attitude "everything is allowed unless explicitly forbidden."

It goes without saying that the first policy is safer. If you make a mistake with the first (more restrictive) ruleset, you're more likely to lock people out of your system accidentally than you are to let them in when you don't want them.

Configuration files

The main configuration file is */etc/rc.firewall*. It's unlikely to match your needs exactly. There are two possibilities:

- You can edit it to match your requirements.

- You can create your own configuration file with your rules.

Which do you choose? If you're making only minor modifications, it's easier to edit it. If you're taking things seriously, though, you'll end up with something that no longer bears much of a relationship with the original file. Upgrades are easier if you have your own file.

If you create your own file, you can tell */etc/rc.conf* its name, and */etc/rc.firewall* will read it. Either way, the rules are the same. In the following section we'll go through the default */etc/rc.firewall* file. There's nothing stopping you from copying them to another file and editing them to match your requirements.

Reading the file is somewhat complicated by a number of environment variables that are set in the system startup scripts. We'll see the important ones below. It's also helpful to know that ${fwcmd} gets replaced by the name of the firewall program, */sbin/ipfw*. The other ones are described in */etc/default/rc.conf*:

```
firewall_enable="NO"                  # Set to YES to enable firewall functionality
firewall_script="/etc/rc.firewall"    # Which script to run to set up the firewall
firewall_type="UNKNOWN"               # Firewall type (see /etc/rc.firewall)
firewall_quiet="NO"                   # Set to YES to suppress rule display
firewall_logging="NO"                 # Set to YES to enable events logging
firewall_flags=""                     # Flags passed to ipfw when type is a file
```

To set up the firewall, first decide the kind of profile you need and set the variable firewall_type accordingly. The current version of */etc/rc.firewall* defines four kinds of usage profile:

- The *open* profile is effectively a disabled firewall. It allows all traffic. You might use this if you're having trouble setting up the firewall and need to disable it temporarily.

- The *client* profile is a good starting point for a system that does not provide many publicly accessible services to the Net. We'll look at it in the next section.

- The *simple* profile, despite its name, is intended for a system that does provide a number of publicly accessible services to the Net. We'll look at it on page 391.

- The *closed* profile allows only local traffic via the loopback interface.

In addition, you can set firewall_type to the name of a file describing the firewall configuration.

All configurations start with a call to setup_loopback, which adds the following rules:

```
${fwcmd} add 100 pass all from any to any via lo0
${fwcmd} add 200 deny all from any to 127.0.0.0/8
${fwcmd} add 300 deny ip from 127.0.0.0/8 to any
```

These rules allow all local traffic and stop traffic coming in with a fake local address.

The client profile

At the beginning of the client profile you'll find a number of variables you need to set. In the following example they're set to match *freebie.example.org* and our example network:

```
[Cc][Ll][Ii][Ee][Nn][Tt])
    ############
    # This is a prototype setup that will protect your system somewhat against
    # people from outside your own network.
    ############

    # set these to your network and netmask and ip
    net="223.147.37.0"
    mask="255.255.255.0"
    ip="223.147.37.1"            freebie.example.org
```

Figure 22-1: Client profile in /etc/rc.firewall

The first line matches the text client whether written in upper or lower case. Then we have:

```
    setup_loopback

    # Allow any traffic to or from my own net.
    ${fwcmd} add pass all from ${ip} to ${net}:${mask}
    ${fwcmd} add pass all from ${net}:${mask} to ${ip}
```

These rules allow any traffic in the local network.

```
    # Allow TCP through if setup succeeded
    ${fwcmd} add pass tcp from any to any established
```

If a TCP connection has already been established, allow it to continue. Establishing a TCP connection requires other rules, which we shall see below.

```
    # Allow IP fragments to pass through
    ${fwcmd} add pass all from any to any frag
```

Fragmented packets are difficult to recognize, and if we block them, strange things might happen. They're usually not a significant security risk.

```
    # Allow setup of incoming email
    ${fwcmd} add pass tcp from any to ${ip} 25 setup

    # Allow setup of outgoing TCP connections only
    ${fwcmd} add pass tcp from ${ip} to any setup
```

```
# Disallow setup of all other TCP connections
${fwcmd} add deny tcp from any to any setup
```

The preceding three rules allow external systems to establish a TCP connection for delivering mail (first rule), but nothing else (third rule). The second rule allows setup of TCP connections to the outside world.

```
# Allow DNS queries out in the world
${fwcmd} add pass udp from ${ip} to any 53 keep-state

# Allow NTP queries out in the world
${fwcmd} add pass udp from ${ip} to any 123 keep-state

# Everything else is denied as default.
```

These two rules allow DNS and NTP queries. The keyword `keep-state` causes *ipfw* to build a short-lived dynamic rule matching this particular combination of end points and protocol. This means that we don't need to open traffic in the other direction. Previously, the rule set for DNS queries consisted of these two rules:

```
$fwcmd add pass udp from any 53 to ${ip}
$fwcmd add pass udp from ${ip} to any 53
```

This allows all DNS traffic in both directions. By contrast, `keep-state` allows only the reply traffic for specific queries to pass the firewall. You don't need this for TCP—the `established` keyword does the same thing— but UDP doesn't have the concept of a connection, so the firewall needs to keep track of the traffic.

There are no more rules, so the default *deny* rule prevents any other kind of traffic.

The simple profile

Despite the name, the *simple* profile is really a (simple) server profile. It assumes that the machine is a gateway, and that it supplies DNS and NTP services to the outside world (for example, to the *client* machine we just looked at). This profile is more appropriate for the system *gw.example.org*, so we'll use its addresses.

```
# set these to your outside interface network and netmask and ip
oif="tun0"
onet="139.130.136.133"
omask="255.255.255.255"
oip="139.130.136.133"

# set these to your inside interface network and netmask and ip
iif="ep0"
inet="223.147.37.0"
imask="255.255.255.0"
iip="223.147.37.0"
```

These addresses and networks correspond to the PPP link and the local ethernet, respectively.

```
# Stop spoofing
${fwcmd} add deny all from ${inet}:${imask} to any in via ${oif}
${fwcmd} add deny all from ${onet}:${omask} to any in via ${iif}
```

These two rules stop any packets purporting to come from the local network that arrive via the external network, and any packets purporting to come from the remote network that arrive via the local interface. These packets would have been faked, an action known as *spoofing*.

```
# Stop RFC1918 nets on the outside interface
${fwcmd} add deny all from any to 10.0.0.0/8 via ${oif}
${fwcmd} add deny all from any to 172.16.0.0/12 via ${oif}
${fwcmd} add deny all from any to 192.168.0.0/16 via ${oif}
```

RFC 1918 defines networks that should not be routed. These rules enforce that requirement.

At this point in the file there are also some other addresses that should not be routed. A check is made for address translation, because non-routed addresses are typically used by NAT environments.

```
# Allow TCP through if setup succeeded
${fwcmd} add pass tcp from any to any established

# Allow IP fragments to pass through
${fwcmd} add pass all from any to any frag

# Allow setup of incoming email
${fwcmd} add pass tcp from any to ${oip} 25 setup

# Allow access to our DNS
${fwcmd} add pass tcp from any to ${oip} 53 setup
${fwcmd} add pass udp from any to ${oip} 53
${fwcmd} add pass udp from ${oip} 53 to any

# Allow access to our WWW
${fwcmd} add pass tcp from any to ${oip} 80 setup
```

These rules add to what we saw for the *client* profile: in addition to email, we allow incoming DNS and WWW connections.

```
# Reject&Log all setup of incoming connections from the outside
${fwcmd} add deny log tcp from any to any in via ${oif} setup

# Allow setup of any other TCP connection
${fwcmd} add pass tcp from any to any setup
```

Here, we don't just reject TCP setup requests from the outside world, we log them as well.

```
# Allow DNS queries out in the world
${fwcmd} add pass udp from ${oip} to any 53 keep-state

# Allow NTP queries out in the world
${fwcmd} add pass udp from ${oip} to any 123 keep-state

# Everything else is denied as default.
```

Finally, we allow DNS and NTP queries via UDP, and deny everything else from the outside world.

user-defined profiles

If the profile isn't one of the recognized keywords, */etc/rc.firewall* checks if there's a file with that name. If so, it uses it as a command file to pass to *ipfw*:

```
elif [ "${firewall}" != "NONE" -a -r "${firewall}" ]; then
    ${fwcmd} ${firewall_flags} ${firewall_type}
```

Note that you can't put comment lines in the file defined by `${firewall}`.

Entries in /etc/rc.conf

When you have decided what kind of firewall configuration best suits your network, note that fact in */etc/rc.conf*. Set the value of `firewall_enable` to **YES** to enable the firewall, and the value of `firewall_type` to indicate the type of firewall. For our example network, `client` is probably the most appropriate type:

```
firewall_enable="YES"            # Set to YES to enable firewall functionality
firewall_script="/etc/rc.firewall"   # Which script to set up the firewall
firewall_type="client"           # Firewall type (see /etc/rc.firewall)
```

If you have decided to write your own file rather than modify */etc/rc.firewall*, set `firewall_type` to the name of the file.

Trying it out

You'll probably find that your first attempt at firewall configuration won't be the optimum. You'll probably discover requirements that you hadn't thought of and that are now being denied by the default rule. Be prepared to spend some time getting everything to work, and *do this at the system console*. There's no good alternative.

IP aliasing

In our reference network on page 294, we assumed that our local network had a valid assigned IP address. Sometimes, this isn't possible. In fact, in the Real World it's pretty well impossible to get a complete class C network for a system with only five systems on it. You have the alternative of getting a subset of a class C network (in this case, eight addresses would do) from your ISP, or using just one address and running software that makes all traffic from the network to the outside world look as if it's coming from that system. The latter approach, called *network address translation (NAT)* or *IP aliasing*, can be significantly cheaper: ISPs often charge good money for additional addresses. On the down side, NAT restricts you in some ways. Any connection between a machine on a NAT network and the global Internet must start from the machine on the NAT network, because the translation doesn't exist until the connection is set up. This also means that you can't connect two machines on different NAT networks.

Network address translation involves three machines: one on the global Internet with real Internet addresses, one on a private subnet with unroutable addresses, and one in the middle that performs the translation. In our reference network (see page 294), let's consider connecting *andante*, the laptop, to the Internet with *presto* acting as address translator. *andante* is not part of the local network, so it gets an address in one of the address spaces specified by RFC 1918 (192.168.0.0 to 192.168.255.255, 172.16.0.0 to 172.31.255.255, or 10.0.0.0 to 10.255.255.255). In this example, it has the address 192.168.27.17, and we can assume that it got this address from a DHCP server on *presto*. A connection to a remote web site *http://www.FreeBSD.org* might look like this:

Figure 22-2: Accessing the Web via NAT

In this diagram, the IP addresses are above the boxes, the interface names above the connection lines, and the port numbers below the connection lines. The connection must be started by *andante*, because there is no way to route to it directly from outside the local link. It finds the address of *www.FreeBSD.org* (216.136.204.117) and sends it out its default route, in this case the only interface, *wi0*. *presto* gets the packet on interface *xl0* and routes it out through interface *dc0*.

So far, that's nothing special—it's what any router does. The difference is that *presto* changes the source address and port number. On the wireless link, *andante*'s address is 192.168.27.17, and the port number for this connection is 2731. On the remote link, the IP address becomes 223.147.37.2, *presto*'s own address, and the port number in this case is 3312. Theoretically, the "changed" port address could be the same as the original, since there is no relationship. The destination IP address and port number can't change, of course, or the packet would never get to its destination.

On return, the reverse happens: *www.FreeBSD.org* replies to *presto*, which recognizes the port number, converts it to *andante*'s IP address and source port, and sends it to *andante* on the local network.

IP aliasing software

There are a number of ways to perform IP aliasing with FreeBSD. If you're connecting to the outside world via User PPP (see Chapter 20, page 348), you can use the -alias keyword to tell PPP to alias *all* packets coming from the network to the address of the tunnel interface. In our reference network, this would be the address 139.130.136.133.

This particular form of IP aliasing has some limitations: it works only for a single User PPP connection to the outside world, and it's global in its functionality. One alternative is the *Network Address Translation Daemon*, or *natd*, which uses divert sockets to translate addresses. It works well in conjunction with the firewall software we looked at above.

natd

To set up *natd* for the example above, perform the following steps:

- Even if you don't plan to run an IP firewall, build and boot a custom kernel with the following options:

```
options IPFIREWALL
options IPDIVERT
```

  If you are running a firewall, configure the firewall normally, but be sure to include the IPDIVERT option.

- Make sure your interfaces are running. For example, if you're running Kernel PPP and you want to specify *ppp0* as your interface, start *pppd* before starting *natd*.

- What you do next differs a little depending on whether you are also running a firewall or not. If you're not, you're better off with a separate script, which you might call */etc/rc.nat*, with the following content:

```
/sbin/ipfw -f flush
/sbin/ipfw add divert natd all from any to any via dc0
/sbin/ipfw add pass all from any to any
```

- If you want to combine NAT with real firewall rules, you need only the second line of the previous example. Set up the firewall as described above, and put the NAT line at the start of the section of */etc/rc.firewall* that you have chosen, so that *natd* sees all packets before they are dropped by the firewall. After *natd* translates the IP addresses, the firewall rules are run again on the translated packet, with the exception of the divert rules. The *client* configuration is the most likely one to suit your needs if you're using NAT. After the example in figure 22-1 on 390, you might add:

```
# set these to your network and netmask and ip
net="192.0.2.0"
mask="255.255.255.0"
ip="192.0.2.1"

setup_loopback

/sbin/ipfw add divert natd all from any to any via dc0

# Allow any traffic to or from my own net.
${fwcmd} add pass all from ${ip} to ${net}:${mask}
${fwcmd} add pass all from ${net}:${mask} to ${ip}
```

- Add the following to */etc/rc.conf*:

```
firewall_enable=YES
gateway_enable="YES"            # Set to YES if this host is a gateway.
natd_enable="YES"
natd_interface="dc0"
firewall_script="/etc/rc.nat"   # script for NAT only
firewall_type="client"          # firewall type if running a firewall
```

The interface name in the second line, *dc0*, is the name of the external interface (the one with the real IP addresses).

If you're using NAT but not a firewall, you don't need to specify a `firewall_type`, because that relates to */etc/rc.firewall*. You do need to specify the name of the script to run, however.

- Enable your firewall as shown above in the firewall section. If you don't intend to reboot now, just run */etc/rc.firewall* (or */etc/rc.natd*) by hand from the console, and then start *natd*:

```
# sh /etc/rc.nat                              for NAT only
# firewall_type=client sh /etc/rc.firewall    for NAT and firewall
# natd dc0
```

The expression `firewall_type=client` tells the Bourne shell to set the value of the variable `firewall` just for this command. If you're using *csh* or *tcsh*, use the following sequence:

```
(setenv firewall_type=client; sh /etc/rc.firewall)
```

Never start this script from an X terminal or across the network. If you do, you can lock yourself out of the session in the middle of the script, causing */etc/rc.firewall* to stop at this point, blocking all accesses to the system.

Proxy servers

For some purposes, a good alternative or adjunct to a packet filtering firewall and NAT is a *proxy server* that converts requests for specific protocols. In the example in the previous section, which was accessing a web server, we could also have run a proxy server on *presto*. Particularly in conjunction with web servers, a proxy server has the advantage that it can cache data locally, thus reducing network load.

There are a couple of other differences between NAT and proxy servers: *natd* does not know much about the data it passes. Proxy servers know a lot about it. This makes proxy servers less suitable as a general security or address translation mechanism. In addition, the client must know about the proxy server, whereas it does not need to know anything about NAT and firewalls. A typical connection looks like this:

Figure 22-3: Accessing the Web via a proxy server

This looks very similar to Figure 22-1. The only thing that appears to have changed is the port number on *presto*'s *xl0* interface. In fact, there's more than that: in Figure 22-1, *andante* establishes a connection with *www.FreeBSD.org*. Here it establishes a connection with *presto.example.org*.

Installing squid

A good choice of web proxy server is *squid*, which is available in the Ports Collection. Install it in the normal manner:

```
# cd /usr/ports/www/squid
# make install
```

squid is not the easiest thing in the world to set up, and it's hampered by sub-standard documentation. The man page is *squid(8)*, but most of the information is in the configuration file */usr/local/etc/squid/squid.conf*. By default, it is set up to do nothing. It has over 3,000 lines of mostly comments. I suggest the following changes:

- Set the value `http_proxy` to the number of the port you want to use. By default, *squid* uses port 3128, but many proxies use port 8080, and that's the port that most web browsers expect too. If you are not running a web server on the machine, you can also use the *http* port, 80. Add:

  ```
  http_port 8080 80
  ```

- The variable `http_access` defines who can access the web server. By default, it denies all requests except from the local manager, so you must set it if you expect to get any results from the server. An appropriate setting might be:

  ```
  acl local src 192.168.27.0/255.255.255.0
  acl exampleorg src 223.147.37.0/24

  http_access allow local
  http_access allow exampleorg
  ```

  This defines two access control lists, one for the NAT network we looked at in the previous section (`local`), and one for the globally visible network 223.147.37.0 (`exampleorg`). The first `acl` statement specifies the network in the form *address/netmask*, while the second specifies it with the number of significant bits in the net mask. The `http_access` statements then allow access for each of them.

- If you're using the *ftp* proxy, it's probably a good idea to change the default name with which *squid* performs anonymous *ftp*. By default it's `Squid@`, but that looks silly. Change it by setting:

  ```
  ftp_user squid@example.org
  ```

- *squid* doesn't expect any line of the *ftp* file listing to be more than 32 characters long. That's pretty conservative. You can make it larger like this:

```
ftp_list_width 120
```

- By default, *squid* caches any object less than 4 MB in size on disk. If you're doing a lot of *ftp* work, this can seriously degrade the cache performance for *http*. You can reduce it to, say, 256 kB with:

```
maximum_object_size 256 KB
```

- The system starts *squid* as user root, which is not the best for security: proxy servers are a popular target for intruders on the Internet. You should change it to run as user and group www:

```
cache_effective_user www
cache_effective_group www
```

Starting squid

Before you can start *squid*, you must first create the cache directories. If not, you can start it, and it doesn't complain, but it doesn't run either. Later you might find something like this in the log file */var/log/messages*:

```
Dec 21 15:26:51 presto squid[23800]: Squid Parent: child process 23802 started
Dec 21 15:26:53 presto (squid):        Failed to verify one of the swap directories
, Check cache.log   for details.  Run 'squid -z' to create swap directories
if needed, or if running Squid for the first time.
Dec 21 15:26:53 presto kernel: pid 23802 (squid), uid 65534: exited on signal 6
Dec 21 15:26:53 presto squid[23800]: Squid Parent: child process 23802 exited due to
 signal 6
Dec 21 15:26:56 presto squid[23800]: Squid Parent: child process 23805 started
```

The log files are in */usr/local/squid/log*, and the cache files should be in */usr/local/squid/cache*. To create them, enter:

```
# squid -z
2002/12/21 15:30:35| Creating Swap Directories
```

Finally, you can start *squid*:

```
# squid
```

On system restart, *squid* will be started automatically from the script in */usr/local/etc/rc.d/squid.sh*.

Browser proxy configuration

As mentioned earlier, proxies aren't transparent to the application. You have to set up your software to talk to the proxy. To do that, you need to configure the web browser accordingly. For example, with *galeon* you select Settings→Preferences→Advanced→Network and get the following screen:

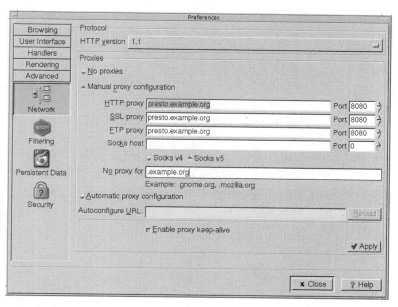

Figure 22-4: Galeon proxy settings

squid understands the individual protocols that it supports, so it can tell the difference between, say, an *http* request on port 8080 and an *ftp* request on the same port. Nevertheless, consider whether it's a good idea to use *squid* for *ftp*. It doesn't speed up access the first time you fetch the file, and if you access each file only once, you don't have any gain through using *squid*. On the other hand, the *ftp* data can pollute the cache.

Setting proxy information for ftp

ftp understands proxies, and uses them for non-interactive connections only. Put the following statement in your *.profile* file:

```
export http_proxy=presto.example.org:8080
export ftp_proxy=presto.example.org:8080
```

23

Network debugging

The chances are quite good that you'll have some problems somewhere when you set up your network. FreeBSD gives you a large number of tools with which to find and solve the problem.

In this chapter, we'll consider a methodology of debugging network problems. In the process, we'll look at the programs that help debugging. It will help to have your finger in Chapter 16 while reading this section.

How to approach network problems

Recall from Chapter 16 that network software and hardware operate on at least four layers. If one layer doesn't work, the ones above won't either. When solving problems, it obviously makes sense to start at the bottom and work up.

Most people understand this up to a point. Nobody expects a PPP connection to the Internet to work if the modem can't dial the ISP. On the other hand, a large number of messages to the FreeBSD-questions mailing list show that many people seem to think that once this connection has been established, everything else will work automatically. If it doesn't, they're puzzled.

Unfortunately, the Net isn't that simple. In fact, it's too complicated to give a hard-and-fast methodology at all. Much network debugging can look more like magic than anything rational. Nevertheless, a surprising number of network problems can be solved by using the steps below. Even if they don't solve your problem, read through them. They might give you some ideas about where to look.

Link layer problems

To test your link layer, start with *ping*. *ping* is a relatively simple program that sends an *ICMP echo packet* to a specific IP address and checks the reply. *ICMP*, is the *Internet Control Message Protocol*, is used for error reporting and testing. See *TCP/IP Illustrated*, by Richard Stevens, for more information.

A typical *ping* output might look like:

```
$ ping bumble
PING bumble.example.org (223.147.37.156): 56 data bytes
64 bytes from 223.147.37.156: icmp_seq=0 ttl=255 time=1.137 ms
64 bytes from 223.147.37.156: icmp_seq=1 ttl=255 time=0.640 ms
64 bytes from 223.147.37.156: icmp_seq=2 ttl=255 time=0.671 ms
64 bytes from 223.147.37.156: icmp_seq=3 ttl=255 time=0.612 ms
^C
--- bumble.example.org ping statistics ---
4 packets transmitted, 4 packets received, 0% packet loss
round-trip min/avg/max/stddev = 0.612/0.765/1.137/0.216 ms
```

In this case, we are sending the messages to the system *bumble.example.org*. By default, *ping* sends messages of 56 bytes. With the IP header, this makes packets of 64 bytes. By default, *ping* continues until you stop it—notice the ^C indicating that this invocation was stopped by pressing **Ctrl-C**.

The information that *ping* gives you isn't much, but it's useful:

- It tells you how long it takes for each packet to get to its destination and back.

- It tells you how many packets didn't make it.

- It also prints a summary of packet statistics.

But what if this doesn't work? You enter your *ping* command, and all you get is:

```
$ ping wait
PING wait.example.org (223.147.37.4): 56 data bytes
^C
--- wait.example.org ping statistics ---
5 packets transmitted, 0 packets received, 100% packet loss
```

Obviously, something's wrong here. We'll look at it in more detail below. This is *very* different, however, from this situation:

```
$ ping presto
^C
```

In the second case, even after some time, nothing happened at all. *ping* didn't print the PING message, and when we hit **Ctrl-C** there was no further output. This is indicative of a name resolution problem: *ping* can't print the first line until it has found the IP address of the system, in other words, until it has performed a DNS lookup. If we wait long enough, it will time out, and we get the message ping: cannot resolve presto: Unknown host. If this happens, use the IP address, not the name. DNS is an application, so we won't try to debug it until we've debugged the link and network layers.

If things don't work out, there are two possibilities:

- If both systems are on the same network, it's a link layer problem. We'll look at that first.

- If the systems are on two different networks, it might be a network layer problem. That's more complicated: we don't know which network to look at. It could be either of the networks on which the systems are located, or it could also be a problem with one of the networks on the way. How do you find out where your packets get lost? First you check the link layer. If it checks out OK, and the problem still exists, continue with the network layer on page 406.

So what can cause link layer problems? There are a number of possibilities:

- One of the interfaces (source or destination) could be misconfigured. They should both have the same range of network addresses. For example, the following two interface configurations cannot talk to each other directly, even if they're on the same physical network:

```
machine 1
dc0: flags=8843<UP,BROADCAST,RUNNING,SIMPLEX,MULTICAST> mtu 1500
        inet 223.147.37.81 netmask 0xffffff00 broadcast 223.147.37.255

machine 2
xl0: flags=8943<UP,BROADCAST,RUNNING,PROMISC,SIMPLEX,MULTICAST> mtu 1500
        options=3<RXCSUM,TXCSUM>
        inet 192.168.27.1 netmask 0xffffff00 broadcast 192.168.27.255
```

- If you see something like this on an Ethernet interface, it's pretty clear that it has a cabling problem:

```
xl0: flags=8943<UP,BROADCAST,RUNNING,PROMISC,SIMPLEX,MULTICAST> mtu 1500
        options=3<RXCSUM,TXCSUM>
        inet 192.168.27.1 netmask 0xffffff00 broadcast 192.168.27.255
        media: Ethernet autoselect (none)
        status: no carrier
```

In this case, check the physical connections. If you're using UTP, check that you have the right kind of cable, normally a "straight-through" cable. If you accidentally use a crossover cable where you need a straight-through cable, or vice versa, you will not get any connection. Also, many hubs and switches have a "crossover" switch that achieves the same result.

- If you're on an RG-58 thin Ethernet, the most likely problem is a break in the cabling. You can check the static resistance between the central pin and the external part of the connector with a multimeter. It should be approximately 25Ω. If it's 50Ω, it indicates that there is a break in the cable, or that one of the terminators has been disconnected.

- If your interface is configured correctly, and you're using a 10 Mb/s card, check whether you are using the correct connection to the network. Some older Ethernet boards support multiple physical connections (for example, both BNC and UTP). For example, if your network runs on RG58 thin Ethernet, and your interface is set to

AUI, you may still be able to send data on the RG58, but you won't be able to receive any.

The method of setting the connection depends on the board you are using. PCI boards are not normally a problem, because the driver can set the parameters directly, but ISA boards can drive you crazy. In the case of very old boards, such as the Western Digital 8003, you may need to set jumpers. In others, you may need to run the setup utility under DOS, and with others you can set it with the *link* flags to *ifconfig*. For example, on a 3Com 3c509 "combo" board, you can set the connection like this:

```
# ifconfig ep0 -link0            set BNC
# ifconfig ep0 link0 -link1      set AUI
# ifconfig ep0 link0 link1       set UTP
```

This example is correct for the *ep* driver, but not necessarily for other Ethernet boards: each board has its own flags. Read the man page for the board for the correct flags.

- If your interface looks OK, the next thing to do is to see whether you can send data to other machines on the network. If so, of course, you should continue your search on the machine that isn't responding. If none are working, you probably have a cabling problem.

On a wireless network, you need to check for a number of additional problems. *ifconfig* should show something like this:

```
wi0: flags=8843<UP,BROADCAST,RUNNING,SIMPLEX,MULTICAST> mtu 1500
        inet6 fe80::202:2dff:fe04:93a%wi0 prefixlen 64 scopeid 0x3
        inet 192.168.27.17 netmask 0xffffff00 broadcast 192.168.27.255
        ether 00:02:2d:21:54:4c
        media: IEEE 802.11 Wireless Ethernet autoselect (DS/11Mbps)
        status: associated
        ssid "FreeBSD IBSS" 1:""
        stationname "FreeBSD WaveLAN/IEEE node"
        channel 3 authmode OPEN powersavemode OFF powersavesleep 100
        wepmode OFF weptxkey 1
        wepkey 2:64-bit 0x123456789a 3:128-bit 0x123456789abcdef123456789ab
```

There are many things to check here:

- Do you have the same operating mode? This example shows a card operating in BSS or IBSS mode. By contrast, you might see this:

    ```
    media: IEEE 802.11 Wireless Ethernet autoselect (DS/11Mbps <adhoc, flag0>)
    ```

In this case, the interface is operating in so-called "Lucent demo ad-hoc" mode, which is not the same thing as "ad-hoc" mode (which in turn is better called IBSS mode). IBSS mode ("ad-hoc") and BSS mode are compatible. IBSS mode and "Lucent demo ad-hoc" mode are not. See Chapter 17, page 306 for further details.

- Is the status `associated`? The alternative is `no carrier`. Some cards, including this one, show `no carrier` when communicating with a station operating in IBSS mode, but they never show `associated` unless they are really associated.

- If the card is not associated, check the frequencies and the network name.

- Check the WEP (encryption) parameters to ensure that they match. Note that *ifconfig* does not display the WEP key unless you are `root`.

  Your card may show `associated` even if the WEP key doesn't match. In such a case, it knows about the network, but it can't communicate with it.

After checking all these things, you should have a connection. But you may not be home yet:

- If you have a connection, check if *all* packets got there. Lost packets could mean line quality problems. That's not very likely on an Ethernet, but it's very possible on a PPP or DSL link. There's an uncertainty about dropped packets: you might hit **Ctrl-C** after the last packet went out, but before it came back. If the line is very slow, you might lose multiple packets. Compare the sequence number of the last packet that returns with the total number returned. If it's one less, all the packets except the ones at the end made it.

- Check that each packet comes back only once. If not, there's definitely something wrong, or you have been pinging a broadcast address. That looks like this:

```
$ ping 223.147.37.255
PING 223.147.37.255 (223.147.37.255): 56 data bytes
64 bytes from 223.147.37.1: icmp_seq=0 ttl=255 time=0.428 ms
64 bytes from 223.147.37.88: icmp_seq=0 ttl=255 time=0.785 ms (DUP!)
64 bytes from 223.147.37.65: icmp_seq=0 ttl=64 time=1.818 ms (DUP!)
64 bytes from 223.147.37.1: icmp_seq=1 ttl=255 time=0.426 ms
64 bytes from 223.147.37.88: icmp_seq=1 ttl=255 time=0.442 ms (DUP!)
64 bytes from 223.147.37.65: icmp_seq=1 ttl=64 time=1.099 ms (DUP!)
64 bytes from 223.147.37.126: icmp_seq=1 ttl=255 time=45.781 ms (DUP!)
```

  FreeBSD systems do not respond to broadcast *ping*s, but most other systems do, so this effectively counts the number of non-BSD machines on a network.

- Check the times. A *ping* across an Ethernet should take between about 0.2 and 2 ms, a *ping* across a wireless connection should take between 2 and 12 ms, a *ping* across an ISDN connection should take about 30 ms, a *ping* across a 56 kb/s analogue connection should take about 100 ms, and a *ping* across a satellite connection should take about 250 ms in each direction. All of these times are for idle lines, and the time can go up to over 5 seconds for a slow line transferring large blocks of data across a serial line (for example, *ftp*ing a file). In this example, some line traffic delayed the response to individual pings.

Network layer problems

Once we know the link layer is working correctly, we can turn our attention to the next layer up, the network layer. Well, first we should check if the problem is still with us.

We need additional tools for the network layer. *ping* is a useful tool for telling you whether data is getting through to the destination, and if so, how much is getting through. But what if your local network checks out just fine, and you can't reach a remote network? Or if you're losing 40% of your packets to *foo.bar.org*, and the remaining ones are taking up to 5 *seconds* to get through. Where's the problem? Based on the recent "upgrade" your ISP performed, and the fact that you've had trouble getting to other sites, you suspect that the performance problems might be occurring in the ISP's net. How can you find out?

As we saw while investigating the link layer, a complete failure is often easier to fix than a partial failure. If nothing at all is getting through, you probably have a routing problem. Check the routing table with *netstat*. On *bumble*, you might see:

```
$ netstat -r
Routing tables

Internet:
Destination          Gateway            Flags   Refs       Use  Netif Expire
default              gw                 UGSc       0         8  xl0
localhost            localhost          UH         2       525  lo0
223.147.37           link#1             UC         6         0  xl0
sat-gw               00:80:c6:f9:d3:fa  UHLW       0         0  xl0    1150
bumble               00:50:da:cf:17:d3  UHLW       0        24  lo0
presto               00:80:c6:f9:a6:c8  UHLW       0         5  xl0    1200
freebie              00:50:da:cf:07:35  UHLW       6    760334  xl0    1159
223.147.37.255       ff:ff:ff:ff:ff:ff  UHLWb      1       403  xl0
```

The default route is via *gw*, which is correct. The first thing is to ensure that you can *ping gw*; that's a link level issue, so we'll assume that you can. But what if you try to *ping* a remote system and you see something like this?

```
# ping rider.fc.net
PING rider.fc.net (207.170.123.194): 56 data bytes
36 bytes from gw.example.org (223.147.37.5): Destination Host Unreachable
Vr HL TOS  Len   ID Flg  off TTL Pro  cks      Src        Dst
 4  5 00 6800 c5da    0 0000   fe  01 246d 223.147.37.2  207.170.123.194

36 bytes from gw.example.org (223.147.37.5): Destination Host Unreachable
Vr HL TOS  Len   ID Flg  off TTL Pro  cks      Src        Dst
 4  5 00 6800 c5e7    0 0000   fe  01 2460 223.147.37.2  207.170.123.194

^C
--- rider.fc.net ping statistics ---
2 packets transmitted, 0 packets received, 100% packet loss
```

These are ICMP messages from *gw* indicating that it does not know where to send the data. This is almost certainly a routing problem; on *gw* you might see something like:

```
$ netstat -r
Routing tables

Internet:
Destination          Gateway            Flags    Refs      Use  Netif Expire
localhost            localhost          UH          1      123  lo0
free-gw.example.ne   exorg-gw.example.  UH         23        0  ppp0
223.147.37           link#1             UC         11        0  dc0
sat-gw               00:80:c6:f9:d3:fa  UHLW        5  1295329  dc0    1027
bumble               00:50:da:cf:17:d3  UHLW        2   760207  dc0     802
flame                08:00:20:76:6c:7b  UHLW        2   426341  dc0     532
wantadilla           00:02:44:17:f8:da  UHLW       36 19778224  dc0    1073
presto               00:80:c6:f9:a6:c8  UHLW        1  1122321  dc0     742
freebie              00:50:da:cf:07:35  UHLW       24  3279563  lo0
air-gw               00:00:b4:33:6d:a2  UHLW        4     2484  dc0     653
kimchi               00:00:21:ca:6e:f1  UHLW        0        1  dc0     829
223.147.37.127       link#1             UHLW        0        5  dc0
fumble               link#1             UHLW        3 51246373  dc0
```

The problem here is that there is no default route. Add it with the *route* command:

```
# route add default free-gw.example.net
# netstat -r
Routing tables

Internet:
Destination          Gateway            Flags    Refs      Use  Netif Expire
default              free-gw.example.ne UGSc       24     5724  ppp0
localhost            localhost          UH          1      123  lo0
...etc
```

See Chapter 17, page 309, for more details, including how to ensure that the routes will be added automatically at boot time.

But what if the routes look right, you don't get any ICMP messages, and no data gets through? You don't always get ICMP messages when the data can't get through. The logical next place to look is *free-gw.example.net*, but there's a problem with that: as the administrator of *example.org*, you don't have access to *example.net*'s machines. You can call them up, of course, but before you do you should be reasonably sure it's their problem. You can find out more information with *traceroute*.

traceroute

traceroute sends UDP packets to the destination, but it modifies the *time-to-live* field in the IP header (see page 280) so that, initially at any rate, they don't get there. As we saw there, the time-to-live field specifies the number of hops that a packet can go before it is discarded. When it is, the system that discards it should send back an ICMP *destination unreachable* message. *traceroute* uses this feature and sends out packets with time-to-live set first to one, then to two, and so on. It prints the IP address of the system that sends the "destination unreachable" message and the time it took, thus giving something like a two-dimensional *ping*. Here's an example to *hub.FreeBSD.org*:

```
$ traceroute hub.freebsd.org
traceroute to hub.freebsd.org (204.216.27.18), 30 hops max, 40 byte packets
 1  gw (223.147.37.5)  1.138 ms  0.811 ms  0.800 ms
 2  free-gw.example.net (139.130.136.129)  131.913 ms  122.231 ms  134.694 ms
 3  Ethernet1-0.way1.Adelaide.example.net (139.130.237.65)  118.229 ms  120.040 ms
118.723 ms
 4  Fddi0-0.way-core1.Adelaide.example.net (139.130.237.226)  171.590 ms  117.911 ms
 123.513 ms
 5  Serial5-0.lon-core1.Melbourne.example.net (139.130.239.21)  129.267 ms  226.927
ms  125.547 ms
 6  Fddi0-0.lon5.Melbourne.example.net (139.130.239.231)  144.372 ms  133.998 ms  13
6.699 ms
 7  borderx2-hssi3-0.Bloomington.mci.net (204.70.208.121)  962.258 ms  482.393 ms  7
54.989 ms
 8  core2-fddi-1.Bloomington.mci.net (204.70.208.65)  821.636 ms  *  701.920 ms
 9  bordercore3-loopback.SanFrancisco.mci.net (166.48.16.1)  424.254 ms  884.033 ms
645.302 ms
10  pb-nap.crl.net (198.32.128.20)  435.907 ms  438.933 ms  451.173 ms
11  E0-CRL-SFO-02-E0X0.US.CRL.NET (165.113.55.2)  440.425 ms  430.049 ms  447.340 ms
12  T1-CDROM-00-EX.US.CRL.NET (165.113.118.2)  553.624 ms  460.116 ms  *
13  hub.FreeBSD.ORG (204.216.27.18)  642.032 ms  463.661 ms  432.976 ms
```

By default, *traceroute* tries each hop three times and prints out the times as they happen, so if the reponse time is more than about 300 ms, you'll notice it as it happens. If there is no reply after a timeout period (default 5 seconds), *traceroute* prints an asterisk (*). You'll also occasionally notice a significant delay at the beginning of a line, although the response time seems reasonable. In this case, the delay is probably caused by a DNS reverse lookup for the name of the system. If this becomes a problem (maybe because the global DNS servers aren't reachable), you can turn off DNS reverse lookup using the –n flag.

If you look more carefully at the times in the example above, you'll see three groups of times:

1. The times to *gw* are round 1 ms. This is typical of an Ethernet network.

2. The times for hops 2 to 6 are in the order of 100 to 150 ms. This indicates that the link between *gw.example.org* and *free-gw.example.net* is running PPP over a telephone line. The delay between *free-gw.example.net* and *Fddi0-0.lon5.Melbourne.example.net* is negligible compared to the delay across the PPP link, so you don't see much difference.

3. The times from *borderx2-hssi3-0.Bloomington.mci.net* to *hub.FreeBSD.ORG* are significantly higher, between 400 and 1000 ms. We also note a couple of dropped packets. This indicates that the line between *Fddi0-0.lon5.Melbourne.example.net* and *borderx2-hssi3-0.Bloomington.mci.net* is overloaded. The length of the link (about 13,000 km) also plays a role: that's a total distance of 26,000 km, which take about 85 ms to transfer. If this were a satellite connection, things would be much slower: the total distance from ground station to satellite and back to the ground is 72,000 km, which takes a total of 240 ms to propagate.

Back to our problem. If we see something like the output in the previous example, we know that there's no reason to call up the people at *example.net*: it's not their problem. This might just be overloading on the global Internet. On the other hand, what about this?

```
$ traceroute hub.freebsd.org
traceroute to hub.freebsd.org (204.216.27.18), 30 hops max, 40 byte packets
 1  gw (223.147.37.5)  1.138 ms  0.811 ms  0.800 ms
 2  * * *
 3  * * *
^C
```

You've fixed your routing problems, but you still can't get data off the system. There are a number of possibilities here:

- The link to the next system may be down. The solution's obvious: bring it up and try again.

- *gw* may not be configured as a gateway. You can check this with:

  ```
  $ sysctl net.inet.ip.forwarding
  net.inet.ip.forwarding: 1
  ```

  For a router, this value should be 1. If it's 0, change it with:

  ```
  # sysctl -w net.inet.ip.forwarding=1
  net.inet.ip.forwarding: 0 -> 1
  ```

  See page 313 for further details, including how to ensure that this *sysctl* is set correctly when the system starts.

- You may be trying to use a non-routable IP address such as those in the range 192.168.*x*.*x*. You can't do that. If you don't have enough globally visible IP address, you'll need to run some kind of aliasing package, such as NAT. See Chapter 22, page 393, for further details.

- Maybe there is something wrong with routing to your network. This is a difficult one to check, but in the case of the reference network, one possibility is to repeat the *traceroute* from the machine *gw*: *gw*'s external address on the *tun0* interface is 139.130.136.133, which is on the ISP's network. As a result, they are not affected by a routing problem for network 223.147.37.*x*. If this proves to be the case, contact your ISP to solve it.

- Maybe there is something wrong with the other end; if everything else fails, you may have to call the admins at *example.net* even if you have no hard evidence that it's their problem.

But maybe the data gets one hop further:

```
$ traceroute hub.freebsd.org
traceroute to hub.freebsd.org (204.216.27.18), 30 hops max, 40 byte packets
 1  gw (223.147.37.5)  1.138 ms  0.811 ms  0.800 ms
 2  free-gw.example.net (139.130.136.129)  131.913 ms  122.231 ms  134.694 ms
 3  * * *
 4  * * *
^C
```

In this case, there is almost certainly a problem at *example.net*. This would be the correct time to use the telephone.

High packet loss

But maybe data *is* getting through. Well, some data, anyway. Consider this *ping* session:

```
$ ping freefall.FreeBSD.org
PING freefall.FreeBSD.org (216.136.204.21): 56 data bytes
64 bytes from 216.136.204.21: icmp_seq=0 ttl=244 time=496.426 ms
64 bytes from 216.136.204.21: icmp_seq=1 ttl=244 time=491.334 ms
64 bytes from 216.136.204.21: icmp_seq=2 ttl=244 time=479.077 ms
64 bytes from 216.136.204.21: icmp_seq=3 ttl=244 time=473.774 ms
64 bytes from 216.136.204.21: icmp_seq=4 ttl=244 time=733.429 ms
64 bytes from 216.136.204.21: icmp_seq=5 ttl=244 time=644.726 ms
64 bytes from 216.136.204.21: icmp_seq=7 ttl=244 time=490.331 ms
64 bytes from 216.136.204.21: icmp_seq=8 ttl=244 time=839.671 ms
64 bytes from 216.136.204.21: icmp_seq=9 ttl=244 time=773.764 ms
64 bytes from 216.136.204.21: icmp_seq=10 ttl=244 time=553.067 ms
64 bytes from 216.136.204.21: icmp_seq=11 ttl=244 time=454.707 ms
64 bytes from 216.136.204.21: icmp_seq=12 ttl=244 time=472.212 ms
64 bytes from 216.136.204.21: icmp_seq=13 ttl=244 time=448.322 ms
64 bytes from 216.136.204.21: icmp_seq=14 ttl=244 time=441.352 ms
64 bytes from 216.136.204.21: icmp_seq=15 ttl=244 time=455.595 ms
64 bytes from 216.136.204.21: icmp_seq=16 ttl=244 time=460.040 ms
64 bytes from 216.136.204.21: icmp_seq=17 ttl=244 time=476.943 ms
64 bytes from 216.136.204.21: icmp_seq=18 ttl=244 time=514.615 ms
64 bytes from 216.136.204.21: icmp_seq=23 ttl=244 time=538.232 ms
64 bytes from 216.136.204.21: icmp_seq=24 ttl=244 time=444.123 ms
64 bytes from 216.136.204.21: icmp_seq=25 ttl=244 time=449.075 ms
^C
--- 216.136.204.21 ping statistics ---
27 packets transmitted, 21 packets received, 22% packet loss
round-trip min/avg/max/stddev = 441.352/530.039/839.671/113.674 ms
```

In this case, we have a connection. But look carefully at those sequence numbers. At one point, four packets in a row (sequence 19 to 22) get lost. How high a packet drop rate is still acceptable? 1% or 2% is probably still (barely) acceptable. By the time you get to 10%, though, things look a lot worse. 10% packet drop rate doesn't mean that your connection slows down by 10%. For every dropped packet, you have a minimum delay of one second until TCP retries it. If that retried packet gets dropped too—which it will every 10 dropped packets if you have a 10% drop rate—the second retry takes another three seconds. If you're transmitting packets of 64 bytes over a 33.6 kb/s link, you can normally get about 60 packets through per second. With 10% packet loss, the time to get these packets through is about eight seconds, a throughput loss of 87.5%.

With 20% packet loss, the results are even more dramatic. Now 12 of the 60 packets have to be retried, and 2.4 of them will be retried a second time (for three seconds delay), and 0.48 of them will be retried a third time (six seconds delay). This makes a total of 22 seconds delay, a throughput degradation of nearly 96%.

Theoretically, you might think that the degradation would not be as bad for big packets, such as you might have with file transfers with *ftp*. In fact, the situation is worse then: in most cases the packet drop rate rises sharply with the packet size, and it's common enough that *ftp* times out completely before it can transfer a file.

To get a better overview of what's going on, let's look at another program, *tcpdump*.

tcpdump

tcpdump is a program that monitors a network interface and displays selected information that passes through it. It uses the *Berkeley Packet Filter* (*bpf*), an optional component of the kernel. It's included in recent versions of the GENERIC kernel, but it's possible to remove it. If you don't configure the Berkeley Packet Filter, you get a message like:

```
tcpdump: /dev/bpf0:  device not configured
```

tcpdump poses a potential security problem: you can use it to read anything that goes over the network. As a result, you must be root to run it. The simplest way to run it is without any parameters. This causes *tcpdump* to monitor and display all traffic on the first active network interface, normally Ethernet:

```
# tcpdump
tcpdump: listening on ep0
1: 13:27:57.757157 arp who-has wait.example.org tell presto.example.org
2: 13:28:06.740047 0:4c:a5:0:0:0 2:0:0:0:45:0 4011 80:
                        c93c c06d c589 c06d c5ff 007b 007b 0038
                        5ccb 1d03 06ee 0000 5613 0000 1093 cb15
                        2512 b7e2 de6b 0ead c000 0000 0000 0000
                        0000 0000 0000
3: 13:28:06.740117 freebie.example.org.ntp > 223.147.37.255.ntp: v3 bcast strat 3 p
oll 6  prec -18
4: 13:28:08.004715 arp who-has wait.example.org tell presto.example.org
5: 13:28:10.987453 bumble.example.org.who > 223.147.37.255.who: udp 84
6: 13:28:13.790106 freebie.example.org.6000 > presto.example.org.1089: P 536925467:
   536925851(384) ack 325114346 win 17280 <nop,nop,timestamp 155186 1163778,nop,no
   p,[|tcp]> (DF)
7: 13:28:13.934336 arp who-has freebie.example.org tell presto.example.org
8: 13:28:13.934444 arp reply freebie.example.org is-at 0:a0:24:37:d:2b
9: 13:28:13.935903 presto.example.org.1089 > freebie.example.org.6000: . ack 536925
851 win 16896 <nop,nop,timestamp 1190189 155186,nop,nop,[|tcp]> (DF)
10: 13:28:13.936313 freebie.example.org.6000 > presto.example.org.1089: P 536925851
   :536926299(448) ack 325114346 win 17280 <nop,nop,timestamp 155186 1190189,nop,no
   p,[|tcp]> (DF)
```

This output looks confusing at first. Let's look at it in more detail:

- The first message shows the interface on which *tcpdump* listens. By default, it is the first running interface that it finds. *tcpdump* searches the list of interfaces in the sequence that *ifconfig -a* displays. Generally you can assume that it will find the primary Ethernet interface. If you want to listen on another interface, specify it on the command line. For example, to listen on a PPP interface, you would enter

  ```
  # tcpdump -i tun0
  ```

- At the beginning of each message is a timestamp, with a resolution of 1 μs. These times are relatively accurate; you'll frequently see time differences of less than 1 ms. In this example, the last two messages are 108 μs apart. These times are important: a lot of network problems are performance problems, and there's a big difference in performance between a net where a reply takes 100 μs and one in which a reply takes 100 ms.

- To make things easier, I have put a line number in *italics* at the beginning of each line. It doesn't appear in the *tcpdump* printout.

- Line 1 shows an *ARP* request: system *presto* is looking for the Ethernet address of *wait*. It would appear that *wait* is currently not responding, since there is no reply.

- Line 2 is not an IP message at all. *tcpdump* shows the Ethernet addresses and the beginning of the packet. We don't consider this kind of request in this book.

- Line 3 is a broadcast *ntp* message. We looked at *ntp* on page 155.

- Line 4 is another attempt by *presto* to find the IP address of *wait*.

- Line 5 is a broadcast message from *bumble* on the rwho port, giving information about its current load averages and how long it has been up. See the man page *rwho(1)* for more information.

- Line 6 is from a TCP connection between port 6000 on *freebie* and port 1089 on *presto*. It is sending 384 bytes (with the sequence numbers 536925467 to 536925851; see page 282), and is acknowledging that the last byte it received from *presto* had the sequence number 325114346. The window size is 17280.

- Line 7 is another ARP request. *presto* is looking for the Ethernet address of *freebie*. How can that happen? We've just seen that they have a TCP connection. In fact, ARP information expires after 20 minutes. It's quite possible that all connections between *presto* and *freebie* have been dormant for this period, so *presto* needs to find *freebie*'s IP address again.

- Line 8 is the ARP reply from *freebie* to *presto* giving its Ethernet address.

- Line 9 shows a reply from *presto* on the connection to *freebie* that we saw on line 6. It acknowledges the data up to sequence number 536925851, but doesn't send any itself.

- Line 10 shows another 448 bytes of data from *freebie* to *presto*, and acknowledges the same sequence number from *presto* as in line 6.

Packet loss revisited

Getting back to our packet loss problem, the following example shows the result of communicating on a less-than-perfect *ssh* connection to *hub.FreeBSD.org*, specifically between port 1019 on *freebie* and port 22, the *ssh* port, on *hub*. To make things more readable, the names have been truncated to *freebie* and *hub*. In real-life output, they would be reported as *freebie.example.org* and *hub.FreeBSD.org*. In addition, *tcpdump* reports a *tos* (type of service) field, which has also been removed. It doesn't interest us here.

```
# tcpdump -i ppp0 host hub.freebsd.org
14:16:35.990506 freebie.1019 > hub.22: P 20:40(20) ack 77 win 17520 (DF)
14:16:36.552149 hub.22 > freebie.1019: P 77:97(20) ack 40 win 17520 (DF)
14:16:36.722290 freebie.1019 > hub.22: . ack 97 win 17520 (DF)
14:16:39.344229 freebie.1019 > hub.22: P 40:60(20) ack 97 win 17520 (DF)
14:16:41.321850 freebie.1019 > hub.22: P 40:60(20) ack 97 win 17520 (DF)
```

The first line shows *freebie* sending bytes 20 to 40 of the stream to *bub*, and also acknowledging receipt of everything up to byte 77 of the stream from *hub*. On the next line, *hub* sends bytes 77 to 97 and acknowledges receiving up to byte 40 of the stream from *freebie*. *freebie* then sends another 20 bytes and acknowledges what it has received from *hub*.

After two seconds, *freebie* has not received an acknowledgment from *hub* that its data has been received, so on the last line it sends the packet again.

```
14:16:42.316150 hub.22 > freebie.1019: P 97:117(20) ack 60 win 17520 (DF)
14:16:42.321773 freebie.1019 > hub.22: . ack 117 win 17520 (DF)
```

This is the missing acknowledgment—it came another second later, along with some more data. *freebie* acknowledges receiving it, but doesn't send any more data.

```
14:16:47.428694 freebie.1019 > hub.22: P 60:80(20) ack 117 win 17520 (DF)
14:16:48.590805 freebie.1019 > hub.22: P 80:100(20) ack 117 win 17520 (DF)
14:16:49.055735 freebie.1019 > hub.22: P 100:120(20) ack 117 win 17520 (DF)
14:16:49.190703 hub.22 > freebie.1019: P 137:157(20) ack 100 win 17520 (DF)
```

Five seconds later, *freebie* sends more data, up to byte 120 to *hub*. *hub* replies with its own data an acknowledgment up to byte 100. Unfortunately, the data it sent (bytes 137 to 157) don't line up with the last previously received data (byte 117 at 14:16:42.316150): bytes 117 to 137 are missing. *freebie* thus repeats the previous acknowledgment and then continues sending its data:

```
14:16:49.190890 freebie.1019 > hub.22: . ack 117 win 17520 (DF)
14:16:49.538607 freebie.1019 > hub.22: P 120:140(20) ack 117 win 17520 (DF)
14:16:49.599395 hub.22 > freebie.1019: P 157:177(20) ack 120 win 17520 (DF)
```

Here, *hub* has sent yet more data, now acknowledging the data that *freebie* sent at 14:16:49.055735. It still hasn't sent the data in the byte range 117 to 136, so *freebie* resends the last acknowledgment again and continues sending data:

```
14:16:49.599538 freebie.1019 > hub.22: . ack 117 win 17520 (DF)
14:16:49.620506 freebie.1019 > hub.22: P 140:160(20) ack 117 win 17520 (DF)
14:16:50.066698 hub.22 > freebie.1019: P 177:197(20) ack 140 win 17520 (DF)
```

Again *hub* has sent more data, still without sending the missing packet. *freebie* tries yet again, and then continues sending data:

```
14:16:50.066868 freebie.1019 > hub.22: . ack 117 win 17520 (DF)
14:16:51.820708 freebie.1019 > hub.22: P 140:160(20) ack 117 win 17520 (DF)
14:16:52.308992 hub.22 > freebie.1019: . ack 160 win 17520 (DF)
14:16:55.251176 hub.22 > freebie.1019: P 117:217(100) ack 160 win 17520 (DF)
```

Finally, *hub* resends the missing data, with bytes from 117 to 217. *freebie* is now happy, and acknowledges receipt of all the data up to 217. That's all we transmitted, so after about 1.5 seconds the two systems exchange final acknowledgments:

```
14:16:55.251358 freebie.1019 > hub.22: . ack 217 win 17420 (DF)
14:16:56.690779 hub.login > freebie.1015: . ack 3255467530 win 17520
14:16:56.690941 freebie.1015 > hub.login: . ack 1 win 17520 (DF)
```

This connection is less than perfect. Why? You can use *traceroute* to find out where it's happening, but unless the place is within your ISP's network, you can't do much about it.

Transport and application layers

If you have got this far, the chances are that things will now work. Problems in transport layer are rare. About the only things that can still cause problems are the individual applications. We'll look at some of these in the relevant chapters.

One particular problem is the Domain Name Service. This is such an integral part of the Internet Protocols that people tend to forget that it's really an application. If you get a timeout accessing a web URL, for example, there's a good chance that DNS is causing the problem. Take a look at Chapter 21, *The Domain Name Service*, for some ideas.

Ethereal

tcpdump is a powerful tool, but the examples above show that the output isn't the easiest thing in the world to read. An alternative is *ethereal*, a program in the Ports Collection (*/usr/ports/net/ethereal*) that displays the data in much more detail, as Figure 23-1 shows.

The screen is divided into three windows:

- The top part shows individual packets (numbered 51 to 54 in this example). The line in inverse video has been selected for display in more detail.

- The middle window shows the full packet. By clicking with the mouse on the boxes on the left, you can expand or reduce the amount of information being displayed.

- The bottom window shows the raw data as hexadecimal and ASCII.

In practice, you'd probably want to scale the window much larger than in this example.

This image shows part of the password for a *telnet* login session being returned. It illustrates one of the reasons you should never use *telnet* to connect across the Internet.

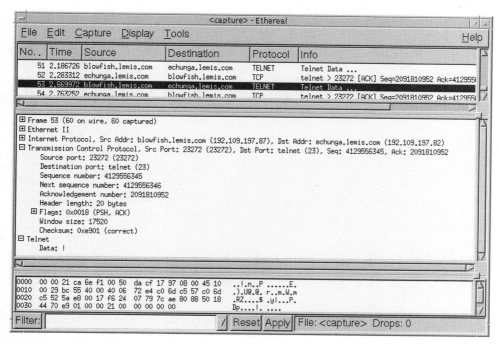

Figure 23-1: ethereal display

24

Basic network access: clients

Finally we have set up the network connections, and everything is working. What can we do with the network? In this part of the book, we'll take a look at some of the more important services that make up the application layer.

The Internet protocols perform most services with a pair of processes: a *client* at one end of the link that actively asks for services, and a *server* at the other end of the link that responds to requests and performs the requested activity. These terms are also used to describe computer systems, but here we're talking about processes, not systems. In this chapter, we'll look at the client side of things, and in Chapter 25, *Basic network access: servers* we'll look at the corresponding servers.

Probably the single most important network service is the *Hypertext Transfer Protocol* or *HTTP*, the service that web browsers use to access the Web. We'll look at web browsers in the next section.

The next most important service is probably the *Simple Mail Transfer Protocol* or *SMTP*, the primary service for sending mail round the Internet. There's also the *Post Office Protocol* or *POP*, which is used by systems unable to run SMTP. This topic is so important that we'll devote Chapters 26 and 27 to it.

To use a remote machine effectively, you need better access than such specialized servers can give you. The most powerful access is obviously when you can execute a shell on the remote machine; that gives you effectively the same control over the machine as you have over your local machine. A number of services are available to do this. In the olden days, you would use *telnet* or *rlogin* to log into another machine. These programs are

417

still with us, but security concerns make them effectively useless outside a trusted local network. We'll look at them briefly on page 430.

The preferred replacement is *ssh*, which stands for *secure shell*. In fact, it's not a shell at all, it's a service to communicate with a remote shell. It encrypts the data sent over the network, thus making it more difficult for crackers to abuse. We'll look at it in detail on page 419.

Another important service is the ability to move data from one system to another. There are a number of ways of doing this. The oldest programs are *rcp* and *ftp*. These programs have the same security concerns as *telnet* and *rlogin*, though *ftp* still has some uses. More modern copying programs use *scp*, which is based on *ssh*. We'll look at file copy programs on page 432. In addition, *rsync* is a useful program for maintaining identical copies files on different systems. We'll look at it on page 437.

A somewhat different approach is the *Network File System* or *NFS*, which mounts file systems from another machine as if they were local. We look at NFS clients on page 441.

The World Wide Web

For the vast majority of the public, the Internet and the *World Wide Web* are the same thing. FreeBSD is an important contender in this area. Some of the world's largest web sites, including Yahoo! (*http://www.yahoo.com/*) run FreeBSD. Even Microsoft runs FreeBSD on its Hotmail service (*http://www.hotmail.com/*), though they have frequently denied it, and for image reasons they are moving to their own software.

Web browsers

A *web browser* is a program that retrieves documents from the Web and displays them. The base FreeBSD system does not include a web browser, but a large number are available in the Ports Collection. All web browsers seem to have one thing in common: they are buggy. They frequently crash when presented with web pages designed for Microsoft, and in other cases they don't display the page correctly. In many cases this is due to poorly designed web pages, of course.

Currently, the most important web browsers are:

- *netscape* was once the only game in town, but it's now showing its age. In addition, many web sites only test their software with Microsoft, and their bugs cause problems with *netscape*.

- *mozilla* is derived from the same sources as *netscape*, but comes in source form. It has now reached the stage where it is less buggy than *netscape*. A number of other browsers, such as *galeon* and *skipstone*, are based on *mozilla*. They're all available in the Ports Collection. *galeon* is included in the *instant-workstation* port described in Chapter 6.

- *konqueror* is included with the KDE port.

- *Opera* is a new browser that some people like. The version in the Ports Collection is free, but it makes up for it by giving you even more advertisements than the web pages give you anyway. You can buy a version that doesn't display the advertisements.

- *lynx* is a web browser for people who don't use X. It displays text only.

You may note two omissions from this list. Microsoft's *Internet Explorer* is not available for FreeBSD. Not many people have missed it. Also, *mosaic*, the original web browser, is now completely obsolete, and it has been removed from the Ports Collection.

In addition to these browsers, *StarOffice* and *OpenOffice* include integrated browsers. You may find you prefer them.

This book does not deal with how to use a web browser: just about everybody knows how to use one. You can also get help from just about any browser; just click on the text or icon marked Help or ?.

ssh

ssh is a *secure shell*, a means of executing programs remotely using encrypted data transfers. There are a number of different implementations of *ssh*: there are two different protocols, and the implementations are complicated both by bugs and license conditions. FreeBSD comes with an implementation of *ssh* called *OpenSSH*, originally developed as part of the OpenBSD project.

Using *ssh* is simple:

```
$ ssh freebie
The authenticity of host 'freebie.example.org (223.147.37.1)' can't be established.
DSA key fingerprint is 08:f7:c4:14:48:0b:14:06:0e:2c:93:4b:1f:f6:ce:b5.
Are you sure you want to continue connecting (yes/no)? yes
Warning: Permanently added 'freebie.example.org' (DSA) to the list of known hosts.
grog@freebie.example.org's password:        as usual, doesn't echo
Last login: Mon May 13 14:21:11 2002
Copyright (c) 1980, 1983, 1986, 1988, 1990, 1991, 1993, 1994
        The Regents of the University of California.  All rights reserved.
FreeBSD 5.0-RELEASE (FREEBIE) #3: Sun Jan  5 13:25:02 CST 2003

Welcome to FreeBSD!
$ tty
/dev/ttyp3
$
```

Once you get this far, you are connected to the machine in almost the same manner as if you were directly connected. This is particularly true if you are running X. As the output of the *tty* command shows, your "terminal" is a *pseudo-tty* or *pty* (pronounced "pity"). This is the same interface that you have with an *xterm*.

It's worth looking in more detail at how the connection is established:

- The first line (*The authenticity...*) appears once *ssh* has established preliminary contact with the remote system. It indicates that you're connected, but that the local system has no information about the remote system. Theoretically you could be connected to a different machine masquerading as the machine you want to connect to. *ssh* saves the fingerprint in ˜/.ssh/known_hosts and checks it every time you connect to that machine thereafter.

- The reference to DSA keys indicates that *ssh* is using the *ssh* Version 2 protocol. We'll look at the differences between the protocols below.

- The password prompt is for the same password as you would see locally. The slightly different format is to clarify exactly which password you should enter. Again, a number of exploits are possible where you might find yourself giving away a password to an intruder, so this caution is justified.

When you log in via *ssh*, there's a chance that your TERM environment variable is set incorrectly. See table 7-3 on page 130 for more details. Remember that TERM describes the display at your end of the link. There is no display at the other end, but the other end needs to know the *termcap* parameters for your display. If you're running an *xterm*, this shouldn't be a problem: the name xterm propagates to the other end. If you're using a character-oriented display (*/dev/ttyvx*), however, your TERM variable is probably set to cons25, which many systems don't know. If systems refuse to start full-screen modes when you connect from a virtual terminal, try setting the TERM variable to ansi.

To exit *ssh*, just log out. If you run into problems, however, like a hung network, you can also hit the combination **Enter ˜. Enter**, which always drops the connection.

Access without a password

Sending passwords across the Net, even if they're encrypted, is not a complete guarantee that nobody else can get in: there are a number of brute-force ways to crack an encrypted password. To address this issue, *ssh* has an access method that doesn't require passwords: instead it uses a technique called *public key cryptography*. You have two keys, one of which you can give away freely, and the other of which you guard carefully. You can encrypt or decrypt with either key: data encrypted with the public key can be decrypted with the private key, and data encrypted with the private key can be decrypted with the public key.

Once you have these keys in place, you can use the *challenge-response* method for authentication. To initiate an *ssh* connection, *ssh* sends your public key to the *sshd* process on the remote system. The remote system must already have a copy of this key. It uses it to encrypt a random text, a *challenge*, which it sends back to your system. The *ssh* process on your system decrypts it with your private key, which is not stored anywhere else, and sends the decrypted key back to the remote *sshd*. Only your system can decode the challenge, so this is evidence to the remote *sshd* that it's really you.

By default, the private key for Version 1 of the protocol is stored in the file *~/.ssh/identity*, and the public key is stored in the file *~/.ssh/identity_pub*. For Version 2, you have a choice of two different encryption schemes, *DSA* and *RSA*. The corresponding private and public keys are stored in the files *~/.ssh/id_dsa*, *~/.ssh/id_dsa.pub*, *~/.ssh/id_rsa* and *~/.ssh/id_rsa.pub* respectively. If you have the choice between DSA keys and RSA keys for protocol Version 2, use DSA keys, which are considered somewhat more secure. You still should have an RSA key pair in case you want to connect to a system that doesn't support DSA keys.

There's still an issue of unauthorized local access, of course. To ensure that somebody doesn't compromise one system and then use it to compromise others, you need a kind of password for your private keys. To avoid confusion, *ssh* refers to it as a *passphrase*. If *ssh* finds keys in the *~/.ssh* directory, it attempts to use them:

```
$ ssh hub
Enter passphrase for key '/home/grog/.ssh/id_rsa': (no echo)
Last login: Sat Jul 13 17:27:33 2002 from wantadilla.lemis
Copyright (c) 1980, 1983, 1986, 1988, 1990, 1991, 1993, 1994
        The Regents of the University of California.  All rights reserved.
FreeBSD 5.0-STABLE (HUB) #7: Thu Jun 26 12:44:34 PDT 2003
(etc)
```

Creating and distributing keys

You create keys with the program *ssh-keygen*. Here's an example of generating all three keys:

```
$ ssh-keygen -t rsa1
Generating public/private rsa1 key pair.
Enter file in which to save the key (/home/grog/.ssh/identity): (ENTER pressed)
Enter passphrase (empty for no passphrase): (no echo)
Enter same passphrase again:  (no echo)
Your identification has been saved in /home/grog/.ssh/identity.
Your public key has been saved in /home/grog/.ssh/identity.pub.
The key fingerprint is:
02:20:1d:50:78:c5:7c:56:7b:1d:e3:54:02:2c:99:76 grog@bumble.example.org
$ ssh-keygen -t rsa
Generating public/private rsa key pair.
Enter file in which to save the key (/home/grog/.ssh/id_rsa): (ENTER pressed)
Enter passphrase (empty for no passphrase):  (no echo)
Enter same passphrase again:  (no echo)
Your identification has been saved in /home/grog/.ssh/id_rsa.
Your public key has been saved in /home/grog/.ssh/id_rsa.pub.
The key fingerprint is:
95:d5:01:ca:90:04:7d:84:f6:00:32:7a:ea:a6:57:2d grog@bumble.example.org
$ ssh-keygen -t dsa
Generating public/private dsa key pair.
Enter file in which to save the key (/home/grog/.ssh/id_dsa): (ENTER pressed)
Enter passphrase (empty for no passphrase):  (no echo)
Enter same passphrase again:  (no echo)
Your identification has been saved in /home/grog/.ssh/id_dsa.
Your public key has been saved in /home/grog/.ssh/id_dsa.pub.
The key fingerprint is:
53:53:af:22:87:07:10:e4:5a:2c:21:31:ec:29:1c:5f grog@bumble.example.org
```

Before you can use these keys, you need to get the public keys on the remote site in the file ˜/.ssh/authorized_keys. Older versions of ssh used a second file, ˜/.ssh/authorized_keys2, for protocol Version 2, but modern versions store all the keys in the one file ˜/.ssh/authorized_keys. There are a number of ways to get the keys in these files. If you already have access to the machine (via password-based authentication, for example), you can put them there yourself. Typically, though, you'll have to get somebody else involved. To make it easier, the public keys are in ASCII, so you can send them by mail. The three public keys generated above look like this:

```
1024 35 1101242842742748033454498238668225412306578450520406221165673293206460199556
75122355303533111871087331545657731342576330585478662959267146045449332197956451897
839276314768175285909667395039795936492323578351726210382756436676090411475643317216
9229141313001215744263830327567324716340068628306033945779068664 grog@bumble.exampl
e.org
ssh-dss AAAAB3NzaC1kc3MAAACBAIltWeRXnqD9HqOLn5kugPSWHicJiu1r0I9dHg8F5m2PpmupyRYSmDzs
cAcsxifo50+1yXk3Vf4P1+EDsAwkyqFlujuMVeKoTYcOi1yrnLDWIDiAeIzt1BQ6ONwbXqxwWKCq1eo1tXxO
rTxw84VboHUuq4XFdt+yPJs8QdxLhj+jAAAAFQC1JL+tU19+UR+c45JGom6ae29d7wAAAIAvNgdN6rTitMjD
CglN7Rq3/8WgI1kzh20XURbCeln2yYsFifcImKb0sUYD2qsB5++gogzsse2IxyIECRCuyCOOFXIQ7WqkvjTp
/T+fuwGPIlho8eeNDRKKABUhHjkuApnoYLIC1O5uyciJ+dIbGaRtGFJr0da7KlkjOLkiv3sR1gAAAIAwgKfW
sRSQJyRZTkKGIHxn3EWTvSicnIRYza+HTaMuMFHMTkNMZBjhei6EoCFpV9B1QB9MlIZgf6WXM2DlmtdUbpm7
KFA669/LZT2LvxbtGP/B++7s0PMs0AgKrKgUxnhVweufMZlPvPPPOz4QS1ZZ5kYhN+lu0S8yuioXYNlDtA==
  grog@bumble.example.org
ssh-rsa AAAAB3NzaC1yc2EAAAABIwAAAIEA1/W3oa1ZEs58KRWMzsrZWMXzPfwoqQ+Z59p6SJlzhevsXG1P
AVWra2wcRz1utKFBjkDpJfEe+09L7h8VAx1aYCHji50tKI8F8YT8OuWGH+UqF/37Wl292SsXsb8g80yyymSf
xgOM/HegvOuHQu46MfaPj9ddfcgY06z3ufcmXts= grog@bumble.example.org
```

In the original, each key is on a single line.

Obviously you don't want anybody messing with your *authorized_keys* files, so *ssh* requires that the files belong to you and are only writeable by you. These two files typically contain multiple keys; to add a new one, just append it to the end of the file. For example, if you receive a new key and store it in the file *newkey*, copy it like this:

```
$ cat newkey >> ~/.ssh/authorized_keys
```

Authenticating automatically

Having to supply the passphrase can become a nuisance and even a serious problem. If you want to run *ssh* from scripts, it may not even be possible to supply the passphrase. *ssh* has another feature available here: it has an *authentication agent* that keeps track of the keys.

The authentication agent is called *ssh-agent*, and you add keys with *ssh-add*. Due to the manner in which it is started, *ssh-agent* needs to be the ancestor of the shell you are running, and of the *ssh-add* command. Otherwise you see error messages like this:

```
$ ssh-agent
SSH_AUTH_SOCK=/tmp/ssh-cwT9aBbV/agent.42902; export SSH_AUTH_SOCK;
SSH_AGENT_PID=42903; export SSH_AGENT_PID;
echo Agent pid 42903;
$ ssh-add
Could not open a connection to your authentication agent.
```

To solve this problem, execute the agent in your current environment with *eval*, then run *ssh-add*:

```
$ eval `ssh-agent`
$ ssh-add
Enter passphrase for /home/grog/.ssh/id_rsa: (enter the passphrase)
Identity added: /home/grog/.ssh/id_rsa (/home/grog/.ssh/id_rsa)
Identity added: /home/grog/.ssh/id_dsa (/home/grog/.ssh/id_dsa)
Identity added: /home/grog/.ssh/identity (grog@zaphod.example.org)
```

You can use *ssh-add*'s -l flag to list which keys the authentication agent currently knows about:

```
$ ssh-add -l
1024 02:20:1d:50:78:c5:7c:56:7b:1d:e3:54:02:2c:99:76 grog@zaphod.example.org (RSA1)
1024 95:d5:01:ca:90:04:7d:84:f6:00:32:7a:ea:a6:57:2d /home/grog/.ssh/id_rsa (RSA)
1024 53:53:af:22:87:07:10:e4:5a:2c:21:31:ec:29:1c:5f /home/grog/.ssh/id_dsa (DSA)
```

If you're using a Bourne-style shell such as *bash*, you can automate a lot of this by putting the following commands in your *.bashrc* or *.profile* file:

```
if      tty > /dev/null; then
        ssh-add -l > /dev/null
        if [ $? -ne 0 ]; then
                eval `ssh-agent`
        fi
fi
```

This first uses the *tty* command to check if this is an interactive shell, then checks if you already have an authentication agent. If it doesn't, it starts one. Don't start a new authentication agent if you already have one: you'd lose any keys that the agent already knows. This script doesn't add keys, because this requires your intervention and could be annoying if you had to do it every time you start a shell.

Setting up X to use ssh

If you work with X, you have the opportunity to start a large number of concurrent *ssh* sessions. It would be annoying to have to enter keys for each session, so there's an alternative method: start X with an *ssh-agent*, and it will pass the information on to any *xterms* that it starts. Add the following commands to your *.xinitrc*:

```
eval `ssh-agent`
ssh-add < /dev/null
```

When you run *ssh-add* in this manner, without an input file, it runs a program to prompt for the passphrase. By default it's */usr/X11R6/bin/ssh-askpass*, but you can change it by setting the SSH_ASKPASS environment variable. */usr/X11R6/bin/ssh-askpass* opens a window and prompts for a passphrase. From then on, anything started under the X session will automatically inherit the keys.

ssh tunnels

Tunneling is a technique for encapsulating an IP connection inside another IP connection. Why would you want to do that? One reason is to add encryption to an otherwise unencrypted connection, such as *telnet* or *POP*. Another is to get access to a service on a system that does not generally supply this service to the Internet.

Let's consider using *http* first. Assume you are travelling, and you want to access your private web server back home. Normally a connection to the http port of *presto.example.com* might have the following parameters:

andante	IP 192.1.7.245	IP 223.147.37.2	*presto*
	Port 9132	Port 80	

But what if the server is firewalled from the global Internet, so you can't access it directly? That's when you need the *ssh* tunnel. The *ssh* tunnel creates a local connection at each end and a separate secure connection across the Internet:

	Tunnel A					Tunnel B		
andante	127.1		*192.1.7.245*	*150.101.248.57*			127.1	*presto*
	4096		*3312*	*22*			80	

The *ssh* connection is shown in `fixed italic` font. It looks just like any other *ssh* connection. The differences are the local connections at each end: instead of talking to presto port 80 (http), you talk to port 4096 on your local machine. Why 4096? It's your choice; you can use any port above 1024. If you're on *andante*, you can set up this tunnel with the command:

```
$ ssh -L 4096:presto.example.org:80 presto.example.org
```

To do the same thing from the *presto* end, you'd set up a *reverse tunnel* with the -R option:

```
$ ssh -R 4096:presto.example.org:80 andante.example.org
```

These commands both set up a tunnel from port 4096 on *andante* to port 80 on the host *presto.example.org*. You still need to supply the name of the system to connect to; it doesn't have to be the same. For example, you might not be able to log in to the web server, but you could access your machine back home, and it has access to the web server. In this case, you could connect to your machine at home:

```
$ ssh -L 4096:presto.example.org:80 freebie.example.org
```

In addition to setting up the tunnel, *ssh* can create a normal interactive session. If you don't want this, use the -f option to tell *ssh* to go into the background after authentication. You can also specify a command to execute, but this is no longer necessary for protocol version 2. If you don't want to execute a command, use the -N option:

```
$ ssh -L 4096:presto.example.org:80 presto.example.org -f -N
```

If you're running protocol version 1, you can use *sleep* with an appropriately long timeout, in this example 1 hour:

```
$ ssh -L 4096:presto.example.org:80 presto.example.org -f sleep 3600
```

Tunneling X

Running X clients on the remote machine is special enough that *ssh* provides a special form of tunneling to deal with it. To use it, you must tell *ssh* the location of an *.Xauthority* file. Do this by adding the following line to the file ˜*/.ssh/environment*:

```
XAUTHORITY=/home/yourname/.Xauthority
```

The name must be in fully qualified form: *ssh* does not understand the shortcut ˜/ to represent your home directory. You don't need to create ˜*/.Xauthority*, though: *ssh* can do that for you.

Once you have this in place, you can set up X tunneling in two different ways. To start it from the command line, enter something like:

```
$ ssh -X -f website xterm
```

As before, the -f option tells *ssh* to go into the background. The -X option specifies X tunneling, and *ssh* runs an *xterm* on the local machine. The DISPLAY environment variable points to the (remote) local host:

```
$ echo $DISPLAY
localhost:13.1
```

Other uses of tunnels

Tunneling has many other uses. Another interesting one is bridging networks. For example, *http://unix.za.net/gateway/documentation/networking/vpn/fbsd.html* describes how to set up a VPN (Virtual Private Network) using User PPP and an *ssh* tunnel.

Configuring ssh

It can be a bit of a nuisance to have to supply all these parameters to *ssh*, but you don't have to: you can supply information for frequently accessed hosts in a configuration file. On startup, *ssh* checks for configuration information in a number of places. It checks for them first in the command-line options, then in you configuration file ˜*/.ssh/config*, and finally in the system-wide configuration file */etc/ssh/ssh_config*. The way it treats duplicate information is pretty much the opposite of what you'd expect: unlike most other programs, options found in a configuration file read in later do *not* replace the options found in an earlier file. Options on the command line replace those given in configuration files.

In practice, such conflicts happen less often than you might expect. The file */etc/ssh/ssh_config*, the main configuration file for the system, normally contains only comments, and by default you don't even get a local *~/.ssh/config*.

ssh_config can contain a large number of options. They're all described in the man page *ssh_config(8)*, but it's worth looking at some of the more common ones. In this section we'll look at some of the more common configuration options.

- The entry Host is special: the options that follow, up to the end of the file or the next following Host argument, relate only to hosts that match the arguments on the Host line.

- Optionally, *ssh* can compress the data streams. This can save a lot of traffic, but it can also increase CPU usage, so by default it is disabled. You can do this by passing the -C flag to *ssh*, but you can also do so by setting Compression yes in the configuration file.

- You can *escape* out of an *ssh* session to issue commands to *ssh* with the EscapeChar. By default it's the *tilde* character, ~. Other programs, notably *rlogin*, use this character as well, so you may want to change it. You can set this value from the *ssh* command line with the -e option.

- To forward an X11 connection, as shown above, you can also set the ForwardX11 variable to yes. This may be useful if you frequently access a remote machine and require X forwarding. This also sets the DISPLAY environment variable correctly to go over the secure channel.

- By default, *ssh* sends regular messages to the remote *sshd* server to check if the remote system has gone down. This can cause connections to be dropped on a flaky connection. Set the KeepAlive option to no to disable this behaviour.

- Use the LocalForward parameter to set up a tunnel. The syntax is similar to that of the -L option above: on *andante*, instead of the command line:

  ```
  $ ssh -L 4096:presto.example.org:80 presto.example.org
  ```

  you would put the following in your *~/.ssh/config*:

  ```
  host presto.example.org
  LocalForward 4096 presto.example.org:80
  ```

  Note that the first port is separated from the other two parameters by a space, not a colon.

- Similarly, you can set up a reverse tunnel with the RemoteForward parameter. On *presto*, instead of the command line:

```
$ ssh -R 4096:presto.example.org:80 andante.example.org
```

you would put the following in your *~/.ssh/config*:

```
host andante.example.org
RemoteForward 4096 presto.example.org:80
```

- By default, *ssh* uses password authentication if it can't negotiate a key pair. Set PasswordAuthentication to no if you don't want this.

- Normally *ssh* connects to the server on port 22 (ssh). If the remote server uses a different port, specify it with the Port keyword. You can also use the -p option on the *ssh* command line.

- By default, *ssh* attempts to connect using protocol 2, and if that doesn't work, it tries to connect using protocol 1. You can override this default with the Protocol keyword. For example, to reverse the default and try first protocol 1, then protocol 2, you would write:

```
Protocol        1,2
```

- By default, *ssh* refuses to connect to a known host if its key fingerprint changes. Instead, you must manually remove the entry for the system from the *~/.ssh/known_hosts* or *~/.ssh/known_hosts2* file. This can indicate that somebody is faking the remote machine, but more often it's because the remote machine has really changed its host key, which it might do at every reboot. If this gets on your nerves, you can add this line to your configuration file:

```
StrictHostKeyChecking   no
```

This doesn't stop the warnings, but *ssh* continues:

```
@@@@@@@@@@@@@@@@@@@@@@@@@@@@@@@@@@@@@@@@@@@@@@@@@@@@@@@@@@@@@@@@@
@    WARNING: REMOTE HOST IDENTIFICATION HAS CHANGED!      @
@@@@@@@@@@@@@@@@@@@@@@@@@@@@@@@@@@@@@@@@@@@@@@@@@@@@@@@@@@@@@@@@@
IT IS POSSIBLE THAT SOMEONE IS DOING SOMETHING NASTY!
Someone could be eavesdropping on you right now (man-in-the-middle attack)!
It is also possible that the DSA host key has just been changed.
The fingerprint for the DSA key sent by the remote host is
95:80:4c:fb:cc:96:1b:36:c5:c9:2b:cb:d1:d4:16:68.
Please contact your system administrator.
Add correct host key in /home/grog/.ssh/known_hosts2 to get rid of this message.
Offending key in /home/grog/.ssh/known_hosts2:39
```

- *ssh* assumes that your user name on the remote system is the same as the name on the local system. If that's not the case, you can use the User keyword to specify the remote user name. Alternatively, you can use the format:

```
$ ssh newuser@remotehost.org
```

Summary of files in ~/.ssh

In addition to the files we have discussed, you will find two other files in the ~/.ssh directory:

- *known_hosts* contains the key fingerprints of all hosts to which you have connected. The example on page 419 shows how *ssh* adds a key.

- *random_seed* is a seed used to generate the keys.

In summary, then, you can expect the following files in your ~/.ssh:

```
drwx------  2 grog  grog    512 Jan 18 21:04 .                     directory
-rw-r--r--  1 grog  grog   1705 Oct 26  1999 authorized_keys        keys
-rw-r--r--  1 grog  grog    844 Jan 27 22:18 authorized_keys2       keys, Version 2 only
-rw-r--r--  1 grog  grog     25 Oct 20 01:35 environment            environment for sshd
-rw-------  1 grog  grog    736 Jul 19 15:40 id_dsa                 DSA private key
-rw-r--r--  1 grog  grog    611 Jul 19 15:40 id_dsa.pub             DSA public key
-rw-------  1 grog  grog    951 Jul 19 15:40 id_rsa                 RSA private key
-rw-r--r--  1 grog  grog    231 Jul 19 15:40 id_rsa.pub             RSA public key
-rw-------  1 grog  grog    536 Jul 19 15:39 identity               RSA1 private key
-rw-r--r--  1 grog  grog    340 Jul 19 15:39 identity.pub           RSA1 public key
-rw-------  1 grog  grog   1000 Jul 25  1999 known_hosts            list of known hosts
-rw-------  1 grog  grog    512 Jul 25  1999 random_seed            for key generation
```

Note particularly the permissions and the ownership of the files and the directory itself. If they are wrong, *ssh* won't work, and it won't tell you why not. In particular, the directory must not be group writeable.

Troubleshooting ssh connections

A surprising number of things can go wrong with setting up *ssh* connections. Here are some of the more common ones:

- After some delay, you get the message:

  ```
  ssh: connect to address 223.147.37.76 port 22: Operation timed out
  ```

  This probably means that the remote host is down, or that you can't reach it due to network problems.

- You get the message:

  ```
  ssh: connect to address 223.147.37.65 port 22: Connection refused
  ```

  This means that the remote host is up, but no *sshd* is running.

- You have set up keys, but you still get a message asking for a password.

  This can mean a number of things: your *ssh-agent* isn't running, you haven't added the keys, the other end can't find them, or the security on the keys at the other end is incorrect. You can check the first two like this:

```
$ ssh-add -l
Could not open a connection to your authentication agent.
```

This message means that you haven't run *ssh-agent*. Do it like this:

```
$ eval `ssh-agent`
Agent pid 95180
$ ssh-add -l
The agent has no identities.
$ ssh-add
Enter passphrase for /home/grog/.ssh/id_rsa: no echo
Identity added: /home/grog/.ssh/id_rsa (/home/grog/.ssh/id_rsa)
Identity added: /home/grog/.ssh/id_dsa (/home/grog/.ssh/id_dsa)
Identity added: /home/grog/.ssh/identity (grog@freebie.lemis.com)
$ ssh-add -l
1024 02:20:1d:50:78:c5:7c:56:7b:1d:e3:54:02:2c:99:76 grog@zaphod.example.org (RSA1)
1024 95:d5:01:ca:90:04:7d:84:f6:00:32:7a:ea:a6:57:2d /home/grog/.ssh/id_rsa (RSA)
1024 53:53:af:22:87:07:10:e4:5a:2c:21:31:ec:29:1c:5f /home/grog/.ssh/id_dsa (DSA)
```

In this case, all three keys are set correctly. If you have, say, only an RSA1 (protocol
Version 1) key, and the other end doesn't support protocol Version 1, *ssh* will ask for
a password.

- You get a message like this:

```
@@@@@@@@@@@@@@@@@@@@@@@@@@@@@@@@@@@@@@@@@@@@@@@@@@@@@@@@@@@
@    WARNING: REMOTE HOST IDENTIFICATION HAS CHANGED!    @
@@@@@@@@@@@@@@@@@@@@@@@@@@@@@@@@@@@@@@@@@@@@@@@@@@@@@@@@@@@
IT IS POSSIBLE THAT SOMEONE IS DOING SOMETHING NASTY!
Someone could be eavesdropping on you right now (man-in-the-middle attack)!
It is also possible that the DSA host key has just been changed.
The fingerprint for the DSA key sent by the remote host is
95:80:4c:fb:cc:96:1b:36:c5:c9:2b:cb:d1:d4:16:68.
Please contact your system administrator.
Add correct host key in /home/grog/.ssh/known_hosts2 to get rid of this message.
Offending key in /home/grog/.ssh/known_hosts2:39
```

There are two possible reasons for this message. As the message states, one is that
somebody is trying to intercept the connection, and the other one is that the remote
system has changed its host key. The latter is by far the more common. To fix this
problem, you have two choices:

1. Edit your *~/.ssh/known_hosts2* file and remove references to the remote system.
    The message suggests changing line 39, but you might have more than one key
    for this system in this file. If one is wrong, there's a good chance that any others
    will be too, so you should remove all references.

2. Add the following line to your *~/.ssh/config* file:

    ```
    StrictHostKeyChecking  no
    ```

    It doesn't remove the warning, but it allows you to connect anyway.

ssh includes debugging options that may help debug problems setting up connections.
Use the −v option, up to three times, to get *ssh* to display largely undocumented
information about what is going on. The output is pretty verbose; with three −v options
you get nearly 200 lines of information.

telnet

As mentioned above, *telnet* is an older, unencrypted program that connects to a shell on a remote system. You might find it of use when connecting to a system that doesn't have *ssh*. Be very careful not to use valuable passwords, since they are transmitted in the clear. Apart from that, you use it pretty much in the same way as *ssh*:

```
$ telnet freebie
Trying 223.147.37.1...
Connected to freebie.example.org.
Escape character is '^]'.
login: grog
Password: (no echo)

FreeBSD/i386 (wantadilla.example.org) (ttypj)

Last login: Mon Oct 14 17:51:57 from sydney.example.org
Copyright (c) 1980, 1983, 1986, 1988, 1990, 1991, 1993, 1994
        The Regents of the University of California.  All rights reserved.

FreeBSD 5.0-RELEASE (FREEBIE) #0: Tue Dec 31 19:08:24 CST 2002

You have new mail.
If I have seen farther than others, it is because I was standing on the
shoulders of giants.
                -- Isaac Newton

In the sciences, we are now uniquely privileged to sit side by side
with the giants on whose shoulders we stand.
                -- Gerald Holton

If I have not seen as far as others, it is because giants were standing
on my shoulders.
                -- Hal Abelson

In computer science, we stand on each other's feet.
                -- Brian K. Reid
$ tty
/dev/ttyp9
$
```

Once you get this far, you are connected to the machine in an almost identical manner as if you were directly connected. This is particularly true if you are running X. As the output of the *tty* command shows, your "terminal" is a *pseudo-tty* or *pty* (pronounced "pity"). This is the same interface that you will have with an *xterm*.

It's worth looking in more detail at how the connection is established:

- The first line (*Trying...*) appears as soon as *telnet* has resolved the IP address.

- The next three lines appear as soon as it has a reply from the other end. At this point, there can be a marked delay before *telnet* continues. *telnet* performs a reverse DNS lookup to find the name of your system. If you get a delay here, it could be an indication that your reverse lookup is not working correctly. After DNS times out, it will continue normally, but the delay is a nuisance.

- Logging in is almost exactly the same as logging in locally. Normally you won't be able to log in directly as root, unless you have set /dev/ptyx as secure in your /etc/ttys (see page 197 for further details). It's not a good idea to set your ptys as secure. Use su instead if you want to become root.

When you log in via *telnet*, there's a good chance that your TERM environment variable will be set incorrectly. See Table 7-3 on page 130 for more details. TERM describes the display at your end of the display, not the other end. If you're running an *xterm*, this shouldn't be a problem: probably the name *xterm* will propagate to the other end. If you're using a character-oriented display (/dev/ttyvx), however, your TERM variable will probably be set to cons25, which many systems don't know. If the remote system refuses to start programs in full-screen modes, try setting the TERM variable to ansi.

To exit *telnet*, you just log off. If you run into problems, however, like a hung network, you can also hit **Ctrl-]** to enter *telnet* command mode, and from there enter quit:

```
$ ^]
telnet> quit
$
```

If you hit **Ctrl-]** by accident, just hit **Enter** to return to the *telnet* session.

Secure telnet

Recent releases of FreeBSD *telnet* include a secure connection option. You can recognize it by the different messages that appear when you connect:

```
$ telnet freebie
Trying 223.147.37.1...
Connected to freebie.example.org.
Escape character is '^]'.
Trying SRA secure login:
User (grog):
Password:
[ SRA accepts you ]
```

There's no particular reason to use this version of *telnet*; it's non-standard, and you're still better off with *ssh*.

Using telnet for other services

The way we have used *telnet* so far, it connects to the default port, telnet (number 23, as you can see in the file /etc/services). This isn't the only possibility, though: you can tell *telnet* which port to connect to. In Chapter Chapter 27, *Electronic mail: servers*, we'll see how to communicate with *sendmail* using *telnet* on port smtp page 502, and how to communicate with *POP* on port pop, page 504. There are many other such uses.

Copying files

The other basic function involves copying files between systems. The traditional tools are *ftp* and *rcp*. Neither use encryption, so it's preferable to use *scp*, a variant of *ssh*. Nevertheless, *ftp* has its uses. About the only use for *rcp* is on systems that don't support *scp*, or systems where security is not an issue, and *scp* is so slow that it's not practical. The good news: you use *rcp* in pretty much the same manner as *scp*: *scp* was designed to be compatible with *rcp*, so you don't need to learn anything else if you want to use it.

scp

scp is a variant of *ssh* used for remote copying. The same access considerations apply as for *ssh*. The syntax for copying is similar to the syntax used by NFS: to copy a file */var/log/messages* from *presto* to the file *prestomessages* on the local machine, you might enter:

```
$ scp presto:/var/log/messages prestomessages
```

As with *ssh*, if you need to authenticate as a different user, you can use the form *user@system*. *scp* does not support the -l option to specify the user name.

scp has a number of options reminiscent of *cp*:

- Use the -p option to preserve modification times and permissions where possible. Note that this means you can't use *ssh*'s -p option to specify an alternative port. *scp* uses the -P option for this instead.

- Use the -r option to recursively copy directories.

You don't have to supply full path names to *scp*; you can write things like:

```
$ scp remotehost:file .
```

This looks for a file called *file* in your home directory on the remote machine and copies it to your current local directory. Note the difference: there is no way for *scp* to know a different remote directory, so relative paths are always relative to the home directory on that machine.

ftp

ftp is the Internet File Transfer Program, and is the standard way to transfer large files long distances across the Net. It works for small files and short distances too, but you may find that *scp* or *NFS* are better alternatives in these areas.

One serious drawback in duplicating files across the net is that you need to have permission to access the remote system. Traditionally, you need a user ID to access a system. Of course, the file server could have a specific user ID without a password, but that would throw the system open to attack from crackers. *ftp* solves this problem by recognizing the special user ftp. This user name used to be anonymous, but it turned out to be a problem to spell. *ftp* servers still accept the name anonymous as well. Login is special: you don't need a password, but by convention, to help the system administrators with their bookkeeping, you should enter your real user ID in place of the password when logging in as ftp. A typical session might look like:

```
$ ftp ftp.freebsd.org
Connected to ftp.beastie.tdk.net.
cd 220 ftp.beastie.tdk.net FTP server (Version 6.00LS) ready.
331 Guest login ok, send your email address as password.
230- The FreeBSD mirror at Tele Danmark Internet.
More messages omitted
Name (grog): ftp
331 Guest login ok, send ident as password.
Password:                        user name does not echo
230 Guest login ok, access restrictions apply.
Remote system type is UNIX.
Using binary mode to transfer files.
ftp> bin                  to ensure binary transfer
200 Type set to I.
ftp> cd /pub/FreeBSD/ports/distfiles
250 CWD command successful.
ftp> get xtset-1.0.tar.gz
local: xtset-1.0.tar.gz remote: xtset-1.0.tar.gz
229 Entering Extended Passive Mode (|||58059|)
150 Opening BINARY mode data connection for 'xtset-1.0.tar.gz' (4239 bytes).
100% |*********************************| 4239       5.49 KB/s    00:00
226 Transfer complete.
4239 bytes received in 00:00 (5.49 KB/s)
ftp> ^D
221 Goodbye.
```

There are a number of things to note about this transfer:

- The server may have multiple names, and the one you use may not be its canonical name (the name specified in the server's DNS A record—see page 363). By convention, the first part of the name of an *ftp* server is *ftp*. Here we connected to the server with the name *ftp.FreeBSD.org*, but the canonical name of the server is *ftp.beastie.tdk.net*.

- Some versions of *ftp* transmit in ASCII mode by default: they change every incidence of the ASCII line feed character (the C language constant \n) to the sequence \r\n (they prepend an ASCII carriage return character). This permits you to print the results on normal printers, but makes a terrible mess of binary files. Transmitting in binary form always works. As the message shows, the FreeBSD *ftp* server uses binary mode, but it doesn't harm to enter the `bin` command. The message `Type set to I.` is *ftp*'s way of telling you that it has set binary transmission mode.

* The line of **** is an indication of the progress of the transfer. It's specific to BSD; other *ftp* clients don't show you anything here.

Specifying file names as URIs

This transmission is fairly typical, and it's the traditional way to do it. FreeBSD has another method, though, which can be of use: instead of the interactive approach, you can specify the file name as a URI, and you can use *ftp* to download HTTP documents from a web server. For example, the last transfer can be simplified to:

```
$ ftp ftp://ftp.freebsd.org/pub/FreeBSD/ports/distfiles/xtset-1.0.tar.gz
Connected to ftp.beastie.tdk.net.
220 ftp.beastie.tdk.net FTP server (Version 6.00LS) ready.
331 Guest login ok, send your email address as password.
...
230 Guest login ok, access restrictions apply.
Remote system type is UNIX.
Using binary mode to transfer files.
200 Type set to I.
250 CWD command successful.
250 CWD command successful.
250 CWD command successful.
250 CWD command successful.
local: xtset-1.0.tar.gz remote: xtset-1.0.tar.gz
229 Entering Extended Passive Mode (|||59779|)
150 Opening BINARY mode data connection for 'xtset-1.0.tar.gz' (4239 bytes).
100% |*************************************|  4239        5.82 KB/s    00:00
226 Transfer complete.
4239 bytes received in 00:00 (5.81 KB/s)
221 Goodbye.
```

Note that this method implies anonymous *ftp*: you don't have to log in.

In the same way, you can download a web page like this:

```
$ ftp http://www.FreeBSD.org/index.html
Requesting http://www.FreeBSD.org/index.html
100% |*************************************| 26493       12.20 KB/s    00:02
26493 bytes retrieved in 00:02 (12.17 KB/s)
```

Note that in this case you can't just specify the URI as *http://www.FreeBSD.org/*: you must specify the real file name.

Other ftp commands

ftp has about sixty commands, some of which can be of use. We'll look at the most useful commands in the following sections.

mget

Frequently you need to copy more than a single file. For example, if you currently have *gcc-2.5.0* and want to get *gcc-2.5.8*, you will discover the following files on the file server:

```
ftp> ls
200 PORT command successful.
150 Opening ASCII mode data connection for /bin/ls.
-rw-rw-r-- 1 117 1001    43367 Nov  1 02:37 gcc-2.5.0-2.5.2.diff.gz
-rw-rw-r-- 1 117 1001     1010 Nov  1 02:37 gcc-2.5.1-2.5.2.diff.gz
-rw-rw-r-- 1 117 1001    78731 Nov 11 13:53 gcc-2.5.2-2.5.3.diff.gz
-rw-rw-r-- 1 117 1001    13931 Nov 17 09:27 gcc-2.5.3-2.5.4.diff.gz
-rw-rw-r-- 1 117 1001    76271 Nov 27 16:48 gcc-2.5.4-2.5.5.diff.gz
-rw-rw-r-- 1 117 1001     8047 Dec  3 09:22 gcc-2.5.5-2.5.6.diff.gz
-rw-rw-r-- 1 117 1001  5994481 Nov 27 16:49 gcc-2.5.5.tar.gz
-rw-rw-r-- 1 117 1001    10753 Dec 12 19:15 gcc-2.5.6-2.5.7.diff.gz
-rw-rw-r-- 1 117 1001    14726 Jan 24 09:02 gcc-2.5.7-2.5.8.diff.gz
-rw-rw-r-- 1 117 1001  5955006 Dec 22 14:16 gcc-2.5.7.tar.gz
-rw-rw-r-- 1 117 1001  5997896 Jan 24 09:03 gcc-2.5.8.tar.gz
226 Transfer complete.
ftp>
```

In other words, you have the choice of transferring 6 MB of software in *gcc-2.5.8.tar.gz* or seven incremental patch files with a total of less than 250 kB. On the other hand, copying the diffs requires typing all these long, complicated file names, so you might decide it's easier just to duplicate the whole 6 MB.

There is an easier way: *mget* (multiple get) duplicates files matching a wild card. You could perform the complete transfer with:

```
ftp> mget gcc-2*diff.gz
mget gcc-2.5.0-2.5.2.diff.gz?y
200 PORT command successful.
150 Opening BINARY mode data connection for
   gcc-2.5.0-2.5.2.diff.gz (43667 bytes).
226 Transfer complete.
43667 bytes received in 19 seconds (2.298 Kbytes/s)
mget gcc-2.5.1-2.5.2.diff.gz?n      we don't need this one
mget gcc-2.5.2-2.5.3.diff.gz?y
200 PORT command successful.
150 Opening BINARY mode data connection for
   gcc-2.5.2-2.5.3.diff.gz (78731 bytes).
226 Transfer complete.
78731 bytes received in 33 seconds (2.835 Kbytes/s)
... etc
```

prompt

Using *mget* saves a lot of network bandwidth and copies the files faster, but it has one disadvantage: *ftp* prompts you for each file name, so you have to wait around to answer the prompts. If you don't, *ftp* disconnects after 15 minutes of inactivity. It would be simpler to perform all the *mget*s without any intervention. This is where the *prompt* command comes in.

The *prompt* command specifies whether to issue certain prompts or not—the *mget* command is one example. This command is a toggle—in other words, if prompting is on, *prompt* turns it off, and if prompting is off, *prompt* turns it on. If prompting is off, the *mget* command in the previous example would have gone through with no interruptions.

In the previous example, you don't really want to transfer the file *gcc-2.5.1-2.5.2.diff.gz*, because you don't need it to perform the patches: you can upgrade from 2.5.0 to 2.5.2 directly with the file *gcc-2.5.0-2.5.2.diff.gz*. On the other hand, not copying the file would mean sitting around for the duration of the transfer and answering the prompt for each file, and the file is only 1 kB long. In this case, it is reasonable to copy it as well—in other cases, you may need to consider alternatives.

reget

Sooner or later, you will lose a connection in the middle of a transfer. According to Murphy's law, this will usually happen with a big file, and it will be shortly before the transfer is finished. You may be able to save the day with *reget*, which picks up the transfer where it left off. The semantics are the same as for *get*.

Unfortunately, not all versions of *ftp* have the *reget* command, and on many systems that do have the command, it doesn't work correctly. If you *do* decide to use it, you should first make a copy of the partially copied file, in case something goes wrong.

user

Normally, *ftp* attempts to log in using the user name of the user who started the *ftp* program. To make establishing connections easier, *ftp* checks for a file called *.netrc* when performing a login sequence. *.netrc* contains information on how to log in to specific systems. A typical *.netrc* might look like:

```
machine freebie        login grog       password foo
machine presto         login grog       password bar
machine bumble         login grog       password baz
machine wait           login grog       password zot
default                login ftp        password grog@example.org
```

Lines starting with the keyword *machine* specify login name (*grog* in this example) and password for each system. The last line is the important one: if the system is not mentioned by name, *ftp* attempts a login with user name ftp and password grog@example.org. Though this may be of use with systems you don't know, it causes a problem: if you want to connect to a machine without anonymous *ftp*, you will need to explicitly tell *ftp* not to attempt an auto-login. Do this with the −n option:

```
$ ftp -n ftp.remote.org
```

The *.netrc* file is a security risk: it contains all your passwords in readable form. Make sure it is secured so that only you can read or write it.

ftp is not overly clear about login failures. For example,

```
$ ftp ftp.tu-darmstadt.de
Connected to ftp.tu-darmstadt.de.
220 rs3.hrz.th-darmstadt.de FTP server (Version 4.1) ready.
331 Password required for grog.
530 Login incorrect.
Login failed.
Remote system type is UNIX.
Using binary mode to transfer files.
ftp>
```

This error message is not very obvious: although you're not logged in, you still get the same prompt, and *ftp* produces enough verbiage that it's easy to oversee that the login attempt failed. To complete the login, use the *user* command:

```
ftp> user ftp
331 Guest login ok, send ident as password.
Password:                          username does not echo
230 Guest login ok, access restrictions apply.
```

sftp

sftp is yet another *ssh*-based program. It's designed to be as compatible as possible with *ftp*, so you use it in exactly the same manner. As with other *ssh*-related commands, you need to authenticate in an *ssh*-specific manner. In addition, it has an *exec* command, which allows you to run programs on the remote machine.

To use *sftp*, the remote machine must be able to run the *sftp-server* server. It is normally started from *sshd*. See page 454 for more details.

rsync

Frequently you want to keep identical copies of files on different machines. You can copy them, of course, but if there are only small changes in large files, this can be relatively inefficient. You can perform this task more efficiently with *rsync*, which is designed to keep identical copies of files on two different systems and to optimize network bandwidth while doing so. It's in the Ports Collection. Install in the normal manner:

```
# cd /usr/ports/net/rsync
# make install
```

By default, *rsync* uses *ssh* to perform the transfer, so you need to have *ssh* configured correctly. In particular, you should be using *ssh-agent* authentication.

You can use *rsync* like *scp*: the syntax is compatible up to a point. For example, you could copy a file from a remote system with:

```
$ rsync presto:/var/log/messages prestomessages
```

You don't need to install *rsync* just for that, of course: you can do exactly the same thing with *scp*. *rsync* has one advantage over *scp*, however, even in this case. The first time you copy the file, there's no difference. But files like */var/log/messages* grow at the end, and the rest doesn't change. That's an ideal situation for *rsync*: it uses an algorithm that recognizes common parts of files (not necessarily at the beginning) and optimizes the transfer accordingly. The first time you run the program, you might see:

```
$ rsync -v /var/log/messages freebie:/var/tmp
messages
wrote 80342 bytes   read 36 bytes   53585.33 bytes/sec
total size is 80255   speedup is 1.00
$ rsync -v /var/log/messages freebie:/var/tmp
messages
wrote 535 bytes   read 726 bytes   840.67 bytes/sec
total size is 80255   speedup is 63.64
```

This example used the option –v to show details of what was transferred; otherwise you wouldn't see any output at all. The first time round, the entire file was copied, so there was no speedup. The second time, though, almost nothing needed to be copied, so the transfer was over 60 times as fast.

Copying directory hierarchies

rsync has a bewildering number of options for synchronizing directories. Consider the case where you maintain web pages locally, but your main web server is co-located somewhere else. After updating the local web pages, you can run a script to update the remote pages with commands like:

```
rsync -LHzav --exclude=RCS --exclude="*~" ~grog/public_html/* website:htdocs/grog
rsync -LHztpgov --exclude="*~" website:htdocs
```

The first *rsync* command synchronizes the local directory *˜grog/public_html* to the remote directory *htdocs/grog* on the system *website*. It includes all subdirectories with the exception of the *RCS* directories. The second command synchronizes the top level web directory only, and not the subdirectories, many of which shouldn't be maintained on the remote site. In each case, files ending in ˜ are excluded (these are normally *Emacs* backup files), and in the second case the *RCS* subdirectories are also excluded. Let's look more carefully at all those options:

• –L copies symbolic links (which the documentation refers to as "soft links") as separate files. If you don't include this option, symbolic links to files within the directory hierarchy will work, but links outside the hierarchy may be broken (depending on whether a file of that name exists on the destination system or not). In this example, a number of files are really located elsewhere, so it makes sense to copy them as files.

- −H is pretty much the opposite of −L: by default, *rsync* doesn't check whether it has already copied a file, so if it finds another link to it, it will create a new file on the remote machine. −H tells it to keep track of links and simply create another link to any file it has already copied on the destination machine. This can only work if the two links have been copied by the same invocation of *rsync*.

- The option −z tells *rsync* to compress data. This can significantly reduce traffic.

- The option −a ("archive") is in fact a shorthand notation for a total of seven other options. We'll see some of them below. The others are:

  - −r: copy subdirectories recursively.

  - −l: create symbolic links where necessary. In this example, it's overruled by the −L option.

  - −D: copy device nodes (only for root).

  The other options are −p, −t, −g and −o. We don't want to copy subdirectories in the second example, so we state them explicitly. Together, they roughly correspond to the −p (preserve) option to some other copy programs.

- The option −p tells *rsync* to set the permissions of the remote copy to be the same as those of the original file.

- The option −t tells *rsync* to preserve the modification times of the original file on the remote copy.

- The option −g tells *rsync* to set the group ownership of the remote copy to be the same as those of the original file.

- The option −o tells *rsync* to set the ownership of the remote copy to be the same as those of the original file.

- We've already seen the −v option: it gives information on what *rsync* is doing.

When copying directories with *rsync*, it's relatively easy to end up with the files in the wrong directory level: either they're in the parent directory, or in a subdirectory of the same name. Consider the following command to synchronize a mail folder to a laptop:

```
$ cd /home/grog
$ rsync -zHLav presto:/home/grog/Mail Mail
```

This would seem to duplicate the directory */home/grog/Mail* on the remote system to a directory of the same name on the local system. In fact, it moves the contents of the host */home/grog/Mail* to */home/grog/Mail/Mail* on the local machine. To do what you expect, write:

```
$ rsync -zHLav presto:/home/grog/Mail .
```

Using an rsync server

The use of *rsync* that we've seen so far doesn't require a server, but it does require an *ssh*. *rsync* also offers a different means of access that uses a server, *rsyncd*. This method is intended more for access to systems for which you don't have a password, something like anonymous *ftp*.

We'll look at setting up an *rsync* server on page 454. The client side is relatively simple. Use two colons when referring to the remote system. For example, you might enter:

```
$ rsync freebie::
This is freebie.example.org.  Be gentle.

groggy              Greg's web pages
tivo                TiVo staging area
```

The first line is simply an identification message, referred to as a message of the day in the documentation. The others represent directory hierarchies that the server makes available, along with a comment about their purpose. The documentation calls them modules. As we'll see on page 454, they correspond to directories on the server machine, though the names don't need to be related.

To find out what is in these directories, you can use the following kind of command, which specifies a particular module, but no destination:

```
$ rsync freebie::groggy
This is freebie.example.org.  Be gentle.

drwxr-xr-x          5632 2002/10/24 12:40:38 .
-rw-r--r--          3855 2002/03/16 13:51:12 20feb99.html
-rw-r--r--          2363 2002/03/16 13:51:12 7mar1999.html
-rw-r--r--          8345 2002/03/16 13:51:12 AOSS-programme-orig.html
-rw-r--r--         11590 2002/03/16 13:51:12 AOSS-programme.html
-rw-r--r--          1798 2002/03/16 13:51:12 BSDCon-2002.html
-rw-r--r--          1953 2002/03/16 13:51:12 Essey-20020222.html
...etc
```

To transfer a file, specify its name and a destination:

```
$ rsync -v freebie::groggy/AOSS-programme.html .
This is freebie.example.org.  Be gentle.

AOSS-programme.html
wrote 98 bytes  read 11744 bytes  23684.00 bytes/sec
total size is 11590  speedup is 0.98
```

This example uses the -v option to show what *rsync* has done; without it, there would be no output.

If you want to transfer the entire module, use the -r or -a options we looked at above:

```
$ rsync -r -v freebie::groggy .
This is freebie.example.org.  Be gentle.

receiving file list ... done
skipping non-regular file "Images/20001111"
20feb99.html
7mar1999.html
AOSS-programme-orig.html
AOSS-programme.html
BSDCon-2002.html
...etc
```

The Network File System

The *Network File System*, or *NFS*, is the standard way to share UNIX files across a network.

We've already seen that UNIX file systems are accessible in a single tree by *mount*ing them on a specific directory. NFS continues this illusion across the network.

From a user point of view, there is little difference: you use the same *mount* command, and it performs what looks like the same function. For example, if system *presto*'s system administrator wants to mount *freebie*'s file systems */*, */usr* and */home*, he could enter:

```
# mkdir /freebie
# mount freebie:/ /freebie
# mount freebie:/usr /freebie/usr
# mount freebie:/home /freebie/home
```

You'll note how to specify the file systems: the system name, a colon (:), and the file system name. This terminology predates URIs; nowadays, people would probably write nfs://freebie/usr.

Note also that you don't need to create */freebie/usr* and */freebie/home*: assuming that the directories */usr* and */home* exist on once you have mounted */freebie*, they will become visible.

If you look at NFS more closely, things don't look quite as similar to disks as they do at first sight. You access local file systems via the disk driver, which is part of the kernel. You access NFS file systems via the NFS processes.

Older implementations of NFS had a plethora of processes. If you're used to such systems, don't let the lack of processes make you think that there's something missing.

NFS client

You don't need any particular software to run as an NFS client, but the program *nfsiod* greatly improves performance. It's started at bootup time if you specify nfs_client_enable="YES" in your */etc/rc.conf*, but you can also start it manually if it's not running:

```
# nfsiod -n 6
```

The parameter -n 6 tells *nfsiod* how many copies of itself to start. The default is four. Each *nfsiod* can handle a concurrent I/O request, so if you find that your performance isn't what you would like it to be, and the CPU time used by each *nfsiod* is similar, then you might like to increase this value. To ensure it's done automatically at boot time, add the following to */etc/sysctl.conf*:

```
vfs.nfs.iothreads=6
```

We'll look at */etc/rc.conf* and */etc/sysctl.conf* in more detail in Chapter 29.

Mounting remote file systems

As we've seen, we mount NFS files with the same *mount* command that we use for local file systems. This is another illusion: *mount* is just a front-end program that determines which program to start. In the case of local file systems, it will start *mount_ufs*, and for NFS file systems it will start *mount_nfs*.

There are a number of options you may wish to use when mounting NFS file systems. Unfortunately, the options that *mount_nfs* uses are not the same as the options you would use in */etc/fstab*. Here's an overview:

Table 24-1: NFS mount options

fstab option	mount_nfs option	Meaning
bg	-b	Continue attempting the mount in the background if it times out on the initial attempt. This is a very good idea in */etc/fstab*, because otherwise the boot process waits until all mounts have completed. If you've just had a power failure, this can cause deadlocks otherwise.
nfsv2	-2	Use NFS Version 2 protocol. By default, *mount_nfs* tries NFS Version 3 protocol first, and falls back to Version 2 if the other end can't handle Version 3. Don't use NFS Version 2 unless you have to.

fstab option	mount_nfs option	Meaning
retry=*num*	-R*num*	Retry up to *num* times before aborting an I/O operation.
-o ro	-o ro	Mount the file system for read-only access.
-o rw	-o rw	Mount the file system for read and write access.
-R *num*	-R *num*	Retry the mount operation up to *num* times. If you have chosen soft mounting, fail I/O operations after *num* retries. The default value is 10.
-r *size*	-r *size*	Set the read data block size to *size* bytes. *size* should be a power of 2 between 1024 and 32768. The default value is 8192. Use smaller block sizes for UDP mounts if you have frequent "fragments dropped due to timeout" messages on the client.
soft	-s	If operations on the file system time out, don't retry forever. Instead, give up after *Retry* timeouts. See option -R.
-t *num*	-t *num*	Time out and retry an operation if it doesn't complete with in *num*/10 seconds. The default value is 10 (1 second).
tcp	-T	Use TCP instead of UDP for mounts. This is more reliable, but slightly slower. In addition, not all implementations of NFS support TCP transport.
-w *size*	-w *size*	Set the write data block size to *size* bytes. *size* should be a power of 2 between 1024 and 32768. The default value is 8192. Use smaller block sizes for UDP mounts if you have frequent "fragments dropped due to timeout" messages on the server.

Normally, the only options that are of interest are -o ro, if you specifically want to restrict write access to the file system, and soft, which you should always use.

> Purists claim that soft compromises data integrity, because it may leave data on the server machine in an unknown state. That's true enough, but in practice the alternative to soft mounting is to reboot the client machine. This is not only a nuisance, it *also* compromises data integrity. The only solution that doesn't always compromise data integrity is to wait for the server machine to come back online. It's unlikely that anybody will wait more than a few hours at the outside for a server to come back.

A typical mount operation might be:

```
# mount -o soft presto:/usr /presto/usr
```

Where to mount NFS file systems

You can mount an NFS file system just about anywhere you would mount a local file system. Still, a few considerations will make life easier. In this discussion, we'll assume that we have a large number of file systems mounted on *freebie*, and we want to make them accessible to *presto*.

- If you have a "special" file system that you want to mount on multiple systems, it makes sense to mount it on the same mount point on every system. *freebie* has two file systems, */S* and */src*, which contain source files and are shared between all systems on the network. It makes sense to mount the file system on the same directory.

- *freebie* has a CD-ROM changer, and mounts the disks on */cdrom/1* to */cdrom/7*. *presto* finds that too confusing, and mounts one of them on */cdrom*.

- Some other file systems can't be mounted in the same place. For example, *freebie:/usr* can't be mounted on */usr*. Mount them on directories that match the system name. For example, mount *freebie:/usr* on */freebie/usr*.

After doing this, you might find the following file systems mounted on *freebie*:

```
# df
Filesystem   1024-blocks      Used    Avail Capacity  Mounted on
/dev/ad0s1a        30206     26830      960     97%   /
/dev/ad0s1e      1152422   1016196    44034     96%   /usr
/dev/da0h         931630    614047   243052     72%   /src
/dev/da1h        2049812   1256636   629192     67%   /home
procfs                 4         4        0    100%   /proc
/dev/cd0a         656406    656406        0    100%   /cdrom/1
/dev/cd1a         664134    664134        0    100%   /cdrom/2
/dev/cd2a         640564    640564        0    100%   /cdrom/3
/dev/cd3a         660000    660000        0    100%   /cdrom/4
/dev/cd4a         525000    525000        0    100%   /cdrom/5
/dev/cd5a         615198    615198        0    100%   /cdrom/6
/dev/cd6a         278506    278506        0    100%   /cdrom/7
```

On *presto*, you might see:

```
# df
Filesystem        1024-blocks      Used     Avail Capacity  Mounted on
/dev/da0s1a             29727     20593      6756     75%   /
/dev/da0s1e           1901185    742884   1006207     42%   /usr
procfs                      4         4         0    100%   /proc
freebie:/               30206     26830       960     97%   /freebie
freebie:/usr          1152422   1016198     44032     96%   /freebie/usr
freebie:/home         2049812   1256638    629190     67%   /home
freebie:/src           931630    614047    243052     72%   /src
freebie:/S            3866510   1437971   2119219     40%   /S
freebie:/cdrom/1       656406    656406         0    100%   /cdrom
```

Mounting NFS file systems automatically

If you want to mount NFS files automatically at boot time, make an entry for them in the file */etc/fstab*. You can even do this if you don't necessarily want to mount them: just add the keyword noauto, and *mountall* will ignore them at boot time. The advantage is that you then just need to specify, say,

```
# mount /src
```

instead of:

```
# mount -s freebie:/src /src
```

See the description of */etc/fstab* on page 566 for more information.

NFS strangenesses

NFS mimics a local file system across the network. It does a pretty good job, but it's not perfect. Here are some things that you should consider.

No devices

NFS handles disk files and directories, but not devices. Actually, it handles devices too, but not the way you would expect.

In a UNIX file system, a device is more correctly known as a *device node*: it's an inode that *describes* a device in terms of its major and minor numbers (see page 195). The device itself is implemented by the device driver. NFS exports device nodes in UFS file systems, but it doesn't interpret the fact that these devices are on another system. If you refer to the devices, one of three things will happen:

- If a driver for the specified major number exists on your local system, and the devices are the same on both systems, you will access the local device. Depending on which device it is, this could create some subtle problems that could go undetected for quite a while.

- If a driver for the specified major number exists on your local system, and the devices are different on the two systems, you will still access the local device with the same major and minor numbers, if such a device exists. The results could be very confusing.

- If no driver for the specified major number exists on your local system, the request will fail. This can still cause considerable confusion.

If the NFS server system runs *devfs*, the device nodes are not exported. You won't see anything unless there are leftover device nodes from before the time of migration to *devfs*.

Just one file system

NFS exports file systems, not directory hierarchies. Consider the example on page 444. *presto* has mounted both *freebie:/* and *freebie:/usr*. If it were just to mount *freebie:/*, we would see the directory */freebie/usr*, but it would be empty.

Things can get even stranger: you can mount a remote file system on a directory that is not empty. Consider the following scenario:

*   You install FreeBSD on system *freebie*. In single-user mode, before mounting the other file systems, you create a directory */usr/bin* and a file */usr/bin/vi*. Since the */usr* file system isn't mounted, this file goes onto the root file system.

*   You go to multi-user mode and mount the other file systems, including the file system for */usr*. You can no longer see the */usr/bin/vi* you put there in single-user mode. It hasn't gone away, it's just masked.

*   On *presto*, you mount the file system *freebie:/* on */freebie*. If you list the contents of the directory */freebie/usr*, you will see the original file *vi*, and not the contents that the users on *freebie* will see.

25

Basic network access: servers

In the previous chapter, we saw how to use clients to access other systems. This is only half the picture, of course. At the other end of the link, we need *servers* to provide this service. For each client, there is a server (a daemon) whose name is usually derived from the client name by adding a d to it:

Table 25-1: Server daemons for basic services

Client	Server
ssh	*sshd*
telnet	*telnetd*
sftp	*sftp-server*
ftp	*ftpd*
rsync	*rsyncd*
(browser)	*httpd*
(NFS)	*nfsd*

In addition to these servers, we look at a few others in other chapters:

- We've already looked at *X servers* briefly in Chapter 8, *Taking control*, and we'll see more in Chapter 28, *XFree86 in depth*.

- Chapter 21 discussed DNS *name servers*.

- Chapter 27 discusses *Mail Transport Agents* or *MTAs*, also referred to as *mail servers*.

Some servers don't need any configuration, and about all you need to do is to start them. Others, like web servers, can be very complicated. None of the complication is related to FreeBSD. For example, the issues involved in configuring *apache* are the same whether you run it with FreeBSD, NetBSD, Linux or Solaris. There are several good books, each at least the size of this one, on the detailed setup of some of these servers. In this chapter we'll look at how to get the servers up and running in a basic configuration, and where to turn for more information.

Running servers from inetd

If you look at */etc/services*, you'll find that there are over 800 services available, most of which are only supported on a small number of machines. It's not always the best idea to start up a daemon for every possible service you may want to offer. IP supplies an alternative: *inetd*, the *Internet daemon*, sometimes called a *super-server*, which listens on multiple ports. When a request arrives on a specific port, *inetd* starts a daemon specific to the port. For example, FreeBSD supports anonymous ftp, but most people don't receive enough requests to warrant having the ftp daemon, *ftpd*, running all the time. Instead, *inetd* starts an *ftpd* when a request comes in on port 21.

At startup, *inetd* reads a configuration file */etc/inetd.conf* to determine which ports to monitor and what to do when a message comes in. Here's an excerpt:

```
# $FreeBSD: src/etc/inetd.conf,v 1.58 2002/08/09 17:34:13 gordon Exp $
#
# Internet server configuration database
#
#ftp     stream  tcp     nowait  root    /usr/libexec/lukemftpd  ftpd -l -r
#ftp     stream  tcp     nowait  root    /usr/libexec/ftpd       ftpd -l
#ftp     stream  tcp6    nowait  root    /usr/libexec/ftpd       ftpd -l
#telnet  stream  tcp     nowait  root    /usr/libexec/telnetd    telnetd
#telnet  stream  tcp6    nowait  root    /usr/libexec/telnetd    telnetd
#shell   stream  tcp     nowait  root    /usr/libexec/rshd       rshd
#shell   stream  tcp6    nowait  root    /usr/libexec/rshd       rshd
#login   stream  tcp     nowait  root    /usr/libexec/rlogind    rlogind
#login   stream  tcp6    nowait  root    /usr/libexec/rlogind    rlogind
#exec    stream  tcp     nowait  root    /usr/libexec/rexecd     rexecd
#shell   stream  tcp6    nowait  root    /usr/libexec/rshd       rshd
```

This file has the following format:

- The first column is the service on which *inetd* should listen. If it starts with a # sign, it's a comment, and *inetd* ignores it. You'll note in this example that all the listed services have been commented out. Unless you run the daemon independently of *inetd*, a request for one of these services will be rejected with the message:

```
Unable to connect to remote host: Connection refused
```

- The next three columns determine the nature of the connection, the protocol to use, and whether *inetd* should wait for the process to complete before listening for new connections. In the example, all the services are TCP, but there are entries both for tcp (the normal TCP protocol for IP Version 4) and tcp6 (the same service for IP Version 6).

- The next column specifies the user as which the function should be performed.

- The next column is the full pathname of the program (almost always a daemon) to start when a message comes in. Alternatively, it might be the keyword internal, which specifies that *inetd* should perform the function itself.

- All remaining columns are the parameters to be passed to the daemon.

Older versions of UNIX ran *inetd* as part of the startup procedure. That isn't always necessary, of course, and for security reasons the default installation of FreeBSD no longer starts it. You can change that by adding the following line to your */etc/rc.conf*:

```
inetd_enable="YES"                      # Run the network daemon dispatcher (YES/NO).
```

To enable services in */etc/inetd.conf*, it may be enough to remove the comment from the corresponding line. This applies for most the services in the example above. In some cases, though, you may have to perform additional steps. For example, *lukemftpd*, an alternative *ftpd*, and *nntpd*, the *Network News Transfer Protocol*, are not part of FreeBSD: they're in the Ports Collection. Also, *nntpd* is intended to run as user usenet, which is not in the base system.

The other daemons are not mentioned in */etc/inetd.conf*:

- The preferred way to run *sshd* is at system startup. As we'll see, the startup is quite slow, so it's not a good idea to run it from */etc/inetd.conf*, though it is possible—see the man page if you really want to.

- *sftp-server* is the server for *sftp*. It gets started from *sshd*.

- *httpd*, the Apache Web Server, also has quite a long startup phase that makes it impractical to start it from */etc/inetd.conf*. Note also that *httpd* requires a configuration file. We'll look at that on page 455.

- By contrast, it's perfectly possible to start *rsyncd* from *inetd*. It's not included in the standard */etc/inetd.conf* file because it's a port. Yes, so are *lukemftpd* and *nntpd*. It's just a little inconsistent. This is the line you need to put in */etc/inetd.conf* to start *rsyncd*.

```
rsync  stream  tcp     nowait  root    /usr/local/bin/rsync rsync --daemon
```

The name *rsync* is not a typo. *rsync* and *rsyncd* are the same thing; it's the --daemon option that makes *rsync* run as a daemon.

inetd doesn't notice alterations to */etc/inetd.conf* automatically. After modifying the file, you must send it a SIGHUP signal:

```
# killall -HUP inetd
```

You can write -1 instead of -HUP. This causes *inetd* to re-read */etc/inetd.conf*.

Instead of starting daemons via *inetd*, you can start them at boot time. *inetd* is convenient for servers that don't get run very often, but if you make frequent connections, you can save overhead by running the servers continuously. On the other hand, it's not practical to start *rshd*, *rlogind*, *rexecd* or *telnetd* at boot time: they're designed to be started once for each session, and they exit after the first connection closes. We'll look at starting the other daemons in the following sections, along with their configuration.

Configuring ftpd

Normally you'll run *ftpd* from *inetd*, as we saw above. If you want to run it directly, perform the following steps:

- Add the following line in */etc/rc.local*:

```
echo -n 'starting local daemons:'
# put your local stuff here
echo " ftpd" && ftpd -D
```

The option -D tells *ftpd* to run as a daemon. You will possibly want other options as well; see the discussion below.

- Comment out the *ftp* line in */etc/inetd.conf* by adding a hash mark (#) in front of it:

```
# ftp     stream  tcp    nowait  root    /usr/libexec/ftpd       ftpd -l
```

- Either reboot, or cause *inetd* to re-read its configuration file:

```
# killall -1 inetd                              send a SIGHUP
```

If you don't perform this step, *inetd* keeps the *ftp* port open, and *ftpd* can't run.

For security reasons, you will probably want to add options such as logging and anonymous *ftp*. We'll look at how to do that in the next two sections.

anonymous ftp

Anonymous *ftp* gives you a couple of security options:

- It restricts access to the home directory of user *ftp*. From the point of view of the remote user, *ftp*'s home directory is the root directory, and he cannot access any files outside this directory. Note that this means that you can't use symbolic links outside the *ftp* directory, either.

- It restricts access to the machine generally: the user doesn't learn any passwords, so he has no other access to the machine.

In addition, you can start *ftpd* in such a manner that it will allow only anonymous *ftp* connections.

There are a number of preparations for anonymous *ftp*:

- Decide on a directory for storing anonymous ftp files. The location will depend on the amount of data you propose to store there. By default, it's */var/spool/ftp*.

- Create a user ftp, with the anonymous *ftp* directory as the home directory and the shell */dev/null*. Using */dev/null* as the shell makes it impossible to log in as user *ftp*, but does not interfere with the use of anonymous *ftp*. *ftp* can be a member of group *bin* or you can create a new group *ftp* by adding the group to */etc/group*. See page 145 for more details of adding users, and the man page *group(5)* for adding groups.

- Create subdirectories *˜ftp/bin* and *˜/ftp/pub*. It is also possible to create a directory for incoming data. By convention its name is *˜ftp/incoming*. This is a very bad idea if you're connected to the global Internet: it won't be long before people start using your system as a server for illicit data. Only use this option if you have some other method of stopping unauthorized access.

  Set the ownership of the directories like this:

```
dr-xr-xr-x    2 ftp     ftp       512 Feb 28 12:57 bin
drwxrwxrwx    2 ftp     ftp       512 Oct  7 05:55 incoming
drwxrwxr-x   20 ftp     ftp       512 Jun  3 14:03 pub
```

  This enables read access to the *pub* directory and read-write access to the *incoming* subdirectory.

- If you have a lot of files that are accessed relatively infrequently, it's possible you will find people on the Net who copy all the files that they see in the directory. Sometimes you'll find multiple connections from one system copying all the files in parallel, which can cause bandwidth problems. In some cases, you might find it more appropriate to distribute the names individually, and to limit access to reading the directories. You can do this by setting the permissions of *pub* and its subdirectories like this:

```
d--x--x--x   20 ftp     ftp       512 Jun  3 14:03 pub
```

  This allows access to the files, but not to the directory, so the remote user can't find the names of the files in the directory.

- Copy the following files to *˜ftp/bin*: */usr/bin/compress*, */usr/bin/gzip*, */usr/bin/gunzip*, */bin/ls*, */usr/bin/tar* and */usr/bin/uncompress*. The view of anonymous *ftp* users is restricted to the home directory, so all programs that are to be executed must also be in this directory.

You can ("hard") link the files if you want (and if the directory is on the same file system), but symbolic links will fail, since they contain path names that do not point to the correct place when running in the anonymous *ftp* environment.

Restricting access and logging

A number of *ftpd* options make it easier to control and monitor *ftp* access:

- The -1 option logs each session, whether successful or not, to *syslogd* with the facility LOG_FTP. To enable this logging, your */etc/syslog.conf* should contain a line like

```
ftp.*                                                           /var/log/ftpd
```

In addition, the file */var/log/ftpd* must exist. If it doesn't, create it with:

```
# touch /var/log/ftpd
```

The -1 option has two levels: if you specify it once, it logs connections only. If you specify it twice, it also lists the files that are transferred.

- The -S option logs all anonymous transfers to the file */var/log/ftpd*.

- You can restrict access to *only* anonymous *ftp* with the -A option.

There are a number of other options; see the man page *ftpd(8)* for further details.

In addition to these options, when a real user establishes a connection, *ftpd* checks the user's shell. If it is not listed in */etc/shells*, *ftpd* will deny the connection. This can be useful if you don't want specific users to access the system: give them a different shell, such as */usr/bin/sh* instead of */bin/sh*, and ensure that */usr/bin/sh* is not in */etc/shells*.

Log file format

The format of the log files is a little unusual. You'll see things like:

```
Oct 12 16:32:04 freebie ftpd[8691]: ANONYMOUS FTP LOGIN FROM adam.adonai.net, leec@a
donainet
Oct 12 18:33:32 freebie ftpd[9007]: connection from gateway.smith.net.au
Oct 12 18:33:37 freebie ftpd[9007]: ANONYMOUS FTP LOGIN FROM gateway.smith.net.au, m
ike
Oct 12 21:36:28 freebie ftpd[9369]: connection from grisu.bik-gmbh.de
Oct 12 21:36:29 freebie ftpd[9369]: ANONYMOUS FTP LOGIN FROM grisu.bik-gmbh.de, harv
est@
Oct 12 21:36:37 1997!harvest@!grisu.bik-gmbh.de!/pub/cfbsd/README!9228!1
Oct 12 21:37:05 freebie ftpd[9371]: connection from grisu.bik-gmbh.de
Oct 12 21:37:06 freebie ftpd[9371]: ANONYMOUS FTP LOGIN FROM grisu.bik-gmbh.de, harv
est@
Oct 13 09:38:19 freebie ftpd[13514]: connection from 151.197.101.46
Oct 13 09:38:21 freebie ftpd[13514]: ANONYMOUS FTP LOGIN FROM 151.197.101.46, bmc@ho
vercraft.willscreek.com
Oct 13 09:38:58 1997!bmc@hovercraft.willscreek.com!151.197.101.46!/pub/cfbsd/dear-re
viewer!8890!1
Oct 13 09:41:42 1997!bmc@hovercraft.willscreek.com!151.197.101.46!/pub/cfbsd/txt/26-
netdebug.txt.gz!12188!1
Oct 13 09:42:05 1997!bmc@hovercraft.willscreek.com!151.197.101.46!/pub/cfbsd/txt/C-p
```

```
ackages.txt.gz!37951!1
Oct 13 09:59:07 freebie ftpd[14117]: connection from 151.197.101.46
Oct 13 09:59:08 freebie ftpd[14117]: ANONYMOUS FTP LOGIN FROM 151.197.101.46, bmc@ho
vercraft.willscreek.com
Oct 13 09:59:24 1997!bmc@hovercraft.willscreek.com!151.197.101.46!/pub/cfbsd/txt/D-b
iblio.txt.gz!1815!1
```

This log excerpt shows three kinds of message:

- The messages starting with the text `connection from` occur when an *ftp* connection is made. They don't mean that any permission to access has been given. These messages are logged by the `-l` option.

- The `ANONYMOUS FTP LOGIN` messages show that somebody has logged in anonymously. The name follows, not always in the required username format. The standard *ftpd* does not enforce this requirement; you may find something that does in the Ports Collection. These messages are logged by the `-S` option.

- The lines full of `!` marks show files being transferred. The `!` marks delimit the fields, which are:

  - The year, as an extension of the timestamp.

  - The user ID.

  - The IP address of the system to which the data is transferred.

  - The name of the file transferred.

  - The number of bytes transferred.

Running sshd

Normally you start *sshd* from the system configuration file */etc/rc.conf*:

```
sshd_enable="YES"                    # Enable sshd
```

That's all you need to do for *sshd*. You can also start it simply with:

```
# sshd
```

sshd reads a configuration file */etc/ssh/sshd_config*. Like its companion */etc/ssh/ssh_config*, it contains mainly commented-out lines showing the default values. Most of them don't require change, but the following entries may be of interest:

- `Protocol` states which *ssh* protocols to use, and in which order. By default, *sshd* tries protocol 2 first, and falls back to protocol 1 if protocol 2 fails. You might consider setting it to use only protocol 2.

- When `PermitRootLogin` is set to `yes`, you can log in as `root` via *ssh*. Normally it's disabled.

- Set `PasswordAuthentication` to no if you want all access to be via key exchange (see page 420 for more details).

- If you want to run *sftp-server*, add the following line to */etc/ssh/sshd_config*:

```
Subsystem       sftp    /usr/libexec/sftp-server
```

It should be present by default.

rsyncd

As we've seen, *rsyncd* is just another name for *rsync*. You don't need to do any specific configuration to start it: it gets started from *sshd*, so all you need to do is to ensure that *sshd* gets started.

Starting *rsyncd* isn't enough, though: it needs configuration. Create a file */usr/local/etc/rsyncd.conf* with contents something like this:

```
motd file = /usr/local/etc/rsyncd.txt
log file = /var/log/rsyncd.log
transfer logging = true

[groggy]
        path = /home/grog/public_html
        uid = grog
        read only = yes
        list = yes
        comment = Greg's web pages
        hosts allow = 223.147.37.0/24

[tivo]
        path = /var/tivo
        uid = grog
        read only = no
        list = yes
        comment = TiVo staging area
        hosts allow = tivo.example.org
```

This is the configuration file used in the server examples in Chapter 24. It consists of two parts: a *global* part at the beginning, with settings that apply to all modules, and one or more *module* parts describing files that the server will supply.

The global options here specify the *motd file*, a file whose contents are printed when you list modules (the "be gentle" message in the examples), and that transfers should be logged to */var/log/rsyncd.log*. The log output looks something like this:

```
2002/10/24 13:31:49 [16398] send presto.example.org [192.109.197.74] groggy () slash
dot/topicscience.gif 1083
2002/10/24 13:31:49 [16398] send presto.example.org [192.109.197.74] groggy () slash
dot/topicsecurity.gif 3034
2002/10/24 13:31:49 [16398] send presto.example.org [192.109.197.74] groggy () slash
dot/topictv.jpg 951
2002/10/24 13:31:49 [16398] send presto.example.org [192.109.197.74] groggy () slide
.pdf 40470
2002/10/24 13:31:49 [16398] send presto.example.org [192.109.197.74] groggy () stock
whip.html 1602
```

The next part of the configuration file describes *modules*, directory hierarchies that *rsyncd* makes available. If you're used to Microsoft-style configuration files, this will seem relatively familiar. The module names are enclosed in square brackets ([]), and they don't have to have any relationship with the name of the directory. In this case we have two modules. Both have a *comment*, a descriptive text printed out when you list the modules, and both allow listing the name of the module (list = yes). In addition:

- Module groggy makes available the directory */home/grog/public_html*, my web pages, for read-only access. *rsyncd* accesses the module as user grog. Any host on the 256 address block starting with 223.147.37.0 can access the data.

- Module tivo makes available the directory */var/tivo* for read-write access, but only to the host *tivo.example.org*. Again *rsyncd* accesses the data as user grog.

There are a large number of other options for *rsyncd*, but this example shows the most important ones. See the man page *rsyncd.conf(5)* for more information.

Setting up a web server

FreeBSD is a system of choice for running web servers, so it's not surprising that a large number are available. Probably the most popular is *apache*, which is available in the Ports Collection. Install with:

```
# cd /usr/ports/www/apache13
# make install
```

In future versions, the name *apache13* will change. Apache comes with a lot of documentation in HTML format (of course), which is installed in */usr/local/share/doc/apache/manual*. You might find it useful to put a symbolic link to it in your web home directory:

```
# cd /usr/local/www/data
# ln -s /usr/local/share/doc/apache/manual apachedoc
```

After this, you can access the documentation at (for example) *http://www.example.org/apachedoc/*.

Configuring apache

The Apache port uses the following directories:

- The configuration files are in the directory hierarchy */usr/local/etc/apache*. The port installs prototype configuration files, but they need to be modified.

- By default, the web pages are in */usr/local/www/data*. This is the "root" directory for the web pages: the file */usr/local/www/data/foo.html* on *www.example.org* will have the URL *http://www.example.org/foo.html*. You may find it a good idea to change the directory to the */var* file system in a location such as */var/www/data*. We'll look at how to do that with the DocumentRoot entry in the configuration file.

- Icons for Apache's own use are stored in */usr/local/www/icons*. You can't access these icons by URI, so don't put your own images here.

- CGI scripts are stored in */usr/local/www/cgi-bin*.

The configuration file

The *apache* configuration file is */usr/local/etc/apache/httpd.conf*. Older versions of *apache* also used the files */usr/local/etc/apache/access.conf* and */usr/local/etc/apache/srm.conf*. The division between these three files was relatively arbitrary, and the current recommendation is to not use these files, but to put their content in */usr/local/etc/apache/httpd.conf* instead. See the *apache* documentation if you need to change the other files.

httpd.conf

Probably the best way to understand *httpd.conf* is to read through it. It's pretty long and contains a large number of comments. Most entries can be left the way there are, so we won't list the entire file here: instead we'll look at the parameters that may need change. We'll look at the system-wide features in the following list, and host-related features in the next section.

- ServerType states whether you start it from *inetd* or standalone (the default). It's not a good idea to start *httpd* from *inetd*, so you should leave this entry unchanged.

- ServerRoot claims to be the path to the configuration files, but in fact the files are stored in the subdirectory *etc/apache* of this directory. You shouldn't need to change it.

- The comments about ScoreBoardFile suggest that you should check to see if the system creates one. Don't bother: FreeBSD doesn't create this file, and you don't need to worry about it.

- The Keep-Alive extension to HTTP, as defined by the HTTP/1.1 draft, allows persistent connections. These long-lived HTTP sessions allow multiple requests to be sent over the same TCP connection, and in some cases have been shown to result in an almost 50% speedup in latency times for HTML documents with lots of images.

- The parameters MinSpareServers, MaxSpareServers, StartServers, MaxClients and MaxRequestsPerChild are used for server tuning. The default values should work initially, but if you have a lot of Web traffic, you should consider changing them.

- The next area of interest is a large list of *modules*. A lot of *apache* functionality is optional, and you include it by including a module. We'll look at this in more detail below.

- The parameter ProxyRequests allows Apache to function as a *proxy server*. We'll look at this in more detail below.

- The parameters starting with Cache apply only to proxy servers, so we'll look at them below as well.

- The Listen parameter defines alternate ports on which Apache listens.

- DirectoryIndex is a list of names that *httpd* recognizes as the main page ("index") in the directory. Traditionally it's *index.html*. This is the means by which *httpd* changes a directory name into an index. It searches for the names in the order specified. For example, if you're using PHP, DirectoryIndex gets set to the string index.php index.php3 index.html, and that's the sequence in which it looks for a page.

The file ends with a commented out VirtualHost section. We'll look at it in detail in the next section, along with a number of parameters that appear elsewhere in the configuration file, but that relate to virtual hosts.

Virtual hosts

Running and maintaining a web server is enough work that you might want to use the same server to host several sets of web pages, for example for a number of different organizations. *apache* calls this feature *virtual hosts*, and it offers a lot of support for them. Theoretically, all your hosts can be virtual, but the configuration file still contains additional information for a "main" server, also called a "default" server. The default configuration does not have any virtual servers at all, though it does contain configuration information.

There's a good reason to keep the "main" server information: it serves as defaults for all virtual hosts, which can make the job of adding a virtual host a lot easier.

Consider your setup at *example.org*: you may run your own web pages and also a set of pages for *biguser.com* (see page 310). To do this, you add the following section to */usr/local/etc/apache/httpd.conf*:

```
<VirtualHost *>
ServerAdmin grog@example.org
DocumentRoot /usr/local/www/biguser        where we put the web pages
ServerName www.biguser.com                 the name that the server will claim to be
ServerAlias biguser.com                    alternative server name
ErrorLog /var/log/biguser/error_log
TransferLog /var/log/biguser/access_log
Options +FollowSymLinks
Options +SymLinksIfOwnerMatch
</VirtualHost>
```

If you look at the default configuration file, you'll find most of these parameters, but not in the context of a VirtualHost definition. They are the corresponding parameters for the "main" web server. They have the same meaning, so we'll look at them here.

- ServerAdmin is the mail ID of the system administrator. For the main server, it's set to you@your.address, which obviously needs to be changed. You don't necessarily need a ServerAdmin for each virtual domain; that depends on how you run the system.

- DocumentRoot is the name of the directory that will become the root of the web page hierarchy that the server provides. By default, for the main server it's */usr/local/www/data*, which is not really a very good place for data that changes frequently. You might prefer to change this to */var/www*, as some Linux distributions do. This is one parameter that you must supply for each virtual domain: otherwise the domain would have the same content as the main server. In this case, it's the location of the files in *http://www.example.com/*.

- Next you can put information about individual data directories. The default server first supplies defaults for all directories:

```
<Directory />
    Options FollowSymLinks
    AllowOverride None
</Directory>
```

The / in the first line indicates the local directory to which these settings should apply. For once, this is really the root directory and not DocumentRoot: they're system-wide defaults, and though you don't have to worry about *apache* playing around in your root file system, that's the only directory of which all other directories are guaranteed to be a subdirectory. The Options directive ensures that the server can follow symbolic links belonging to the owner. Without this option, symbolic links would not work. We'll look at the AllowOverride directive in the discussion of the *.htaccess* file below.

There's a separate entry for the data hierarchy:

```
<Directory "/usr/local/www/data">
    Options Indexes FollowSymLinks MultiViews
    AllowOverride None
    Order allow,deny
    Allow from all
</Directory>
```

In this case, we have two additional options:

- Indexes allows *httpd* to display the contents of a directory if no index file, with a name defined in DirectoryIndex, is present. Without this option, if there is no index file present, you will not be able to access the directory at all.

- MultiViews allows content-based multiviews, which we don't discuss here.

Note that if you change the name of the default data directory, you should also change the name on the Directory invocation.

We'll look at the remaining entries in more detail when we see them again in the discussion of the *.htaccess* file.

- Normally you should set ServerName. For example, *www.example.org* is a CNAME for *freebie.example.org* (see page 370), and if you don't set this value, clients will access *www.example.org*, but the server will return the name *freebie.example.org*.

- *httpd* can maintain two log files, an *access log* and an *error log*. We'll look at them in the next section. It's a good idea to keep separate log files for each domain.

- You should have a default `VirtualHost` entry. People can get quite confused if they select an invalid name (for example, *http://www.big-user.com*) and get the (default) web page for *http://www.example.org*. The default page should not match any other host. Instead, it should indicate that the specified domain name is invalid.

- For the same reason, it's a good idea to have a `ServerAlias` entry for the same domain name without initial *www*. The entry in the example above serves the same pages for *www.biguser.com* and *biguser.com*.

- The directive `Options +SymLinksIfOwnerMatch` limits following symbolic links to those links that belong to the same owner as the link. Normally the `Options` directive specifies all the options: it doesn't merge the default options. The + sign indicates that the option specified should be added to the defaults.

After restarting *apache*, it handles any requests to *www.biguser.com* with these parameters. If you don't define a virtual host, the server will access the main web pages (defined by the main `DocumentRoot` in entry */usr/local/etc/apache/access.conf*).

Log file format

httpd logs accesses and errors to the files you specify. It's worth understanding what's inside them. The following example shows five log entries. Normally each entry is all on a very long line.

```
p50859b17.dip.t-dialin.net - -           name of system, more
[01/Nov/2002:07:06:12 +1030]             date of access
"GET /Images/yaoipower.jpeg HTTP/1.1"    HTML command
200                                      status (OK)
19365                                    length of data transfer

aceproxy3.acenet.net.au - -
[01/Nov/2002:07:35:34 +1030]
"GET /Images/randomgal.big.jpeg HTTP/1.0"
304 -                                    status (cached)

218.24.24.27 - -                         system without reverse DNS
[01/Nov/2002:07:39:55 +1030]
"GET /scripts/root.exe?/c+dir HTTP/1.0"  looking for an invalid file
404 284                                  status (not found)

218.24.24.27 - -
[01/Nov/2002:07:39:56 +1030]
"GET /MSADC/root.exe?/c+dir HTTP/1.0" 404 282

218.24.24.27 - -
[01/Nov/2002:07:39:56 +1030]
"GET /c/winnt/system32/cmd.exe?/c+dir HTTP/1.0" 404 292

218.24.24.27 - -
[01/Nov/2002:07:40:00 +1030]
"GET /_vti_bin/..%255c../..%255c../..%255c../winnt/system32/cmd.exe?/c+dir HTTP/1.0"
404 323
```

The fields in the log file are separated by blanks, so empty entries are replaced by a – character. In this example, the second and third fields are always empty. They're used for identity checks and authorization.

To get the names of the clients, you need to specify the HostnameLookups on directive. This requires a DNS lookup for every access, which can be relatively slow.

Although we specified hostname lookups, the last four entries don't have any name: the system doesn't have reverse DNS. They come from a Microsoft machine infected with the *Nimda* virus and show an attempt to break into the web server. There's not much you can do about this virus; it will probably be years before it goes away. Apart from nuisance value, it has never posed any threat to *apache* servers.

Access control

Sometimes you want to restrict access to a web server, either for specific directories or for the web site as a whole. *apache* has a number of options to limit access. One possibility is to set options in */usr/local/etc/apache/httpd.conf* to cover an individual host, but this is seldom useful. It's more likely that you will want to restrict access to specific directories, and it's easier to do that in the file *.htaccess* in the same directory.

For *apache* to even look at *.htaccess*, you need to change the configuration file, however: by default, it disables the use of *.htaccess* altogether, as we saw above:

```
<Directory />
    Options FollowSymLinks
    AllowOverride None
</Directory>
```

For it to work, you'll have to change the AllowOverride parameter to some other value. There are five categories of entries that you can allow in *.htaccess* files:

1. AuthConfig allows *.htaccess* to include authorization directives.

2. FileInfo allows the use of directives controlling document types.

3. Indexes allows the use of directives controlling directory indexing.

4. Limit allows the use of directives controlling host access.

5. Options allows the use of directives controlling specific directory features.

You can find more details in */usr/local/share/doc/apache/manual/mod/core.html*.

The most common use of the *.htaccess* is to require that users authorize themselves before accessing a directory. In this case, the browser will pop up a window like this:

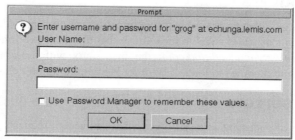

To achieve this, add something like this to your *.htaccess* file:

```
AuthType Basic
AuthName grog
AuthDBUserFile /usr/local/etc/apache/passwd
Require valid-user
```

This method is similar to normal login authentication. You need a password file, which you can create and update with *dbmmanage*:

```
# dbmmanage /usr/local/etc/apache/passwd adduser grog
New password:
Re-type new password:
User grog added with password encrypted to OzREW8Xx5hUAs using crypt
# dbmmanage /usr/local/etc/apache/passwd adduser guest
New password:
Re-type new password:
User guest added with password encrypted to hFCYwd23ftHE6 using crypt
```

This adds passwords for users grog and guest. The AuthName suggests a name to authenticate, but Require valid-user states that it can be any user. Even if you don't care which user logs in, you need to specify an AuthName line. If you *do* insist that only user grog can log in, you can write:

```
Require user grog
```

This will fail the authentication for any other user. You can also specify a list of users or groups. For example, you might add the following line:

```
AuthGroupFile /usr/local/etc/apache/group
Require group bigshots
```

/usr/local/etc/apache/group might then contain:

```
bigshots:   davidb davidp gordon grog liz malcolm
```

This will allow any of the users specified on this line to access the directory.

Apache modules

apache offers a large quantity of optional functionality, which it provides in the form of dynamically loadable *modules*. We've seen above that there are two long lists of module names in */usr/local/etc/apache/httpd.conf*; the first starts with LoadModule and tells *httpd* which dynamic modules to load. The order is important; don't change it.

Proxy web servers

Apache is capable of operating as a proxy server: it can accept requests for web pages of other systems. This can be an alternative to a general IP aliasing package such as *natd* (see page 393) if you need it only for web access. It's also useful in conjunction with *caching*.

Unfortunately, by default the current version of Apache does not support proxy servers. You need to rebuild the package manually after enabling it in the configuration file. See the file *INSTALL* in the port build directory for more details. This file will be present after building Apache from source, and it will have a name like */usr/ports/www/apache13/work/apache_1.3.23/src/INSTALL*. In addition to reinstalling the server with code for proxy serving, you must set ProxyRequests to On to enable the proxy server.

Caching

One reason for enabling the proxy server is to *cache* data requests. Caching keeps pages requested through the proxy and presents them again if they are requested again. This is particularly useful if the server serves a large number of people who communicate with each other and are thus likely to request many of the same pages.

The Cache parameters are commented out by default. If you uncomment them, you should uncomment them all execpt possibly NoCache. When setting these values, change the name of the directory CacheRoot. A good name might be */usr/local/www/proxy*.

Running apache

When you install *apache*, it installs the file */usr/local/etc/rc.d/apache.sh*, which automatically starts *apache* at boot time. If you don't want to start it automatically, remove this file. You can start and stop *apache* manually with the *apachectl* program, which takes a command parameter:

```
# apachectl start              start httpd
# apachectl stop               stop httpd
# apachectl restart            restart httpd, or start if not running
# apachectl graceful           restart httpd "gracefully," or start if not running
# apachectl configtest         do a configuration syntax test
```

The difference between a normal and a "graceful" restart is that the graceful restart waits for existing connections to complete before restarting the individual server processes. Unless you're in a big hurry, use the graceful restart.

NFS server

A number of processes are needed to provide NFS server functionality:

- The *NFS daemon*, *nfsd*, is the basic NFS server.

- The *mount daemon*, *mountd*, processes mount requests from clients.

- The *NFS lock daemon*, *rpc.lockd*, processes lock requests for NFS file systems. There are still a lot of problems with this function on all platforms. It's best to avoid it if you can.

- The *status monitoring daemon*, *rpc.statd*, provides a status monitoring service.

In addition:

- Since NFS uses *Remote procedure calls* (*RPC*), the *rpcbind* daemon must be running. *rpcbind* is not part of NFS, but it is required to map RPC port numbers to IP service numbers. In previous releases of FreeBSD, this function was performed by the *portmap* daemon. It has not been renamed, it has been replaced.

- The server needs a file */etc/exports* to define which file systems to export and how to export them. We'll look at this in the next section.

/etc/exports

A number of security implications are associated with NFS. Without some kind of authentication, you could mount any file system on the Internet.

NFS was developed at a time when users were relatively trusted. As a result, the security precautions are not overly sophisticated. */etc/exports* describes one file system per line. The format is:

file system   *options*   *systems*

systems is a list of systems allowed to mount the file system. The only required field is the name of the file system, but if you're on the Internet, you should at least limit the number of systems that can mount your file systems. By default any system on the Net can mount your file systems.

There are a number of options. Here are the more important ones:

- The -maproot option describes how to treat root. By default, root does not have special privileges on the remote system. Instead, NFS changes the user ID to user nobody, which is user 65534 (or -2). You can change this with the -maproot option. For example, to map root to the real root user for a specific file system, you would add -maproot=0 to the line describing the file system.

- The -mapall option maps the user IDs of other users. This is relatively uncommon. See the man page *exports(5)* for more details.

- The -ro option restricts access to read-only.

- The -network option restricts the access to systems on the specified network.

- The -alldirs option allows remote clients to mount any directory in the file system directly. Without this option, remote clients can only mount the root directory of the exported file system. We'll see an example where -alldirs can be of use during the discussion of diskless booting on page 543.

If you come from a System V background, you'll notice that the mechanism is different. */etc/exports* corresponds in concept roughly to System V's */etc/dfs/dfstab* file, except that the *share* statement does not exist.

Updating /etc/exports

To grant access to a file system, it's not enough to change the contents of */etc/exports*: you also need to tell *mountd* that you have done so. You do this by the relatively common method of sending a hangup signal (SIGHUP) to *mountd*:

```
# killall -HUP mountd
```

A typical */etc/exports* for *presto* might be:

```
/          -maproot=0                    presto bumble wait gw
/usr       -maproot=0      -alldirs      -network 223.147.37.0
```

This allows root access to both file systems. Only the trusted systems *presto*, *bumble*, *wait* and *gw* are allowed to access the root file system, whereas any system on the local network may access */usr*. Remote systems may mount any directory on the */usr* file system directly.

Samba

BSD UNIX and the Internet grew up together, but it took other vendors a long time to accept the Internet Protocols. In that time, a number of other protocols arose. We've already mentioned X.25 and SNA, currently both not supported by FreeBSD. The protocols that grew up in the DOS world are more widespread, in particular Novell's *IPX* and Microsoft's *Common Internet File System*, or *CIFS*. CIFS was previously known as *SMB (Server Message Block)*.

IPX support is relatively rudimentary. FreeBSD includes an IPX routing daemon, *IPXrouted*. See the man page *IPXrouted(8)* for further information. IPX is going out of use, so it's unlikely that support for it will improve. By contrast, Microsoft's CIFS is still alive and kicking. In the rest of this chapter we'll look at the standard implementation, *Samba*. This chapter describes only the FreeBSD side of the setup; you'll need to follow the Microsoft documentation for setting up the Microsoft side of the network.

Samba is a collection of software components that implement the SMB protocol over TCP/IP. You can use it to interface with all current Microsoft environments. It is part of the Ports Collection, in */usr/ports/net/samba*. You can get more information from *Using Samba*, by Jay Ts, Robert Eckstein and David Collier-Brown. At *http://samba.org/* you can get even more information, including support and a mailing list.

Samba includes a number of programs, most of which we don't touch on here. The ones we look at are:

- *smbd*, a daemon that provides file and print services to SMB clients.

- *nmbd*, which provides name services for NetBIOS.

- *smbpasswd*, which sets up network passwords for *Samba*.

- *smbclient*, a simple ftp-like client that is useful for accessing SMB shared files on other servers, such as Windows for Workgroups. You can also use it to allow a UNIX box to print to a printer attached to any SMB server.

- *testparm*, which tests the *Samba* configuration file, *smb.conf*.

- *smbstatus* tells you who is using the *smbd* daemon.

Installing the Samba software

Install *Samba* from the port:

```
# cd /usr/ports/net/samba
# make install
```

This operation installs the Samba binaries in */usr/local/bin*, the standard location for additional binaries on a BSD system, and the daemons *smbd* and *nmbd* in */usr/local/sbin*. These locations are appropriate for FreeBSD, but they are *not* the locations that the Samba documentation recommends. It also installs the man pages in */usr/local/man*, where the *man* program can find them. Finally, it installs a sample configuration file in */usr/local/etc/smb.conf.default*. We'll look at how to configure Samba below.

There are a number of security implications for the server, since it handles sensitive data. To maintain an adequate security level,

- Ensure that the software is readable by all and writeable only by `root`. *smbd* should be executable by all. Don't make it *setuid*. If an individual user runs it, it runs with their permissions.

- Put server log files in a directory readable and writable only by `root`, since they may contain sensitive information.

- Ensure that the *smbd* configuration file in */usr/local/etc/smb.conf* is secured so that only `root` can change it.

  The Samba documentation recommends setting the directory readable and writeable only by `root`. Depending on what other configuration files you have in */etc/local/etc*, this could cause problems.

smbd and nmbd: the Samba daemons

The main component of Samba is *smbd*, the SMB daemon. In addition, you need the Samba name daemon, *nmbd*, which supplies NetBIOS name services for Samba. *smbd* requires a configuration file, which we'll look at below, while you don't normally need one for *nmbd*. By default, *nmbd* maps DNS host names (without the domain part) to NetBIOS names, though it can perform other functions if you need them. In this chapter we'll assume the default behaviour. See the man page *nmbd(8)* for other possibilities.

You have two choices of how to run *smbd* and *nmbd*: you can start them at boot time from */usr/local/etc/rc.d/samba.sh*, or you can let *inetd* start them. The Samba team recommends starting them at boot time

When you install Samba from the Ports Collection, it installs a file */usr/local/etc/rc.d/samba.sh.sample*. You just need to rename it to */usr/local/etc/rc.d/samba.sh*. As the name suggests, it's a shell script. You can modify it if necessary, but it's usually not necessary.

The man page for *smbd* gives a number of parameters to specify the configuration file and the log file. As long as you stick to the specified file names, you shouldn't need to change anything: by default, *smbd* looks for the configuration file at */usr/local/etc/smb.conf*, and this file contains the names of the other files.

Running the daemons from inetd

To run the daemons from *inetd*,

* Edit */etc/inetd.conf*. You should find the following two lines towards the bottom of the file with a # in front. Remove the # to show the lines as they are here. If your */etc/inetd.conf* doesn't contain these lines, add them.

```
netbios-ssn stream tcp nowait      root   /usr/local/sbin/smbd   smbd
netbios-ns  dgram  udp wait        root   /usr/local/sbin/nmbd   nmbd
swat        stream tcp nowait/400  root   /usr/local/sbin/swat   swat
```

  swat is an administration tool that we don't discuss here.

* Either reboot, or send a HUP signal to cause *inetd* to re-read its configuration file:

```
# killall -1 inetd
```
                                                  send a SIGHUP

The configuration file

The Samba configuration file describes the services that the daemon offers. The port installs a sample configuration file in */usr/local/etc/smb.conf.default*. You can use it as the basis of your own configuration file, which must be called */usr/local/etc/smb.conf*: simply copy the file, and then edit it as described below.

The configuration file is divided into sections identified by a label in brackets. Most labels correspond to a service, but there are also three special labels: [global], [homes] and [printers], all of which are optional. We look at them in the following sections.

The [global] section

As the name suggests, the [global] section defines parameters that either apply to the server as a whole, or that are defaults for the other services. The interesting ones for us are:

- The workgroup parameter defines the Microsoft workgroup to which this server belongs. Set it to match the Microsoft environment. In these examples, we'll assume:

  ```
  workgroup = EXAMPLE
  ```

- The printing entry specifies what kind of printer support *Samba* provides. Current versions of *Samba* support CUPS. If you are using CUPS (not described in this book), you don't need to do anything. Otherwise set:

  ```
  printcap name = /etc/printcap
  printing = bsd
  ```

- guest account is the account (in UNIX terms: user ID) to use if no password is supplied. You probably want to define a guest account, since many Microsoft clients don't use user IDs. Ensure that the privileges are set appropriately. Alternatively, alter the parameter to point to an existing user.

- Modern versions of Microsoft use a simple form of password encryption; older versions used none. Currently, *Samba* defaults to no encryption. Set encrypt passwords to yes.

- Microsoft uses its own version of host name resolution, which doesn't involve DNS. Optionally, *Samba* will map Microsoft names to DNS. To enable this option, set dns proxy to yes.

- By default, the log file is specified as */var/log/log.%m*. The text %m is replaced by the name of the remote machine, so you get one log file per machine. Unfortunately, the name doesn't make it clear that this is a *Samba* log file. It's better to change this entry to:

  ```
  log file = /var/log/samba.log.%m
  ```

- socket options is hardly mentioned in the documentation, but it's very important: many Microsoft implementations of TCP/IP are inefficient and establish a new TCP connection more often than necessary. Select the socket options TCP_NODELAY and IPTOS_LOWDELAY, which can speed up the response time of such applications by over 95%.

The [homes] section

The [homes] section allows clients to connect to their home directories without needing an entry in the configuration file. If this section is present, and an incoming request specifies a service that is not defined in the configuration file, Samba checks if it matches a user ID. If it does, and if the specified password is correct, Samba creates a service that supplies the user's home directory.

The following options are of interest in the [homes] section:

- writeable can be yes or no, and specifies whether the user is allowed to write to the directory.

- create mode specifies the permission bits (in octal) to set for files that are created.

- public specifies whether other users are allowed access to this directory. In combination with a guest user, this can be a serious security liability.

The [printers] section

The [printers] section describes printing services. It doesn't need the names of the printers: if it doesn't find the specified service, either in the configuration file or in the [homes] section, if it exists, it looks for them in the */etc/printcap* file.

The *Samba* documentation claims that *Samba* can recognize BSD printing system automatically, but this is not always correct. Ensure that you have the following entries:

```
printing = bsd                          in the [global] sectionW
print command = lpr -r -P'%p' '%s'      in the [printers] sectionW
```

Note the printable option in the [printers] section: this is the option that distinguishes between printers ("yes") and file shares ("no").

Other sections: service descriptions

Samba takes any section name except for [global], [homes] or [printers] as the definition of a service. A typical example might be:

```
[ftp]
  comment = ftp server file area
  path = /var/spool/ftp/pub
  read only = yes
  public = yes
  write list = grog
```

This entry defines access to the anonymous *ftp* section. Anybody can read it, but only user grog can write to it.

Setting passwords

Samba uses a separate password file, */usr/local/private/secrets.tdb*. To set up users, use
the *smbpasswd* command, which copies the information from the system password file:

```
# smbpasswd -a grog
New SMB password:
Retype new SMB password:                         as usual, no echo
Password changed for user grog.
```

Testing the installation

Once you have performed the steps described above, you can proceed to test the
installation. First, run *testparm* to check the correctness of the configuration file:

```
$ testparm
Load smb config files from /usr/local/etc/smb.conf
Processing section "[homes]"
Processing section "[printers]"
Processing section "[ftp]"
Processing section "[src]"
Processing section "[grog]"
Loaded services file OK.
Press enter to see a dump of your service definitions          Press Enter

Global parameters:
lots of information which could be of use in debugging

[homes]
        comment = Home Directories
        read only = No

[printers]
        comment = All Printers
        path = /var/spool/samba
        guest ok = Yes
        printable = Yes
        browseable = No

[ftp]
        comment = ftp server file area
        path = /var/spool/ftp/pub
        write list = grog
        guest ok = Yes

[grog]
        path = /home/grog
        valid users = grog
        read only = No
```

As you see, *testparm* spells out all the parameters that have been created, whether
explicitly or by default. If you run into problems, this is the first place to which to return.

Next, check that you can log in with *smbclient*. If you're running the servers as daemons,
start them now. If you're starting them from *inetd*, you don't need to do anything.

```
$ smbclient -L freebie -U grog
added interface ip=223.147.37.1 bcast=223.147.37.255 nmask=255.255.255.0
Password:                               as usual, no echo
Domain=[EXAMPLE] OS=[Unix] Server=[Samba 2.2.7a]

        Sharename       Type        Comment
        ---------       ----        -------
        homes           Disk        Home Directories
        ftp             Disk        ftp server file area
        grog            Disk
        IPC$            IPC         IPC Service (Samba Server)
        ADMIN$          Disk        IPC Service (Samba Server)

        Server                      Comment
        ---------                   -------
        FREEBIE                     Samba Server
        PRESTO                      Samba Server

        Workgroup                   Master
        ---------                   -------
        EXAMPLE                     PRESTO
```

If you get this far, your password authentication is working. Finally, try to access the shares. Samba services are specified in Microsoft format: *system**service*. To make this worse, UNIX interprets the \ character specially, so you would need to repeat the character. For example, to access the ftp service on *freebie*, you would have to enter \\\\freebie\\ftp. Fortunately, *smbclient* understands UNIX-like names, so you can write //freebie/ftp instead.

To test, start *smbclient* from another system:

```
$ smbclient //freebie/ftp -U grog
added interface ip=223.147.37.1 bcast=223.147.37.255 nmask=255.255.255.0
Password:                               as usual, no echo
Domain=[EXAMPLE] OS=[Unix] Server=[Samba 2.2.7a]
smb: \> ls
  .                             DR        0  Wed Jan 29 12:06:29 2003
  ..                            D         0  Sat Oct 26 10:36:29 2002
  instant-workstation-1.0.tar.gz       9952  Mon Mar 19 11:49:01 2001
  xtset-1.0.tar.gz                     4239  Mon Aug  5 16:44:14 2002
  gpart-0.1h.tbz.tgz                  27112  Tue Aug 27 10:07:59 2002
```

If you get this far, Samba is working. The next step is to attach to the services from the Microsoft machines. That's not a topic for this book. Note, however, that Samba only works with TCP/IP transport, not with NetBEUI.

Displaying Samba status

You can display the status of Samba connections with *smbstatus*. For example,

```
$ smbstatus
Samba version 2.2.7a
Service    uid    gid     pid    machine
-------------------------------------------
ftp        grog   example 37390  freebie  (223.147.37.1) Mon Mar 31 13:48:13 2003

No locked files
```

26

Electronic mail: clients

Electronic mail, usually called *email*, *e-mail* or simply *mail*, is a method of sending messages to other people on the Net. As with other network services, there are two parts to mail software:

- The user interface to the mail system is the client, the *Mail User Agent*, or *MUA*. It interacts with the user and handles incoming and outgoing mail. People frequently use the word *mailer* when referring to MUAs. In this chapter we'll look at my favourite MUA, *mutt*, and we'll briefly touch on what others are available.

- The server part is the *Mail Transfer Agent*, or *MTA*. As the name suggests, it is responsible for moving mail from one system to another. We'll look at MTAs in the next chapter, Chapter 27, *Electronic mail: servers*.

Mail formats

Email is defined by a number of Internet standards, the so-called *RFC*s, or *Requests For Comments*. You can browse the RFCs at *http://www.faqs.org/rfcs/*. Here are the most important ones.

- RFC 2821 is a recent update to the venerable RFC 821, which dates from the early 1980s. It defines the *Simple Mail Transfer Protocol* or *SMTP*. It specifies how to send mail round the network. For most people it's not very interesting, but it does impose some restrictions such as the basic line length limit. Apart from this problem (which Microsoft abuses), most mail systems adhere to SMTP.

- Similarly, RFC 2822 replaces RFC 822. It defines the basic format of a mail message. It defines the headers (To:, Cc:, Subject: and so on) and a simple body made up of US-ASCII text, the message itself. This was fine for when it was written, but it can't handle the more complex formats used nowdays, such as images, binary files or embedded messages. It also can't handle non-US character sets, which causes problems in particular in countries like Russia, Israel and Japan.

- RFC 2045, RFC 2046, RFC 2047, RFC 2048 and RFC 2049 together describe the *Multipurpose Internet Mail Extensions*, better known as *MIME*. They define how to encode non US-ASCII text and attachments so that they can be represented in ASCII and hence sent by RFC 2822, and also how to divide the single RFC 2822 body into multiple parts using ASCII separators.

  A number of UNIX MUAs have inadequate MIME support. Find one which does the job properly. On the other hand, if your target audience typically does not use MIME-aware MUAs, avoid sending MIME messages.

Mail user agents

A *mail user agent* is a program that interfaces between the user and the mail system. It allows the user to read, forward and reply to incoming mail, and to send his own mail. It usually has facilities for creating and maintaining *folders*, where you can keep received mail messages. For most UNIX MUAs, a folder is the same thing as a file, but some MUAs keep mail messages as individual files, and the folder corresponds to a directory.

mail

The oldest MUA you're likely to meet is *mail*. It's a very basic, character-oriented program, but nevertheless it has its advantages. You can use it in scripts to send mail. For example, if you have a job running and producing copious output, where you want to save the output, you might normally write something like:

```
$ longjob 2>&1 > logfile
```

This command runs *longjob*. The sequence 2>&1 redirects the error output to the standard output, and the > writes them to the file *logfile*. While this is a good way to solve the problem, you might find that you have a lot of such jobs, or that you tend to forget the log files and leave them cluttering up your disks. An alternative is to send mail to yourself. You can do this with the following command:

```
$ longjob 2>&1 | mail me
```

In this case, *me* is your user ID. When the job finishes, you get a mail message with the output of the commands. *cron* (see page 151) uses this method to send you its output.

Other MUAs

mail has a number of limitations: it doesn't deal very well with long mail messages, it's difficult to keep an overview of large quantities of mail, like most people seem to accumulate, and it can't handle *MIME*.

Many more sophisticated MUAs have been written since *mail*. Some of the more popular ones, which are also available in the Ports Collection, are:

- *elm* is one of the oldest full-screen MUAs. Its age is showing: it has a few annoying problems that make it less desirable now that there's a choice.

- *pine* is not *elm*—that's what the acronym stands for. It's quite like *elm*, nonetheless.

- *mutt* is also similar to *elm* and *pine*. It's my current favourite, and we'll look at it in the next section.

- *exmh* is built on Rand's *mh* MUA. Some people like it, but it seems relatively easy to configure it to mutilate messages.

- *xfmail* is an X-based MUA, which you might prefer to the text-based MUAs we're talking about here.

- *sylpheed* is a more recent X-based MUA. You may prefer it to *xfmail*.

Files, folders or directories?

There are two schools of thought about how to store mail:

- Traditional MUAs represent folders as files. They store all the messages in a folder in that single file. This is sometimes called the *mbox* method. *mail*, *elm* and *pine* do it this way.

- Other MUAs, including *exmh*, *xfmail* and *sylpheed*, represent a folder as a directory. Each message in the folder is then a file by itself.

- *mutt* can use either method, but the default is the mbox method.

Which method should you use? Both have their advocates. The directory and file approach is more robust (if you trash a file, you only lose one message, not all of them), and it enables you to have the same message in multiple folders. On the other hand, it also imposes a lot higher overhead. Current versions of *ufs*, at least on FreeBSD, have a default block size of 16 kB and a fragment size of 2 kB. That means that all files have a length that is a multiple of 2 kB, and so the average waste of space is 1 kB. In addition, each file uses an inode. If you have a lot of mail, this can add up to a lot of wasted space. For example, I currently have 508,649 saved mail messages, which take up a total of 2.1 GB, almost exactly 4 kB per message. If I stored them in a directory structure, I would lose about another 500 MB of space, or 25%. The file system on which the messages are stored is 9.5 GB in size and has 1.2 million inodes; nearly half of them would be used for the mail messages.

mutt

In this section, we'll take a detailed look at *mutt*. Start it by typing in its name. Like most UNIX MUAs, *mutt* runs on a character-oriented terminal, including of course an *xterm*. We'll take a look into my mailbox. By default, when starting it up you get a display like the one shown in Figure 26-1.

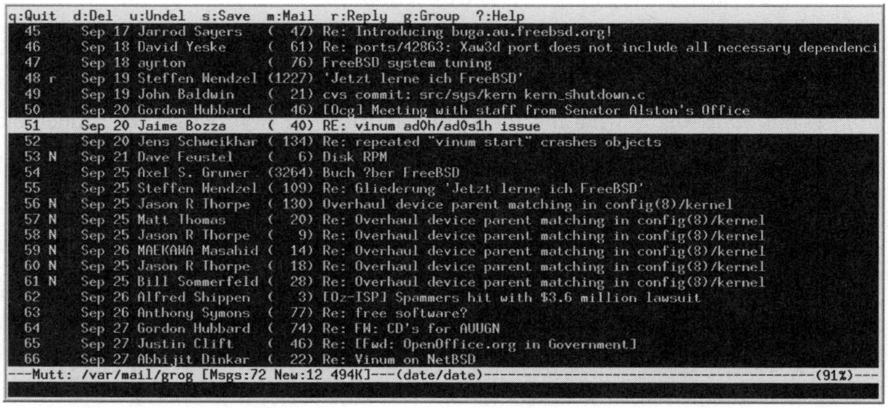

```
q:Quit  d:Del  u:Undel  s:Save  m:Mail  r:Reply  g:Group  ?:Help
   45       Sep 17 Jarrod Sayers    (  47) Re: Introducing buga.au.freebsd.org!
   46       Sep 18 David Yeske      (  61) Re: ports/42863: Xaw3d port does not include all necessary dependenci
   47       Sep 18 ayrton           (  76) FreeBSD system tuning
   48 r     Sep 19 Steffen Wendzel (1227) 'Jetzt lerne ich FreeBSD'
   49       Sep 19 John Baldwin     (  21) cvs commit: src/sys/kern kern_shutdown.c
   50       Sep 20 Gordon Hubbard   (  46) [Ocg] Meeting with staff from Senator Alston's Office
   51       Sep 20 Jaime Bozza      (  40) RE: vinum ad0h/ad0s1h issue
   52 N     Sep 20 Jens Schweikhar (134) Re: repeated "vinum start" crashes objects
   53 N     Sep 21 Dave Feustel     (   6) Disk RPM
   54       Sep 25 Axel S. Gruner  (3264) Buch ?ber FreeBSD
   55       Sep 25 Steffen Wendzel ( 109) Re: Gliederung 'Jetzt lerne ich FreeBSD'
   56 N     Sep 25 Jason R Thorpe   ( 130) Overhaul device parent matching in config(8)/kernel
   57 N     Sep 25 Matt Thomas      (  20) Re: Overhaul device parent matching in config(8)/kernel
   58 N     Sep 25 Jason R Thorpe   (   9) Re: Overhaul device parent matching in config(8)/kernel
   59 N     Sep 26 MAEKAWA Masahid (  14) Re: Overhaul device parent matching in config(8)/kernel
   60 N     Sep 25 Jason R Thorpe   (  18) Re: Overhaul device parent matching in config(8)/kernel
   61 N     Sep 25 Bill Sommerfeld ( 28) Re: Overhaul device parent matching in config(8)/kernel
   62       Sep 26 Alfred Shippen   (   3) [Oz-ISP] Spammers hit with $3.6 million lawsuit
   63       Sep 26 Anthony Symons   (  77) Re: free software?
   64       Sep 27 Gordon Hubbard   (  74) FW: CD's for AUUGN
   65       Sep 27 Justin Clift     (  46) Re: [Fwd: OpenOffice.org in Government]
   66       Sep 27 Abhijit Dinkar   (  22) Re: Vinum on NetBSD
---Mutt: /var/mail/grog [Msgs:72 New:12 494K]---(date/date)----------------------------(91%)---
```

Figure 26-1: mutt main menu

mutt sets reverse video by default. You can change the way it displays things, however. On page 481 we'll see how to change it to the style shown in one shown in Figure 26-2.

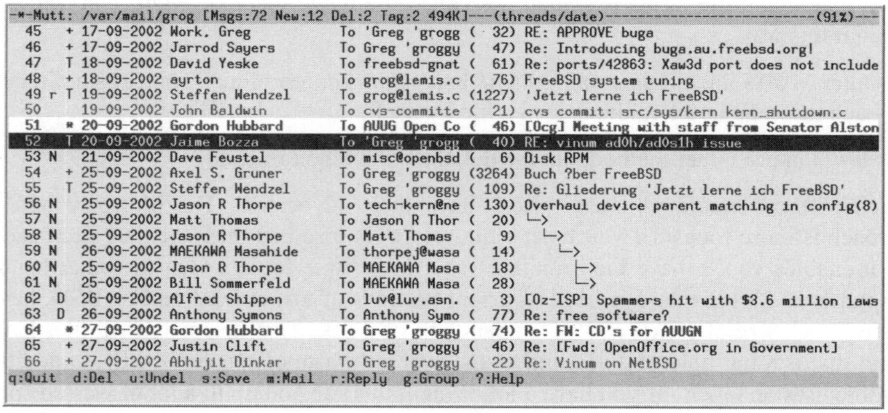

```
-*-Mutt: /var/mail/grog [Msgs:72 New:12 Del:2 Tag:2 494K]---(threads/date)----------------(91%)---
   45    + 17-09-2002 Work, Greg        To 'Greg 'grogg (  32) RE: APPROVE buga
   46    + 17-09-2002 Jarrod Sayers     To 'Greg 'groggy (  47) Re: Introducing buga.au.freebsd.org!
   47    T 18-09-2002 David Yeske       To freebsd-gnat ( 61) Re: ports/42863: Xaw3d port does not include
   48    + 18-09-2002 ayrton            To grog@lemis.c (  76) FreeBSD system tuning
   49 r  T 19-09-2002 Steffen Wendzel   To grog@lemis.c (1227) 'Jetzt lerne ich FreeBSD'
   50      19-09-2002 John Baldwin      To cvs-committe (  21) cvs commit: src/sys/kern kern_shutdown.c
   51    * 20-09-2002 Gordon Hubbard    To AUUG Open Co (  46) [Ocg] Meeting with staff from Senator Alston
   52    T 20-09-2002 Jaime Bozza       To 'Greg 'grogg (  40) RE: vinum ad0h/ad0s1h issue
   53 N    21-09-2002 Dave Feustel      To misc@openbsd (   6) Disk RPM
   54    + 25-09-2002 Axel S. Gruner    To Greg 'groggy (3264) Buch ?ber FreeBSD
   55    T 25-09-2002 Steffen Wendzel   To Greg 'groggy ( 109) Re: Gliederung 'Jetzt lerne ich FreeBSD'
   56 N    25-09-2002 Jason R Thorpe    To tech-kern@ne ( 130) Overhaul device parent matching in config(8)
   57 N    25-09-2002 Matt Thomas       To Jason R Thor (  20) └→
   58 N    25-09-2002 Jason R Thorpe    To Matt Thomas  (   9)  └→
   59 N    26-09-2002 MAEKAWA Masahide  To thorpej@wasa ( 14)   └→
   60 N    25-09-2002 Jason R Thorpe    To MAEKAWA Masa ( 18)   ├→
   61 N    25-09-2002 Bill Sommerfeld   To MAEKAWA Masa ( 28)   └→
   62 D    26-09-2002 Alfred Shippen    To luv@luv.asn. (   3) [Oz-ISP] Spammers hit with $3.6 million laws
   63 D    26-09-2002 Anthony Symons    To Anthony Symo ( 77) Re: free software?
   64    * 27-09-2002 Gordon Hubbard    To Greg 'groggy (  74) Re: FW: CD's for AUUGN
   65    + 27-09-2002 Justin Clift      To Greg 'groggy (  46) Re: [Fwd: OpenOffice.org in Government]
   66    + 27-09-2002 Abhijit Dinkar    To Greg 'groggy (  22) Re: Vinum on NetBSD
q:Quit  d:Del  u:Undel  s:Save  m:Mail  r:Reply  g:Group  ?:Help
```

Figure 26-2: mutt main menu

The display of Figure 26-2 shows a number of things:

- The line at the top specifies the name of the file ("folder") that contains the mail messages (*/var/mail/grog*), the number of messages in the folder, and its size. It also states the manner in which the messages are sorted: first by *threads*, then by date. We'll look at threads further down.

- The bottom line gives a brief summary of the most common commands. Each command is a single character. You don't need to press **Enter**.

- The rest of the screen contains *index lines*, information about the messages in the folder. The first column gives the message a number, then come some flags:

  - In the first column, we can see r next to some messages. This indicates that I have already replied to these messages.

  - In the same column, N signalizes a *new* message (an unread message that has arrived after the last invocation of *mutt* finished).

  - The symbol D means that the message has been marked for deletion. It won't be deleted until you leave *mutt* or update the display with the **$** command, and until then you can undelete it with the **u** command

  - The symbol + means that the message is addressed to me, and only to me. We'll see below how *mutt* decides who I am.

  - The symbol T means that the message is addressed to me and other people.

  - The symbol C means that the message is addressed to other people, and that I have been copied.

  - The symbol F means that the message is from me.

  - The symbol * means that the message is *tagged*: certain operations work on all tagged messages. We'll look at that on page 481.

- The next column is the date (in international notation in this example, but it can be changed).

- The next column is the name of the sender, or, if I'm the sender, the name of the recipient.

- The next column is the name of the recipient. This is often me, of course, but frequently enough it's the name of a mailing list. You'll notice that this is a column I have added; it's not in the default display.

- The next column gives the size of the message. The format is variable: you can specify number of lines (as in the example), or the size in kilobytes.

- The last column is usually the subject. For messages 56 to 61, it's a series of line drawings. This is *threading*, and it shows a relationship between a collection of messages on the same topic. Message 56 was the original message in the thread, message 57 is a reply to message 56, and so on. Messages 60 and 61 are both replies to message 59. *mutt* automatically collects all messages in a thread in one place.

You'll notice in the example that the lines are of different intensity. In the original, these are different colours, and they're a matter of personal choice; they highlight specific kinds of message. I use different colours to highlight messages on different topics. If you're interested in the exact colours, see *http://ezine.daemonnews.org/200210/ports.html*, which contains an early version of this text.

The index line for message 52 appears to be in reverse video. In fact, it's in white on a blue background, a colour I don't use for anything else. This is the *cursor*, which you can position either with the cursor up and cursor down keys, or with the *vi*-like commands **j** (move down) or **k** (move up). In the default display, it is in normal video (i.e. not reversed, or doubly reversed). You can also move between pages with the left and right cursor commands. Many commands, such as **r** (reply) or **Enter** (read), operate on the message on which the cursor is currently positioned. For example, if you press **Enter** at this point, you'll see a display like that in Figure 26-3.

```
52/72   T Jaime Bozza                RE: vinum ad0h/ad0s1h issue                       -- (50%)
Date: Fri, 20 Sep 2002 08:13:44 -0500
From: "Jaime Bozza" <jbozza@thinkburst.com>
To: "'Greg 'groggy' Lehey'" <grog@FreeBSD.org>
Cc: <freebsd-stable@FreeBSD.ORG>
Subject: RE: vinum ad0h/ad0s1h issue
X-Mailer: Microsoft Outlook, Build 10.0.4024

>I think I now understand the problem here.  Try the following patch
>and tell me if it solves the problem:
>
>---- vinumio.c   2 May 2002 08:43:44 -0000        1.52.2.6
>+++ vinumio.c  19 Sep 2002 05:10:27 -0000

Tried patch.  System no longer reads ad0h/ad2h, but after the second
'vinum start', the system shows 0 drives ('vinum ld' lists nothing.)

The third 'vinum start' reads ad0s1h/ad2s1h again.  Additional starts
cycle between the two (no drives, correct drives.)

>The problem here is that vinum_scandisk() tries to read from each
>slice.  If it doesn't find any (for example, on a dedicated disk), it
>tries the compatibility slice.  That normally works fine, but if all
i:Exit  -:PrevPg  <Space>:NextPg v:View Attachm.  d:Del  r:Reply  j:Next ?:Help
```

Figure 26-3: mutt message display

Here, the display has changed to show the contents of the message. The top line now tells you the sender of the message, the subject, and how much of the message is displayed, in this case 50%. As before, the bottom line tells you the most common commands you might need in this context: they're not all the same as in the menu display.

The message itself is divided into three parts: the first 6 lines are a selection of the *headers*. The headers can be quite long. They include information on how the message got here, when it was sent, who sent it, who it was sent to, and much more. We'll look at them in more detail on page 484.

The headers are separated from the message body by an empty line. The first part, which *mutt* displays in **bold**, is *quoted* text: by putting a > character before each line, the sender has signalized that the text was written by another person, often the person to whom it is addressed: this message is a reply, and the text is what he is replying to. Normally there is an attribution above the text, but it's missing in this example. We'll see attributions below in the section on replying.

If the message is longer than one screen, press **SPACE** to page down and – (hyphen) to page up. In general, a 25 line display is inadequate for reading mail. On an X display, choose as high a window as you can.

Creating a new message

To create a new message, press **m**. *mutt* starts your favourite editor for you. How does it know which one? If you specify the name of the editor in your *.muttrc* file, or set your EDITOR environment variable to the name of your editor, it starts that editor; otherwise it starts *vi*. On page 481 we'll look at what to put in *.muttrc*.

In this case, we start *emacsclient*. *emacsclient* isn't really an editor at all: it simply finds an *Emacs* process and latches on to it. This is much faster than starting a new instance of *Emacs*: it's practically instantaneous, whereas even on fast modern machines, starting *Emacs* causes a brief delay. To exit the client, you use the key combination **c-x c-#**.

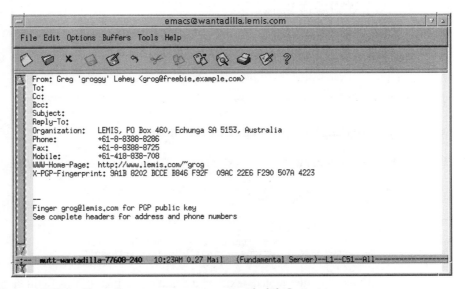

Figure 26-4: Creating a new message: initial state

Fill out the name of the intended recipient in the appropriate place, and enter the text of the message below the headers, leaving one line of space. Apart from this, most of the actions involved in sending a new mail message are the same as those in replying to an existing message, so we'll look at both activities together in the next section.

Replying to a message

To reply to a message, in this case the message shown in Figure 26-3, simply press **r**.
Before entering any text, the editor screen looks like Figure 26-5.

```
File  Edit  Options  Buffers  Tools  Help

From: Greg 'groggy' Lehey <grog@freebie.example.com>
To: Jaime Bozza <jbozza@thinkburst.com>
Cc:
Bcc:
Subject: Re: vinum ad0h/ad0s1h issue
Reply-To:
In-Reply-To: <009201c260a7$8c356670$6401010a@bozza>
Organization:   LEMIS, PO Box 460, Echunga SA 5153, Australia
Phone:          +61-8-8388-8286
Fax:            +61-8-8388-8725
Mobile:         +61-418-838-708
WWW-Home-Page:  http://www.lemis.com/~grog
X-PGP-Fingerprint: 9A1B 8202 BCCE B846 F92F  09AC 22E6 F290 507A 4223

On Friday, 20 September 2002 at  8:13:44 -0500, Jaime Bozza wrote:
> >I think I now understand the problem here.  Try the following patch
> >and tell me if it solves the problem:
> >
> >--- vinumio.c   2 May 2002 08:43:44 -0000         1.52.2.6
> >+++ vinumio.c   19 Sep 2002 05:10:27 -0000
>
> Tried patch.  System no longer reads ad0h/ad2h, but after the second
> 'vinum start', the system shows 0 drives ('vinum ld' lists nothing.)
>
> The third 'vinum start' reads ad0s1h/ad2s1h again.  Additional starts
> cycle between the two (no drives, correct drives.)
--:--  mutt-current-41952-2        (Fundamental Server)--L20--Top-----------------
```

Figure 26-5: Replying to a message: initial state

You'll notice that *mutt* automatically "quotes" the text. The original text started with:

```
>I think I now understand the problem here.  Try the following patch
>and tell me if it solves the problem:
>
>--- vinumio.c   2 May 2002 08:43:44 -0000         1.52.2.6
>+++ vinumio.c   19 Sep 2002 05:10:27 -0000
Tried patch.  System no longer reads ad0h/ad2h, but after the second
'vinum start', the system shows 0 drives ('vinum ld' lists nothing.)
```

This message itself starts with quoted text, which indicates that it was written by
somebody else. There should be a line at the top stating who wrote it, but it's missing
here. The text from the submitter starts with `Tried patch`. When you reply, however,
all this text is quoted again. The first line attributes the text below. You'll notice that this
reply also includes a selection of headers for the *outgoing* message. This can be very
convenient if you want to tailor your headers to the message you're sending, or just to add
other recipients.

This is a reply to a technical question, so I change the `From:` header to my `FreeBSD.org`
address and copy the original mailing list. I also remove irrelevant text and add a reply,
as shown in Figure 26-6. It wasn't necessary to reformat the original text, since it was
relatively short. The quoting method makes lines grow, though, and many MUAs have

difficulty with long lines, so it's a good idea to reformat long paragraphs. See *http://www.lemis.com/email.html* for more details.

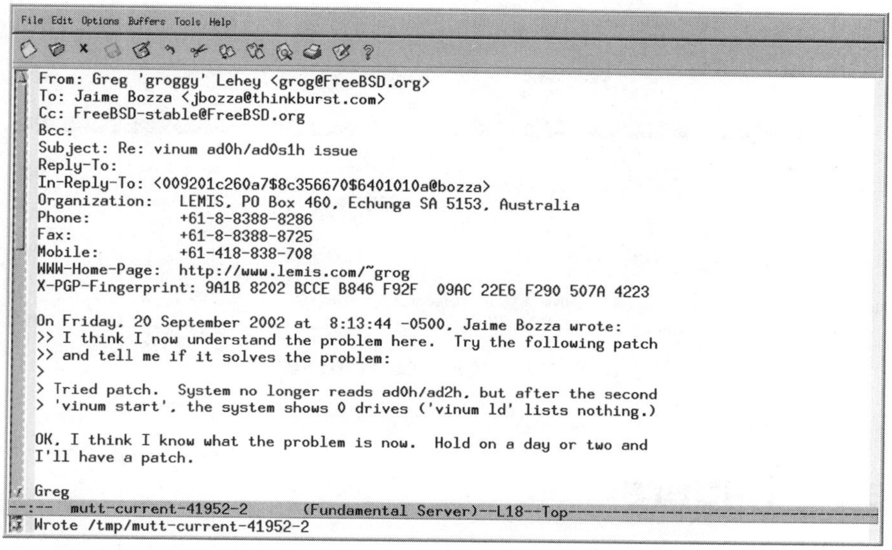

Figure 26-6: Replying to a message: after editing

In this example, I reply with the **r** (reply to sender) command. I could also do a *group reply* with the **g** key, which would include all the original recipients, so it wouldn't be necessary to add the mailing list again.

Next, I leave the editor with **c-x c-#** and return to the screen in Figure 26-7. Here I have another opportunity to change some of the headers before sending the message. You'll note what seem to be a couple of additional headers in this display: PGP and Fcc:. In fact, they're not headers at all. PGP states what parts of the message, if any, should be encrypted with *pgp* or *gpg*. In this case, Clear (the default) means not to encrypt anything.

Fcc: is also not a header. It specifies the name of a folder in which to save the outgoing message. We'll look at folders in the next section.

After making any further changes to the headers, I send the message with the **y** command, after which I return to the previous display.

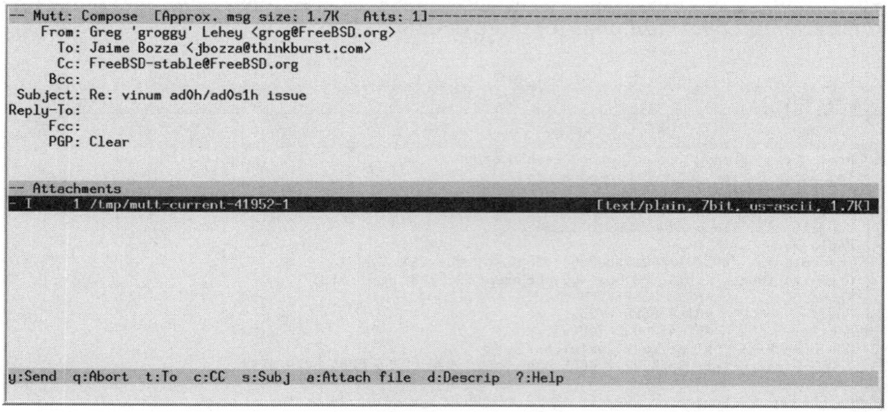

```
-- Mutt: Compose [Approx. msg size: 1.7K   Atts: 1]----------------------------------
    From: Greg 'groggy' Lehey <grog@FreeBSD.org>
      To: Jaime Bozza <jbozza@thinkburst.com>
      Cc: FreeBSD-stable@FreeBSD.org
     Bcc:
 Subject: Re: vinum ad0h/ad0s1h issue
Reply-To:
     Fcc:
     PGP: Clear

-- Attachments
-  I     1 /tmp/mutt-current-41952-1                         [text/plain, 7bit, us-ascii, 1.7K]




y:Send   q:Abort   t:To   c:CC   s:Subj   a:Attach file   d:Descrip   ?:Help
```

Figure 26-7: Replying to a message: ready to send

Using folders

mutt can handle multiple folders. It defaults to your incoming mail folder, sometimes called an *inbox*. On BSD, it is a single file in */var/mail* with the same name as your user ID. We saw that above at the top of the index screen: mine is called */var/mail/grog*.

mutt stores other folders as single files in the directory *~/Mail*, in other words a subdirectory of your home directory. Many MUAs use this method, but not all of them: some use the directory *~/mail* instead. By default, when you write a mail message, the outgoing message gets copied to a file in this directory. In the previous section, the Compose menu contained the pseudo-header Fcc: =jbozza. This refers to the file *~/Mail/jbozza*: *mutt* uses the shorthand = to refer to the mail directory.

To keep incoming mail, you use the **s** (save) command, which sets a default folder name from the name of the sender, the same name as when saving sent messages. You can thus reply a message, saving a copy in the folder, then save the original message, without explicitly mentioning a folder name at all.

To read messages in a folder, you can tell *mutt* to read it directly on startup:

```
$ mutt -f =fred
```

Alternatively you can change folders with the **c** command.

Deleting messages

Once you've finished reading a message, you may want to delete it. You can do this by entering **d**. The D flag appears on the left of the line, but nothing much else happens. The message doesn't get deleted until you exit *mutt*, or until you enter **$**.

When you save a message to a folder, it is automatically deleted from the current folder. If you don't want to do that, or if you have accidentally deleted a message, you can *undelete* it by entering **u**.

Finished reading a thread? You can delete the entire thread by entering **^D** (**Control-D**).

Tagging messages

We've seen that you can delete an entire thread with a single keystroke. What about other operations on multiple messages? There are a couple of useful possibilities. You select the messages under the cursor by entering **t**. In the example above, messages 51 and 64 are tagged. You can reply to all tagged messages in one reply by pressing **;r**. In this case, *mutt* ignores the message under the cursor and replies only to the tagged messages, reply to all people on the To: headers of each message. Similarly, you can do a group reply to all the tagged messages with **;g**, and you can delete them all with **;d**.

Configuring mutt

We've already see that there are a lot of things that you can change about *mutt*'s behaviour. They are described in a file *˜/.muttrc* (the file *.muttrc* in your home directory). Here are a few of the more interesting entries in my *.muttrc*:

```
source /usr/local/etc/Muttrc
```

The file */usr/local/etc/Muttrc* contains the default definitions for running *mutt*. Put this at the top of your *.muttrc* file so that the following definitions can override any previous definitions. This file also contains a large number of comments about how to set each variable, and what it does: it's over 3,000 lines long.

```
source ~/.mail_aliases
```

˜/.mail_aliases is the name of an *alias file*, a file with abbreviations for frequently used mail addresses. We'll look at them on page 484.

```
set alternates="greg.lehey@auug.org.au|groggy@|grog@|auugexec@|core@free"
```

This string is a regular expression that *mutt* uses to determine whether mail is addressed to me. If it matches, it sets one of the flags discussed above: + if the message is sent only to me, T if I am mentioned on the To: header, and C if I am mentioned on the Cc: header.

```
my_hdr Organization:   LEMIS, PO Box 460, Echunga SA 5153, Australia
my_hdr Phone:          +61-8-8388-8286
```

These lines and more become headers in messages I send; you can see them in the examples above.

```
set editor=emacsclient
```

This line overrides the default editor in EDITOR. We've already seen the use of *emacsclient*.

```
set pager_index_lines=10
```

This tells *mutt* to keep ten lines of the index when displaying a message. Figure 26-8 shows what the display looks like when this is set. Clearly this isn't much use with a 25 line display. If, on the other hand, you have a larger X display, it can be very convenient to have a selection of the index at the top of the screen.

```
set hdr_format="%4C %Z %{%d-%m-%Y} %-20.20L %-15.15t (%4l) %s" # format of the index
set status_on_top        # put the status bar at the top
set sort=threads
set date_format="%A, %e %B %Y at %k:%M:%S %Z"
```

These variables tell *mutt* how to display the message index. They account for the difference in layout (but not colour) between the default screen and the custom screen. hdr_format is a *printf*-like format string that describes the layout, status_on_top reverses the information lines at the top and bottom of the display, sort=threads sets a threaded display by default (you can change it by pressing **o**), and date_format is set to international conventions.

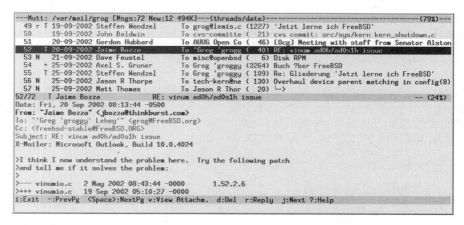

Figure 26-8: Reading a message with pager_index_lines set

```
set edit_hdrs                    # let me edit the message header when composing
set fast_reply                   # skip initial prompts when replying
set attribution="On %d, %n wrote:"
set charset="iso-8859-15"        # character set for your terminal
set sendmail_wait=-1
```

These variables specify how to write and reply to mail messages:

- edit_hdrs tells *mutt* to include the headers in the message you write, as shown in the preceding examples.

- fast_reply tells *mutt* not to prompt for a number of the headers. This is faster, and it's not necessary when you have the headers in the message you're writing.

- *attribution* describes the format of the attribution at the beginning of a reply, the text On Friday, 20 September 2002 at 8:13:44 -0500, Jaime Bozza wrote: in the example above.

- charset specifies the character set to use for the message. This should correspond to the character set of the fonts on your display, otherwise things may look strange. ISO 8859-15 is the new Western European character set that includes the character for the Euro. You'll still see many message with the older Western European character set, ISO 8859-1, which is otherwise very similar.

- Finally, sendmail_wait tells *mutt* whether it should wait for the mail to be sent before continuing. This can take some time if your MTA has to perform numerous DNS lookups before it can send the message. Setting this variable to -1 tells *mutt* not to wait.

```
ignore *
unignore  From: Date: To: Cc: Subject: X-Mailer: Resent-From:
hdr_order Date: From: To: Cc: Subject: X-Mailer: Resent-From:
```

These specifications tell *mutt* to ignore all headers except for specific ones, and to sort them in the order specified, no matter what order they occur in in the message.

Colours in mutt

Finally, *.muttrc* contains definitions to describe the colour of the display. Many of these are personal preferences, so I'll just show a couple. Each definition specifies the foreground colour, then the background colour:

```
color normal black white
```

This is the basic default colour, overriding the reverse video shown above.

```
color hdrdefault brightblack white
color quoted brightblack white
```

This tells *mutt* to highlight headers and quoted text in bold.

```
color status black yellow
```

This tells *mutt* to display the status bars in black on a yellow background.

```
color index blue white FreeBSD
```

This tells *mutt* to display any messages with the text FreeBSD in blue on white, like messages 48 and 49 in the example above.

There are many more variables you can set to customize your *mutt* display. Read */usr/local/etc/Muttrc* for more details.

Mail aliases

You'll find that some people have strange mail IDs: they are unusual, confusing, or just plain difficult to type. Most MUAs give you the option of setting up *aliases*, short names for people you often contact. In *mutt*, you can put the aliases in the *%.muttrc* file, or you can put them in a separate file and tell *mutt* when to find them in the *%.muttrc* file, as illustrated above. The aliases file contains entries like this:

```
alias questions FreeBSD-questions@FreeBSD.org (FreeBSD Questions)
alias stable FreeBSD Stable Users <FreeBSD-stable@FreeBSD.org>
```

The format is straightforward:

- First comes the keyword alias. Aliases can be placed in *%.muttrc*, so the word alias is used to distinguish them from other commands.

- Next is the alias name (questions and stable in this example).

- Next comes the mail ID in one of two forms: either the name followed by the mail ID in angle brackets (<>), or the mail ID followed by the name in parentheses (()).

In *mutt*, you can add aliases to this file automatically with the **a** command, which offers default values relating to the current message.

Mail headers

In the message display above we saw only a selection of the mail headers that a message might contain. Sometimes it's interesting to look at them in more detail, especially if you're having mail problems. To look at the complete headers, press the h key. Figure 26-9 shows the complete headers of our message 52.

- The first line shows the name of the sender and the date it arrived at this machine. The date is in local time. In this case, the name of the sender is a mailing list, not the original sender.

```
52/72   T Jaime Bozza              RE: vinum ad0h/ad0s1h issue                    -- (65%)
From owner-freebsd-stable@FreeBSD.ORG  Sat Sep 21 10:24:14 2002
Return-Path: <owner-freebsd-stable@FreeBSD.ORG>
Delivered-To: grog@lemis.com
Received: from mx2.freebsd.org (mx2.FreeBSD.org [216.136.204.119])
        by wantadilla.lemis.com (Postfix) with ESMTP id 195CC81743
        for <grog@lemis.com>: Sat, 21 Sep 2002 10:23:04 +0930 (CST)
Received: from hub.freebsd.org (hub.FreeBSD.org [216.136.204.18])
        by mx2.freebsd.org (Postfix) with ESMTP
        id EA28F55A31: Fri, 20 Sep 2002 06:16:47 -0700 (PDT)
        (envelope-from owner-freebsd-stable@FreeBSD.ORG)
Received: by hub.freebsd.org (Postfix, from userid 538)
        id E817237B404: Fri, 20 Sep 2002 06:16:44 -0700 (PDT)
Received: from localhost (localhost [127.0.0.1])
        by hub.freebsd.org (Postfix) with SMTP
        id B3AD72E8008: Fri, 20 Sep 2002 06:16:44 -0700 (PDT)
Received: by hub.freebsd.org (bulk_mailer v1.12); Fri, 20 Sep 2002 06:16:44 -0700
Delivered-To: freebsd-stable@freebsd.org
Received: from mx1.FreeBSD.org (mx1.FreeBSD.org [216.136.204.125])
        by hub.freebsd.org (Postfix) with ESMTP
        id 502E637B401: Fri, 20 Sep 2002 06:16:43 -0700 (PDT)
Received: from mail.thinkburst.com (juno.geocomm.com [204.214.64.110])
        by mx1.FreeBSD.org (Postfix) with ESMTP
        id BE5E143E42: Fri, 20 Sep 2002 06:16:42 -0700 (PDT)
        (envelope-from jbozza@thinkburst.com)
Received: from mailgate.thinkburstmedia.com (gateway.thinkburstmedia.com [204.214.64.100])
        by mail.thinkburst.com (Postfix) with ESMTP
        id 210F1367C2: Fri, 20 Sep 2002 08:17:03 -0500 (CDT)
Received: from sigma.geocomm.com (sigma.geocomm.com [10.1.1.5])
        by mailgate.thinkburstmedia.com (Postfix) with ESMTP
        id B53F220F03: Fri, 20 Sep 2002 08:16:41 -0500 (CDT)
Received: by sigma.geocomm.com (Postfix, from userid 805)
        id A787D24544: Fri, 20 Sep 2002 08:16:41 -0500 (CDT)
Received: from bozza (dhcp00.geocomm.com [10.1.1.100])
        by sigma.geocomm.com (Postfix) with ESMTP
        id 3CF7A2453E: Fri, 20 Sep 2002 08:16:41 -0500 (CDT)
From: "Jaime Bozza" <jbozza@thinkburst.com>
To: "'Greg 'groggy' Lehey'" <grog@FreeBSD.org>
Cc: <freebsd-stable@FreeBSD.ORG>
Subject: RE: vinum ad0h/ad0s1h issue
Date: Fri, 20 Sep 2002 08:13:44 -0500
Message-ID: <009201c260a7$8c356670$6401010a@bozza>
MIME-Version: 1.0
Content-Type: text/plain:
        charset="US-ASCII"
Content-Transfer-Encoding: 7bit
X-Priority: 3 (Normal)
X-MSMail-Priority: Normal
X-Mailer: Microsoft Outlook, Build 10.0.4024
X-MimeOLE: Produced By Microsoft MimeOLE V5.50.4910.0300
In-Reply-To: <20020919051420.GH37454@wantadilla.lemis.com>
Importance: Normal
X-Sanitizer: ThinkBurst Media, Inc. mail filter
Sender: owner-freebsd-stable@FreeBSD.ORG
List-ID: <freebsd-stable.FreeBSD.ORG>
List-Archive: <http://docs.freebsd.org/mail/> (Web Archive)
List-Help: <mailto:majordomo@FreeBSD.ORG?subject=help> (List Instructions)
List-Subscribe: <mailto:majordomo@FreeBSD.ORG?subject=subscribe%20freebsd-stable>
List-Unsubscribe: <mailto:majordomo@FreeBSD.ORG?subject=unsubscribe%20freebsd-stable>
X-Loop: FreeBSD.ORG
Precedence: bulk
X-Spam-Status: No, hits=-102.0 required=5.0 tests=IN_REP_TO,A_FROM_IN_AUTO_WLIST version=2.01
Status: RO
Content-Length: 1602
Lines: 40

i:Exit  -:PrevPg  <Space>:NextPg  v:View Attachm.  d:Del  r:Reply  j:Next  ?:Help
```

Figure 26-9: Complete headers

- The next line (Return-Path:) is used to indicate the address to which error messages should be sent if something goes wrong with delivery. The FreeBSD mailing lists specify the list owner to avoid spamming senders with multiple error messages, which can easily happen when you send messages to a large mailing list.

- The `Delivered-To:` header specifies the user to whom the message was delivered.

- The next group of headers shows how the message got from the source to the destination, in reverse chronological order. There are a total of 11 `Received:` headers, making up more than half the total number of lines. This is because it went via a mailing list. Normal mail messages have only one or two `Received:` headers.

  The first `Received:` header is split over three lines. It shows the most recent step of the message's journey to its destination. It shows that it was received from *mx2.freebsd.org* by *wantadilla.lemis.com*, and that *wantadilla.lemis.com* was running *postfix*. It also shows the time the message arrived at *wantadilla*, Sat, 21 Sep 2002 at 10:23:04. The time zone is 9½ hours ahead of UTC, and the message ID is 195CC81743.

- The following `Received:` headers trace back to the origin of the message, via *hub.freebsd.org*, where it went through three transformations. Before that, it went through *mail1.thinkburst.com*, *mailgate.thinkburstmedia.com*, *sigma.geocomm.com* and *dhcp00.geocomm.com*. By pure coincidence, every one of these systems was running *postfix*. Each header contains a message ID, the name of the server and its IP address. In one case, though, the name looks different:

  ```
  Received: from mailgate.thinkburstmedia.com (gateway.thinkburstmedia.com [204
  .214.64.100])
  ```

  The first name is the name that the server claims to be, and the second is the name returned by a reverse DNS lookup of the server IP address.

- The next five headers are the "normal" headers: sender, recipient, copied recipients and date. This example shows why they are in colour; they can appear in a large number of different places.

- We've just seen eleven different message IDs. So why the header `Message-Id:`? That's exactly the reason: the other eleven IDs are local to the system they pass through. The line beginning with `Message-Id:` gives a definitive message ID that can be used for references.

- The next three headers relate to MIME and describe the version and the manner in which the message has been encoded (7 bit plain ASCII text).

- The next four headers start with X-. They are *official custom headers*, and we'll see more below. The RFCs deliberately don't define their meaning. Clearly these ones are used by Microsoft software to communicate additional information, including the fact that the MUA that created this mail message was Microsoft Outlook.

- The `In-Reply-To:` header shows the ID of the message to which this is a reply. *mutt* uses this field to thread the messages in the index.

- The next two fields, `Importance:` is also not defined by the standards. It may be a Microsoft "extension." This is not an abuse of the standards: the RFCs allow use of any undefined header, and the X- convention is only provided to make certain that a specific set of headers remains undefined.

- Next comes the Sender: header is the address of the *real sender*. Although this message is From: Jaime Bozza, it was resent from the FreeBSD-stable mailing list. This header documents the fact.

- The following List- headers are also not defined by the standards. They're used as comments by the mailing list software.

- X-Loop is used by the mailing list software to avoid mailing loops. The mailing list software recognizes an X-Loop header with its own name to mean that it has somehow sent a message to itself.

- The Precedence: header is used internally by *sendmail* to determine the order in which messages should be sent. bulk is a low priority.

- The X-Spam-Status: header is added by *spamassassin*, which is used to detect spam. This message has been given a clean bill of health.

- The final headers are added by *mutt* when it updates the mail folder, for example when it exits. Other MUAs add similar headers.

  The Status: flag is used by the MUA to set flags in the display. The letters each have their own meaning: R means that the message has been read, and O means that it is old (in other words, it was already in the mail folder when the MUA last exited).

- The Content-Length: header specifies the *approximate* length of the message (without the headers) in bytes. It is used by some MUAs to speed things up.

- The Lines: header states the length of the message in lines.

How to send and reply to mail

In the impersonal world of the Internet, your mail messages are the most tangible thing about you. Send out a well thought out, clear and legible message, and you leave a good impression. Send out a badly formulated, badly formatted and badly spelt message, and you leave a bad impression.

So what's good and what's bad? That's a matter of opinion (and self-expression), of course. We've seen some of the following things already:

- Unless there's a very good reason, avoid proprietary formats. Most MUAs can handle them nowadays, but some can't. For example, some people set up Microsoft MUAs to use HTML as the standard format. Many other MUAs have difficulty with HTML, though *mutt* can display it with the help of a web browser. Microsoft MUAs are also often configured to send out mail in Microsoft Word format, which is illegible to just about anybody without a Microsoft system.

- When sending "conventional" mail, ensure that you adhere to the standards. Again, Microsoft mailers are often bad in this respect: without telling you, they may either transform paragraphs into one long line, or they break lines into two, one long and one short. The resulting appearance of the message looks like (taking this paragraph as an example):

```
When sending ``conventional'' mail, ensure that you adhere to the standards.
  Again, Microsoft mailers are often bad in this respect: without telling yo
u, they may either transform paragraphs into one long line, or they break li
nes into two, one long and one short.  The resulting appearance of the messa
ge looks like (taking this paragraph as an example):
```

Figure 26-10: One line per paragraph

```
When sending ``conventional'' mail, ensure that you adhere to the
standards.
Again, Microsoft mailers are often bad in this respect: without
telling you,
they may either transform paragraphs into one long line, or they
break lines
into two, one long and one short.  The resulting appearance of the
message looks
like (taking this paragraph as an example):
```

Figure 26-11: Alternate long and short lines

This can happen to you without you knowing. If you get messages from other people that appear to be garbled, your MUA may be reformatting them on arrival, in which case it is possibly reformatting them before transmission.

- When replying, ensure that you use a quote convention as shown above. Place your reply text directly below the part of the text to which you are replying.

- Messages tend to grow as more and more replies get added. If large parts of the original text are irrelevant, remove them from the reply.

- Leave an empty line between the original text and your reply, and leave a space after the > quote character. Both make the message more legible. For example, compare these two fragments:

```
> rdkeys@csemail.cropsci.ncsu.edu writes:
>>Not to pick at nits.... but, I am still confused as to what EXACTLY
>>is the ``stable'' FreeBSD.  Please enlighten me, and tell me the
>>reasoning behind it.
>OK, I'll take a shot at this.  To really understand what 2.2-STABLE is,
>you have to have some idea of how the FreeBSD team uses 'branches'.  In
>particular, we are talking about branches as implemented by the CVS
```

Figure 26-12: Less legible reply

```
> rdkeys@csemail.cropsci.ncsu.edu writes:
>> Not to pick at nits.... but, I am still confused as to what EXACTLY
>> is the ``stable'' FreeBSD.  Please enlighten me, and tell me the
>> reasoning behind it.
>
> OK, I'll take a shot at this.  To really understand what 2.2-STABLE is,
> you have to have some idea of how the FreeBSD team uses 'branches'.  In
> particular, we are talking about branches as implemented by the CVS
```

Figure 26-13: More legible reply

- What about salutations? You'll see a lot of messages out there that don't start with "Dear Fred," and either aren't even signed or just have the name of the author. This looks rather rude at first, but it has become pretty much a standard on the Net. There's a chance that this will change in the course of time, but at the moment it's the way things are, and you shouldn't assume any implicit rudeness on the part of people who write in this manner.

- At the other end of the scale, some people add a standard signature block to each message. You can do this automatically by storing the text in a file called `~/.signature`. If you do this, consider that it appears in *every* message you write, and that it can get on people's nerves if it's too long or too scurrile.

- Make sure that your user ID states who you are. It doesn't make a very good impression to see mail from foobar@greatguru.net (The greatest guru on Earth), especially if he happens to make an incorrect statement. There are better ways to express your individuality.

Using MIME attachments

MIME allows you to attach all sorts of data to a mail message, including images and sound clips. It's a great advantage, but unfortunately many people refuse to use it, perhaps because the UNIX community haven't got their act together. Credit where credit's due, this is one area where Microsoft is ahead of the UNIX crowd.

Nevertheless, you can do a lot of things wrong with MIME attachments. Here are some of the more common ones, most of which are default for Microsoft MUAs.

- *Use HTML attachments only for web pages*. Many MUAs allow you to send messages in text/html format by default. HTML is not an appropriate format for mail messages: it's intended for the Web. Of course, if you want to send somebody a web page, this is the way to do it.

- *Don't use proprietary attachments*. From time to time, I get attachments that assume that I have the same software as the sender. Typical ones are application/octet-stream with Microsoft proprietary formats (for example, one of the Microsoft Word formats), and application/mac-binhex40, which is used by Mac MUAs for images. If the recipients don't have this software, they can't use the attachment.

- *Don't send multiple copies in different formats*. Some MUAs send both a text/plain and a text/html attachment bundled up in a multipart/alternative attachment. This wastes space and can cause a lot of confusion.

- *Specify the correct attachment type*. If you send a web page as an attachment, be sure that it is specified as text/html. The receiving MUA can use this to display the attachment correctly. If you specify it, say, as text/plain, the MUA displays it with all the formatting characters, which doesn't improve legibility. If you send a *.gif* image as image/gif, the MUA can display the image directly. Otherwise the user needs to save the message and perform possibly complex conversions to see the image.

Microsoft-based MUAs frequently make this mistake. You may receive attachments of the type `application/octet-stream`, which really describes the encoding, not the content, but the name might end in `.doc`, `.gif` or `.jpg`. Many MUAs assume that these attachments are Microsoft Word documents or GIF and JPEG images respectively. This is contrary to the standards and could be used to compromise the security of your system.

27

Electronic mail:
servers

In the previous chapter, we looked at email from a user perspective. The other part of a mail system is the *Mail Transfer Agent*, or *MTA*. As the name suggests, MTAs perform the transfer of mail from one system to another. Specifically, they perform three related tasks:

- They send outgoing mail, in other words mail that originates from their system. If the destination system is not available, they look for an alternative system, and if none is available, they retry delivery at a later date. Typically an MTA will retry every 30 minutes for five days before giving up.

- They receive incoming mail, possibly for multiple domain names. They may be quite picky about how they perform this task: since the advent of spam, a number of techniques have developed. We'll look at some in the section on *postfix* configuration.

- They *relay* mail. Consider the case where a sending MTA can't reach the destination MTA and chooses an alternative. The alternative MTA is called a *relay*, and it must be prepared to deliver the mail to the final recipient at a later time. Until a few years ago, MTAs performed relaying by default, but the advent of spam has changed that radically.

Mail has been around for a long time now, well over 25 years. In that time, many mail systems have come and gone. One seems to have been around for ever: the *sendmail* MTA. *sendmail* has an unparalleled reputation. On the one hand, it can do just about anything, but on the other hand, its configuration file is one of the most arcane ever to be seen. Still, it's holding well against the competition, and it is still actively being developed.

The definitive book on *sendmail*, called the "bat book" after its cover, was written by Bryan Costales and others (O'Reilly)—see Appendix A, *Bibliography* for more details. It is over 1000 pages long. Obviously this book can't compete with it.

The good news about *sendmail* is: it works. It is possible to install *sendmail* and run it with no configuration whatsoever. The less good news is that in the past few years it has been constantly changing, and any information I write here is liable to be out of date by the time you read it. As a result, I recommend:

> If **sendmail** *works for you, use it. If you have difficulties, use* **postfix** *instead.*

The following sections show how to configure a mail system using *postfix*. In general, *sendmail* is quite similar. You'll find every detail in the bat book, and the original *sendmail* distribution, available from *http://www.sendmail.org/* , contains instructions for experts.

How mail gets delivered

Ideally, to send mail, the source MTA contact the destination MTA and sends the message. In practice, this doesn't always work. Here's the general method:

- Each time an MTA receives a message not addressed to its system, this MTA collects all MX records for the destination that are not higher than its own MX record.

- If the MTA finds any MX records, it attempts to send to one of them, starting at the lowest preference.

- If the lowest MX record points to the MTA's own machine, then there's a mail misconfiguration: the MTA doesn't know what to do with it locally, but the MX is telling it to deliver it locally. When this happens, the MTA reject the message ("mail loops back to myself").

- If there are no MX records at all (which implies that the MTA doesn't have one either), most, but not all versions of sendmail will look up an A record for the system name. If they find one, they will try to deliver there, and only there.

- If all else fails, the MTA rejects the message ("can't find the destination").

MTA files

MTAs use three different kinds of files:

- Configuration files tell the MTA what to do. Typical configuration issues include what name to present to the outside world, and when to accept mail for delivery and when to reject it. The issue of spam (unsolicited commercial email) makes this quite a complicated issue. *postfix* keeps its configuration files in the directory */usr/lo-cal/etc/postfix*, and *sendmail* keeps them in */etc/mail*.

- Outgoing *postfix* mail is stored in the directory hierarchy */var/spool/postfix*, while *sendmail* currently stores its mail in the hierarchies */var/spool/mqueue* and */var/spool/clientmqueue*.

- Incoming mail is stored in the directory */var/mail*. Normally each user gets a file that corresponds to his user name.

Who gets the mail?

According to RFC 2822, a mail ID is something like `grog@example.org`. This looks very much like a user ID, the @ sign, and the name of a machine. This similarity is intended, but it's still only a similarity. Consider the system manager of *example.org*. At different times he might send mail from *freebie.example.org*, *bumble.example.org*, and *wait.example.org*. If the mail ID were associated with the machine, he would have three different mail IDs: `fred@freebie.example.org`, `fred@bumble.example.org` and `fred@wait.example.org`. It would make things a whole lot simpler (and easier to type) if his mail ID were simply `fred@example.org`. This name change is called *masquerading*.

One way to do this would be to associate the name `example.org` as a CNAME with one of the machines—say *wait.example.org*. This would work, but it would mean that mail would always have to come from and go to *wait.example.org*. If for any reason that machine were inaccessible, the mail would not get through. In practice, it's possible to run MTAs on more than one machine. DNS solves this problem with a special class of record, the MX record (*mail exchanger*). MX records can point to more than one machine, so if one machine is not accessible, the mail can be sent to another. We saw how to add them on page 370. MX records are not directly associated with any particular machine, though they point to the names of machines that run an MTA.

Postfix

postfix is in the Ports Collection, not the base system, so before you can use it, you must install it. It is an *interactive* port: at various points in the installation process it asks for input. The first is a menu offering optional additional configurations, as shown in Figure 27-1. For the configuration in this book, you don't need anything in addition to what the menu suggests; just select OK and continue.

Some time later you get the informational messages:

```
Added group "postfix".
Added group "maildrop".
Added user "postfix".
You need user "postfix" added to group "mail".
Would you like me to add it [y]? Enter pressed
Done.
```

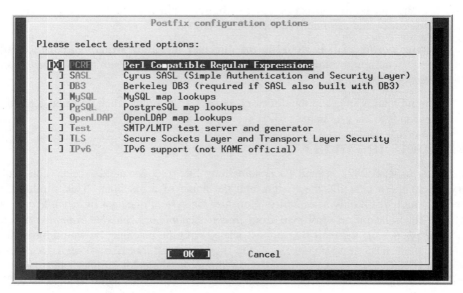

Figure 27-1: Postfix configuration menu

The build continues for a while, and finally you get the information:

```
Installed HTML documentation in /usr/local/share/doc/postfix
===>    Generating temporary packing list
Would you like to activate Postfix in /etc/mail/mailer.conf [n]? y
```

The output goes on to explain which flags to set in your system configuration file *etc/rc.conf*. In particular, it tells you to set sendmail_enable and finishes by saying "This will disable Sendmail completely." This may look strange, especially if you don't have any *sendmail*-related entries in */etc/rc.conf*. Why should setting sendmail_enable to YES disable *sendmail*? Well, it's a somewhat unfortunate choice of naming, and it's possible it will change, but the answer is in the details: sendmail_enable should really be called something like mail_enable. The other *sendmail* parameters turn off all *sendmail*-related components.

Configuring postfix

postfix requires only one configuration file, */usr/local/etc/postfix/main.cf*. This file contains a large number of comments: with a little experience you can configure it without any outside help. In this section, we'll look at some of the entries of interest.

```
# The mail_owner parameter specifies the owner of the Postfix queue
# and of most Postfix daemon processes.  Specify the name of a user
# account THAT DOES NOT SHARE ITS USER OR GROUP ID WITH OTHER ACCOUNTS
# AND THAT OWNS NO OTHER FILES OR PROCESSES ON THE SYSTEM.  In
# particular, don't specify nobody or daemon. PLEASE USE A DEDICATED USER.
#
mail_owner = postfix
```

Older MTAs used to run as `root`, which made it easier to write exploits transmitted by mail. Modern MTAs use a dedicated user ID. As we saw above, the `postfix` user gets added to your password files when you install it. *sendmail* uses another user ID, `smmsp`. Don't change this entry.

Host and domain names

A significant portion of the configuration file defines host names. By default, the variable `myhostname` is the fully qualified host name of the system, for example `freebie.example.org`. You should normally leave it like that; it's not identical to the name that will appear on outgoing mail.

The next variable is `mydomain`, which defaults to the domain name of the system. Again, you won't normally want to change it.

Then comes the variable `myorigin`, which is the name that appears on outgoing mail. It defaults to `myhostname`, which is probably not a good choice. As suggested above, a better name would be the domain name, `mydomain`. Make the following changes to *main.cf*:

```
# The myorigin parameter specifies the domain that locally-posted
# mail appears to come from. The default is to append $myhostname,
# which is fine for small sites.  If you run a domain with multiple
# machines, you should (1) change this to $mydomain and (2) set up
# a domain-wide alias database that aliases each user to
# user@that.users.mailhost.
#
#myorigin = $myhostname
myorigin = $mydomain
```

In the original configuration file, the last line is present, but it is "commented out": it starts with the # character. Just remove this character.

The next variable of interest is `mydestination`. This is a list of host and domain names for which the MTA considers itself the final destination (in other words, it accepts mail for final delivery). By default, it accepts mail addressed to the name of the machine (`$myhostname` in postfix parlance) and also `localhost.$mydomain`, the local host name for this domain. In particular, it does *not* accept mail addressed to the domain, so if you send mail as `fred@example.org`, any reply will bounce. To fix this, add `$mydomain` to the list.

You might also want to accept mail for other domains. For example, if you also wanted to accept mail for *beispiel.org*, you would add that name here as well. The result might look like this:

```
#mydestination = $myhostname, localhost.$mydomain
#mydestination = $myhostname, localhost.$mydomain $mydomain
mydestination = $myhostname, localhost.$mydomain, $mydomain,
        beispiel.org
```

For the mail for *beispiel.org* to actually be delivered to this machine, the lowest priority MX record for *beispiel.org* must point to this host.

Further down, we'll see a feature called *virtual hosting*. This is a way to allocate email addresses to people without a UNIX account on this machine. It works at the user level, not the domain name level.

Relaying mail

One of the favourite tricks of spammers is to send their mail via another system to give it the aura of respectability. This is doubly annoying for the "other" system: first, it gives it the reputation of being a spammer, and secondly it often incurs expense, either for data charges or simply from congestion. *postfix* has a number of tricks to help. The first specifies which networks to trust: *postfix* will relay mail coming from these networks. You could consider this to be "outgoing" mail, though the methods *postfix* uses don't make this assumption. By default, *postfix* trusts your network and the localhost network 127.0.0.0/8, in other words with a net mask 255.0.0.0. But how does it know the net mask for your network? There are two possibilities: you tell it, or it guesses.

postfix is pretty simplistic when it comes to guessing. It takes the default net mask for the address class, so if your IP address is, say, 61.109.235.17 (a "class A" network), it will accept mail from any network whose first octet is 61. I know of at least 20 sources of spam in that range. In almost every case, you should specify the network and mask explicitly:

```
mynetworks = 223.147.37.0/24, 127.0.0.0/8
```

This is a good choice where you know the name of the originating networks, for example systems that expect you to handle the mail connection to the outside world. But what if you want to accept mail from anywhere addressed to specific domains? Consider this "incoming" mail, though again that's not the way *postfix* looks at it. For example, maybe you're a backup MX for *beispiel.de*, so you want to accept any mail sent to that domain. In that case, you want to relay mail to this domain no matter where it comes from. For this case, use the relay_domains variable, a list of domain names for which *postfix* will always relay. You might put this in your *main.cf*:

```
relay_domains = $mydestination, $mydomain, beispiel.de
```

You can also use the permit_mx_backup variable to accept mail for any domain that lists you as a secondary MX. This is very dangerous: you don't have any control over who lists you as a secondary MX, so any spammer could take advantage of this setting and use you for a relay.

Aliases revisited

On page 484 we looked at how to set up individual aliases for use with *mutt*. *postfix* and *sendmail* also have an alias facility, this time at the system level. The system installs a file called */etc/mail/aliases*. It's there by default, so there's no particular reason to move it. The default */etc/mail/aliases* looks like:

```
# Basic system aliases -- these MUST be present
MAILER-DAEMON: postmaster
postmaster: root

# General redirections for pseudo accounts
bin:       root
daemon:    root
games:     root
ingres:    root
nobody:    root
system:    root
toor:      root
uucp:      root

# Well-known aliases -- these should be filled in!
# root:
# manager:
# dumper:
# operator:

root:     grog
```

Each line contains the name of an alias, followed by the name of the user who should receive it. In this case, mail addressed to the users bin, daemon, games, ingres, nobody, system, toor and uucp will be sent to root instead. Note that the last line redefines root to send all mail to a specific user.

You must run the *newaliases* program after changing */etc/aliases* to rebuild the aliases database. Don't confuse this with the *newalias* program, which is part of the *elm* MUA.

A couple of other uses of aliases are:

- You can also use an alias file for spam protection. If you want to subscribe to a mailing list, but you are concerned that spammers might get hold of the contents of the mailing list, you could subscribe as an alias and add something like:

  ```
  frednospamplease:  fred
  ```

  If you do get spam to that name, you just remove the alias (and remember never to have any dealings with the operator of the mailing list again).

- Another use of aliases is for *majordomo*, the mailing list manager we'll look at on page 505.

By default, *postfix* doesn't have a specific alias file. *main.cf* contains:

```
#alias_maps = dbm:/etc/aliases
#alias_maps = hash:/etc/aliases
#alias_maps = hash:/etc/aliases, nis:mail.aliases
#alias_maps = netinfo:/aliases
```

The texts dbm, hash and netinfo describe the kind of lookup to perform. For *sendmail* compatibility, we want hash. Assuming you also want to run *majordomo*, add the line:

```
alias_maps = hash:/etc/mail/aliases,hash:/usr/local/majordomo/aliases.majordomo
```

Rejecting spam

One of the biggest problems with email today is the phenomenon of *spam*, unsolicited
email. Currently the law and ISPs are powerless against it. Hopefully the community
will find solutions to the problem in the future, but at the moment keeping spam to
manageable proportions is a battle of wits. There are a number of ways to combat it, of
course:

- Reject mail from domains known to be spammers. *postfix* helps here with a file
  called */usr/local/etc/postfix/access*, which contains names of domains to reject.

  There are a couple of problems with this approach:

  - It's relatively easy to register a domain, so you may find the same spam coming
    from a different location.

  - It's relatively easy to *spoof* a domain name. Mail is regularly relayed, so you
    have to go by the name on the From line. But you can forge that, so you often see
    mail from yahoo.com or hotmail.com that has never been near those ISPs.
    Obviously it doesn't help to complain to the ISP.

- Of course, if the names are spoofed, you can still find out where the message really
  came from from the headers, as we saw on page 484. Or can we? There are two
  issues there: firstly, if the message has gone by another system, a *relay*, you can't rely
  on the headers further back than one hop. Anything beyond that can be forged.

  In the olden days, MTAs would accept mail for relaying from any system: they were
  so-called *open relays*. Spammers have found this very useful, and now most systems
  have restricted relaying to specific trusted systems. There are still a large number of
  open relays on the net, though.

  This is a problem that could theoretically happen to you: if your system is an open
  relay, you could end up delivering spam without even knowing it. By default, all
  current MTAs supplied with FreeBSD refuse to relay, but it's possible to
  (mis)configure them to be open relays. Be aware of the problems.

  But what if you get a message like this?

```
Received: from femail.sdc.sfba.home.com (femail.sdc.sfba.home.com [24.0.95.82])
        by wantadilla.lemis.com (Postfix) with ESMTP id BCBFF6ACC0
        for <webmaster@lemis.com>; Tue, 19 Jun 2001 13:50:57 +0930 (CST)
Received: from u319 ([24.21.217.142]) by femail2.sdc1.sfba.home.com
        (InterMail vM.4.01.03.20 201-229-121-120-20010223) with SMTP
        id <20010619042005.FBWM26828.femail2.sdc1.sfba.home.com@u319>;
        Mon, 18 Jun 2001 21:20:05 -0700
From: britneyvideo1234@yahoo.com
To:
Subject: stolen britney spears home video!!!
Date: Thu, 19 Jun 2025 13:52:44 -0200
```

This message *has* come from the domain *home.com*, though it's claiming to come
from *yahoo.com*, but the IP address of the originating MTA does not resolve to a
name. The format of the Received: headers is:

announced-name (*real-name* [*real-IP*])

The first header is correct: the name it claims to be (*femail.sdc.sfba.home.com*) matches the reverse lookup. In the second case though, *u319* is not a valid fully-qualified domain name, and there is no second name: the reverse lookup failed. Some MTAs use the word *unknown* in this case, and some even add a warning.

Why should the IP of an MTA not resolve? It's ideal for spammers, of course: it makes them almost impossible to trace. In this case, it's probable that the IP range belongs to *home.com*, because they accepted the message for relaying, but the lack of a valid reverse lookup says nothing for their professionalism.

- A number of commercial and public service sites maintain a list of known spam sites. You can use them to decide whether to accept a mail message.

- The previous example shows another obvious point: this message has been forged to appear to come from yahoo.com. All messages that really come from Yahoo! have a header of this nature:

```
Received: from web11207.mail.yahoo.com (web11207.mail.yahoo.com [216.136.131.189])
        by mx1.FreeBSD.org (Postfix) with SMTP id 4079E43E65
        for <freebsd-arch@freebsd.org>; Mon,  7 Oct 2002 10:39:14 -0700 (PDT)
        (envelope-from gathorpe79@yahoo.com)
```

So if you can recognize messages claiming to come from yahoo.com, but without this kind of header, there's a good chance that they're spam.

So how do we use this information to combat spam? *postfix* helps for the first three, but we need other tools for the last.

The rules for blocking unwanted messages are not included in */usr/local/etc/postfix/main.cf*. Instead, they're in */usr/local/etc/postfix/sample-smtpd.cf*. Copy those you want to the bottom of your */usr/local/etc/postfix/main.cf*. Specifically, the variables of interest are smtpd_helo_restrictions (which relates to the sending MTA, which could be a relay), and smtpd_sender_restrictions, which relates to the (claimed) original sender. See *sample-xmtpd.cf* for details of all possible restrictions. The more interesting ones are:

- reject_unknown_client: reject the request if the client hostname is unknown, i.e. if the DNS reverse lookup fails.

- reject_maps_rbl: reject if the client is listed under $maps_rbl_domains. We'll discuss this below.

- reject_invalid_hostname: reject hostname with bad syntax.

- reject_unknown_hostname: reject hostname without DNS A or MX record.

- reject_unknown_sender_domain: reject sender domain without A or MX record. This is probably a forged domain name.

- `check_sender_access maptype:mapname`. Look the sender address up in the specified map and decide whether to reject it. We'll look at this in more detail below.

- `reject_non_fqdn_hostname`: reject HELO hostname that is not in FQDN form.

- `reject_non_fqdn_sender`: reject sender address that is not in FQDN form.

Rejecting known spam domains

If you have identified domains that you would rather not hear from again, use the form `check_sender_access maptype:mapname`. By default, the map is stored in */usr/local/etc/postfix/access.db*. Add the following text to *main.cf*:

```
smtpd_sender_restrictions = hash:/usr/local/etc/postfix/access
```

Note that the `.db` is missing from the name. Now add this line to the file */usr/local/etc/postfix/access*, creating it if necessary:

```
spamdomain.com                    550       Mail rejected.  Known spam site.
```

This form rejects messages from this domain with SMTP error code 550 and the message that follows.

As we have seen, *postfix* reads the file */usr/local/etc/postfix/access.db*, not */usr/local/etc/postfix/access*. Use the *postmap* program to create or update */usr/local/etc/postfix/access.db*:

```
# postmap /usr/local/etc/postfix/access
```

The changes to */usr/local/etc/postfix/main.cf* depend on other items as well, so we'll look at them at the end of this discussion.

To judge by the name, *spamdomain.com* is probably a hard-core spam producer. But there are others, notably large ISPs with little or no interest in limiting spam, and they also have innocent users who will also be blocked. If you find out about it, you can make exceptions:

```
spamdomain.com              550       Mail rejected.  Known spam site.
innocent@spamdomain.com OK
```

Don't forget to re-run *postmap* after updating *alias*. One way is to create a *Makefile* in */usr/local/etc/postfix* with the following contents:

```
access.db:      access
        /usr/local/sbin/postmap access
```

Then add the following line to */etc/crontab*:

```
1  *  *  *  *  root    (cd /usr/local/etc/postfix; make) 2>/dev/null >/dev/null
```

This checks the files every hour and rebuilds */usr/local/etc/postfix/access.db* if necessary.

Rejecting sites without reverse lookup

A very large number of spam sites don't have reverse lookup on their IP addresses. You can reject all such mail: after all, it's misconfigured. Just add the `reject_un-known_sender_domain` keyword to the `smtpd_sender_restrictions`. Unfortunately, some serious commercial enterprises also don't have reverse lookup. It's your choice whether you want to accept mail from them and open the flood gates to spam, or to ignore them. The FreeBSD project has chosen the latter course: if you don't have reverse lookup, you will not be able to send mail to FreeBSD.org.

Rejecting listed sites

Another alternative is to reject sites that have been listed on a public list of spam sites, sometimes referred to as an *rbl* (*Realtime Blackhole List*). The example given in the configuration file is *http://www.mail-abuse.org/* , but there are others as well. They maintain a list of spam sites that you can query before accepting every message.

I don't like these sites for a number of reasons:

• They slow things down.

• They frequently cost money.

• They have a habit of blocking large quantities of address space, including domains who are not in any way related with the spammers. I don't know anything about MAPS, so I can't comment on whether they do this sort of thing.

If you want to use this kind of service, add the following two lines to your *main.cf*:

```
smtpd_client_restrictions = reject_maps_rbl
maps_rbl_domains = rbl.maps.vix.com
```

The name *rbl.maps.vix.com* comes from the sample file. Replace it with information from your rbl supplier.

Recognizing spoofed messages

There's only so much that *postfix* can do to restrict spam. The Ports Collection contains a couple of other useful tools, *procmail* and *spamassassin*, which together can reject a lot of spam. It involves a fair amount of work, unfortunately. Take a look at the ports if you're interested.

Sender restrictions: summary

The restrictions above are interdependent. I would recommend rejecting senders based on address and lack of reverse lookup. To do that, add just the following lines to your *main.cf*:

```
smtpd_sender_restrictions = reject_unknown_sender_domain,
         hash:/usr/local/etc/postfix/access
```

Running postfix at boot time

By default, the system starts *sendmail* at boot time. You don't need to do anything
special. Just set the following parameters in */etc/rc.conf* :

```
sendmail_enable="YES"
sendmail_flags="-bd"
sendmail_outbound_enable="NO"
sendmail_submit_enable="NO"
sendmail_msp_queue_enable="NO"
```

The flags have the following meanings:

- `sendmail_enable` is a bit of a misnomer. It should be called `mail_enable`.

- `-bd` means *become daemon*: *postfix* runs as a daemon and accepts incoming mail.

  sendmail uses an additional parameter, usually something like `-q30m`. This tells
  sendmail how often to retry sending mail (30 minutes in this example). *postfix*
  accepts this option but ignores it. Instead, you tell it how often to retry mail ("run the
  queue") with the `queue_run_delay` parameter in the configuration file, which is set
  to 1000 seconds, about 16 minutes. A retry attempt takes up local and network
  resources, so don't set this value less than about 15 minutes.

- The other parameters are only there to stop the system from running *sendmail* as
  well.

Talking to the MTA

The *Simple Mail Transfer Protocol*, or *SMTP*, is a text-based protocol. If you want, you
can talk to the MTA directly on the `smtp` port. Try this with *telnet*:

```
$ telnet localhost smtp
Trying ::1...
telnet: connect to address ::1: Connection refused        attempt to connect with IPv6
Trying 127.0.0.1...
Connected to localhost.
Escape character is '^]'.
220 freebie.example.org ESMTP Postfix on FreeBSD, the professional's choice
ehlo freebie.example.org                                  say who you are
250-freebie.example.org                                   name
250-PIPELINING                                            and list of available features
250-SIZE 10240000
250-ETRN
250 8BITMIME
mail from: grog@example.org                               who the mail is from
250 Ok
rcpt to: grog@example.org                                 and who it goes to
250 Ok
data                                                      start the message body
354 End data with <CR><LF>.<CR><LF>
Test data                                                 The message
```

```
                    .                              End of message
250 Ok: queued as 684F081471
quit                                               and exit
221 Bye
Connection closed by foreign host.
```

This rather cumbersome method is useful if you're having trouble with *postfix*.

Downloading mail from your ISP

As we discussed before, the Internet wasn't designed for dialup use. Most protocols assume that systems are up a large proportion of the time: down time indicates some kind of failure. This can cause problems delivering mail if you are not permanently connected to the Internet.

If you have an MX record that points to another system that is permanently connected, this doesn't seem to be a problem: the mail will be sent to that system instead. When you connect, the mail can be sent to you.

How does the mail system know when you connect? Normally it doesn't. That's the first problem. Most systems set up their MTA to try to deliver mail every 30 to 120 minutes. If you are connected that long, the chances are good that the mail will be delivered automatically, but you don't know when.

One possibility here is to tell the remote MTA when you're connected. You can do this with the SMTP ETRN command. Telnet to the smtp port on the system where the mail is queued:

```
$ telnet mail.example.net  smtp
Trying 139.130.237.17...
Connected to mail.example.net.
Escape character is '^]'.
220 freebie.example.org ESMTP Sendmail 8.8.7/8.8.7 ready at Mon, 5 May 1997
12:55:10 +0930 (CST)

etrn freebie.example.org
250 Queuing for node freebie.example.org started
quit
221 mail.example.net closing connection
Connection closed by foreign host.
```

The mail starts coming after the message Queuing for node freebie.example.org started. Depending on how much mail it is, it might take a while, but you don't need to wait for it.

Another alternative is the *Post Office Protocol*, or *POP*. POP was designed originally for Microsoft-style computers that can't run daemons, so they have to explicitly request the other end to download the data. POP is an Internet service, so you need the cooperation of the other system to run it. We'll look at POP in the next section.

POP: the Post Office Protocol

The Post Office Protocol is a means for transferring already-delivered mail to another
site. It consists of two parts, the client and the server. A number of both clients and
servers are available. In this discussion, we'll look at the server *popper* and the client
fetchmail, both of which are in the Ports Collection.

popper: the server

Install *popper* from the Ports Collection in the usual manner:

```
# cd /usr/ports/mail/popper
# make install
```

popper is designed to be started only via *inetd*. To enable it, edit */etc/inetd.conf*. By
default, it contains the following line:

```
#pop3    stream  tcp     nowait  root    /usr/local/libexec/popper        popper
```

This line is *commented out* with the # character. Remove that character to enable the
service. Then cause *inetd* to re-read its configuration file:

```
# killall -1 inetd                          send a SIGHUP
```

To test the server, telnet to the pop3 port. You can't do much like this, but at least you
can confirm that the server is answering:

```
$ telnet localhost pop3
Trying ::1...
telnet: connect to address ::1: Connection refused
Trying 127.0.0.1...
Connected to localhost.
Escape character is '^]'.
+OK QPOP (version 2.53) at freebie.example.com starting.   <11755.1028797120@freebie.
example.com>
quit
+OK Pop server at freebie.example.com signing off.
Connection closed by foreign host.
```

fetchmail: the client

Install *fetchmail* from the Ports Collection. To run it, just specify the name of the server
from which you want to load the mail.

```
$ fetchmail hub
querying hub
Enter mailserver password:                      doesn't echo
QPOP (version 2.3) at hub.freebsd.org starting.  <27540.876902406@hub.freebsd.org>
5 messages in folder, 4 new messages.
reading message 1...
flushing message 2
reading message 2....
flushing message 3
reading message 3...
flushing message 4
```

```
reading message 4...
flushing message 5
reading message 5....
```

fetchmail and *popper* are relatively simple to use if you have to, but they add another level of complexity to the mail system, and they require additional work in a system that is designed to be automatic. In addition, *fetchmail* is not a speed demon: if you have a lot of mail to transfer, be prepared to wait much longer than an SMTP MTA would take.

Mailing lists: majordomo

majordomo is a mail list manager. If you run mailing lists, you probably want to use majordomo: it saves you manually modifying the mailing lists. As usual, you can find *majordomo* in the Ports Collection, in the directory */usr/ports/mail/majordomo*. When installing, you'll notice a message:

```
To finish the installation, 'su' to root and type:

        make install-wrapper

If not installing the wrapper, type

        cd /usr/local/majordomo; ./wrapper config-test

(no 'su' necessary) to verify the installation.
./install.sh -o root -g 54  -m 4755 wrapper /usr/local/majordomo/wrapper
```

With the exception of the last line, this comes from the original *majordomo* installation procedure. The last line is the port performing the `make install-wrapper` for you. You don't need to do anything else, and you can ignore the messages.

After installation, you still need to perform some configuration:

- Customize */usr/local/majordomo/majordomo.cf*. This should be easy enough to read, and you may not need to change anything. Once you have it up and running, you might like to consider changing the `default_subscribe_policy`.

- Define your lists in */usr/local/majordomo/aliases.majordomo*. This file contains a single list, `test-1`, which you should remove once you have things up and running.

- Ensure that there is a mail user `majordomo-owner` on the system. The best way to handle this is to add an entry in */etc/mail/aliases* (see page 496):

```
majordomo-owner:        root
```

  Since `root` should be an alias for your mail ID, this will mean that you get the mail for `majordomo-owner` as well. Don't run *postmap* or *newaliases* yet.

- Add */usr/local/majordomo/aliases.majordomo* to the list *postfix* aliases. We looked at this point above; you need at least the bold text part of the following line in */usr/local/etc/postfix/main.cf*:

```
alias_maps = hash:/etc/mail/aliases,hash:/usr/local/majordomo/aliases.majordomo
```

- Run *postmap*.
- Restart *postfix*:

  ```
  # postfix reload
  ```

This isn't absolutely necessary, but it will take *postfix* a few minutes to notice otherwise.

That's all you need to do. You don't need to start any processes to run *majordomo*: it gets started automatically when a mail message is received.

28

XFree86 in depth

The information in Chapter 6 should be enough to get X up and running. There's a lot more to X than that, however, enough to fill many books. In this chapter we'll look at some of the more interesting topics:

- The next section describes the technical background of running X displays.

- On page 516 we'll look at setting up the *XF86Config* file.

- On page 523 we'll look at using more than one monitor with X.

- On page 524 we'll look at using X in a network.

X configuration: the theory

Setting up your *XF86Config* file normally takes a few minutes, but sometimes you can run into problems that make grown men cry. In the rest of this chapter, we'll look at the technical background:

- How display boards and monitors work.

- How to set up XFree86 to work with your hardware.

- How to tune your hardware for maximum display performance.

- How to fry your monitor.

I mean the last point seriously: conventional wisdom says that you can't damage hardware with a programming mistake, but in this case it is possible. Read the section on how monitors work, and don't start tuning until you understand the dangers involved.

How TVs and monitors work

You don't have to be a computer expert to see the similarity between monitors and TVs: current monitor technology is derived from TV technology, and many older display boards have modes that can use TVs instead of monitors. Those of us who were on the microcomputer scene 20 to 25 years ago will remember the joy of getting a computer display on a portable TV, a "glass tty" connected by a serial line running at 300 or 1200 bps.

There are at least two ways to create pictures on a cathode ray tube: one is derived from oscilloscopes, where each individual character is scanned by the electron beam, rather like writing in the sand with your finger. Some early terminals used this technology, but it has been obsolete for several decades.

TVs and monitors display the picture by scanning equally spaced lines across the entire screen. Like in a book, the first line starts at the top left of the screen and goes to the top right. Each successive line starts slightly below the previous line. This continues until the screen is full. The picture is formed by altering the intensity of the electron beam as it scans the lines.

To perform this scan, the TV has two *deflection units*: one scans from left to right, and the other scans, much more slowly, from top to bottom. Not surprisingly, these units are called the *horizontal* and *vertical* deflection units. You may also encounter the terms *line* and *frame* deflection.

Figure 28-1 shows the resultant pattern.

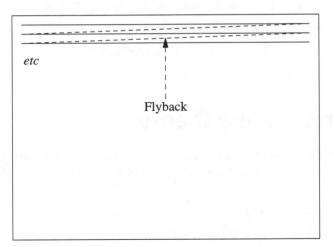

Figure 28-1: Scanning pattern on the monitor

The tube can only move the electron beam at a finite speed. When the electron beam reaches the right hand side of the screen, it needs to be deflected back again. This part of the scan is called the *horizontal flyback*, and it is not used for displaying picture data. The actual time that the hardware requires for the flyback depends on the monitor, but it is in the order of 5% to 10% of the total line scan time. Similarly, when the vertical deflection reaches the bottom of the screen, it performs a *vertical flyback*, which is also not used for display purposes.

It's not enough to just deflect, of course: somehow you need to ensure that the scanning is synchronized with the incoming signal, so that the scan is at the top of the screen when the picture information for the top of the screen arrives. You've seen what happens when synchronization doesn't work: the picture runs up and down the screen (incorrect vertical synchronization) or tears away from the left of the screen (incorrect horizontal synchronization). Synchronization is achieved by including synchronization pulses in the horizontal and vertical flyback periods. They have a voltage level outside the normal picture data range to ensure that they are recognized as synchronization pulses.

As if that wasn't enough, the video amplifier, the part of the TV that alters the intensity of the spot as it travels across the screen, needs time to ensure that the flyback is invisible, so there are brief pauses between the end of the line and the start of the sync pulse, and again between the end of the sync pulse and the beginning of the data. This process is called *blanking*, and the delays are called the *front porch* (before the sync pulse) and the *back porch* (after the sync pulse). Figure 28-2 depicts a complete scan line.

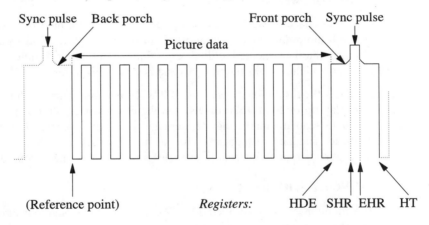

Figure 28-2: Scan line and register values

The register information at the bottom of the picture refers to the video controller registers. We'll look at how to interpret them on page 511.

That, in a nutshell, is how horizontal deflection works. Vertical deflection works in almost the same way, just slower, with one minor exception. This basic display mechanism was developed for TVs in the 1930s, at a time when terms like high-tech (or even electronics) hadn't even been invented, and even today we're stuck with the low data rates that they decided upon in those days. Depending on the country, conventional TVs display only 25 or 30 frames (pages of display) per second. This would cause an unpleasant flicker in the display. This flicker is minimized with a trick called *interlacing*: instead of displaying the frame in one vertical scan, the odd and even lines are displayed in two alternating half frames, which doubles the apparent vertical frequency.

How monitors differ from TVs

So how do we apply this to computer displays? Let's look at the US standard NTSC system—the international PAL and SECAM systems are almost identical except for the number of lines and a minor difference in the frequencies. NTSC specifies 525 lines, but that includes the vertical flyback time, and in fact only about 480 lines are visible. The aspect ratio of a normal TV is 4:3, in other words the screen is one-third wider than it is high, so if we want square pixels,[1] we need to have one-third more pixels per line. This means that we can display 640 pixels per line on 480 lines.[2] This resolution is normally abbreviated to "640x480." PAL and SECAM have lower vertical frequencies, which allows a nominal 625 lines, of which about 600 are displayed. Either way, these values have two huge disadvantages: first, the resolution is barely acceptable for modern graphics displays, and secondly they are interlaced displays. Older PC display hardware, such as the CGA and some EGA modes, was capable of generating these signal frequencies, but normal graphic cards can no longer do it. Instead, dedicated TV output cards are available if that's what you want to do.

The first problem is interlace: it works reasonably for TVs, but it's a pain for computer displays—there's still more flicker than a real 50 Hz or 60 Hz display. Modern display boards can still run in interlace mode, but don't even think about doing so unless you're forced to—the resultant picture looks out of focus and is very tiring to read.

The second problem is the resolution: nowadays, 1024x768 is a minimum resolution, and some monitors display up to 2048x1536 pixels. On the other hand, even 60 Hz refresh rate is barely adequate: read any marketing literature and you'll discover that 72 Hz is the point at which flicker suddenly disappears. To get high-resolution, high refresh rate displays, you need some very high internal frequencies—we'll look at that further down.

How to fry your monitor

Remember that a monitor is just a glorified TV? Well, one of the design constraints of real TVs is that they have only a single horizontal frequency and only a single vertical frequency. This simplifies the hardware design considerably: the horizontal deflection uses a tuned circuit to create both the deflection frequency and the high voltage required to run the tube. This circuit is comprised of a transformer (the *line transformer*) and a condenser. Run a line transformer even fractionally off its intended frequency and it runs much less efficiently and use more current, which gets converted to heat. If you run a conventional monitor off spec for any length of time, it will burn out the line transformer.

---

1. A square pixel is one with the same height and width. They don't have to be that way, but it makes graphics software much simpler.
2. Does this look familiar?

You don't have to roll your own X configuration to burn out the monitor: 20 years ago, the standard display boards were CGAs and HDAs,[1] and they had different horizontal frequencies and thus required different monitors. Unfortunately, they both used the same data connector. If you connected an HDA (18.43 kHz horizontal frequency) to a CGA monitor (15.75 kHz, the NTSC line frequency), you would soon see smoke signals.

All modern PC monitors handle at least a range of horizontal frequencies. This doesn't mean that an out of spec signal can't damage them—you might just burn out something else, frequently the power supply. Most better monitors recognize out-of-spec signals and refuse to try to display them; instead, you get an error display. Unfortunately, there are plenty of other monitors, especially older or cheaper models, which don't protect themselves against out of spec signals. In addition, just because the monitor displays correctly doesn't mean that it is running in spec. The moral of the story:

> *Never run your monitor out of spec. If your display is messed up, there's a good chance that the frequencies are out, so turn off the monitor.*

Monitors aren't the only thing that you can burn out, of course. If you try hard, you can also burn out chips on some display boards by running them at frequencies that are out of spec. In practice, though, this doesn't happen nearly as often.

Another difference between TVs and monitors is the kind of signal they take. A real TV includes a receiver, of course, so you have an antenna connection, but modern TVs also have connections for inputs from VCRs, which are usually two audio signals and a video signal. The video signal contains five important components: the *red*, *green* and *blue* signals, and the horizontal and vertical sync pulses. This kind of signal is called *composite video*. By contrast, most modern monitors separate these signals onto separate signal lines, and older boards, such as the EGA, even used several lines per colour. Unfortunately, there is no complete agreement about how these signals should work: the polarity of the sync pulses can vary, and some boards cheat and supply the sync pulses on the green signal line. This is mainly of historical interest, but occasionally you'll come across a real bargain 20" monitor that only has three signal connections, and you may not be able to get it to work—this could be one of the reasons.

The CRT controller

The display controller, usually called a CRT (Cathode Ray Tube) controller, is the part of the display board that creates the signals we've just been talking about. Early display controllers were designed to produce signals that were compatible with TVs: they had to produce a signal with sync pulses, front and back porches, and picture data in between. Modern display controllers can do a lot more, but the principles remain the same.

The first part of the display controller creates the framework we're looking for: the horizontal and vertical sync pulses, blanking and picture information, which is represented as a series of points or *dots*. To count, we need a pulse source, which also

---

1. Color Graphics Adapter and Hercules Display Adapter.

determines the duration of individual dots, so it is normally called a *dot clock*. For reasons lost in history, CRT controllers start counting at the top left of the display, and not at the vertical sync pulse, which is the real beginning of the display. To define a line to the horizontal deflection, we need to set four CRTC registers to tell it—see the diagram on page 509:

- The *Horizontal Display End* register (HDE) specifies how many dots we want on each line. After the CRTC has counted this many pixels, it stops outputting picture data to the display.

- The *Start Horizontal Retrace* register (SHR) specifies how many dot clock pulses occur before the sync pulse starts. The difference between the contents of this register and the contents of the HDE register defines the length of the front porch.

- The *End Horizontal Retrace* register (EHR) defines the end of the sync pulse. The width of the sync pulse is the difference between the contents of this register and the SHR register.

- The *Horizontal Total* register (HT) defines the total number of dot clocks per line. The width of the back porch is the difference between the contents of this register and the EHR register.

In addition, the *Start Horizontal Blanking* and *End Horizontal Blanking* registers (SHB and EHB) define when the video signals are turned off and on. The server sets these registers automatically, so we don't need to look at them in more detail.

The control of the vertical deflection is similar. In this case, the registers are *Vertical Display End* (VDE), *Start Vertical Retrace* (SVR), *End Vertical Retrace* (EVR), *Vertical Total* (VT), *Start Vertical Blanking* (SVB), and *End Vertical Blanking* (EVB). The values in these registers are counted in lines.

VGA hardware evolved out of older 8 bit character-based display hardware, which counted lines in characters, not dot clocks. As a result, all of these registers are 8 bits wide. This is adequate for character displays, but it's a problem when counting dots: the maximum value you can set in any of these registers is 255. The designers of the VGA resorted to a number of nasty kludges to get around this problem: the horizontal registers count in groups of 8 dot clocks, so they can represent up to 2048 dot clocks. The vertical registers overflow into an overflow register. Even so, the standard VGA can't count beyond 1024 lines. Super VGAs vary in how they handle this problem, but typically they add additional overflow bits. To give you an idea of how clean the VGA design is, consider the way the real Vertical Total (total number of lines on the display) is defined on a standard VGA. It's a 10 bit quantity, but the first 8 bits are in the VT register, the 9th bit is in bit 0 of the overflow register, and the 10th bit is in bit 5 of the overflow register.

The XF86Config mode line

One of the steps in setting up XFree86 is to define these register values. Fortunately, you don't have to worry about which bits to set in the overflow register: the mode lines count in dots, and it's up to the server to convert the dot count into something that the display board can understand. A typical Mode line looks like:

```
Modeline "640x480a" 28 640 680 728 776 480 480 482 494
```

These ten values are required. In addition, you may specify modifiers at the end of the line. The values are:

- A label for the resolution line. This must be enclosed in quotation marks, and is used to refer to the line from other parts of the *XF86Config* file. Traditionally, the label represents the resolution of the display mode, but it doesn't have to. In this example, the resolution really is 640x480, but the a at the end of the label is a clue that it's an alternative value.

- The clock frequency, 28 MHz in this example.

- The Horizontal Display End, which goes into the HDE register. This value and all that follow are specified in dots. The server mangles them as the display board requires and puts them in the corresponding CRTC register.

- The Start Horizontal Retrace (SHR) value.

- The End Horizontal Retrace (EHR) value.

- The Horizontal Total (HT) value.

- The Vertical Display End (VDE) value. This value and the three following are specified in lines.

- The Start Vertical Retrace (SVR) value.

- The End Vertical Retrace (EVR) value.

- The Vertical Total (VT) value.

This is pretty dry stuff. To make it easier to understand, let's look at how we would set a typical VGA display with 640x480 pixels. Sure, you can find values for this setup in any release of XFree86, but that doesn't mean that they're the optimum for *your system*. We want a non-flicker display, which we'll take to mean a vertical frequency of at least 72 Hz, and of course we don't want interlace. Our monitor can handle any horizontal frequency between 15 and 40 kHz: we want the least flicker, so we'll aim for 40 kHz.

First, we need to create our lines. They contain 640 pixels, two porches and a sync pulse. The only value we really know for sure is the number of pixels. How long should the porches and the sync pulses be? Good monitor documentation should tell you, but most monitor manufacturers don't seem to believe in good documentation. The documented values vary significantly from monitor to monitor, and even from mode to mode: they're not as critical as they look. Here are some typical values:

Horizontal sync pulse: 1 to 4 μs, front porch 0.18 to 2.1 μs, back porch 1.25 to 3.56 μs.

As we'll see, the proof of these timing parameters is in the display. If the display looks good, the parameters are OK. I don't know of any way to damage the monitor purely by modifying these parameters, but there are other good reasons to stick to this range. As a rule of thumb, if you set each of the three values to 2 μs to start with, you won't go too far wrong. Alternatively, you could start with the NTSC standard values: the standard specifies that the horizontal sync pulse lasts for 4.2 to 5.1 μs, the front porch must be at least 1.27 μs. NTSC doesn't define the length of the back porch—instead it defines the total line blanking, which lasts for 8.06 to 10.3 μs. For our purposes, we can consider the back porch to be the length of the total blanking minus the lengths of the front porch and the sync pulse. If you take values somewhere in the middle of the ranges, you get a front porch of 1.4 μs, a sync pulse of 4.5 μs, and total blanking 9 μs, which implies a back porch of 9 - 1.4 - 4.5 = 3.1 μs.

For our example, let's stick to 2 μs per value. We have a horizontal frequency of 40 kHz, or 25 μs per line. After taking off our 6 μs for flyback control, we have only 19 μs left for the display data. To get 640 pixels in this time, we need one pixel every 19 ÷ 640 μs, or about 30 ns. This corresponds to a frequency of 33.6 MHz. This is our desired dot clock.

The next question is: do we have a dot clock of this frequency? Maybe. This should be in your display board documentation, but I'll take a bet that it's not. Never mind, the XFree86 server is clever enough to figure this out for itself. At the moment, let's assume that you do have a dot clock of 33 MHz.

> If you don't have a suitable clock, you'll have to take the next lower clock frequency that you do have: you can't go any higher, since this example assumes the highest possible horizontal frequency.

You now need to calculate four register values to define the horizontal lines:

- The first value is the Horizontal Display End, the number of pixels on a line. We know this one: it's 640.

- You calculate SHR by adding the number of dot clocks that elapse during the front porch to the value of HDE. Recall that we decided on a front porch of 2 μs. In this time, a 33 MHz clock counts 66 cycles. So we add 66, right? Wrong. Remember that the VGA registers count in increments of 8 pixels, so we need to round the width of the front porch to a multiple of 8. In this case, we round it to 64, so we set SHR to 640 + 64 = 704.

- The next value we need is EHR, which is SHR plus the width of the horizontal retrace, again 64 dot clocks, so we set that to 704 + 64 = 768.

- The final horizontal value is HT. Again, we add the front porch—64 dot clocks—to EHR and get 768 + 64 = 832.

At this point, our vestigial mode line looks like:

```
Modeline "640x480"   28   640 704 768 832
```

Next, we need another four values to define the vertical scan. Again, of the four values we need, we only know the number of lines. How many lines do we use for the porches and the vertical sync? As we've seen, NTSC uses about 45 lines for the three combined, but modern monitors can get by with much less. Again referring to the Multisync manual, we get a front porch of betwwen 0.014 and 1.2 ms, a sync pulse of between 0.06 and 0.113 ms, and a back porch of between 0.54 and 1.88 ms. But how many lines is that?

To figure that out, we need to know our *real* horizontal frequency. We were aiming at 40 kHz, but we made a couple of tradeoffs along the way. The real horizontal frequency is the dot clock divided by the horizontal total, in this case 33 MHz ÷ 832, which gives us 39.66 kHz—not too bad. At that frequency, a line lasts 1÷39660 seconds, or just over 25 μs, so our front porch can range between ½ and 48 lines, our sync pulse between 2 and 5 lines, and the back porch between 10 and 75 lines. Do these timings make any sense? No, they don't—they're just values that the monitor can accept.

To get the highest refresh rate, we can go for the lowest value in each case. It's difficult to specify a value of ½, so we'll take a single line front porch. We'll take two lines of sync pulse and 10 lines of back porch. This gives us:

- VDE is 480.

- SVR is 481.

- EVR is 483.

- VT is 493.

Now our mode line is complete:

```
Modeline "640x480" 28   640 704 768 832   480 481 483 493
```

Now we can calculate our vertical frequency, which is the horizontal frequency divided by the Vertical Total, or 39.66 ÷ 493 kHz, which is 80.4 Hz—that's not bad either. By comparison, if you use the default value compiled into the server, you get a horizontal frequency of 31.5 kHz and a vertical frequency of only 60 Hz.

If you know the technical details of your monitor and display board, it really is that simple. This method doesn't require much thought, and it creates results that work.

Note that the resultant mode line may not work on other monitors. If you are using a laptop that you want to connect to different monitors or overhead display units, don't use this method. Stick to the standard frequencies supplied by the X server. Many overhead projectors understand only a very small number of frequencies, and the result of using a tweaked mode line is frequently that you can't synchronize with the display, or that it cuts off a large part of the image.

XF86Config

The main configuration file for XFree86 is called *XF86Config*. It has had a long and varied journey through the file system. At the time of writing, it's located at */usr/X11R6/lib/X11/XF86Config*, but previously it has been put in */etc/X11/XF86Config*, */etc/XF86Config* or */usr/X11R6/etc/X11/XF86Config*, and the server still looks for it in many of these places. If you're upgrading a system, you should ensure that you don't have old configuration files in one of the alternative places.

As we saw on page 102, there are a couple of ways to automatically create an *XF86Config* file. On that page we saw how to do it with *xf86cfg*. An alternative way is to run the X server in configuration mode:

```
# X -configure
XFree86 Version 4.2.0 / X Window System
(protocol Version 11, revision 0, vendor release 6600)
Release Date: 18 January 2002
        If the server is older than 6-12 months, or if your card is
        newer than the above date, look for a newer version before
        reporting problems.  (See http://www.XFree86.Org/)
Build Operating System: FreeBSD 5.0-CURRENT i386 [ELF]
Module Loader present
Markers: (--) probed, (**) from config file, (==) default setting,
        (++) from command line, (!!) notice, (II) informational,
        (WW) warning, (EE) error, (NI) not implemented, (??) unknown.
(==) Log file: "/var/log/XFree86.0.log", Time: Sat Apr  6 13:51:10 2002
List of video drivers:
        atimisc
(the list is long, and will change; it's omitted here)
(++) Using config file: "/root/XF86Config.new"


Your XF86Config file is /root/XF86Config.new

To test the server, run 'XFree86 -xf86config /root/XF86Config.new'
```

Note that *X* does not place the resultant configuration file in the default location. The intention is that you should test it first and then move it to the final location when you're happy with it. As generated above, it's good enough to run XFree86, but you'll possibly want to change it. For example, it only gives you a single resolution, the highest it can find. In this section we'll look at the configuration file in more detail, and how to change it.

XF86Config is divided into several sections, as shown in Table 28-1. We'll look at them in the order they appear in the generated *XF86Config* file, which is not the same order as in the man page.

Table 28-1: XF86Config sections

Section	Description
ServerLayout	Describes the overall layout of the X configuration. X can handle more than one display card and monitor. This section is the key to the other sections
Files	Sets the default font and RGB paths.
ServerFlags	Set some global options.
Module	Describes the software modules to load for the configuration.
InputDevice	Sets up keyboards, mice and other input devices.
Monitor	Describes your monitor to the server.
Device	Describes your video hardware to the server.
Screen	Describes how to use the monitor and video hardware.

The server layout

The ServerLayout section describes the relationships between the individual hardware components under the control of an X server. For typical hardware, X -configure might generate:

```
Section "ServerLayout"
        Identifier      "XFree86 Configured"
        Screen       0  "Screen0" 0 0
        InputDevice     "Mouse0" "CorePointer"
        InputDevice     "Keyboard0" "CoreKeyboard"
EndSection
```

This shows that the server has one screen and two input devices. The names Mouse0 and Keyboard0 suggest that they're a mouse and a keyboard, but any name is valid. These entries are pointers to sections elsewhere in the file, which must contain definitions for Screen0, Mouse0 and Keyboard0.

Normally you only have one screen, one mouse and one keyboard, so this section might seem rather unnecessary. As we will see when we look at multiple monitor configurations, it's quite important to be able to describe these relationships.

The Files section

The *Files* section of the *XF86Config* file contains the path to the RGB database file, which should never need to be changed, and the default font path. You may want to add more font paths, and some ports do so: the FontPath lines in your *XF86Config* are concatenated to form a search path. Ensure that each directory listed exists and is a valid font directory.

The standard *Files* section looks like:

```
Section "Files"
        RgbPath         "/usr/X11R6/lib/X11/rgb"
        ModulePath      "/usr/X11R6/lib/modules"
        FontPath        "/usr/X11R6/lib/X11/fonts/misc/"
        FontPath        "/usr/X11R6/lib/X11/fonts/Speedo/"
        FontPath        "/usr/X11R6/lib/X11/fonts/Type1/"
        FontPath        "/usr/X11R6/lib/X11/fonts/CID/"
        FontPath        "/usr/X11R6/lib/X11/fonts/75dpi/"
        FontPath        "/usr/X11R6/lib/X11/fonts/100dpi/"
EndSection
```

If you are running a high-resolution display, this sequence may be sub-optimal. For example, a 21" monitor running at 1600x1200 pixels has a visible display of approximately 16" wide and 12" high, exactly 100 *dpi* (*dots per inch*, really pixels per inch). As a result, you'll probably be happier with the 100 dpi fonts. You can change this by swapping the last two lines in the section:

```
        FontPath        "/usr/X11R6/lib/X11/fonts/100dpi/"
        FontPath        "/usr/X11R6/lib/X11/fonts/75dpi/"
EndSection
```

Don't just remove the 75 dpi fonts: some fonts may be available only in the 75 dpi directory.

Sometimes the server complains:

```
Can't open default font 'fixed'
```

This is almost certainly the result of an invalid entry in your font path. Try running *mkfontdir* in each directory if you are certain that each one is correct. The *XF86Config* man page describes other parameters that may be in this section of the file.

The ServerFlags section

The ServerFlags section allows you to specify a number of global options. By default it is not present, and you will probably not find any reason to set it. See the man page *XF86Config(5)* for details of the options.

The Module section

The Module section describes binary modules that the server loads:

```
Section "Module"
        Load    "extmod"
        Load    "xie"
        Load    "pex5"
        Load    "glx"
        Load    "GLcore"
        Load    "dbe"
        Load    "record"
        Load    "type1"
EndSection
```

We won't look at modules in more detail; see the XFree86 documentation.

The InputDevice section

The *InputDevice* section specifies each input device, typically mice and keyboards. Older versions of XFree86 had separate Mouse and Keyboard sections to describe these details. The default XF86Config looks something like this:

```
Section "InputDevice"
        Identifier   "Keyboard0"
        Driver       "keyboard"
EndSection

Section "InputDevice"
        Identifier   "Mouse0"
        Driver       "mouse"
        Option       "Protocol" "auto"
        Option       "Device" "/dev/mouse"
EndSection
```

There's not much to be said for the keyboard. Previous versions of XFree86 allowed you to set things like *NumLock* handling and repeat rate, but the former is no longer needed, and the latter is easier to handle with the *xset* program.

Mice are still not as standardized as keyboards, so you still need a Protocol line and a device name. The defaults shown here are correct for most modern mice; the mouse driver can detect the mouse type correctly. If you're using the mouse daemon, *moused*, change this entry to the *moused* device, */dev/sysmouse*.

If you're using a serial mouse or one with only two buttons, *and* if you're not using *moused*, you need to change the device entries and specify the Emulate3Buttons option. That's all described in the man page, but in general it's easier to use *moused*.

The Monitor section

Next comes the description of the monitor. Modern monitors can identify themselves to the system. In that case, you get a section that looks like this:

```
Section "Monitor"
        Identifier   "Monitor0"
        VendorName   "IBM"
        ModelName    "P260"
        HorizSync    30.0 - 121.0
        VertRefresh  48.0 - 160.0
```

This tells the server that the monitor is an IBM P260, that it can handle horizontal frequencies between 30 kHz and 121 kHz, and vertical frequencies between 48 Hz and 160 Hz. Less sophisticated monitors don't supply this information, so you might end up with an entry like this:

```
Section "Monitor"
        Identifier   "Monitor0"
        VendorName   "Monitor Vendor"
        ModelName    "Monitor Model"
EndSection
```

This may seem like no information at all, but in fact it does give the identifier. Before you use it, you should add at least the horizontal and vertical frequency range, otherwise the server assumes it's a standard (and obsolete) VGA monitor capable of only 640x480 resolution.

This is also the place where you can add mode lines. For example, if you have created a mode line as described in the first part of this chapter, you should add it here:

```
Section "Monitor"
        Identifier   "right"
        VendorName   "iiyama"
        ModelName    "8221T"
        HorizSync    24.8 - 94.0
        VertRefresh  50.0 - 160.0

ModeLine    "640x480"    73    640  672  768  864    480  488  494  530
# 62 Hz!
ModeLine    "800x600"   111    800  864  928 1088    600  604  610  640
# 143 Hz
ModeLine    "1024x768"  165   1024 1056 1248 1440    768  771  781  802
# 96 Hz
ModeLine    "1280x1024" 195   1280 1312 1440 1696   1024 1031 1046 1072 -hsync -vsync
# 76 Hz
ModeLine    "1600x1200" 195   1600 1616 1808 2080   1200 1204 1207 1244 +hsync +vsync
# 56 Hz!
ModeLine    "1920x1440" 200   1920 1947 2047 2396   1440 1441 1444 1483 -hsync +vsync
# 61 Hz
ModeLine    "1920x1440" 220   1920 1947 2047 2448   1440 1441 1444 1483 -hsync +vsync
        EndSection
```

It's possible to have multiple mode lines for a single frequency, and this even makes sense. The examples for 1920x1440 above have different pixel clocks. If you use this monitor with a card with a pixel clock that only goes up to 200 MHz, the server chooses the first mode line. If you use a card with up to 250 MHz pixel clock, it uses the second and gets a better page refresh rate.

The X server has a number of built-in mode lines, so it's quite possible to have a configuration file with no mode lines at all. The names correspond to the resolutions, and there can be multiple mode lines with the same name. The server chooses the mode line with the highest frequency compatible with the hardware.

The Device section

The *Device* section describes the video display board:

```
Section "Device"
        ### Available Driver options are:-
        ### Values: <i>: integer, <f>: float, <bool>: "True"/"False",
        ### <string>: "String", <freq>: "<f> Hz/kHz/MHz"
        ### [arg]: arg optional
        #Option     "SWcursor"              # [<bool>]
        #Option     "HWcursor"              # [<bool>]
```

```
       #Option      "PciRetry"                # [<bool>]
       #Option      "SyncOnGreen"             # [<bool>]
       #Option      "NoAccel"                 # [<bool>]
       #Option      "ShowCache"               # [<bool>]
       #Option      "Overlay"                 # [<str>]
       #Option      "MGASDRAM"                # [<bool>]
       #Option      "ShadowFB"                # [<bool>]
       #Option      "UseFBDev"                # [<bool>]
       #Option      "ColorKey"                # <i>
       #Option      "SetMclk"                 # <freq>
       #Option      "OverclockMem"            # [<bool>]
       #Option      "VideoKey"                # <i>
       #Option      "Rotate"                  # [<str>]
       #Option      "TexturedVideo"           # [<bool>]
       #Option      "Crtc2Half"               # [<bool>]
       #Option      "Crtc2Ram"                # <i>
       #Option      "Int10"                   # [<bool>]
       #Option      "AGPMode"                 # <i>
       #Option      "DigitalScreen"           # [<bool>]
       #Option      "TV"                      # [<bool>]
       #Option      "TVStandard"              # [<str>]
       #Option      "CableType"               # [<str>]
       #Option      "NoHal"                   # [<bool>]
       #Option      "SwappedHead"             # [<bool>]
       #Option      "DRI"                     # [<bool>]
       Identifier   "Card0"
       Driver       "mga"
       VendorName   "Matrox"
       BoardName    "MGA G200 AGP"
       BusID        "PCI:1:0:0"  .
EndSection
```

This example shows a Matrox G200 AGP display board. It includes a number of options that you can set by removing the comment character (#). Many of these options are board dependent, and none of them are required. See the X documentation for more details.

Note particularly the last line, BusID. This is a hardware-related address that tells the X server where to find the display board. If you move the board to a different PCI slot, the address will probably change, and you will need to re-run *X -configure* to find the new bus ID.

If your display board is older, much of this information will not be available, and you'll have to add it yourself. Unlike older monitors, it's hardly worth worrying about older boards, though: modern boards have become extremely cheap, and they're so much faster than older boards that it's not worth the trouble.

The Screen section

The final section is the Screen section, which describes the display on a monitor. The default looks something like this:

```
Section "Screen"
       Identifier "Screen0"
       Device     "Card0"
       Monitor    "Monitor0"
       SubSection "Display"
               Depth      1
       EndSubSection
       SubSection "Display"
```

```
            Depth     4
        EndSubSection
        SubSection "Display"
            Depth     8
        EndSubSection
        SubSection "Display"
            Depth     15
        EndSubSection
        SubSection "Display"
            Depth     16
        EndSubSection
        SubSection "Display"
            Depth     24
        EndSubSection
EndSection
```

The first three lines describe the relationship between the screen display, the video board that creates it, and the monitor on which it is displayed. Next come a number of subsections describing the possible bit depths that the screen may have. For each display depth, you can specify which mode lines you wish to use. Modern display hardware has plenty of memory, so you'll probably not want to restrict the display depth. On the other hand, you may want to have multiple mode lines. Your display card and monitor are good enough to display 2048x1536 at 24 bits per pixel, but occasionally you'll get images (in badly designed web pages, for example) so miniscule that you'll want to zoom in, maybe going all the way back to 640x480 in extreme cases. You can toggle through the available resolutions with the key combinations **Ctrl-Alt-Numeric +** and **Ctrl-Alt-Numeric -**. You're probably not interested in pixel depths lower than 640x480, so your Screen section might look like:

```
Section "Screen"
        Identifier "Screen0"
        Device     "Card0"
        Monitor     "Monitor0"
        DefaultDepth     24
        SubSection "Display"
            Depth     24
            Modes     "2048x1536" "1600x1200" "1024x768"  "640x480"
        EndSubSection
EndSection
```

This section includes a DefaultDepth entry for the sake of example. In this case, it's not strictly needed, because there's only one pixel depth. If there were more than one Display subsection, it would tell *xinit* which depth to use by default.

Multiple monitors and servers

We've seen above that X provides for more than one monitor per server. If you have multiple display cards and monitors, let the server generate the *XF86Config* file: it generates a file that supports all identified devices. The resultant server layout section might look like this:

```
Section "ServerLayout"
        Identifier      "XFree86 Configured"
        Screen       0  "Screen0" 0 0
        Screen       1  "Screen1" RightOf "Screen0"
        Screen       2  "Screen2" RightOf "Screen1"
        InputDevice     "Mouse0" "CorePointer"
        InputDevice     "Keyboard0" "CoreKeyboard"
EndSection
```

The file will also have multiple monitor, device and screen sections. The server can't know about the real physical layout of the screen, of course, so you may have to change the ordering of the screens. When you run the server without any other specifications, it is assigned server number 0, so these screens will be numbered *:0.0*, *:0.1* and *:0.2*.

Multiple servers

It's also possible to run more than one X server on a single system, even if it only has a single monitor. There can be some good reasons for this: you may share a system amongst your family members, so each of them can have their own server. Alternatively, you may have a laptop with a high-resolution display and need to do a presentation on overhead projectors that can't handle more than 1024x768 pixels. It's not practical to simply switch to a lower resolution, because the overall screen size doesn't change, and it's difficult to avoid sliding the image around when you move the cursor.

For each server, you require one virtual terminal—see page 109 for more details. If you're using the same hardware, you can also use the same *XF86Config* file. The only difference is in the way in which you start the server. For example, you could start three X servers, one with the *fvwm2* window manager, one with *KDE* and one with *GNOME*, with the following script:

```
xinit &
xinit .xinitrc-kde -- :1 &
xinit .xinitrc-gnome -- :2 -xf86config XF86Config.1024x768 &
```

Due to different command line options, you must use *xinit* here, and not *startx*. The first *xinit* starts a server with the default options: it reads its commands from *.xinitrc*, it has the server number 0, and it reads its configuration from the default *XF86Config* file. The second server reads its commands from *.xinitrc-kde*, it has the server number 1, and it reads its configuration from the default *XF86Config* file. The third server reads its commands from *.xinitrc-gnome*, it has the server number 2, and the configuration file is *XF86Config.1024x768*. Assuming that you reserve virtual terminals */dev/ttyv7*, */dev/ttyv8* and */dev/ttyv9* for the servers, you can switch between them with the key combinations **Ctrl-Alt-F8**, **Ctrl-Alt-F9** and **Ctrl-Alt-F10**.

X in the network

X is a network protocol. So far we have looked at the server. The clients are the individual programs, such as *xterm*, *emacs* or a web browser, and they don't have to be on the same machine. A special notation exists to address X servers and screens:

System name **:** *server number* **.** *screen number*

When looking at X client-server interaction, remember that the server is the software component that manages the display. This means that you're always sitting at the server, not at the client. For example, if you want to start an *xterm* client on *freebie* and display it on *presto*, you'll be sitting at *presto*. To do this, you could type in, on *presto*,

```
$ ssh freebie xterm -ls -display presto:0 &
```

The flag -ls tells *xterm* that this is a *login shell*, which causes it to read in the startup files.

For this to work, you must tell the X server to allow the connection. There are two things to do:

- Use *xhost* to specify the names of the systems that have access:

  ```
  $ xhost freebie presto bumble wait gw
  ```

  This enables access from all the systems on our reference network, including the one on which it is run. You don't need to include your own system, which is enabled by default, but if you do, you can use the same script on all systems on the network.

- *xhost* is not a very robust system, so by default *startx* starts X with the option -nolisten tcp. This completely blocks access from other systems. If you want to allow remote clients to access your X server, modify */usr/X11R6/bin/startx*, which contains the text:

  ```
  listen_tcp="-nolisten tcp"
  ```

  Change this line to read:

  ```
  listen_tcp=
  ```

  This enables remote connections the next time you start the server.

Multiple monitors across multiple servers

We saw above that a server can handle multiple monitors, and a system can handle multiple servers. One problem with multiple monitors is that most computers can only handle a small number of display boards: a single AGP board and possibly a number of PCI boards. But PCI boards are difficult to find nowadays, and they're slower and have less memory.

If you have a number of machines located physically next to each other, you have the alternative of running X on each of them and controlling everything from one keyboard and mouse. You do this with the *x11/x2x* port. For example: *freebie*, *presto* and *bumble* have monitors next to each other, and *presto* has two monitors. From left to right they are *freebie:0.0*, *presto:0.0*, *presto:0.1* and *bumble:0.0*. The keyboard and mouse are connected to *presto*. To incorporate *freebie:0.0* and *bumble:0.0* in the group, enter these commands on *presto*:

```
$ DISPLAY=:0.0 x2x -west -to freebie:0 &
$ DISPLAY=:0.1 x2x -east -to bumble:0 &
```

After this, you can move to the other machines by moving the mouse in the corresponding direction. It's not possible to continue to a further machine, but it is possible to connect in other directions (*north* and *south*) from each monitor on *presto*, which in this case would allow connections to at least six other machines. Before that limitation becomes a problem, you need to find space for all the monitors.

Stopping X

To stop X, press the key combination **Ctrl-Alt-Backspace**, which is deliberately chosen to resemble the key combination **Ctrl-Alt-Delete** used to reboot the machine. **Ctrl-Alt-Backspace** stops X and returns you to the virtual terminal in which you started it. If you run from *xdm*, it redisplays a login screen.

29

Starting and
stopping the system

Before you can run FreeBSD, you need to start it up. That's normally pretty straightforward: you turn the machine on, a lot of things scroll off the screen, and about a minute later you have a `login:` prompt or an X login window on the screen. Sometimes, though, the process is of more interest. You have a number of options when booting, and it's also a source of a number of problems, so it pays to understand it. In this chapter we'll look at the following topics:

• In the next section, we'll look at the startup process in more detail.

• On page 529 we'll look at how to control the boot process.

• If something goes wrong, and the system doesn't come up, those messages that scrolled off the screen are very important. We'll look at what they mean on page 529.

• It's not so obvious that you need to adhere to a procedure when shutting down the system. We'll look at the hows and whys on page 541.

• There are a number of ways of starting the system for particular applications. On page 542 we'll look at how to run FreeBSD without a disk.

Starting the system

When you power up the system, or when you reboot, a number of actions occur before
the system is up and running. Starting the system is usually called "bootstrapping," after
the story of Baron von Munchhausen pulling himself up by his own bootstraps. The
following sequence describes the sequence on the PC architecture, but there are only
relatively minor differences on other platforms.

- First, the BIOS[1] performs tests that check that the machine is working correctly and
  determines the hardware configuration. This *Power On Self Test* or *POST* has
  nothing to do with FreeBSD.

- Next, the BIOS bootstrap loads the *Master Boot Record* from the first sector of the
  first disk on the system (C: in BIOS parlance) into memory and executes it. This
  step is the same for all operating systems on PCs.

- It's up to this bootstrap to decide which operating system to boot. The bootstrap in
  the MBR may or may not be part of the FreeBSD system. FreeBSD can install two
  different MBRs, as we saw on page 66. The standard MBR works without
  intervention, while the boot manager gives you the choice of booting from any
  partition on the disk.

- The FreeBSD bootstrap first loads the second-level bootstrap, *BTX*, from the next 15
  sectors on disk and executes it.

- The second-level boot locates the third-level bootstrap, called *loader*, and loads it into
  memory. *loader* is an intelligent bootstrap component that allows preloading of
  multiple kernel components. See the man page *loader(8)* for more information. By
  default, *loader* locates the kernel, the file */boot/kernel/kernel* on the root file system,
  and loads it into memory. You can interrupt the loader at this point, for example to
  load different or additional files.

- The kernel performs its own tests to look for hardware it knows about. It's quite
  verbose about this, and prints messages about both the hardware it finds and the
  hardware it doesn't find. This operation is called *probing*. Most kernels are built to
  recognize a large selection of hardware, so it's normal to have more "not found"
  messages than "found" messages.

- After the probe, the kernel starts two processes. The first, process 0, is the *swapper*
  and is responsible for emergency clearing of memory when the standard virtual
  memory algorithms aren't fast enough.

- Process 1 is called *init*. As the name suggests, it is responsible for starting up the
  system and daemons. When coming up in the default multi-user mode, it spawns a
  shell to execute the shell script */etc/rc*.

---

1. More accurately, the system firmware. The firmware is called *BIOS* (*Basic Input/Output System*) on the i386
   architecture, *SRM* on the Alpha architecture, and *Open Firmware* on a number of other architectures.

- */etc/rc* first reads in the description files */etc/defaults/rc.conf*, which contains defaults for a number of configuration variables, and */etc/rc.conf*, which contains your modifications to the defaults. It then proceeds to perform the steps necessary to bring up the system, first starting virtual disk drivers, mounting swap space and checking the file system integrity if necessary.

- When */etc/rc* exits, *init* reads the file */etc/ttys* and starts processes as determined there. It spends the rest of its life looking after these processes.

Things you can do before booting

You can do a number of things before you boot the system:

- The most obvious thing to do is to decide what you're going to boot. The boot loader gives you the chance to load different operating systems or different FreeBSD kernels and modules. We'll look at that below.

- You can also set a number of options for the kernel loader, including specification of hardware and software characteristics. We'll look at that on page 532.

What are you going to boot?

If you have multiple operating systems on your system, you can use the boot manager described on page 64, to choose which one to boot. For example, if you have two disks, the first of which contains four partitions, the first stage of the boot looks something like this:

```
F1: FreeBSD
F2: Windows
F3: Linux
F4: FreeBSD
F5: Drive 1

Default: F1
```

After 10 seconds, the boot manager attempts to load the bootstrap from the default partition; you can choose any of the selections by pressing the corresponding function key. If you press **F5**, you get a menu showing the partitions on the second disk, with F5 to return to the first disk.

If you choose to boot FreeBSD, the bootstrap loaders load, and you see something like:

```
/                                        this is a "twirling baton"
BTX loader 1.00  BTX version is 1.01
BIOS drive A: is disk0
BIOS drive C: is disk1
BIOS drive D: is disk1
BIOS 639kB/130048kB available memory
```

These messages are printed by *BTX*. If you're loading from disk, the / character at the end of the previous line keeps changing through -, \, and | before going back to / again, giving the impression that the character is rotating. This display, called a *twirling baton*, is your indication that the system hasn't crashed and burned. It's normal for it to take a few seconds before the baton starts to twirl.

Next, *loader* prints its prompt:

```
FreeBSD/i386 bootstrap loader, Revision 0.8
(grog@freebie.example.com, Thu Jun 13 13:06:03 CST 2002)
Loading /boot/defaults/loader.conf

Hit [Enter] to boot immediately, or any other key for command prompt.
Booting [kernel] in 6 seconds...              this counts down from 10 seconds
```

At this point, you would normally continue with the boot, either by pressing the **Enter** key or just waiting the 10 seconds. We'll see what happens then on page 533.

Sometimes you may want to change software or hardware characteristics. In this case, you press the "any other key" (by tradition the space bar) and enter commands to the loader.

Loader commands

There are two ways to communicate with the loader:

- A number of files in the directory */boot* on the root file system tell the loader what to do. Most are not intended to be changed, but you can create a file called */boot/loader.conf*, into which you can enter commands to override the commands in */boot/defaults/loader.conf*. We'll look at this below.

- In addition, the file */boot/device.hints* takes the place of many configuration file entries and allows you to set hardware characteristics such as information about IRQ, DMA, I/O address and other settings for the hardware. You can change these values during booting.

  The CD-ROM installation installs */boot/device.hints*, but a kernel install does not. You'll find it in the *conf* directory for your architecture. For example, */usr/src/sys/i386/conf* includes the configuration file *GENERIC* and the corresponding hints file *GENERIC.hints*. Install it like this:

  ```
  # cp /usr/src/sys/i386/conf/GENERIC.hints /boot/device.hints
  ```

  The hints file contains entries of the following nature:

  ```
  hint.sio.0.at="isa"
  hint.sio.0.port="0x3F8"
  hint.sio.0.flags="0x10"
  hint.sio.0.irq="4"
  hint.sio.1.at="isa"
  hint.sio.1.port="0x2F8"
  hint.sio.1.irq="3"
  hint.sio.2.at="isa"
  ```

```
hint.sio.2.disabled="1"
hint.sio.2.port="0x3E8"
hint.sio.2.irq="5"
hint.sio.3.at="isa"
hint.sio.3.disabled="1"
hint.sio.3.port="0x2E8"
hint.sio.3.irq="9"
```

These entries describe the serial port configuration. They replace the older method of hard coding the information in the kernel. For example, the hints above contain the configuration information contained in these lines of the Release 4 configuration file:

```
device          sio0    at isa? port IO_COM1 flags 0x10 irq 4
device          sio1    at isa? port IO_COM2 irq 3
device          sio2    at isa? disable port IO_COM3 irq 5
device          sio3    at isa? disable port IO_COM4 irq 9
```

The corresponding line in the Release 5 configuration file is:

```
device          sio              # 8250, 16[45]50 based serial ports
```

More importantly, though, this means that you don't need to recompile the kernel if you change the hardware addresses.

* You can enter commands directly to the command prompt.

When you hit the space bar, you get the following prompt:

```
Type '?' for a list of commands, 'help' for more detailed help.
ok ?
Available commands:
  reboot            reboot the system
  heap              show heap usage
  bcachestat        get disk block cache stats
  boot              boot a file or loaded kernel
  autoboot          boot automatically after a delay
  help              detailed help
  ?                 list commands
  show              show variable(s)
  set               set a variable
  unset             unset a variable
  more              show contents of a file
  lsdev             list all devices
  include           read commands from a file
  ls                list files
  load              load a kernel or module
  unload            unload all modules
  lsmod             list loaded modules
  pnpscan           scan for PnP devices
```

The most important of these commands are set, show, load, unload and boot. We'll see some examples of their use in the following sections. Note, however, that if you have accidentally hit the "any" key during boot and just want to continue with the boot, you just have to enter **boot**.

loader.conf

Much of the behaviour of the loader is controlled by entries in */boot/defaults/loader.conf*. You shouldn't change this file, though: put changes in a file */boot/loader.conf*, which may not exist. There are a large number of possible entries; in */boot/defaults/loader.conf* you'll see the default values, frequently commented out because the loader already knows the defaults. Here are some of the more interesting ones:

```
kernel="kernel"

verbose_loading="NO"                      # Set to YES for verbose loader output

#autoboot_delay="10"                      # Delay in seconds before autobooting
#console="vidconsole"                     # Set the current console
#currdev="disk1s1a"                       # Set the current device
module_path="/boot/kernel;/boot/modules;/modules"       # Set the module search path
#prompt="\${interpret}"                   # Set the command prompt
#root_disk_unit="0"                       # Force the root disk unit number
#rootdev="disk1s1a"                       # Set the root filesystem
```

- The `kernel` entry gives the name of the kernel, relative to the kernel directory */boot/kernel*. Sometimes it might be of interest to change this value, for example when testing.

- `console=vidconsole` tells the loader where to output its messages. `vidconsole` is short for *video console*; you can also select `comconsole` if you have a serial terminal connected to a specified serial port.

- `currdev` specifies where to look for the root file system. If you have multiple BIOS partitions on a disk, you can select the correct one with this value.

There are many more options to the loader; read the man page for more details.

Loading other modules at boot time

By default, *loader* loads only the kernel. That may not be what you want. You might want to load a different kernel, or you may want to load a kld as well.

There are two ways to do this. If you only want to do this once, you can interrupt the boot sequence by pressing the space bar, and tell *loader* what to do:

```
Booting [kernel] in 6 seconds...           this counts down from 10 seconds
(space bar hit)
Type '?' for a list of commands, 'help' for more detailed help.
ok unload                                  not the kernel we wanted
OK load /boot/kernel.old/kernel            load the old kernel
/boot/kernel.old/kernel text=0x3e474c data=0x52f00+0x81904 syms=[0x4+0x4cab0+0x4+0x5
b458]
OK load /boot/kernel.old/vinum.ko          and the old vinum module
/boot/kernel.old/vinum.ko text=0x149a4 data=0xaf75c+0x164 syms=[0x4+0x11e0+0x4+0xcac]
ok boot                                    then start the kernel
Copyright (c) 1992-2002 The FreeBSD Project.
Copyright (c) 1979, 1980, 1983, 1986, 1988, 1989, 1991, 1992, 1993, 1994
       The Regents of the University of California. All rights reserved.
FreeBSD 5.0-RELEASE #0: Sat 15 Feb 16:30:26 CST 2003
    grog@monorchid.example.org:/usr/src/sys/i386/compile/BUMBLE
Preloaded elf kernel "/boot/kernel.old/kernel" at 0xc072a000.
```

```
Preloaded elf module "/boot/kernel.old/vinum.ko" at 0xc072a0bc.
Timecounter "i8254"  frequency 1193182 Hz
(etc)
```

This example shows two separate activities: one is changing the kernel from */boot/kernel/kernel* to */boot/kernel.old/kernel*, and the other is loading the *vinum* kld. You don't need to reload the kernel to load the *vinum* module.

Automatic kld load

The method described above is cumbersome if you want to load the kld every time you boot. In this case, it's easier to add the following line to */boot/loader.conf*:

```
vinum_load="YES"
```

To see what commands you can use, look in */boot/defaults/loader.conf*, where you would find all normal configuration entries commented out.

```
...
ccd_load="NO"            # Concatenated disk driver
vinum_load="NO"          # Concatenated/mirror/raid driver
md_load="NO"             # Memory disk driver (vnode/swap/malloc)
...
```

Don't change this file; it's designed to be replaced on upgrade, and any changes would get lost when you upgrade.

Running the kernel

The next step in the boot process is to run the kernel. This is what happens by default if you do nothing at the Booting [kernel] prompt, or if you press **Enter**. If you have interrupted the boot process, you continue with the command:

```
ok boot
```

The following example shows the output of booting an Abit BP6 dual processor motherboard. This board also has four IDE controllers on board, and the system had two SCSI host adapters connected to it.

The loader transfers control to the kernel it has preloaded. Messages from the kernel are in high-intensity text (brighter than normal). This is the most common time to see them, though they sometimes appear during normal machine operation. These messages also get copied to the kernel message buffer, and you can retrieve the most recent messages with the *dmesg* program. In the course of time, other messages may fill the buffer, and you will no longer be able to find the boot messages with *dmesg*, so one of the final steps in the startup saves the content of the boot messages in the file */var/run/dmesg.boot*, which should always contain the complete startup messages. In the case of laptops, the message buffer normally does not get cleared on shutdown, not even if the power goes down, so you may find logs for multiple boots.

Once it has finished loading, the kernel prints some summary information and then calls all configured drivers to examine the hardware configuration of the machine on which it is running. This is called *probing* for the devices. If you have time, it's a good idea to confirm that it's correct. Much of it appears so quickly that you can't read it, but once the boot is complete, you can examine it with the *dmesg* command. If something goes wrong, it *won't* scroll off the screen. The place where it stops is then of interest.

Under normal circumstances, we see something like:

```
Copyright (c) 1992-2002 The FreeBSD Project.
Copyright (c) 1979, 1980, 1983, 1986, 1988, 1989, 1991, 1992, 1993, 1994
     The Regents of the University of California. All rights reserved.
FreeBSD 5.0-RELEASE #0: Sat 15 Feb 16:30:26 CST 2003
     grog@monorchid.example.org:/usr/src/sys/i386/compile/BUMBLE
Preloaded elf kernel "/boot/kernel/kernel" at 0xc0663000.
```

Here the kernel identifies itself with information about the release number, when and where it was built, and where it was loaded from.

```
Timecounter "i8254"  frequency 1193182 Hz
CPU: Pentium II/Pentium II Xeon/Celeron (467.73-MHz 686-class CPU)
   Origin = "GenuineIntel"  Id = 0x665  Stepping = 5
   Features=0x183fbff<FPU,VME,DE,PSE,TSC,MSR,PAE,MCE,CX8,APIC,SEP,MTRR,PGE,MCA,CMOV,P
AT,PSE36,MMX,FXSR>
real memory  = 134217728 (128 MB)
avail memory = 123465728 (117 MB)
```

The lines above identify the basic hardware. There is one time counter (some motherboards have two), the CPU is a Celeron, Pentium II or Xeon, and it runs at 466 MHz. This information is relatively reliable. The real memory value is the size of RAM. Some older systems reserve 1 kB of RAM in real mode, but this should not have any effect on the value of real memory. Available memory is the memory available to users after the kernel has been loaded and initialized.

On some older machines, the kernel reports only 16 MB although the system has more memory. This is due to BIOS incompatibilities, and occurs surprisingly often on big-name machines. To fix it, build a custom kernel that specifies the memory size explicitly—see the description of the MAXMEM parameter, which is described in the verbose configuration file */usr/src/sys/i386/conf/NOTES*.

This machine is in fact a multiprocessor with two CPUs, so we see:

```
Programming 24 pins in IOAPIC #0
IOAPIC #0 intpin 2 -> irq 0
IOAPIC #0 intpin 16 -> irq 10
IOAPIC #0 intpin 17 -> irq 9
IOAPIC #0 intpin 18 -> irq 11
FreeBSD/SMP: Multiprocessor System Detected: 2 CPUs
  cpu0 (BSP): apic id:  0, version: 0x00040011, at 0xfee00000
  cpu1 (AP):  apic id:  1, version: 0x00040011, at 0xfee00000
  io0 (APIC): apic id:  2, version: 0x00170011, at 0xfec00000
```

The IOAPIC is the *I/O Advanced Programmable Interrupt Controller* used by SMP machines only. It reassigns some interrupt requests. This information is provided in case you need to debug the kernel. None of this appears for a normal machine.

```
Initializing GEOMetry subsystem
Pentium Pro MTRR support enabled
npx0: <math processor> on motherboard                  numeric coprocessor, on chip
npx0: INT 16 interface
```

The *GEOM*etry subsystem is a disk I/O system that was introduced in FreeBSD Release 5. This processor is a P6 class processor, so it has *Memory Type Range Registers* or *MTRR*s, which are used to optimize memory usage.

Next we look at the other chips on the motherboard, starting with the so-called "chipset," the processor support chips.

```
pcib0: <Intel 82443BX (440 BX) host to PCI bridge> at pcibus 0 on motherboard
pci0: <PCI bus> on pcib0
agp0: <Intel 82443BX (440 BX) host to PCI bridge> mem 0xe0000000-0xe3ffffff at devic
e 0.0 on pci0
pcib1: <PCIBIOS PCI-PCI bridge> at device 1.0 on pci0
pci1: <PCI bus> on pcib1
```

This motherboard has an Intel 82443 BX chipset with two PCI buses. Next we see some of the devices on the motherboard:

```
pci1: <Matrox MGA G200 AGP graphics accelerator> at 0.0
isab0: <Intel 82371AB PCI to ISA bridge> at device 7.0 on pci0
isa0: <ISA bus> on isab0                                       ISA bus
atapci0: <Intel PIIX4 ATA33 controller> port 0xf000-0xf00f at device 7.1 on pci0
ata0: at 0x1f0 irq 14 on atapci0                              primary IDE controller
ata1: at 0x170 irq 15 on atapci0                            secondary IDE controller
uhci0: <Intel 82371AB/EB (PIIX4) USB controller> port 0xc000-0xc01f irq 10 at device
 7.2 on pci0                                                   USB controller
usb0: <Intel 82371AB/EB (PIIX4) USB controller> on uhci0 USB bus
usb0: USB revision 1.0
uhub0: Intel UHCI root hub, class 9/0, rev 1.00/1.00, addr 1
uhub0: 2 ports with 2 removable, self powered
Timecounter "PIIX"  frequency 3579545 Hz
pci0: <bridge, PCI-unknown> at device 7.3 (no driver attached)
```

The system doesn't know which devices are implemented internally in the chipset, which are separate chips on the mother board, and which are on plug-in boards. So far it has found the IDE controllers, but not the disks; it'll look for them later.

Next we find two Symbios SCSI host adapters:

```
sym0: <875> port 0xc400-0xc4ff mem 0xec002000-0xec002fff,0xec003000-0xec0030ff irq 1
0 at device 9.0 on pci0
sym0: Symbios NVRAM, ID 7, Fast-20, SE, NO parity
sym0: open drain IRQ line driver, using on-chip SRAM
sym0: using LOAD/STORE-based firmware.
sym0: SCAN FOR LUNS disabled for targets 0.
sym1: <875> port 0xc800-0xc8ff mem 0xec001000-0xec001fff,0xec000000-0xec0000ff irq 9
 at device 13.0 on pci0
sym1: No NVRAM, ID 7, Fast-20, SE, parity checking
```

The first Symbios adapter is on IRQ 10. It is on ID 7, like most SCSI host adapters, and it doesn't support parity. The second board is on IRQ 9 and does support parity, but it doesn't have a BIOS. This is not a problem for FreeBSD, which doesn't use the BIOS, but if it were in the system by itself, the POST would not find it. In this case, the BIOS on the other Symbios board does in fact find the second host adapter.

```
dc0: <Macronix 98715AEC-C 10/100BaseTX> port 0xe000-0xe0ff mem
0xe7800000-0xe78000ff irq 11 at device 11.0 on pci0
dc0: Ethernet address: 00:80:c6:f9:a6:c8
miibus0: <MII bus> on dc0
dcphy0: <Intel 21143 NWAY media interface> on miibus0
dcphy0:  10baseT, 10baseT-FDX, 100baseTX, 100baseTX-FDX, auto
```

This is a Macronix Ethernet card with associated PHY interface at IRQ 11.

After that, we return to on-board peripherals, in this case two additional IDE controllers and legacy ISA peripherals:

```
atapci1: <HighPoint HPT366 ATA66 controller> port 0xd800-0xd8ff,0xd400-0xd403,0xd000
-0xd007 irq 11 at device 19.0 on pci0
ata2: at 0xd000 on atapci1                                          Third IDE controller
atapci2: <HighPoint HPT366 ATA66 controller> port 0xe400-0xe4ff,0xe000-0xe003,0xdc00
-0xdc07 irq 11 at device 19.1 on pci0
ata3: at 0xdc00 on atapci2                                          Fourth IDE controller
orm0: <Option ROMs> at iomem 0xc0000-0xc7fff,0xc8000-0xc87ff on isa0
fdc0: ready for input in output                                    Floppy controller
fdc0: cmd 3 failed at out byte 1 of 3
```

The floppy driver command failure here is caused by the lack of any floppy drive on this machine.

```
atkbdc0: <Keyboard controller (i8042)> at port 0x60,0x64 on isa0
atkbd0: <AT Keyboard> flags 0x1 irq 1 on atkbdc0                    keyboard
kbd0 at atkbd0
vga0: <Generic ISA VGA> at port 0x3c0-0x3df iomem 0xa0000-0xbffff on isa0
sc0: <System console> at flags 0x100 on isa0                        system console
sc0: VGA <16 virtual consoles, flags=0x300>
sio0 at port 0x3f8-0x3ff irq 4 flags 0x10 on isa0                   first serial port
sio0: type 16550A                                                  it's a buffered UART
sio1 at port 0x2f8-0x2ff irq 3 on isa0                             second serial port
sio1: type 16550A
sio2 not found at 0x3e8                                            no more serial I/O ports
sio3 not found at 0x2e8
```

UNIX starts counting device numbers from 0, whereas Microsoft starts counting from 1. Devices /dev/sio0 through /dev/sio3 are known as *COM1:* through *COM4:* in the Microsoft world.

```
ppc0: <Parallel port> at port 0x378-0x37f irq 7 on isa0            parallel port controller
ppc0: Generic chipset (NIBBLE-only) in COMPATIBLE mode
plip0: <PLIP network interface> on ppbus0
lpt0: <Printer> on ppbus0                                          line printer on parallel port
lpt0: Interrupt-driven port
ppi0: <Parallel I/O> on ppbus0                                     alternate I/O on the same port
```

Next, on this multiprocessor board, we get some SMP-specific messages. The system tests the IO-APIC, which can sometimes cause problems, and then starts the second processor:

```
APIC_IO: Testing 8254 interrupt delivery
APIC_IO: routing 8254 via IOAPIC #0 intpin 2
SMP: AP CPU #1 Launched!
```

Finally, the system detects the disks connected to this machine:

```
ad0: 19574MB <WDC WD205BA> [39770/16/63] at ata0-master UDMA33
ad4: 19574MB <WDC WD205BA> [39770/16/63] at ata0-master UDMA66
Waiting 15 seconds for SCSI devices to settle
(noperiph:sym0:0:-1:-1): SCSI BUS reset delivered.
da0 at sym1 bus 0 target 3 lun 0
da0: <SEAGATE ST15230W SUN4.2G 0738> Fixed Direct Access SCSI-2 device
da0: 20.000MB/s transfers (10.000MHz, offset 15, 16bit), Tagged Queueing Enabled
da0: 4095MB (8386733 512 byte sectors: 255H 63S/T 522C)
da1 at sym1 bus 0 target 0 lun 0
da1: <SEAGATE ST15230W SUN4.2G 0738> Fixed Direct Access SCSI-2 device
da1: 20.000MB/s transfers (10.000MHz, offset 15, 16bit), Tagged Queueing Enabled
da1: 4095MB (8386733 512 byte sectors: 255H 63S/T 522C)
```

Here, we have four disks, one each on the first and third IDE controllers, both as master, and two on the second SCSI host adapter. There is nothing on the first host adapter.

Finally, the system starts Vinum and mounts the root file system and the swap partition:

```
Mounting root from ufs:/dev/ad0s1a
vinum: loaded
vinum: reading configuration from /dev/ad0s1h
vinum: updating configuration from /dev/ad4s2h
swapon: adding /dev/ad0s1b as swap device
swapon: /dev/vinum/swap: No such file or directory
Automatic reboot in progress...
```

At this point, the system is up and running, but it still needs to start some services. The remaining messages come from processes, not from the kernel, so they are in normal intensity.

```
add net default: gateway 223.147.37.5
Additional routing options: tcp extensions=NO TCP keepalive=YES.
routing daemons:.
Mounting NFS file systems.
additional daemons: syslogd
Doing additional network setup: portmap.
Starting final network daemons: rwhod.
setting ELF ldconfig path: /usr/lib /usr/lib/compat /usr/X11R6/lib /usr/local/lib
setting a.out ldconfig path: /usr/lib/aout /usr/lib/compat/aout /usr/X11R6/lib/aout
starting standard daemons: inetd cron
Initial rc.i386 initialization:.
rc.i386 configuring syscons: blank_time.
Local package initialization:.
Additional TCP options:.
Tue Apr 23 13:59:05 CST 2000
```

At this point, the kernel has finished probing, and it transfers control to the shell script */etc/rc*. From this point on the display is in normal intensity. */etc/rc* first reads the configuration information in */etc/defaults/rc.conf* and */etc/rc.conf* (see page 552). Next, it checks the consistency of the file systems. Normally you'll see messages like this for each file system in */etc/fstab*:

```
/dev/da0s1a: FILESYSTEM CLEAN; SKIPPING CHECKS
/dev/da0s1a: clean, 6311 free (367 frags, 743 blocks, 0.9% fragmentation)
/dev/da0s1e: FILESYSTEM CLEAN; SKIPPING CHECKS
/dev/da0s1e: clean, 1577 files, 31178 used, 7813 free (629 frags, 898 blocks, 1.6% fr
agmentation)
```

If your system has crashed, however, either due to a software or hardware problem, or because it was not shut down correctly, it will perform a file system check (*fsck*), which can take quite a while, up to an hour on very big file systems. You'll see something like:

```
WARNING: / was not properly dismounted
/dev/da0s1a: 6311 free (367 frags, 743 blocks, 0.9% fragmentation)
```

On a large file system, *fsck* can take a long time to complete, up to several hours in extreme cases. By default, the system does not need to wait for it to terminate; the *fsck* continues in the background. This is a relatively new feature in FreeBSD, so you can turn it off in case you have problems with it. See page 554 for more details.

Next, */etc/rc* invokes the first of three network start invocations. This one initializes the interfaces, sets the routes and starts the firewall if necessary:

```
Doing initial network setup: hostname.
dc0: flags=8843<UP,BROADCAST,RUNNING,SIMPLEX,MULTICAST> mtu 1500
        inet 223.147.37.81 netmask 0xffffff00 broadcast 223.147.37.255
        inet6 fe80::280:c6ff:fef9:a6c8%dc0 prefixlen 64 scopeid 0x1
        ether 00:80:c6:f9:a6:c8
        media: autoselect (100baseTX <full-duplex>) status: active
        supported media: autoselect 100baseTX <full-duplex> 100baseTX 10baseT/UTP <f
ull-duplex> 10baseT/UTP 100baseTX <hw-loopback> none
lo0: flags=8049<UP,LOOPBACK,RUNNING,MULTICAST> mtu 16384
        inet 127.0.0.1 netmask 0xff000000

add net default: gateway 223.147.37.5
Additional routing options:.
routing daemons:.
```

In this example, there were no additional routing options and no routing daemons. The messages accordingly have nothing between the character : and the final period. You'll see this relatively frequently.

Next, */etc/rc* mounts the network file systems, cleans up */var/run* and then starts *syslogd*:

```
Mounting NFS file systems.
Additional daemons: syslogd.
```

Then it checks if we have a core dump. If so, it tries to save it to */var/crash*.

```
checking for core dump...savecore: no core dump
```

Saving the core dump may fail if there isn't enough space in */var/crash*. If this happens, you can clean up and save the dump later, as long as you haven't used enough swap space to overwrite the dump.

Next comes the second pass of the network startup, which starts our choice of *named*, *ntpdate*, *ntpd*, *timed*, *portmap*, *ypserv*, *rpc.ypxfrd*, *rpc.yppasswdd*, *ypbind*, *ypset*, *keyserv* and *rpc.ypupdated*:

```
Doing additional network setup: named xntpd portmap.
starting.   named 8.1.2 Sun May  9 13:04:13 CST 1999  grog@freebie.example.org:/usr
/obj/usr.sbin/named
master zone "example.org" (IN) loaded (serial 1997010902)
master zone "37.147.223.in-addr.arpa" (IN) loaded (serial 1996110801)
listening on [223.147.37.149].53 (ep0)
listening on [127.0.0.1].53 (lo0)
Forwarding source address is [0.0.0.0].1063
Ready to answer queries.
```

With the exception of the first line, all the messages come from *named*. They may come in the middle of the first line, rather than waiting for the end of the line.

Next, */etc/rc* enables quotas if asked, and then runs the third network pass, which starts our choice of *mountd*, *nfsd*, *rpc.lockd*, *rpc.statd*, *nfsiod*, *amd*, *rwhod* and *kerberos*:

```
Starting final network daemons: mountd nfsd rpc.statd nfsiod rwhod.
```

Now we're almost done. */etc/rc* rebuilds a couple of internal databases (for use by the *ps* command and some others), then it sets the default paths for *ldconfig*:

```
setting ELF ldconfig path: /usr/lib /usr/lib/compat /usr/X11R6/lib /usr/local/lib
setting a.out ldconfig path: /usr/lib/aout /usr/lib/compat/aout
/usr/X11R6/lib/aout
/usr/local/lib/aout
```

Next, it starts your choice of *inetd*, *cron*, *printer*, *sendmail* and *usbd*:

```
starting standard daemons: inetd cron sendmail.
```

The last thing that */etc/rc* does is to check for other startup files. These could be in the files specified in the variable local_startup, or in the file */etc/rc.local*. In our case, there are none, so all we see is:

```
Local package initialization:.
```

Finally, we're done. */etc/rc* stops, and *init* processes */etc/ttys*, which starts *getty* processes on specified terminals. On the console, we see:

```
Mon May 13 13:52:00 CST 2002

FreeBSD (freebie.example.org) (ttyv0)

login:
```

At this point, we're at the beginning of Chapter 7 (page 111).

Single-user mode

Sometimes it's inconvenient that multiple users can access the system. For example, if you're repartitioning a disk, you don't want other people walking all over the disk while you're doing so. Even if you're the only user on the system, daemons may be doing things in the background. To avoid this problem, you can stop the boot process before most of the daemons have been started and enter *single-user mode*. To do this, set the boot_single variable, or specify the -s flag at boot time:

```
ok boot -s
```

As soon as the device probes have been completed, the system startup is interrupted, and you are prompted for a shell. Only the root file system is accessible, and it is mounted read-only. The reason for this is that the file system may be damaged and require repair before you can write to it. If you do need to write to the root file system, you should first check the consistency of the file system with *fsck*, after which you can mount it with the -u (update) option. For example,

```
npx0 on motherboard
npx0: INT 16 interface                             end of the probes (high intensity display)
Enter pathname of shell or RETURN for sh:          hit Enter
erase ^H, kill ^U, intr ^C
# fsck -y /dev/ad0s1a                              check the integrity of the root file system
** /dev/ad0s1a
** Last Mounted on /
** Root file system
** Phase 1 - Check Blocks and Sizes
** Phase 2 - Check Pathnames
** Phase 3 - Check Connectivity
** Phase 4 - Check Reference Counts
** Phase 5 - Check Cyl groups
1064 files, 8190 used, 6913 free (61 frags, 1713 blocks, 0.4% fragmentation)
# mount -u /                                       remount root file system read/write
# mount /usr                                       mount any other file systems you need
```

To leave single-user mode and enter multi-user mode, just enter **Ctrl-D**:

```
# ^D
Skipping file system checks...
(the rest of the boot sequence)
```

System V and Linux have the concept of *run levels*, which are controlled by *init*. Single-user mode corresponds to run level 1 or S, and multi-user mode corresponds roughly to System V run level 3 or Linux run level 4. Nothing corresponds with the other System V run levels, in particular run level 2, which starts a System V system without networking.

Networking is such an integral part of FreeBSD that this is just not practicable. FreeBSD *init* now understands a syntax similar to the System V *init*. Table 29-1 shows the supported levels. For example, to read in the */etc/ttys* file, you could enter:

```
# init q
```

Table 29-1: init levels

Level	Signal	Action
0	SIGUSR2	Halt and turn the power off
1	SIGTERM	Go to single-user mode
6	SIGINT	Reboot the machine
c	SIGTSTP	Block further logins
q	SIGHUP	Rescan the ttys(5) file

You can also enter single-user mode from a running FreeBSD system with the *shutdown* command, which we'll look at in the next section.

Password protecting single-user mode

If you run a secure environment, you could be concerned about the fact that you can start up in single-user mode without entering a password. That's the default—normally, if somebody can access your system console, a password is no longer much use, and it can be a nuisance—but you can change it. Find this entry in */etc/ttys*, and change the word secure to insecure:

```
# If you want to be asked for password, change "secure" to "insecure" here
console none                                    unknown off insecure
```

If you do this, you will be in real trouble if you forget the root password.

Shutting down and rebooting the system

FreeBSD uses a number of sophisticated techniques to achieve its high performance. In particular, when you write data to a disk, the system doesn't put it on the disk immediately: it waits for more data to arrive, which reduces the number of disk accesses by up to several orders of magnitude and thus improves performance dramatically.

The result of turning power off before the data is written is equally dramatic. You may just lose the data, but if the data is information on a change in file system structure, your file system will be damaged. To check for this, the system runs a program called *fsck* (File System Check) at startup. *fsck* can repair minor damage, but it's obviously a better idea to avoid damage by ensuring that the system is shut down in an orderly way.

Never stop your machine by just turning off the power. The results could be devastating.

The correct way to shut a system down is with the *shutdown* command. To quote the man page *shutdown(8)*:

> Shutdown provides an automated shutdown procedure for super-users to nicely notify users when the system is shutting down, saving them from system administrators, hackers, and gurus, who would otherwise not bother with such niceties.

This command has a number of useful options:

- Use the -r option to reboot the computer. You sometimes need to do this, for example after installing a new kernel.

- Use the -h option to stop the machine. This isn't the default.

- Without an option, shutdown attempts to put the machine in single-user mode. This doesn't always work as well as booting in single-user mode.

- *shutdown* requires a time parameter to tell it when to actually perform the shutdown. This is useful in a multi-user environment, but normally you'll want to shut down immediately, so *shutdown* understands the keyword now.

In the normal case, where you want to stop the machine immediately so you can turn the power off, you type:

```
# shutdown -h now
Feb  4 12:38:36 freebie shutdown: halt by grog:
Feb  4 12:38:39 freebie syslogd: exiting on signal 15
syncing disks... done
The operating system has halted.
Please press any key to reboot.
```

Be sure to wait for this message before you turn off the power.

FreeBSD without disks

Disks are getting much cheaper and their capacity is continually increasing, so it's easy to think that there would never be a reason to want to run FreeBSD without a disk at all. Still, there are reasons:

- Disks are unreliable. For a machine that you want to keep running for a long time, the most likely hardware failure is a disk failure.

- Disks are noisy. There are places where you might not want the noise.

- Disks are sensitive. You may not want to place them in some environments.

- You may find systems administration easier if all the configuration files are in one place.

- The "sweet spot" for hard disk prices, the place where you get the most storage for your dollar, is currently around 80 GB, about 10 times what it was five years before. You may not want that much disk space for any one machine, but for a group, it might make more sense to have a disk for the whole group on one machine.

There are a number of ways to run a system without a disk. You can replace the disk with something else, such as a flash card, floppy disk or CD-ROM drive, or you can access a remote disk via a network. We'll consider network booting in the following section, and we'll look at the disk replacement strategy on page 549.

Network booting

Network booting is not a new idea. It was the original reason for Sun's *Network File System*, which we looked at in Chapters 24 and 25. Nowadays people normally use NFS for additional shared file systems; in the case of net booting, you mount your own private NFS file system as your root file system. Clearly, the first thing you need to do is to create this file system.

Next, you need to find a way to boot the system. There are a few possibilities here:

- You can boot a minimal system from floppy disk or CD-ROM and use this to mount the file systems remotely. This is different from running the system from floppy or CD-ROM: in this case, the disk device serves effectively as a bootstrap, and the operating system is located elsewhere.

- You can create a boot PROM for your network card and use that to boot.

- You can use PXE if your card supports it.

Whichever method you use, you need to set up a network interface very early. In Chapter 17 we saw that the network setup is part of the system initialization, and that the configuration is stored in */etc/rc.conf*. For a network boot, the network must be running before the kernel can be loaded, so that method won't work here. Instead, we use *DHCP*, which we looked at on page 302. We could also use the *bootpd* daemon, but it's more limited, so it's better to use *DHCP*.

If you use floppy or CD-ROM, you could theoretically load the bootstrap from that device. This isn't the same as the alternative we'll see on page 549, where we load the kernel from floppy or CD: here we only load the bootstrap and then load the kernel from the network. This minor difference has significant implications on the ease of system administration.

The next step is to actually transfer the data. We do this with *TFTP*, the *Trivial File Transfer Protocol*. As the name suggests, *TFTP* is a relatively simple replacement for *FTP*. In particular, it knows almost nothing about security. If you use *TFTP*, make sure that it can't be accessed from outside your network, for example by using a firewall. The default firewall rules block *TFTP*.

In the following sections we'll look at the example of setting up *bumble.example.org* as a diskless machine.

Setting up the file systems

There are a number of ways to put the files on the NFS server:

- You might copy the files in the root and */usr* file systems of the server machine.

- You could install FreeBSD on a separate disk and NFS mount it where the remote system can access it. By itself, this doesn't have much of an advantage over having a local disk on the machine, but it's possible to install a number of systems on a single disk and have different machines access the different installations.

- You could combine those two methods and copy a freshly installed system to a file system where you need it.

We'll look at refining this technique after the system is up and running.

Building a diskless kernel

You still need to build a special kernel for diskless workstations. The following entries in the configuration file are relevant:

```
# Kernel BOOTP support

options         BOOTP               # Use BOOTP to obtain IP address/hostname
options         BOOTP_NFSROOT       # NFS mount root filesystem using BOOTP info
options         BOOTP_NFSV3         # Use NFS v3 to NFS mount root
options         BOOTP_COMPAT        # Workaround for broken bootp daemons.
options         BOOTP_WIRED_TO=fxp0 # Use interface fxp0 for BOOTP
```

Only the first two are required. If you use BOOTP_WIRED_TO, make sure that the interface name matches the network card you are using.

Build the kernel, as described on page 616. To install, you need to set the DESTDIR variable to specify the directory in which you want to install the kernel:

```
# make install DESTDIR=/src/nodisk/bumble
```

Configuring TFTP

Next we need to set up *TFTP* to deliver the kernel to the system. The first question is whether the firmware on the Ethernet card can load the kernel directly or not. Some boot PROMs run in 16 bit 8086 mode, which limits their addressing capability to 640 kB. That's too small for any FreeBSD kernel, and if you try to load the kernel directly you'll get a message like this:

```
File transfer error: Image file too large for low memory.
```

In this case, you'll need to load a loader, such as *pxeboot*.

As a minor concession to security, the *tftpd* daemon refuses to access files outside its data directory hierarchy, which by convention is called */tftpboot*. You can use symbolic links, however. It makes more sense to have the kernel in the same place as on machines with disks, namely in */boot/kernel/kernel* on the root file system, so we create symbolic links:

```
# mkdir /tftpboot
# ln -s /src/nodisk/bumble/boot/kernel/kernel /tftpboot/kernel.bumble
# ln -s /boot/pxeboot /tftpboot/pxeboot
```

We also need to ensure that we can start the *TFTP* daemon, *tftpd*. Unless you're constantly booting, there's no need to have it running constantly: just enable it in */etc/inetd.conf*, which has the following entries in the distribution file:

```
#tftp   dgram   udp    wait    root    /usr/libexec/tftpd    tftpd -s /tftpboot
#tftp   dgram   udp6   wait    root    /usr/libexec/tftpd    tftpd -s /tftpboot
```

These are entries for IPv4 and IPv6 respectively. We enable *tftpd* by uncommenting the first line (removing the # character) and sending a HUP signal to *inetd*:

```
# killall -1 inetd
```
                                                    send a SIGHUP

Configuring DHCP

We already looked at *dhcpd*'s configuration file */usr/local/etc/dhcpd.conf* on page 302, In addition to the information we looked at there, we need to know what file to load, which system to load it from, and where the root file system is located. For our diskless system *bumble* we might add the text in bold to the configuration we saw on page 303:

```
subnet 223.147.37.0 netmask 255.255.255.0 {
    range 223.147.37.90 223.147.37.110;
    option domain-name-servers freebie.example.com, presto.example.com;
    option domain-name "example.com";
    option routers gw.example.com;
    option subnet-mask 255.255.255.0;
    option broadcast-address 223.147.37.255;
    default-lease-time 86400;
    max-lease-time 259200;
    host sydney {
        hardware ethernet 0:50:da:cf:7:35;
    }

    host bumble {
        hardware ethernet 0:50:da:cf:17:d3;
        next-server presto.example.com;           only if on a different machine
        filename "/tftpboot/bumble/kernel.bumble"; for direct booting
        filename "/tftpboot/pxeboot";              for PXE
        option root-path 223.147.37.1:/src/nodisk/bumble;
    }
}
```

There are a few things to note here:

- The `next-server` line tells where the *TFTP* server is located. If it's the same as the machine running the *DHCP* server, you don't need this specification.

- As we've seen, hardware restrictions may make it impossible to load the kernel directly. In this case you need to load a loader. The only one that FreeBSD currently supplies is *pxeboot*.[1] Choose one of the two `filename` lines.

- You have to specify the root path as an IP address, because no name services are available when the root file system is mounted.

Other Ethernet bootstraps

If your Ethernet card doesn't have a boot ROM, you can make one with the *net/etherboot* port, or you can copy the necessary information to a floppy disk or CD-R and use that to start the bootstrap. In either case, you first build the port and then copy the data to your selected medium. For example, to create a boot disk for a Compex RL2000 card, a 10 Mb/s PCI NE-2000 clone, you first look up the card in */usr/ports/net/etherboot/work/etherboot-5.0.5/src/NIC*, where you read:

```
# Compex RL2000
compexrl2000     ns8390              0x11f6,0x1401
```

This information is mainly for the build process; you just need to know the `compexrl2000`, which is the name of the driver.

```
# cd /usr/ports/net/etherboot
# make all
# cd work/ether*/src
# cat bin/boot1a.bin bin32/compexrl2000.lzrom > /dev/fd0
```

bin/boot1a.bin is a disk bootstrap intended to load and start *compexrl2000.lzrom*. You can also put *compexrl2000.lzrom* in an EPROM. This requires a little more care, and the information is subject to change. You can find detailed information about how to proceed at the web site *http://etherboot.sourceforge.net/doc/html/documentation.html*.

etherboot uses NFS, not TFTP. As a result, things change: you can use absolute path names, and you can't use symbolic links. An entry in *dhcpd.conf* for this method might look like this:

```
host bumble {
  hardware ethernet 00:80:48:e6:a0:61;
  filename "/src/nodisk/bumble/boot/kernel/kernel";
  fixed-address bumble.example.org;
  option root-path "192.109.197.82:/src/nodisk/bumble";
}
```

When booting in this manner, you don't see any boot messages. The boot loader outputs several screens full of periods, each indicating a downloaded block. It finishes like this:

---

1. See *http://www.freebsd.org/doc/en_US.ISO8859-1/articles/pxe/index.html* for documentation for setting up *pxeboot* on FreeBSD.

```
..............................done
.
```

After that, nothing appears on the screen for quite some time. In fact, the boot is proceeding normally, and the next thing you see is a login prompt.

Configuring the machine

Setting up a diskless machine is not too difficult, but there are some gotchas:

- Currently, locking across NFS does not work properly. As a result, you may see messages like this:

```
Dec 11 14:18:50 bumble sm-mta[141]: NOQUEUE: SYSERR(root): cannot flock(/var/run/
sendmail.pid, fd=6, type=2, omode=40001, euid=0): Operation not supported
```

One solution to this problem is to mount */var* as an MD (memory) file system. This is what currently happens by default, though it's subject to change: at startup, when the system detects that it is running diskless (via the sysctl vfs.nfs.disk-less_valid), it invokes the configuration file */etc/rc.diskless1*. This file in turn causes the file */etc/rc.diskless2* to be invoked later in the startup procedure. Each of these files adds an MD file system. In the course of time, this will be phased out and replaced by the traditional configuration via */etc/fstab*, but at the moment this file has no provision for creating MD file systems.

You should probably look at these files carefully: they may need some tailoring to your requirements.

- It is currently not possible to add swap on an NFS file system. *swapon* (usually invoked from the startup scripts) reports, incorrectly:

```
Dec 11 14:18:46 bumble savecore: 192.109.197.82:/src/nodisk/swap/bumble: No such
file or directory
```

This, too, will change; in the meantime, it *is* possible to mount swap on files, even if they are NFS mounted, but not on the NFS file system itself. This means that the first of the following entries in */etc/fstab* will not work, but the second will:

```
192.109.197.82:/src/nodisk/swap/bumble  none swap  sw        0       0
/src/nodisk/swap/bumble                 none swap  sw        0       0
echunga:/src           /src             nfs    rw             0       0
```

The reason here is the third line: */src/nodisk/swap/bumble* is NFS mounted, so this is a swap-to-file situation. For this to work, you may have to add the following line at the end of your */etc/rc.diskless2*:

```
swapon -a
```

This is because the standard system startup mounts swap before mounting additional NFS file systems. If you place the swap file on the root file system, it will still work, but frequently you will want the root file system to be read-only to be able to share it between several machines.

- If the machine panics, it's not possible to take a dump, because you have no disk. The only alternative would be a kernel debugger.

Sharing system files between multiple machines

In many cases, you may have a number of machines that you want to run diskless. If you have enough disk (one image for each machine), you don't have anything to worry about, but often it may be attractive to share the system files between them. There are a lot of things to consider here:

- Obviously, any changeable data specific to a system can't be shared.

- To ensure that things don't change, you should mount shared resources read-only.

- Refer to Table 32-1 on page 594 for an overview of FreeBSD installed directories. Of these directories, only */etc* and */usr/local/etc* must be specific for a particular system, though there are some other issues:

  - Installing ports, for example, will install ports for all systems. That's not necessarily a bad thing, but if you have two systems both installing software in the same directory, you can expect conflicts. It's better to designate one system, possibly the host with the disk, to perform these functions.

  - If you share */boot* and make some configuration changes, the options will apply to all systems.

  - When building system software, you can use the same */usr/src* and */usr/obj* directories as long as all systems maintain the same release of FreeBSD. You can even have different kernels: each kernel build directory carries the name of the configuration file, which by convention matches the name of the system.

The big problem is */etc*. In particular, */etc/rc.conf* contains information like the system name. One way to handle this is to have a separate */etc* directory for each system. This may seem reasonable, because */etc* is only about 1.5 MB in size. In fact, this implies mounting the entire root file system with the other top-level directories, and that means more like 60 MB.

Disk substitutes

The other alternative to network booting is to find a local substitute for the disk. This is obviously the only alternative for a stand-alone machine. There are a number of alternatives:

- For really small systems, you can use *PicoBSD*, a special small version of FreeBSD that fits on a single floppy disk. It requires a fair amount of memory as RAM disk, and obviously it's very limited.

  PicoBSD is good for some special applications. As the FreeBSD kernel grows, it's becoming more and more difficult to get even the kernel onto a single floppy, let alone any application software. Still, you can find a number of different configurations in the source tree in */usr/src/release/picobsd*. Be prepared for some serious configuration work.

- Alternatively, you can boot from CD-R or CD-ROM. In this case, you can have up to 700 MB of data, enough for a number of applications. It's possible to run programs directly from the CD, but there's little advantage to having files on CD instead of on disk. The most likely application for this alternative is for systems where the reliability of rotating media is insufficient, where the CD is used only for booting, and after that the system runs from RAM disk.

- Yet another alternative is *Flash memory*, often abbreviated simply as *Flash*, which we looked at in Chapter 8, on page 159. Flash is available in sizes up to several hundred megabytes, and Compact Flash cards look like disks to their interface. They don't fit IDE connectors, but adapters are available.

  Flash memory is intended mainly for reading. It is much slower to write than to read, and it can only take a certain number of write cycles before it fails. Clearly it's a candidate for read-only file systems.

30

FreeBSD
configuration files

One of the outstanding things about UNIX is that all system configuration information is stored in text files, usually in the directory */etc* or its subdirectories. Some people consider this method primitive by comparison with a flashy GUI configuration editor or a "registry," but it has significant advantages. In particular, you see the *exact* system configuration. With a GUI editor, the real configuration is usually stored in a format that you can't read, and even when you can, it's undocumented. Also, you can see more of the configuration at a time: a GUI editor usually presents you with only small parts of the configuration, and it's difficult to see the relationships ("standing outside and looking in through a window").

In the Microsoft world, one of the most common methods of problem resolution is to reinstall the system. This is a declaration of bankruptcy: it's very slow, you're liable to cause other problems on the way, and you never find out what the problem was. If you have problems with your FreeBSD system configuration, ***don't reinstall the system***. Take a look at the configuration files, and there's a good chance that you'll find the problem there.

Many configuration files are the same across all versions of UNIX. This chapter touches on them briefly, but in many case you can get additional information in books such as the *UNIX System Administration Handbook*, by Evi Nemeth, Garth Snyder, Scott Seebass, and Trent R. Hein. In all cases, you can get more information from section 5 of the man pages.

In the following section, we'll first look at */etc/rc.conf*, the main configuration file. We'll look at the remaining configuration files on page 566.

/etc/rc.conf

/etc/rc.conf is the main system configuration file. In older releases of FreeBSD, this file
was called */etc/sysconfig*.

/etc/rc.conf is a shell script that is intended to be the one file that defines the
configuration of your system—that is to say, what the system needs to do when it starts
up. It's not quite that simple, but nearly all site-dependent information is stored here.
We'll walk through the version that was current at the time of writing. The files will
change as time goes on, but most of the information will remain relevant.

/etc/rc.conf is completely your work. When you install the system, there is no such file:
you create it, usually implicitly with the aid of *sysinstall*. The system supplies a script
/etc/defaults/rc.conf that contains default values for everything you might put in
/etc/rc.conf, and which the other configuration files read to get their definitions. When
the system starts, it first reads */etc/defaults/rc.conf*. Commands at the end of this file
check for the existence of the file */etc/rc.conf* and read it in if they find it, so that the
definitions in */etc/rc.conf* override the defaults in */etc/defaults/rc.conf*. This makes it
easier to upgrade: just change the file with the defaults, and leave the site-specific
configuration alone. You may still need to change some things, but it'll be a lot easier.

In this section we'll walk through */etc/defaults/rc.conf*. As we do, we'll build up two
different */etc/rc.conf* files, one for a server and one for a laptop connected with an
802.11b wireless card. To avoid too much confusion, I show the text that goes into
/etc/rc.conf in **constant width bold** font, whereas the text in */etc/defaults/rc.conf* is
in constant width font.

```
#!/bin/sh
#
# This is rc.conf - a file full of useful variables that you can set
# to change the default startup behavior of your system.  You should
# not edit this file!  Put any overrides into one of the ${rc_conf_files}
# instead and you will be able to update these defaults later without
# spamming your local configuration information.
#
# The ${rc_conf_files} files should only contain values which override
# values set in this file.  This eases the upgrade path when defaults
# are changed and new features are added.
#
# All arguments must be in double or single quotes.
#
# $FreeBSD: src/etc/defaults/rc.conf,v 1.159 2002/09/05 20:14:40 gordon Exp $
```

The claim that all arguments must be in double or single quotes is incorrect. Both this
file and */etc/rc.conf* are Bourne shell scripts, and you only need quotes if the values you
include contain spaces. It's a good idea to stick to this convention, though, in case the
representation changes.

Note the version information on the previous line (1.159). Your */etc/defaults/rc.conf* will
almost certainly have a different revision. If you have a CVS repository on line (see
Chapter 31), you can see what is changed with the following commands:

```
$ cd /usr/src/etc/defaults
$ cvs diff -wu -r1.159 rc.conf
```

Continuing,

```
##############################################################
###  Important initial Boot-time options  ###################
##############################################################
rc_ng="YES"                      # Set to NO to disable new-style rc scripts.
rc_info="YES"                    # Enables display of informational messages at boot.
rcshutdown_timeout="30"          # Seconds to wait before terminating rc.shutdown
```

FreeBSD Release 5 has a new method of system startup, called *RCng* (run commands,
next generation). This method was originally introduced in NetBSD. Don't change these
values unless you know *exactly* what you are doing. If you make a mistake, you may find
it impossible to start the system.

```
swapfile="NO"                    # Set to name of swapfile if aux swapfile desired.
```

Normally you set up entries for swap partitions in */etc/fstab*. This entry refers only to
swapping on files, not for partitions. It requires the *md* driver, which we looked at on
page 245.

```
apm_enable="NO"                  # Set to YES to enable APM BIOS functions (or NO).
apmd_enable="NO"                 # Run apmd to handle APM event from userland.
apmd_flags=""                    # Flags to apmd (if enabled).
```

These parameters cover *APM, Advanced Power Management.*

```
devd_enable="NO"          # Run devd, to trigger programs on device tree changes.
pccard_enable="NO"        # Set to YES if you want to configure PCCARD devices.
pccard_mem="DEFAULT"      # If pccard_enable=YES, this is card memory address.
pccard_beep="2"           # pccard beep type.
pccard_ifconfig="NO"      # Specialized pccard ethernet configuration (or NO).
pccardd_flags="-z"        # Additional flags for pccardd.
pccard_conf="/etc/defaults/pccard.conf" # pccardd(8) config file
pccard_ether_delay="5"    # Delay before trying to start dhclient in pccard_ether
```

These parameters control *devd*, the *device daemon* used primarily for hot-pluggable
devices such as USB and PC Card, and *pccardd*, the daemon for the old PC Card code.
See page 159 for more details of *devd*, and page 161 for a brief description of *pccardd*
and the old PC Card code.

If you're running PC Card devices, you would start *devd*. That's what we put in the
/etc/rc.conf for *andante*:

```
devd_enable="YES"
```

Next comes a list of directories that are searched for startup scripts:

```
local_startup="/usr/local/etc/rc.d /usr/X11R6/etc/rc.d" # startup script dirs.
script_name_sep=" "              # Change if startup scripts' names contain spaces
```

If you come from a System V background, you would expect to find these scripts in the directories such as */etc/rc2.d*.

```
rc_conf_files="/etc/rc.conf /etc/rc.conf.local"
```

`rc_conf_files` is a list of files to read after this file. You'll recognize */etc/rc.conf*, which we discussed above. */etc/rc.conf.local* is an idea that hasn't completely died, but there's a good chance that it will. You'd be best off not to use it until you're sure it's going to stay.

For obvious reasons, this is one entry in */etc/defaults/rc.conf* that you can't override in */etc/rc.conf*. If you really want to search other files, you'll have to modify */etc/defaults/rc.conf*. It's still not a good idea.

```
fsck_y_enable="NO"          # Set to YES to fsck -y if the initial preen fails.
background_fsck="YES"       # Attempt to run fsck in the background
extra_netfs_types="NO"      # List of network extra filesystem types for delayed
                            # mount at startup (or NO).
```

On system startup, the system checks the integrity of all file systems. It does this in a number of steps:

- First, it checks the *superblock*, the key to the file system, to see whether it was unmounted before the system stopped. If so, it assumes that the file systems are consistent and continues with the startup.

- If any file system was not unmounted, the system probably crashed or was turned off without proper shutdown. The file system could contain inconsistent data, so the startup scripts run *fsck* against the file system.

- If you're running with soft updates and checkpointing, you may be able to perform the *fsck* in the *background*, in other words in parallel with other activities. If you have a good reason, you can inhibit this behaviour by setting `background_fsck` to NO.

- If the file system is badly damaged, the "standard strength" fsck may not be able to recover the file system. In this case, the normal action is to drop into single-user mode and let a human take a look at it.

The usual first action of the human is to run *fsck* with the -y option, meaning "answer *yes* to all questions from *fsck*". If you set `fsck_y_enable` to YES, the startup scripts will perform this task for you. It's still possible that the check will fail, so this is not enough to ensure that you will always pass *fsck*, but it helps.

```
##############################################################
###   Network configuration sub-section  ####################
##############################################################
### Basic network and firewall/security options: ###
hostname=""                     # Set this!
```

hostname is the fully qualified name of the host. Always set it in */etc/rc.conf*. See page 302 for more details. In our */etc/rc.conf* we'll put:

```
hostname="gw.example.org"
hostname="andante.example.org"
```

Continuing in */etc/defaults/rc.conf*,

```
nisdomainname="NO"                    # Set to NIS domain if using NIS (or NO).
```

If you're using Sun's NIS, set this. We don't discuss NIS in this book.

```
dhcp_program="/sbin/dhclient"    # Path to dhcp client program.
dhcp_flags=""                    # Additional flags to pass to dhcp client.
```

The settings for the *DHCP* client, *dhclient*. Normally you won't need to change them. We talked about *DHCP* on page 302.

```
firewall_enable="NO"             # Set to YES to enable firewall functionality
firewall_script="/etc/rc.firewall" # Which script to run to set up the firewall
firewall_type="UNKNOWN"          # Firewall type (see /etc/rc.firewall)
firewall_quiet="NO"              # Set to YES to suppress rule display
firewall_logging="NO"            # Set to YES to enable events logging
```

Parameters for the *ipfw* firewall. See page 389, where we set the following flags in the */etc/rc.conf* for *gw*:

```
firewall_enable="YES"            # Set to YES to enable firewall functionality
firewall_type="client"           # Firewall type (see /etc/rc.firewall)
```

You don't normally run firewalls on laptops, though there's no technical reason why not. The problem with firewalls on laptops is that the configuration files are dependent on where the system is located, which makes it a pain for systems that frequently change locations. As a result, we won't add any firewall parameters to the */etc/rc.conf* for *andante*.

```
ip_portrange_first="NO"          # Set first dynamically allocated port
ip_portrange_last="NO"           # Set last dynamically allocated port
```

These values are used to set the numbers of ports that are dynamically allocated. Normally they won't need changing.

```
ipsec_enable="NO"                # Set to YES to run setkey on ipsec_file
ipsec_file="/etc/ipsec.conf"     # Name of config file for setkey
```

Parameters for IPSec. We don't discuss IPSec in this book.

```
natd_program="/sbin/natd"        # path to natd, if you want a different one.
natd_enable="NO"                 # Enable natd (if firewall_enable == YES).
natd_interface=""                # Public interface or IPaddress to use.
natd_flags=""                    # Additional flags for natd.
```

Parameters for *natd*. See page 395 for more details. In the example there, we'll add
these lines to *gw*'s */etc/rc.conf*:

```
firewall_enable=YES
gateway_enable="YES"            # Set to YES if this host is a gateway.
natd_enable="YES"
natd_interface="dc0"
firewall_script="/etc/rc.nat"   # script for NAT only
firewall_type="client"          # firewall type if running a firewall
```

Continuing with */etc/defaults/rc.conf*,

```
ipfilter_enable="NO"            # Set to YES to enable ipfilter functionality
ipfilter_program="/sbin/ipf"    # where the ipfilter program lives
ipfilter_rules="/etc/ipf.rules" # rules definition file for ipfilter, see
                                # /usr/src/contrib/ipfilter/rules for examples
ipfilter_flags=""               # additional flags for ipfilter
ipnat_enable="NO"               # Set to YES to enable ipnat functionality
ipnat_program="/sbin/ipnat"     # where the ipnat program lives
ipnat_rules="/etc/ipnat.rules"  # rules definition file for ipnat
ipnat_flags=""                  # additional flags for ipnat
ipmon_enable="NO"               # Set to YES for ipmon; needs ipfilter or ipnat
ipmon_program="/sbin/ipmon"     # where the ipfilter monitor program lives
ipmon_flags="-Ds"               # typically "-Ds" or "-D /var/log/ipflog"
ipfs_enable="NO"                # Set to YES to enable saving and restoring
                                # of state tables at shutdown and boot
ipfs_program="/sbin/ipfs"       # where the ipfs program lives
ipfs_flags=""                   # additional flags for ipfs
```

These entries define defaults for *ipfilter*, another firewall package, *ipnat*, another NAT
package, *ipmon*, an IP monitor package, and *ipfs*, a utility for saving the state tables of
ipfilter, *ipnat* and *ipfilter*. We don't discuss any of them in this book.

```
tcp_extensions="NO"             # Disallow RFC1323 extensions (or YES).
log_in_vain="0"                 # >=1 to log connects to ports w/o listeners.
tcp_keepalive="YES"             # Enable stale TCP connection timeout (or NO).
# For the following option you need to have TCP_DROP_SYNFIN set in your
# kernel.  Please refer to LINT and NOTES for details.
tcp_drop_synfin="NO"            # Set to YES to drop TCP packets with SYN+FIN
                                # NOTE: this violates the TCP specification
icmp_drop_redirect="NO"         # Set to YES to ignore ICMP REDIRECT packets
icmp_log_redirect="NO"          # Set to YES to log ICMP REDIRECT packets
```

These are some of the more obscure IP configuration variables. You can find more about
them in *tcp(4)* and *icmp(4)*.

```
network_interfaces="auto"       # List of network interfaces (or "auto").
cloned_interfaces=""            # List of cloned network interfaces to create.
#cloned_interfaces="gif0 gif1 gif2 gif3" # Pre-cloning GENERIC config.
ifconfig_lo0="inet 127.0.0.1"   # default loopback device configuration.
#ifconfig_lo0_alias0="inet 127.0.0.254 netmask 0xffffffff" # Sample alias entry.
#ifconfig_ed0_ipx="ipx 0x00010010"  # Sample IPX address family entry.
```

In previous releases of FreeBSD, you had to set network_interfaces to a list of the
interfaces on the machine. Nowadays the value auto enables the startup scripts to find
them by themselves, so you don't need to change this variable. You still need to set the
interface addresses, of course. For *gw*, we add the following entry to */etc/rc.conf*:

```
ifconfig_ed0="inet 223.147.37.5    netmask 255.255.255.0"
```

We don't need to do anything here for *andante*: its Ethernet interface is a PC Card card. We looked at that on page 304.

If you're using DHCP, you don't have an address to specify, of course. You still need to tell the startup scripts to use DHCP, however. Do it like this:

```
ifconfig_ed0="DHCP"
```

Continuing,

```
# If you have any sppp(4) interfaces above, you might also want to set
# the following parameters.  Refer to spppcontrol(8) for their meaning.
sppp_interfaces=""              # List of sppp interfaces.
#sppp_interfaces="isp0"         # example: sppp over ISDN
#spppconfig_isp0="authproto=chap myauthname=foo myauthsecret='top secret' hisauthnam
e=some-gw hisauthsecret='another secret'"
gif_interfaces="NO"             # List of GIF tunnels (or "NO").
#gif_interfaces="gif0 gif1"     # Examples typically for a router.
                                # Choose correct tunnel addrs.
#gifconfig_gif0="10.1.1.1 10.1.2.1"     # Examples typically for a router.
#gifconfig_gif1="10.1.1.2 10.1.2.2"     # Examples typically for a router.
```

These are parameters for the *sppp* implementation for *isdn4bsd* and the *Generic Tunnel Interface*, both of which we won't discuss here. See the man pages *spp(4)* and *gif(4)* for more details.

```
# User ppp configuration.
ppp_enable="NO"                 # Start user-ppp (or NO).
ppp_mode="auto"                 # Choice of "auto", "ddial", "direct" or "dedicated".
                                # For details see man page for ppp(8). Default is auto.
ppp_nat="YES"                   # Use PPP's internal network address translation or NO.
ppp_profile="papchap"           # Which profile to use from /etc/ppp/ppp.conf.
ppp_user="root"                 # Which user to run ppp as
```

These parameters relate to running user PPP, which we discussed in Chapter 20, on page 348.

```
### Network daemon (miscellaneous) ###
syslogd_enable="YES"            # Run syslog daemon (or NO).
syslogd_program="/usr/sbin/syslogd" # path to syslogd, if you want a different one.
syslogd_flags="-s"              # Flags to syslogd (if enabled).
#syslogd_flags="-ss"            # Syslogd flags to not bind an inet socket
```

You should always run syslogd unless you have a very good reason not to. In previous releases of FreeBSD, syslogd_flags was empty, but security concerns have changed that, and now by default *syslogd* is started with the −s flag, which stops *syslogd* from accepting remote messages. If you specify the −ss flag, as suggested in the comment, you will also not be able to log to remote systems.

Sometimes it's very useful to log to a remote system. For example, you might want all systems in *example.org* to log to *gw*. That way you get one set of log files for the entire network. To do this, you would add the following line at the beginning of */etc/syslog.conf* on each machine:

```
*.*                                           @gw
```

For this to work, add the following to */etc/rc.conf* on *gw*:

```
syslogd_flags=""
```

Next come some parameters relating to *inetd*, the *Internet Daemon*, sometimes called the *super-server*. It's responsible for starting services on behalf of remote clients.

```
inetd_enable="NO"              # Run the network daemon dispatcher (YES/NO).
inetd_program="/usr/sbin/inetd" # path to inetd, if you want a different one.
inetd_flags="-wW"              # Optional flags to inetd
```

We looked at *inetd* on page 448. Normally you will want to have it enabled, but you won't need to change the flags. Add this line to the */etc/rc.conf* for both *gw* and *andante*:

```
inetd_enable="YES"
```

Continuing, we see:

```
named_enable="NO"              # Run named, the DNS server (or NO).
named_program="/usr/sbin/named" # path to named, if you want a different one.
#named_flags="-u bind -g bind"  # Flags for named
```

These parameters specify whether we should run the name server, and what flags we should use if we do. See page 366 for more details. Previous versions of *named* required a flag to specify the location of the configuration file, but the location FreeBSD uses has now become the standard, so we no longer need to specify any flags. All we put in */etc/rc.conf* for *gw* is:

```
named_enable="YES"                       # Run named, the DNS server (or NO).
```

Continuing with */etc/defaults/rc.conf*,

```
kerberos4_server_enable="NO"          # Run a kerberos IV master server (or NO).
kerberos4_server="/usr/sbin/kerberos" # path to kerberos IV KDC
kadmind4_server_enable="NO"           # Run kadmind (or NO)
kadmind4_server="/usr/sbin/kadmind"   # path to kerberos IV admin daemon
kerberos5_server_enable="NO"          # Run a kerberos 5 master server (or NO).
kerberos5_server="/usr/libexec/kdc"   # path to kerberos 5 KDC
kadmind5_server_enable="NO"           # Run kadmind (or NO)
kadmind5_server="/usr/libexec/k5admind" # path to kerberos 5 admin daemon
kerberos_stash="NO"                   # Is the kerberos master key stashed?
```

Set these if you want to run Kerberos. We don't discuss Kerberos in this book.

```
rwhod_enable="NO"              # Run the rwho daemon (or NO).
rwhod_flags=""                 # Flags for rwhod
```

Set this if you want to run the *rwhod* daemon, which broadcasts information about the system load.

```
rarpd_enable="NO"               # Run rarpd (or NO).
rarpd_flags=""                  # Flags to rarpd.
bootparamd_enable="NO"          # Run bootparamd (or NO).
bootparamd_flags=""             # Flags to bootparamd
xtend_enable="NO"               # Run the X-10 power controller daemon.
xtend_flags=""                  # Flags to xtend (if enabled).
```

These entries relate to the *rarpd*, *bootparamd* and the X-10 daemons, which we don't discuss in this book. See the respective man pages.

```
pppoed_enable="NO"              # Run the PPP over Ethernet daemon.
pppoed_provider="*"             # Provider and ppp(8) config file entry.
pppoed_flags="-P /var/run/pppoed.pid"   # Flags to pppoed (if enabled).
pppoed_interface="fxp0"         # The interface that pppoed runs on.
```

pppoed is the *PPP Over Ethernet* daemon. We discussed it briefly on page 348.

```
sshd_enable="NO"                # Enable sshd
sshd_program="/usr/sbin/sshd"   # path to sshd, if you want a different one.
sshd_flags=""                   # Additional flags for sshd.
```

sshd is the *Secure Shell Daemon* which we talked about on page 453. You don't need to change anything here to run *ssh*, but if you want to connect to this system with *ssh*, you'll need to run *sshd*. In *gw*'s */etc/rc.conf* we put:

sshd_enable="YES"

Next, we see:

```
amd_enable="NO"                 # Run amd service with $amd_flags (or NO).
amd_flags="-a /.amd_mnt -l syslog /host /etc/amd.map /net /etc/amd.map"
amd_map_program="NO"            # Can be set to "ypcat -k amd.master"
```

These entries relate to the automounter, which we don't discuss in this book. See *amd(8)* for details.

```
nfs_client_enable="NO"          # This host is an NFS client (or NO).
nfs_access_cache="2"            # Client cache timeout in seconds
nfs_server_enable="NO"          # This host is an NFS server (or NO).
nfs_server_flags="-u -t -n 4"   # Flags to nfsd (if enabled).
mountd_enable="NO"              # Run mountd (or NO).
mountd_flags="-r"               # Flags to mountd (if NFS server enabled).
weak_mountd_authentication="NO" # Allow non-root mount requests to be served.
nfs_reserved_port_only="NO"     # Provide NFS only on secure port (or NO).
nfs_bufpackets="DEFAULT"        # bufspace (in packets) for client (or DEFAULT)
rpc_lockd_enable="NO"           # Run NFS rpc.lockd needed for client/server.
rpc_statd_enable="NO"           # Run NFS rpc.statd needed for client/server.
rpcbind_enable="NO"             # Run the portmapper service (YES/NO).
rpcbind_program="/usr/sbin/rpcbind" # path to rpcbind, if you want a different one.
rpcbind_flags=""                # Flags to rpcbind (if enabled).
rpc_ypupdated_enable="NO"       # Run if NIS master and SecureRPC (or NO).
```

These are flags for NFS. Some of them have changed from previous releases of FreeBSD. In particular, single_mountd_enable is now called mountd_enable, and *portmap* has been replaced by *rpcbind*, so portmap_enable is now called rpcbind_enable, portmap_program is now called rpcbind_program and `portmap_flag` is now called `rpcbind_flags`. See page 441. We set the following values in */etc/rc.conf* for *gw*:

```
nfs_client_enable="YES"         # This host is an NFS client (or NO).
nfs_server_enable="YES"         # This host is an NFS server (or NO).
```

For *andante*, we enable only the client (the first line). Next, we see:

```
keyserv_enable="NO"             # Run the SecureRPC keyserver (or NO).
keyserv_flags=""                # Flags to keyserv (if enabled).
```

These entries refer to the Secure RPC key server, which we don't discuss in this book. See the man pages *keyserv(8)* for more details.

```
### Network Time Services options: ###
timed_enable="NO"               # Run the time daemon (or NO).
timed_flags=""                  # Flags to timed (if enabled).
ntpdate_enable="NO"             # Run ntpdate to sync time on boot (or NO).
ntpdate_program="/usr/sbin/ntpdate"  # path to ntpdate, if you want a different one.
ntpdate_flags="-b"              # Flags to ntpdate (if enabled).
ntpd_enable="NO"                # Run ntpd Network Time Protocol (or NO).
ntpd_program="/usr/sbin/ntpd"   # path to ntpd, if you want a different one.
ntpd_flags="-p /var/run/ntpd.pid"   # Flags to ntpd (if enabled).
```

timed, *ntpdate* and *ntpd* are three different ways of synchronizing your machine with the current date and time. As we saw on page 155, we'll use *ntpd*. We add the following line to */etc/rc.conf* for each system:

```
ntpd_enable="YES"               # Run ntpd Network Time Protocol (or NO).
```

Continuing with */etc/defaults/rc.conf*,

```
# Network Information Services (NIS) options: All need rpcbind_enable="YES" ###
nis_client_enable="NO"          # We're an NIS client (or NO).
nis_client_flags=""             # Flags to ypbind (if enabled).
nis_ypset_enable="NO"           # Run ypset at boot time (or NO).
nis_ypset_flags=""              # Flags to ypset (if enabled).
nis_server_enable="NO"          # We're an NIS server (or NO).
nis_server_flags=""             # Flags to ypserv (if enabled).
nis_ypxfrd_enable="NO"          # Run rpc.ypxfrd at boot time (or NO).
nis_ypxfrd_flags=""             # Flags to rpc.ypxfrd (if enabled).
nis_yppasswdd_enable="NO"       # Run rpc.yppasswdd at boot time (or NO).
nis_yppasswdd_flags=""          # Flags to rpc.yppasswdd (if enabled).
```

More parameters for configuring NIS. As mentioned above, this book does not deal with NIS.

```
### Network routing options: ###
defaultrouter="NO"              # Set to default gateway (or NO).
static_routes=""                # Set to static route list (or leave empty).
gateway_enable="NO"             # Set to YES if this host will be a gateway.
```

See page 309 for more information on routing. On *gw* we add the following line to */etc/rc.conf*:

```
defaultrouter="139.130.136.133"  # Set to default gateway (or NO).
gateway_enable="YES"             # Set to YES if this host will be a gateway.
```

andante gets its routing information from *DHCP*, so we don't need to do anything here.

```
router_enable="NO"           # Set to YES to enable a routing daemon.
router="/sbin/routed"        # Name of routing daemon to use if enabled.
router_flags="-q"            # Flags for routing daemon.
mrouted_enable="NO"          # Do multicast routing (see /etc/mrouted.conf).
mrouted_flags=""             # Flags for multicast routing daemon.
```

These parameters relate to the routing daemons *routed* and *mrouted*. In the configurations we considered, you don't need them.

```
ipxgateway_enable="NO"       # Set to YES to enable IPX routing.
ipxrouted_enable="NO"        # Set to YES to run the IPX routing daemon.
ipxrouted_flags=""           # Flags for IPX routing daemon.
```

IPX is a Novell proprietary networking protocol designed to be similar to IP. FreeBSD supplies the daemon *IPXrouted* (note the capitalization) which handles IPX routing tables. See the man page *IPXrouted(8)* for further details.

```
arpproxy_all="NO"            # replaces obsolete kernel option ARP_PROXYALL.
forward_sourceroute="NO"     # do source routing
accept_sourceroute="NO"      # accept source routed packets to us
### ATM interface options: ###
atm_enable="NO"              # Configure ATM interfaces (or NO).
#atm_netif_hea0="atm 1"      # Network interfaces for physical interface.
#atm_sigmgr_hea0="uni31"     # Signalling manager for physical interface.
#atm_prefix_hea0="ILMI"      # NSAP prefix (UNI interfaces only) (or ILMI).
#atm_macaddr_hea0="NO"       # Override physical MAC address (or NO).
#atm_arpserver_atm0="0x47.0005.80.999999.9999.9999.9999.999999999999.00"
#atm_scsparp_atm0="NO"       # Run SCSP/ATMARP on network interface (or NO).
atm_pvcs=""                  # Set to PVC list (or leave empty).
atm_arps=""                  # Set to permanent ARP list (or leave empty).
### ISDN interface options: (see also: /usr/share/examples/isdn) ###
isdn_enable="NO"             # Enable the ISDN subsystem (or NO).
isdn_fsdev="NO"              # Output device for fullscreen mode
isdn_flags="-dn -d0x1f9"     # Flags for isdnd
isdn_ttype="cons25"          # terminal type for fullscreen mode
isdn_screenflags="NO"        # screenflags for ${isdn_fsdev}
isdn_trace="NO"              # Enable the ISDN trace subsystem (or NO).
isdn_traceflags="-f /var/tmp/isdntrace0"  # Flags for isdntrace
```

A few miscellaneous IP options and parameters for ATM and ISDN. This book doesn't discuss any of them.

```
### Miscellaneous network options: ###
icmp_bmcastecho="NO"         # respond to broadcast ping packets
```

This parameter relates to the so-called *smurf* "denial of service" attack: according to the RFCs, a machine should respond to a ping to its broadcast address. But what happens if somebody pings a remote network's broadcast address across the Internet, as fast as he can? Each system on the remote network will reply, completely overloading the outgoing Internet interface. Yes, this is silly, but there are silly people out there. If you leave this parameter as it is, your system will not be vulnerable. See *http://www.cert.org/advisories/CA-98.01.smurf.html* for more details.

Next come a large number of options for *IPv6*, the new Internet protocol standard. This book doesn't deal with IPv6, and they're liable to change, so they're not printed here. Next, we find:

```
###########################################################
### System console options ###############################
###########################################################
keymap="NO"                     # keymap in /usr/share/syscons/keymaps/*
keyrate="NO"                    # keyboard rate to: slow, normal, fast
keybell="NO"                    # bell to duration.pitch or normal or visual
keychange="NO"                  # function keys default values
cursor="NO"                     # cursor type {normal|blink|destructive}
scrnmap="NO"                    # screen map in /usr/share/syscons/scrnmaps/*
font8x16="NO"                   # font 8x16 from /usr/share/syscons/fonts/*
font8x14="NO"                   # font 8x14 from /usr/share/syscons/fonts/*
font8x8="NO"                    # font 8x8 from /usr/share/syscons/fonts/*
blanktime="300"                 # blank time (in seconds) or "NO" to turn it off.
saver="NO"                      # screen saver: Uses /boot/kernel/${saver}_saver.ko
```

These parameters describe the use of alternate keyboard mappings when using the standard character-based terminals only. See the files in */usr/share/syscons/keymaps* for key map files, and */usr/share/syscons/fonts* for alternate fonts. These parameters have no effect on the X-based displays that this book assumes. You can enable a screen saver by setting the variable saver to YES.

```
moused_enable="NO"              # Run the mouse daemon.
moused_type="auto"             # See man page for available settings.
moused_port="/dev/psm0"        # Set to your mouse port.
moused_flags=""                 # Any additional flags to moused.
mousechar_start="NO"            # if 0xd0-0xd3 default range is occuped in your
                                # language code table, specify alternative range
allscreens_flags=""             # Set this vidcontrol mode for all virtual screens
allscreens_kbdflags=""          # Set this kbdcontrol mode for all virtual screens
```

Parameters for *moused*, a mouse driver for the character-based terminals, and global flags for virtual screens. If you're using an X server, you should run *moused*. On *andante*, we add this line to */etc/rc.conf* :

moused_enable="YES"

Next follow some definitions for the alternative console driver *pcvt*, which we don't look at here, followed by a section describing the mail configuration:

```
###########################################################
### Mail Transfer Agent (MTA) options ####################
###########################################################
mta_start_script="/etc/rc.sendmail"
                                # Script to start your chosen MTA
# Settings for /etc/rc.sendmail:
sendmail_enable="NO"            # Run the sendmail inbound daemon (YES/NO).
sendmail_flags="-L sm-mta -bd -q30m" # Flags to sendmail (as a server)
sendmail_submit_enable="YES"    # Start a localhost-only MTA for mail submission
sendmail_submit_flags="-L sm-mta -bd -q30m -ODaemonPortOptions=Addr=localhost"
                                # Flags for localhost-only MTA
sendmail_outbound_enable="YES"  # Dequeue stuck mail (YES/NO).
sendmail_outbound_flags="-L sm-queue -q30m" # Flags to sendmail (outbound only)
sendmail_msp_queue_enable="YES" # Dequeue stuck clientmqueue mail (YES/NO).
sendmail_msp_queue_flags="-L sm-msp-queue -Ac -q30m"
```

Since FreeBSD Release 5, the *sendmail* MTA is no longer enabled by default. If you have been running *sendmail* on an older release of FreeBSD, add an entry to */etc/rc.conf* to keep it running.

```
##############################################################
###  Miscellaneous administrative options  #################
##############################################################
cron_enable="YES"               # Run the periodic job daemon.
cron_program="/usr/sbin/cron"   # Which cron executable to run (if enabled).
cron_flags=""                   # Which options to pass to the cron daemon.
```

Run *cron*, the daemon responsible for running things at specific times. See page 151 for a description of *cron*. Leave this enabled unless you have a good reason not to.

```
lpd_enable="NO"                 # Run the line printer daemon.
lpd_program="/usr/sbin/lpd"     # path to lpd, if you want a different one.
lpd_flags=""                    # Flags to lpd (if enabled).
```

See page 263 for a discussion of printing. In older releases of FreeBSD, lpd_enable was set to YES. Now, to run *lpd*, we need to put the following line in */etc/rc.conf* for both *gw* and *adagio*:

```
lpd_enable="YES"                # Run the line printer daemon.
```

Next, we see:

```
usbd_enable="NO"                # Run the usbd daemon.
usbd_flags=""                   # Flags to usbd (if enabled).
```

Run *usbd*, the *Universal Serial Bus* or *USB* daemon. See the man pages *usbd(8)* and *usb(4)* for more information.

```
dumpdev="NO"                    # Device name to crashdump to (if enabled).
dumpdir="/var/crash"            # Directory where crash dumps are to be stored
savecore_flags=""               # Used if dumpdev is enabled above, and present.
```

These parameters specify how to take dumps when the system panics. See page 83 for details. As mentioned there, it is preferable to set this value in */boot/loader.conf*: that way you can still get a dump if your system panics before reading */etc/rc.conf*, so we don't change anything here.

Continuing with */etc/defaults/rc.conf*,

```
enable_quotas="NO"              # turn on quotas on startup
check_quotas="YES"              # Check quotas on startup
accounting_enable="NO"          # Turn on process accounting
ibcs2_enable="NO"               # Ibcs2 (SCO) emulation loaded at startup
ibcs2_loaders="coff"            # List of additional Ibcs2 loaders
sysvipc_enable="NO"             # Load System V IPC primitives at startup
linux_enable="NO"               # Linux binary compatibility loaded at startup
svr4_enable="NO"                # SysVR4 emulation loaded at startup
osf1_enable="NO"                # Alpha OSF/1 emulation loaded at startup
```

We don't discuss quotas or accounting in this book. We looked at the parameters *ibcs2_enable* on page 164 and *linux_enable* on page 163. We also don't discuss System V and OSF-1 emulation.

```
clear_tmp_enable="NO"                    # Clear /tmp at startup.
```

In the old days, the startup sequence automatically deleted everything in the file system */tmp*. Sometimes this wasn't desirable, so now it's your choice. Change this value to YES if you want the old behaviour.

Note that if you use a */tmp* based on MFS (memory file system), this variable has no effect. The contents of MFS file systems disappear on reboot.

```
ldconfig_insecure="NO"                   # Set to YES to disable ldconfig security checks
ldconfig_paths="/usr/lib/compat /usr/X11R6/lib /usr/local/lib"
                                         # shared library search paths
ldconfig_paths_aout="/usr/lib/compat/aout /usr/X11R6/lib/aout /usr/local/lib/aout"
                                         # a.out shared library search paths
```

ldconfig maintains the dynamic library cache required for finding libraries when starting most processes. Potentially this can be a security issue, and *ldconfig* makes a number of security checks before accepting libraries. If you really want to, you can disable these checks by setting *ldconfig_insecure*. The two other variables are lists of the directories that are searched to find *ELF* and *a.out* dynamic libraries, respectively. See page 636 for more details. You would normally not remove anything from these lists, but you might want to add something.

```
kern_securelevel_enable="NO"             # kernel security level (see init(8)),
kern_securelevel="-1"                    # range: -1..3 ; '-1' is the most insecure
update_motd="YES"                        # update version info in /etc/motd (or NO)
```

The kernel runs with five different levels of security. Any super-user process can raise the security level, but only *init* can lower it. The security levels are:

-1. Permanently insecure mode: always run the system in level 0 mode. This is the default initial value.

0. Insecure mode: the immutable and append-only flags may be turned off. All devices may be read or written subject to their permissions.

1. Secure mode: the immutable and append-only flags may not be turned off. Disks for mounted filesystems, */dev/mem* and */dev/kmem* may not be opened for writing.

2. Highly secure mode. This is the same as secure mode with the addition that disks may not be opened for writing (except by *mount(2)*), whether or not they are mounted. This level precludes tampering with filesystems by unmounting them, but it also prevents running *newfs(8)* while the system is multi-user.

3. Network secure mode. This is the same as highly secure mode with the addition that IP packet filter rules (see page 389) can not be changed and dummynet configuration can not be adjusted. We don't discuss dummynet in this book.

To set the secure level to anything except -1, set the variable `kern_securelevel` to the value you want, and set `kern_securelevel_enable` to YES.

```
start_vinum="NO"                    # set to YES to start vinum
```

We looked at *Vinum* on page 221. There we put the following text into */etc/rc.conf* to start it on booting:

```
start_vinum="YES"                   # set to YES to start vinum
```

Finally we have a few miscellaneous entries:

```
unaligned_print="YES"        # print unaligned access warnings on the alpha
entropy_file="/entropy"      # Set to NO disables caching entropy through reboots
entropy_dir="/var/db/entropy"# Set to NO to disable caching entropy via cron.
entropy_save_sz="2048"       # Size of the entropy cache files.
entropy_save_num="8"         # Number of entropy cache files to save.
harvest_interrupt="YES"      # Entropy device harvests interrupt randomness
harvest_ethernet="YES"       # Entropy device harvests ethernet randomness
harvest_p_to_p="YES"         # Entropy device harvests point-to-point randomness
dmesg_enable="YES"           # Save dmesg(8) to /var/run/dmesg.boot
```

`unaligned_print` is a diagnostic tool for the Alpha processor; there's a good chance it will go away. `dmesg_enable` saves the boot messages to the file */var/run/dmesg.boot*. Leave it this way; the messages are often useful for reference, and after a certain number of messages, they get flushed from the kernel internal message buffer.

The other messages are used for configuring entropy harvesting for the *random number devices*, */dev/random* and */dev/urandom*. See *random(4)* for further details. Under normal circumstances you shouldn't change them.

Our /etc/rc.conf

To summarize the changes from the defaults, */etc/rc.conf* for *gw* should now contain the following entries:

```
hostname="gw.example.org"
firewall_enable="YES"           # Set to YES to enable firewall functionality
firewall_type="client"          # Firewall type (see /etc/rc.firewall)
natd_enable="YES"               # Enable natd (if firewall_enable == YES).
natd_interface="tun0"           # Public interface or IPaddress to use.
syslogd_flags=""                # Allow logging from other systems
inetd_enable="YES"              # Run inetd
named_enable="YES"              # Run named, the DNS server (or NO).
sshd_enable="YES"               # Enable sshd
nfs_client_enable="YES"         # This host is an NFS client (or NO).
nfs_server_enable="YES"         # This host is an NFS server (or NO).
ntpd_enable="YES"               # Run ntpd Network Time Protocol (or NO).
defaultrouter="139.130.136.133" # Set to default gateway (or NO).
gateway_enable="YES"            # Set to YES if this host will be a gateway.
lpd_enable="YES"                # Run the line printer daemon.
start_vinum="YES"               # set to YES to start vinum
```

The corresponding */etc/rc.conf* for *andante* should now contain the following entries:

```
hostname="andante.example.org"
inetd_enable="YES"              # Run inetd
nfs_client_enable="YES"         # This host is an NFS client (or NO).
ntpd_enable="YES"               # Run ntpd Network Time Protocol (or NO).
moused_enable="YES"             # Run the mouse daemon
lpd_enable="YES"                # Run the line printer daemon.
start_vinum="YES"               # set to YES to start vinum
```

Files you need to change

rc.conf is only part of the story, of course. The */etc* directory contains a large number of other files, nearly all of them relating to the configuration. Some of them, like */etc/amd.map* and */etc/dm.conf*, are intended for specific subsystems that we don't discuss here. In general, they have comments in them to explain their purpose, and they have a man page in section 5 of the manual.

Most of the files in */etc* are intended to be left the way they are. Some, however, will definitely need changing, and there are others that you may need to change. In this section we'll look at the ones you almost certainly need to change, and on page 568 we'll look at the ones you may have to change. On page 576 we'll look at the some of the more interesting ones you should normally leave alone.

/etc/exports

/etc/exports is a list of file systems that should be NFS exported. We looked at it on page 463. See also the man page *exports(5)*.

/etc/fstab

/etc/fstab contains a list of file systems known to the system. The script */etc/rc* starts *mount* twice during system startup first to mount the local file systems, and later to mount the NFS file system. *mount* will mount all file systems in */etc/fstab* unless they are explicitly excluded.

Here's a typical */etc/fstab*, from host *freebie.example.org*:

```
# File system     Mount point             fstype  flags
/dev/ad0s1a       /                       ufs     rw              1 1
/dev/ad0s1b       none                    swap    sw              0 0
/dev/ad0s1e       /usr                    ufs     rw              2 2
/dev/da0b         none                    swap    sw              0 0
/dev/da0h         /src                    ufs     rw              2 2
/dev/da1h         /home                   ufs     rw              2 2
/dev/da2b         none                    swap    sw              0 0
/dev/da2e         /S                      ufs     rw,noauto       2 2
/dev/da3a         /mod                    ufs     rw,noauto       0 0
proc              /proc                   procfs  rw              0 0
/dev/cd0a         /cdrom/1                cd9660  ro,noauto       0 0
/dev/cd1a         /cdrom/2                cd9660  ro,noauto       0 0
/dev/cd2a         /cdrom/3                cd9660  ro,noauto       0 0
/dev/cd3a         /cdrom/4                cd9660  ro,noauto       0 0
```

```
/dev/cd4a        /cdrom/5        cd9660  ro,noauto              0 0
/dev/cd5a        /cdrom/6        cd9660  ro,noauto              0 0
/dev/cd6a        /cdrom/7        cd9660  ro,noauto              0 0
/dev/cd7a        /cdrom/8        cd9660  ro,noauto              0 0
presto:/         /presto         nfs     soft,rw,noauto         0 0
presto:/usr      /presto/usr     nfs     soft,rw,noauto         0 0
presto:/home     /presto/home    nfs     soft,rw,noauto         0 0
bumble:/         /bumble         nfs     soft,rw,noauto         0 0
bumble:/usr      /bumble/usr     nfs     soft,rw,noauto         0 0
wait:/C          /C              nfs     soft,rw,noauto         0 0
wait:/           /wait           nfs     soft,rw,noauto,tcp     0 0
```

This information has the following meaning:

- The first column contains either the name of a device (for swap, *ufs* and *cd9660* file systems), the name of a file system (for NFS file systems), or proc for the *proc* file system.

- The lines beginning with # are *commented out*: *mount* ignores them completely.

- The second column is either a mount point or the keyword none in the case of a partition that is not mounted, such as swap.

- The third column is the kind of file system (or swap).

- The fourth column are flags relating to the particular file system being mounted. We'll look at them below.

- The fifth column is used by *dump(8)* to determine how often to dump the file system. 0 means not to dump the file system. *dump* only understands ufs file systems, so this field should be 0 for all other file systems.

- The sixth column is the *pass number* for running *fsck* at boot time. Again, 0 means "don't run *fsck*." Normally you set pass 1 only for the root file system, and pass 2 for other file systems.

The flags are worth a closer look. Some of the more common are:

Table 30-1: Mount flags

Flag	Purpose
ro	Mount read-only.
rw	Mount read/write.
sw	Mount as swap.
noauto	Don't mount automatically.
soft	For an NFS mount, fail if the request times out. If you don't specify this option, NFS will keep retrying for ever.
tcp	For NFS only, mount with TCP transport rather than the standard UDP transport. This feature is supported almost only by BSD systems—check whether the other end offers TCP transport.

For NFS mount flags, see Chapter 24, page 442.

Why are there so many entries with the noauto keyword? If you don't bother to mount them, why bother to mention them?

If file system has an entry in */etc/fstab*, *mount* is clever enough to get all the information it needs from this file. You just need to specify the name of the mount point or the name of the special device (for *ufs* and *cd9660*) or the remote file system (for NFS). This is particularly useful for *cd9660*, the CD file system type. Without an entry in */etc/fstab*, you would have to write something like the following to mount a CD-ROM.

```
# mount -t cd9660 -o ro /dev/cd0a /cdrom
```

With the entry, you can simplify this to:

```
# mount /cdrom
```

/etc/group

/etc/group defines the groups known to the system. You normally update it when adding users, for example with *vipw* or *adduser*, though you can also edit it directly. See page 113 for more details.

/etc/namedb/named.conf

/etc/named/named.conf is the main configuration file for *named*, the Domain Name Service daemon. We looked at it in Chapter 21. Previous versions of *named* used a different form of configuration file stored in */etc/named.boot*.

/etc/mail

The directory */etc/mail* contains configuration information for some MTAs, including *sendmail*.

/etc/master.passwd

/etc/master.passwd is the real password file. Like */etc/group*, you update with *vipw* or *adduser*. See page 144 for more details.

Files you might need to change

You don't need to customize any of the following files to get the system up and running. You may find it necessary to change them to do specific things, however.

/etc/crontab

/etc/crontab describes the jobs to be performed by *cron* on behalf of the system. You don't have to use this file at all; you can use each user's *crontab* files instead. Note that this file has a slightly different format from the other *crontab* files. A user's *crontab* contains entries like this:

```
0       0       *       *       *       /home/grog/Scripts/rotate-log
```

This line runs the script */home/grog/Scripts/rotate-log* at midnight every day. If you put this entry into */etc/crontab*, you need to tell *cron* which user to run it as. Do this by putting the name of the user before the command:

```
0       0       *       *       *       grog    /home/grog/Scripts/rotate-log
```

See page 151 for more details about *cron*.

/etc/csh.cshrc, /etc/csh.login, /etc/csh.logout

These are default initialization files for *csh*. See the man page *csh(1)* for more details.

/etc/dhclient.conf

/etc/dhclient.conf describes the client side of DHCP services. Normally it's empty. We discussed *dhcp* on 302.

/etc/disktab

/etc/disktab contains descriptions of disk geometries for *disklabel*. This is almost obsolete.

/etc/ftpusers

/etc/ftpusers is a list of users who are *not* allowed to connect to this system using *ftp*. It's a strong contender for the prize for the worst-named file in the system.

/etc/hosts

For a small network, especially if you're not permanently connected to the Internet, you have the option of placing the addresses of the systems you want to talk to in a file called */etc/hosts*. This file is simply a list of IP addresses and host names, for example:

```
# Local network host addresses
#
# loopback address for all systems
127.1 loopback local localhost
###### domain example.com.
#
223.147.37.1    freebie freebie.example.org     # FreeBSD 3.0
223.147.37.2    presto.example.org presto       # 66 MHz 486 (BSD UNIX)
```

Before the days of DNS, this was the way to resolve IP addresses. It only works locally, and even there it's a pain to maintain: you need to propagate every update to every machine on the network. As we saw in Chapter 21, it's far preferable to run *named*, even if you're not connected to the Internet.

/etc/hosts.equiv

/etc/hosts.equiv is a list of hosts whose users may use *rsh* to access this system without supplying a password. *rsh* is now obsolete, so it's unlikely you'll need to change this file. See the description of *ssh* on page 419 for a replacement.

/etc/hosts.lpd

/etc/hosts.lpd is a list of hosts that can use the *lpd* spooler on this system.

/etc/inetd.conf

/etc/inetd.conf is the configuration file for *inetd*, the Internet daemon. It dates back to the original implementation of TCP/IP in 4.2BSD, and the format is the same for all versions of UNIX. We have looked at various modifications to this file throughout the network part of the book. See the index (*inetd.conf*) and the man page *inetd.conf(5)* for further details. FreeBSD now disables all services by default to limit security exposures, so there's a good chance you'll have to edit this file.

/etc/login.access

/etc/login.access is a file that limits remote access by individual users. We don't look at it in more detail here.

/etc/login.conf

/etc/login.conf describes user parameters set at login time.

In UNIX tradition, root has been the owner of the universe. This is rather primitive, and the 4.3BSD Net/2 relase introduced *login classes*, which determine session accounting, resource limits and user environment settings. Many programs use the database described in */etc/login.conf* to set up a user's login environment and to enforce policy, accounting and administrative restrictions. The login class database also provides the means to authenticate users to the system and to choose the type of authentication.

When creating a user, you may optionally enter a class name, which should match an entry in */etc/login.conf*—see page 146 for more details. If you don't, the system uses the entry default for a non-root user. For the root user, the system uses the entry root if it is present, and default otherwise.

The structure of the login configuration database is relatively extensive. It describes a number of parameters, many of which can have two values: a *current* value and a *maximum* value. On login, the system sets the values to the –cur (current) value, but the user may, at his option, increase the value to the –max (maximum) value. We'll look at the default entry for an example.

```
default:\
        :passwd_format=md5:\
        :copyright=/etc/COPYRIGHT:\
        :welcome=/etc/motd:\
        :setenv=MAIL=/var/mail/$,BLOCKSIZE=K,FTP_PASSIVE_MODE=YES:\
        :path=/sbin /bin /usr/sbin /usr/bin /usr/games /usr/local/sbin /usr/local/bi
n /usr/X11R6/bin ~/bin:\
        :nologin=/var/run/nologin:\
        :cputime=unlimited:\
        :datasize=unlimited:\
        :stacksize=unlimited:\
        :memorylocked=unlimited:\
        :memoryuse=unlimited:\
        :filesize=unlimited:\
        :coredumpsize=unlimited:\
        :openfiles=unlimited:\
        :maxproc=unlimited:\
        :sbsize=unlimited:\
        :vmemoryuse=unlimited:\
        :priority=0:\
        :ignoretime@:\
        :umask=022:
```

As in the password file, the fields are delimited by colons (:). In this example, though, lines are *continued* by placing a backslash (\) at the end of each line except the last. This usage is common in UNIX. Unlike Microsoft usage, a backslash is never used to represent a directory.

This entry defines the following parameters:

- passwd_format controls the password format used for new passwords. It takes the values des, md5 or blf. See the *login.conf(5)* manual page for more information about login capabilities.

- Processes may use as much CPU time as they want. If you change this, you can stop processes that use more than a specific amount of CPU time.

- The current maximum sizes of the user data segment and the stack are set to 64 MB. The entry doesn't define maximum values for these parameters.

- The user may lock a maximum of 10 MB of memory per process.

- The total memory use per process may not exceed 100 MB.

- There is no limit on the size of data files or core dump files that the user may create.

- The user may have up to 64 processes.

- Each process may have up to 64 open files. For some programs, this could be a limitation.

- The user *need not* have a home directory to log in. The @ symbol specifies that the preceding symbol (requirehome) should be undefined. As a result, the system does not require the home directory.

- By default, the *umask* is set to 022. See page 184 for more details of *umask*.

- The system uses the default authentication scheme for this user.

See the man page *login.conf(5)* for further details.

/etc/motd

/etc/motd (*message of the day*) is a file whose contents are printed out at login. You can put any message you like in it. See page 114 for an example.

/etc/newsyslog.conf

/etc/newsyslog.conf contains configuration information for the *newsyslog* command: which log files to archive, how many copies, and whether to compress. See *newsyslog(8)* for further details. If you generate a lot of logging information, you may need to modify this file to avoid overflowing the file system with your */var/log* directory.

/etc/nsswitch.conf

/etc/nsswitch.conf tells the resolver how to perform name resolution. This file format comes from Solaris and replaces the older */etc/host.conf*. It gives you the flexibility to use both */etc/hosts* and DNS lookups, for example. You specify the lookup sequence for hostnames with a line like this:

```
hosts:    files dns
```

The word hosts here specifies the type of lookup (for host names, not NIS, password entries or something else). The keyword file represents the */etc/hosts* file in this case. This file is not installed by default; see the man page *nsswitch.conf(8)* if you need to use it.

/etc/pccardd.conf

/etc/pccardd.conf and its companion */etc/defaults/pccardd.conf* are the configuration files for *pccardd*. We looked at them in detail in Chapter 17, on page 304.

/etc/periodic.conf

/etc/periodic.conf controls how to perform the maintenance jobs that *cron* runs during the night:

```
# Perform daily/weekly/monthly maintenance.
1     3     *     *     *     root     periodic daily
15    4     *     *     6     root     periodic weekly
30    5     1     *     *     root     periodic monthly
```

Like */etc/rc.conf*, */etc/periodic.conf* is an optional file which overrides the default file */etc/defaults/periodic.conf*. You don't need to change it at all, but you may find it worthwhile. Read the man page *periodic.conf(5)* or the file */etc/defaults/periodic.conf* for more details.

/etc/printcap

/etc/printcap describes the printers connected to a system. See page 265 for more details.

/etc/profile

/etc/profile is a default startup file for Bourne-style shells. See page 130 for more details.

/etc/rc.firewall

/etc/rc.firewall is used to initialize the packet filtering firewall *ipfw*. See page 389 for further details.

/etc/resolv.conf

/etc/resolv.conf is used by the *resolver* library to locate name servers to perform DNS lookups. See 366 for more details.

/etc/syslog.conf

/etc/syslog.conf is the configuration file for *syslogd*. See *syslogd.conf(5)* for further details.

/etc/ttys

/etc/ttys is a file that describes terminals and pseudo-terminals to *init*. We've looked at it in a number of places: check the index.

Here's an excerpt from the default */etc/ttys*:

```
# This entry needed for asking password when init goes to single-user mode
# If you want to be asked for password, change "secure" to "insecure" here
console none                                        unknown off secure
```

The system console. This is not a real terminal: it can be moved from one device to another. By default, it corresponds to */dev/ttyv0* (the next entry).

```
ttyv0   "/usr/libexec/getty Pc"             cons25  on  secure
```

This is the first virtual terminal, the one that you get automatically at boot time. To change to the others, press **Alt-F***x*, where *x* is between 1 and 16. This will give you one of the others:

```
# Virtual terminals
ttyv1   "/usr/libexec/getty Pc"             cons25  on secure
ttyv2   "/usr/libexec/getty Pc"             cons25  on secure
ttyv3   "/usr/libexec/getty Pc"             cons25  on secure
(etc)
ttyv8   "/usr/X11R6/bin/xdm -nodaemon"      xterm   off secure
```

Each virtual terminal can support either a login or an X server. The default */etc/ttys* enables *getty* on the first eight virtual terminals and reserves */dev/ttyv8* for X. If you don't enable *xdm* on this terminal, you start X with *startx*.

The default kernel supports sixteen virtual terminals, the maximum possible value. The kernel configuration parameter MAXCONS (defined in */usr/src/sys/conf/NOTES*) allows you to reduce this number.

```
# Serial terminals
ttyd0    "/usr/libexec/getty std.9600"    unknown off secure
ttyd1    "/usr/libexec/getty std.9600"    unknown off secure
ttyd2    "/usr/libexec/getty std.9600"    unknown off secure
ttyd3    "/usr/libexec/getty std.9600"    unknown off secure
```

These are the serial ports on your machine. It doesn't matter if it contains names that correspond to non-existent hardware, such as */dev/ttyd3*, as long as you don't try to enable them.

```
# Pseudo terminals
ttyp0         none             network
ttyp1         none             network
```

There's a whole list of these. The purpose here is to tell network programs the properties of the terminal: in particular, they're not secure, which means that you're not allowed to log in on them as root.

/boot/device.hints

The file */boot/device.hints* contains configuration information that was previously stored in the kernel configuration file, and which could not be changed except by building and running a new kernel. Now it can be set at boot time. For these changes to apply, you may still need to reboot, but you no longer need a new kernel.

The information in */boot/device.hints* consists of structured variables. For example, consider a third ISA serial I/O port, called */dev/sio2* in FreeBSD. By default, this port gets IRQ 4, the same as */dev/sio0*. This just plain doesn't work, so you will have to find a different IRQ. The hints for this device start with the text hint.sio.2. The default */boot/device.hints* contains the following parameters for this device:

```
hint.sio.2.at="isa"
hint.sio.2.disabled="1"
hint.sio.2.port="0x3E8"
hint.sio.2.irq="5"
```

In sequence, these "hints" state that the device is connected to the ISA bus, that it is disabled (in other words, the kernel does not probe for it), that its device registers are at address 0x3e8, and that it interrupts at IRQ 5. Modern motherboards configure this device via the BIOS. You may find that on your system it's more appropriate to run at IRQ 11. In this case, in */boot/device.hints*, you would remove the "disabled" line and change the irq line:

```
hint.sio.2.at="isa"
hint.sio.2.port="0x3E8"
hint.sio.2.irq="11"
```

In some cases, you can change these flags at run time with the *kenv* command. For example, to change the flags of the first serial port to 0x90 to run a serial debugger, you might enter:

```
# kenv hint.sio.0.flags
0x0
# kenv hint.sio.0.flags=0x90
hint.sio.0.flags="0x90"
```

Wiring down SCSI devices

Another example is so-called *wiring down* SCSI and ATA devices. We looked at this issue on page 202. By default, FreeBSD assigns SCSI unit numbers in the order in which it finds the devices on the SCSI bus. If you remove or add a disk drive, the numbers change, and you may have to modify your */etc/fstab* file. To avoid this problem, you can *wire down* your SCSI devices so that a given bus, target, and unit (*LUN*) always come on line as the same device unit.

The unit assignment begins with the first non-wired down unit for a device type. Units that are not specified are treated as if specified as LUN 0. For example, if you wire a disk as sd3, the first non-wired disk is assigned sd4.

The following example shows configuration file entries for a system with three Adaptec 2940 class host adapters, one of them with two buses. The first has a disk on ID 0 that we want to call */dev/da0*, the second has a tape on ID 6 that we want to call */dev/sa0*, the first bus of the third adapter has a disk on ID 3 that we want to call */dev/da2*, and the second bus of the third adapter has a disk on ID 1 that we want to call */dev/da1*.

```
hint.scbus.0.at="ahc0"              scbus0 is ahc0
hint.scbus.1.at="ahc1"              scbus1 is ahc1 bus 0 (only one)
hint.scbus.1.bus="0"
hint.scbus.3.at="ahc2"              scbus3 is ahc2 bus 0
hint.scbus.3.bus="0"
hint.scbus.2.at="ahc2"              scbus2 is ahc2 bus 1
hint.scbus.2.bus="1"
hint.da.0.at="scbus0"              da0 is on scsbus0, target 0, unit 0
hint.da.0.target="0"
hint.da.0.unit="0"
hint.da.1.at="scbus3"              da1 is on scsbus3, target 1
hint.da.1.target="1"
hint.da.2.at="scbus2"              da2 is on scsbus2, target 3
hint.da.2.target="3"
hint.sa.1.at="scbus1"              sa1 is on scsbus1, target 6
hint.sa.1.target="6"
```

If there are any other devices connected to the host adapters, they are assigned other names in sequence, starting at */dev/da3* and */dev/sa2*.

This arrangement corresponds to the earlier syntax in the kernel configuration file:

```
controller      scbus0 at ahc0          # Single bus device
controller      scbus1 at ahc1 bus 0    # Single bus device
controller      scbus3 at ahc2 bus 0    # Twin bus device
controller      scbus2 at ahc2 bus 1    # Twin bus device
disk            da0 at scbus0 target 0 unit 0
disk            da1 at scbus3 target 1
disk            da2 at scbus2 target 3
tape            sa1 at scbus1 target 6
device   cd0 at scbus?
```

Files you should not change

The files in the following section are there as a kind of reference information. Normally you should not change them, though there might be exceptional circumstances where it makes sense to change them.

/etc/gettytab

/etc/gettytab describes profiles for *getty*. You probably don't need it; check the man page if you're interested.

/etc/manpath.config

/etc/manpath.config is a configuration file for *man*. You don't usually need to change this file.

/etc/netconfig

/etc/netconfig is new in FreeBSD Release 5. It is similar to the file of the same name in UNIX System V, but it's only used for C library RPC code. In general, you don't need to worry about this file unless you're upgrading from an older release of FreeBSD. If it's not here, a number of network functions, including NFS, will not work.

/etc/networks

/etc/networks was once a list of networks in the Internet. Although this sounds like a good idea, it is almost useless: if you connect to the Internet, you should use a name server, which supplants this file.

/etc/passwd

/etc/passwd is the old-style password file. It is now present only for programs that expect to read user information from it, and it no longer contains passwords. Don't change this file; the programs *vipw*, *adduser* and *pwd_mkdb* do it automatically. See page 144 for more details.

/etc/protocols

/etc/protocols is a list of known protocols that run on the IP layer. Consider this file to be read-only.

/etc/pwd.db

/etc/pwd.db is a machine-readable form of the user database with the passwords removed. We looked at it on page 144. Like */etc/passwd*, it is generated automatically.

/etc/rc

/etc/rc is the main script that starts up the system. It uses the other files whose names start with */etc/rc* to perform specific initialization. See page 528 for more details.

/etc/rc.i386

/etc/rc.i386 is used to initialize features specific to the Intel 386 architecture, such as SCO and Linux emulation. You don't normally need to look at or change this file.

/etc/rc.network and /etc/rc.network6

The main scripts for starting the network are */etc/rc.network*, which in earlier FreeBSD releases was called */etc/network*, and */etc/rc.network6*, which starts IPv6 services. You normally don't change these files: they read all the necessary definitions from */etc/rc.conf*, and that's the file you should change.

/etc/rc.pccard

/etc/rc.pccard sets up laptops using the PC Card bus.

/etc/rc.serial

/etc/rc.serial sets default values for serial devices.

/etc/shells

/etc/shells is a list of valid shells, used by *ftp* and some other programs. *ftpd* refuses to open a session for a user whose shell is not mentioned in this file. This prevents people from starting an *ftp* session as a daemon, which frequently have no passwords. *chpass* will not let you change your shell to a shell not included in this file. See page 452 for more details. It is usually updated when you install a new shell from the Ports Collection.

/etc/services

/etc/services contains a list of the IP services that this system supports.

/etc/spwd.db

/etc/spwd.db is a machine-readable form of the user database with the passwords intact. We looked at it on page 144.

/etc/termcap

/etc/termcap (*terminal capabilities*) describes terminal control sequences. By default, programs use the value of the TERM environment variable to look up the terminal capabilities in this database. See page 128 for more details.

/etc/periodic

The directory */etc/periodic* contains three directories used by *cron* at regular intervals: *daily*, *weekly* and *monthly*. The directories contain a number of files for performing specific tasks. For example, */etc/periodic/daily* contains the following files:

```
-rwxr-xr-x  5 grog  lemis  1269 Apr 26  2001 100.clean-disks
-rwxr-xr-x  4 grog  lemis  1449 Nov 21 13:55 110.clean-tmps
-rwxr-xr-x  5 grog  lemis  1092 Sep 15  2000 120.clean-preserve
-rwxr-xr-x  5 grog  lemis   695 Sep 15  2000 130.clean-msgs
-rwxr-xr-x  5 grog  lemis  1056 Sep 15  2000 140.clean-rwho
-rwxr-xr-x  1 grog  lemis   595 Jan  9 07:11 150.clean-hoststat
-rwxr-xr-x  5 grog  lemis  1742 Nov 15  2001 200.backup-passwd
-rwxr-xr-x  5 grog  lemis   996 Sep 15  2000 210.backup-aliases
-rwxr-xr-x  5 grog  lemis   679 Sep 15  2000 300.calendar
-rwxr-xr-x  5 grog  lemis  1211 May 31  2001 310.accounting
-rwxr-xr-x  5 grog  lemis   710 Sep 15  2000 330.news
-rwxr-xr-x  5 grog  lemis   516 Jul 26  2002 400.status-disks
-rwxr-xr-x  5 grog  lemis   548 Sep 15  2000 420.status-network
-rwxr-xr-x  5 grog  lemis   687 Sep 15  2000 430.status-rwho
-rwxr-xr-x  3 grog  lemis  1362 Dec  9 07:15 440.status-mailq
-rwxr-xr-x  5 grog  lemis   768 Jul 26  2002 450.status-security
-rwxr-xr-x  3 grog  lemis  1633 Dec  9 07:15 460.status-mail-rejects
-rwxr-xr-x  1 grog  lemis  1489 Jan  7 07:10 470.status-named
-rwxr-xr-x  5 grog  lemis   723 Jul 26  2002 500.queuerun
-rwxr-xr-x  5 grog  lemis   712 Jun  2  2001 999.local
```

The files are executed in the order of their names, so the names consist of two parts: a number indicating the sequence, and a name indicating the function. This method is new with FreeBSD Release 3. In older releases of FreeBSD, these functions were performed by files with the names */etc/daily*, */etc/weekly* and */etc/monthly*. See page 151 for more details of *cron*.

Obsolete configuration files

In the course of time, a number of configuration files have come and gone. This can be tricky if you're updating a system: some old configuration files could remain and either confuse you by not working the way you expect, or cause incorrect operation by some side effect of the presence of the file.

/etc/host.conf

/etc/host.conf described the order in which to perform name resolution. It has been replaced by */etc/nsswitch.conf*, which has a different syntax.

/etc/named.boot

Previous versions of *named*, the DNS daemon, used */etc/named.boot* as the main configuration file. Newer versions use */etc/namedb/named.conf*, and the format is very different.

/etc/netstart

/etc/netstart was a script called by */etc/rc* to start up the network. Its name has now been changed to */etc/rc.network*. FreeBSD still includes a file */etc/netstart*, but its only purpose is to start the network in single-user mode.

/etc/sysconfig

/etc/sysconfig was a file that contained all the site-specific configuration definitions. Its name has been changed to */etc/rc.conf*.

31

Keeping up to date

FreeBSD is constantly changing. The average time that elapses between changes to the source tree is in the order of a few minutes. Obviously you can't keep up to date with that pace of change.

In the following three chapters we'll look at how to keep up to date. In this chapter, we'll look at:

- FreeBSD releases: how the FreeBSD project comes to terms with the rapid rate of change, and how it keeps the system stable despite the changes.

- How the system sources are stored, and how you can update them.

In Chapter 32, *Updating the system software*, we'll look at how to upgrade FreeBSD to a new release, with particular reference to upgrades to FreeBSD Release 5, and in Chapter 33, *Custom kernels*, we'll look at building special kernels.

FreeBSD releases and CVS

The FreeBSD project keeps the entire operating system sources in a single master source tree, called a *repository*, which is maintained by the *Concurrent Versions System*, or *CVS*. It's included in most multi–CD-ROM distributions of FreeBSD. The repository contains all versions of FreeBSD back to Release 2.0 and the last release from the Computer Sciences Research Group of the University of California at Berkeley, 4.4BSD-Lite, upon which it was based. For copyright reasons FreeBSD Release 1 was not included, because at the time, as the result of the lawsuits described on page 8, it was not permitted to distribute it freely. That situation changed in early 2002, but it's now too late to include FreeBSD Release 1 in the repository.

CVS is built on top of the *Revision Control System*, or *RCS*. *RCS* keeps multiple versions of files, called *revisions*, in a single RCS file. Each revision has a number indicating its relationship to the other revisions. The oldest revision has the number 1.1, the next oldest has the number 1.2, and so on. The RCS file contains the most recent revision of the file along with instructions for creating any other revision.

In addition to this linear sequence, it's possible to update a specific revision in more than one way. The obvious way to update revision 1.2 would create revision 1.3; but it's also possible to create *branches*, which get numbers like 1.2.1.1. Updating revision 1.2.1.1 would create revision 1.2.1.2, and so on. By contrast, the revisions with a two-part number are collectively called the *trunk* of the tree.

Symbolic names or tags

In addition to the numeric identifiers, each of which relates only to a single file, RCS allows you to attach *symbolic names* to specific revisions. CVS generally calls these names *tags*, and that's the term you'll see most often. FreeBSD uses tags to indicate the revisions corresponding to a particular release. For example, in the directory */usr/src/sys/kern*, revision 1.13 of *kern_clock.c*, revision 1.12 of *kern_fork.c* and revision 1.21.4.1 of *kern_exec.c* participate in RELENG_2_1_0_RELEASE. We'll look at tags in more detail on page 588.

RCS stores its files either in the same directory as the working files it is tracking, or in a subdirectory *RCS* if it exists. To avoid file name conflicts, *RCS* appends the characters *,v* to the RCS file, so the working file *main.c* would correspond to the RCS file *main.c,v*. For more details of *RCS*, see the man page.

CVS is an extension to *RCS* that allows concurrent access, making it more suitable for projects involving more than one person. Unlike *RCS*, it stores its RCS files in a separate directory hierarchy, called a *repository*. Each directory in the working tree contains a subdirectory *CVS* with information on the location of the repository, the revisions of the working files and a tag if the revision isn't on the trunk.

If you're a serious developer, there are a number of advantages to keeping a copy of the repository. If you're a casual user, it's probably overkill.

FreeBSD releases

There are four main versions of FreeBSD, each intended for use by different people:

FreeBSD-RELEASE

FreeBSD-RELEASE is the latest version of FreeBSD that has been released for general use. It contains those new features that are stable, and it has been through extensive testing. You can get it on CD-ROM. FreeBSD-RELEASEs are given a release number that uniquely identifies them, such as 5.0. There are three or four releases a year. A new branch is made for each release of FreeBSD.

FreeBSD-STABLE

FreeBSD-STABLE is an updated version of FreeBSD-RELEASE to which all possible bug fixes have been applied, to make it as stable as possible. Fixes are made on a daily basis. It is based on the same source branch as FreeBSD-RELEASE, so it has all the features and fewer bugs. It may contain additional features, but new features are tested in the -CURRENT branch first.

Due to the frequent updates, FreeBSD-STABLE is not available on CD-ROM.

Security fix releases

Despite the name, FreeBSD-STABLE is subject to some problems. Every change to a source tree has the potential to go wrong. In many cases, you're more interested in keeping your system running than you are in getting minor bug fixes. FreeBSD also maintains a second "stable" branch consisting of the release and only very important bug fixes, including security updates. This branch does not have a well-defined name, but it's generally referred to as the *security branch*.

FreeBSD-CURRENT

FreeBSD-CURRENT is the very latest version of FreeBSD, located on the trunk of the tree. All new development work is done on this branch of the tree. FreeBSD-CURRENT is an ever-changing snapshot of the working sources for FreeBSD, including work in progress, experimental changes and transitional mechanisms that may or may not be present in the next official release of the software. Many users compile almost daily from FreeBSD-CURRENT sources, but there are times when the sources are uncompilable, or when the system crashes frequently. The problems are always resolved, but others can take their place. On occasion, keeping up with FreeBSD-CURRENT can be a full-time business. If you use -CURRENT, you should be prepared to spend a lot of time keeping the system running. The following extract from the RCS log file for */usr/src/Makefile* should give you a feel for the situation:

```
$ cvs log Makefile
...
revision 1.152
date: 1997/10/06 09:58:11;  author: jkh;  state: Exp;  lines: +41 -13
Hooboy!

Did I ever spam this file good with that last commit.  Despite 3
reviewers, we still managed to revoke the eBones fixes, TCL 8.0 support,
libvgl and a host of other new things from this file in the process of
parallelizing the Makefile.  DOH!  I think we need more pointy hats - this
particular incident is worthy of a small children's birthday party's worth of
pointy hats. ;-)

I certainly intend to take more care with the processing of aged diffs
in the future, even if it does mean reading through 20K's worth of them.
I might also be a bit more anal about asking for more up-to-date changes
before looking at them. ;)
```

This example also shows the list of the symbolic names for this file, and their corresponding revision numbers. There is no symbolic name for -CURRENT, because it is located on the trunk. That's the purpose of the line head:, which shows that at the time of this example, the –CURRENT revision of this file was 1.270.

So why use –CURRENT? The main reasons are:

*   You might be doing development work on some part of the source tree. Keeping "current" is an absolute requirement.

*   You may be an active tester, which implies that you're willing to spend time working through problems to ensure that FreeBSD-CURRENT remains as sane as possible. You may also wish to make topical suggestions on changes and the general direction of FreeBSD.

*   You may just want to keep an eye on things and use the current sources for reference purposes.

People occasionally have other reasons for wanting to use FreeBSD-CURRENT. The following are *not* good reasons:

*   They see it as a way to be the first on the block with great new FreeBSD features. This is not a good reason, because there's no reason to believe that the features will stay, and there is good reason to believe that they will be unstable.

*   They see it as a quick way of getting bug fixes. In fact, it's a way of *testing* bug fixes. Bug fixes will be retrofitted into the -STABLE branch as soon as they have been properly tested.

*   They see it as the newest officially supported release of FreeBSD. This is incorrect: FreeBSD-CURRENT is *not* officially supported. The support is provided by the users.

If you do decide to use –CURRENT, read the suggestions on page 621.

Snapshots

FreeBSD-CURRENT *is* available in the form of ISO (CD-ROM) images. From time to time, at irregular intervals when the tree is relatively stable, the release team makes a *snapshot* release from the –CURRENT source tree. They are also available on CD-ROM from some vendors; check the online handbook for details. This is a possible alternative to online updates if you don't want the absolute latest version of the system.

Getting updates from the Net

There are a number of possibilities to keep up with the daily modifications to the source tree. The first question is: how much space do you want to invest in keeping the sources? Table 31-1 shows the approximate space required by different parts of the sources. Note that the repository keeps growing faster than the source tree, because it includes all old revisions as well.

Table 31-1: Approximate source tree sizes

Component	Size (MB)
Repository *src/sys*	250
Repository *src*	1000
Repository *ports*	300
Source tree */usr/src/sys*	110
Source tree */usr/src*	450
Source tree */usr/ports*	200
Object tree */usr/obj*	160

The size of */usr/src/sys* includes the files involved in a single kernel build. You can remove the entire kernel build directory, but if you want to be able to analyze a panic dump, you should keep the *kernel.debug* file in the kernel build directory. This changes the size of */usr/src* as well, of course. The other object files get built in the directory */usr/obj*. Again, you can remove this directory tree entirely if you want, either with the *rm* command or with make clean. Similarly, the size of */usr/ports* includes a few ports. It will, of course, grow extremely large (many gigabytes) if you start porting all available packages.

If you're maintaining multiple source trees (say, for different versions), you still only need one copy of the repository.

CVSup

CVSup is a software package that distributes updates to the repository. You can run the client at regular intervals—for example, with *cron* (see page 151) to update your repository.

To get started with *CVSup*, you need the following:

- A source tree or repository, which doesn't have to be up to date. This is not absolutely necessary, but the initial setup will be faster if you do it this way.

- A copy of the *cvsup* program. Install it with *pkg_add* from the CD-ROM (*/cdrom/packages/Latest/cvsup.tbz*).

- A *cvsupfile*, a command file for *cvsup*. We'll look at this below.

- A *mirror site* from which you can load or update the repository. We'll discuss this below as well.

The *cvsupfile* contains a description of the packages you want to download. You can find all the details in the online handbook, but the following example shows a reasonably normal file:

```
*default release=cvs
*default host=cvsup9.freebsd.org
*default base=/src/cvsup
*default prefix=/home/ncvs
*default delete
*default use-rel-suffix
*default compress
src-all
ports-all
doc-all
```

The lines starting with *default specify default values; the lines that do not are collections that you want to track. This file answers these implicit questions:

- Which files do you want to receive? These are the names of the *collections* in the last three lines: all of the sources, ports and documentation.

- Which versions of them do you want? By default, you get updates to the repository. If you want a specific version, you can write:

  ```
  *default tag=version
  ```

  version is a *release tag* that identifies the version you want, or . (a period) to represent the -CURRENT version. We'll discuss release tags on page 588.

  Alternatively, you might ask for a version as of a specific date. For example:

  ```
  *default date=97.09.13.12.20
  ```

  This would specify that you want *the version* as it was on 13 September 1997 at 12:20. In this case, *version* defaults to . (a period).

- Where do you want to get them from? Two parameters answer this question: host=cvsup9.freebsd.org specifies the name of the host from which to load the files, and release=cvs specifies to use the *cvs* release. The *release* option is obsolescent, but it's a good idea to leave it in there until it is officially removed.

- Where do you want to put them on your own machine? This question is answered by the line *default prefix=/home/ncvs. We're tracking the repository in this example, so this is the name of the repository. If we were tracking a particular release, we would use *default prefix=/usr. The collections are called *doc*, *ports* and *src*, so we refer to the parent directory in each case.

- Where do you want to put your status files? This question is answered by the line *default base=/src/cvsup.

In addition, the file contains three other lines. *default delete means that *cvsup* may delete files where necessary. Otherwise you run the risk of accumulating obsolete files. *default compress enables compression of the data transmitted, and *default use-rel-suffix specifies how *cvsup* should handle list files. It's not well-documented, but it's necessary. Don't worry about it.

Which CVSup server?

In this example, we've chosen one of the backup US servers, *cvsup9.FreeBSD.org*. In practice, this may not be the best choice. A large number of servers are spread around the world, and you should choose the one topographically closest to you. This isn't the same thing as being geographically closest—I live in Adelaide, South Australia, and some ISPs in the same city are further away on the Net than many systems in California. Look on the web site *http://www.FreeBSD.org* for an up-to-date list.

Running *cvsup*

cvsup is a typical candidate for a *cron* job. I rebuild the –CURRENT tree every morning at 3 am. To do so, I have the following entry in */root/crontab*:

```
# Get the latest and greatest FreeBSD stuff.
0 3 * * * ./extract-updates
```

The file */root/extract-updates* contains, amongst other things,

```
cvsup -g -L2 /src/cvsup/cvs-cvsupfile
```

/src/cvsup/cvs-cvsupfile is the name of the *cvsupfile* we looked at above. The other parameters to *cvsup* specify *not* to use the GUI (–g), and –L2 specifies to produce moderate detail about the actions being performed.

Getting individual releases

The example *cvsupfile* above is useful if you're maintaining a copy of the repository. If you just want to maintain a copy of the sources of one version, say Release 5.0, use the following file instead:

```
*default tag=RELENG_5_0_0_RELEASE
*default release=cvs
*default host=cvsup9.freebsd.org
*default base=/usr                      for /usr/doc, /usr/ports, /usr/src
*default prefix=/home/ncvs
*default delete
*default use-rel-suffix
*default compress
src-all
```

Be careful with tags. They must exist in the repository, or *cvsup* will replace what you have with nothing: it will delete all the files. In our original *cvsupfile*, we had two additional sets, ports-all and *doc-all*. These sets don't have the same release tags, so if you left them in this file, you would lose all the files in the */usr/doc* and */usr/ports* directory hierarchies.

Creating the source tree

If you're tracking the repository, you're not finished yet. Once you have an up-to-date repository, the next step is to create a source tree. By default, the source tree is called */usr/src*, though it's very common for */usr/src* to be a symbolic link to a source tree on a different file system. You create the tree with *cvs*.

Before you check anything out with *cvs*, you need to know:

1. What do you want to check out? You specify this with a module name, which usually corresponds with a directory name (for example, *src*). There are a number of top-level modules, including *doc*, *ports*, *src* and *www*.

2. Which version do you want to check out? By default, you get the latest version, which is FreeBSD-CURRENT. If you want a different version, you need to specify its *tag*.

3. Possibly, the date of the last update that you want to be included in the checkout. If you specify this date, *cvs* ignores any more recent updates. This option is often useful when somebody discovers a recently introduced bug in -CURRENT: you check out the modules as they were before the bug was introduced. You specify the date with the -D option, as we'll see below.

Release tags

FreeBSD identifies releases with two or more numbers separated by periods. Each number represents a progressively smaller increment in the functionality of the release. The first number is the base release of FreeBSD. The number is incremented only when significant functionality is added to the system. The second number represents a less significant, but still important difference in the functionality, and the third number is only used when a significant bug requires rerelease of an otherwise unchanged release. Before Release 3 of FreeBSD, a fourth number was sometimes also used.

Tags for released versions of FreeBSD follow the release numbers. For release *x.y.z* you would look for the tag RELENG_*x*_*y*_*z*_RELEASE. For example, to get the current state of the FreeBSD 5.0 source tree, you would look for the tag RELENG_5_0_0_RELEASE.

Tags for the -STABLE branch are simpler: they just have the release number, for example RELENG_4. The security branch has an additional number, for example RELENG_4_7.

Some tags diverge from this scheme. In particular, CSRG and bsd_44_lite both refer to the original 4.4BSD sources from Berkeley. If you feel like it, you can extract this source tree as well.

To find out what tags are available, do:

```
# cd $CVSROOT/src
# rlog Makefile,v | less
RCS file: /home/ncvs/src/Makefile,v
RCS file: /home/ncvs/src/Makefile,v
Working file: Makefile
head: 1.270
branch:
locks: strict
access list:
symbolic names:
        RELENG_5_0_0_RELEASE: 1.271                    5.0-RELEASE
...
        RELENG_4_7_0_RELEASE: 1.234.2.18               4.7-RELEASE
        RELENG_4_7: 1.234.2.18.0.2                     4.7 security fixes only
        RELENG_4_7_BP: 1.234.2.18                      branch point for 4.7
        RELENG_4_6_2_RELEASE: 1.234.2.12               4.6.2-RELEASE
        RELENG_4_6_1_RELEASE: 1.234.2.12               4.6.1-RELEASE
        RELENG_4_6_0_RELEASE: 1.234.2.12               4.6-RELEASE
...
        RELENG_4: 1.234.0.2                            4-STABLE
...
        RELEASE_2_0: 1.30                              2.0-RELEASE
        BETA_2_0: 1.30
        ALPHA_2_0: 1.29.0.2
        bsd_44_lite: 1.1.1.1                           4.4BSD-Lite
        CSRG: 1.1.1
keyword substitution: kv
total revisions: 179;    selected revisions: 179
description:
```

This example shows the same file we saw on page 583. This time we use the *rlog* command, which is part of *RCS*, to look at the revision log. Normally you'd use cvs*log*, but that only works in a checked out source tree.

There are a number of ways to tell *cvs* the name of its repository: if you already have a *CVS* subdirectory, it will contain files *Root* and *Repository*. The name of the repository is in *Root*, not in *Repository*. When you first check out files, you won't have this directory, so you specify it, either with the –d option to *cvs* or by setting the CVSROOT environment variable. As you can see in the example above, it's convenient to set the environment variable, since you can use it for other purposes as well.

The repository contains a number of directories, usually one for each collection you track. In our case, we're tracking the source tree and the Ports Collection, so:

• *CVSROOT* contains files used by CVS. It is not part of the source tree.

• *ports* contains the Ports Collection.

• *src* contains the system sources.

The directories *ports* and *src* correspond to the directories */usr/ports* and */usr/src* for a particular release. To extract the *src* tree of the most up-to-date version of FreeBSD-CURRENT, do the following:

```
# cd /usr
# cvs co src 2>&1 | tee /var/tmp/co.log
```

To check out any other version, say, everything for Release 4.6, you would enter:

```
# cd /usr
# cvs co -r RELENG_4_6_RELEASE src 2>&1 | tee /var/tmp/co.log
```

If you need to check out an older version, for example if there are problems with the most recent version of –CURRENT, you could enter:

```
# cvs co  -D "10 December 2002" src/sys
```

This command checks out the kernel sources as of 10 December 2002. During checkout, *cvs* creates a subdirectory *CVS* in each directory. *CVS* contains four files. We'll look at typical values when checking out the version of the directory */usr/src/usr.bin/du* for Release 4.6, from the repository at */home/ncvs*:

- *Entries* contains a list of the files being maintained in the parent directory, along with their current versions. In our example, it would contain:

  ```
  /Makefile/1.4.2.1/Sun Jul  2 10:45:29 2000//TRELENG_4_6_0_RELEASE
  /du.1/1.15.2.7/Thu Aug 16 13:16:47 2001//TRELENG_4_6_0_RELEASE
  /du.c/1.17.2.3/Thu Jul 12 08:46:53 2001//TRELENG_4_6_0_RELEASE
  D
  ```

  Note that *cvs* prepends a T to the version name.

- *Repository* contains the name of the directory in the repository that corresponds to the current directory. This corresponds to *$CVSROOT/directory*. In our example, it would contain src/usr.bin/du.

- *Root* contains the name of the root of the repository. In our example, it would contain /home/ncvs.

- *Tag* contains the *version tag* of the source tree. This is the RCS tag prefixed by a T. In this case, it is TRELENG_4_6_0_RELEASE.

cvs co produces a lot of output—at least one line for each directory, and one line for each file it checks out. Here's part of a typical output:

```
U src/usr.sbin/mrouted/rsrr_var.h
U src/usr.sbin/mrouted/vif.c
U src/usr.sbin/mrouted/vif.h
cvs checkout: Updating src/usr.sbin/mrouted/common
U src/usr.sbin/mrouted/common/Makefile
cvs checkout: Updating src/usr.sbin/mrouted/map-mbone
U src/usr.sbin/mrouted/map-mbone/Makefile
cvs checkout: Updating src/usr.sbin/mrouted/mrinfo
U src/usr.sbin/mrouted/mrinfo/Makefile
cvs checkout: Updating src/usr.sbin/mrouted/mrouted
U src/usr.sbin/mrouted/mrouted/Makefile
cvs checkout: Updating src/usr.sbin/mrouted/mtrace
U src/usr.sbin/mrouted/mtrace/Makefile
cvs checkout: Updating src/usr.sbin/mrouted/testrsrr
U src/usr.sbin/mrouted/testrsrr/Makefile
```

The flag at the beginning of the line indicates what action *cvs* took for the file. The meanings are:

- U means that *cvs* updated this file. Either it didn't exist previously, or it was an older version.

- You won't normally see P on a local update. It implies that *cvs* patched the file to update it. Otherwise it has the same meaning as U.

- ? means that *cvs* found the file in the directory, but it doesn't exist in the repository.

- M means that *cvs* found that the file in your working directory has been modified since checkout, but it either didn't need to change it, or it was able to apply the changes cleanly.

- C found that the file in your working directory has been modified since checkout, and it needed to change it, but it was not able to apply the changes cleanly. You will have to resolve the conflicts manually.

After checkout, check the log file for conflicts. For each conflict, you must check the files manually and possibly recover the contents. See the man page *cvs(1)* for more details.

Updating an existing tree

Once you have checked out a tree, the ground rules change a little. Next time you do a checkout, files may also need to be deleted. Apart from that, there isn't much difference between checkout and updating. To update the */usr/src* directory after updating the repository, do:

```
# cd /usr/src
# cvs update -Pd
```

Note that this time we can start in */usr/src*: we now have the *CVS/* subdirectories in place, so *cvs* knows what to do without being given any more information.

Using a remote CVS tree

A CVS tree takes up a lot of space, and it's getting bigger all the time. If you don't check out very often, you may find it easier to use *anonymous CVS*, where the tree is on a different system. FreeBSD provides the server *anoncvs.FreeBSD.org* for this purpose.

For example, to check out the *-CURRENT* source tree, perform the following steps:

```
$ cd /usr                                                        go to the parent directory
$ CVSROOT=:pserver:anoncvs@anoncvs.FreeBSD.org:/home/ncvs        set the server path
$ cvs login                                                      You only need to do this once
Logging in to :pserver:anoncvs@anoncvs.freebsd.org:2401/home/ncvs
CVS password:                                                    enter anoncvs; it doesn't echo
$ cvs co src
cvs server: Updating src
U src/COPYRIGHT
U src/Makefile
U src/Makefile.inc1
(etc)
```

32

Updating the system software

In the previous chapter, we looked at how to get an up-to-date FreeBSD source tree. Once you have the sources, you can build various components of the system. The main tool we use for this purpose is *make*, which we looked at on page 167. The best way to think of upgrading the system is that everything is a matter of changing files. For the purposes of this discussion, you can divide the files on your system into the following categories:

- The *userland*, that part of the system software that is not the kernel. Unlike some other operating systems, FreeBSD expects to keep userland and kernel at the same release level. We'll look at the interaction between kernel and userland below.

- The kernel. You may build a new kernel without updating the sources, of course, if you want to add functionality to the kernel. In this chapter we'll look at upgrading the kernel in the context of a complete system upgrade. We'll consider building a custom kernel in the next chapter, Chapter 33, *Custom kernels*.

- Support for booting the machine, which is currently performed as a separate step.

- Configuration files relating to your system. Some of them, such as */etc/fstab* and */etc/rc.conf*, overlap with the previous category.

- The Ports Collection. This doesn't have to be done at the same time as userland and kernel, though if you upgrade to a significant new version of FreeBSD, it's a good idea to upgrade the ports as well. We looked at upgrading ports on page 178.

- Your own files. They have nothing to do with a software upgrade.

You can make upgrading less onerous by planning in advance. Here are some suggestions:

- Keep system files and user files on different file systems.

- Keep careful records of which configuration files you change, for example with *RCS*, the *Revision Control System*. This proves to be the most complicated part of the entire upgrade process.

The only files that are upgraded are on the traditional root file system and */usr*. No others are affected by an upgrade. Table 32-1, an abridged version of Table 10-2 on page 188, gives an overview of where the system files come from.

Table 32-1: FreeBSD directory hierarchy

directory name	Usage	Populated by
/bin	Executable programs of general use.	*make world*
/boot	Files used when booting the system.	*make install* in */usr/src/sys*.
/dev	Directory of device nodes.	System startup (*devfs*)
/etc	Configuration files used at system startup.	Install from CD-ROM only, *mergemaster*, administrator
/sbin	System executables needed at system startup time.	*make world*
/usr/X11R6	The X11 windowing system.	X-based programs in the Ports Collection
/usr/bin	Standard executable programs that are not needed at system start.	*make world*
/usr/compat	A directory containing code for emulated systems, such as Linux.	Ports Collection
/usr/games	Games.	*make world*
/usr/include	Header files for programmers.	*make world*
/usr/lib	Library files.	*make world*
/usr/libexec	Executable files that are not started directly by the user.	*make world*
/usr/libdata	Miscellaneous files used by system utilities.	*make world*
/usr/local	Additional programs that are not part of the operating system.	Ports collection
/usr/obj	Temporary object files created when building the system.	*make world*
/usr/ports	The Ports Collection.	*sysinstall, cvs*
/usr/sbin	System administration programs that are not needed at system startup.	*make world*

directory name	Usage	Populated by
/usr/share	Miscellaneous read-only files, mainly informative.	*make world*
/usr/src	System source files.	*sysinstall, cvs*

Upgrading kernel and userland

The core part of a system upgrade consists of a synchronized update of both kernel and userland. It's relatively simple to do, but depending on the speed of the machine, it may keep the computer busy for several hours. In general, you build and install the userland first, then you build and install the kernel.

The traditional way to build the userland is:

```
# cd /usr/src
# make world
```

This operation performs a number of functions, which can be influenced by variables you pass to *make*. Without any variables, *make world* performs the following steps:

- It removes the old build directories and creates new ones. You can skip this step by setting the NOCLEAN variable. Don't set NOCLEAN unless you know exactly why you are doing so, since it can cause inconsistencies that come back to bite you later. In particular, if you do have problems after building the world in this manner, you should first go back and perform a complete rebuild without NOCLEAN.

- It rebuilds and installs build tools, including *make*, the C compiler and the libraries.

- It builds the rest of the system, with the exception of the kernel and the boot tools.

- It installs everything. You can omit this stage by building the buildworld target instead of world.

It does this by building a number of subtargets. Occasionally, you might find it useful to build them individually: *make world* can pose a chicken-and-egg problem. It creates the userland, and *make kernel* makes the kernel. Userland and kernel belong together, and if you upgrade the userland first, you may find that the new userland takes advantage of differences in the newer version of the kernel. A typical situation is when a new system call is added to the kernel. In this case, you may find processes exiting with a signal 12 (invalid system call). If this happens, you may have to perform the upgrade with the sequence:

```
# make buildworld
# make kernel
(reboot)
# make installworld
```

You'll find information about such requirements in the file */usr/src/UPDATING*. Table 32-2 gives an overview of the more useful targets to the top-level *Makefile*.

Table 32-2: Targets for top-level *Makefile*

Target	Purpose
buildworld	Rebuild everything, including glue to help do upgrades.
installworld	Install everything built by buildworld.
world	Perform buildworld and installworld.
update	Update your source tree.
most	Build user commands, no libraries or include files.
installmost	Install user commands, but not libraries or include files.
reinstall	If you have a build server, you can NFS mount the source and object directories and do a make reinstall on the *client* to install new binaries from the most recent build on the server.
buildkernel	Build a kernel for your architecture. By default, use the GENERIC kernel configuration file. You can select a different configuration file, say MYKERNEL, with: # **make buildkernel KERNCONF=MYKERNEL** By default, this target builds all the KLDs (Kernel Loadable Modules), which significantly increases the time it takes. If you know that your KLDs will not change, or that you won't be using any, you can skip building them by specifying the –DNO_MODULES flag.
installkernel	Install a kernel you have built with buildkernel.
reinstallkernel	Install a kernel you have built with buildkernel. Don't rename the previous kernel directory to *kernel.old*. Use this target when the previous kernel is not worth keeping.
kernel	Build and install a kernel.

Another issue is that the system configuration might have changed. For example, in early 2002 the default configuration for *sendmail* changed. The process added a daemon user and group, both called smmsp. To install the userland, this user already needed to be present.

The solution to this issue is called *mergemaster*, a script that helps you to upgrade the configuration files. We'll look at it in more detail below, but at this point you should know that you need to run it with the –p (*pre-build*) option:

```
# mergemaster -p
```

As we've seen in table 32-1, the `installworld` target changes a number of directories. Sometimes, though, it leaves old binaries behind: it doesn't remove anything that it doesn't replace. The result can be that you end up using old programs that have long passed their use-by date. One solution to this problem is to look at the last modification date of each program in the directories. For example, if you see:

```
$ ls -lrt /usr/sbin
-r-xr-xr-x  1 root    wheel         397 Jul 14 11:36 svr4
-r-xr-xr-x  1 root    wheel         422 Jul 14 11:29 linux
-r-xr-xr-x  1 root    wheel      142080 Jul 13 17:20 sshd
...
-r-xr-xr-x  1 root    wheel       68148 Jul 13 17:16 uuchk
-r-xr-xr-x  1 root    wheel        6840 Jan  5  2002 ispppcontrol
-r-xr-xr-x  1 root    wheel       27996 Apr 21  2001 k5stash
-r-xr-xr-x  1 root    wheel       45356 Apr 21  2001 ktutil
-r-xr-xr-x  1 root    wheel       11124 Apr 21  2001 kdb_util
-r-xr-xr-x  1 root    wheel        6768 Apr 21  2001 kdb_init
```

It's fairly clear that the files dated April 2001 have not just been installed, so they must be out of date. You can use a number of techniques to delete them; one might be:

```
# find . -mtime +10 | xargs rm
```

This command removes all files in the current directory (.) that are older than 10 days (+10). Of course, this method will only work if you haven't installed anything in these directories yourself. You shouldn't have done so; that's the purpose of the directory hierarchy */usr/local*, to ensure that you keep system files apart from ports and private files.

Be careful with */usr/lib*: a number of ports refer to libraries in this directory hierarchy, and if you delete them, the ports will no longer work. In general there's no problem with old libraries in */usr/lib*, unless they take up too much space, so you're safer if you don't clean out this directory hierarchy.

Note that you need to specify the KERNCONF parameter to all the targets relating to kernel builds.

Upgrading the kernel

There are two reasons for building a new kernel: it might be part of the upgrade process, which is what we'll look at here, or you may build a kernel from your current sources to add functionality to the system. We'll look at this aspect in Chapter 33.

One point to notice is that if you're upgrading from an older custom configuration file, you could have a lot of trouble. We'll see a strategy for minimizing the pain on page 616. In addition, when upgrading to FreeBSD Release 5 from an older release of FreeBSD, you need to install a file */boot/device.hints*, which you can typically copy from */usr/src/sys/i386/conf/GENERIC.hints*:

```
# cp /usr/src/sys/i386/conf/GENERIC.hints /boot/device.hints
```

See page 608 for more details.

When upgrading the kernel, you might get error messages like this one:

```
# config GENERIC
config: GENERIC:71: devices with zero units are not likely to be correct
```

Alternatively, you might get a clearer message:

```
# config GENERIC
../../conf/files: coda/coda_fbsd.c must be optional, mandatory or standard
Your version of config(8) is out of sync with your kernel source.
```

Apart from that, you might find that the kernel fails to link with lots of undefined references. This, too, could mean that the *config* program is out of synchronization with the kernel modules. In each case, build and install the new version of *config*:

```
# cd /usr/src/usr.sbin/config
# make depend all install clean
```

You need to *make clean* at the end since this method will store the object files in non-standard locations.

Upgrading the boot files

At the time of writing, it's still necessary to install the files in */boot* separately. It's possible that this requirement will go away in the future. There are two steps: first you build and install the boot files in the */boot* directory, then you install them on your boot disk. Assuming your system disk is the SCSI disk */dev/da0*, you would perform some of the following steps.

```
# cd /usr/src/sys              build directory
# make install                 build and install the bootstraps
# bsdlabel -B da0              Either, for a dedicated disk
# bsdlabel -B da0s1            Or, for a PC disk slice
# boot0cfg -B da0             Or, booteasy for a dedicated PC disk
```

If you have a dedicated disk, which is normal on a non-Intel platform, use the first *bsdlabel* invocation to install the bootstrap (*boot1*) at the beginning of the disk. Otherwise, install *boot1* at the beginning of your FreeBSD slice and use *boot0cfg* to install the *boot0* boot manager at the beginning of the disk.

Upgrading the configuration files

Currently, the system build procedure does not install the configuration files in */etc*. You need to do that separately. There are two possible methods:

- Do it manually:

  1. Backup the old configuration files. They're not very big, so you can probably make a copy on disk somewhere.

  2. Install pristine new configuration files:

     ```
     # cd /usr/src/etc/
     # make install
     ```

  3. Compare the files and update the new ones with information from your configuration.

- Use *mergemaster*, a semi-automatic method of doing effectively the same thing.

The simple method is: run *mergemaster* with the options -i and -a, which tell it to run automatically (in other words, not to stop and ask questions), and to install new files automatically. That doesn't mean intelligently: you may run into problems anyway.

mergemaster produces a lot of output, and some of it in the middle is important, so you should save the output to disk with the *tee* command. The first time you try, you might see:

```
# mergemaster -ia 2>&1 | tee -a /var/tmp/merge

*** Creating the temporary root environment in /var/tmp/temproot
 *** /var/tmp/temproot ready for use
 *** Creating and populating directory structure in /var/tmp/temproot

set - `grep "^[a-zA-Z]" /usr/src/etc/locale.deprecated`; while [ $# -gt 0 ] ; do
for dir in /usr/share/locale /usr/share/nls /usr/local/share/nls; do test -d /va
r/tmp/temproot/${dir} && cd /var/tmp/temproot/${dir}; test -L "$2" && rm -rf "$2";
 test -L "$1" && test -d "$1" && mv "$1" "$2"; done; shift; shift; done
mtree -deU -f /usr/src/etc/mtree/BSD.root.dist -p /var/tmp/temproot/
./bin missing (created)
./boot missing (created)
...
./vm missing (created)
mtree -deU -f /usr/src/etc/mtree/BSD.sendmail.dist -p /var/tmp/temproot/
mtree: line 10: unknown user smmsp
*** Error code 1

Stop in /usr/src/etc.

   *** FATAL ERROR: Cannot 'cd' to /usr/src/etc and install files to
       the temproot environment
```

These messages are somewhat misleading. First, the files that are created are all in */var/tmp/temproot*. In addition, the message Cannot 'cd' to /usr/src/etc does not refer to any problem with that directory; it's just an indication that it can't continue with the installation due to the previous errors.

The real issue here is that the user smmsp doesn't exist. As we saw above, this user was added some time in 2002 to address some mail security problems. It's in the new */etc/master.passwd* file, but it's not in the one on the system. But how do you merge the two files? One way would to be to use *mergemaster* with the -p option, but then *mergemaster* prompts you for every single file that it finds to be different, usually about 300 of them. In addition, the editing facilities are relatively basic. It's better to edit the file in advance with an editor.

Merging the password file

As we saw on page 145, the password file is quite complicated. Depending on how much work you want to do, you have a couple of possibilities:

- You can choose to completely replace the old */etc/master.passwd* with the new one. This will cause all added user names and passwords to disappear, so unless this is just a test machine, it's unlikely you'll want to follow this path.

- You can take advantage of the fact that, with the exception of root, the distribution */etc/master.passwd* contains no "real" users. You can merge the entries for real users with the entries in the distribution */etc/master.passwd*. This works relatively well, but it removes the passwords of the system users, so you have to set them again. We'll look at how to do that below.

The distribution version of */etc/master.passwd* looks something like this:

```
# $FreeBSD: src/etc/master.passwd,v 1.33 2002/06/23 20:46:44 des Exp $
#
root::0:0::0:0:Charlie &:/root:/bin/csh
toor:*:0:0::0:0:Bourne-again Superuser:/root:
...etc
```

The individual fields are separated by colons (:). We'll look at only the fields that interest us in the following expansion. It's easier to look at if they're separated by spaces; numerically, they're the first, second, eighth, ninth and tenth fields. For a description of the other fields, see the man page *master.passwd(4)*.

User	password	GECOS	home directory	shell
root		Charlie &	/root	/bin/csh
toor	*	Bourne-again Superuser	/root	
daemon	*	Owner of many processes	/root	/sbin/nologin
operator	*	System &	/	/sbin/nologin
bin	*	Binaries Commands	/	/sbin/nologin
tty	*	Tty Sandbox	/	/sbin/nologin
kmem	*	KMem Sandbox	/	/sbin/nologin
games	*	Games pseudo-user	/usr/games	/sbin/nologin
news	*	News Subsystem	/	/sbin/nologin
man	*	Mister Man Pages	/usr/share/man	/sbin/nologin
sshd	*	Secure Shell Daemon	/var/empty	/sbin/nologin
smmsp	*	Sendmail Submission	/var/spool/clientmqueue	/sbin/nologin
mailnull	*	Sendmail Default User	/var/spool/mqueue	/sbin/nologin
bind	*	Bind Sandbox	/	/sbin/nologin
xten	*	X-10 daemon	/usr/local/xten	/sbin/nologin
pop	*	Post Office Owner	/nonexistent	/sbin/nologin
www	*	World Wide Web Owner	/nonexistent	/sbin/nologin
nobody	*	Unprivileged user	/nonexistent	/sbin/nologin

The first field is the name of the user. In the course of time, a number of pseudo-users have been added to reduce exposure to security issues. The main issue in merging the files is to add these users. If you don't have the user in your current */etc/master.passwd*, you can add the line from the distribution file.

The second field contains the *password*. In the distribution file, it's usually *, which means it needs to be set before you can log in at all. Only root has no password; you need to be able to log in as root to set passwords. By contrast, in your installed */etc/master.passwd*, you will almost certainly have a password, and in general you will want to keep it.

The home directory entry has not changed much. You'll notice directory names like */nonexistent* and */var/empty*. The former is a fake, the latter a directory that can't be changed. It's possible that this entry will change from one release to another, and it's important to get it correct.

For many accounts, the *shell* field contains the name */sbin/nologin*, which prints the text "This account is currently not available" and exits. Currently only root has a real shell, but that could change.

To update the */etc/master.passwd*, you can use the following method:

- *Make a copy of your old /etc/master.passwd!*

- Maintain a strict separation of the original lines from the distribution file and your own entries. This will help you with the next update.

- Copy the entire distribution */etc/master.passwd* to the top of your */etc/master.passwd* file. At this point you will have a number of duplicates.

- Check the entries for root. You can probably remove the distribution entry and leave your entry in the file, preserving the password and shell. In this case, you should make an exception to the separation between distribution and local additions: due to the way the name lookups work, if you put user root below user toor ("root" spelt backwards, and the same user with possibly a different shell), all files will appear to belong to toor instead of to root.

- Check what other entries you have for user ids under 1000. You can probably remove them all, but if you have installed ports that require their own user ID, you will need to keep them.

- You should be able to keep all the entries for users with IDs above and including 1000, with the exception of user nobody (ID 65534). Use the entry from the distribution file for nobody.

Once you have merged the files, you need to run *pwd_mkdb* to rebuild the password files */etc/passwd*, */etc/pwd.db* and */etc/spwd.db*. */etc/passwd* is gradually going out of use, but you probably have one on your system, and some ports use it, so it's preferable to recreate it. Do this with the -p option to *pwd_mkdb*:

```
# pwd_mkdb -p /etc/master.passwd
```

Merging /etc/group

In addition to */etc/master.passwd*, you will probably need to upgrade */etc/group*. In this case, the main issue is to add users to the wheel group. The distribution */etc/group* looks like this:

```
# $FreeBSD: src/etc/group,v 1.27 2002/10/14 20:55:49 rwatson Exp $
#
wheel:*:0:root
daemon:*:1:
kmem:*:2:
sys:*:3:
tty:*:4:
operator:*:5:root
mail:*:6:
bin:*:7:
news:*:8:
man:*:9:
games:*:13:
staff:*:20:
sshd:*:22:
smmsp:*:25:
mailnull:*:26:
guest:*:31:
bind:*:53:
uucp:*:66:
xten:*:67:
dialer:*:68:
network:*:69:
www:*:80:
nogroup:*:65533:
nobody:*:65534:
```

Again, new groups have appeared for security reasons. Use a similar method to the one you used for */etc/master.passwd*:

- *Make a copy of your old /etc/group!*

- Maintain a strict separation of the original lines from the distribution file and your own entries. This will help you with the next update.

- Copy the entire distribution */etc/group* to the top of your */etc/group* file. At this point you will have a number of duplicates.

- Check the entries for wheel. You can probably remove the distribution entry and leave your entry in the file, preserving the users.

- In addition, you may have some users in other groups. For example, installing *postfix* adds the user postfix to group mail. You need to preserve these users.

You don't need to do anything special after updating */etc/group*. You can now continue with *mergemaster*.

Mergemaster, second time around

Before running *mergemaster* again, you should delete the contents of */var/tmp/temproot*. Otherwise you might see something like:

```
*** The directory specified for the temporary root environment,
    /var/tmp/temproot, exists.  This can be a security risk if untrusted
    users have access to the system.
```

mergemaster does not delete the old directories: you should do so yourself. If this file already exists, *mergemaster* ignores it and creates a new directory with a name like */var/tmp/temproot.0917.02.18.06*. The numbers are a representation of the date and time of creation.

mergemaster doesn't make it easy to remove the */var/tmp/temproot* directory. You may see:

```
# rm -rf /var/tmp/temproot
rm: /var/tmp/temproot/var/empty: Operation not permitted
rm: /var/tmp/temproot/var: Directory not empty
rm: /var/tmp/temproot: Directory not empty
```

The problem here is that the directory */var/empty* has been set *immutable*. Change that with the *chflags* command and try again:

```
# find /var/tmp/temproot|xargs chflags noschg
# rm -rf /var/tmp/temproot
```

Run *mergemaster* in the same way as before, saving the output. If you haven't deleted the old */var/tmp/temproot* directory, you might see:

```
# mergemaster -ia 2>&1 | tee -a /var/tmp/merge
*** Creating the temporary root environment in /var/tmp/temproot.1102.15.01.14
 *** /var/tmp/temproot.1102.15.01.14 ready for use
 *** Creating and populating directory structure in /var/tmp/temproot.1102.15.01.14

set - `grep "^[a-zA-Z]" /usr/src/etc/locale.deprecated`; while [ $# -gt 0 ] ; do
for dir in /usr/share/locale  /usr/share/nls  /usr/local/share/nls; do  test -d /va
r/tmp/temproot.1102.15.01.14/${dir} && cd /var/tmp/temproot.1102.15.01.14/${dir};  t
est -L "$2" && rm -rf "$2";  test  -L "$1" && test -d "$1" && mv "$1" "$2";  done;
   shift; shift;  done
mtree -deU  -f /usr/src/etc/mtree/BSD.root.dist -p /var/tmp/temproot.1102.15.01.14/
./bin missing (created)
./boot missing (created)
./boot/defaults missing (created)
./boot/kernel missing (created)
./boot/modules missing (created)
./
...
install -o root -g wheel -m 644 /dev/null  /var/tmp/temproot.1102.15.01.14/var/run/u
tmp
install -o root -g wheel -m 644 /usr/src/etc/minfree  /var/tmp/temproot.1102.15.01.1
4/var/crash
cd /usr/src/etc/..; install -o root -g wheel -m 444  COPYRIGHT /var/tmp/temproot.110
2.15.01.14/
cd /usr/src/etc/../share/man; make makedb
makewhatis /var/tmp/temproot.1102.15.01.14/usr/share/man
```

```
*** Beginning comparison

 *** Temp ./etc/defaults/rc.conf and installed have the same CVS Id, deleting
 *** Temp ./etc/defaults/pccard.conf and installed have the same CVS Id, deleting
   *** ./etc/defaults/periodic.conf will remain for your consideration
 *** Temp ./etc/gnats/freefall and installed have the same CVS Id, deleting
 *** Temp ./etc/isdn/answer and installed have the same CVS Id, deleting
 *** Temp ./etc/isdn/isdntel.sh and installed have the same CVS Id, deleting
 ...

*** Comparison complete

*** Files that remain for you to merge by hand:
/var/tmp/temproot.1102.15.01.14/etc/defaults/periodic.conf
/var/tmp/temproot.1102.15.01.14/etc/mail/freebsd.mc
/var/tmp/temproot.1102.15.01.14/etc/mail/freebsd.cf
/var/tmp/temproot.1102.15.01.14/etc/mail/sendmail.cf
/var/tmp/temproot.1102.15.01.14/etc/mail/freebsd.submit.cf
/var/tmp/temproot.1102.15.01.14/etc/mail/mailer.conf
/var/tmp/temproot.1102.15.01.14/etc/mtree/BSD.include.dist
/var/tmp/temproot.1102.15.01.14/etc/mtree/BSD.local.dist
/var/tmp/temproot.1102.15.01.14/etc/mtree/BSD.usr.dist
/var/tmp/temproot.1102.15.01.14/etc/mtree/BSD.var.dist
/var/tmp/temproot.1102.15.01.14/etc/pam.d/su
/var/tmp/temproot.1102.15.01.14/etc/periodic/security/100.chksetuid
/var/tmp/temproot.1102.15.01.14/etc/periodic/security/200.chkmounts
/var/tmp/temproot.1102.15.01.14/etc/periodic/security/500.ipfwdenied
/var/tmp/temproot.1102.15.01.14/etc/periodic/security/600.ip6fwdenied
/var/tmp/temproot.1102.15.01.14/etc/periodic/security/700.kernelmsg
/var/tmp/temproot.1102.15.01.14/etc/rc.d/local
/var/tmp/temproot.1102.15.01.14/etc/crontab
/var/tmp/temproot.1102.15.01.14/etc/inetd.conf
/var/tmp/temproot.1102.15.01.14/etc/motd
/var/tmp/temproot.1102.15.01.14/etc/syslog.conf


*** You chose the automatic install option for files that did not
    exist on your system.  The following were installed for you:
       /etc/periodic/security/510.ipfdenied
       /etc/periodic/security/security.functions
       /etc/mac.conf
```

You're not done yet: there are 21 files above that need looking at. There's a good chance that you've never heard of some of them, let alone changed them. If you *know* for a fact that you have never changed them, for example if you have religiously kept track of your changes with RCS, you don't need to bother: *mergemaster* errs on the side of safety. You may have changed others, though. The most obvious one above is */etc/crontab*, which contains system-wide commands to be executed by *cron*. To compare them, use *diff*:

```
$ diff -wu /etc/crontab /var/tmp/temproot.1102.15.01.14/etc/crontab
--- /var/tmp/crontab    Sat Nov  2 16:27:02 2002
+++ /var/tmp/temproot.1102.15.01.14/etc/crontab Sat Nov  2 15:01:16 2002
@@ -1,6 +1,6 @@
 # /etc/crontab - root's crontab for FreeBSD
 #
-# $FreeBSD: src/etc/crontab,v 1.21 1999/12/15 17:58:29 obrien Exp $
+# $FreeBSD: src/etc/crontab,v 1.31 2001/02/19 02:47:41 peter Exp $
 #
 SHELL=/bin/sh
 PATH=/etc:/bin:/sbin:/usr/bin:/usr/sbin
@@ -10,19 +10,18 @@
 #
 */5     *       *       *       *       root    /usr/libexec/atrun
```

```
 #
+# save some entropy so that /dev/random can reseed on boot
+*/11    *       *       *       *       operator /usr/libexec/save-entropy
+#
 # rotate log files every hour, if necessary
 0       *       *       *       *       root    newsyslog
 #
 # do daily/weekly/monthly maintenance
-59      1       *       *       *       root    periodic daily
-30      3       *       *       6       root    periodic weekly
+1       3       *       *       *       root    periodic daily
+15      4       *       *       6       root    periodic weekly
 30      5       1       *       *       root    periodic monthly
 #
 # time zone change adjustment for wall cmos clock,
-# does nothing if you have UTC cmos clock.
+# does nothing, if you have UTC cmos clock.
 # See adjkerntz(8) for details.
-# 1,31 0-5      *       *       *       root    adjkerntz -a
+1,31   0-5      *       *       *       root    adjkerntz -a
-0,30   *        *       *       *       build   /home/build/build_farm/build_test 2>
 /home/build/cron.err
-0      21       *       *       *       root    /usr/local/bin/cleanup
-0      7        *       *       *       grog    /home/grog/bin/update-FreeBSD-cvs
-1      *        *       *       *       root    (cd /usr/local/etc/postfix; make) 2
 >/dev/null >/dev/null
```

The lines starting with – show lines only in the old file, which is still in */etc/crontab*. The lines starting with + show lines only in the new file, which is in */var/tmp/temp-root.1102.15.01.14/etc/crontab*. There are a number of changes here: the CVS ID ($FreeBSD$) has changed from 1.21 to 1.31, and the times of the periodic maintenance have changed. In the meantime, though, you have added other tasks (the bottom four lines), and you have also commented out the periodic invocation of *adjkerntz*. These are the changes you need to make to the new */etc/crontab* before you install it.

There's a simpler possibility here, though: the only real change that would then be left in */etc/crontab* is the change in the starting times for the daily and weekly housekeeping. Does that matter? If you want, you don't need to change anything: the old */etc/crontab* is fine the way it is.

There's a whole list of files that you're likely to change from the defaults. Here are some more likely candidates:

- You may find it necessary to change */etc/syslog.conf*. If so, you may have to merge by hand, but it shouldn't be too difficult.

- You will almost certainly change */etc/fstab*. About the only reason why you might need to merge changes would be if the file format changes, which it hasn't done for over 20 years.

- */etc/motd* contains the login greeting. There's never a reason to take the new version.

- */etc/inetd.conf* can be a problem: as new services are introduced, it changes. At the same time, you may have added services via ports, or enabled services in the manner we will see on page 448. You definitely need to merge this one yourself.

- If you're using *postfix*, don't install the distribution version of */etc/mail/mailer.conf*. It will reenable *sendmail*, which can cause significant problems.

- If you have changed anything in */etc/sysctl.conf*, you'll need to move the changes to the new file.

33

Custom kernels

So far, everything we've done has been with the standard GENERIC kernel distributed with FreeBSD. You may find it an advantage to install a custom kernel:

- • As we saw in Chapter 2, GENERIC doesn't support everything that FreeBSD knows about. For example, if you want to install a Yoyodyne frobulator, you'll need to install special support for it.[1]

- • It will take less time to boot because it does not have to spend time probing for hardware that you do not have.

- • A custom kernel often uses less memory. The kernel is the one system component that must always be present in memory, so unused code ties up memory that would otherwise be available to the virtual memory system. On a system with limited RAM, you can save some memory by building a custom kernel, but don't overestimate the savings: a minimal kernel might save 500 kB over the GENERIC kernel supplied with the system.

- • In addition, there are several kernel options that you can tune to fit your needs.

- • Finally, on page 621 we'll look at things to think about if you want to run the -CURRENT version of FreeBSD.

In older releases of BSD, you needed to build a new kernel for just about anything you wanted to change, even things as simple as a different IRQ for a device. FreeBSD has evolved quite a bit since then, and it's becoming increasingly less necessary to build a custom kernel. You will certainly need to do so if you want to enable kernel-wide

---

1. In fact, the developer working on the Yoyodyne has defected to the Free Software Foundation. See the GNU General Public License for further details.

options, such as extra consistency checking, but in many cases you have more flexible alternatives:

- If you just need to add device support, you may be able to load a *Kernel Loadable Module*, or *kld*. See page 619 for more information on klds.

- If you want to change ISA parameters such as I/O address, IRQ or DMA settings, you no longer need to build a new kernel: the kernel configuration file no longer knows about such parameters. Instead, they're in the file */boot/device.hints*, that we'll look at below.

- A number of kernel options have been replaced by the *sysctl* interface. For example, the GENERIC kernel does not perform packet routing by default. In older releases of FreeBSD, you had to build a new kernel with the option GATEWAY. Nowadays you can turn this feature on and off at will with a *sysctl* command. We'll look at sysctls on page 620.

Configuring a kernel has changed a lot since the early days of FreeBSD, but it's not done yet. The information in this chapter represents a snapshot in the evolution of building kernels. The goal of these changes is to make it unnecessary to build a kernel at all except to upgrade to a new release.

Building a new kernel

FreeBSD is distributed in source, and building a kernel primarily involves compiling the source files needed for the kernel. To build a kernel, you perform the following steps:

- Install the system source, if you haven't already done so. We looked at that in Chapter 31.

- Define your kernel configuration in a *kernel configuration file*. This file defines parameters to use during the build process. We'll look at how to do this starting on page 610.

- Change to the directory */usr/src* and run *make kernel*. This builds and installs the kernel and all modules. We'll look at it in more detail on page 616, where we'll also see alternatives that give more control over the process.

Configuring I/O devices

A lot of the configuration file relates to the I/O devices that you may connect to your machine. In older releases of FreeBSD, it was often necessary to specify some of the IRQ, DMA channel, board memory, and I/O addresses for the devices you configure, particularly for ISA boards. Since Release 5 of FreeBSD, this is no longer the case. Instead, you modify the file */boot/device.hints*, which we looked at on page 574.

The kernel installation does not install */boot/device.hints* automatically. If it doesn't exist, copy it from the configuration directory:

```
# cp -p /usr/src/sys/i386/conf/GENERIC.hints  /boot/device.hints
```

The kernel build directory

The kernel sources are kept in the directory */usr/src/sys*. The symbolic link */sys* also points to this directory. There are a number of subdirectories of */usr/src/sys* that represent different parts of the kernel, but for our purposes, the most important of them are the architecture dependent directories such as */usr/src/sys/i386/conf* (for the i386 architecture), */usr/src/sys/alpha/conf* (for the Alpha architecture), or */usr/src/sys/sparc64/conf* (for the SPARC64 architecture) where you edit your custom kernel configuration. In addition, the old style kernel build described below builds the kernel in the directory */usr/src/sys/i386/compile*, */usr/src/sys/alpha/compile* or */usr/src/sys/sparc64/compile* respectively. Notice the logical organization of the directory tree: each supported device, file system, and option has its own subdirectory. In the rest of this chapter, we'll look at the i386 architecture. Most of this applies to other architectures as well.

If your system doesn't have the directory */usr/src/sys*, the kernel source has not been installed. If you have a CD-ROM, the sources are on the first CD-ROM in the directory */src*. To install from the CD-ROM, perform the following steps:

```
# mkdir -p /usr/src/sys
# ln -s /usr/src/sys /sys
# cd /
# cat /cdrom/src/ssys.[a-h]* | tar xzvf -
```

The symbolic link */sys* for */usr/src/sys* is not strictly necessary, but it's a good idea: some software uses it, and otherwise you may end up with two different copies of the sources.

By definition, the files on CD-ROM are out of date. See Chapter 31 for details of how to get the current, up-to-date sources.

Next, move to the directory *i386/conf* and copy the *GENERIC* configuration file to the name you want to give your kernel. For example:

```
# cd /usr/src/sys/i386/conf
# cp GENERIC FREEBIE
```

Traditionally, this name is in all capital letters and, if you are maintaining multiple FreeBSD machines with different hardware, it's a good idea to name it after your machine's hostname. In this example we call it *FREEBIE*.

Now, edit *FREEBIE* with your favourite text editor. Change the comment lines at the top to reflect your configuration or the changes you've made to differentiate it from *GENERIC*:

```
#
# FREEBIE -- My personal configuration file
#
# For more information on this file, please read the handbook section on
# Kernel Configuration Files:
#
#    http://www.FreeBSD.org/doc/en_US.ISO8859-1/books/handbook/kernelconfig-config.html
#
# The handbook is also available locally in /usr/share/doc/handbook
# if you've installed the doc distribution, otherwise always see the
# FreeBSD World Wide Web server (http://www.FreeBSD.org/) for the
# latest information.
#
# An exhaustive list of options and more detailed explanations of the
# device lines is also present in the ../../conf/NOTES and NOTES files.
# If you are in doubt as to the purpose or necessity of a line, check first
# in NOTES.
#
# $FreeBSD: src/sys/i386/conf/FREEBIE,v 1.369 2002/10/19 16:54:07 rwatson Exp $

machine        "i386"
cpu            "I486_CPU"
cpu            "I586_CPU"
cpu            "I686_CPU"
ident          FREEBIE
maxusers       0
```

The configuration file

The directory */sys/i386/conf* contains a number of configuration files:

GENERIC   General-purpose configuration file

LINT   This file used to be a "complete" configuration file with comments, used for testing and documentation. Since FreeBSD Release 5, it no longer exists. You can create it from the files *NOTES* and */usr/src/sys/conf/NOTES* with the command:

        $ make LINT

NOTES   A complete pseudo-configuration file with copious comments. This file is descended from *LINT*, but it also includes device hints. You can't use it for building kernels. Instead, create the file *LINT* as described above.

        NOTES contains only platform-specific information. Most of the information is in the platform-independent file */usr/src/sys/conf/NOTES*.

OLDCARD   A configuration file for laptops that use PCCARD controllers. At the time of writing, PCCARD support has largely been rewritten, but the new code does not support some of the devices that the old code supports. This configuration file uses the old PCCARD code instead of the new code. When the new code is complete, it will go away.

The general format of a configuration file is quite simple. Each line contains a keyword and one or more arguments. Anything following a # is considered a comment and ignored. Keywords that contain numbers used as text must be enclosed in quotation marks.

One of the results of this simplicity is that you can put in options that have absolutely no effect. For example, you could add a line like this:

```
options        APPLE_MAC_COMPATIBILITY
```

You can build a kernel with this option. It will make no difference whatsoever. Now it's unlikely that you'll think up a non-existent option like this, but it's much more possible that you'll misspell a valid option, especially finger-twisters like SYSVSHM, with the result that you don't compile in the option you wanted. The *config* program warns if you use unknown options, so take these warnings seriously.

Kernel options change from release to release, so there's no point in describing them all here. In the following sections we'll look at some of the more interesting ones; for a complete list, read *LINT* or the online handbook. See above for details of how to create *LINT*.

Naming the kernel

Every kernel you build requires the keywords machine, cpu, and ident. For example,

```
machine        "i386"                  For i386 architecture
machine        "alpha"                 For alpha architecture
machine        "sparc64"               For SPARC 64 architecture
cpu            "I486_CPU"
cpu            "I586_CPU"
cpu            "I686_CPU"
ident          FREEBIE
```

machine

The keyword machine describes the machine architecture for which the kernel is to be built. Currently it should be i386 for the Intel architecture, and alpha for the AXP architecture. Don't confuse this with the processor: for example, the i386 architecture refers to the Intel 80386 and all its successors, including lookalikes made by AMD, Cyrix and IBM.

cpu cpu_type

cpu describes which CPU chip or chips this kernel should support. For the i386 architecture, the possible values are I386_CPU, I486_CPU, I586_CPU and I686_CPU, and you can specify any combination of these values. For a custom kernel, it is best to specify only the CPU you have. If, for example, you have an Intel Pentium, use I586_CPU for *cpu_type*.

If you're not sure what processor type you have, look at the output from the *dmesg* command when running the GENERIC kernel. For example:

```
CPU: AMD Athlon(tm) XP processor 1700+ (1462.51-MHz 686-class CPU)
  Origin = "AuthenticAMD"  Id = 0x662  Stepping = 2
  Features=0x383f9ff<FPU,VME,DE,PSE,TSC,MSR,PAE,MCE,CX8,SEP,MTRR,PGE,MCA,CMOV,PAT,PS
E36,MMX,FXSR,SSE>
  AMD Features=0xc0480000<<b19>,AMIE,DSP,3DNow!>
```

This shows that the processor, an AMD Athlon XP, is a "686 class" CPU, so to run a kernel on this processor, you must set I686_CPU in the config file.

Since Release 5 of FreeBSD, it is no longer possible to build a single kernel with support for both the 80386 processor and later processors: the code for the later processors is optimized to use instructions that the 80386 processor does not have. Choose either I386_CPU or any combination of the others.

ident machine_name

ident specifies a name used to identify the kernel. In the file *GENERIC* it is GENERIC. Change this to whatever you named your kernel, in this example, FREEBIE. The value you put in ident will print when you boot up the kernel, so it's useful to give a kernel a different name if you want to keep it separate from your usual kernel (if you want to build an experimental kernel, for example). As with machine and cpu, enclose your kernel's name in quotation marks if it contains any numbers.

This name is passed to the C compiler as a variable, so don't use names like DEBUG, or something that could be confused with another machine or CPU name, like vax.

Kernel options

There are a number of global kernel options, most of which you don't need to change. In the following section, we'll look at some of the few exceptions.

Configuring specific I/O devices

There are some devices that the GENERIC kernel does not support. In older releases of FreeBSD, you needed to build a new kernel to support them. This is seldom the case any more: most devices can be supported by *kld*s. Work is under way to support the remainder. In case of doubt, look at the file *HARDWARE.TXT* on the installation CD-ROM.

maxusers number

This value sets the size of a number of important system tables. It is still included in the kernel configuration file, but you no longer need build a new kernel to change it. Instead, you can set it at boot time. For example, you might add the following line to your */boot/loader.conf* file:

```
maxusers="64"
```

See 532 for more details of */boot/loader.conf.*

maxusers is intended to be roughly equal to the number of simultaneous users you expect to have on your machine, but it is only used to determine the size of some system tables. The default value 0 tells the kernel to autosize the tables depending on the amount of memory on the system. If the autosizing doesn't work to your satisfaction, change this value. Even if you are the only person to use the machine, you shouldn't set maxusers lower than the default value 32, especially if you're using X or compiling software. The reason is that the most important table set by maxusers is the maximum number of processes, which is set to 20 + 16 * maxusers, so if you set maxusers to one, you can only have 36 simultaneous processes, including the 18 or so that the system starts up at boot time, and the 15 or so you will probably create when you start X. Even a simple task like reading a man page can start up nine processes to filter, decompress, and view it. Setting maxusers to 32 will allow you to have up to 532 simultaneous processes, which is normally ample. If, however, you see the dreaded *proc table full* error when trying to start another program, or are running a server with a large number of simultaneous users, you can always increase this number and reboot.

> maxusers does *not* limit the number of users who can log into the machine. It simply sets various table sizes to reasonable values considering the maximum number of users you will likely have on your system and how many processes each of them will be running. It's probable that this parameter will go away in future.

Multiple processors

FreeBSD 5.0 supports most modern multiprocessor systems. The GENERIC kernel does not support them by default. For i386, set the following options:

```
# To make an SMP kernel, the next two are needed
options         SMP                     # Symmetric MultiProcessor Kernel
options         APIC_IO                 # Symmetric (APIC) I/O
```

For Alpha, only the first line is necessary:

```
options         SMP                     # Symmetric MultiProcessor Kernel
```

An SMP kernel will not run on a single processor Intel machine without an *IOAPIC (I/O Advanced Programmable Interrupt Controller)* chip. Be sure to disable the cpu "I386_CPU" and cpu "I486_CPU" options for SMP kernels.

Debug options

FreeBSD is a very stable operating system. No software is perfect, however, and sometimes it crashes. When it does, it provides a number of facilities to help fix the problem. Some of these are dependent on kernel build options.

Even if you have no intention of debugging a kernel problem yourself, you should set debug symbols when you build a kernel. They cost nothing except disk space, and if you are short on disk space, you can remove most of the files after the build.

To set the debug symbols, remove the leading # mark from this line in the configuration file:

```
makeoptions     DEBUG=-g                    # Build kernel with gdb(1) debug symbols
```

Under normal circumstances this makes no difference: the build process still installs the kernel without the debug symbols, and it has no effect on performance. If, however, you have a crash, the kernel with debug symbols is available in the kernel build directory, in this case */usr/src/sys/i386/compile/FREEBIE/kernel.debug*, to assist analysis of the problem. Without this file it will be very difficult to find it.

So why is it commented out? Without debug symbols, your build directory will take about 50 MB of disk space. With debug symbols, it will be about 250 MB. The FreeBSD Project couldn't agree to change it.

Other debugging options

If you run into trouble with your system, there are a number of other debugging options that you can use. The following are the more important ones:

```
options         DDB
options         BREAK_TO_DEBUGGER
options         DDB_UNATTENDED          # Don't drop into DDB for a panic
options         GDB_REMOTE_CHAT         # Use gdb remote debugging protocol
options         KTRACE
options         DIAGNOSTIC
options         INVARIANTS
options         INVARIANT_SUPPORT
options         WITNESS                 #Enable checks to detect deadlocks and cycles
options         WITNESS_SKIPSPIN        #Don't run witness on spinlocks for speed
```

These options provide support for various debugging features.

DDB

Specify DDB to include the kernel debugger, *ddb*. If you set this option, you might also want to set the BREAK_TO_DEBUGGER option,

BREAK_TO_DEBUGGER

Use the option BREAK_TO_DEBUGGER if you have installed the kernel debugger and you have the system console on a serial line.

DDB_UNATTENDED

If you have a panic on a system with *ddb*, it will not reboot automatically. Instead, it will enter *ddb* and give you a chance to examine the remains of the system before rebooting. This can be a disadvantage on systems that run unattended: after a panic, they would wait until somebody comes past before rebooting. Use the DDB_UNATTENDED option to cause a system with *ddb* to reboot automatically on panic.

GDB_REMOTE_CHAT

ddb supports remote debugging from another FreeBSD machine via a serial connection. See the online handbook for more details. To use this feature, set the option GDB_REMOTE_CHAT.

KTRACE

Set KTRACE if you want to use the system call trace program *ktrace*.

DIAGNOSTIC

A number of source files use the DIAGNOSTIC option to enable extra sanity checking of internal structures. This support is not enabled by default because of the extra time it would take to check for these conditions, which can only occur as a result of programming errors.

INVARIANTS and INVARIANT_SUPPORT

INVARIANTS is used in a number of source files to enable extra sanity checking of internal structures. This support is not enabled by default because of the extra time it would take to check for these conditions, which can only occur as a result of programming errors.

INVARIANT_SUPPORT option compiles in support for verifying some of the internal structures. It is a prerequisite for INVARIANTS. The intent is that you can set INVARIANTS for single source files (by changing the source file or specifying it on the command line) if you have INVARIANT_SUPPORT enabled.

WITNESS and WITNESS_SKIPSPIN

One of the big changes in FreeBSD Release 5 relates to the manner in which the kernel performs resource locking. As a result, the danger exists of *deadlocks*, locks that can't be undone without rebooting the machine. WITNESS checks for the danger of deadlocks and warns if it finds a potential deadlock ("lock order reversal"). This is a very expensive debugging option: it can slow the machine down by an order of magnitude, so don't use it unless you have to.

A compromise that doesn't use quite so much processor power is the combination of WITNESS with WITNESS_SKIPSPIN, which avoids spin locks. It can still catch most problems.

Preparing for upgrades

When changing the configuration file, consider that it probably won't be the only time you make these changes. At some time in the future, you'll upgrade the system, and you'll have to build your custom kernel all over again. But the GENERIC kernel configuration file will have changed as well. You have two choices: incorporate the modifications to GENERIC into your configuration file, or incorporate your modifications to the old GENERIC file into the new GENERIC configuration file. It turns out that the latter path is easier.

To prepare for this approach, try to change as little as possible in the body of the configuration file. Instead, add all your changes to the end, along with a comment so that you can readily recognize the changes. For example, you might append:

```
# Added by grog, 24 October 2002
# Comment out WITNESS, WITNESS_SKIPSPIN and SCSI_DELAY above

options        SMP                      # Symmetric MultiProcessor Kernel
options        APIC_IO                  # Symmetric (APIC) I/O

options        BREAK_TO_DEBUGGER

options        SCSI_DELAY=3000          #Delay (in ms) before probing SCSI

options        CAMDEBUG
options        MSGBUF_SIZE=81920
# options      TIMEREQUESTS             # watch for delays

device         snp                      #Snoop device - to look at pty/vty/etc..
```

That won't be all, of course. Look at that option SCSI_DELAY. That option already exists in the configuration file (with a value of 15 seconds instead of 3). If you leave both, *config* will issue a warning. You need to comment out the first occurrence, as the comment at the top indicates.

Building and installing the new kernel

The traditional way to build a BSD kernel was, assuming a configuration file called *FREEBIE*:

```
# cd /usr/src/sys/i386/conf
# config FREEBIE
# cd ../compile/FREEBIE
# make depend all install
```

At the time of writing, this still works, but it will go away at some time in the future. It has the disadvantage that you need to know your architecture, and the kernel is built in the source tree, which is not a good idea. The new kernel build method starts from */usr/src*, the same directory as all other build operations, and it builds the kernel in the */usr/obj* hierarchy.

You'll need about 250 MB of free space on */usr/obj* to build a kernel. If you're really tight on space, you can reduce this value to about 50 MB by omitting the makeoptions DEBUG=-g specification, but if you have problems with the system at some later stage, it will be much more difficult to find what is causing them.

There are a number of alternative commands for building the kernel:

```
# cd /usr/src
# make kernel KERNCONF=FREEBIE                build and install kernel and klds
# make buildkernel KERNCONF=FREEBIE          build kernel and klds
# make installkernel KERNCONF=FREEBIE        install prebuilt kernel and klds
# make reinstallkernel KERNCONF=FREEBIE      reinstall kernel and klds
# make kernel KERNCONF=FREEBIE -DNO_MODULES  build and install kernel only
```

The easiest way is make kernel, which is subdivided into the buildkernel and installkernel steps. You can perform these steps individually if you want. If you use the reinstallkernel target instead of the installkernel target, the */boot/kernel.old* hierarchy remains unchanged. This is useful when a previous kernel build failed to boot.

If you know the klds are not going to change, you can speed things up by not building them again. Use the -DNO_MODULES flag in combination with any of the other targets to inhibit building or installing the klds, as shown in the last example. Don't do this the first time you build the kernel: if you have mismatches between the kernel and the klds, you may find it impossible to start the system. On the other hand, if you find the kernel doesn't boot, and you want to change the configuration file and rebuild it from the same sources, you can save some time like this.

The first step in building the kernel is to run the *config* program. You no longer have to do this yourself; the buildkernel and kernel targets do it for you. *config* creates a directory in which to build the kernel and fills it with the necessary infrastructure, notably the kernel *Makefile* and a number of header files.

It's possible to get error messages at this stage if you have made a mistake in the config file. If the *config* command fails when you give it your kernel description, you've probably made a simple error somewhere. Fortunately, *config* will print the line number that it had trouble with, so you can quickly find it with an editor. For example:

```
config: line 17: syntax error
```

One possibility is that you have mistyped a keyword. Compare it to the entry in the GENERIC or LINT kernel definitions.

The next step is to compile all the source files and create a kernel and a set of matching *kld*s. It can take some time, up to an hour on a slow machine. It's also possible to have errors, and unfortunately they are usually *not* self-explanatory. If the *make* command fails, it usually signals an error in your kernel description that is not obvious enough for *config* to catch. A common one is when you omit an entry from the configuration file which is a prerequisite for an entry which is present. For example, if you have SCSI disks (device da), you require the scbus device as well, and if you have just about any kind of Ethernet card, you require the miibus device as well:

```
device          scbus         # SCSI bus (required)
device          da            # Direct Access (disks)

device          miibus        # MII bus support
device          fxp           # Intel EtherExpress PRO/100B (82557, 82558)
```

If you leave scbus or miibus out of the configuration, *config* will not complain, but the kernel link phase will fail with lots of unresolved references.

If you can't resolve the problem after comparing your configuration file with *GENERIC*, send mail to questions@FreeBSD.ORG with your kernel configuration, and it should be diagnosed very quickly. A description of how to interpret these errors has been in the works for a long time, but currently it's still deep magic.

Rebooting

Next, shutdown the system and reboot load the new kernel:

```
# shutdown -r now
```

If the new kernel does not boot, or fails to recognize your devices, don't panic. Reset the machine, and when the boot prompt appears, press the space bar to interrupt the boot. Then boot the old kernel:

```
Ok unload                                    remove the kernel that the loader has loaded
Ok load /boot/kernel.old/kernel              load the previous kernel
Ok boot
```

When reconfiguring a kernel, it is always a good idea to keep on hand a kernel that is known to work. There are two points here:

- If your kernel doesn't boot, you don't want to save it to *kernel.old* when you build a new one. It's no use, and if the new kernel doesn't boot either, you'll be left without a runnable kernel. In this case, use the reinstallkernel target mentioned above:

  ```
  # make buildkernel KERNCONF=FREEBIE          build kernel and klds
  # make reinstallkernel KERNCONF=FREEBIE      reinstall kernel and klds
  ```

- You could still make a mistake and type make install, throwing away your last good kernel. It's easy enough to end up with a completely unbootable system like this. It's a good idea to keep another kernel copy with a name like *kernel.save*, which the installation procedure does not touch.

After booting with a good kernel you can check over your configuration file and try to build it again. One helpful resource is the */var/log/messages* file which records, among other things, all of the kernel messages from every successful boot. Also, the *dmesg* command prints the most recent kernel messages from the current boot. After some time the original messages are overwritten, so the system startup procedure saves the messages at boot time in the file */var/run/dmesg.boot*. Note that most laptops maintain the previous contents of the kernel message buffer when rebooted, so the beginning of the output of *dmesg* may relate to an earlier boot. Check through to the end before jumping to conclusions.

Making device nodes

FreeBSD Release 5 comes with *devfs*, the *device file system*. One great advantage of *devfs* is that it automatically creates device nodes for the hardware it finds, so you no longer need to run the */dev/MAKEDEV* script supplied with older releases of FreeBSD.

Kernel loadable modules

As we saw at the beginning of the chapter, you may not have to build a new kernel to implement the functionality you want. Instead, just load it into the running kernel with a *Kernel Loadable Module* (*kld*). The directory */boot/kernel/modules* contains a number of klds. To load them, use *kldload*. For example, if you wanted to load SCO UNIX compatibility, you would enter:

```
# kldload ibcs2
```

This loads the module */boot/kernel/modules/ibcs2.ko*. Note that you don't need to specify the directory name, nor the *.ko* extension.

To find what modules are loaded, use *kldstat*:

```
# kldstat
Id Refs Address    Size    Name
 1    5 0xc0100000 1d08b0  kernel
 2    2 0xc120d000 a000    ibcs2.ko
 3    1 0xc121b000 3000    ibcs2_coff.ko
 5    1 0xc1771000 e000    linux.ko
 6    1 0xc177f000 bf000   vinum.ko
```

You can also unload some klds, but not all of them. Use *kldunload* for this purpose:

```
# kldunload vinum
```

You can't unload a kld which has active resources. In the case of *vinum*, for example, you can only unload it when none of its volumes are mounted.

sysctl

sysctl is a relatively new kernel interface that allows access to specific variables in the kernel. Some of these variables are read-only: you can look, but not touch. Others are changeable.

sysctl variables are usually referred to simply as *sysctls*. Each *sysctl* has a name in "Management Information Base" (*MIB*) form, consisting of a hierarchical arrangement of names separated by periods (.). The first component of the name indicates the part of the kernel to which it relates. The following examples give you an idea of how to use the *sysctl* program:

```
$ sysctl kern.ostype
FreeBSD
$ sysctl kern                          list all sysctls starting with kern
$ sysctl -a                            list all sysctls
# sysctl net.inet.ip.forwarding=1      turn IP forwarding on
net.inet.ip.forwarding: 0 -> 1
```

Some of the more interesting *sysctls* are:

```
kern.ostype: FreeBSD
kern.osrelease: 5.0-RELEASE
kern.version: FreeBSD 5.0-RELEASE #0: Thu Jan 16 15:03:31 CST 2003
    grog@freebie.example.org:/usr/src/sys/GENERIC
kern.hostname: freebie.example.org
kern.boottime: { sec = 1007165073, usec = 570637 } Fri Jan 17 10:34:33 2003
kern.bootfile: /boot/kernel/kernel
kern.init_path: /sbin/init:/sbin/oinit:/sbin/init.bak:/stand/sysinstall
kern.module_path: /boot/kernel;/boot/kernel;/boot/modules;/modules
kern.coredump: 1
kern.corefile: /var/tmp/%N.core
kern.msgbuf: nreach TCP 213.46.243.23:25370 139.130.136.138:25 in via ppp0
net.inet.ip.fw.enable: 1
hw.machine: i386
hw.model: Pentium II/Pentium II Xeon/Celeron
hw.ncpu: 1
hw.byteorder: 1234
hw.physmem: 129949696
hw.usermem: 100556800
hw.pagesize: 4096
hw.floatingpoint: 1
hw.machine_arch: i386
hw.ata.ata_dma: 1
hw.ata.wc: 1
hw.ata.tags: 0
hw.ata.atapi_dma: 0
compat.linux.osname: Linux
compat.linux.osrelease: 2.2.12
compat.linux.oss_version: 198144
```

Many of these need no description, but some are less obvious:

- kern.msgbuf shows the contents of the kernel message buffer, which is also listed by the *dmesg* program.

- `kern.corefile` specifies a template for the name of the core dump file generated when a process fails. By default the core file ends up in the current working directory—whatever that might be. By specifying an absolute path name, you can ensure that any core file will go into a specific directory. The text %N is replaced by the name of the program.

Living with FreeBSD-CURRENT

Keeping up with FreeBSD-CURRENT requires work on your part. You should be on the `FreeBSD-current@FreeBSD.org` mailing list, which you can join via majordomo. See page 17 for details of how to use majordomo.

Build kernels with debug symbols

FreeBSD-CURRENT is not as stable as the released releases. To prepare yourself for possible problems, you should build kernels that include debug symbols. The resultant kernel is about 30 MB in size, but it will make debugging with *ddb* (the kernel debugger) or *gdb* much easier. Even if you don't intend to do this yourself, the information will be of great use to anybody you may call in to help. We looked at how to build a debug kernel on page 614.

Solving problems in FreeBSD-CURRENT

You *will* run into problems with FreeBSD-CURRENT. When it happens, please first read the mailing list and possibly the mail archives and see if the problem has been reported. If it hasn't, try to investigate the problem yourself. Then send mail to `FreeBSD-current` describing the problem and what you have done to solve it.

If you experience a panic, please don't just send a message to `FreeBSD-current` saying "My kernel panics when I type *foo*." Remember that you're asking somebody to use their spare time to look at the problem. Make it easy for them:

1. Update to the absolutely latest sources, unless emails have been warning against this.

2. If you have any local patches, back them out.

3. Recompile, from scratch, your kernel with *ddb* and with complete symbols (see above).

4. Report all details from the panic. At an absolute minimum, give all information from `show reg` and `trace`.

5. Try to dump the system.

6. If you're successful, follow the procedure discussed in the following section to find out something about how the problem occurred.

If you don't do at least this, there isn't much chance that a mail message to `FreeBSD-current` will have much effect.

Analyzing kernel crash dumps

When the kernel panics, and you have dumping enabled, you'll usually see something like this on the console:

```
Fatal trap 9: general protection fault while in kernel mode
instruction pointer    = 0x8:0xc01c434b
stack pointer          = 0x10:0xc99f8d0c
frame pointer          = 0x10:0xc99f8d28
code segment           = base 0x0, limit 0xfffff, type 0x1b
                       = DPL 0, pres 1, def32 1, gran 1
processor eflags       = interrupt enabled, resume, IOPL = 0
current process        = 2638 (find)
interrupt mask         = net tty bio cam
trap number            = 9
panic: general protection fault

syncing disks... 7 7 7 7 7 7 7 7 7 7 7 7 7 7 7 7 7 7 7 7 7
giving up on 6 buffers
Uptime: 17h53m13s

dumping to dev #ad/1, offset 786560
dump ata0: resetting devices .. done
```

You don't need to write this information down: it is saved in the dump.

When you reboot, the system startup scripts find that you have a dump in the designated dump device (see above) and copy it and the current kernel to */var/crash*, assuming the directory exists and there's enough space for the dump. You'll see something like this in the directory:

```
# cd /var/crash
# ls -l
-rw-r--r--  1 root  wheel          3 Dec 29 10:09 bounds
-rw-r--r--  1 root  wheel    4333000 Dec 29 10:10 kernel.22
-rw-r--r--  1 root  wheel          5 Sep 17  1999 minfree
-rw-------  1 root  wheel  268369920 Dec 29 10:09 vmcore.22
```

The important files here are *kernel.22*, which contains a copy of the kernel running when the crash occurred, and *vmcore.22*, which contains the contents of memory. The number 22 indicates that the sequence number of the dump. It's possible to have multiple dumps in */var/crash*. Note that you can waste a lot of space like that.

The file *bounds* contains the number of the next dump (23 in this case), and *minfree* specifies the minimum amount of free space (in kilobytes) to leave on the file system after you've copied the dump. If this can't be guaranteed, *savecore* doesn't save the dump.

savecore copies the kernel from which you booted. As we've seen, it typically isn't a debug kernel. In the example above, we installed */usr/src/sys/i386/conf/FREEBIE/kernel*, but the debug version was */usr/src/sys/i386/conf/FREEBIE/kernel.debug*. This is the one you need. The easiest way to access it is to use a symbolic link:

```
# ln -s /usr/src/sys/i386/conf/FREEBIE/kernel.debug .
# ls -lL
-rw-r--r--  1 root   wheel            3 Dec 29 10:09 bounds
-rwxr-xr-x  1 grog   lemis     16796546 Dec 18 14:21 kernel.debug
-rw-r--r--  1 root   wheel      4333000 Dec 29 10:10 kernel.22
-rw-r--r--  1 root   wheel            5 Sep 17  1999 minfree
-rw-------  1 root   wheel    268369920 Dec 29 10:09 vmcore.22
```

As you can see, it's much larger.

Next, run *gdb* against the kernel and the dump:

```
# gdb -k kernel.debug vmcore.22
```

The first thing you see is a political message from the Free Software Foundation, followed by a repeat of the crash messages, a listing of the current instruction (always the same) and a prompt:

```
#0  dumpsys () at ../../kern/kern_shutdown.c:473
473                 if (dumping++) {
(kgdb)
```

Due to the way C, *gdb* and FreeBSD work, the real information you're looking for is further down the stack. The first thing you need to do is to find out exactly where it happens. Do that with the *backtrace* command:

```
(kgdb) bt
#0  dumpsys () at ../../kern/kern_shutdown.c:473
#1  0xc01c88bf in boot (howto=256) at ../../kern/kern_shutdown.c:313
#2  0xc01c8ca5 in panic (fmt=0xc03a8cac "%s") at ../../kern/kern_shutdown.c:581
#3  0xc033ab03 in trap_fatal (frame=0xc99f8ccc, eva=0)
    at ../../i386/i386/trap.c:956
#4  0xc033a4ba in trap (frame={tf_fs = 16, tf_es = 16, tf_ds = 16,
    tf_edi = -1069794208, tf_esi = -1069630360, tf_ebp = -912290520,
    tf_isp = -912290568, tf_ebx = -1069794208, tf_edx = 10, tf_ecx = 10,
    tf_eax = -1, tf_trapno = 9, tf_err = 0, tf_eip = -1071889589, tf_cs = 8,
    tf_eflags = 66182, tf_esp = 1024, tf_ss = 6864992})
    at ../../i386/i386/trap.c:618
#5  0xc01c434b in malloc (size=1024, type=0xc03c3c60, flags=0)
    at ../../kern/kern_malloc.c:233
#6  0xc01f015c in allocbuf (bp=0xc3a6f7cc, size=1024)
    at ../../kern/vfs_bio.c:2380
#7  0xc01effa6 in getblk (vp=0xc9642f00, blkno=0, size=1024, slpflag=0,
    slptimeo=0) at ../../kern/vfs_bio.c:2271
#8  0xc01eded2 in bread (vp=0xc9642f00, blkno=0, size=1024, cred=0x0,
    bpp=0xc99f8e3c) at ../../kern/vfs_bio.c:504
#9  0xc02d0634 in ffs_read (ap=0xc99f8ea0) at ../../ufs/ufs/ufs_readwrite.c:273
#10 0xc02d734e in ufs_readdir (ap=0xc99f8ef0) at vnode_if.h:334
#11 0xc02d7cd1 in ufs_vnoperate (ap=0xc99f8ef0)
    at ../../ufs/ufs/ufs_vnops.c:2382
#12 0xc01fbc3b in getdirentries (p=0xc9a53ac0, uap=0xc99f8f80)
    at vnode_if.h:769
#13 0xc033adb5 in syscall2 (frame={tf_fs = 47, tf_es = 47, tf_ds = 47,
    tf_edi = 134567680, tf_esi = 134554336, tf_ebp = -1077937404,
    tf_isp = -912289836, tf_ebx = 672064612, tf_edx = 134554336,
    tf_ecx = 672137600, tf_eax = 196, tf_trapno = 7, tf_err = 2,
    tf_eip = 671767876, tf_cs = 31, tf_eflags = 582, tf_esp = -1077937448,
    tf_ss = 47}) at ../../i386/i386/trap.c:1155
#14 0xc032b825 in Xint0x80_syscall ()
#15 0x280a1eee in ?? ()
#16 0x280a173a in ?? ()
```

```
#17 0x804969e in ?? ()
#18 0x804b550 in ?? ()
#19 0x804935d in ?? ()
(kgdb)
```

The rest of this chapter is only of interest to programmers with a good understanding of C. If you're not a programmer, this is about as far as you can go. Save this information and supply it to whomever you ask for help. It's usually not enough to solve the problem, but it's a good start, and your helper will be able to tell you what to do next.

Climbing through the stack

The backtrace outputs information about *stack frames*, which are built when a function is called. They're numbered starting from the most recent frame, #0, which is seldom the one that interests us. In general, we've had a panic, the most important frame is the function that calls panic:

```
#3  0xc033ab03 in trap_fatal (frame=0xc99f8ccc, eva=0)
    at ../../i386/i386/trap.c:956
```

The information here is:

- #3 is the frame number. This is a number allocated by *gdb*. You can use it to reference the frame in a number of commands.

- 0xc033ab03 is the return address from the call to the next function up the stack (panic in this case).

- trap_fatal is the name of the function.

- (frame=0xc99f8ccc, eva=0) are the parameter values supplied to trap_fatal.

- ../../i386/i386/trap.c:956 gives the name of the source file and the line number in the file. The path names are relative to the kernel build directory, so they usually start with ../../.

In this example, the panic comes from a user process. Starting at the bottom, depending on the processor platform, you may see the user process stack. You can recognize them on an Intel platform by the addresses below the kernel base address 0xc0000000. On other platforms, the address might be different. In general, you won't get any symbolic information for these frames, since the kernel symbol table doesn't include user symbols.

Climbing up the stack, you'll find the system call stack frame, in this example at frames 14 and 13. This is where the process involved the kernel. The stack frame above (frame 12) generally shows the name of the system call, in this case getdirentries. To perform its function, getdirentries indirectly calls ffs_read, the function that reads from a UFS file. ffs_read calls bread, which reads into the buffer cache. To do so, it allocates a buffer with getblk and allocbuf, which calls malloc to allocate memory for buffer cache. The next thing we see is a stack frame for trap: something has gone wrong inside malloc. trap determines that the trap in unrecoverable and calls trap_fatal, which in turn calls panic. The stack frames above show how the system prepares to dump and writes to disk. They're no longer of interest.

Finding out what really happened

In general, you start analyzing a panic dump in the stack frame that called panic, but in the case of the fatal trap that we have here, the most important stack frame is the one below trap, in this case frame 5. That's where things went wrong. Select it with the frame command, abbreviated to f, and list the code with list (or l):

```
(kgdb) f 5
#5  0xc01c434b in malloc (size=1024, type=0xc03c3c60, flags=0)
    at ../../kern/kern_malloc.c:233
233             va = kbp->kb_next;
(kgdb) l
228                     }
229                         freep->next = savedlist;
230                         if (kbp->kb_last == NULL)
231                             kbp->kb_last = (caddr_t)freep;
232                     }
233                 va = kbp->kb_next;
234                 kbp->kb_next = ((struct freelist *)va)->next;
235     #ifdef INVARIANTS
236             freep = (struct freelist *)va;
237             savedtype = (const char *) freep->type->ks_shortdesc;
(kgdb)
```

You might want to look at the local (automatic) variables. Use info local, which you can abbreviate to i loc:

```
(kgdb) i loc
type = (struct malloc_type *) 0xc03c3c60
kbp = (struct kmembuckets *) 0xc03ebc68
kup = (struct kmemusage *) 0x0
freep = (struct freelist *) 0x0
indx = 10
npg = -1071714292
allocsize = -1069794208
s = 6864992
va = 0xffffffff <Address 0xffffffff out of bounds>
cp = 0x0
savedlist = 0x0
ksp = (struct malloc_type *) 0xffffffff
(kgdb)
```

The line where the problem occurs is 233:

```
233             va = kbp->kb_next;
```

Look at the structure kbp:

```
(kgdb) p *kbp
$2 = {
  kb_next = 0xffffffff <Address 0xffffffff out of bounds>,
  kb_last = 0xc1a31000 "",
  kb_calls = 83299,
  kb_total = 1164,
  kb_elmpercl = 4,
  kb_totalfree = 178,
  kb_highwat = 20,
  kb_couldfree = 3812
}
```

The problem here is that the pointer kb_next is set to 0xffffffff. It should contain a valid address, but as *gdb* observes, this isn't not valid.

So far we have found that the crash is in malloc, and that it's caused by an invalid pointer in an internal data structure. malloc is a function that is used many times a second by all computers. It's unlikely that the bug is in malloc. In fact, the most likely cause is that a function that has used memory allocated by malloc has overwritten its bounds and hit malloc's data structures.

What do we do now? To quote *fortune*:

```
         The seven eyes of Ningauble the Wizard floated back to his hood
as he reported to Fafhrd: "I have seen much, yet cannot explain all.
The Gray Mouser is exactly twenty-five feet below the deepest cellar in
the palace of Gilpkerio Kistomerces.  Even though twenty-four parts in
twenty-five of him are dead, he is alive.

         "Now about Lankhmar.  She's been invaded, her walls breached
everywhere and desperate fighting is going on in the streets, by a
fierce host which out-numbers Lankhmar's inhabitants by fifty to one --
and equipped with all modern weapons.  Yet you can save the city."

         "How?" demanded Fafhrd.

         Ningauble shrugged.  "You're a hero.  You should know."
                -- Fritz Leiber, from "The Swords of Lankhmar"
```

From here on, you're on your own. If you get this far, the FreeBSD-hackers mailing list may be interested in giving suggestions.

Bibliography

While the manual pages provide the definitive reference for individual pieces of the FreeBSD operating system, they are notorious for not illustrating how to put the pieces together to make the whole operating system run smoothly.

Since the last edition of this book, a number of other books on FreeBSD have appeared. We'll look at them first, though you can consider most of them to be an alternative to this book.

Books on BSD

The following books relate specifically to BSD, most of them to FreeBSD.

FreeBSD: An Open-Source Operating System For Your Personal Computer. Annelise Anderson, The Bit Tree Press, 2001. An introductory book, particularly suitable for Microsoft users.

Advanced UNIX Programming, by Warren W. Gay. Sams Publishing, 2000. This book uses FreeBSD as the basis for an in-depth programming course.

The Berkeley UNIX Environment, by R. Nigel Horspool. Prentice-Hall Canada Inc, 1992. This book predates FreeBSD, but it includes a lot of information for the advanced user.

Absolute BSD, by Michael Lucas. No Starch Press, 2002.

The FreeBSD Corporate Networker's Guide, by Ted Mittelstaedt. Addison-Wesley, 2001. An introduction to FreeBSD for Microsoft system administrators.

FreeBSD: The Complete Reference, by Roderick W. Smith. McGraw-Hill/Osborne, 2003.

The FreeBSD Handbook, edited by Murray Stokely and Nik Clayton. Wind River systems, 2001. A print version of the online handbook.

FreeBSD Unleashed, by Michael Urban and Brian Tiemann. Sams Publishing, 2002. An introduction to FreeBSD with detailed descriptions of shell programming, Gnome and Perl programming.

Users' guides

These books are good general texts. They have no particular emphasis on BSD.

UNIX for the Impatient, by Paul W. Abrahams and Bruce R. Larson. Second Edition, Addison-Wesley, 1996. An excellent not-too-technical introduction to UNIX in general. Includes a section on X11.

Learning the Unix Operating System: A Concise Guide for the New User, by Jerry Peek, Grace Todino-Gonguet, John Strang. 5th Edition, O'Reilly & Associates, Inc., 2001. A good introduction for beginners.

UNIX Power Tools, by Shelley Powers, Jerry Peek, Tim O'Reilly, Mike Loukides, O'Reilly & Associates, Inc., 3rd Edition October 2002. A superb collection of interesting information. Recommended for everybody, from beginners to experts.

Administrators' guides

Building Internet Firewalls, by D. Brent Chapman and Elizabeth Zwicky. O'Reilly & Associates, Inc., 1995.

DNS and BIND, by Paul Albitz, Cricket Liu. 4th Edition, O'Reilly & Associates, Inc., 2001

Firewalls and Internet Security: Repelling the Wily Hacker, by William R. Cheswick and Steven M. Bellovin. Second edition, Addison-Wesley, 2003.

Essential System Administration, by Æleen Frisch. Third edition, O'Reilly & Associates, Inc., 2003. Includes coverage of FreeBSD 4.7.

TCP/IP Network Administration, by Craig Hunt. Third Edition. O'Reilly & Associates, 2002

UNIX System Administration Handbook, by Evi Nemeth, Garth Snyder, Scott Seebass, and Trent R. Hein. 3nd edition, Prentice Hall, 2001. An excellent coverage of four real-life systems, including FreeBSD 3.4.

Managing NFS and NIS, by Hal Stern, Mike Eisler and Ricardo Labiaga. 2nd Edition, O'Reilly & Associates, Inc., 2001

Using Samba, by Jay Ts, Robert Eckstein and David Collier-Brown. 2nd Edition, O'Reilly & Associates, Inc., 2003.

Programmers' guides

X Window System Toolkit, by Paul Asente. Digital Press.

The Annotated C++ Reference Manual, by Margaret A. Ellis and Bjarne Stroustrup. Addison-Wesley, 1990.

C: A Reference Manual, by Samuel P. Harbison and Guy L. Steele, Jr. 3rd edition, Prentice Hall, 1991.

"Porting UNIX to the 386" in *Dr. Dobb's Journal*, William Jolitz. January 1991-July 1992.

Porting UNIX Software, by Greg Lehey. O'Reilly & Associates, 1995.

The Design and the Implementation of the 4.4BSD Operating System. Marshall Kirk McKusick, Keith Bostic, Michael J. Karels, John S. Quarterman . Addison-Wesley, 1996. The definitive description of the 4.4BSD kernel and communications.

The Standard C Library, by P. J. Plauger. Prentice Hall, 1992.

TCP/IP illustrated, by W. Richard Stevens and Gary R. Wright (Volume 2 only). Prentice-Hall, 1994–1996. A three-volume work describing the Internet Protocols. Volume 2 includes code from the 4.4BSD-Lite implementation, most of which is very similar to the FreeBSD implementation.

UNIX Network Programming, by W. Richard Stevens. Prentice-Hall, 1998. A two-volume introduction to network programming.

Writing Serial Drivers for UNIX, by Bill Wells. *Dr. Dobb's Journal*, 19(15), December 1994. pp 68-71, 97-99.

Hardware reference

RS-232 made easy, second edition. Martin D. Seyer, Prentice-Hall 1991. A discussion of the RS-232 standard.

ISA System Architecture, by Tom Stanley. 3rd edition, Addison-Wesley, 1995.

PCI System Architecture, by Tom Stanley. 3rd edition, Addison-Wesley, 1995.

The Undocumented PC, by Frank Van Gilluwe. Addison-Wesley, 1994.

The 4.4BSD manuals

The original 4.4BSD manual set includes the man pages and a number of documents on various aspects of programming, user programs and system administration. With a few minor exceptions, you can find the latest versions in */usr/share/man* (the man pages) and */usr/share/doc* (the other documents). If you want the original 4.4BSD versions, you can check them out of the repository.

If you prefer a bound version, O'Reilly and Associates published the original five-volume set of documentation for 4.4BSD as released by the CSRG in 1994, including the AT&T historical documents. Compared to FreeBSD, much of this documentation is severely out of date, and it's also out of print, though you should still be able to find it second-hand. It comprises the following volumes:

- *4.4BSD Programmer's Reference Manual.* These are sections 2, 3, 4 and 5 of the man pages for 4.4BSD.

- *4.4BSD Programmer's Supplementary Documents.* You can find the latest versions of most of these documents in */usr/share/doc/psd*.

- *4.4BSD User's Reference Manual.* This book contains sections 1, 6 and 7 of the 4.4BSD man pages.

- *4.4BSD User's Supplementary Documents.* You can find the latest versions of most of these documents in */usr/share/doc/usd*.

- *4.4BSD System Manager's Manual.* Contains section 8 of the manual and a number of other documents. You can find the latest versions of most of these documents in */usr/share/doc/smm*.

Getting FreeBSD on CD-ROM

FreeBSD is available on CD-ROM from a number of suppliers:

Daemon News Mall
560 South State Street, Suite A2
Orem, UT 84058
USA
Phone: +1 800 407-5170
Fax: +1 801 765-0877
Email: *sales@bsdmall.com*
WWW: *http://www.bsdmall.com/*

Everything Linux
PO Box 243
Croydon NSW 2132
Australia
Phone: 0500 500 368
         02 8752 6666
Fax: 02 9712 3977
Email: *sales@everythinglinux.com.au*
WWW: *http://www.everythinglinux.com.au/*

FreeBSD Mall, Inc.
3623 Sanford Street
Concord, CA 94520-1405
USA
Phone: +1 925 674-0783
Fax: +1 925 674-0821
Email: *<info@freebsdmall.com>*
WWW: *http://www.freebsdmall.com/*

FreeBSD Services Ltd
11 Lapwing Close
Bicester
OX26 6XR
United Kingdom
WWW: *http://www.freebsd-services.com/*

Hinner EDV
St. Augustinus-Straße 10
D-81825 München
Germany
Phone: (089) 428 419
WWW: *http://www.hinner.de/linux/freebsd.html*

Ingram Micro
1600 E. St. Andrew Place
Santa Ana, CA 92705-4926
USA
Phone: 1 (800) 456-8000
WWW: *http://www.ingrammicro.com/*

The Linux Emporium
Hilliard House, Lester Way
Wallingford
OX10 9TA
United Kingdom
Phone: +44 1491 837010
Fax: +44 1491 837016
WWW: *http://www.linuxemporium.co.uk/bsd.html*

UNIXDVD.COM LTD
57 Primrose Avenue
Sheffield
S5 6FS
United Kingdom
WWW: *http://www.unixdvd.com/*

In addition, in the USA Frys Electronics and CompUSA carry boxed sets of FreeBSD
and documentation.

The evolution of FreeBSD

FreeBSD has been around for ten years. During this time, it has evolved significantly, and it continues to evolve. In this chapter we'll look at what has changed, particularly in more recent times. If you're planning to install one of the older releases of FreeBSD, for example on old hardware that is too small for modern releases, refer to Appendix A, *Bibliography*, for copies of older editions of this book.

FreeBSD Releases 1 and 2

Release 1.0 of FreeBSD appeared in December 1993. It was substantially an improved and debugged version of 386/BSD, based on the 4.3BSD Net/2 tape. FreeBSD Release 2 was released in January 1995. The big difference from Release 1 was that it was based on 4.4BSD Lite, one of the results of the lawsuit we discussed on page 8. There were no major differences from Release 1.

FreeBSD Release 3

FreeBSD Release 3.0 was released in September 1998. It represented the biggest change in FreeBSD since the code base was moved to 4.4BSD. A number of new features were introduced, which made upgrading a little more complicated than is normally the case. In particular, the following new features were of note:

- It introduced support for the Compaq/Digital Equipment *AXP* (also known as *ALPHA*) processor.

- On the Intel architecture, FreeBSD supported multiple processors.

- A new SCSI driver, *CAM*, was introduced. This required some modifications to the kernel configuration, and the device names changed. At present this means that FreeBSD device names are different from the NetBSD or OpenBSD names for the same devices. We'll look at CAM in more detail below.

- The IDE driver first supported DMA. We discussed DMA on page 32. The entire IDE driver was replaced in a later release.

- A new console driver was introduced.

- This release of FreeBSD started phasing out *loadable kernel modules*, described on page 163. Since then, they have been replaced by *kernel loadable modules* (*kld*s). Does this sound like word play? Well, there's a solid technical background: you can tell the bootstrap to load *kld*s along with the kernel. We'll look at them below.

- A new, more flexible bootstrap (the program that loads the kernel) was introduced.

- The default object file format changed from *a.out* to *ELF*. FreeBSD supported the ELF format for some time previously, initially to emulate Linux, but now it is the native format as well. FreeBSD still supports *a.out* binaries.

The CAM SCSI driver

FreeBSD Release 3.0 included a new SCSI driver, based on the ANSI ratified *Common Access Method* or *CAM* specification, which defines a software interface for talking to SCSI and ATAPI devices. The FreeBSD driver is not completely CAM compliant, but it follows many of the precepts of CAM. More importantly, it addresses many of the shortcomings of the previous SCSI layer and provides better performance and reliability, and eases the task of adding support for new controllers.

For most users, the most obvious difference between the old SCSI driver and CAM is the way they named SCSI devices. In the old driver, disks were called *sdn*, and tapes were called *stn*, where *n* was a small positive number. The CAM driver calls disks *dan* (for *direct access*), and tapes are called *san* (for *serial access*).

In addition, a new program, *camcontrol*, enables you to administrate the SCSI chain at a more detailed level then previously: for example, it is now possible to add devices to a chain after the system has started. See the man page for more details.

Kernel loadable modules

Older releases of FreeBSD supplied *Loadable Kernel Modules* or *LKM*s, object files that could be loaded and executed in the kernel while the kernel was running.

The ELF kernel and the new bootstrap introduced with FreeBSD Release 3 allow you to load additional modules at boot time. To do so, however, the format of the modules needed to be changed. To avoid (too much) confusion, the name changed from *loadable kernel module* to *kernel loadable module (kld)*.

Table B-1: Differences between LKMs and klds

Parameter	LKM	kld
Directory	*/lkm*	*/boot/kernel*
Load program	*modload*	*kldload*
Unload program	*modunload*	*kldunload*
List program	*modstat*	*kldstat*

Some other details have changed as well. *kldload* knows an internal path for finding *kld*s, so you don't need to specify the path unless it's in a non-standard location. It also assumes that the name of the *kld* ends in *.ko*, and you don't need to specify that either. For example, to load the Linux emulator as an LKM, you entered:

```
# modload /lkm/linux_mod.o
```

To load the *kld*, you enter:

```
# kldload linux
```

kldload searches for klds in a number of places. Table B-1 shows the default path, */boot/kernel*. If you boot from a different kernel, for example */boot/kernel.old/kernel*, the path will change to */boot/kernel.old*. Up to Release 4 of FreeBSD, it searched */modules* as well. At the time of writing, this directory is still in the search path, but it may be phased out. It's a bad idea to store kernel code where it might be loaded by different kernels.

The ELF object format

When UNIX was written, the world was simple. The kernel of the Third Edition of UNIX, in January 1973, had a little over 7,000 lines of code in total. The FreeBSD 5.0 kernel has approximately 300 times as much code. The original UNIX object format was correspondingly simple: it had provision for only three data segments. It was named after the name of the output from the assembler, *a.out*.

In the course of time, binaries required additional features, in particular the ability to link to dynamic libraries. UNIX System V introduced a new object file format, *COFF*, but BSD objected to some of the details of COFF and remained with *a.out* and used some rather dirty tricks to link to dynamic libraries. The change to *ELF* enabled a much cleaner interface.

Since Release 3, FreeBSD uses *ELF* as the default executable format, but the Intel port supported execution of *a.out* binaries until Release 5. The Alpha port was created after the change to *ELF* and does not support *a.out* at all.

What happened to my libraries?

One detail of the change from *a.out* to *ELF* can make life difficult: ELF and *a.out* executables need different libraries, each with their own format, but frequently with the same name. For example, the system now knows the following versions of the standard C library, which is required by every program:

- *libc.a* is a static library used for including the library routines into the program at link time.

- *libc_p.a* is a static library containing profiled versions of the library routines for inclusion into the program at link time.

- *libc_pic.a* is a static library containing position-independent versions of the library routines for inclusion into the program at link time.

- *libc_r.a* is a static library containing reentrant versions of the library routines for inclusion into the program at link time.

- *libc.so* is a symbolic link to the current version of a dynamic library for linking at run time. This link is only used for ELF programs.

- *libc.so.3* is a version of an ELF dynamic library for linking at run time. The number *3* changes with the release.

- *libc.so.3.1* is a version of an *a.out* dynamic library for linking at run time. The number *3.1* changes with the release.

Don't worry if these names don't make much sense to you; unless you're writing programs, all you need to know is that an ELF system uses */usr/lib/libc.so* at run time.

/usr/lib contains a large number of libraries. It would be possible, but messy, to find an alternative arrangement for the name conflicts, and leave the rest of the names unchanged. Instead, the conversion process moves all *a.out* libraries to a subdirectory *aout*, so an *a.out* executable now looks for */usr/lib/aout/libc.so.3.0*. An ELF executable looks for */usr/lib/libc.so.3*.

But how does the system know to look in a different place? It uses a *hints file* generated by the *ldconfig* program. When the system starts, it takes a list of directory names from */etc/rc.conf* and runs *ldconfig* to search the directories for *a.out* libraries and to generate the hints file. In Release 2 of FreeBSD, the standard */etc/rc.conf* contained the following definition:

```
ldconfig_paths="/usr/lib/compat /usr/X11R6/lib /usr/local/lib" # search paths
```

In Release 3.0, this changed to:

```
ldconfig_paths="/usr/lib/compat /usr/X11R6/lib /usr/local/lib"
                    # shared library search paths
ldconfig_paths_aout="/usr/lib/compat/aout /usr/X11R6/lib/aout /usr/local/lib/aout"
                    # a.out shared library search paths
```

Upgrading from Release 2 of FreeBSD

If you're still using Release 2, you might run into some minor problems. The following discussion applies when upgrading to Release 3 or any later release: part of the upgrade process from Release 2 to Release 3 changes this entry in */etc/rc.conf*, so there should be no problem with normal libraries. A couple of problems may still occur, however:

- Some programs refer to library names that are symbolic links. The upgrade process doesn't always handle symbolic links correctly, so you may find that the link points to the wrong place. For example, you might have this in a 2.2.7 system */usr/lib/compat*:

```
/usr/lib/compat:
total 1
-r--r--r--  1 root   wheel   8417 Jan 21 18:37 libgnumalloc.so.2.0
-r--r--r--  1 root   wheel   8398 Jan 21 18:37 libresolv.so.2.0
lrwxr-xr-x  1 root   wheel     31 Jan 21 18:36 libtermcap.so.3.0 -> /usr/lib/libte
rmcap.so.2.1
lrwxr-xr-x  1 root   wheel     31 Jan 21 18:36 libtermlib.so.3.0 -> /usr/lib/libte
rmlib.so.2.1
-r--r--r--  1 root   wheel   8437 Jan 21 18:37 liby.so.2.0
```

  After updating, you could end up with this:

```
/usr/lib/compat/aout:
total 1
-r--r--r--  1 root   wheel   8417 Jan 21 18:37 libgnumalloc.so.2.0
-r--r--r--  1 root   wheel   8398 Jan 21 18:37 libresolv.so.2.0
lrwxr-xr-x  1 root   wheel     31 Jan 21 18:36 libtermcap.so.3.0 -> /usr/lib/libte
rmcap.so.2.1
lrwxr-xr-x  1 root   wheel     31 Jan 21 18:36 libtermlib.so.3.0 -> /usr/lib/libte
rmlib.so.2.1
-r--r--r--  1 root   wheel   8437 Jan 21 18:37 liby.so.2.0
```

  In other words, the libraries have been moved, but the symbolic links are absolute and still point to the old place. The system doesn't install absolute symbolic links, so it doesn't make any attempt to correct them. You need to fix the problem manually. In this example, we replace the symbolic links with relative symbolic links:

```
# cd /usr/lib/compat/aout
# rm libtermcap.so.3.0
# ln -s libtermcap.so.2.1 libtermcap.so.3.0
# rm libtermlib.so.3.0
# ln -s libtermlib.so.2.1 libtermlib.so.3.0
```

- If you have modified your *etc/rc.conf* significantly, the update may fail, and your *a.out* hints file will still point to the old locations. In this case edit *etc/rc.conf* as shown above.

```
# cd /usr/X11R6/lib
# mkdir aout
# cp -p lib* aout
```

FreeBSD Version 4

FreeBSD Release 4.0 appeared in March 2000. It included a number of significant changes from Release 3. At the time of writing, FreeBSD Release 4 is still a current release, in parallel with Release 5.

First, the good news: the differences between Release 3 and Release 4 aren't as far-reaching or as complicated as the differences between Release 2 and Release 3. Still, there are a couple of things that you need to know. There are also a few things that make installation easier. You can get a blow-by-blow description of the changes from the file */usr/src/UPDATING*. This document discusses the following more important new features:

- From Release 4, FreeBSD no longer has block devices. See page 640 for more details.

- The base operating system now includes *OpenSSH*. This may conflict with the *ports/security/ssh* port: the base *OpenSSH* is installed in */usr/bin* and the port goes into */usr/local/bin*. Most paths have */usr/bin* in the path before */usr/local/bin*, so problems may arise. If you don't want OpenSSH, add the following line to */etc/make.conf*:

  ```
  NO_OPENSSH=yes
  ```

  You will also need to enable OpenSSH in */etc/rc.conf* if you want to run the new servers. You may need to move your host key and other config files from */usr/local/etc* to */etc/ssh*.

  OpenSSH has different command line parsing, available options and default settings from *ssh*, so you should take some care in its operation. Perform a full audit of all configuration settings.

- *sendmail.cf* has moved from */etc/sendmail.cf* to */etc/mail/sendmail.cf*. In addition to moving this file, you may need to adjust */etc/rc.conf*.

- *xntpd* has been updated to Revision 4. The name of the daemon has changed from *xntpd* to *ntpd*, so you may need to update your */etc/rc.conf* file. The *ntp.conf* files are compatible with the old release, unless you are using a local reference clock. You can find more details about *ntp4* at *http://www.ntp.org/*.

- There is a new driver for ATA (IDE) drives. See page 641 for more details.

- Release 3 supported both the old and the new names for SCSI devices, for example */dev/sd0* and */dev/da0*. The old names are no longer there in Release 4, so if you're upgrading you should check your */etc/fstab* and */etc/rc.conf* and change the names where necessary.

- *bad144* support for old WD and ESDI drives has been removed.

- The *mfs* driver has been replaced with the *md* driver. Accordingly the MFS_ROOT and MFS_ROOT_SIZE kernel configuration options have been replaced by MD_ROOT and MD_ROOT_SIZE. See the *GENERIC* or *LINT* configuration files for more details.

- Some Ethernet drivers no longer supports hard wired addresses in the config file. This is part of an on-going process to remove static hardware information from the kernel and to enable learning it at boot time.

- */var/cron/log* has been moved to */var/log/cron* to get all the log files in one place.

- User-visible TCP timers are now expressed in units of 1ms, instead of 500ms, so if you've customized any timer values under net.inet.tcp, multiply them by 500 to preserve TCP's behavior.

- The *bpfilter* device has been renamed to *bpf*.

- *Vinum* now supports a simplified interface. See the man page *vinum(8)* for details.

- A new driver, *ida*, was introduced for the Compaq Smart Raid array.

- The *lpt* driver has been rewritten using *ppbus*. See *ppbus(4)* for details.

- Linux threads options has gone away (they are now standard in the FreeBSD kernel).

- From Release 4, FreeBSD supports *PAM* (*Pluggable Authentication Modules*). This requires a new file */etc/pam.conf*. If you don't have this (for example, if you're upgrading from an older release of FreeBSD, and you don't install the file), you'll get relatively harmless error messages.

- For improved security, FreeBSD Release 4 runs *named* as a new user and group, both called bind.

- The floppy tape driver *ft* has been removed from the kernel. There is no replacement: this driver was always very non-standard, and the hardware that it supports is unreliable and obsolete.

- There are new keyboard and video card drivers. We'll look at them in more detail on page 641.

No more block devices

From the beginnings of UNIX, users were confused by the fact that a disk drive could appear in two different ways, either a *block device* or a *character device*, also called a *raw disk*. For example, your root partition might have been one of these:

```
$ ls -l /dev/wd0a /dev/rwd0a
crw-r-----  1 root  operator  3,  0 Oct 19  1997 /dev/rwd0a
brw-r-----  1 root  operator  0,  0 Oct 19  1997 /dev/wd0a
```

A raw device always accesses the drive directly. As a result, you're limited to the way the drive is organized: the transfer must start on a sector[1] boundary and must be an integral number of sectors long. By contrast, block devices are *buffered*: instead of accessing the disk directly, the system transfers data via an area of memory called *buffer cache*. You access the copy of the data in buffer cache. This has the advantages that you can access it much more quickly if it is in cache, and you don't have to pay any attention to sector boundaries. Still, having two different kinds of device is confusing, and it's obvious why we should want to simplify things.

But why are block devices going away, and not the raw disks? Until recently, for example, Linux didn't have any raw disk access, only block devices. There are a number of reasons to prefer to keep the raw disks:

- If you want to access disks in an aligned fashion, it's faster: you don't have to go via buffer cache. This also saves memory.

- If you have an error on a write to a raw device, you get an error indication immediately. On a block device, the error may not occur until after the process has terminated, too late to try to recover.

- The buffer cache isn't going away, only the device interface. It's very seldom that you'll find a need to access disk devices directly from user context. The most common access is via a file system or as swap. In the former case, the file system provides the buffering, and in the latter case it's counterproductive, since swap always writes entire pages. The only other access to disk devices is from system programs like *disklabel*, *newfs* and *mount*, all of which have always accessed the raw device.

For most users, the biggest difference is that you will never use a name like */dev/rda0a* again; instead, it will become */dev/da0a*. If you are upgrading, you must run */dev/MAKEDEV* to recreate the device nodes.

Note that in Release 5 of FreeBSD, */dev/MAKEDEV* is no longer needed.

---

1. Data on disk used to be stored in units called *sectors*. Modern disks store data in a number of different ways, but this is not visible outside the drive. The externally visible unit of data is still a sector of 512 bytes.

New ATA (IDE) disk driver

There is a new driver, *ata*, for *ATA* (*AT attachment*) drives, which were formerly called IDE. It supports not only disks but also ATAPI CD-ROM and DVD drives, ZIP drives and tape streamers.

In the process, the name of the devices has changed: disk drives are now called *ad*, CD-ROM drives are called *acd*, LS-120 floppies are called *afd*, and tapes are called *ast*.

For a transition period, the *wd* driver remains available, but you shouldn't use it unless you have very good reasons, for example if you have old or unusual hardware that has trouble with the *ad* driver.

New console driver

FreeBSD Release 4 includes a new console driver. The configuration file entries have changed. See the GENERIC configuration file for more details.

FreeBSD Release 5

FreeBSD Release 5 is the latest release of FreeBSD. It has a number of new features, most of which are transparent to the user. There's a complete list in the release notes, which you should certainly read if you're upgrading the system, but here are some highlights:

- SMP (symmetric multiprocessor) support has been rewritten from scratch. This will ultimately give much better performance and scalability, though currently the performance potential has not been fully realized. We looked at some of the visible differences on page 148.

- The *kqueue* event notification facility is a new interface that is able to replace *poll* and *select*. It offers improved performance as well as the ability to report many different types of events. Support for monitoring changes in sockets, pipes, fifos, and files are present, as well as for signals and processes.

- A large number of kernel configuration options have been turned into boot-time tunable variables, and the need to build specific kernels has become much more seldom.

- The *Kernel-Scheduled Entity* (*KSE*) project offers multi-threading in the kernel.

- Support for the 80386 processor has been removed from the GENERIC kernel, as this code seriously pessimizes performance on other IA32 processors.

  The I386_CPU kernel option to support the 80386 processor is now mutually exclusive with support for other IA32 processors; this should slightly improve performance on the 80386 due to the elimination of run time processor type checks.

Custom kernels that will run on the 80386 can still be built by changing the cpu options in the kernel configuration file to only include I386_CPU.

- Support has been added for 64 bit SPARC and IA 64 (Itanium) processors.

- The system includes the *device file system*, or *devfs*. In older releases of FreeBSD, as in other versions of UNIX, the directory */dev* contained *device nodes*, entries that looked like files but which in fact described a possible device on the system. The problem was that there was no good way to keep the device nodes in sync with the kernel, and problems occurred where the hardware corresponding to a device node didn't exist (a "Device not configured" error), or where the device node corresponding to the hardware did not exist (a "no such file or directory" error). *devfs* solves this problem by creating at boot time the device nodes for the hardware the system finds.

- The disk I/O access system has been rearranged and made more flexible with the *GEOM* framework.

- A number of file system enhancements have been made. The standard UFS file system now supports snapshots and background file system checking after a crash, significantly reducing reboot time after a crash.

- UFS has been significantly enhanced as *UFS2*. It supports files larger than 1 TB and extended file attributes.

- The PCMCIA code has been rewritten and now supports CardBus devices.

- The default kernel no longer supports *a.out* file format. You can still execute these files by loading the *aout.ko* KLD.

- FreeBSD now supports the *Advanced Configuration and Power Interface (ACPI)*, the replacement for *APM*.

- It is now possible to increase the size of ufs file systems with the *growfs* command.

- *Vinum* now supports the root file system. See Chapter 12 for details.

- *disklabel*, the program which creates disk labels, has been split into multiple programs depending on the platform: on PCs it is now called *bsdlabel*, and on SPARC64 it is called *sunlabel*. Some options have changed. In particular, the -r option no longer exists. See page 215 for further details.

Index

T

About the author

Greg Lehey was born in Australia and went to school in Malaysia and England before studying Chemistry in Germany and Chemical Engineering in England. He spent most of his professional career in Germany, where he worked for computer manufacturers such as Univac, Tandem, and Siemens-Nixdorf, the German space research agency, nameless software houses and a large user. Finally he worked for himself as a consultant. He returned to Australia in 1997.

In the course of 30 years in the industry he has performed most jobs, ranging from kernel development to product management, from systems programming to systems administration, from processing satellite data to programming petrol pumps, from the production of CD-ROMs of ported free software to DSP instruction set design. Apart from this book, he is also the author of "Porting UNIX Software" (O'Reilly and Associates, 1995). About the only thing he hasn't done is writing commercial applications software. He is available for short-term contracts and can be reached by mail at grog@FreeBSD.org or grog@lemis.com. Alternatively, browse his home page at *http://www.lemis.com/grog/*.

When he can drag himself away from his collection of UNIX workstations, he is involved in performing baroque and classical woodwind music on his collection of original instruments, exploring the Australian countryside with his family on their Arabian and Peruvian horses, or exploring new cookery techniques or ancient and obscure European languages.

Related Titles Available from O'Reilly

Unix Administration

CVS Pocket Reference, *2nd Edition*

DNS & BIND, *4th Edtion*

DNS & BIND Cookbook

Essential CVS

Essential System Administration, *3rd Edition*

Essential System Administration Pocket Reference

Postfix: The Definitive Guide

qmail

sendmail, *3rd Edition*

sendmail Cookbook

System Performance Tuning, *2nd Edition*

The Unix CD Bookshelf, *Version 3.0*

Unix Backup & Recovery

Unix Basics

GNU Emacs Pocket Reference

Learning GNU Emacs, *2nd Edition*

Learning the bash Shell, *2nd Edition*

Learning the Korn Shell

Learning the Unix Operating System, *5th Edition*

Learning the vi Editor, *6th Edition*

sed & awk Pocket Reference, *2nd Edition*

sed & awk, *2nd Edition*

Unix in a Nutshell, System V Edition, *3rd Edition*

Using csh & tcsh

Unix Tools

Effective awk Programming, *3rd Edition*

lex & yacc, *2nd Edition*

Managing Projects with make, *2nd Edition*

Practical PostgreSQL

Unix Power Tools, *3rd Edition*

Writing GNU Emacs Extensions

O'REILLY®

Our books are available at most retail and online bookstores.
To order direct: 1-800-998-9938 • *order@oreilly.com* • *www.oreilly.com*
Online editions of most O'Reilly titles are available by subscription at *safari.oreilly.com*

Keep in touch with O'Reilly

1. Download examples from our books

To find example files for a book, go to:

www.oreilly.com/catalog

select the book, and follow the "Examples" link.

2. Register your O'Reilly books

Register your book at *register.oreilly.com*

Why register your books?
Once you've registered your O'Reilly books you can:

- Win O'Reilly books, T-shirts or discount coupons in our monthly drawing.
- Get special offers available only to registered O'Reilly customers.
- Get catalogs announcing new books (US and UK only).
- Get email notification of new editions of the O'Reilly books you own.

3. Join our email lists

Sign up to get topic-specific email announcements of new books and conferences, special offers, and O'Reilly Network technology newsletters at:

elists.oreilly.com

It's easy to customize your free elists subscription so you'll get exactly the O'Reilly news you want.

4. Get the latest news, tips, and tools

www.oreilly.com

- "Top 100 Sites on the Web"—PC Magazine
- CIO Magazine's Web Business 50 Awards

Our web site contains a library of comprehensive product information (including book excerpts and tables of contents), downloadable software, background articles, interviews with technology leaders, links to relevant sites, book cover art, and more.

5. Work for O'Reilly

Check out our web site for current employment opportunities:

jobs.oreilly.com

6. Contact us

O'Reilly & Associates, Inc.
1005 Gravenstein Hwy North
Sebastopol, CA 95472 USA
TEL: 707-827-7000 or 800-998-9938
       (6am to 5pm PST)
FAX: 707-829-0104

order@oreilly.com
For answers to problems regarding your order or our products. To place a book order online, visit:

www.oreilly.com/order_new

catalog@oreilly.com
To request a copy of our latest catalog.

booktech@oreilly.com
For book content technical questions or corrections.

corporate@oreilly.com
For educational, library, government, and corporate sales.

proposals@oreilly.com
To submit new book proposals to our editors and product managers.

international@oreilly.com
For information about our international distributors or translation queries. For a list of our distributors outside of North America check out:

international.oreilly.com/distributors.html

adoption@oreilly.com
For information about academic use of O'Reilly books, visit:

academic.oreilly.com